Statistical
Record
OF Women
Worldwide

Statistical Record of Women Worldwide

Compiled and Edited by
LINDA SCHMITTROTH

 **Gale Research Inc.** • *DETROIT* • *LONDON*

Linda Schmittroth, *Editor*

Gale Research Inc. Staff

Mary Beth Trimper, *Production Manager*
Evi Seoud, *Assistant Production Manager*

Arthur Chartow, *Art Director*
Bonnie Gornie, *Graphic Designer*
Yolanda Y. Latham, *Keyliner*

Library of Congress Cataloging-in-Publication Data

Statistical record of women worldwide / compiled and edited
by Linda Schmittroth.
   p. cm.
   Includes bibliographical references and index.
   ISBN 0-8103-8349-7
   1. Women—Statistics. I. Schmittroth, Linda.
HQ1150.S73 1991   305.4'021—dc20   91-4175

A CIP catalogue record for this book is available from the British Library.

The paper used in this publication meets the minimum requirements
of American National Standard for Information Sciences—Permanence
Paper for Printed Library Materials, ANSI Z39.48-1984. ∞™

Copyright© 1991
Gale Research Inc.
835 Penobscot Bldg.
Detroit, MI 48226-4094

ISBN 0-8103-8349-7
Printed in the United States of America
Published simultaneously in the United Kingdom
by Gale Research International Limited
(An affiliated company of Gale Research Inc.)

TABLE OF CONTENTS

Crime, Law Enforcement, and Legal Justice continued:

Health and Medical Care continued:

Health and Medical Care continued:

Income, Spending, and Wealth continued:

Labor, Employment, and Occupations continued:

Population and Vital Statistics continued:

Population and Vital Statistics continued:

Sports and Recreation continued:

PREFACE

Strong and continued growing interest in the field of women's studies is seen in government, the media, and academia, as well as among business marketers, and interest in the topic has lately expanded to encompass women abroad. Students, researchers, government officials, journalists, and the concerned public are hungry for information of all kinds on the topic of women. The need for easy-to-use statistics on any subject from multiple sources is particularly acute. *Statistical Record of Women Worldwide* seeks to address these needs by bringing together actual statistical data on the lives and status of women throughout the world from a wide variety of sources — government and non-government, U.S. and international, published and unpublished — in a single accessible and affordable compilation.

MULTIPLICITY OF SOURCES

The data arranged herein have been collected from periodical literature, government documents, reports and studies from associations, companies, institutions, research centers, organizations, and other materials that provide statistical information on women regularly or incidentally. Coverage is approximately 50% U.S. and 50% international. In short, *Statistical Record of Women Worldwide* is not a repackaging of U.S. Census Bureau information; rather, it is a compilation of data from many sources illustrating the condition of women around the world.

COMPARATIVE AND HISTORICAL DATA

Because statistical data are often more meaningful when comparisons can be made, data for men, data by race/ethnicity, and for girls are presented in this book whenever feasible. Further, to point to progress or its lack in the improvement of the lot of women, U.S. data are often presented in an historical context; due to space limitations, such data generally go back no further than 1970. Space constraints also preclude presentation of international data in an historical context. When available, forecast data are also presented.

COVERAGE OF TOPICS NATIONALLY AND INTERNATIONALLY

When consulting this volume, the reader will note that some topics are covered in more detail than others. This is a reflection of the general availability of the published data. There is no shortage of data on topics such as labor, population, education, and health; religion and sexuality, however, are areas for which little information was uncovered (although there are numerous informal magazine surveys, a few of which are reproduced in this book as a guide for interested readers). The Census Bureau's proposal to include a question about religious affiliation in the census of 1970 brought a storm of protest that such a question was a violation of the constitutional guarantee of freedom of religion. Perhaps some of the same sentiment is involved when it comes to providing information about sexuality.

Because data collection methods and accuracy vary from country to country, international coverage in this book for the most part is limited to data collected and standardized by international sources rather than individual foreign national sources. (In this respect, it is interesting to note that only 75 of the World Health Organization's 164 member states are able to measure maternal mortality, although maternal mortality accounts for the largest or near-largest proportion of deaths among women of reproductive age in most of the developing world.)

GEOGRAPHIC SCOPE OF THIS VOLUME
AND A NOTE ABOUT FOOTNOTES

The geographic scope of this book ranges from individual cities and states to the United States as a whole, from major world areas to individual countries. Individual countries and U.S. cities and states are indexed in the "Subject and Geographic Index" at the end of this book. It should be noted that, particularly in the case of international data, footnotes are often so voluminous that space does not permit reproducing them all in this book. The user is urged to consult the original source, clearly identified at the end of each entry, if questions arise.

ARRANGEMENT OF CHAPTERS

The status of a woman in a society is often defined in terms of her level of income, employment, education, health and fertility, and the roles she plays in the family and society. With this in mind, chapters in the book are divided into such topics as *Income, Spending, and Wealth; Labor, Employment, and Occupations; Education; Health and Medical Care; Domestic Life;* and *Public Life*. Other topics include *Crime, Law Enforcement, and Legal Justice; Business and Economics; The Military; Population and Vital Statistics; Religion; Sexuality;* and *Sports and Recreation*. Within each chapter are subheadings that group tables together under broad subjects. Each table has a sequential entry number above a brief headline outlining its scope. Subject access is facilitated by a comprehensive "Table of Contents," which lists each table title within a chapter, and by a detailed "Subject and Geographic Index." For a detailed explanation, refer to the *How to Use This Book* section.

ACKNOWLEDGMENTS

The editor acknowledges with gratitude the following people, who graciously consented to offer advice and suggestions at the conceptualization stage of this project on topics of greatest interest and sources to consult:

Jane Cramer, Government Documents Librarian, Brooklyn College;

Elizabeth Dunn, Reference Librarian;

Judi Fouts, Librarian, Dallas Public Library, and Owner, *Finders Keepers Out of Print Book Service*;

Lynn C. Hattendorf, Assistant Reference Librarian, University of Illinois at Chicago;

Constance McCarthy, Assistant Head, Reference Department, Northwestern University Library;

Edna Reinhold, Manager, Collection Development, St. Louis Public Library; and

Luke Swindler, Social Sciences Bibliographer, University of North Carolina, Chapel Hill.

The editor is also grateful to all the women whose enthusiasm and labor made this book possible: proofreader Virginia Snyder Semrow; proofreader and mother's helper Ann Lane; courier Peggy Polo; research assistant Zohre Raein; and sense reader Mary McCall. Thank you to cheerleader Sara Schmittroth and her father, John, for his inspiration. Thank you to Barbara Beach and Christine Hammes at Gale Research Inc. for their assistance. Thanks also to Arsen Darnay for sharing his computer expertise.

HOW TO USE THIS BOOK

Entries in the *Statistical Record of Women Worldwide* are arranged into 14 chapters, as outlined on the Contents pages. Within each chapter, tables are arranged under broad subject headings and are assigned a sequential entry number. A sample entry illustrating and explaining the types of information typically provided in an entry is shown below.

Access to entries is facilitated by the alphabetical Subject and Geographic Index appearing at the end of this volume. An explanation of this index follows the sample entry.

SAMPLE ENTRY

The boldfaced number preceding each portion of the sample entry designates an item of information that might be included in an entry. Each item is explained in the paragraph preceded by the corresponding number that follows the sample entry.

(1) *Sequential Entry Number.* The entries in this volume are numbered sequentially, beginning with the first entry in *Attitudes and Opinions* and ending with the last entry in *Sports and Recreation*. Both the sequential entry number and the page number are used in the Subject and Geographic Index (the entry number being surrounded by brackets) to refer to an entry.

(2) *Headline*. A brief headline outlines the scope of the table.

(3) *Explanatory Note*. Usually a one-sentence explanation of table details such as the universe included.

(4) *Legend*. Defines who or what are to be enumerated below.

(5) *Data*. Statistical information appears here, usually in the form of percentages or numbers (this is clearly indicated on the table). For quick retrieval of data on women from the body of the table, "female" or "women" is highlighted in boldface. In some cases, where data does not easily lend itself to the tabular format, summaries of data are provided in text form.

(6) *Source Notes*. Here appears a description of the source from which the editor took the data. A fuller description of the source is provided in the List of Sources Consulted at the end of the book.

(7) *Primary Source*. Here appears a description of where the source obtained the data.

(8) *Also in Source*. Since the data are in most cases *extracts* from the published sources, here appears information on what other data is to be found in the cited source.

Other information that might appear after *Also in Source* includes general notes about the table, footnotes from the cited source, and references to related reading on the topic.

SUBJECT AND GEOGRAPHIC INDEX

A comprehensive Subject and Geographic Index is provided at the end of this volume. Headings used in the index are based on references by subject to every table in the book with appropriate page and entry numbers; in addition, extensive cross-references and related terms are provided. Unless otherwise

SAMPLE ENTRY

★ 218 ★

Higher Education Attainment in Selected Countries

Total population age 24 and percentages of the total that are graduates from higher education institutions.

Sex and country	Year	Population age 24	Higher Education Graduates		
			All fields	Sciences	Engineering
Females					
Japan	1988	817,000	12.4%	0.6%	0.3%
USA	1986	2,092,000	24.0%	2.2%	0.6%
Canada	1987	234,275	23.3%	2.1%	0.4%
England	1986	466,700	13.0%	2.4%	0.3%
West Germany	1985	504,700	10.0%	0.7%	0.2%
France	1987	425,061	14.5%	2.1%	0.6%
Males					
Japan	1988	849,000	33.4%	2.5%	8.8%
USA	1986	1,947,000	25.0%	3.7%	4.3%
Canada	1987	234,525	20.6%	3.5%	2.9%
England	1986	477,000	16.0%	3.6%	3.3%
West Germany	1985	534,100	15.3%	1.9%	3.9%
France	1987	426,554	14.3%	3.6%	2.8%

Source: Selected from "International Comparisons of Higher Education Attainment" and "Number of Graduates from Higher Education Institutions, by Sex, Field of Study, and Country," *The Condition of Education 1990: Volume 2: Postsecondary Education*, Table 2:8, p. 34,117 (Washington, D.C.: National Center for Educational Statistics, 1990). Primary source: Data collected for the Organization for Economic Cooperation and Development Indicators Project on Higher Education. Also in source: Total numbers of higher education graduates.

specified, it should be assumed that the subjects relate to women. Subject terms that relate to a table that is international in scope will be followed by "worldwide"; subject terms followed by "United States" refer to tables that feature the United States and are international in scope. Subject terms followed by neither of these refer to U.S. tables only. Every country that appears in the book is also listed in the index, followed by subject terms and appropriate page and entry numbers. States, cities, institutions, and individuals that appear in a table are also listed in the index with page and entry numbers. Here it should be noted that the source conventions for naming countries were sometimes used in the presentation of data; thus, for example, some tables refer to Burma and others refer to Myanmar, the name by which Burma is now known. In such cases, every attempt has been made to ensure that appropriate "see also" references are provided.

LIST OF SOURCES CONSULTED

Here appears detailed information on the sources from which the data for this book were collected, as well as information on other works for further reading and study.

SPECIAL NOTES ON THE CLASSIFICATION OF COUNTRIES, LEVELS OF EDUCATION IN INTERNATIONAL SOURCES, AND INTERPRETATION OF DATA

The United Nations uses the following country classifications (among others):[1]

Developing countries: Latin America and the Caribbean area, Africa (other than South Africa), Asia (excluding Japan), and Cyprus, Malta, and Yugoslavia.

Developed market economies: North America, southern and western Europe (excluding Cyprus, Malta, and Yugoslavia), Australia, Japan, New Zealand, and South Africa.

---

1   *1989 Report on the World Social Situation*, p. viii (New York: United Nations, 1989).

Centrally planned economies: China, Eastern Europe, and Union of Soviet Socialist Republics.

Please consult the *1988 Demographic Yearbook*, p. 41-42 (New York: United Nations, 1988) for a complete list of countries included under such designations as Eastern Africa, Middle Africa, and so on.

Levels of education as defined by UNESCO:

- *Education preceding the first level* provides education for children who are not old enough to enter a school at the first level (e.g., at nursery school, kindergarten, infant school).

- *Education at the first level* provides the basic elements of education (e.g., at elementary or primary school).

- *Education at the second level* is based on at least four years' previous instruction at the first level and provides general or specialized instruction or both (e.g., at middle, secondary, or high school, teacher- training at this level, or training of a vocational or technical nature at this level).

- *Education at the third level* (International Standard Classification of Education [ISCED] levels 5, 6, and 7) requires as a minimum condition of admission the successful completion of education at the second level or evidence of the attainment of an equivalent level of knowledge (e.g., at university, teacher's college, or higher professional school).

While censuses of population have been conducted for at least five thousand years, it is only in the last twenty years or so that there has existed technology enabling the collection of detailed information specifically on women. The collection and interpretation of such a vast amount of data are always subject to error. Particularly in the case of international statistics, the contributions of women to the family, society, and socioeconomic development are often grossly underestimated and sometimes completely disregarded in official statistics. The rationale for the exclusion of whole areas of productive activity, such as the fruits of subsistence farming (which still comprises most of the world's farming activity and is primarily the work of women) is summarized in the 1953 revision of the United Nations' System of National Accounts thus: "primary production and the consumption of their own produce by nonprimary producers is of little or no importance." Data on female labor force participation in developing countries are still considered to be of poor quality, being affected by variables such as male respondents being less likely to report female economic activity and male interviewers making assumptions about female respondents (for example, assuming they are housewives). The official statistics on women worldwide should be approached as general rather than infallible guidelines to what is known about the lives and status of women and girls worldwide.

Statistical
Record
OF Women
Worldwide

ATTITUDES AND OPINIONS

Abortion

★ 1 ★

Abortion Demonstrations

Respondents were asked how they feel about anti-abortion demonstrators blocking entrances to abortion clinics.

Characteristic of respondent	Feelings toward demonstrations				
	Support strongly	Support	Oppose	Oppose strongly	Don't know/ no answer
U.S. Total	4%	18%	37%	30%	11%
Sex					
Female	3%	17%	38%	30%	11%
Male	5%	19%	36%	30%	11%
Age					
18 to 29 years	3%	19%	35%	31%	11%
30 to 44 years	5%	21%	36%	28%	10%
45 to 64 years	3%	16%	39%	30%	12%
65 years and older	3%	12%	41%	32%	12%

Source: "Attitudes toward abortion demonstrations by demographic characteristics, United States, 1989," *Sourcebook of Criminal Justice Statistics 1989,* 1989, p. 164. Primary source: Table provided to SOURCEBOOK staff by the Media General/Associated Press Poll. Percents may not add to 100 due to rounding.

★ 2 ★

Abortion: 1977-1989

Questions and responses of women and men about abortion, 1977-1989.

Question	Sex	Response	Year									
			1977	1978	1980	1982	1983	1984	1985	1987	1988	1989
Should it be possible for a pregnant woman to obtain a legal abortion if the woman wants if for any reason?	F	Yes	37%	32%	41%	41%	34%	37%	35%	36%	36%	38%
		No	63%	68%	59%	59%	66%	63%	65%	64%	64%	62%
		Sample	814	865	790	831	862	842	815	793	555	562
	M	Yes	39%	35%	41%	42%	35%	40%	39%	44%	36%	43%
		No	61%	65%	59%	58%	65%	60%	61%	56%	64%	57%
		Sample	665	619	616	605	653	578	666	601	381	427

[Continued]

★ 2 ★

Abortion: 1977-1989
[Continued]

Question	Sex	Response	Year									
			1977	1978	1980	1982	1983	1984	1985	1987	1988	1989
Should it be possible for a pregnant woman to obtain a legal abortion if there is a strong chance of serious defect in the baby?	F	Yes	87%	82%	82%	84%	78%	79%	78%	78%	79%	80%
		No	13%	18%	18%	16%	22%	21%	22%	22%	21%	20%
		Sample	817	868	801	832	865	844	818	804	550	564
	M	Yes	84%	82%	85%	85%	80%	82%	80%	81%	79%	83%
		No	16%	18%	15%	15%	20%	18%	20%	19%	21%	17%
		Sample	670	629	618	615	649	577	668	610	394	431
Should it be possible for a pregnant woman to obtain a legal abortion if the woman's own health is seriously endangered by the pregnancy?	F	Yes	90%	91%	88%	91%	89%	88%	87%	86%	88%	90%
		No	10%	9%	12%	9%	11%	12%	13%	14%	12%	10%
		Sample	817	861	808	840	865	847	818	799	549	566
	M	Yes	91%	90%	93%	93%	90%	91%	92%	91%	90%	90%
		No	9%	10%	7%	7%	10%	9%	8%	9%	10%	10%
		Sample	671	631	621	626	655	584	673	619	393	437
Should it be possible for a pregnant woman to obtain a legal abortion if she is married and does not want any more children?	F	Yes	45%	39%	46%	47%	36%	41%	38%	38%	39%	41%
		No	55%	61%	54%	53%	64%	59%	62%	62%	61%	59%
		Sample	801	860	791	829	861	845	816	800	560	560
	M	Yes	49%	42%	48%	51%	43%	45%	44%	46%	41%	49%
		No	51%	58%	52%	49%	57%	55%	56%	54%	59%	51%
		Sample	661	623	616	607	659	575	672	611	389	431
Should it be possible for a pregnant woman to obtain a legal abortion if the family has a very low income and cannot afford any more children?	F	Yes	54%	46%	50%	52%	42%	45%	42%	43%	42%	45%
		No	46%	54%	50%	48%	58%	55%	58%	57%	58%	55%
		Sample	809	854	787	830	856	837	818	798	556	559
	M	Yes	53%	50%	53%	52%	46%	48%	46%	49%	42%	51%
		No	47%	50%	47%	48%	54%	52%	54%	51%	58%	49%
		Sample	669	615	621	611	651	577	670	607	385	433
Should it be possible for a pregnant woman to obtain a legal abortion if she became pregnant as a result of rape?	F	Yes	84%	83%	81%	86%	82%	79%	80%	78%	80%	82%
		No	16%	17%	19%	14%	18%	21%	20%	22%	20%	18%
		Sample	804	861	797	830	853	827	810	793	542	558
	M	Yes	84%	83%	86%	88%	84%	83%	83%	84%	83%	85%
		No	16%	17%	14%	12%	16%	17%	17%	16%	17%	15%
		Sample	665	620	614	609	651	579	664	606	382	433
Should it be possible for a pregnant woman to obtain a legal abortion if she is not married and does not want to marry the man?	F	Yes	49%	39%	49%	49%	38%	42%	40%	39%	38%	41%
		No	51%	61%	51%	51%	62%	58%	60%	61%	62%	59%
		Sample	795	852	787	822	848	841	817	800	551	560
	M	Yes	51%	44%	47%	49%	41%	47%	43%	46%	41%	51%
		No	49%	56%	53%	51%	59%	53%	57%	54%	59%	49%
		Sample	664	621	617	610	645	579	669	610	381	425

Source: Selected from *An American Profile—Opinions and Behavior, 1972-1989*, p. 549-69 (Detroit: Gale Research Inc., 1990). Primary source: General Social Survey. Also in source: data by race and age.

★3★

French Women on RU486.

The opinions of 506 women aged 18-44 interviewed in France in October, 1988, on the topic of RU486, a pill that causes abortion without surgery.

Statement regarding RU486:	Agree	Disagree	Don't Know
With this pill there are fewer risks to the health of women who abort:	54%	21%	25%
It is a way to abort too easily; one doesn't take time to weigh the pros and cons:	53%	38%	9%
To abort with the aid of a pill is less traumatic for women:	76%	15%	9%
With such a pill, there is a danger of increasing the number of abortions:	62%	29%	9%
There is a risk that some women would use it in place of regular contraception:	53%	36%	11%
With this abortion pill, women have taken a great additional stride in their liberation:	63%	29%	8%

Source: Selected from *Index to International Public Opinion, 1988-1989*, p. 425-26 (New York: Greenwood Press, 1988/89). Primary source: Institut Francais d'Opinion Francais (France).

★4★

Overturning Roe vs Wade

Respondents asked whether they would like to see the Supreme Court completely overturn its Roe vs Wade decision establishing a constitutional right to an abortion.

Respondent characteristic	Yes	No	No opinion
U.S. Total	33%	61%	6%
Sex			
Female	35%	58%	7%
Male	32%	63%	5%
Age			
18 to 29 years	35%	61%	4%
30 to 49 years	26%	68%	6%
50 years and older	40%	51%	9%

Source: "Attitudes toward overturning the 1973 Supreme Court ruling on abortion by demographic characteristics, United States, 1989," *Sourcebook of Criminal Justice Statistics 1989*, 1989, p. 164. Primary source: George Gallup, Jr., *The Gallup Report*, Report No. 289 (Princeton, NJ: The Gallup Poll, October 1989), p. 17. Also in source: data by other characteristics of respondents.

Athletes

★5★

Strength of Women Athletes' Feminist Views

Answers of female athletes to the question: "If feminism is defined as being committed to equality for women in all aspects of life, how strong would you say your feminist views are?" (N=1,650).

Response	Percent
Very strong	41%
Strong	25%
Somewhat strong	20%
Not very strong	6%
I do not consider myself a feminist	8%

Source: Miller Lite Report on Women in Sports, December 1985, p. 15. Based on a random sample of 7,000 members of the Women's Sports Foundation.

★6★

Women in Sports

General opinions of female athletes on women in sports.

Statement	Agree Strongly	Agree Somewhat	Disagree Somewhat	Disagree Strongly
Women's sports should be kept separate from men's so that women are free to develop their own skills.	23%	46%	23%	8%
In this society, a woman is often forced to choose between being an athlete and being feminine.	20%	37%	21%	21%
Girls should be allowed to play contact sports like football if they want to.	36%	37%	17%	10%
Intense athletic involvement complicates romantic relationships.	8%	33%	26%	33%
Female athletes exhibit higher levels of aggression than their non-athletic counterparts.	16%	36%	26%	22%
A woman athlete's sexual orientation is no one's business but her own.	76%	17%	4%	3%
Participation in racially mixed sports/fitness groups often reduces prejudice.	49%	42%	6%	3%
Women have something to teach men about humane competition.	36%	42%	16%	5%
Participation in sports diminishes a woman's femininity.	3%	3%	12%	82%

[Continued]

★ 6 ★

Women in Sports
[Continued]

Statement	Agree Strongly	Agree Somewhat	Disagree Somewhat	Disagree Strongly
There is too much pressure today for women to be just like men in sports and athletics.	10%	32%	36%	22%
American women athletes are going to have to take steroids and drugs to compete successfully internationally.	1%	3%	12%	84%
If young girls compete successfully on the athletic field, they will be better able to compete successfully in later life.	57%	36%	5%	2%
What a woman does is feminine.	40%	31%	20%	9%
Compared to other women athletes, women of color are less able to convert their athletic success into commercial success off the field.	12%	38%	30%	20%

Source: Miller Lite Report on Women in Sports, December 1985, p. 11. Based on a random sample of 7,000 members of the Women's Sports Foundation.

Crime and Punishment

★ 7 ★

Death Penalty

Question: "Do you favor or oppose the death penalty for people convicted of:?" Percent in favor.

Characteristic of respondent	Offense and % in favor of death penalty					
	Murder	Rape	Hijacking an airplane	Attempt to assassinate President	Spying for a foreign nation in peacetime	Drug dealers not con- victed of murder
Total United States	79%	51%	49%	63%	42%	38%
Sex						
Female	75%	48%	42%	60%	35%	36%
Male	83%	55%	58%	66%	50%	40%
Age						
18 to 29 years	83%	59%	47%	66%	45%	31%
30 to 49 years	80%	49%	46%	62%	38%	35%
50 years and older	77%	48%	55%	62%	45%	47%
Race						
White	82%	53%	51%	66%	43%	39%

[Continued]

★ 7 ★

Death Penalty
[Continued]

Characteristic of respondent	Offense and % in favor of death penalty					
	Murder	Rape	Hijacking an airplane	Attempt to assassinate President	Spying for a foreign nation in peacetime	Drug dealers not con- victed of murder
Nonwhite	61%	45%	41%	44%	38%	33%
Black	57%	40%	40%	42%	38%	28%

Source: "Attitudes toward the death penalty for persons convicted of murder and other offenses," *Sourcebook of Criminal Justice Statistics - 1988,* 1989, p. 223. Primary source: George Gallup, Jr., *The Gallup Report,* Report No. 280 (Princeton, NJ: The Gallup Poll, January 1989), pp. 28,29. Table adapted by SOURCEBOOK staff. By demographic characteristics, United States, 1988. Responses of "no opinion" were omitted by the Source.

★ 8 ★

Walking Alone at Night and Safety at Home

Question: "Is there any area near where you live...where you would be afraid to walk alone at night? How about at home at night...do you feel safe and secure?"

Characteristic of respondent	Afraid to walk alone at night		Feel safe at home	
	Yes	No	Yes	No
Total United States	43%	57%	90%	10%
Sex				
Female	59%	41%	86%	14%
Male	25%	75%	94%	6%
Age				
18 to 29 years	45%	55%	89%	11%
30 to 49 years	32%	68%	91%	9%
50 years and older	52%	48%	89%	11%
Race				
White	41%	59%	91%	9%
Nonwhite	55%	45%	82%	18%
Black	53%	47%	81%	19%

Source: "Attitudes toward walking alone at night and safety at home," *Sourcebook of Criminal Justice Statistics - 1988,* 1989, p. 211. Primary source: George Gallup, Jr., *The Gallup Report,* Report Nos. 282-283 (Princeton, NJ: The Gallup Poll, March/April 1989), p. 8. Table adapted by SOURCEBOOK staff. Also in source: data by education, politics, income, and religion.

Economic Matters

★ 9 ★

Taxes

Answers in 1988 to the question: "Which Do You Think Is the Worst Tax?"

Respondent	Federal Income Tax	Social Security	State Income Tax	State Sales Tax	Local Property Tax	Don't Know/ No Answer
Total Public	26%	17%	9%	15%	24%	9%
Females	27%	16%	7%	15%	24%	11%
Males	26%	17%	10%	16%	24%	7%

Source: "Changing Public Attitudes on Governments and Taxes, 1989," Table 5 (Washington, D.C., Advisory Commission on Intergovernmental Relations, 1988). Also in source: data for other years and by other characteristics of respondents.

★ 10 ★

Women's Attitudes About Money

Comparison of responses to statements about money: 1977 and 1988, based on a *Ms* magazine survey.

Statement	1977	1988
Can money buy happiness? or love? "Money can't buy happiness."		
Agree	66%	73%
Disagree	34%	27%
"When poverty comes in at the door, love flies out by the window."		
Agree	49%	32%
Disagree	51%	68%
Assuming you have enough money, how easy is it for you to spend it on the following?		
Percent who say "very easy" to spend on:		
Gifts	47%	51%
Small self-indulgences	46%	47%
Clothes for yourself	33%	44%
Treating others to dinner	32%	42%
Travel	36%	40%
Giving to a cause	18%	39%
Pension plan	not asked	39%
Entertainment	43%	38%
Paying someone to clean house	18%	27%
Costly luxury items	6%	7%

Source: "Smart Money: Ignorance is no longer bliss. Women are seeking financial expertise and economic independence," *Ms* 108 (November 1989): 51+. Approximately 23,000 women responded to the 1988 survey.

★ 11 ★

Women's Perception of Social Security Policies

Attitudes about Social Security policies for women by age and race, based on a survey of Chicago-area women.

Attitude	All Women	Age			Race	
		25-34	35-44	45-54	White	Non-white
Social Security policies toward women are:						
Fair	17%	17%	17%	19%	17%	19%
Unfair	44%	41%	47%	47%	43%	50%
Don't know	38%	42%	36%	34%	40%	31%
Total	1,874	844	571	459	833	326
Social security policies are unfair because:						
Benefits are too limited	47%	43%	50%	50%	43%	60%
Unequal treatment of women	72%	74%	74%	68%	72%	74%
Taxes	90%	89%	90%	91%	90%	89%
Total	832	348	268	216	625	208

Source: Selected from "Attitudes about Social Security Policies for Women by Age and Race, for Chicago-Area Women," *Widows and Dependent Wives: From Social Problem to Federal Program,* p. 194-95 (New York: Praeger, 1986. Primary source: Chicago area commitments study, compiled by K. Norr. Also in source: other attitudes regarding Social Security. Figures are percentage distributions.

Home, Family, Community

★ 12 ★

Importance of Family Life

Question: How would you rate the importance of having a good family life? Number surveyed: Women = 499; men = 502.

Characteristic of respondent	Very important	Somewhat important	Very unimportant	No opinion
U.S. Total	89%	10%	[1]	1%
Sex:				
Female	92%	7%	[1]	1%
Male	86%	14%	[1]	[1]
Age:				
18-29 years	90%	10%	[1]	[1]
30-49 years	87%	13%	[1]	[1]
50 and older	91%	7%	1%	1%

Source: George Gallup, Jr., *The Gallup Poll,* Report Nos. 282/283 (Princeton, NJ: The Gallup Poll, March/April, 1989), p. 39. Also in source: Other characteristics of respondents; trend since 1981. *Note:* 1. Less than 1%.

★ 13 ★

Importance of Values

Question: How would you rate the importance of following a strict moral code?
Number surveyed: women = 499; men = 502.

Characteristic of respondent	Very important	Somewhat important	Very unimportant	No opinion
U.S. Total	60%	36%	1%	3%
Sex:				
Women	66%	29%	1%	4%
Men	54%	42%	1%	3%
Age:				
18-29 years	53%	44%	2%	1%
30-49 years	58%	40%	1%	1%
50 and older	66%	26%	1	8%

Source: George Gallup, Jr., *The Gallup Report,* Report Nos. 282/283 (Princeton, NJ: The Gallup Poll, March/April, 1989), p. 38. Also in source: other characteristics of respondents; trend since 1981. *Note:* 1. Less than 1%.

★ 14 ★

Maternal Fears For Children

Mother's fears about their children. "Mothers worry more about immediate events over which they have little realistic control, and have less concern in areas in which parents can have influence" (e.g., "drugs, depression, too much TV, poor school performance, sexual promiscuity, or delinquency") (source).

Fear	% who worried
Abduction Actual incidence of kidnapping by non-family member: "about 1.5 per 10,000,000"	72%
Cancer Rate of cancer-related deaths in children under 15: 3 per 100,000	50%
Ear infections	64%
Reaction to immunizations	56%
Eating the right foods	64%
Homicide	41%
Sexual abuse	55%
Accidents	18%
Drugs	13%

Source: Gunnar B. Stickler, Margery Salter, Daniel D. Broughton, Anthony Alario, Norah M. Guttrecht, and Sidney W. Maurer, "Parents' Fears About Their Children Compared with Actual Risks," (abstract, Mayo Clinic and Mayo Foundation, Rochester, MN; and Rhode Island Hospital, Providence, RI, 1990). Four hundred mothers ages 16 to 52 rated how much they worried about a variety of issues.

★ 15 ★

Most Important Problem Facing the Community

Question: "What do you think is the most important problem facing the community you live in?" Responses by sex and race, 1986.

Problem	Total US	Sex		Race	
		Female	Male	White	Black
War	0%	0%	0%	0%	0%
Taxes	3%	3%	4%	4%	1%
Unemployment	17%	16%	18%	16%	17%
Economy, inflation	6%	5%	6%	6%	1%
Politicians inept	2%	1%	2%	2%	2%
Nuclear sites	0%	0%	0%	0%	0%
Environment, pollution	3%	3%	3%	3%	0%
Road maintenance	1%	2%	1%	1%	0%
Development	2%	2%	3%	3%	0%
Population, traffic	2%	1%	3%	2%	0%
Mass transit	0%	0%	0%	0%	0%
Welfare	1%	0%	1%	1%	0%
Health, AIDS	0%	1%	0%	0%	1%
Farmers	2%	2%	2%	3%	0%
Social Security, elderly	0%	0%	0%	0%	0%
Poor	1%	2%	0%	1%	1%
Crime	8%	8%	7%	7%	10%
Oil	1%	1%	2%	1%	0%
Homeless	1%	1%	0%	1%	2%
Minorities, race relations	1%	0%	1%	1%	0%
Education	3%	3%	2%	3%	0%
Housing	2%	2%	3%	2%	7%
Immigrants	1%	0%	1%	1%	0%
Gangs	1%	1%	1%	0%	6%
Labor	0%	0%	0%	0%	0%
Youth	0%	0%	0%	0%	0%
Morality, values	1%	2%	1%	1%	3%
Indifference, nobody cares	1%	1%	1%	1%	0%
Drugs	13%	14%	12%	12%	18%
Alcohol	1%	1%	0%	1%	0%

Source: "Attitudes toward the most improtant problem facing respondent's community," *Sourcebook of Criminal Justice Statistics - 1988,* 1989, p. 183. Primary source: Table adapted by SOURCEBOOK staff from tables provided by The New York Times/CBS News Poll.

★ 16 ★

Religious Influence on Menstrual Attitudes

Some results of a study of 121 women (18 Orthodox Mikveh attenders, 23 Orthodox Jewish non-attenders, 35 Protestants, and 45 Catholics) comparing their menstrual attitudes and symptoms.

A study of 121 women (18 Orthodox Mikveh attenders, 23 Orthodox Jewish Mikveh non-attenders, 35 Protestant, and 45 Catholic) compared menstrual attitudes and symptoms. Among the findings:

1. **Forty-one percent** of Mikveh attenders and **43.5%** of non-attenders acknowledged that their religion dictates that "menstruation makes women unclean," as compared to **2.2%** of Catholics and **0%** of Protestants.

2. **Fifty-two percent** of non-Mikveh attenders and **17.7%** of Mikveh attenders acknowledged the dictate that "men should be protected from menstruating women," as compared to **4.4%** of Catholics and **0%** of Protestants.

3. **Four percent** of non-Mikveh attenders (1) and **2.2%** of Catholics (1) endorsed the belief that "menstruation makes women less holy than men."

4. **Ninety-four percent** of Mikveh attenders and **43.5%** of non-attenders endorsed the belief that "women should refrain from sex during menstruation," compared to **20%** of Protestants and **13.3%** of Catholics.

Source: Barbara Olasov Rothbaum, PhD, and Joan Jackson, PhD, "Religious Influence on Menstrual Attitudes and Symptoms," *Women and Health* 161(1) (1990): 63-77.

★ 17 ★

Women's Fears of Becoming Homeless

Percentage of women who feared becoming homeless, by household income, based on a *Ms* magazine survey.

Household income	Percent who fear becoming homeless
Less than $15,000	44%
$15,000 to $24,999	41%
$25,000 to $34,999	28%
$35,000 to $49,999	24%
$50,000 to $74,999	20%
More than $75,000	14%

Source: "Smart Money: Ignorance is no longer bliss. Women are seeking financial expertise and economic independence," *Ms* 108 (November 1989): 51+. Approximately 23,000 women responded to the survey that appeared in November, 1988.

Politics and Government

★ 18 ★

Attitudes Toward Ronald Reagan

Question: Do you approve or disapprove of the way Ronald Reagan is handling his job as president? Number of respondents = 605 women, 608 men. Results of a telephone survey conducted December 27-29, 1988.

Characteristic of Respondent	Approve	Disapprove	No opinion
National total	63%	29%	8%
Sex:			
Women	59%	32%	9%
Men	67%	26%	7%
Age:			
18-29 years	71%	22%	7%
30-49 years	63%	30%	7%
50 and older	56%	33%	11%
65 and older	51%	38%	11%
Politics:			
Republican	93%	5%	2%
Democratic	38%	51%	11%
Independent	58%	31%	11%

Source: George Gallup, Jr., *The Gallup Report*, Report No. 280 (Princeton, NJ: The Gallup Poll, January 1989, p. 13). Also in source: other characteristics of respondents.

★ 19 ★

Candidate's Opinion on Abortion

Question: How important is a candidate's opinion when you decide how to vote in an election for governor or state legislture? Number surveyed: women = 621; men = 613.

Characteristic of respondent	One of the most important	Very important	Somewhat important	Not too important	No opinion
U.S. Total	14%	29%	32%	23%	2%
Sex:					
Female	17%	32%	31%	18%	2%
Male	11%	25%	33%	29%	2%
Age:					
18-29 years	16%	30%	36%	17%	1%

[Continued]

★ 19 ★

Candidate's Opinion on Abortion
[Continued]

Characteristic of respondent	One of the most important	Very important	Somewhat important	Not too important	No opinion
30-49 years	13%	27%	34%	25%	1%
50 and older	13%	30%	27%	26%	4%

Source: George Gallup, Jr., *The Gallup Report*, Report No. 289 (Princeton, NJ: The Gallup Poll, October 1989). Also in source: other characteristics of respondents; trend since 1979.

★ 20 ★

Government Efficiency

Answers to questions about how often government performs its duties efficiently and at the best possible cost.

Level of government	Almost all of the time	Most of the time	Some of the time	Hardly ever	Don't Know/ No Answer
Total Public					
Local government	5%	41%	37%	13%	4%
State government	3%	33%	47%	13%	4%
Federal government	2%	23%	48%	23%	4%
Females					
Local government	6%	44%	36%	10%	4%
State government	3%	34%	49%	10%	4%
Federal government	2%	24%	48%	22%	4%
Males					
Local government	5%	38%	37%	16%	4%
State government	3%	31%	46%	16%	4%
Federal government	2%	21%	49%	24%	4%

Source: "Changing Public Attitudes on Governments and Taxes, 1989," Tables 10, 11, and 12 (Washington, D.C., Advisory Commission on Intergovernmental Relations, 1988). Also in source: data for other years and by other characteristics of respondents.

Pornography

★ 21 ★

Pornography: 1973-1989

Responses to questions regarding pornography: 1973-1989.

Statements	Percent Agreeing with Statement by Year										
	1973	1975	1976	1978	1980	1983	1984	1986	1987	1988	1989
There should be laws against the distribution of pornography whatever the age.											
Female	48%	46%	48%	51%	49%	50%	49%	52%	51%	52%	49%
Male	36%	34%	32%	34%	32%	31%	30%	31%	26%	34%	30%
There should be laws against the distribution of pornography to persons under 18.											
Female	43%	44%	45%	44%	46%	46%	49%	45%	46%	44%	47%
Male	54%	53%	58%	56%	61%	64%	63%	65%	69%	60%	64%
There should be no laws forbidding the distribution of pornography.											
Female	9%	9%	6%	5%	5%	4%	3%	4%	3%	4%	3%
Male	10%	13%	11%	10%	8%	5%	7%	4%	5%	6%	7%
Number Surveyed:											
Female	786	813	808	878	805	893	853	843	815	546	581
Male	683	658	657	637	631	681	593	612	629	429	437
Sexually graphic materials lead to a breakdown in morals.											
Female	63%	60%	64%	64%	71%	66%	73%	72%	72%	71%	75%
Male	48%	53%	54%	54%	57%	56%	54%	58%	57%	58%	56%
Number Surveyed:											
Female	755	735	752	834	754	851	808	794	771	529	547
Male	661	618	627	617	604	655	579	591	603	412	419
Sexually graphic materials lead people to commit rape.											
Female	61%	65%	65%	67%	66%	66%	67%	66%	67%	69%	74%
Male	46%	50%	50%	53%	51%	51%	49%	54%	50%	51%	52%
Number Surveyed:											
Female	737	717	743	806	737	832	788	782	748	511	542
Male	653	618	613	610	591	644	560	578	580	398	413

Source: Selected from *An American Profile—Opinions and Behavior, 1972-1989,* p. 600,620,623 (Detroit: Gale Research Inc., 1990). Also in source: data by race and age. Primary source: General Social Survey. Question not asked in 1972, 1974, 1977, 1982, 1985.

Weapons

★ 22 ★

Banning Handguns

Respondents were asked, "Do you think there should or should not be a law that would ban the possession of handguns except by the police and other authorized persons?"

Characteristic of Respondent	Should	Should not	No opinion
U.S. Total	37%	59%	4%
Sex			
Female	45%	49%	6%
Male	28%	70%	2%
Age			
18 to 29 years	37%	60%	3%
30 to 49 years	34%	64%	2%
50 years and older	40%	54%	6%

Source: "Attitudes toward banning the possession of handguns except by the police and other authorized person, by demographic characteristics, United States, 1988," *Sourcebook of Criminal Justice Statistics 1989*, 1989, p. 177. Primary source: George Gallup, Jr., *The Gallup Report*, Report No. 275 (Princeton, NJ: The Gallup Poll, August 1988), p. 4. Table adapted by SOURCEBOOK staff. Also in source: data by other characteristics of respondents.

★ 23 ★

Banning Specific Gun Types

Respondents were asked if they would favor or oppose Federal legislation banning the manufacture, sale, and possession of cheap handguns, plastic, and assault guns.

Respondent characteristic	Ban cheap handguns		Ban plastic guns		Ban assault guns	
	Favor	Oppose	Favor	Oppose	Favor	Oppose
U.S. Total	71%	25%	75%	20%	72%	23%
Sex						
Female	73%	21%	75%	18%	74%	19%
Male	68%	30%	74%	22%	70%	27%
Age						
18 to 29 years	69%	29%	72%	26%	66%	29%
30 to 49 years	74%	24%	80%	17%	77%	20%
50 years and older	66%	26%	71%	20%	71%	21%

Source: "Attitudes toward Federal laws banning the manufacture, sale, and possession of firearms, by demographic characteristics, United States, 1989," *Sourcebook of Criminal Justice Statistics 1989*, 1989, p. 174. Primary source: George Gallup, Jr., *The Gallup Report*, Report Nos. 282-283 (Princeton, NJ: The Gallup Poll, March/April 1989), p. 4. Table adapted by SOURCEBOOK staff. "No opinion" category was omitted by Source.

Work

★ 24 ★

Supervisor Support for Child Care Needs

Employee perceptions on supervisor support for child care needs. Question: To what extent does your supervisor support you and your child-care needs?

Respondent	To a great extent	To some extent	To a small extent	Not at All
Women	32%	31%	20%	17%
Men	23%	32%	19%	27%

Source: John P. Fernandez, *The Politics and Reality of Family Care in Corporate America,* 1990, (Lexington, Mass: Lexington Books, 1990). Data were collected through a self-administered questionnaire; N=14,064 women and 12,140 men.

★ 25 ★

Teachers' Attitudes Toward Teaching

Responses of female public school teachers to survey questions concerning their willingness to each again, 1961 to 1986.

	1961	1966	1971	1976	1981	1986
Number of teachers, in thousands	1,408	1,710	2,055	2,196	2,184	2,207
Percentage female	68.7%	69.0%	65.7%	67.0%	66.9%	68.8%
Willingness to teach again						
Certainly would	49.9%	52.6%	44.9%	37.5%	21.8%	22.7%
Probably would	26.9%	25.4%	29.5%	26.1%	24.6%	26.3%
Chances about even	12.5%	12.9%	13.0%	17.5%	17.6%	19.8%
Probably would not	7.9%	7.1%	8.9%	13.4%	24.0%	22.0%
Certainly would not	2.8%	2.0%	3.7%	5.6%	12.0%	9.3%

Source: Selected from "Selected characteristics of public school teachers: Spring 1961 to spring 1986," *Digest of Education Statistics,* p. 72 (Washington, D.C.: National Center for Education Statistics, 1989). Primary source: National Education Association, *Status of the American Public School Teacher 1985-1986.* 1987. Washington, D.C.: NEA. Also in source: other characteristics of teachers. Data are based upon sample surveys of public school teachers. Because of rounding, percents may not add to 100.0.

Working Women

★ 26 ★

How Women Feel About Their Work

The attitudes of working women toward work, according to a survey of 1,000 working women over age 18 conducted for *Ladies' Home Journal*.

1. **Fifty-seven percent**, primarily women with young children, blue-collar jobs, and salaries under $15,000 a year, said they work because they have to.

2. **Twenty-seven percent**, primarily executives, said they work "because it makes them feel productive."

3. **Seven percent** work to be around people; **5%** work to "have something to do."

4. Of the **13%** who are their own bosses, most are professionals or over sixty.

5. **Two percent** said their bosses were "incompetent." **Thirty-four percent** felt they could do the boss's job.

6. **Seventy-nine percent** said they had not been held back because of their sex. **Eighteen percent** said they have been discriminated against. Although **86%** said they had never been sexually harassed at work, **more than one woman in ten** said she had been sexually harassed at work. Those most likely to say they had been harassed were those women under 45, earning between $15,000 and $35,000, living in the South or West.

7. The question, "If you were harassed, what did you do about it?" elicited the following answers:

   Dealt with the harasser myself (**61%**)
   Complained to personnel office or other authority (**21%**)
   Complained to my boss (**15%**)
   Left the job (**14%**)
   Ignored it because I didn't want to get in trouble or lose my job (**9%**)

Source: Selected from "The Roper Poll of the American Woman, Nine to Five," *Ladies' Home Journal* 106:March, 1989: 83+.

★ 27 ★

Opinions on Working Women: 1977-1989

Opinions on various issues relating to working women. Key to response codes: SA = Strongly agree; AG = Agree; DS = Disagree; SD = Strongly disagree; N = Number surveyed.

Statement	Sex	Response[1]	Year				
			1977	1985	1986	1988	1989
A working mother can establish just as secure and warm a relationship with her children as a mother who does not work.	F	SA	21%	28%	27%	29%	28%
		AG	34%	39%	40%	40%	41%
		DS	28%	24%	24%	22%	26%
		SD	17%	8%	8%	8%	5%

[Continued]

★ 27 ★

Opinions on Working Women: 1977-1989
[Continued]

Statement	Sex	Response[1]	Year				
			1977	1985	1986	1988	1989
		N	824	836	846	544	567
	M	SA	9%	13%	15%	17%	14%
		AG	33%	40%	41%	38%	45%
		DS	40%	'34%	37%	35%	32%
		SD	18%	13%	7%	10%	9%
		N	681	682	614	433	423
It is much better for everyone involved if the man is the achiever outside the home and the woman takes care of the home and family.	F	SA	18%	9%	11%	8%	9%
		AG	46%	37%	37%	31%	30%
		DS	29%	36%	38%	41%	40%
		SD	8%	18%	15%	19%	21%
		N	823	833	836	540	559
	M	SA	19%	11%	7%	11%	11%
		AG	50%	40%	41%	35%	32%
		DS	27%	41%	43%	41%	46%
		SD	4%	8%	9%	13%	11%
		N	680	669	608	424	418
A preschool child is likely to suffer if his or her mother works.	F	SA	19%	11%	11%	11%	9%
		AG	43%	36%	35%	32%	34%
		DA	32%	39%	42%	44%	45%
		SD	6%	14%	11%	14%	12%
		N	821	828	836	541	558
	M	SA	23%	15%	10%	11%	9%
		AG	51%	48%	48%	45%	46%
		DA	24%	33%	36%	37%	38%
		SD	3%	4%	6%	7%	7%
		N	677	671	606	424	416
Do you approve or diapprove of a married woman earning money in business or industry if she had a husband?	F	Approve	65%	86%	77%	79%	79%
		Disapprove	35%	14%	23%	21%	21%
		N	824	822	832	536	563
	M	Approve	68%	87%	79%	82%	79%
		Disapprove	32%	13%	21%	18%	21%
		N	682	666	610	425	419

[Continued]

★ 27 ★

Opinions on Working Women: 1977-1989
[Continued]

Statement	Sex	Response[1]	Year				
			1977	1985	1986	1988	1989
It is more important for a wife to help her husband's carrer than to have one herself.	F	SA	15%	7%	7%	4%	5%
		AG	45%	31%	30%	25%	24%
		DA	32%	42%	44%	46%	46%
		SD	7%	20%	18%	25%	25%
		N	812	814	836	536	559
	M	SA	12%	6%	5%	6%	6%
		AG	40%	31%	29%	28%	21%
		DA	42%	51%	52%	51%	60%
		SD	6%	12%	14%	15%	13%
		N	660	658	600	430	406

Source: Selected from *An American Profile—Opinions and Behavior, 1972-1989*, p. 529-48 (Detroit: Gale Research Inc., 1990). Primary source: General Social Survey. Also in source: data by race and age.

Youth and Young Adults

★ 28 ★

College Freshmen on Marijuana: 1970-1989

Percent of college freshmen agreeing strongly or somewhat that marijuana should be legalized.

Year	Legalize marijuana		
	Total	Female	Male
1970	38.4%	35.2%	41.0%
1971	38.7%	35.0%	41.7%
1972	46.6%	43.0%	49.6%
1973	48.2%	45.2%	50.9%
1974	46.7%	43.4%	49.7%
1975	47.2%	43.3%	50.7%
1976	48.9%	46.1%	51.6%
1977	52.9%	49.2%	56.6%
1978	49.5%	47.1%	52.1%
1979	46.0%	43.6%	48.6%
1980	39.3%	36.6%	42.1%
1981	34.0%	31.9%	36.3%
1982	29.4%	26.4%	32.5%
1983	25.7%	23.1%	28.4%
1984	22.9%	20.3%	25.8%
1985	21.8%	18.9%	24.8%
1986	21.3%	18.0%	25.0%
1987	19.3%	15.9%	23.1%

[Continued]

★ 28 ★

College Freshmen on Marijuana: 1970-1989
[Continued]

Year	Legalize marijuana		
	Total	Female	Male
1988	19.3%	16.4%	22.8%
1989	16.7%	13.7%	20.1%

Source: "College freshmen reporting that marihuana should be legalized, by sex, United States, 1968-89," *Sourcebook of Criminal Justice Statistics 1989,* 1989, p. 195. Primary source: Alexander W. Astin, Kenneth C. Green, and William S. Korn, *The American Freshman: Twenty Years Trends,* Higher Education Research Institute (Los Angeles: University of California, 1987), pp. 50, 74, 98; Alexander W. Astin et al., *The American Freshman: National Norms for Fall 1987,* Higher Education Research Institute (Los Angeles: University of California, 1987), pp 29, 45, 61; Alexander W. Astin et al., *The American Freshman: National Norms for Fall 1988,* Higher Education Research Institute (Los Angeles: University of California, 1988), pp. 29, 45, 61; Alexander W. Astin, William S. Korn, and Ellyne R. Berz, *The American Freshman: National Norms for Fall 1989,* Higher Education Research Institute (Los Angeles: University of California, 1989), pp. 25, 41, 57; and data provided by the Higher Education Research Institute, University of California, Los Angeles. Table adapted by SOURCEBOOK staff. Also in source: data for 1968 and 1969. The American Freshman Survey is conducted annually by the Cooperative Institution Research Program of the Higher Education Research Institute at the University of California, Los Angeles. Approximately 200,000 full-time students entering the freshman classes at a nationally-representative sample of two-year and four-year colleges and universities are surveyed.

★ 29 ★

College Freshmen on Various Topics
Survey responses of over 200,000 freshmen, fall 1989.

	Women	Men	Total
Agree strongly or somewhat that:			
Government is not doing enough to protect the consumer	71.5%	64.7%	68.4%
Government is not doing enough to promote disarmament	76.2%	58.8%	68.1%
Government is not doing enough to control pollution	87.6%	84.8%	86.3%
Taxes should be raised to reduce the federal deficit	25.5%	32.6%	28.8%
There is too much concern in the courts for the rights of criminals	65.5%	71.9%	68.5%
Military spending should be increased	19.6%	30.2%	24.5%
Abortion should be legal	65.5%	63.6%	64.7%
The death penalty should be abolished	23.8%	18.4%	21.3%
It is all right for two people who like each other to have sex even if they've known each other for a very short time	36.4%	65.1%	49.7%
Married women's activities are best confined to home and family	20.4%	32.3%	25.9%
Marijuana should be legalized	13.7%	20.1%	16.7%
Busing to achieve racial balance in schools is all right	56.0%	56.1%	56.0%
It is important to have laws prohibiting homosexual relationships	35.1%	57.3%	45.4%
Colleges should not invest in companies that do business in South Africa	44.2%	54.1%	48.8%
The chief benefit of college is that it increases one's earning power	66.8%	75.6%	70.9%
Employers should be allowed to require employees or job applicants to take drug tests	78.9%	76.5%	77.8%
The best way to control AIDS is through widespread, mandatory testing	67.5%	66.9%	67.2%
Just because a man thinks that a woman has "led him on" does not entitle him to have sex with her	92.8%	79.0%	86.4%

[Continued]

★ 29 ★

College Freshmen on Various Topics
[Continued]

	Women	Men	Total
Only volunteers should serve in the armed forces	50.7%	52.3%	51.5%
The government should do more to control the sale of handguns	87.6%	67.2%	78.2%
A national health-care plan is needed to cover everybody's medical costs	79.0%	72.1%	75.8%

Source: Chronicle of Higher Education Almanac, September 5, 1990, p. 14. Primary source: *The American Freshman: National Norms for Fall 1989*, by Alexander W. Astin, published by American Council on Education and University of California at Los Angeles. The statistics are based on a survey of 216,362 freshmen entering 403 two-year and four-year institutions in the fall of 1989. The figures were statistically adjusted to represent the total population of 1.6 million first-time, full-time freshmen. Because of rounding or multiple responses, figures may add to more than 100%.

★ 30 ★

College Students' Attitudes Toward Alcohol Abuse on Campus

Question: ...how much of a problem is alcohol abuse by students on this campus...?

Characteristic of respondent	Serious problem	Somewhat of a problem	Not too much of a problem	No problem at all	No opinion
Total United States	14%	39%	32%	7%	8%
Sex					
Female	11%	45%	28k%	7%	9%
Male	16%	34%	34%	8%	8%
Age					
18 years and under	21%	29%	40%	7%	3%
19 to 20 years	12%	47%	28%	6%	7%
21 to 22 years	14%	36%	36%	8%	6%
23 years and over	10%	38%	25%	10%	17%
Race					
White	13%	41%	31%	8%	7%
Nonwhite	16%	28%	34%	7%	15%
Class					
Freshman	18%	30%	34%	10%	8%
Sophomore	12%	40%	33%	9%	6%
Junior	9%	50%	32%	4%	5%
Senior	12%	51%	22%	4%	11%

Source: Selected from "College students' attitudes toward alcohol abuse as a problem on campus," *Sourcebook of Criminal Justice Statistics - 1988,* 1989, p. 188. Primary source: George Gallup, Jr., *The Gallup Report,* Report No. 265 (Princeton, NJ: The Gallup Poll, October 1987), p. 48. Also in source: Data by region, parents' income, alcohol or drug user. This survey was conducted by the Gallup Organization, Inc. for "Newsweek on Campus."

★ 31 ★

College Students' Attitudes Toward Drug Abuse

Question: ...how much of a problem is drug abuse by students on this campus...?

Characteristic of respondent	Serious problem	Somewhat of a problem	Not too much of a problem	No problem at all	No opinion
Total United States	7%	31%	34%	9%	19%
Sex					
Female	5%	35%	30%	9%	21%
Male	9%	27%	38%	10%	16%
Age					
18 years and under	8%	33%	35%	10%	14%
19 to 20 years	7%	29%	39%	8%	17%
21 to 22 years	7%	43%	23%	11%	16%
23 years and over	6%	23%	32%	9%	30%
Race					
White	6%	32%	35%	10%	17%
Nonwhite	10%	27%	25%	8%	30%
Class					
Freshman	8%	29%	33%	12%	18%
Sophomore	8%	23%	39%	10%	20%
Junior	6%	39%	38%	6%	11%
Senior	4%	47%	21%	10%	18%

Source: Selected from "College students' attitudes toward drug abuse as a problem on campus," *Sourcebook of Criminal Justice Statistics - 1988,* 1989, p. 188. Primary source: George Gallup, Jr., *The Gallup Report,* Report No. 265 (Princeton, NJ: The Gallup Poll, October 1987), p. 48. Also in source: data by region, parents' income, alcohol or drug user.

★ 32 ★

Eighth Graders' Attitudes About Selected Classes

Eighth graders' attitudes about selected classes: 1988.

| Class subject and attitude | Percent who agree with statement | | |
	All 8th graders	Female	Male
Mathematics			
Look forward to	56.6%	54.6%	58.7%
Afraid to ask questions	20.9%	23.2%	18.6%
Useful in my future	88.0%	86.9%	89.0%
English class			
Look forward to	56.9%	61.6%	52.0%
Afraid to ask questions	15.4%	15.3%	15.6%
Useful in my future	84.1%	87.6%	80.6%
Social studies class			
Look forward to	58.5%	55.0%	62.1%
Afraid to ask questions	15.1%	16.1%	14.1%

[Continued]

★ 32 ★

Eighth Graders' Attitudes About Selected Classes
[Continued]

Class subject and attitude	Percent who agree with statement		
	All 8th graders	Female	Male
Useful in my future	59.1%	57.3%	61.0%
Science class			
Look forward to	61.3%	57.5%	65.1%
Afraid to ask questions	14.9%	15.5%	14.2%
Useful in my future	68.7%	65.2%	72.3%

Source: Selected from "Eighth graders' attitudes about selected classes, by selected student and school characteristics: 1988," *Digest of Education Statistics,* p. 130 (Washington, D.C.: National Center for Education Statistics, 1989). Primary source: U.S. Department of Education, National Center for Education Statistics, "National Education Longitudinal Study of 1988" survey. Also in source: other characteristics of students and schools. Data are preliminary.

★ 33 ★

High-School Students' Satisfaction with School

Student satisfaction with various aspects of the local high school, 1990.

Aspect	Satisfied	Dissatisfied	Neutral
Classroom Instruction			
Female	30%	7%	13%
Male	25%	5%	12%
Number and Variety of Course Offerings			
Female	27%	16%	9%
Male	23%	10%	9%
Grading Practices and Policies			
Female	28%	9%	14%
Male	22%	7%	12%
School Rules, Regulations, Policies			
Female	19%	18%	13%
Male	15%	14%	12%
Library or Learning Center			
Female	29%	8%	13%
Male	23%	7%	12%
Laboratory Facilities			
Female	23%	10%	14%
Male	20%	8%	12%
Provisions for Special Help in Reading, Math, Etc.			
Female	19%	8%	11%
Male	15%	5%	11%
Adequacy of Programs in Career Education and Planning			
Female	21%	14%	13%
Male	17%	9%	13%

Source: Selected from "Student Satisfaction with Various Aspects of the Local High School," *ACT High School Profile Report,* p. 4 (Iowa City: American College Testing Program, 1990). Also in source: other aspects.

★ 34 ★

Importance of Values to Young Adults

Percent of high school seniors in 1972 and 1982, and four years later, who felt that certain life values were "very important," by sex: 1972-1976 and 1982-1986.

Value	Percent of 1972 seniors				Percent of 1982 seniors			
	1972		1976		1982		1986	
	Female	Male	Female	Male	Female	Male	Female	Male
Being successful in work	83.0	86.5	69.7	80.3	85.5	88.2	77.2	84.0
Having steady work	73.7	82.3	62.1	79.3	84.4	88.0	76.3	84.2
Having lots of money	9.8	26.0	9.4	17.7	24.1	41.3	16.9	27.8
Being a community leader	8.0	14.9	4.2	9.2	5.9	11.3	4.5	9.5
Correcting inequalities	31.1	22.5	17.1	16.2	11.7	11.8	10.9	10.7
Having children	-	-	-	-	47.0	37.0	56.2	41.4
Having a happy family life	85.7	78.6	86.4	84.2	86.3	81.6	87.8	86.8
Providing better opportunities for children	66.2	66.6	58.8	59.8	68.7	71.0	67.4	68.4
Living closer to parents or relatives	8.2	6.8	11.9	7.7	15.7	15.0	19.8	12.9
Moving from area	14.6	14.3	6.4	6.7	12.8	14.4	7.4	9.0
Having strong friendships	78.7	81.2	72.1	76.1	79.1	80.4	75.0	76.5
Having leisure time	-	-	60.1	65.4	68.8	70.2	68.9	70.1

Source: "Percent of high school seniors in 1972 and 1982, and four years later, who felt that certain life values were "very important," by sex: 1972-1976 and 1982-1986," *Youth Indicators 1988: Trends in the Well-Being of American Youth*, Volume 1, August 1988, p. 122. Primary source: U.S. Department of Education, National Center for Education Statistics, National Longitudinal Study and High School and Beyond Surveys.

★ 35 ★

Teens' Attitudes Toward Problems Facing Young People

Question: "What do you feel is the biggest problem facing people your age?"

Characteristic of respondent	Problem								
	Drug abuse	Alcohol abuse	Teenage pregnancy	Peer pressures	AIDS	Problems w/ parents	Maturity, independence	Unemployment	Teenager suicide
Total United States	54%	12%	11%	10%	5%	2%	2%	2%	2%
Sex									
Female	52%	14%	19%	12%	5%	3%	1%	1%	2%
Male	55%	10%	3%	8%	5%	2%	3%	3%	1%
Age									
13 to 15 years	53%	10%	10%	9%	4%	3%	3%	1%	2%
16 to 17 years	54%	15%	12%	11%	7%	1%	1%	3%	1%
City size									
Metropolitan	53%	8%	10%	12%	6%	5%	2%	2%	3%
Suburban	58%	14%	10%	9%	6%	1%	3%	3%	2%
Nonmetropolitan	51%	12%	12%	9%	4%	2%	2%	2%	1%
Race									

[Continued]

★ 35 ★

Teens' Attitudes Toward Problems Facing Young People
[Continued]

Characteristic of respondent	Problem								
	Drug abuse	Alcohol abuse	Teenage pregnancy	Peer pressures	AIDS	Problems w/ parents	Maturity, indepen-dence	Unemploy-ment	Teenager suicide
White	54%	14%	9%	10%	5%	2%	2%	2%	2%
Nonwhite	55%	2%	25%	12%	6%	4%	3%	1	1

Source: Selected from "Teenager attitudes toward problems facing young people," *Sourcebook of Criminal Justice Statistics - 1988,* 1989, p. 187. Primary source: George Gallup, Jr., *The Gallup Report,* Report No. 265 (Princeton, NJ: The Gallup Poll, October 1987), p. 43. Table adapted by SOURCEBOOK staff. Also in source: data by region. *Note:* 1. Less than 1%.

BUSINESS AND ECONOMICS

Corporate Officers/Executives

★ 36 ★

Executive Mothers

Female executives by marital status and presence of children.

Characteristic of female executive	%
Married, no children	9%
Married or divorced, with children	39%
Single	52%

Source: Elizabeth Ehrlich, "The Mommy Track: Juggling Kids and Careers in Corporate America Takes a Controversial Turn," *Business Week*, March 20, 1989, p. 126+. Primary source: Korn/Ferry International.

★ 37 ★

Minority Women Managers

Some statistics on minority women in management, 1988.

Percent of all employed managers who were black and female: **2.9%**
Number of black women employed in management: **407,000**
- black women in accounting and auditing management: **64,000**
- black women in education and related managment: **29,000**
- black women in public administration management: **28,000**

Percent of employed Hispanic women who were managers: **6.7%**
Percent of all employed managers who were female and Hispanic: **1.6%**
Number of Hispanic women employed in management: **221,000**
- Hispanic women in public administration management: **11,000**
- Hispanic women in financial management: **9,000**

Source: Facts on Working Women, No. 89-4, December 1989, p. 6.

★ 38 ★

The Glass Ceiling: Progress of Women Managers

Proportion of women managers at the nation's 1,000 largest companies, 1979 and 1990.

Year	% Female
1979	1%
1990	3%

Source: "Ten Years Later, the Glass Ceiling Gleams," *Newsweek*, September 3, 1990, p. 52. Primary source: Korn/Ferry International and UCLA Anderson Graduate School of Management. Based on a survey of 698 top executives at the 1,000 biggest companies.

★ 39 ★

Women CEOs

Number of chief executives of America's 1,000 largest public corporations, ranked by market value: **986.**

Number who are women: **2.**

Source: "The Corporate Elite: The Chief Executives of the 1000 most valuable publicly held U.S. Companies," *Business Week*, October 19, 1990, p. 55+.

★ 40 ★

Women Corporate Officers

Number of directors and highest executives at 799 major companies according to *Fortune* magazine, July 1990.

Sex	Number of Executives
Female	19
Male	3,993

Source: Peter T. Kilborn, "Labor Dept. Wants to Take on Job Bias in the Executive Suite: Threatens U.S. Contracts of Companies That Balk," *New York Times*, July 30, 1990, p. 1.

★ 41 ★

Women Corporate Officers by Race/Ethnicity

Distribution by race/ethnic group of corporate women officers employed in Fortune 1000 companies who responded to a survey in 1986.

Race/ethnicity	% of women corporate officers
White	96.7%
Native American	0.5%
Black	0.9%
Asian	1.9%

Source: Facts on Working Women, No. 89-4, December 1989, p. 7. Primary source: Women's Bureau, from data provided by Heidrick and Struggles, Inc.

★ 42 ★

Women Directors on Fortune Boards

Number of women directors on Fortune boards, 1980-1988.

Year	Total Number of Women Directors	Number of Director-ships held by Women	Number of Companies with Women on Their Boards	Percentage of Companies with Women on Their Boards
1980	317	461	378	29%
1981	336	490	398	30%
1982	336	499	405	31%
1983	367	527	427	33%
1984	313	455	364	36%
1985	339	511	407	41%
1986	395	576	439	44%
1987	424	628	471	47%
1988	426	632	474	47%

Source: Selected from "Historical Data on the Number of Women Directors on Fortune Boards, Selected Years, 1969-88 (in numbers)," *The American Woman 1990-91*, 1990, p. 388 (New York: W.W. Norton & Company, 1990). Primary source: Catalyst, 250 Park Avenue South, New York, NY 10003. Also in source: data for 1969-1979. Statistics for 1984-1988 are based on the new Fortune 1000 classification rather than the former Fortune 1350 classification and thus appear to have declined; figures actually reflect a proportionate increase.

★ 43 ★

Women Executives in High Technology

Number of executives and percent women in high-tech companies.

Job	Executives	Women
Chairman	2,937	1.9%
CEO	27,711	3.3%
VP Marketing	6,782	7.4%
VP Sales	18,681	5.6%
VP International	714	4.6%
VP Finance	18,644	6.8%
VP Information Systems	573	7.0%
VP Personnel	6,008	9.4%
VP Administration	1,453	17.7%
VP Purchasing	4,911	7.5%
VP Research/Development	19,829	3.3%
VP Manufacturing	8,098	3.7%
VP Engineering	2,612	1.1%
VP Tech Transfer	593	2.0%
VP Corporate Development	698	4.7%
VP Strategic Planning	442	5.2%
VP Other	4,231	7.1%
Total	124,917	5.1%

Source: USA Today, July 13, 1990, *Money* section. Primary source: Corp Tech. Based on the executive teams in 29,000 companies that make or develop high-tech products.

★ 44 ★

Women in the Auto Industry

A discussion of women in top management in the auto industry, reported in *Automotive News*.

According to the author, women hold less than **2%** of top management jobs in the auto industry. Some figures on women's representation:

3 vice presidents and **two outside directors** at General Motors are women

1 vice president at Ford Motor Company is a woman; there are **seven women in upper management positions**

Chrysler Corporation has **2 female outside directors and 1 woman vice president**

Mitsubishi has **4 women in upper management positions**

Volkswagen has **1 women in upper management**

Toyota has **no women in executive positions**

Source: Liz Pinto, "Women remain far away from auto industry's top jobs," *Automotive News*, March 11, 1991, p. 1+.

The Media

★ 45 ★

Advertising in Women's Magazines

Shares, by publication, of advertising in leading women's magazines. Shares represent percentages of group total ad pages (6,266) for the first half of 1990.

Title	Shares
Vogue	21.6%
Cosmopolitan	17.5%
Glamour	14.3%
Good Housekeeping	13.3%
Woman's Day	12.0%
McCall's	7.8%
Working Woman	7.6%
Soap Opera Digest	3.3%
Woman	2.4%

Source: Wall Street Journal, July 26, 1990, p. B1, from Publishers Information Bureau.

★ 46 ★

Circulation of Women's Publications

Women's periodicals with paid circulation over 500,000.

Title	Circulation
Canadian Living Magazine	515,756
Chatelaine	1,089,496
Cosmopolitan	2,778,497
Country Woman	650,000
Family Circle	5,212,555
First	2,000,000
Glamour	2,273,039
Good Housekeeping	5,114,774
Health	800,000
Ladies' Home Journal	5,117,712
Mademoiselle	1,141,271
McCall's	5,088,686
New Woman	1,390,830
Playgirl	600,000
SELF Magazine	1,173,440
Shape	794,675
True Story	1,240,252
Woman's Day	4,705,288
Working Woman Magazine	903,704

Source: Selected from *Gale Directory of Publications and Broadcast Media 1991*, p. 2691+ (Detroit: Gale Research Inc., 1991).

★ 47 ★

Media Reviews of Artists' Exhibitions

Percent of review space devoted to female versus male artists by medium, 1984-1987 (selected media).

Medium	Year	Females	Males
Artforum	1984	30%	70%
Art News	1984	32%	68%
Boston Review	1984	45%	55%
Los Angeles Times	1982-86	24%	76%
Los Angeles Herald Examiner	1983-86	10%	90%
Artscene	1982-86	32%	68%
Artweek	1982-86	30%	70%
High Performance, Issues 1-32	to 1986	38%	62%
Flash Art	1986	13%	87%
Artforum	1986	16%	86%[1]
Art in America	1986	24%	76%
Arts	1986	25%	75%

Source: Selected from "Media Review of Exhibitions by Gender," Eleanor Dickinson, "Gender Discrimination in the Art Field: Incomplete and random statistics of number of artists, art faculty, art criticism, art exhibitions, etc. which may be useful in indicating patterns and trends," 1990, p. 9 (Washington, D.C.: Artists Equity Association, 1990). Reprinted by permission. Also in source: data for other media and for 1972-1984. Related Reading: Elsa Honig Fine, "Women in Art," *The American Woman 1990-91*, 1990, p. 238+ (New York: W.W. Norton & Company, 1990). *Note:* 1. Per source.

Women Business Owners

★ 48 ★

Asian American Women Business Owners

Characteristics of businesses and owners, Asian American women business owners, 1982.

Characteristic of business/owner	Percent
Characteristics of businesses:	
Home-based	51%
No employees	88%
1 to 4 employees	8%
Employed women	9%
Employed minorities	7%
Exported goods or services outside U.S.	12%[1]
Sales less than $5,000	47%
Sales between $5,000 and $49,999	39%
Profits less than $5,000	39%
Profits between $5,000 and $19,999	25%
Net loss less than $5,000	19%
100% of 1982 income came from business	20%
Had no initial capital	30%

[Continued]

★ 48 ★

Asian American Women Business Owners
[Continued]

Characteristic of business/owner	Percent
Began with less than $5,000	35%
Had no equity capital	60%
Family as dominant source of equity capital	23%
Firm's initial debt ratio zero	61%
Firms debt between 91% and 100%	8%
Debt sources:	
Bank	46%
Family	33%
Friends	18%
Former owners	15%
Business owned in 1982 survived until 1986	58%
Discontinued operations due to:	
Insufficient profit	42%
Personal reasons	47%
Characteristics of Asian American women business owners:	
Between the ages of 25 and 54	67%
Married	74%
At least 1 year of college	71%
Business owner less than 7 years	87%
Business owner less than 1 year	36%
Founder of the firm	72%
Previously owned another business	12%
Had previous paid employment	86%
Had no managerial experience in paid employment	62%
Had attended business courses or seminars	53%
Role models:	
Had a role model	36%
Had worked for a relative	30%

Source: Facts on Working Women, U.S. Department of Labor Women's Bureau, No. 89-8, December 1989. Primary source: *Minorities, Women, Veterans and the 1982 Characteristics of Business Owners Survey, A Preliminary Analysis*, Faith Ando and Associates, Haverford, Pennsylvania, September 1988; and U.S. Small Business Administration. For a further discussion of the results of the 1982 Characteristics of Business Owners, see Faith H. Ando, "Women in Business," *The American Woman 1990-91: A Status Report*, p. 222-230. *Note:* 1. Approximate figure.

★ 49 ★

Black Women Business Owners
Characteristics of businesses and owners, Black-owned businesses.

Characteristic of business/owner	Percent
Characteristics of businesses:	
Home-based	60%
No employees	96%

[Continued]

★ 49 ★

Black Women Business Owners
[Continued]

Characteristic of business/owner	Percent
1 to 4 employees	3%
Employed women	3%
Employed minorities	4%
Exported goods or services outside U.S.	7%[1]
Sales less than $5,000	57%
Sales between $5,000 and $24,999	34%
Profits less than $5,000	46%
Profits between $5,000 and $19,999	21%
Net loss less than $5,000	24%
100% of 1982 income came from business	18%
Had no initial capital	43%
Began with less than $5,000	44%
Had no equity capital	73%
Family as dominant source of equity capital	12%
Firm's initial debt ratio zero	71%
Firms debt between 91% and 100%	9%
Debt sources:	
Bank	50%
Family	27%
Friends	14%
Business owned in 1982 survived until 1986	50%[1]
Discontinued operations due to:	
Insufficient profit	41%
Personal reasons	47%
Characteristics of black women business owners:	
Between the ages of 25 and 54	71%
Married	55%
At least 1 year of college	51%
Business owner less than 7 years	72%
Business owner less than 1 year	29%
Founder of the firm	72%
Previously owned another business	8%
Had previous paid employment	82%
Had no managerial experience in paid employment	63%
Had attended business courses or seminars	65%
Role models:	
Had close relatives who owned a business	22%
Had worked for the relative	29%
Had a role model	39%

Source: Facts on Working Women, U.S. Department of Labor Women's Bureau, No. 89-7, September 1989. Primary source: *Minorities, Women, Veterans and the 1982 Characteristics of Business Owners Survey, A Preliminary Analysis*, Faith Ando and Associates, Haverford, Pennsylvania, September 1988; and U.S. Small Business Administration. For a further discussion of the results of the 1982 Characteristics of Business Owners, see Faith H. Ando, "Women in Business," *The American Woman 1990-91: A Status Report*, p. 222-230. *Note:* 1. Approximate value.

★ 50 ★

Hispanic Women Business Owners

Characteristics of businesses and owners: Hispanic origin women business owners, 1982.

Characteristic of business/owner	Percent
Characteristics of businesses:	
Home-based	55%
No employees	91%
1 to 4 employees	6%
Employed women and minorities	6%
Exported goods or services outside U.S.	9%
Sales less than $5,000	48%
Sales between $5,000 and $24,999	36%
Profits less than $5,000	45%
Profits between $5,000 and $19,999	26%
Net loss less than $5,000	18%
100% of 1982 income came from business	23%
Had no initial capital	40%
Began with less than $5,000	39%
Had no equity capital	73%
Family as dominant source of equity capital	13%
Firm's initial debt ratio zero	65%
Firms debt between 91% and 100%	12%
Debt sources:	
Bank	51%
Family	32%
Business owned in 1982 survived until 1986	55%
Discontinued operations due to:	
Insufficient profit	43%
Personal reasons	47%
Characteristics of Hispanic women business owners:	
Between the ages of 25 and 54	78%
Married	72%
At least 1 year of college	39%
Business owner less than 7 years	78%
Business owner less than 1 year	29%
Founder of the firm	74%
Previously owned another business	9%
Had previous paid employment	84%
Had no managerial experience in paid employment	69%
Had attended business courses or seminars	49%
Role models:	
Had close relatives who owned a business	29%

[Continued]

★ 50 ★

Hispanic Women Business Owners
[Continued]

Characteristic of business/owner	Percent
Had worked for a relative	29%
Had a role model	39%

Source: Facts on Working Women, U.S. Department of Labor Women's Bureau, No. 89-6, December 1989. Primary source: *Minorities, Women, Veterans and the 1982 Characteristics of Business Owners Survey, A Preliminary Analysis*, Faith Ando and Associates, Haverford, Pennsylvania, September 1988; and U.S. Small Business Administration. For a further discussion of the results of the 1982 Characteristics of Business Owners, see Faith H. Ando, "Women in Business," *The American Woman 1990-91: A Status Report*, p. 222-230.

★ 51 ★

Native American Business Owners

Characteristics of businesses and owners, Native American and Alaska Native businesses.

Characteristic of business/owner	Percent
Characteristics of businesses:	
Home-based	69%
No employees	94%
Employed women	5%
Employed minorities	3%
Exported goods or services outside U.S.	11%
Sales less than $5,000	59%
Sales between $5,000 and $24,999	28%
Profits less than $5,000	49%
Profits between $5,000 and $19,999	25%
Net loss less than $5,000	19%
100% of 1982 income came from business	21%
Had no initial capital	50%[1]
Began with less than $5,000	33%
Had no equity capital	75%
Family as dominant source of equity capital	11%
Firm's initial debt ratio zero	68%
Firm's debt between 91% and 100%	10%
Debt sources:	
Bank	46%
Family	22%
Business owned in 1982 survived until 1986	54%
Discontinued operations due to:	
Insufficient profit	42%
Personal reasons	47%
Characteristics of American Indian/Alaska Native women business owners:	
Between the ages of 25 and 54	82%
Married	70%

[Continued]

★ 51 ★

Native American Business Owners
[Continued]

Characteristic of business/owner	Percent
At least 1 year of college	38%
Business owner less than 7 years	80%
Business owner less than 1 year	31%
Founder of the firm	70%
Previously owned another business	10%
Had previous paid employment	90%
Had no managerial experience in paid employment	63%
Had attended business courses or seminars	45%
Role models:	
Had close relatives who owned a business	23%
Had worked for the relative	31%
Had a role model	39%

Source: Facts on Working Women, U.S. Department of Labor Women's Bureau, No. 89-9, December 1989. Primary source: *Minorities, Women, Veterans and the 1982 Characteristics of Business Owners Survey, A Preliminary Analysis*, Faith Ando and Associates, Haverford, Pennsylvania, September 1988; and U.S. Small Business Administration. For a further discussion of the results of the 1982 Characteristics of Business Owners, see Faith H. Ando, "Women in Business," *The American Woman 1990-91: A Status Report*, p. 222-230. *Note:* 1. Approximate value.

★ 52 ★

States with Largest Sales and Receipts, Women-Owned Businesses

State and rank	Women-owned businesses, 1987					
	All firms		Firms with paid employees			
	Firms (number)	Sales and receipts ($1,000)	Firms (number)	Sales and receipts ($1,000)	Employees (number)	Annual payroll ($1,000)
1. California	559,821	31,026,855	73,164	21,997,497	311,273	4,130,687
2. New York	284,912	29,969,920	43,729	25,172,731	268,070	4,610,254
3. Florida	221,361	16,828,094	39,496	13,562,428	195,448	2,430,236
4. Illinois	177,057	13,884,278	25,464	11,607,789	149,164	2,137,522
5. New Jersey	117,373	13,553,517	19,389	11,470,775	124,665	2,129,396
6. Texas	298,138	13,384,958	40,421	9,716,787	143,861	1,753,064
7. Pennsylvania	167,362	13,339,231	25,631	11,067,283	147,109	1,880,437
8. Massachusetts	111,376	11,139,810	13,885	9,455,887	107,865	1,696,101
9. Indiana	89,949	8,913,422	16,571	8,006,788	115,173	1,397,603
10. Ohio	154,084	8,872,169	22,007	7,220,878	116,798	1,370,860

Source: "Statistics for Women-Owned Firms by State: 1987 and 1982," *Women-Owned Businesses*, 1990, p. 8 (Washington, D.C.: U.S. Bureau of the Census, September 1990).

★ 53 ★

States with the Most Asian American Women Business Owners

The most Asian American women business owners in 1982.

State	Percent of businesses
California	40%
Hawaii	11%
New York	8%
Texas	6%
Illinois	4%
Washington	3%

Source: Facts on Working Women, U.S. Department of Labor Women's Bureau, No. 89-8, December 1989. Primary source: *Minorities, Women, Veterans and the 1982 Characteristics of Business Owners Survey, A Preliminary Analysis*, Faith Ando and Associates, Haverford, Pennsylvania, September 1988; and U.S. Small Business Administration. For a further discussion of the results of the 1982 Characteristics of Business Owners, see Faith H. Ando, "Women in Business," *The American Woman 1990-91: A Status Report*, p. 222-230.

★ 54 ★

States with the Most Black Women Business Owners in 1982

State	Percent of businesses
California	14%
Texas	9%
New York	9%
Maryland	6%
Illinois	5%
Ohio	5%

Source: Facts on Working Women, U.S. Department of Labor Women's Bureau, No. 89-7, September 1989. Primary source: *Minorities, Women, Veterans and the 1982 Characteristics of Business Owners Survey, A Preliminary Analysis*, Faith Ando and Associates, Haverford, Pennsylvania, September 1988; and U.S. Small Business Administration. For a further discussion of the results of the 1982 Characteristics of Business Owners, see Faith H. Ando, "Women in Business," *The American Woman 1990-91: A Status Report*, p. 222-230.

★ 55 ★

States with the Most Hispanic Women Business Owners in 1982

State	Percent of businesses
California	33%
Texas	23%
Florida	12%
New York	6%

[Continued]

★ 55 ★

States with the Most Hispanic Women Business Owners in 1982
[Continued]

State	Percent of businesses
New Mexico	4%
Arizona	3%

Source: Facts on Working Women, U.S. Department of Labor Women's Bureau, No. 89-6, December 1989. Primary source: *Minorities, Women, Veterans and the 1982 Characteristics of Business Owners Survey, A Preliminary Analysis*, Faith Ando and Associates, Haverford, Pennsylvania, September 1988; and U.S. Small Business Administration. For a further discussion of the results of the 1982 Characteristics of Business Owners, see Faith H. Ando, "Women in Business," *The American Woman 1990-91: A Status Report*, p. 222-230.

★ 56 ★

States with the Most Native American Women Business Owners
The six States with the most sole proprietorships owned by American Indian/ Alaska Native women business owners in 1982.

State	Percent of businesses
California	19%
Oklahoma	11%
North Carolina	9%
Alaska	6%
Texas	5%
Colorado	4%

Source: Facts on Working Women, U.S. Department of Labor Women's Bureau, No. 89-9, December 1989. Primary source: *Minorities, Women, Veterans and the 1982 Characteristics of Business Owners Survey, A Preliminary Analysis*, Faith Ando and Associates, Haverford, Pennsylvania, September 1988; and U.S. Small Business Administration. For a further discussion of the results of the 1982 Characteristics of Business Owners, see Faith H. Ando, "Women in Business," *The American Woman 1990-91: A Status Report*, p. 222-230.

★ 57 ★

Women Business Owners

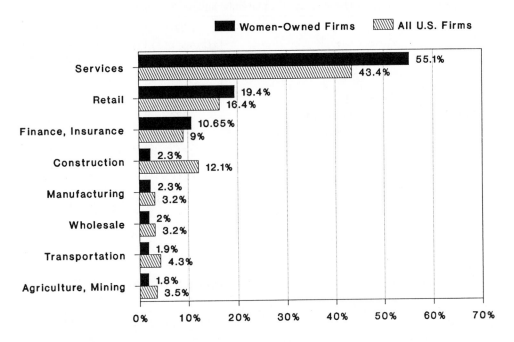

Facts about women-owned businesses, 1987.

Major industry group	All firms		Firms with paid employees			
	Firms (number)	Sales and receipts ($1,000)	Firms (number)	Sales and receipts ($1,000)	Employees (number)	Annual payroll ($1,000)
All industries	4,114,787	278,138,117	618,198	224,006,218	3,102,685	40,884,633
Agricultural services, forestry, fishing	47,979	1,932,818	9,377	1,291,282	24,689	297,919
Mining	26,420	1,933,822	1,942	1,428,180	11,992	271,946
Construction	94,308	20,302,124	36,178	17,832,436	180,338	3,985,259
Manufacturing	93,960	30,914,089	26,989	29,933,879	363,938	6,949,963
Transportation and public utilities	79,768	10,936,278	19,083	9,488,317	106,388	1,798,272
Wholesale trade	82,513	42,804,558	22,691	40,324,930	187,833	4,068,924
Retail trade	798,692	85,417,525	199,302	74,424,387	1,090,697	9,764,491
Finance, insurance, and real estate	437,360	17,833,402	36,741	9,326,301	109,312	1,860,570
Services	2,269,028	61,123,430	253,276	38,670,269	1,015,971	11,624,739
Industries not classified	184,759	4,940,071	12,619	1,286,237	11,527	262,550

Source: "Statistics for Women-Owned Firms by Major Industry Group: 1987 and 1982," *Women-Owned Businesses*, 1990, p. 7 (Washington, D.C.: U.S. Bureau of the Census, September 1990). Also in source: data for 1982.

★ 58 ★

Women-Owned Businesses: 1980-1986

Women-owned businesses by industry (in thousands) and percent change 1980-1986.

Industry	1986 (thousands)	1980 (thousands)	% change 1980-1986
Total	4,121	2,535	62.5%
Agriculture, forestry, fishing	65	31	110.9%
Mining, construction, manufacturing	224	84	165.9%
Transportation, communications, elec. utilities	52	28	86.1%
Wholesale and retail trade	975	825	18.2%
Finance, insurance, real estate	451	355	27.2%
Services	2,355	1,213	94.2%

Source: Facts on Working Women, U.S. Department of Labor Women's Bureau, No. 89-5. December 1989.

★ 59 ★

Women-Owned Firms and Receipts for 10 Largest MSAs

Firms and receipts in 1987.

Metropolitan Statistical Area	Women-Owned Firms-1987	
	Number (thousands)	Receipts (millions)
Los Angeles-Long Beach, CA PMSA	162.4	$10,775
New York, NY PMSA	136.2	$17,314
Chicago, IL PMSA	89.4	$9,195
Washington DC-MD-VA MSA	78.7	$4,940
Philadelphia, PA-NJ PMSA	68.0	$6,749
Houston, TX PMSA	59.9	$2,653
Boston, MA PMSA	59.0	$7,545
Detroit, MI PMSA	58.8	$4,183
Dallas, TX PMSA	55.5	$2,722
Anaheim-Santa Ana, CA PMSA	54.4	$3,266

Source: "Women-Owned Firms and Receipts for 10 Largest Metropolitan Statistical Areas: 1987," Women-Owned Businesses, p. 6 (Washington, D.C.: U.S. Bureau of the Census, September 1990).

★ 60 ★

Women-Owned and Men-Owned Businesses

Characteristics of women-owned businesses and owners compared to men-owned businesses and owners, 1982.

Characteristic of business/owner	Women-Owned	Men-Owned
Characteristics of businesses:		
Home-based	56%	51%
No employees	84%	76%
Employed women	11%	NA

[Continued]

★ 60 ★

Women-Owned and Men-Owned Businesses
[Continued]

Characteristic of business/owner	Women-Owned	Men-Owned
Employed minorities	4%	NA
Business acquired in 1982	20%	15%
Acquired before 1960	6%	11%
Had no initial capital	75%	66%
Did not borrow because capital not required	36%	26%
Characteristics of business owners:		
Between the ages of 25 and 54	69%	67%
Aged 55 to 64	16%	18%
Aged 65 and over	8%	9%
Married	71%	82%
At least a high school education	86%	83%
At least 1 year of college	52%	NA
Owner was original founder of business	75% (approx)	NA
Owner purchased business (not a gift or marital acquisition)	13%	NA
Previously owned another business	14%	22%
Had attended business courses or seminars	63%	NA

Source: Facts on Working Women, U.S. Department of Labor Women's Bureau, No. 89-5, December 1989. Primary source: *1982 Characteristics of Business Owners, CB082-1, Bureau of the Census*, U.S. Department of Commerce, issued August 1987. For a further discussion of the results of the 1982 Characteristics of Business Owners, see Faith H. Ando ,"Women in Business," *The American Woman 1990-91: A Status Report*, p. 222-230.

Women-Owned Businesses

★ 61 ★

Women-Owned Businesses by State

Facts about women-owned businesses, by State, 1987.

Geographic Area	Women-owned businesses, 1987					
	All firms		Firms with paid employees			
	Firms (number)	Sales and receipts ($1,000)	Firms (number)	Sales and receipts ($1,000)	Employees (number)	Annual payroll ($1,000)
United States	4,114,787	278,138,117	618,198	224,006,218	3,102,685	40,884,633
Alabama	48,018	3,624,355	9,184	3,037,188	43,141	525,917
Alaska	13,976	829,326	1,929	617,879	7,215	125,285
Arizona	60,567	2,910,886	8,947	2,192,859	37,881	429,262
Arkansas	35,469	2,007,652	6,415	1,607,384	25,392	261,390
California	559,821	31,026,855	73,164	21,997,497	311,273	4,130,687
Colorado	89,411	4,260,547	12,750	3,277,813	53,798	658,882

[Continued]

★ 61 ★

Women-Owned Businesses by State
[Continued]

| Geographic Area | Women-owned businesses, 1987 | | | | | |
| | All firms | | Firms with paid employees | | | |
	Firms (number)	Sales and receipts ($1,000)	Firms (number)	Sales and receipts ($1,000)	Employees (number)	Annual payroll ($1,000)
Connecticut	60,924	5,319,710	9,297	4,237,344	51,495	825,588
Delaware	9,727	753,238	1,782	602,687	9,617	113,500
District of Colombia	10,987	774,019	1,230	584,863	8,343	156,761
Florida	221,361	16,828,094	39,496	13,562,428	195,448	2,430,236
Georgia	88,050	5,873,682	14,459	4,654,107	67,749	839,127
Hawaii	21,696	856,930	2,404	546,087	9,548	105,425
Idaho	18,973	813,043	3,076	639,282	10,448	105,770
Illinois	177,057	13,884,278	25,464	11,607,789	149,164	2,137,522
Indiana	89,949	8,913,422	16,571	8,006,788	115,173	1,397,603
Iowa	53,592	2,904,611	8,600	2,486,473	41,037	443,039
Kansas	53,505	2,660,785	7,182	2,154,908	31,015	352,572
Kentucky	53,454	3,265,168	8,595	2,648,483	40,767	434,037
Louisiana	55,852	2,961,708	8,386	2,269,000	36,306	410,380
Maine	23,922	1,634,638	4,003	1,368,098	20,711	267,850
Maryland	81,891	5,508,587	10,288	4,416,225	61,829	849,799
Massachusetts	111,376	11,139,810	13,885	9,455,887	107,865	1,696,101
Michigan	133,958	7,889,112	18,565	6,375,374	92,533	1,187,941
Minnesota	88,137	4,991,493	12,368	4,072,685	65,034	783,012
Mississippi	28,976	2,062,007	6,109	1,695,149	24,279	257,563
Missouri	87,658	5,349,139	13,458	4,452,869	64,403	770,351
Montana	17,747	930,377	3,256	754,356	12,538	117,895
Nebraska	32,285	1,649,048	5,048	1,361,036	21,442	234,914
Nevada	18,831	1,413,558	2,869	1,147,722	17,546	228,425
New Hampshire	22,713	1,857,769	3,855	1,544,697	20,036	292,184
New Jersey	117,373	13,553,517	19,389	11,470,775	124,665	2,129,396
New Mexico	25,397	1,166,312	4,182	907,012	15,592	159,938
New York	284,912	29,969,920	43,729	25,172,731	268,070	4,610,254
North Carolina	93,532	6,813,158	15,166	5,698,499	85,825	1,057,189
North Dakota	12,689	571,701	2,268	475,712	8,526	82,007
Ohio	154,084	8,872,169	22,007	7,220,878	116,798	1,370,860
Oklahoma	63,690	2,947,868	8,609	2,206,514	35,516	397,101
Oregon	58,941	4,279,167	9,529	3,657,505	46,222	572,658
Pennsylvania	167,362	13,339,231	25,631	11,067,283	147,109	1,880,437
Rhode Island	14,517	1,340,182	2,488	1,123,399	15,667	227,064
South Carolina	42,604	2,949,555	7,524	2,383,926	37,934	465,061
South Dakota	13,374	726,047	2,233	618,391	9,800	96,082
Tennessee	67,448	4,226,269	11,168	3,370,530	51,353	614,443
Texas	298,138	13,384,958	40,421	9,716,787	143,861	1,753,064

[Continued]

★ 61 ★

Women-Owned Businesses by State
[Continued]

	Women-owned businesses, 1987					
	All firms		Firms with paid employees			
Geographic Area	Firms (number)	Sales and receipts ($1,000)	Firms (number)	Sales and receipts ($1,000)	Employees (number)	Annual payroll ($1,000)
Utah	29,810	1,392,426	3,885	1,093,769	18,478	212,627
Vermont	13,802	766,092	2,508	618,480	10,277	112,946
Virginia	94,416	5,951,516	13,755	4,783,510	72,886	927,966
Washington	90,285	4,689,046	13,218	3,733,756	56,993	709,599
West Virginia	22,549	1,114,228	3,668	890,779	14,567	148,069
Wisconsin	69,185	4,667,000	12,192	3.998,151	62,419	718,192
Wyoming	10,796	523,908	1,993	422,874	7,101	70,662

Source: "Statistics for Women-Owned Firms by State: 1987 and 1982," *Women-Owned Businesses*, 1990, p. 8 (Washington, D.C.: U.S. Bureau of the Census, September 1990). Also in source: data for 1982.

CRIME, LAW ENFORCEMENT, AND LEGAL JUSTICE

Arrests and Convictions

★ 62 ★

Arrest Trends: 1980 and 1989

Arrests, by offense, total and for persons under 18, 1980 and 1989.

Offense charged	Females				Males			
	Total		Under 18		Total		Under 18	
	1980	1989	1980	1989	1980	1989	1980	1989
Total	1,044,420	1,544,336	286,127	289,399	5,608,028	6,950,843	1,123,067	1,027,567
Murder and nonnegligent manslaughter	1,588	1,676	96	114	11,148	12,434	1,093	1,619
Forcible rape	166	254	58	66	19,966	23,352	2,857	3,514
Robbery	7,394	9,567	2,271	2,105	95,427	101,385	29,328	22,812
Aggravated assault	22,252	36,553	3,944	5,135	158,131	242,399	22,970	30,852
Burglary	21,704	25,747	9,825	7,094	313,108	252,673	139,979	79,020
Larceny-theft	227,248	297,334	77,106	75,239	542,147	660,274	214,980	201,295
Motor vehicle theft	8,327	14,424	4,357	5,948	87,859	129,483	38,132	52,770
Arson	1,550	1,588	588	492	11,337	9,853	5,169	4,475
Violent crime[1]	31,400	48,050	6,369	7,420	284,672	379,570	56,248	58,797
Property crime[2]	258,829	339,093	91,876	88,773	954,451	1,052,283	398,260	337,560
Crime Index total[3]	290,229	387,143	98,245	96,193	1,239,123	1,431,853	454,508	396,357
Other assaults	44,009	87,159	11,857	18,586	271,329	465,552	44,268	62,940
Forgery and counterfeiting	16,063	21,176	2,011	1,477	35,701	41,475	4,706	3,233
Fraud	78,017	102,570	1,602	2,379	110,133	124,713	4,225	5,950
Embezzlement	1,689	4,252	190	438	4,308	6,581	557	477
Stolen property; buying, receiving, possessing	9,056	13,632	2,309	2,568	77,936	103,302	24,260	26,421
Vandalism	14,391	20,435	6,574	6,599	151,996	166,520	75,676	67,666
Weapons; carrying, possessing, etc.	7,329	10,085	996	1,555	98,828	122,471	16,854	22,396
Prostitution and commercialized vice	38,366	47,289	1,435	526	18,916	21,274	687	361
Sex offenses (except forcible rape and prostitution)	2,867	4,854	555	760	41,879	58,729	7,668	9,737
Drug abuse violations	51,125	141,303	11,969	8,152	326,050	710,802	59,570	61,346
Gambling	3,077	2,081	52	20	26,913	10,831	874	537
Offenses against family and children	3,383	6,707	400	548	29,182	31,878	749	957
Driving under the influence	87,624	120,806	2,187	1,530	811,636	877,297	18,082	9,773
Liquor laws	44,136	72,298	22,212	24,252	244,801	307,400	74,361	61,972
Drunkenness	58,334	50,174	4,127	2,228	698,853	463,305	26,072	10,542
Disorderly conduct	61,597	90,002	14,034	14,511	346,652	374,538	61,153	57,229
Vagrancy	2,714	2,745	436	224	19,216	19,924	2,630	1,386
All other offenses (except traffic)	166,654	292,207	41,176	39,435	979,416	1,531,171	171,007	147,060

[Continued]

44

★ 62 ★

Arrest Trends: 1980 and 1989
[Continued]

Offense charged	Females				Males			
	Total		Under 18		Total		Under 18	
	1980	1989	1980	1989	1980	1989	1980	1989
Suspicion (not included in totals)	1,225	1,338	352	259	7,995	6,781	1,560	968
Curfew and loitering law violations	11,057	12,963	11,057	12,963	37,349	38,649	37,349	38,649
Runaways	52,703	54,455	52,703	54,455	37,811	42,578	37,811	42,578

Source: Selected from "Total Arrest Trends, Sex, 1980-1989," *Crime in the United States 1989*, p. 177 (August 5, 1990). Also in source: data for males. Based on reports from 5,928 agencies. *Notes:* 1. Violent crimes are offenses of murder, forcible rape, robbery, and aggravated assault. 2. Property crimes are offenses of burglary, larceny-theft, motor vehicle theft, and arson. 3. Includes arson.

★ 63 ★

Average Sentence for Convicted Offenders
Average incarceration sentence lengths imposed, in months, by offense and offender characteristics, 1986.

Offender characteristics	Average sentence length in months for offenders convicted of:						
	All offenses	Violent offenses	Property offenses		Drug offenses	Public order offenses	
			Fraudulent	Other		Regulatory	Other
All offenders[1]	52.0	128.6	32.6	37.4	62.0	41.7	30.5
Sex							
Female	32.2	72.4	23.4	27.9	40.0	34.9	19.9
Male	55.3	133.0	34.4	38.9	64.7	39.9	33.8
Race							
White	51.7	130.6	33.6	39.8	62.4	40.7	31.5
Black	55.3	147.1	30.5	35.0	61.0	34.6	38.0
Other	58.2	91.8	25.5	24.8	71.6	-	30.5
Ethnicity							
Hispanic	49.4	111.9	31.7	36.6	64.3	36.4	22.2
Non-Hispanic	53.9	132.9	32.6	37.8	61.5	40.4	37.8
Age							
16-18 years	38.6	115.1	-	27.2	37.6	-	8.1
19-20 years	37.5	88.7	20.8	23.6	38.5	22.4	24.8
21-30 years	47.6	120.4	27.8	35.1	50.2	44.4	29.0
31-40 years	57.9	144.5	33.2	42.9	67.4	42.7	36.6
Over 40 years	56.7	148.7	37.5	39.4	78.0	32.8	36.0

Source: Selected from "Average incarceration sentence lengths imposed, by offense and offender characteristics, 1986," *Compendium of Federal Justice Statistics, 1986*, 1990, p. 43. Also in source: data by education, marital status, employment status at arrest, annual income, criminal record, drug abuse history. *Note:* 1. Includes offenders for whom these characteristics are unknown.

★ 64 ★

Characteristics of Convicted Offenders

Characteristics of convicted offenders, 1986.

Offender characteristics	Total number of offenders	Percent of offenders convicted of:						
		All offenses	Violent offenses	Property offenses		Drug offenses	Public order offenses	
				Fraudulent	Other		Regulatory	Other
Sex								
Female	5,768	16.6%	6.0%	28.1%	21.7%	12.1%	14.7%	9.5%
Male	29,013	83.4%	94.0%	71.9%	78.3%	87.9%	85.3%	90.5%
Race								
White	22,737	73.4%	55.8%	66.3%	58.4%	81.0%	85.3%	80.9%
Black	7,284	23.5%	30.5%	31.2%	37.7%	17.5%	12.0%	16.2%
Other	951	3.1%	13.7%	2.4%	3.9%	1.5%	2.7%	2.9%
Ethnicity								
Hispanic	6,024	17.9%	9.0%	8.1%	7.0%	26.2%	14.8%	26.7%
Non-Hispanic	27,598	82.1%	91.0%	91.9%	93.0%	73.8%	85.2%	73.3%
Age								
16-18 years	378	1.1%	2.0%	.7%	2.2%	.8%	1.0%	1.3%
19-20 years	1,218	3.5%	5.5%	2.9%	5.7%	3.0%	3.7%	3.4%
21-30 years	12,283	35.4%	44.8%	32.6%	38.8%	38.6%	29.3%	32.1%
31-40 years	11,150	32.1%	30.9%	31.7%	28.8%	37.1%	30.4%	28.2%
Over 40 years	9,709	27.9%	16.8%	32.2%	24.5%	20.5%	35.6%	34.9%

Source: Selected from "Characteristics of convicted offenders, 1986," *Compendium of Federal Justice Statistics, 1986,* 1990, p. 33. Also in source: Data by education, marital status, employment status at arrest, annual income, criminal record, and drug abuse record.

★ 65 ★

Delinquency Cases Disposed of by Juvenile Courts

Delinquency cases disposed of, in thousands, by reason for referral, 1985.

Reason for Referral	Total	Female
	In thousands	
All delinquency offenses	1,117	205
Violent offenses	70	9
Criminal homicide	1	[2]
Forcible rape	4	[2]
Robbery	25	2
Aggravated assault	40	8
Property offenses	470	91
Burglary	133	9
Larceny	296	77
Motor vehicle theft	35	5
Arson	7	1
Delinquency offenses	577	105
Simple assault	84	22
Vandalism	81	8

[Continued]

★ 65 ★

Delinquency Cases Disposed of by Juvenile Courts
[Continued]

Reason for Referral	Total	Female
Drug law violations	74	13
Obstruction of Justice	64	16
Other[1]	274	48

Source: "Delinquency Cases Disposed by Juvenile Courts, by Reason for Referral, 1982 to 1985, and by Sex, 1985," *Statistical Abstract of the United States 1990*, 1990, p. 186. Primary source: U.S. National Center for Juvenile Justice, Pittsburgh, PA, *Juvenile Court Statistics, 1985;* and unpublished data. Also in sources: totals for 1982, 1983, 1984; male breakdown 1985. A delinquency offense is an act committed by a juvenile for which an adult could be prosecuted in a criminal court. Disposition of a case involves taking a definite action such as transferring the case to criminal court, dismissing the case, placing the youth on probation, placing the youth in a facility for delinquent or status offenders, or such actions as fines, restitution, and community service. *Notes:* 1. Includes such offenses as stolen property offenses, trespassing, weapons offenses, other sex offenses, liquor law violations, disorderly conduct, and miscellaneous offenses. 2. Fewer than 500.

★ 66 ★

Drug Arrests

Drug arrest rates per 100,000 inhabitants for drug abuse violations, by type of offense, 1988.

Offense	Rate per 100,000 inhabitants	
	Total	Female
Drug arrests, total	449.9	137.1
Sale and/or manufacture	123.9	35.8
Heroin or cocaine[1]	74.8	21.6
Marijuana	25.4	6.5
Synthetic or manufactured drugs	3.6	1.3
Other dangerous nonnarcotic drugs	20.1	6.4
Possession	326.0	101.3
Heroin or cocaine[1]	153.7	53.9
Marijuana	130.1	30.4
Synthetic or manufactured drugs	8.5	3.3
Other dangerous nonnarcotic drugs	33.9	13.8

Source: "Drug Arrest Rates for Drug Abuse Violations, 1980 to 1988, and by Sex and Region, 1988," *Statistical Abstract of the United States 1990*, 1990, p. 178. Primary source: U.S. Federal Bureau of Investigation, *Crime in the United States*, annual. Also in source: totals for 1980, 1985, 1987; data by region, 1988. Based on Bureau of the Census estimated resident population as of July 1, except 1980, enumerated as of April 1. *Note:* 1. Includes other derivatives such as morphine, heroin, and codeine.

★ 67 ★

Educational Attainment of Arrestees

Number and percent of arrestees completing less than 12 grades of school, by race, selected cities, 1988.

City	% completing less than 12 grades of school					
	Females			Males		
	Black	White	Hispanic	Black	White	Hispanic
San Antonio	[1]	42%	74%	55%	50%	81%
Kansas City	51%	[1]	[1]	58%	70%	[1]
St. Louis	52%	38%	[1]	64%	70%	[1]
Philadelphia	56%	42%	[1]	55%	54%	69%
Dallas	46%	49%	[1]	56%	69%	86%
New Orleans	48%	44%	[1]	60%	34%	[1]
New York	57%	54%	64%	55%	36%	65%
Indianapolis	36%	64%	[1]	60%	68%	[1]
Chicago	48%	[1]	[1]	56%	50%	65%
Detroit	54%	67%	[1]	62%	47%	[1]
Portland	51%	65%	[1]	46%	54%	71%
Birmingham	52%	55%	[1]	49%	57%	[1]
Los Angeles	29%	42%	72%	34%	38%	72%
Phoenix	47%	50%	74%	36%	37%	74%
San Diego	31%	46%	71%	34%	37%	61%
Total arrestees surveyed:	1,533	1,169	438	5,622	2,936	1,794

Source: "Percentage of Arrestees Who Completed Less than 12 Grades of School," *National Institute of Justice/Research in Action,* December 1989, p. 7. Primary source: National Institute of Justice/Drug Use Forecasting Program, Washington, D.C., 1988. Data based on voluntary self-reports, 1988. *Note:* 1. Less than 20 cases.

★ 68 ★

Felony Arrests

Persons arrested for a felony in 12 States, by arrest offense, 1987.

Arrest Offense	Females	Males
Violent offenses	10%	89%
Homicide	10%	90%
Kidnaping	8%	92%
Sexual assault		
Rape	1%	99%
Other	1%	99%
Type unspecified	2%	98%
Robbery	8%	92%
Assault	13%	87%
Other violent	14%	86%
Property offenses	16%	82%
Burglary	10%	90%
Larceny/theft	24%	76%
Motor vehicle theft	9%	91%
Arson	16%	84%
Fraud	35%	65%

[Continued]

★ 68 ★

Felony Arrests
[Continued]

Arrest Offense	Females	Males
Stolen property	12%	80%
Other property	7%	93%
Drug offenses	15%	85%
Public-order offenses	11%	89%
Weapons	5%	95%
Other public-order	13%	87%

Source: Jacob Perez, "Tracking Offenders, 1987", *Bureau of Justice Statistics Bulletin*, October 1990, Table 10, p. 6. Detail may not add to total because of rounding.

★ 69 ★

Juveniles in Custody: 1983-1987
Juveniles held in public and private custody, 1983-1987.

Characteristic	Public Custody			Private Custody		
	1983	1985	1987	1983	1985	1987
Number of residents[1,2]	50,799	51,402	56,097	31,473	34,112	38,184
Juvenile	48,701	49,322	53,503	31,390	34,080	38,143
Female	6,519	6,773	7,231	9,148	10,236	11,804
Male	42,182	42,549	46,272	22,242	23,844	26,399
Average age (years)	15.4	15.4	15.8	14.9	14.9	14.8

Source: "Juveniles Held in Public and Private Custody—Residents and Facilities: 1983 to 1987," *Statistical Abstract of the United States 1990*, 1990, p. 186. Primary source: 1983, U.S. Office of Juvenile Justice and Delinquency Prevention, *Children in Custody: Advance Report on the 1982 Census of Public Juvenile Facilities*; and *Children in Custody: Advance Report on the 1982 Census of Private Juvenile Facilities*; 1985, U.S. Bureau of Justice Statistics, *Census of public and Private Juvenile Detention, Correctional, and Shelter Facilities, 1975-85*; and U.S. Office of Juvenile Justice and Delinquency Prevention, *1987 Children in Custody: Census of Public and Private Juvenile Custody Facilities*. Public and private facilities for juveniles include detention centers, shelters, reception and diagnostic centers, training schools, halfway houses, group homes, ranches, forestry camps, and farms. *Notes:* 1. Includes adults. 2. Data for February 1, 1983, and 1985, and February 2, 1987. 3. Includes races not reported and races not shown. 4. Based on juvenile residents only.

★ 70 ★

Likelihood of Being Prosecuted for Sexual Offenses
Likelihood of being prosecuted after arrest for a felony in 7 States, 1987.

Arrest offense	% of arrested persons pro- secuted
Sexual assault, other	86%
Sexual assault, type unspecified	80%
Rape	74%

Source: Jacob Perez, "Tracking Offenders, 1987, *Bureau of Justice Statistics Bulletin*, October 1990, Table 2, p. 3.

★ 71 ★

Persons Arrested and Prison Population: Selected Countries

Persons arrested and prison population, number and number per 100,000 population, by country, 1975 and 1980.

Country or area	Year	Persons apprehended				Prison population			
		Number		Per 100,000 pop.		Number		Per 100,000 pop.	
		Female	Male	Female	Male	Female	Male	Female	Male
Africa									
Mauritius	1975	8	453	2	106	29	1,851	6.6	432.0
	1980	12	544	2	115	38	1,712	7.8	363.4
Morocco	1975	-	-	-	-	883	16,588	10.2	191.8
	1980	-	-	-	-	1,501	19,731	15.5	203.4
Senegal	1975	-	8,685	-	368	-	-	-	-
	1980	-	7,361	-	262	-	-	-	-
South Africa	1975	-	-	-	-	5,639	84,894	43.8	672.3
	1980	-	-	-	-	5,443	94,621	37.7	667.5
Uganda	1975	-	-	-	-	99	9,981	1.8	180.6
North America									
Bahamas	1975	468	3,160	457	3,110	269	1,654	263.0	1,628.0
	1980	387	2,869	366	2,708	648	3,141	612.5	3,011.5
Barbados	1975	-	-	-	-	4	226	3.1	192.2
	1980	-	-	-	-	12	248	9.2	210.0
Belize	1975	-	1,846	-	-	18	803	-	-
	1980	-	2,523	-	3,553	-	842	-	1,185.9
Canada	1975	78,508	641,819	689	5,665	-	-	-	-
Costa Rica	1980	-	-	-	-	73	2,288	6.5	198.7
Honduras	1975	752	11,352	49	732	-	-	-	-
	1980	1,423	11,333	77	612	-	-	-	-
Jamaica	1975	-	-	-	-	0	93	0.0	9.3
	1980	-	-	-	-	0	14	0.0	1.3
Panama	1980	1,489	-	156	-	-	-	-	-
St. Lucia	1980	-	-	-	-	13	980	20.5	1,725.4
Trinidad and Tobago	1975	-	4,838	-	938	102	2,509	-	-
	1980	-	5,215	-	954	164	2,223	29.9	406.8
United States	1975	1,546,518	7,727,081	1,398	7,334	16,639	377,839	15.0	358.6
	1980	1,705,377	8,735,623	1,459	7,879	22,535	489,602	19.3	441.6
South America									
Argentina	1975	21,120	166,592	162	1,281	828	15,675	6.3	120.5
	1980	14,978	116,152	106	827	872	20,027	6.1	142.6
Chile	1975	7,549	54,504	145	1,064	129	1,012	2.4	19.8
	1980	7,673	54,438	137	988	59	867	1.1	15.7
Colombia	1975	7,943	84,826	69	732	-	-	-	-

[Continued]

★ 71 ★

Persons Arrested and Prison Population: Selected Countries
[Continued]

Country or area	Year	Persons apprehended				Prison population			
		Number		Per 100,000 pop.		Number		Per 100,000 pop.	
		Female	Male	Female	Male	Female	Male	Female	Male
	1980	7,513	81,711	58	632	1,465	31,084	11.4	240.5
Peru	1975	-	-	-	-	296	11,870	3.9	155.4
	1980	-	-	-	-	770	16,598	9.0	190.5
Suriname	1975	23	1,279	13	700	-	-	-	-
	1980	41	973	23	554	-	-	-	-
Uruguay	1975	1,040	9,363	73	668	166	1,851	11.6	132.1
	1980	1,457	7,853	99	547	142	1,768	9.6	123.2
Venezuela	1975	-	-	-	-	410	15,341	6.6	239.5
	1980	-	-	-	-	365	11,766	4.9	154.8
Asia									
Bahrain	1980	-	3,947	-	1,954	-	-	-	-
Bangladesh	1975	505	98,999	1	250	1,049	35,942	2.8	90.9
	1980	1,001	72,716	2	160	2,515	18,663	5.9	41.0
India	1975	28,743	1,396,343	10	434	-	-	-	-
	1980	47,433	1,906,821	14	535	-	-	-	-
Indonesia	1975	-	-	-	-	729	28,022	1.1	41.6
	1980	-	-	-	-	875	34,860	1.2	46.4
Japan	1975	61,432	302,685	108	552	1,081	44,913	1.9	81.8
	1980	74,225	317,888	125	553	1,655	49,051	2.8	85.4
Korea, Republic of	1975	104,422	768,000	597	4,321	-	-	-	-
	1980	74,234	529,086	394	2,747	-	-	-	-
Kuwait	1975	-	-	-	-	31	204	6.8	37.1
	1980	-	-	-	-	22	281	3.7	35.7
Pakistan	1980	-	213,372	-	478	-	-	-	-
Philippines	1975	549	7,702	3	36	-	-	-	-
	1980	194	5,492	1	23	-	-	-	-
Qatar	1975	23	1,651	41	1,437	23	1,225	40.9	1,066.1
	1980	132	3,548	162	2,483	132	2,819	161.8	1,972.7
Singapore	1975	-	5,816	-	503	15	1,382	1.4	119.5
	1980	-	10,118	-	821	25	966	2.1	78.4
Sri Lanka	1980	-	44,213	-	585	-	-	-	-
Thailand	1975	-	329,487	-	1,585	-	-	-	-
	1980	-	180,878	-	775	-	-	-	-
United Arab Emirates	1980	-	17,183	-	2,538	-	-	-	-

[Continued]

★ 71 ★

Persons Arrested and Prison Population: Selected Countries

[Continued]

Country or area	Year	Persons apprehended				Prison population			
		Number		Per 100,000 pop.		Number		Per 100,000 pop.	
		Female	Male	Female	Male	Female	Male	Female	Male
Europe									
Austria	1975	16,847	95,304	424	2,690	-	-	-	-
	1980	20,501	107,840	518	3,037	-	-	-	-
Belgium	1975	488	8,500	10	177	283	6,398	5.7	133.4
	1980	529	8,193	11	170	225	5,525	4.5	114.8
Czechoslovakia	1975	25,503	186,508	336	2,586	-	-	-	-
	1980	20,559	146,496	262	1,963	-	-	-	-
Denmark	1975	-	-	-	-	104	3,278	4.1	130.8
	1980	6,265	38,549	241	1,524	138	3,199	5.3	126.5
Finland	1975	-	-	-	-	98	4,834	4.0	212.2
	1980	15,970	127,990	647	5,539	117	4,372	4.75	189.2
France	1975	-	-	-	-	679	24,634	2.5	95.4
	1980	119,022	567,332	434	2,156	11,079	33,819	40.4	128.5
Germany, Federal Republic	1975	274,146	1,149,822	849	3,894	2,015	48,943	6.2	165.7
	1980	195,278	917,718	607	3,120	1,295	42,821	4.0	145.6
Greece	1975	14,558	193,705	315	4,371	108	2,564	2.3	57.9
	1980	21,522	309,487	438	6,538	135	2,845	2.7	60.1
Ireland	1975	-	-	-	-	20	742	1.2	46.2
	1980	-	-	-	-	21	808	1.2	47.3
Italy	1975	-	-	-	-	980	27,357	3.4	100.2
	1980	-	-	-	-	1,471	27,826	5.0	99.8
Netherlands	1975	13,595	129,454	196	1,889	58	3,042	0.8	44.4
	1980	19,592	182,837	275	2,604	127	3,617	1.8	51.5
Norway	1975	1,217	11,249	60	565	34	1,879	1.7	94.4
	1980	1,209	12,376	59	611	56	1,694	2.7	83.7
Poland	1975	29,187	242,565	167	1,465	3,714	73,647	21.3	444.9
	1980	26,680	236,547	146	1,365	3,845	81,359	21.1	469.4
Portugal	1975	-	-	-	-	144	2,525	2.9	56.7
	1980	-	-	-	-	174	4,869	3.3	103.9
Spain	1975	-	66,265	-	382	294	6,915	1.6	39.8
	1980	-	111,426	-	606	490	14,099	2.6	76.7
Sweden	1975	10,169	88,041	247	2,161	15	139	0.4	3.4
	1980	11,826	89,867	282	2,182	19	185	0.5	4.5
United Kingdom (England and Wales)	1975	-	-	-	-	784	27,199	2.7	99.6
	1980	-	-	-	-	1,030	28,563	3.6	104.8
Yugoslavia	1975	22,401	209,707	207	1,996	-	-	-	-
	1980	16,581	154,101	147	1,401	-	-	-	-

[Continued]

★ 71 ★

Persons Arrested and Prison Population: Selected Countries
[Continued]

Country or area	Year	Persons apprehended				Prison population			
		Number		Per 100,000 pop.		Number		Per 100,000 pop.	
		Female	Male	Female	Male	Female	Male	Female	Male
Oceania									
Australia	1975	-	42,599	-	623	-	-	-	-
	1980	-	51,404	-	701	325	9,427	4.4	128.5
New Zealand	1975	-	-	-	-	111	2,612	7.2	169.0
	1980	23,286	118,852	1,462	7,539	115	2,685	7.2	170.3
Tonga	1975	-	488	-	-	0	204	-	-
	1980	-	779	-	-	0	128	-	-

Source: "Selected series on criminal justice by sex, 1975 and 1980: A. Persons apprehended and prison population," *Compendium of Statistics and Indicators on the Situation of Women, 1986* p. 582-585 (New York: United Nations, 1989). Primary source: First and Second United Nations Surveys of Crime Trends, Operations of Criminal Justice systems and Crime Prevention Strategies, Centre for Social Development and Humanitarian Affairs of the United Nations Secretariat, unpublished data.

★ 72 ★

Sentences for Sexual Assault

Sentences received in 12 States for sexual assault, 1987.

Arrest offense	Number of persons convicted[1]	% of those convicted who were sentenced to:					
		Nonincarceration			Incarceration		
		Total	Probation[2]	Other	Total	Prison	Jail
Sexual assault							
Rape	2,523	20%	13%	6%	80%	48%	32%
Other	1,807	29%	20%	9%	71%	30%	41%
Type unspecified	3,240	20%	16%	5%	80%	47%	33%

Source: Jacob Perez, "Tracking Offenders, 1987," *Bureau of Justice Statistics Bulletin*, October 1990, Table 5, p. 3. Also in source: data for other offenses. Detail may not add to total because of rounding. *Notes:* 1. Number of convictions for which sentencing data were available. 2. Includes dispositions of probation without a verdict.

Crime and Criminals

★ 73 ★

Prison Population: 1970-1990

Number and rate per 100,000 resident population of sentenced prisoners in State and Federal institutions, number and rate female, on December 31, 1970-1987; number and rate on June 30, 1990.

Year	Prison Population		Females	
	Total	Rate per 100,000 population	Number	Rate per 100,000 population
1970	196,429	96	5,635	5
1971	198,061	95	6,329	6
1972	196,092	93	6,269	6
1973	204,211	96	6,004	6
1974	218,466	102	7,389	7
1975	240,593	111	8,675	8
1976	262,833	120	10,039	9
1977[1]	278,141	126	11,044	10
1977[1]	285,456	129	11,212	10
1978	294,396	132	11,583	10
1979	301,470	133	12,005	10
1980	315,974	138	12,331	11
1981	353,167	153	14,227	12
1982	394,374	170	16,329	14
1983	419,820	179	17,429	14
1984	443,398	188	19,205	NA
1985	480,568	200	21,296	NA
1986	522,084	216	24,544	NA
1987	556,748	228	26,586	NA
1990[1]	755,425	289	43,541	NA

Source: "Number and rate (per 100,000 resident population of each sex) of sentenced prisoners in State and Federal institutions on Dec. 31," *Sourcebook of Criminal Justice Statistics - 1988*, p. 612. Primary source: U.S. Department of Justice, Bureau of Justice Statistics, *Prisoners 1925-81*, Bulletin NCJ-85861, p. 2; *Prisoners in 1983*, Bulletin NCJ-92949, p. 2; *Prisoners in 1985*, Bulletin NCJ-101384, p. 2; *Prisoners in 1986*, Bulletin NCJ 104864, p.3, Table 5; and *Correctional Populations in the United States, 1985*, NCJ-103957, Tables 5.1-5.4; *1986*, NCJ-111611, Tables 5.1-5.4; *1987*, NCJ-118762, Tables 5.1-5.4 (Washington, DC: U.S. Dept. of Justice). Table adapted by SOURCEBOOK staff. Figures for 1990 from Russell Snyder, "Record numbers fill U.S. prisons," *Detroit Free Press*, October 8, 1990, p. 3A. *Notes:* 1. Two sets of figures for 1977 are given in source without further explanation.

★ 74 ★

Sexual Harassment in the Workplace: Selected States

Number of Title VII cases filed per 100,000 of female work force: California, Michigan, New York, and Texas.

State and year	No. cases per 100,000 female work force
California	
1985	15.9
1986	16.3
1987	21.0
1988	24.0
Michigan	
1985	5.9
1986	6.5
1987	4.0
1988	3.1
New York	
1981	5.0
1982	7.7
1983	8.0
1984	6.6
1985	8.6
1986	6.3
Texas	
1987	2.2
1988	1.7

Source: Gretchen Morgenson, "Watch that leer, stifle that joke. Corporations and activists crusade against sexual harassment, yet we're told the problem's getting worse. Is it really?", *Forbes* (May 15, 1989): 69+. Also in source: a discussion of sexual harassment and litigation outcomes. These states were chosen by the author because of their large populations and regional diversity.

★ 75 ★

Women in Prison

Characteristics of the female prison population, 1989.

Characteristic	Number or %
Total prison population, year end, 1987	562,623
Female prison inmates as of June 30, 1989	5.4%
Growth of female prison population, first half of 1989	13.0%
Number of female prison inmates in 1980	13,420
Number of female prison inmates in 1989	36,855
Number of male inmates in 1980	316,401
Number of male inmates in 1989	636,710

Source: BJS Data Report, 1989, 1990, p. 79. Primary source: BJS press release, *Prisoners at Midyear 1989*, September 10, 1989.

Crimes and Crime Rates

★ 76 ★

Forcible Rape by Month: 1985-1989

Percent of annual total of forcible rapes, by month, 1985-1989; number of offenses, rate per 100,000 inhabitants, and percent change, 1988-1989.

Months	1985	1986	1987	1988	1989
January	7.2%	7.1%	7.2%	7.4%	7.4%
February	6.6%	6.7%	6.8%	7.3%	6.3%
March	8.2%	7.9%	8.1%	8.0%	7.7%
April	8.3%	8.1%	8.2%	8.0%	8.3%
May	8.9%	8.8%	8.9%	9.0%	8.6%
June	9.0%	9.2%	9.3%	8.7%	8.9%
July	10.1%	9.8%	9.7%	9.9%	10.0%
August	9.9%	10.2%	9.8%	9.8%	9.5%
September	8.8%	9.1%	8.9%	9.0%	8.8%
October	8.5%	8.4%	8.1%	8.4%	8.9%
November	7.7%	7.8%	7.7%	7.6%	8.3%
December	6.9%	7.0%	7.3%	6.8%	7.3%
Total number of offenses				92,486	94,504
Rate per 100,000 inhabitants				37.6	38.1
Percent change				+2.2%	+1.3%

Source: "Forcible Rape by Month, 1985-1989," *Crime in the United States 1989*, p. 14-15 (August 5, 1990). Forcible rape is defined as the carnal knowledge of a female forcibly and against her will. Assaults or attempts to commit rape by force or threat of force are also included; however, statutory rape (without force) and other sex offenses are excluded.

★ 77 ★

State Prison Inmates by Criminal History

State prison inmates, by criminal history and selected characteristics of the inmate: 1986.

Characteristic	Total	Criminal History of Prison Inmates							
		First-timers			Recidivists[1]				
		Total	Non-violent	Violent	Total	Non-violent	Prior violent only	Current violent only	Current and prior violent
Prison inmates, total	447,185	82,791	23,808	58,983	364,393	129,465	49,827	98,946	86,155
Percent distribution:									
Female	4.4%	7.3%	8.8%	6.7%	3.7%	6.4%	2.5%	2.6%	1.7%
Male	95.6%	92.7%	91.2%	93.3%	96.3%	93.6%	97.5%	97.4%	98.3%
Median age	28	29	29	28	28	27	29	28	30
Median age at first arrest	17	22	23	22	16	17	16	16	15
Median age at first confinement	19	24	25	24	18	19	17	19	18
Average number of months served on current confinement	27.3	21.9	21.0	30.6	20.6	19.6	20.7	32.1	32.0

Source: "State Prison Inmates, by Criminal History and Selected Characteristics of the Inmate: 1986," *Statistical Abstract of the United States 1990*, 1990, p. 188. Primary source: U.S. Bureau of Justice Statistics, *Profiles of State Prison Inmates, 1986,* January 1988. Also in source: data by race. Based on a sample survey of about 13,711 inmates. Violent/nonviolent refers to the current or past criminal offense for which the iinmate is or was incarcerated. *Notes:* 1. An individual who has been previously sentenced to probation or incarceration as a juvenile or adult.

★ 78 ★

Teenage Crime Victims

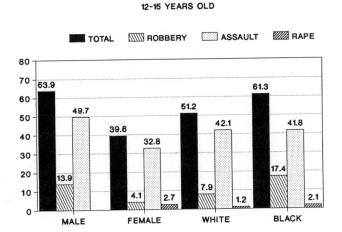

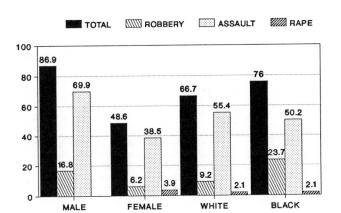

Average annual number of victims of crimes of violence per 1,000 persons, by type of crime and sex: 1982 to 1984.

Age and sex	Total	Robbery	Assault	Rape[1]
		Crimes per 1,000 persons		
12-15 years old	52.0	9.1	41.4	1.5
16-19 years old	67.8	11.5	54.2	2.1
Female				
12-15 years old	39.6	4.1	32.8	2.7
16-19 years old	48.6	6.2	38.5	3.9
Male				
12-15 years old	63.9	13.9	49.7	-
16-19 years old	86.9	16.8	69.9	-

Source: "Average annual number of victims of crimes of violence per 1,000 persons, by type of crime and characteristic of victim: 1982 to 1984," *Youth Indicators 1988: Trends in the Well-Being of American Youth,* Volume 1, August 1988, p. 112. Primary source: U.S. Department of Justice, Bureau of Justice Statistics, *Teenage Victims: A National Crime Survey Report,* November 1986. Also in source: data by race. The victimization rates are annual averages for the period 1982 through 1984. The numerator of a given rate is the sum of the number of victims in 1982, 1983, and 1984. The denominator is the sum of the annual population totals for the 3 years. *Notes:* 1. Crimes of violence include rape, robbery, and assault. Numbers for rape were calculated by subtracting the sum of robbery and assault from the total of violent crimes.

★ 79 ★

Violent Offenders Under the Influence

Characteristics of violent offenders under the influence of drugs or alcohol as reported by victims.

Offender characteristics	Percent of violent crime incidents where victim perceived the offender to be:						
	Total	Not under influence	Under the influence				
			Total	Alcohol only	Drugs only	Both	Not sure which substance
Both sexes	100%	17%	47%	23%	13%	11%	--[1]
Female	100%	34%	27%	17%	6%	3%	1[2]
Male	100%	19%	38%	23%	6%	6%	2%

Source: "Characteristics of violent offenders under the influence of drugs or alcohol as reported by victims," *The Redesigned National Crime Survey: Selected New Data*, Bureau of Justice Statistics Special Report, January 1989. Also in source: data by race, age, and relationship to victim. Percents may not total 100% because of rounding. For incidents with more than one offender, data show incidents in which at least one offender was under the influence. Crimes committed by mixed racial groups are not presented. *Notes:* 1. Less than 0.5%. 2. Estimate is based on 10 or fewer sample cases.

★ 80 ★

Worldwide Crimes and Crime Rates

Volume and types of crime, number of offenders, percent female, selected countries, latest available year.

Country, year, offence	Volume of crime			Offenders	
	Cases known to police	Cases solved	Volume per 100,000	Total	% Female
Argentina: 1986					
Homicides	62	69.35%	0.20	45	13.33%
Sex offenses (including rape)	160	48.12%	0.51	79	8.86%
Rape	53	37.73%	0.17	21	-
Serious assault	184	83.15%	0.59	156	6.41%
Theft	47,613	3.10%	153.59	1,539	11.17%
Fraud	1,336	25.44%	4.30	352	15.05%
Counterfeit currency	104	33.65%	0.33	37	5.40%
Drug offenses	1,573	93.45%	5.07	3,267	8.72%
Australia: 1986					
Homicides	664	85%	4.2	571	13.5%
Sex offenses (including rape)	14,501	74.3%	91.5	4,515	0.06%
Rape	2,403	72%	15.2	1,070	0.06%
Serious assault	12,889	67.9%	81.3	8,180	8.6%
Theft	851,724	26.4%	5,372.9	144,976	12.8%
Fraud	209,999	61.3%	1,324.8	12,748	28.5%
Counterfeit currency	216	18.8%	1.4	112	-
Drug offenses	61,541	99.6%	388.2	44,466	-
Austria: 1986					
Homicides	182	95.1%	2.4	172	16.3%
Sex offenses (including rape)	3,481	79%	46	1,780	4.2%
Rape	368	73.1%	4.8	263	0.4%

[Continued]

★ 80 ★

Worldwide Crimes and Crime Rates
[Continued]

Country, year, offence	Volume of crime			Offenders	
	Cases known to police	Cases solved	Volume per 100,000	Total	% Female
Serious assault	108	96.3%	1.4	107	12.1%
Theft	180,717	28.9%	2,391.2	30,373	24.2%
Fraud	23,871	98.1%	315.8	14,489	21.5%
Counterfeit currency	762	15.7%	10	114	22.8%
Drug offenses	5,157	99.6%	68.2	4,347	19.9%
Burma: 1985					
Homicides	1,963	22.93%	5.56	3,440	2.29%
Sex offenses (including rape)	-	-	-	-	-
Rape	953	15.01%	2.70	1,159	1.93%
Serious assault	15,686	38.16%	44.42	16,772	8.88%
Theft	24,450	52.23%	69.24	758	1.19%
Fraud	4,614	37.08%	13.07	5,479	14.19%
Counterfeit currency	17	11.77%	0.05	26	-
Drug offenses	4,112	14,06%	11.64	5,813	14.95%
Canada: 1986					
Homicides	1,449	86.7%	5.66	1,279	10.6%
Sex offenses (including rape)	23,533	68%	91.95	9,509	1.5%
Rape	-	-	-	-	-
Serious assault	31,735	79%	124.01	19,630	8.5%
Theft	1,315,274	21.8%	5,139.59	251,426	11.9%
Fraud	130,559	71.3%	510.17	41,839	23.9%
Counterfeit currency	2,044	26.6%	7.98	248	8.9%
Drug offenses	56,251	88.4%	219.8	41,606	10.2%
Chile: 1986					
Homicides	744	80.90%	6.04	599	11.35%
Sex offenses (including rape)	4,081	75.56%	33.11	1,733	50.03%
Rape	1,180	72.12%	9.57	311	3.54%
Serious assault	15,971	68.41%	129.56	1,760	7.67%
Theft	107,989	26.97%	876.03	10,217	8.85%
Fraud	8,048	64.29%	65.29	3,273	14.51%
Counterfeit currency	-	-	-	-	-
Drug offenses	1,536	82.66%	12.46	1,305	14.25%
China: 1986					
Homicides	11,510	92.4%	1.1	11.745	9.4%
Sex offenses (including rape)	-	-	-	-	-
Rape	39,121	96.2%	3.7	37,801	-
Serious assault	18,364	97.9%	1.7	24,701	3.6%
Theft	425,845	75.1%	40.4	340,740	2.1%
Fraud	14,663	95.7%	1.4	17,035	5.2%
Counterfeit currency	497	95.6%	-	634	4.9%

[Continued]

★ 80 ★

Worldwide Crimes and Crime Rates
[Continued]

Country, year, offence	Volume of crime			Offenders	
	Cases known to police	Cases solved	Volume per 100,000	Total	% Female
Ethiopia: 1986					
Homicides	3,091	73.15%	7.36	4,522	4.97%
Sex offenses (including rape)	545	96.3%	1.30	898	18.15%
Rape	503	96%	1.19	822	16.18%
Serious assault	10,571	96.16%	25.2	15,700	17.5%
Theft	15,536	97%	37	24,271	8.64%
Fraud	1,706	99.4%	4.06	2,269	8.95%
Counterfeit currency	-	-	-	-	-
Drug offenses	6	100%	0.01	9	22.2%
Finland: 1986					
Homicides	53	94.3%	1.1	57	17.5%
Sex offenses (including rape)	986	76.4%	20	827	1%
Rape	292	65.1%	5.9	216	-
Serious assault	1,820	82.2%	36.9	1,789	7.4%
Theft	109,203	28.9%	2,216.8	55,162	7.8%
Fraud	40,725	81.8%	826.7	43,011	18.9%
Counterfeit currency	-	-	-	-	-
Drug offenses	1,973	92.1%	40.1	2,106	12.2%
France: 1986					
Homicides	2,239	89.90%	4.05	2,580	15.62%
Sex offenses (including rape)	18,933	71.70%	34.25	11,288	8.91%
Rape	2,937	81.58%	5.31	2,548	4.47%
Serious assault	36,549	74.85%	66.12	30,777	9.69%
Theft	2,092,008	15.51%	3,784.44	264,582	16.39%
Fraud	594,517	94.91%	1,075.48	235,762	29.36%
Counterfeit currency	15,838	130.32%(sic)	28.65	2,724	22.28%
Drug offenses	49,086	102.22%(sic)	88.80	45,737	13.08%
Germany, Federal Republic: 1986					
Homicides	2,728	93.9%	4.5	2,734	10.8%
Sex offenses (including rape)	38,713	66.1%	63.4	19,451	9.6%
Rape	5,604	70.8%	9.2	4,030	0.7%
Serious assault	64,097	84.2%	105	67,912	10.8%
Theft	2,748,658	29.3%	4,502.5	519,098	30.9%
Fraud	422,282	90.4%	691.7	262,595	24.3%
Counterfeit currency	523	94.3%	0.9	497	13.7%
Drug offenses	68,694	94.3%	112.5	56,662	16%
Greece: 1986					
Homicides	153	88.9%	1.5	164	6.7%
Sex offenses (including rape)	487	93.6%	4.9	695	22.9%
Rape	124	95.2%	1.2	154	-
Serious assault	5,358	97.7%	53.8	6,013	10.7%
Theft	35,307	18.4%	354.3	7,745	7.6%

[Continued]

Worldwide Crimes and Crime Rates
[Continued]

Country, year, offence	Volume of crime			Offenders	
	Cases known to police	Cases solved	Volume per 100,000	Total	% Female
Fraud	578	79.4%	5.8	535	7.1%
Counterfeit currency	125	87.2%	1.3	137	9.5%
Drug offenses	977	98.1%	9.8	1,735	8.06%
Hong Kong: 1986					
Homicides	71	74.6%	1.3	82	7.3%
Sex offenses (including rape)	1,713	76.1%	31	1,564	6.6%
Rape	72	56.9%	1.3	50	-
Serious assault	7,804	73%	141.3	5,421	8.3%
Theft	51,615	31.4%	934.3	13,387	19.9%
Fraud	1,508	39.3%	27.3	668	11.8%
Counterfeit currency	8	100	0.1	17	11.8%
Drug offenses	4,118	99.7%	74.5	5,296	9%
Hungary: 1986					
Homicides	447	94.3%	4.2	449	16.5%
Sex offenses (including rape)	1,913	75.8%	18	1,325	8.1%
Rape	622	68.9%	5.8	582	0.9%
Serious assault	6,186	83.2%	58.1	5,288	9.5%
Theft	89,969	44.7%	845.6	24,778	14.1%
Fraud	4,623	86.1%	43.4	2,191	20.9%
Counterfeit currency	46	74.5%	0.4	35	8.6%
Drug offenses	116	90.5%	1.1	110	26.4%
India: 1983					
Homicides	25,112	80.4%	3.5	59,802	2%
Sex offenses (including rape)	-	-	-	-	-
Rape	6,019	86.5%	0.8	8,403	1%
Serious assault	-	-	-	-	-
Theft	353,536	39.7%	49.1	240,073	2.2%
Fraud	19,767	64.5%	2.7	16,983	1.7%
Counterfeit currency	809	31.2%	0.1	735	0.5%
Drug offenses	-	-	-	-	-
Ireland, Northern: 1982					
Homicides	362	23%	23.95	44	-
Sex offenses (including rape)	403	42%	26.69	73	-
Rape	80	34%	5.30	18	-
Serious assault	2,159	33%	142.99	746	3%
Theft	51,985	19%	3,422.96	6,839	17%
Fraud	2,713	46%	179.68	495	23%
Counterfeit currency	33	21%	2.19	-	-
Drug offenses	131	57%	8.68	44	11%
Ireland, Republic of: 1981					
Homicides	24	100%	0.70	29	3.4%

[Continued]

★ 80 ★

Worldwide Crimes and Crime Rates
[Continued]

Country, year, offence	Volume of crime			Offenders	
	Cases known to police	Cases solved	Volume per 100,000	Total	% Female
Sex offenses (including rape)	247	77.3%	7.18	134	-
Rape	51	70.6%	1.48	62	-
Serious assault	93	84.9%	2.70	24	-
Theft	74,930	33.9%	2,177.93	9,026	12.2%
Fraud	9,579	39.8%	278.42	1,515	28.7%
Counterfeit currency	1	100%	0.03	1	-
Drug offenses	-	-	-	1,256[1]	9.4%
Israel: 1986					
Homicides	199	65.8%	4.6	214	4.7%
Sex offenses (including rape)	2,036	70.8%	47	1,216	1.8%
Rape	313	86.9%	7.2	265	2.6%
Serious assault	939	84.8%	21.7	1,262	7.6%
Theft	154,296	11.2%	3,563.4	11,024	9.9%
Fraud	12,045	74.9%	278.2	497	23.3%
Counterfeit currency	147	15.6%	3.4	27	14.8%
Drug offenses	5,155	87.2%	119	5,849	10.4%
Japan: 1986					
Homicides	1,676	96.7%	1.4	1,692	18.4%
Sex offenses (including rape)	4,041	82.6%	3.3	2,682	1.2%
Rape	1,750	88.1%	1.4	1.577	1%
Serious assault	21,171	93.8%	17.4	28,380	6.7%
Theft	1,377,045	58.7%	1,131.8	262,375	24.9%
Fraud	64,788	96.9%	53.2	13,379	11%
Counterfeit currency	170	63.5%	0.1	13	7.7%
Drug offenses	2,000	100%	1.6	1,618	28.2%
Korea, Republic of: 1986					
Homicides	565	95.8%	1.37	599	12.9%
Sex offenses (including rape)	15,571	91.7%	37.83	21,625	30.6%
Rape	3,909	96.4%	9.5	5,158	0.4%
Serious assault	24,834	96.4%	60.3	51,083	11.1%
Theft	104,765	58.3%	254.5	66,803	8.6%
Fraud	77,879	82.9%	189.2	74,543	17.8%
Counterfeit currency	25	24%	0.06	7	-
Drug offenses	523	87.4%	1.27	547	20.1%
Kuwait: 1985					
Homicides	92	75%	5.42	79	8%
Sex offenses (including rape)	492	89%	28.99	671	25%
Rape	11	82%	0.65	11	-
Serious assault	351	87%	20.68	457	4%
Theft	2,552	21%	150.36	704	19%
Fraud	514	92%	30.28	523	3%
Counterfeit currency	-	-	-	-	-

[Continued]

★ 80 ★

Worldwide Crimes and Crime Rates
[Continued]

Country, year, offence	Volume of crime			Offenders	
	Cases known to police	Cases solved	Volume per 100,000	Total	% Female
Drug offenses	180	98%	10.61	268	3%
Libya: 1986					
Homicides	44	-	1.25	78	7.69%
Sex offenses (including rape)	492	-	14.05	-	-
Rape	202	-	5.77	375	25.6%
Serious assault	126	-	3.60	241	2.48%
Theft	5,662	-	161.77	3,102	2.15%
Fraud	301	-	8.60	287	6.62%
Counterfeit currency	-	-	-	-	-
Drug offenses	230	-	6.57	495	3.23%
Monaco: 1982[2]					
Homicides	-	-	-	-	-
Sex offenses (including rape)	7	71.42%	25.34	4	-
Rape	-	-	-	-	-
Serious assault	17	88.23%	61.54	22	4.54%
Theft	748	17.91%	2,707.79	192	10.41%
Fraud	146	86.98%	528.52	118	27.96%
Counterfeit currency	5	80%	18.10	5	20%
Drug offenses	12	100%	43.44	33	6.06%
Morocco: 1986					
Homicides	339	83%	1.47	509	24.75%
Sex offenses (including rape)	5,690	90.87%	24.73	6,037	50.37%
Rape	692	90%	3	956	-
Serious assault	39,214	87.93%	170.49	50,392	34.30%
Theft	46,469	54.05%	202.03	22,378	6.42%
Fraud	1,519	90.30%	6.60	1,411	-
Counterfeit currency	47	46%	0.20	16	-
Drug offenses	2,721	100%	11.83	3,816	-
Netherlands: 1986					
Homicides	173	94.2%	1.19	190	-
Sex offenses (including rape)	8,718	48.3%	60	3,704	1%
Rape	1,201	64.8%	8.27	627	0.3%
Serious assault	17,128	72.8%	117.88	13,651	5.9%
Theft	820,728	15.3%	5,648.73	111,980	17.1%
Fraud	4,895	72.7%	33.69	2,867	13.5%
Counterfeit currency	522	48.7%	3.59	313	11.8%
Drug offenses	5,099	100%	35.09	7,603	12.1%
New Zealand: 1986					
Homicides	136	95.6%	4.11	142	12.7%
Sex offenses (including rape)	3,200	63.3%	96.76	1,574	4.6%
Rape	633	74%	19.14	282	-

[Continued]

★ 80 ★

Worldwide Crimes and Crime Rates
[Continued]

Country, year, offence	Volume of crime			Offenders	
	Cases known to police	Cases solved	Volume per 100,000	Total	% Female
Serious assault	4,528	76.8%	136.92	3,001	5.3%
Theft	259,796	21.3%	7,855.74	52.754	22.7%
Fraud	29,088	44.7%	879.57	11,784	34%
Counterfeit currency	119	27.7%	3.60	19	-
Drug offenses	17,328	92.2%	523.97	15,546	16.5%
Norway: 1986					
Homicides	39	90%	0.9	35	2.9%
Sex offenses (including rape)	1,245	40%	29.8	363	1.4%
Rape	255	30%	6.1	67	-
Serious assault	1,143	54%	27.4	486	5.1%
Theft	124,074	14%	2,972.5	6,544	11.2%
Fraud	6,667	53%	159.7	921	21.4%
Counterfeit currency	16	6%	0.4	1	-
Drug offenses	4,583	79%	109.8	1,975	17.6%
Drug offenses	1,631	-	8.5	1,969	13.6%
Peru: 1984					
Homicides	237	77.6%	1.2	-	-
Sex offenses (including rape)	942	54.6%	4.9	1,353	2.30%
Rape	657	53.1%	3.4	-	-
Serious assault	2,008	55.4%	10.5	-	-
Theft	34,336	17.2%	178.9	28,967	3.50%
Fraud	7,660	16.5%	39.9	651	6.14%
Counterfeit currency	16	43.8	0.1	-	-
Philippines: 1981					
Homicides	15,735	-	31.77	13,908	1.81%
Sex offenses (including rape)	1,184	-	2.39	1,159	2.16%
Rape	-	-	-	-	-
Serious assault	22,888	-	46.21	26,110	6.16%
Theft	39,424	-	79.60	48,623	6.02%
Portugal: 1985					
Homicides	421	-	4.2	263	11.8%
Sex offenses (including rape)	251	-	2.5	228	7.5%
Rape	159	-	1.6	139	4.3%
Serious assault	93	-	0.9	71	22.5%
Theft	39,875	-	396.8	7,577	13.3%
Fraud	21,030	-	209.3	23,163	22.4%
Counterfeit currency	1,661	-	16.5	861	14.1%
Drug offenses	1,371	-	13.6	1,934	9.6%
Saudi Arabia: 1986					
Homicides	107	-	1.02	102	3%
Sex offenses (including rape)	2,092	-	19.9	2,900	29%

[Continued]

Worldwide Crimes and Crime Rates
[Continued]

Country, year, offence	Volume of crime			Offenders	
	Cases known to police	Cases solved	Volume per 100,000	Total	% Female
Rape	63	-	0.6	45	-
Serious assault	18	-	0.2	21	-
Theft	6,851	-	65.2	1,662	2%
Fraud	177	-	1.7	227	-
Counterfeit currency	32	-	0.3	34	-
Drug offenses	4,279	-	40.8	6,046	1.4%
Senegal: 1986					
Homicides	82	64[3]	1.21	66	27.27%
Sex offenses (including rape)	591	482	8.77	556	74.28%
Rape	63	63	0.93	83	-
Serious assault	1,868	1,408	27.74	1,227	21.43%
Theft	8,086	4,754	120.11	6,433	5.20%
Fraud	1,014	858	15.06	889	8.09%
Counterfeit currency	24	20	0.35	26	0.03%
Drug offenses	1,424	1,278	21.15	1,666	7.26%
Spain: 1986					
Homicides	879	86.35%	2.32	860	11.28%
Sex offenses (including rape)	5,226	66.03%	13.84	3,223	-
Rape	1,466	53.20%	3.88	768	-
Serious assault	10,122	59.99%	26.81	3,861	6.39%
Theft	514,931	11%	1,364.19	66,236	5.93%
Fraud	21,504	54.25%	56.96	3,239	12.38%
Counterfeit currency	179	100%	0.47	168	-
Drug offenses	13,773	98.17%	36.48	19,203	22.02%
Sri Lanka: 1986					
Homicides	4,378	94.7%	27.2	5,182	15.8%
Sex offenses (including rape)	503	92.4%	3.1	702	2.4%
Rape	257	93.6%	1.5	371	4.5%
Serious assault	6,742	92.8%	41.9	10,233	8.4%
Theft	45,735	56.5%	1,284.2	32,017	3.3%
Fraud	3,522	67.8%	21.8	3,418	8.3%
Counterfeit currency	61	50%	0.3	97	-
Drug offenses	114	95%	0.7	140	0.1%
Sudan: 1986					
Homicides	1,045	24.9%	5	-	2.2%
Sex offenses (including rape)	2,738	40%	13.1	-	6.1%
Rape	601	32%	2.8	-	-
Serious assault	7,335	65%	35.2	-	9.3%
Fraud	15,014	73%	72	-	-
Drug offenses	3,584	74%	17.2	3,584	0.1%

[Continued]

★ 80 ★

Worldwide Crimes and Crime Rates
[Continued]

Country, year, offence	Volume of crime			Offenders	
	Cases known to police	Cases solved	Volume per 100,000	Total	% Female
Switzerland: 1986					
Homicides	136	-	2.08	126	11.1%
Sex offenses (including rape)	3,359	-	51.49	1,732	-
Rape	398	-	6.10	215	-
Serious assault	3,259	-	49.96	3,023	9%
Theft	294,815	-	4,519.55	39,352	16.8%
Fraud	7,180	-	110.07	5,289	14.9%
Counterfeit currency	714	-	10.95	-	-
Drug offenses	15,815	-	242.45	15,815	19%
Syria: 1986					
Homicides	220	94%	2.07	72	31%
Sex offenses (including rape)	548	100%	5.16	474	308%(sic)
Rape	109	100%	1.03	30	15%
Serious assault	7	100%	0.06	-	-
Theft	3,516	59%	33.13	616	132%(sic)
Fraud	377	95%	3.55	19	12%
Counterfeit currency	69	100%	0.65	5	4%
Drug offenses	279	98%	2.63	29	12%
Tunisia: 1985					
Homicides	153	100%	2.10	219	4.56%
Sex offenses (including rape)	5,043	85.84%	69.45	7,249	23.04%
Rape	551	94.73%	7.58	634	-
Serious assault	9,732	95.62%	134.02	12,668	14.13%
Theft	25,320	43.66%	348.70	12,598	4.65%
Fraud	1,108	85.92%	15.25	870	3.10%
Counterfeit currency	147	33.33%	2.02	58	8.62%
Drug offenses	81	100%	1.11	205	-
United Kingdom (England & Wales): 1986					
Homicides	820	93%	1.64	418	10%
Sex offenses (including rape)	22,684	71%	45.44	8,367	2%
Rape	2,288	62%	4.58	415	1%
Serious assault	122,139	71%	244.65	50,162	10%
Theft	2,970,335	29%	5,949.77	329,106	20%
Fraud	133,431	67%	267.27	25,570	22%
Drug offenses	7,332	99%	14.69	21,318	13%
United States: 1986					
Homicides	20,610	70.2%	8.6	16,966	12.1%
Sex offenses (including rape)	-	-	-	211,944	33.2%
Rape	90,430	52.3%	37.5	31,128	1.1%
Serious assault	834,320	59.4%	346.1	293,952	13.2%
Theft	12,265,480	-	5,087.8	1,810,402	22.9%
Fraud	-	-	-	284,790	43.3%

[Continued]

★ 80 ★

Worldwide Crimes and Crime Rates
[Continued]

Country, year, offence	Volume of crime			Offenders	
	Cases known to police	Cases solved	Volume per 100,000	Total	% Female
Counterfeit currency	-	-	-	76,546	33.9%
Drug offenses	-	-	-	691,882	14.5%
Yugoslavia: 1986					
Homicides	1,255	90.3%	5.36	1,344	11.23%
Sex offenses (including rape)	1,620	90.6%	6.92	1,781	1.40%
Rape	1,165	90.2%	4.98	1,284	0.54%
Serious assault	8,311	94.4%	35.49	10,277	7.53%
Theft	157,479	49.4%	672.53	114,947	7.97%
Fraud	13,367	94.8%	57.09	13,520	14.50%
Counterfeit currency	884	88.4%	3.78	542	22.32%
Drug offenses	560	95.1%	2.39	475	5.26%

Source: Selected from *International Crime Statistics 1981-1982* and *1985-86* (Saint Cloud, France: 1982 and 1986). Also in source: % attempts; % minors; % aliens; other types of offenses. *Notes:* 1. Persons charged with 1,118 non-indictable offenses. 2. "Accound (sic) should be taken of the very large tourist population." 3. The figures in this column appear to be whole numbers rather than percentages (editor).

Drugs

★ 81 ★

Cocaine Use Among High School Seniors

Cocaine use in the last 12 months by sex and college plans, 1987-1988.

Year, sex, college plans	Never used	Ever used	Most recent use		
			Within last 30 days	Within last year/not in last 30 days days	Not within last year
1987					
Female	86.4%	13.6%	3.7%	5.5%	4.4%
Male	83.5%	16.5%	4.9%	6.4%	5.2%
College plans:					
None or under 4 years	81.6%	18.4%	5.3%	7.1%	6.0%
Complete 4 years	86.8%	13.2%	3.6%	5.4%	4.2%
1988					
Female	89.6%	10.4%	2.6%	3.9%	3.9%
Male	86.4%	13.6%	4.2%	4.9%	4.5%
College plans:					

[Continued]

★ 81 ★

Cocaine Use Among High School Seniors
[Continued]

Year, sex, college plans	Never used	Ever used	Most recent use		
			Within last 30 days	Within last year/not in last 30 days days	Not within last year
None or under 4 years	84.2%	15.8%	4.6%	5.1%	6.1%
Complete 4 years	90.0%	10.0%	2.8%	3.9%	3.3%

Source: Selected from "Reported majihuana, cocaine, and heroin use and most recent use among high school seniors by sex, region, population density, and college plans, United States, 1987 and 1988," *Sourcebook of Criminal Justice Statistics - 1988*, p. 356. Primary source: Lloyd D. Johnston, Patrick M. O'Malley, and Jerald G. Bachman, *Illicit Drug Use, Smoking, and Drinking by America's High School Students, College Students, and Young Adults, 1975-1987*, U.S. Department of health and Human Services, National Institute on Drug Abuse (Washington, DC: USGPO, 1989), pp. 36, 38, 40; and data provided by U.S. Department of Health and Human Services, National Institute on Drug Abuse. Number surveyed = 16,300.

★ 82 ★

Drug Arrests of Pregnant Women

Characteristics of black and white women reported after delivery for substance abuse in Pinellas County, Florida; total number of women screened was 715 (499 white and 199 black).

Characteristic	White[1] (n = 48)	Black (n = 85)	Total (n = 133)
	Percent		
Low (<$12,000)	23	56	79
Middle ($12,000-$25,000)	20	23	43
High (>$25,000)	5	6	11
Drug use reported			
Alcohol	18	22	40
Marijuana	19	16	35
Cocaine	28	74	102
Opiates	1	0	1
Other	1	4	5

Source: Ira J. Chasnoff, M.D, Harvey J. Landress, A.C.S.W., and Mark kE. Barrett, Ph.D., "The Prevalence of Illicit-Drug or Alcohol Use During Pregnancy and Discrepancies in Mandatory Reporting in Pinellas County, Florida," *New England Journal of Medicine* 332:17 (April 26, 1990), p. 1202-1206. Related reading: Dorothy Roberts, "The Bias in Drug Arrests of Pregnant Women," *New York Times*, August 11, 1990, p. 17. "Florida is one of several states that have sought to protect newborns by requiring that mothers known to have used alcohol or illicit drugs during pregnancy be reported to health authorities" (source). *Notes:* 1. Includes only non-Hispanic white women. 2. The median annual family income in the ZIP Code area where the woman lived was used as an indicator of socioeconomic status.

★ 83 ★

Heroin Use Among High School Seniors

Heroin use in the last 12 months among high school seniors by sex and college plans, 1987-1988.

Year, sex, college plans	Never used	Ever used	Most recent use		
			Within last 30 days	Within last year but not last 30 days	Not within last year
1987					
Female	99.2%	0.8%	0.1%	0.2%	0.5%
Male	98.4%	1.6%	0.3%	0.4%	0.9%
College plans:					
None or under 4 years	98.5%	1.5%	0.2%	0.3%	1.0%
Complete 4 years	99.0%	1.0%	0.2%	0.2%	0.6%
1988					
Female	99.1%	0.9%	0.1%	0.2%	0.6%
Male	98.6%	1.4%	0.3%	0.4%	0.7%
College plans:					
None or under 4 years	98.3%	1.7%	0.4%	0.4%	0.9%
Complete 4 years	99.2%	0.8%	0.1%	0.2%	0.5%

Source: Selected from "Reported majihuana, cocaine, and heroin use and most recent use among high school seniors by sex, region, population density, and college plans, United States, 1987 and 1988," *Sourcebook of Criminal Justice Statistics - 1988,* p. 356. Primary source: Lloyd D. Johnston, Patrick M. O'Malley, and Jerald G. Bachman, *Illicit Drug Use, Smoking, and Drinking by America's High School Students, College Students, and Young Adults, 1975-1987,* U.S. Department of health and Human Services, National Institute on Drug Abuse (Washington, DC: USGPO, 1989), pp. 36, 38, 40; and data provided by U.S. Department of Health and Human Services, National Institute on Drug Abuse. Number surveyed = 16,300.

★ 84 ★

Marijuana Use Among High School Seniors

Marijuana use of high school seniors by sex and college plans, 1987-1988.

Year, sex, college plans	Never used	Ever used	Most recent use		
			Last 30 days	Last year/ not in last 30 days	Not within last year
1987					
Female	52.0%	48.0%	18.6%	15.2%	14.2%
Male	48.0%	52.0%	23.1%	15.5%	13.4%
College plans:					
None or under 4 years	43.0%	57.0%	25.1%	15.5%	16.4%
Complete 4 years	53.6%	46.4%	18.5%	15.5%	12.4%
1988					

[Continued]

★ 84 ★

Marijuana Use Among High School Seniors
[Continued]

Year, sex, college plans	Never used	Ever used	Most recent use		
			Last 30 days	Last year/ not in last 30 days	Not within last year
Female	55.5%	44.5%	15.2%	15.1%	14.2%
Male	50.2%	49.8%	20.7%	15.1%	14.0%
College plans:					
None or under 4 years	46.4%	53.6%	20.4%	15.8%	17.4%
Complete 4 years	56.0%	44.0%	16.4%	14.9%	12.7%

Source: Selected from "Reported majihuana, cocaine, and heroin use and most recent use among high school seniors by sex, region, population density, and college plans, United States, 1987 and 1988," *Sourcebook of Criminal Justice Statistics - 1988,* p. 356. Primary source: Lloyd D. Johnston, Patrick M. O'Malley, and Jerald G. Bachman, *Illicit Drug Use, Smoking, and Drinking by America's High School Students, College Students, and Young Adults, 1975-1987,* U.S. Department of health and Human Services, National Institute on Drug Abuse (Washington, DC: USGPO, 1989), pp. 36, 38, 40; and data provided by U.S. Department of Health and Human Services, National Institute on Drug Abuse. Table adapted by SOURCEBOOK staff. Number surveyed = 16,300.

Law Enforcement

★ 85 ★

Aliens Applying for Temporary Residency
Aliens applying for temporary residency, by age and marital status, 1988.

Characteristic	Pre-1982 Provisions	Special Agricultural Workers
	In thousands	
Total applicants[1]	1,767.0	1,287.8
Female	761.4	217.6
Male	1,005.5	1,070.1
Under 15 years old	136.6	2.7
15-19 years old	141.4	118.0
20-24 years old	234.7	384.2
25-29 years old	349.2	288.1
30-34 years old	335.2	191.0
35-39 years old	227.6	117.7
40-44 years old	137.8	76.9
45-64 yeras old	184.4	105.5
65 years old and over	19.8	3.5
Median age	30.3	27.4

[Continued]

★ 85 ★

Aliens Applying for Temporary Residency
[Continued]

Characteristic	Pre-1982 Provisions	Special Agricultural Workers
Marital status:		
Single	860.7	687.4
Married	732.3	541.8
Other	174.0	58.6

Source: "Alien Amnesty Program—Aliens Applying for Temporary Residency, by Selected Characteristic of the Alien: 1988," *Statistical Abstract of the United States, 1990,* 1990, p. 179. Primary Source: U.S. Immigration and Naturalization Service, *Provisional Legalization Application Statistics, January 27, 1989.* Also in source: data by selected country of citizenship and selected State of residence. Preliminary. Represents applications filed as of January 27, 1989 under the provisions of the Immigration Reform and Control Act of 1986. Applicants may apply under two provisions of the Act-those who have continuously resided in the United States since January 1, 1982 under the pre-1982 provisions, and those who have worked on perishable crops under Special Agricultural Worker provisions. *Notes:* 1. Includes a small number of unknown or not reported cases for which age and sex data were not recorded.

Law Enforcement Personnel

★ 86 ★

Assignments of Female Police Officers

Percentage of female officers in municipal departments by type assignment and city size, 1986.

City Size	Total Females (N=293)	Field (N=292)	CID (N=293)	Vice (N=250)	Admin (N=283)
Million+	9.9%	10.9%	7.9%	9.6%	17.5%
500,000-1,000,000	9.9%	10.3%	6.7%	7.4%	11.6%
250,000-500,000	8.8%	8.9%	7.0%	7.2%	10.8%
100,000-250,000	6.6%	7.1%	5.0%	6.7%	5.7%
50,000-100,000	5.1%	5.3%	5.3%	3.6%	4.1%

Source: Susan E. Martin, "Women on the Move?: A Report on the Status of Women in Policing," *Women & Criminal Justice* (1) 1989, p. 21+. Based on the responses of 319 police agencies serving populations over 50,000.

★ 87 ★

Female Supervisors in Police Departments

Mean percentage of female supervisors (sergeant, lieutenant, and above) in municipal departments by city size and ethnicity, 1986 (N=316).

City Size	White	Minority
Million+	2.5%	1.1%
500,000-1,000,000	2.4%	1.8%
250,000-500,000	3.1%	1.2%
100,000-250,000	2.3%	0.4%
50,000-100,000	1.1%	0.3%

Source: Susan E. Martin, "Women on the Move?: A Report on the Status of Women in Policing," *Women & Criminal Justice* (1) 1989, p. 21+. Also in source: data for 1978. Based on the responses of 319 police agencies serving populations over 50,000.

★ 88 ★

Law Enforcement Employees

Law enforcement employees, total and percent female, 1989.

Population group	Police employees		Police officers		Civilian employees	
	Total	% female	Total	% female	Total	% female
Total agencies: 12,218; population 229,678,000:	676,647	23.2%	496,353	8.3%	180,294	64.2%
Total cities: 9,295; population 153,189,000:	414,038	21.7%	322,293	7.9%	91,745	70.5%

Source: "Law Enforcement Employees, Percent Male and Female, October 31, 1989," *Crime in the United States 1989*, p. 241 (August 5, 1990). Also in source: breakdown by size of city.

★ 89 ★

Minorities in Police Departments

Mean percentage of police in municipal departments by sex and ethnicity, 1986.

Ethnicity	Female	Male
White	5.3%	72.2%
Minority	3.5%	19.0%

Source: Susan E. Martin, "Women on the Move?: A Report on the Status of Women in Policing," *Women & Criminal Justice* (1) 1989, p. 21+. Based on the responses of 319 police agencies serving populations over 50,000.

★ 90 ★

Police in America's Largest Cities

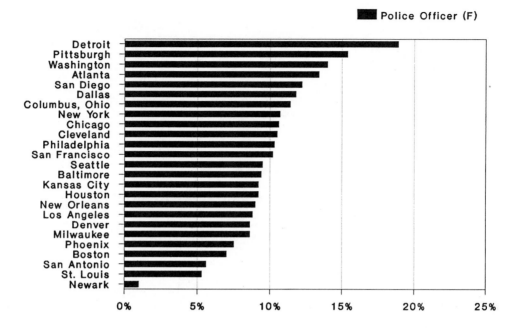

Percentages of female police officers in America's largest cities, 1987.

City	% Female
Detroit	18.9%
Pittsburgh	15.4%
Washington	14.0%
Atlanta	13.4%
San Diego	12.2%
Dallas	11.8%
Columbus, Ohio	11.4%
New York	10.7%
Chicago	10.6%
Cleveland	10.5%
Philadelphia	10.3%
San Francisco	10.2%
Seattle	9.5%
Baltimore	9.4%
Kansas City	9.2%
Houston	9.2%
New Orleans	9.0%
Los Angeles	8.8%
Denver	8.6%
Milwaukee	8.6%
Phoenix	7.5%
Boston	7.0%

[Continued]

★ 90 ★

Police in America's Largest Cities
[Continued]

City	% Female
San Antonio	5.6%
St. Louis	5.3%
Newark	1.0%

Source: "Women: Cops Sue City for Harassment," *Detroit News*, December 9, 1990, p. 1A+. Primary source: 1987 U.S. Justice Department study.

★ 91 ★

Sworn Personnel in State Police Agencies

Race and sex of sworn personnel in State police agencies, 1987.

	Percent of sworn employees		
	Total	Female	Male
Total	100%	4.2%	95.8%
White	88.7%	3.6%	85.1%
Black	6.5%	0.4%	6.1%
Hispanic	3.8%	0.2%	3.7%
Other	0.9%	0.8%	--

Source: "Race and sex of sworn personnel in State police agencies, 1987," *BJS Data Report, 1989*, 1990, p. 58. Table includes both full-time and part-time employees. Breakdown of blacks and whites does not include Hispanics. "Other" includes American Indians, Alaska Natives, Asians, and Pacific Islanders. Detail may not add to total because of rounding.

★ 92 ★

Women in Police Departments

Proportion of women in large and medium-sized police departments.

	1978	1986
Proportion of women sworn personnel	4.2%	8.8%

Source: Susan E. Martin, "Women on the Move?: A Report on the Status of Women in Policing," *Women & Criminal Justice* (1) 1989, p. 21+. Based on the responses of 319 police agencies serving populations over 50,000.

Victims

★ 93 ★

10 Facts About Violence Against Women

Statistics prepared for a congressional hearing on legislation to reduce the growing problem of violent crime against women, 1990.

The most serious crimes against women are rising at a significantly faster rate than total crime: since 1980, rape rates have risen nearly 4 times as fast as the total crime rate.

Every hour, 16 women confront rapists; a woman is raped every 6 minutes.

Every 18 seconds, a woman is beaten; 3 to 4 million women are battered each year.

Since 1974, the rate of assaults against young women between the ages of 20 and 24 has risen almost 50%.

Three out of 4 women will be victims of at least 1 violent crime during their lifetimes.

A woman is 10 times more likely to be raped than to die in a car crash.

Only 50% of rapes are ever reported; of those reported, less than 40% result in arrests.

One third of all domestic violence cases, if reported, would be charged as felony rape or felonious assault.

Each year, more than 1,000,000 women seek medical assistance for injuries caused by battering.

The crime rate against women in the United States is significantly higher than in other countries—the United States has a rape rate which is 13 times higher than England's, nearly 4 times higher than Germany's, and more than 20 times higher than Japan's.

Source: U.S. Senate, Committee on the Judiciary, *One Hundred First Congress Second Session on Legislation to Reduce the Growing Problem of Violent Crime Against Women*, June 20, 1990, Part 1, Serial No. J-101-80, p. 12.

★ 94 ★

Child Abuse Cases Reported: 1960-1986

Number of abused children reported and characteristics (in percent) of child abuse cases, 1976 to 1986.

Item	1976	1977	1978	1979	1980	1981	1982	1983	1984	1985	1986
Number of children reported (in thousands)[1]	669	838	836	988	1,154	1,225	1,262	1,477	1,727	1,928	2,086
Rate per 10,000 children	101	128	129	154	181	194	201	236	273	306	328
Type of maltreatment:											
Deprivation of necessities	70.7%	64.0%	62.9%	63.1%	60.7%	59.4%	62.5%	58.4%	54.6%	53.6%	54.9%
Minor physical injury	18.9%	20.8%	21.2%	15.4%	19.8%	20.4%	16.8%	18.5%	17.7%	17.8%	13.9%

[Continued]

★ 94 ★

Child Abuse Cases Reported: 1960-1986

[Continued]

Item	1976	1977	1978	1979	1980	1981	1982	1983	1984	1985	1986
Sexual maltreatment	3.2%	6.1%	6.65	5.8%	6.8%	7.5%	6.9%	8.5%	13.3%	13.8%	15.7%
Emotional maltreatment	21.6%	25.4%	23.8%	14.9%	13.5%	11.9%	10.0%	10.1%	11.2%	11.5%	8.3%
Other maltreatment	11.2%	11.6%	11.3%	15.8%	14.7%	19.0%	16.3%	16.7%	16.5%	13.8%	21.6%
Characteristics of child involved:											
Age, average (years)	7.7	7.6	7.4	7.5	7.3	7.2	7.1	7.1	7.2	7.2	7.2
Sex:											
Female	50.0%	50.1%	50.6%	50.5%	50.2%	50.5%	50.5%	51.1%	52.0%	52.4%	52.5%
Male	50.0%	49.9%	49.4%	49.5%	49.8%	49.2%	49.5%	48.9%	48.0%	47.6%	47.5%
Characteristics of perpetrator:											
Age, average (years)	32.3	31.7	31.7	32.0	31.4	33.8	31.2	31.3	31.5	31.6	31.7
Sex:											
Female	61.0%	60.8%	61.0%	61.9%	58.8%	60.7%	61.4%	59.6%	57.0%	55.9%	55.9%
Male	39.0%	39.2%	39.0%	38.1%	41.2%	39.3%	38.6%	40.4%	43.0%	44.1%	44.1%
Other maltreatment											

Source: "Child Maltreatment Cases Reported—Summary: 1976 to 1986," *Statistical Abstract of the United States, 1990,* p. 176. Primary source: American Humane Association, Denver, CO, *National Study on Child Neglect and Abuse Reporting,* annual. Because of differences in enumeration methods, a relatively small number of States (5 to 10) can provide only unduplicated reports, whereas most states provide only duplicated counts. *Notes:* 1. Total number of children reported is generally a duplicate count in that a child may be reported and therefore enumerated more than once each year.

★ 95 ★

Crimes Reported to Police

Percent of victimizations reported to the police by type of crime.

Sex	All personal crimes	Crimes of violence	Crimes of theft
Both sexes	33.5%	47.9%	27.5%
Female	34.8%	52.0%	28.8%
Male	32.3%	44.9%	26.1%

Source: Selected from "Percent of victimizations reported to the police, by selected characteristics of victims and type of crime," *Criminal Victimization in the United States, 1988,* p. 81. Also in source: data by race/ethnicity.

★ 96 ★

Female Victims of Violent Crimes

Characteristics of female victims of violent crimes and of violent crimes against females, 1987 or 1989.

Characteristic	Number or %
Female rates of violent victimization, 1987[1]	24%
Aggravated assaults per 1,000 women, 1989	4.0
Aggravated assaults per 1,000 men, 1989	11.9
Violent crimes reported by female victims that were committed by family members or intimates	25%
Violent crimes reported by female victims that were committed by people whom the victims knew	27%

[Continued]

★ 96 ★

Female Victims of Violent Crimes
[Continued]

Characteristic	Number or %
Number of female victims of violence committed by family members or intimates who were injured	50%
Number who received medical treatment	23%
Number who were hospitalized	10%
Number of female murder victims in 1989 who were killed by husbands or boyfriends	28%
Number of female victims of violence who were attacked by a family member or intimate using a weapon	21%

Source: Violent Crime in the United States, March 1991, various pages. *Note:* 1. Rate per 1,000 persons age 12 or older.

★ 97 ★

Hospital Care of Crime Victims

Percent distribution of victimizations in which injured victims received hospital care by type of care, crimes of violence.

Sex and type of crime	Number of victimiza-tions	Emergency room care	Inpatient care
Female			
Crimes of violence[2]	183,080	66.2%	33.8%
Robbery	32,190	59.6%	40.4%[1]
Assault	121,390	68.9%	31.1%
Male			
Crimes of violence[2]	270,860	56.0%	44.0%
Robbery	65,880	52.1%	47.9%
Assault	203,240	56.9%	43.1%

Source: Selected from "Percent distribution of victimizations in which injured victims received hospital care, by selected characteristics of victims, type of crime, and type of hospital care," *Criminal Victimization in the United States, 1988*, p. 71. Also in source: data by race and for other types of crimes and by victim-offender relationship. Data may not add to total shown because of rounding. *Notes:* 1. Estimate is based on about 10 or fewer sample cases. 2. Includes data on rape, not shown separately.

★ 98 ★

Murder Circumstances by Relationship

Percent distribution of murder circumstances by relationship, 1989.

Victim	Total	Felony type	Romantic triangle	Argument over money or property	Other arguments
Husband	2.4%	.3%	5.5%	2.0%	5.4%
Wife	4.1%	.2%	8.1%	1.5%	8.1%
Mother	.7%	.3%	-	.9%	.9%
Father	.9%	.4%	.3%	.7%	1.7%
Daughter	1.4%	.8%	.3%	-	.6%
Son	1.6%	.8%	.3%	.2%	1.2%
Brother	1.0%	.2%	.8%	1.6%	2.0%
Sister	.2%	.1%	-	-	.3%
Other family	2.3%	1.5%	1.3%	3.8%	3.9%
Acquaintances	29.3%	27.5%	53.2%	55.0%	41.1%
Friend	4.7%	3.7%	10.9%	16.0%	7.2%
Boyfriend	1.4%	.1%	1.6%	1.3%	3.5%
Girlfriend	2.6%	.4%	9.6%	2.4%	5.4%
Neighbor	1.2%	1.2%	.8%	2.5%	1.9%
Stranger	13.1%	27.7%	5.7%	7.4%	9.4%
Unknown relationship	33.1%	34.8%	1.8%	4.7%	7.4%

Source: Selected from "Murder Circumstances by Relationship," *Crime in the United States 1989*, p. 12 (August 5, 1990). Also in source: other circumstances. Because of rounding, percentages may not add to totals. "Among all female murder victims in 1989, 28% were slain by husbands or boyfriends."

★ 99 ★

Murder Victims by Age

Murder victims by age and sex, 1989.

Age	Total	Sex	
		Female	Male
Total U.S.	18,954	4,483	14,464
Percent distribution	100%	23.7%	76.3%
Under 18[1]	1,899	616	1,281
18 and over[1]	16,798	3,795	13,002
Infant (under 1)	254	118	134
1 to 4	340	158	182
5 to 9	159	77	82
10 to 14	247	95	152
15 to 19	2,001	328	1,673
20 to 24	3,159	605	2,554
25 to 29	3,300	704	2,596
30 to 34	2,641	585	2,055
35 to 39	1,922	431	1,491
40 to 44	1,279	312	967
45 to 49	847	197	650
50 to 54	639	141	498

[Continued]

★ 99 ★

Murder Victims by Age
[Continued]

Age	Total	Sex	
		Female	Male
55 to 59	466	102	364
60 to 64	430	117	313
65 to 69	313	111	202
70 to 74	262	101	161
75 and over	438	229	209
Unknown	257	72	181

Source: Selected from "Age, Sex, and Race of Murder Victims, 1989," *Crime in the United States 1989*, p. 10 (August 5, 1990). *Note:* 1. Does not include unknown ages.

★ 100 ★

Robbery-Rape Victims

Percentage of male offender-female victim robberies that include rape, by racial composition, number of offenders, victim-offender relationship, and location. Number of robberies in parentheses.

Characteristic of male offender/female victim	Total	Single offender	Multiple offender	Stranger	Non-stranger	Private locations	Public locations
White offender/white victim	2.64% (2,615)	3.52% (1,249)	1.83% (1,366)	2.59% (1,773)	2.61% (804)	3.70% (649)	1.95% (1,746)
White offender/black victim	2.65% (565)	9.43% (53)	1.95% (512)	1.94% (464)	6.74% (89)	3.77% (106)	2.26% (443)
Black offender/white victim	2.60% (1,999)	3.85% (935)	1.50% (1,064)	2.64% (1,668)	2.30% (304)	6.55% (336)	1.72% (1,514)
Black offender/black victim	3.88% (798)	5.54% (505)	1.02% (293)	4.78% (523)	2.46% (244)	6.16% (211)	2.27% (529)

Source: Scott J. South and Richard B. Felson, "The Racial Patterning of Rape," *Social Forces*, September 1990, 69(1):71-93. Also in source: a discussion of interracial and intraracial rapes. Based on data on 1,396 rapes reported in the National Crime Survey.

★ 101 ★

Spouse Murders

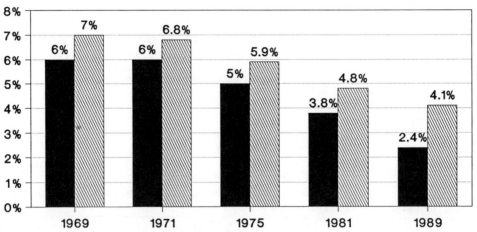

Some statistics on marriage and murder over the last 20 years.

Risk of Being Killed by a Spouse: 1.3 in 100,000. In 1989, 6.5% of all murders were committed by a spouse killing a spouse.

How Many Spouses are Murdered: About 500 to 1,000 husbands are murdered by their wives each year; about 1,000 to 1,300 wives are killed by their husbands.

Most at Risk of Being Killed by a Spouse: Black husbands, 9.7 per 100,000; followed by black wives, 7.1 per 100,000; white wives, 1.3 per 100,000, and white husbands, 0.7 per 100,000.

Age at Which Most Spouses are Murdered: For black husbands and wives, it peaks at age 15-24, then drops sharply. For white women, it peaks at 15-24, then gradually drops to age 55. For white men, chances are low at any age.

Murder Weapons: Firearms were used in 71.5% of the spouse murders between 1976 and 1985, by both men and women. Wives were more likely than husbands to use a knife; husbands were more likely to use a blunt instrument.

Source: James A. Mercy and Linda E. Saltzman, *American Journal of Public Health*, May 1989; U.S. Uniform Crime Report, 1969-1989. Source of chart: U.S. Uniform Crime Reports, as published in *Detroit Free Press*, March 31, 1991, p. 6F. Data for 1989, in chart, are estimated.

★ 102 ★

Victim/Offender Relationship

Victim/offender relationship by race and sex, 1989.

Victim	Total victims/ offenders	Offender						
		Race				Sex		
		White	Black	Other	Unknown	Female	Male	Unknown
Race								
White	5,205	4,462	645	55	43	554	4,608	43
Black	5,064	297	4,741	12	14	837	4,213	14
Other	186	51	22	107	6	25	155	6
Unknown	63	15	15	1	32	1	30	32
Sex								
Female	2,637	1,372	1,188	58	19	245	2,373	19
Male	7,818	3,438	4,220	116	44	1,171	6,603	44
Unknown	63	15	15	1	32	1	30	32

Source: "Victim/Offender Relationship by Race and Sex, 1989," *Crime in the United States 1989*, p. 10 (August 5, 1990). Single victim/single offender.

★ 103 ★

Victimization Rate by Race, Age, and Type of Crime

Victimization rates per 1,000 persons age 12 and over by race and age of victims and type of crime, 1988.

Race, sex, and age	Total population	Rate per 1,000 persons	
		Crimes of violence	Crimes of theft
White Female			
12-15	5,149,780	40.3	127.3
16-19	5,884,210	52.7	126.8
20-24	7,806,880	37.4	112.8
25-34	18,115,920	31.5	79.5
35-49	21,039,490	21.1	70.3
50-64	15,054,910	7.6	37.6
65 and over	15,224,870	2.4	17.9
Black Female			
12-15	1,017,840	46.1	114.2
16-19	1,105,130	72.5	79.5
20-24	1,375,260	58.7	104.8
25-34	2,901,780	44.2	69.5
35-49	2,848,370	20.8	68.2
50-64	1,816,170	16.6	34.1
65 and over	1,448,100	5.1[1]	16.3
White Male			
12-15	5,383,160	70.1	96.4
16-19	5,999,440	84.7	129.2

[Continued]

81

★ 103 ★

Victimization Rate by Race, Age, and Type of Crime
[Continued]

Race, sex, and age	Total population	Rate per 1,000 persons	
		Crimes of violence	Crimes of theft
20-24	7,667,050	77.3	142.0
25-34	18,268,210	36.9	86.1
35-49	20,683,440	22.8	62.5
50-64	13,783,060	11.3	42.4
65 and over	10,814,820	5.7	19.9
Black Male			
12-15	1,042,320	82.6	120.2
16-19	1,111,690	113.3	92.6
20-24	1,138,960	82.5	92.0
25-34	2,448,740	45.5	91.0
35-49	2,324,440	21.7	60.3
50-64	1,465,630	13.0	41.4
65 and over	982,340	10.5[1]	11.9

Source: "Victimization rates for persons age 12 and over, by race, sex, and age of victims and type of crime," *Criminal Victimization in the United States, 1988,* December 1990, p. 22. *Note:* 1. Estimate is based on about 10 or fewer sample cases.

★ 104 ★

Victimization Rates by Age of Victim and Type of Crime

Victimization rates per 1,000 persons age 12 and over, by sex and age of victims and type of crime, 1988.

Sex and age	Total population	Crimes of violence	Completed violent crimes	Attempted violent crimes	Rape
Female					
12-15	6,401,330	41.5	12.2	29.3	.7[1]
16-19	7,205,190	54.7	25.3	29.4	3.4
20-24	9,462,620	39.8	16.4	23.4	3.0
25-34	21,772,870	32.8	14.9	17.8	2.0
35-49	24,702,580	21.2	8.9	12.3	.5[1]
50-64	17,183,600	8.8	4.2	4.7	.3[1]
65 and over	16,878,070	2.7	1.6	1.1	0[1]
Male					
12-15	6,708,590	71.7	24.9	46.7	0[1]
16-19	7,337,660	89.0	32.4	56.6	.5[1]
20-24	9,043,400	78.8	24.5	54.3	0[1]
25-34	21,404,300	37.6	11.9	25.6	0[1]
35-49	23,780,000	22.5	7.2	15.3	.1[1]

[Continued]

★ 104 ★

Victimization Rates by Age of Victim and Type of Crime
[Continued]

Sex and age	Total population	Crimes of violence	Completed violent crimes	Attempted violent crimes	Rape
50-64	15,557,320	11.6	2.7	8.9	.1[1]
65 and over	11,974,860	6.2	2.2	4.0	0[2]

Source: "Victimization rates for persons age 12 and over, by sex and age of victims and type of crime," *Criminal Victimization in the United States, 1988,* December 1990, p. 18. Detail may not add to total shown because of rounding. *Note:* 1. Estimate is based on about 10 or fewer sample cases.

★ 105 ★

Victimization Rates by Residence and Race

Victimization rates for crimes of violence for persons age 12 and over, by type of locality of residence, race, and sex of victims and by type of crime.

Locality, race, and sex	Total population	Crimes of violence	Completed violent crimes	Attempted violent crimes	Rape
All areas					
White male	82,599,220	34.4	10.7	23.7	0.1[1]
White female	88,276,070	22.4	9.1	13.3	0.9
Black male	10,514,160	47.3	18.6	28.7	0.0[1]
Black female	12,512,680	34.6	17.7	16.8	2.6
Metropolitan areas					
Central cities					
White male	20,912,990	46.5	16.1	30.3	0.3[1]
White female	23,357,510	33.1	13.5	19.7	1.6
Black male	5,705,980	54.1	21.1	33.0	0.0[1]
Black female	7,094,430	40.6	21.6	18.9	4.1
Outside central cities					
White male	37,927,140	33.6	10.4	23.2	0.0[1]
White female	39,735,600	19.2	8.0	11.2	0.8
Black male	2,828,100	39.8	17.1	22.7	0.0[1]
Black female	3,135,890	27.1	11.8	15.3	0.6[1]
Nonmetropolitan areas					
White male	23,759,070	25.0	6.4	18.6	0.1[1]

[Continued]

★ 105 ★

Victimization Rates by Residence and Race
[Continued]

Locality, race, and sex	Total population	Crimes of violence	Completed violent crimes	Attempted violent crimes	Rape
White female	25,182,950	17.3	6.7	10.6	0.5[1]
Black male	1,980,080	38.3	13.3	25.0	0.0[1]
Black female	2,282,350	26.1	13.8	12.3	0.7[1]

Source: Selected from "Victimization rates for persons age 12 and over, by type of locality of residence, race, and sex of victims and by type of crime," *Criminal Victimization in the United States, 1988*, p. 32. Also in source: data for other types of crime. Detail may not add to total shown because of rounding. *Note:* 1. Estimate is based on about 10 or fewer sample cases.

★ 106 ★

Victimization Rates by Sex of Head of Household

Victimization rates for violent crimes for persons age 12 and over in female-headed households by relationship of victims to head.

Relationship of victims to female head of household	Total population	Crimes of violence	Completed violent crimes	Attempted violent crimes	Rape
			Rate per 1,000 persons age 12 and over		
Households headed by females					
All female heads	31,941,920	32.9	15.3	17.6	1.6
Female heads living alone	14,000,640	21.7	9.3	12.4	1.1[1]
Female heads living with others	17,941,270	41.6	19.9	21.7	1.9
Husbands	5,133,680	21.2	7.1	14.0	0.3[1]
Own children under age 18	5,238,670	81.7	34.7	47.0	0.7[1]
Own children age 18 and over	6,280,210	54.2	23.0	31.2	1.2[1]
Other relatives	3,462,390	44.9	16.1	28.8	1.7[1]
Nonrelatives	3,361,260	68.9	26.4	42.5	5.2
Households headed by males					
All male heads	63,960,330	23.5	7.1	16.4	0.1[1]
Male heads living alone	9,533,000	47.1	18.6	28.5	0[1]
Male heads living with others	54,427,330	19.4	5.1	14.3	0.1[1]
Wives	46,150,100	9.8	3.6	6.2	0.2[1]
Own children under age 18	13,519,890	47.1	16.1	31.1	0.5[1]
Own children age 18 and over	11,566,190	43.0	15.5	27.5	0.7[1]
Other relatives	4,041,680	38.4	14.0	24.4	0.5[1]
Nonrelatives	4,756,090	73.9	24.3	49.7	2.0[1]

Source: Selected from "Victimization rates for persons age 12 and over, by sex of head of household, relationship of victims to head, and type of crime," *Criminal Victimization in the United States, 1988*, p. 12. Also in source: rate per 1,000 persons age 12 and over for other types of crimes. Detail may not add to total shown because of rounding. *Note:* 1. Estimate is based on about 10 or fewer sample cases.

★ 107 ★

Victimization Rates by Type of Crime

Victimization rate per 1,000 persons age 12 and over, 1988.

Type of crime	Rate per 1,000 persons over 12		
	Total	Female	Male
Crimes of violence	29.6	23.8	35.9
Completed	10.9	10.2	11.7
Attempted	18.7	13.6	24.2
Rape	.6	1.2	.1[1]
Completed	.3	.6	0[1]
Attempted	.3	.5	.1[1]
Robbery	5.3	4.1	6.5
Assault	23.7	18.6	29.3
Crimes of theft	70.5	67.9	73.3
Completed	66.4	63.9	69.1
Attempted	4.1	4.0	4.2
Personal larceny with contact	2.5	2.9	2.0
Personal larceny without contact	68.0	65.0	71.3
Total population age 12 and over	199,412,460	103,606,290	95,806,160

Source: Selected from "Victimization rates for persons age 12 and over, by type of crime and sex of victims," *Criminal Victimization in the United States, 1988,* December 1990, p. 16. Detail may not add to total shown because of rounding. *Note:* 1. Estimate is based on about 10 or fewer sample cases.

★ 108 ★

Victimization Rates by Type of Crime and Race

Victimization rates per 1,000 persons age 12 and over by type of cirme and race of victims, 1988.

Type of crime	Rate per 1,000 persons age 12 and over			
	Female		Male	
	White	Black	White	Black
Crimes of violence	22.4	34.6	34.4	47.3
Completed	9.1	17.7	10.7	18.6
Attempted	13.3	16.8	23.7	28.7
Rape	.9	2.6	.1[1]	0[1]
Robbery	3.6	7.7	5.9	11.4
Assault	17.8	24.3	28.4	35.9

[Continued]

★ 108 ★

Victimization Rates by Type of Crime and Race
[Continued]

Type of crime	Rate per 1,000 persons age 12 and over			
	Female		Male	
	White	Black	White	Black
Crimes of theft	68.4	66.3	73.2	73.1
Completed	64.5	62.1	69.0	68.6
Attempted	3.9	4.2	4.2	4.5
Personal larceny with contact	2.7	3.9	1.6	4.2
Personal larceny without contact	65.8	62.4	71.6	68.9
Total population age 12 and over	88,276,070	12,512,680	82,599,220	10,514,160

Source: Selected from "Victimization rates for persons age 12 and over, by type of crime and sex and race of victims," *Criminal Victimization in the United States, 1988,* December 1990, p. 19. Also in source: data broken down by crimes attempted and completed "with injury," etc. Detail may not add to total shown because of rounding. *Note:* 1. Estimate is based on about 10 or fewer sample cases.

★ 109 ★

Victimization by Type of Crime and Sex of Offender

Number and percent distribution of single-offender victimizations, by type of crime and perceived sex of offender: 1988.

	Number of victimi- zations	% single-offender victimizations		
		Perceived sex of offender		
		Total	Female	Male
Crimes of violence	4,326,370	100%	13.7%	85.6%
Rape	115,820	100%	1.7%[1]	95.0%
Robbery	568,510	100%	11.1%	87.0%
Assault	3,642,040	100%	14.5%	85.1%

Source: Selected from "Percent distribution of single-offender victimizations, by type of crime and perceived sex of offender," *Criminal Victimization in the United States, 1988,* December 1990, p. 46. Also in source: breakdown by types of robbery; data for "Not known and not available." Detail may not add to total shown because of rounding. *Note:* 1. Estimate is based on about 10 or fewer sample cases.

★ 110 ★

Victims Protecting Themselves

Percent of all victimizations in which victims took self-protective measures, violent crimes.

Sex	Crimes of violence	Completed violent crimes	Attempted violent crimes	Rape
Female	74.6%	74.8%	74.4%	85.8%
Male	73.3%	66.8%	76.5%	100.0%[1]

Source: Selected from "Percent of victimizations in which victims took self-protective measures, by selected characteristics of victims and type of crime, *Criminal Victimization in the United States, 1988*, p. 65. Also in source: data by race and age; data for other types of crime. *Note:* 1. Estimate is based on about 10 or fewer sample cases.

DOMESTIC LIFE

Caregiving

★ 111 ★

Caregiving Outside the Household

Distribution by selected characteristics of persons who provided assistance to persons outside their household, by type of assistance, 1986.

Characteristic	Provided assistance with...					
	One or more activities	Personal care	Getting around	Preparing meals	Doing housework	Keeping track of bills and/ or money
Total (in thousands)	15,099	3,790	11,656	6,794	7,475	3,456
Sex						
Female	67.1%	74.0%	66.0%	79.4%	74.9%	64.8%
Male	32.9%	26.0%	34.0%	20.6%	25.1%	35.2%
Relationship to Recipient						
Son	12.0%	11.8%	12.9%	8.0%	10.1%	19.7%
Daughter	22.2%	26.9%	24.2%	27.7%	29.3%	35.2%
Other relative	32.6%	35.6%	31.8%	34.5%	35.2%	31.5%
Nonrelative	33.2%	25.7%	31.1%	29.8%	25.5%	13.6%

Source: The Need for Personal Assistance with Everyday Activities: Recipients and Caregivers, Current Population Reports, Series P-70, Table 1, No. 19, 1990, p. 14. Also in source: data by age, race, Hispanic origin, and labor force participation of persons 15 to 64 years.

★ 112 ★

Caregiving in Middle Age

Percentages of respondents in caregiving roles, by age.

Role	Age of respondent				
	40-44	45-49	50-54	55-59	60-64
Help parents 3 or more hours/week					
Women	20%	12%	9%	8%	14%
Men	12%	12%	5%	10%	3%
Help in-laws 3 or more hours/week					

[Continued]

★ 112 ★

Caregiving in Middle Age
[Continued]

Role	Age of respondent				
	40-44	45-49	50-54	55-59	60-64
Women	5%	6%	2%	3%	1%
Men	4%	5%	0%	4%	5%
Help adult children 3 or more hours/week					
Women	7%	19%	33%	36%	29%
Men	3%	12%	21%	18%	23%
Any parents live with respondent					
Female	3%	6%	6%	8%	8%
Male	2%	3%	4%	0%	9%
Total respondents					
Female	124	86	92	78	125
Male	93	61	56	49	65

Source: Glenna Spitze and John Logan, "More Evidence on Women (and Men) in the Middle," *Research on Aging* 12:2 (June 1990), p. 182+. Based on personal interviews conducted in the Albany-Schenectady-Troy, New York, metropolitan area during a 6-month period from September, 1988, to February, 1989. There were 1,200 persons, age 40 and older, interviewed.

★ 113 ★

Caregiving to a Household Member

Distribution by selected characteristics of persons who provided assistance to a household member, by type of assistance provided, 1986.

Caregiver characteristic	Provided assistance with...					
	One or more activities	Personal care	Getting around	Preparing meals	Doing housework	Keeping track of bills and/ or money
Total (in thousands)	5,791	2,469	2,894	3,734	3,927	1,815
Sex of caregiver						
Female	55.8%	67.8%	53.9%	57.1%	52.3%	70.6%
Male	44.2%	32.2%	46.1%	42.9%	47.7%	29.4%
Age of caregiver						
Under 18 years	9.6%	6.0%	4.3%	8.0%	11.5%	0.3%
18 to 64 years	64.2%	62.9%	68.2%	63.5%	62.5%	62.0%
65 years and over	26.2%	31.1%	27.5%	28.5%	26.0%	37.7%
Relationship to Recipient						
Son	11.9%	7.4%	10.7%	10.6%	11.6%	7.3%
Daughter	18.4%	18.3%	15.2%	20.2%	22.0%	21.6%
Spouse	44.0%	45.0%	49.0%	44.6%	42.3%	38.2%

[Continued]

★ 113 ★

Caregiving to a Household Member
[Continued]

Caregiver characteristic	Provided assistance with...					
	One or more activities	Personal care	Getting around	Preparing meals	Doing housework	Keeping track of bills and/ or money
Other relative	19.9%	22.9%	19.2%	18.4%	17.9%	25.8%
Nonrelative	5.8%	6.3%	5.8%	6.3%	6.2%	7.1%

Source: The need for Personal Assistance with Everyday Activities: Recipients and Caregivers, Current population Reports, Series P-70, Table H, No. 19, 1990, p. 11. Also in source: data by race and Hispanic origin; labor force participation status of persons 15 to 64 years.

★ 114 ★

Child Care Arrangements, Children Under 15

Primary child care arrangements used by employed mohters for children under 15, fall 1987.

Type of arrangement	Number of children in thousands		
	Total	Under 5	5-14 years
Number of children (in thousands)	28,842	9,124	19,718
Care in child's home	5,397	2,726	2,671
By father	2,719	1,395	1,324
By grandparent	750	463	287
By other relative	1,090	298	792
By nonrelative	838	570	268
Care in another home	4,309	3,249	1,059
By grandparent	1,177	792	384
By other relative	593	414	179
By nonrelative	2,539	2,043	496
Organized child care facilities	2,679	2,220	459
Day/group care center	1,806	1,465	341
Nursery school/preschool	873	755	118
Kindergarten/grade school	14,105	90	14,014
Child cares for self	832	24	807
Mother cares for child at work[1]	1,521	814	707

Source: Martin O'Connell and Amara Bachu, *Who's Minding the Kids? Child Care Arrangements: Winter, 1986-87,* Current Population Reports Household Economic Studies, Series P-70, Table B, No. 20, 1990, p. 3. Data on child care arrangements were collected only for the three youngest children under age 15 in the family. *Note:* 1. Includes women working at home or away from home.

★ 115 ★

Child Care Arrangements, Children Under Age 5

Primary child care arrangements used by employed mothers for children under 5, by age of child, fall 1987.

Type of arrangement	Total	Under 1 year	1 to 2 years	3 to 4 years
Number of children (in thousands)	9,124	1,485	3,771	3,868
Care in child's home	29.9%	31.2%	32.7%	26.6%
Care in another home	35.6%	38.4%	41.3%	29.0%
Organized child care facilities	24.3%	14.1%	18.1%	34.3%
Kindergarten/grade school	1.0%	-	-	2.3%
Child cares for self	0.3%	0.4%	0.2%	0.2%
Mother cares for child at work[1]	8.9%	16.0%	7.6%	7.5%

Source: Martin O'Connell and Amara Bachu, *Who's Minding the Kids? Child Care Arrangements: Winter, 1986-87,* Current Population Reports Household Economic Studies, Series P-70, No. 20, 1990, Table E, p. 7. Also in source: detailed breakdown of caregivers/facilities. Data on child care arrangements were collected only for the three youngest children under age 15 in the family. *Note:* 1. Includes women working at home or away from home.

★ 116 ★

Child Care Arrangements, Secondary Care

Children of employed mothers using secondary child care arrangements, by age of child and type of primary arrangement: 1987.

Age of child and type of primary arrangements	All children (thousands)	Using secondary care	
		Number (thousands)	Percent
All Children			
Total	28,842	7,938	27.5%
Care in child's home	5,397	776	14.4%
Care in another home	4,309	627	14.6%
Organized child care facilities	2,679	412	15.4%
Children Under 5 Years			
Total	9,124	1,080	11.8%
Care in child's home	2,726	342	12.5%
Care in another home	3,250	349	10.7%
Organized child care facilities	2,220	320	14.4%

[Continued]

★ 116 ★

Child Care Arrangements, Secondary Care
[Continued]

Age of child and type of primary arrangements	All children (thousands)	Using secondary care	
		Number (thousands)	Percent
Children 5 to 14 Years			
Total	19,718	6,857	34.8%
Care in child's home	2,671	434	16.2%
Care in another home	1,059	278	26.3%
Organized child care facilities	459	91	19.8%

Source: Martin O'Connell and Amara Bachu, *Who's Minding the Kids? Child Care Arrangements: Winter, 1986-87,* Current Population Reports Household Economic Studies, Series P070, No. 20, 1990, p. 18. Primary source: 1984-85 data are from Current Population Reports, Series P-70, No. 9, table F. Also in source: extensive breakdown of data by type of child care; data for Fall 1986 and Winter 1984-85. *Note:* 1. Includes women working at home or away from home.

★ 117 ★

Dependent Persons in Developing Countries: 1988-2020

Numbers of dependent persons (under age 20 and over age 64) per 100 persons of working age, Asia, Africa, Latin America and the Caribbean, 1988-2020.

Region and country	Dependent persons per 100 persons of working age											
	Total[1]			Youth[2]			Elderly[3]			Oldest[4]		
	1988	2005	2020	1988	2005	2020	1988	2005	2020	1988	2005	2020
Asia												
Bangladesh	131.7	100.4	73.8	124.9	93.2	66.1	6.9	7.2	7.8	17.7	17.6	18.2
China	81.3	61.1	62.6	71.4	48.1	42.8	10.0	13.0	19.8	19.2	25.0	23.8
Hong Kong	61.8	55.8	61.0	48.4	36.6	32.9	13.4	19.2	28.1	22.1	33.2	23.7
India	104.1	81.6	67.1	97.1	73.4	56.8	6.9	8.2	10.3	13.9	15.6	16.3
Indonesia	103.4	77.4	65.1	97.8	68.6	53.2	5.6	8.8	11.9	12.6	17.5	20.3
Korea, Republic of	77.7	67.7	61.7	69.7	53.1	45.1	7.9	11.6	16.6	19.1	18.3	20.6
Philippines	120.4	107.7	94.0	113.2	99.2	83.9	7.3	8.5	10.2	18.7	19.7	20.3
Singapore	59.4	52.4	59.2	50.7	38.9	32.9	8.7	13.5	26.3	21.6	23.2	20.0
Thailand	95.9	71.4	65.4	88.2	61.5	51.7	7.7	10.0	13.8	21.1	22.7	21.5
Turkey	109.8	86.1	71.5	100.7	75.5	59.3	9.1	10.6	12.3	20.8	22.2	22.5
Africa												
Kenya	181.4	169.3	139.0	175.5	163.6	133.3	5.9	5.7	5.7	15.9	17.5	18.8
Malawi	165.9	152.6	128.8	158.8	146.8	123.0	7.2	5.8	5.8	19.0	16.4	16.2
Morocco	128.2	99.8	77.8	119.0	90.3	67.2	9.2	9.5	10.6	23.0	23.6	23.1
Tunisia	117.3	86.5	70.0	107.8	76.5	59.1	9.5	10.0	10.9	20.6	22.9	21.8

[Continued]

★ 117 ★

Dependent Persons in Developing Countries: 1988-2020
[Continued]

| Region and country | Dependent persons per 100 persons of working age | | | | | | | | | | | |
| | Total[1] | | | Youth[2] | | | Elderly[3] | | | Oldest[4] | | |
	1988	2005	2020	1988	2005	2020	1988	2005	2020	1988	2005	2020
Zimbabwe	170.9	150.9	126.0	163.5	145.1	120.3	7.5	5.8	5.7	21.8	18.0	17.7
Brazil	107.6	89.7	78.1	99.3	79.5	64.8	8.3	10.2	13.3	19.8	23.3	23.3
Costa Rica	99.9	79.5	70.6	91.8	69.0	55.2	8.1	10.4	15.4	21.0	23.8	23.0
Guatemala	136.3	100.9	80.0	128.8	92.7	70.1	7.5	8.2	10.0	20.0	21.2	22.2
Jamaica	117.0	89.4	73.8	102.4	77.1	60.2	14.6	12.3	13.5	29.5	31.8	25.9
Mexico	122.3	82.2	68.7	113.2	72.3	55.8	9.1	10.0	12.9	26.8	26.1	27.1
Peru	118.2	96.1	79.3	110.2	87.1	68.2	8.0	9.0	11.1	18.9	19.7	21.0
Uruguay	83.7	76.0	68.7	62.5	53.5	47.9	21.3	22.4	20.8	25.9	32.3	29.7

Source: "Support Ratios: 1988, 2005, and 2020," *Aging in the Third World,* International Population Reports, Series P-95, No. 75, September 1988, p. 54. Primary Source: U.S. Bureau of the Census, Center for International Research, International Data Base on Aging. *Notes:* 1. Total - the number of persons aged 0-19 and 65 and over per 100 persons aged 20-64. 2. Youth - the number of persons aged 0-19 per 100 persons aged 20-64. 3. Elderly - the number of persons 65 and over per 100 persons aged 20-64. 4. Oldest - the number of persons 75 and over per 100 persons aged 60 and over.

★ 118 ★

Early Child Care Effects on Infant-Mother Attachment Pattern

The relationship of extrafamilial child care to the infant-mother attachment pattern; sample size was 93 infants.

| Attachment pattern | Child care (hours per week) | | | Total |
	Little/none (0-3 hours)	Moderate (4-19 hours)	High (20-54 hrs)	
	Number/percent of babies			
Secure	24/ 68.6%	35/ 77.8%	5/ 38.5%	64/ 68.8%
Anxious	11/ 31.4%	10/ 22.2%	8/ 61.5%	29/ 31.2%
Total	35/ 100%	45/ 100%	13/ 100%	93/ 100%

Source: Joseph L. Jacobson and Diane E. Wille, "Influence of Attachment and Separation Experience on Separation Distress at 18 Months," *Developmental Psychology* 20:3 (1984), 477-84. Distress in response to brief maternal separations was examined in a sample of 93 predominantly home-reared infants using the Ainsworth strange situation paradigm. At 18 months, the age when separation protest begins to decline, securely attached infants are better able than anxiously attached infants to tolerate brief maternal separations.

★ 119 ★

Personal Assistance Needs, Part I: Females

Women 15 years old and over by need for assistance status and selected characteristics, 1986.

Characteristic of person needing assistance	Total	Needed assistance with--						Did not need assistance
		One or more activities	Personal care	Getting around outside	Preparing meals	Doing housework	Keeping track of bills and/ or money	
Total females 15 years and over, in thousands	97,064	5,655	1,953	3,607	3,417	4,508	1,916	91,409
Age								
Under 65 years	80,812	2,495	741	1,324	1,576	2,062	495	78,317
65 years and over	16,252	3,160	1,211	2,283	1,841	2,446	1,421	13,092
65 to 69 years	5,298	589	142	341	318	476	151	4,709
70 to 74 years	4,183	525	220	358	315	435	182	3,659
75 years and over	6,771	2,046	849	1,583	1,208	1,536	1,087	4,725
Marital Status								
Married, spouse present	52,318	2,065	626	1,113	1,414	1,850	382	50,253
Married, spouse absent, widowed, divorced, separated	22,502	2,986	1,053	2,127	1,642	2,241	1,228	19,515
Never married	22,245	604	274	367	361	418	306	21,641
Living Arrangement								
Family member	80,329	3,630	1,339	2,231	2,508	3,070	1,124	76,699
Not a family member	16,735	2,025	614	1,376	909	1,438	792	14,710
Lives alone	13,018	1,835	529	1,238	767	1,289	692	11,183

Source: Selected from *Current Population Reports,* "The Need for Personal Assistance with Everyday Activities: Recipients and Caregivers," Series P-70, Table 4, No. 19, 1990, p. 27. Also in source: data for males (see separate table); data by race and Hispanic origin; data concerning health status.

★ 120 ★

Personal Assistance Needs, Part II: Males

Men 15 years old and over by need for assistance status and selected characteristics, 1986.

Characteristic of person needing assistance	Total	Needed assistance with...						Did not need assistance
		One or more activities	Personal care	Getting around outside	Preparing meals	Doing housework	Keeping track of bills and/ or money	
Total males 15 years and over, in thousands	88,958	2,551	1,258	1,606	1,413	1,418	1,123	86,407
Age								
Under 65 years	77,547	1,300	642	753	739	759	555	76,247
65 years and over	11,411	1,251	616	853	673	660	569	10,160
65 to 69 years	4,316	301	143	205	166	159	123	4,015
70 to 74 years	3,208	281	115	167	157	132	117	2,927
75 years and over	3,886	669	359	482	350	369	329	3,217
Marital Status								
Married, spouse present	52,318	1,374	763	972	700	624	534	50,945
Married, spouse absent, widowed, divorced, separated	9,819	686	284	369	418	512	310	9,133
Never married	26,821	492	211	264	294	282	279	26,329
Living Arrangement								
Family member	74,537	1,971	1,086	1,322	1,102	962	902	72,566
Not a family member	14,421	580	172	284	311	456	221	13,841
Lives alone	8,889	434	102	188	234	343	143	8,455

Source: Selected from *Current Population Reports,* "The Need for Personal Assistance with Everyday Activities: Recipients and Caregivers," Series P-70, No. 19, Table 4, p. 26. Also in source: data for females (see separate table); data by race and Hispanic origin; data concerning health status.

★ 121 ★

Women as Caregivers: An Overview
Some statistics and predictions on the status of women as caregivers.

According to the Older Women's League, women can expect to spend **17** years caring for children and **18** years helping an elderly parent. **Eighty-nine percent of all women over age 18** will be caregivers to children, parents, or both.

Predictions are that between 1985 and 2020, the over-65 population will number more than 52 million, 1 in 6 persons. If present trends continue, caregivers will be their wives, daughters, nieces and granddaughters. Mainly due to caregiving responsibilities, women average **11.5 years** out of the paid labor force; men average 1.3 years.

Source: Maryanne Sugarman Costa, "Women Who Care Are Women Who Need Relief," *National Business Woman,* Summer 1989, p. 20. Primary Source: "Failing America's Caregivers: A Status Report on Women Who Care," Older Women's League, 730 11th St., NW, Suite 300, Washington, DC 20001. Also in source: a discussion of possible solutions to the long-term care situation, such as improving the working conditions of paid caregivers.

Children

★ 122 ★

Adoptive Children by Race of Mother and Child
Number of adopted children in thousands and percent distribution by race of mother and child, 1970-79 and 1980-87.

Characteristic	Year of adoption		
	All years[1]	1970-79	1980-87
	Number in thousands		
All children[2]	1,081	404	315
	Percent distribution		
Total	100%	100%	100%
Race of adoptive mother			
White	93.2%	96.0%	87.0%
Black	4.5%	3.6%	9.0%
Other	2.3%	0.4%	4.1%
Race of adoptive mother and child[3]			
Same race	92.4%	-	-
White	85.4%	-	-
Black	5.9%	-	-
Other	1.1%	-	-
Different race	7.6%	-	-
White mother, black child	1.2%	-	-
White mother, child of race other than black	4.8%	-	-

[Continued]

★ 122 ★

Adoptive Children by Race of Mother and Child

[Continued]

Characteristic	Year of adoption		
	All years[1]	1970-79	1980-87
Mother of other race, white child	1.6%	-	-
All other	0.0%	-	-

Source: "Number of Unrelated Children Ever Adopted by Women 20-54 Years of Age and Percent Distribution by Selected Characteristics According to Year of Adoption," National Health Interview Survey, 1987, *Advance Data*, January 5, 1990, p. 5. Primary source: National Center for Health Statistics. *Notes:* 1. Includes adopted children for whom date of adoption was not ascertained and children adopted before 1970. 2. Includes adopted children for whom information on specific characteristics is not ascertained; percent distributions based on known cases. 3. Based on adoptive children known to be living in household with adoptive mother at time of survey.

★ 123 ★

Children Living with Mother Only: 1970-1989

Total children and number living with mother only, by race and Hispanic origin, 1970-1989.

	1989	1980	1970	Percent distribution		
				1989	1980	1970
	Numbers in thousands					
All children under 18 years	63,637	63,427	69,162	100%	100%	100%
Living with mother only	13,700	11,406	7,452	21.5%	18.0%	10.8%
White children under 18 years	51,134	52,242	58,790	100%	100%	100%
Living with mother only	8,220	7,059	4,581	16.1%	13.5%	7.8%
Black children under 18 years	9,835	9,375	9,422	100%	100%	100%
Living with mother only	5,023	4,117	2,783	51.1%	43.9%	29.5%
Hispanic children under 18 years[1]	6,973	5,459	4,006	100%	100%	100%
Living with mother only	1,940	1,069	NA	27.8%	19.6%	NA

Source: Selected from *Current Population Reports*, Series P-20, No. 445, "Marital Status and Living Arrangements: March 1989," 1990, p. 3. Also in source: data by other living arrangements and for 1960. Excludes persons under 18 years old who were maintaining households or family groups. *Note:* 1. Persons of Hispanic origin may be of any race.

★ 124 ★

Children in Single-Parent Families in Poverty: Selected Countries

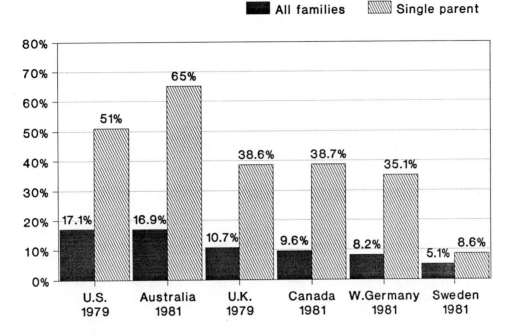

Children in single-parent families living in poverty compared to children in all families in poverty, selected countries.

Country	Year	% of Children in Poor Families	
		Children in All Families in Poverty	Children in Single-Parent Families in Poverty
United States	1979	17.1%	51%
Australia	1981	16.9%	65%
United Kingdeom	1979	10.7%	38.6%
Canada	1981	9.6%	38.7%
West Germany	1981	8.2%	35.1%
Sweden	1981	5.1%	8.6%

Source: "Children in Single-Parent Families Are More Likely to Live in Poverty than Children in All Family Types," *Census and You* 25:12 (December 1990), p. 6. Primary source: *Children's Well-Being: An International Comparison,* International Population Reports, Series P-95, No. 80.

★ 125 ★

Children of Divorce

Percent distribution of divorces by petitioner, according to presence of children under 18 at time of divorce and mean number of children, 1984.

Petitioner			Number of children					Mean number of children
	Total[1]	None	1 or more					
			Total	1	2	3	4 or more	
All marriages								
Wife	61.6%	57.1%	65.7%	65.8%	65.2%	66.3%	66.6%	1.0
Husband	32.3%	36.6%	28.6%	28.7%	28.6%	27.9%	28.4%	0.8
Both or other person	6.0%	6.3%	5.8%	5.5%	6.1%	5.8%	5.1%	0.9

Source: "Percent distribution of divorces by petitioner, according to presence of children under 18 years of age at time of divorce, and mean number of children, all marriages and primary marriages: 30 reporting States, 1984," *Vital and Health Statistics,* "Children of Divorce, Series 21, No. 46, 1989, p. 10. Also in source: data for primary marriages. Based on sample data. See source for a discussion of reporting States. *Note:* 1. Includes number of children not stated.

★ 126 ★

Households with Children: Selected Countries

Households in developed countries that contain children as percentage of all households.

Country	Year	Family households with children as % of all households
Japan	1985	41.7%
Canada	1986	37.9%
United States	1988	35.1%
Australia	1982	33.9%
France	1988	33.9%
United Kingdom	1987	32%
Sweden	1985	28.6%
West Germany	1988	25.2%

Source: "Family Households with Children as Percentage of All Households," *Census and You:* 25:12 (December 1990), p. 6. Primary source: *Children's Well-Being: An International Comparison,* International Population Reports, Series P-95, No. 80.

★ 127 ★

Monthly Family Income/Poverty Status, Children in Day Care

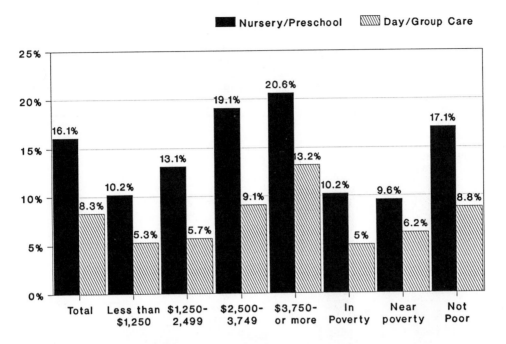

Monthly family income and poverty status of children under 5 in organized care facilities, fall 1987. Numbers in thousands.

Family income/poverty status	Total children	Nursery/ preschool	Day/group care
Total children under 5 in organized care (thousands)	2,220	755	1,465
Monthly family income:			
Less than $1,250	15.5%	10.2%	5.3%
$1,250-$2,499	18.8%	13.1%	5.7%
$2,500-$3,749	28.2%	19.1%	9.1%
$3,750 or more	33.8%	20.6%	13.2%
Poverty status:			
In poverty	15.2%	10.2%	5.0%
Near poverty	15.8%	9.6%	6.2%
Not poor	25.9%	17.1%	8.8%

Source: Martin O'Connell and Amara Bachu, *Who's Minding the Kids? Child Care Arrangements: Winter, 1986-87,* Current Population Reports Household Economic Studies, Series P070, No. 20, 1990, p. 8.

Families

★ 128 ★

Experience of Life Cycle Events

■ Women born 1920-24   ▨ Women born 1940-44

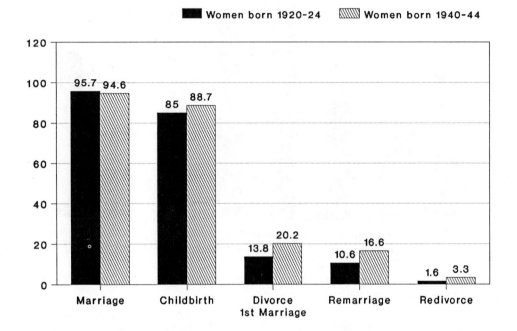

Woman who experienced certain life cycle events, by year of woman's birth: June 1985.

Life Cycle Event	Women born	
	1920-24	1940-44
Marriage	95.7%	94.6%
Childbirth	85.0%	88.7%
Divorce after first marriage	13.8%	20.2%
Remarriage	10.6%	16.6%
Redivorce	1.6%	3.3%

Source: Arthur J. Norton and Louisa F. Miller, "The Family Life Cycle: 1985," *Work and Family Patterns of American Women*, Current Population Reports Special Studies Series P-23, No. 165, 1990, p. 1 (Washington, DC, 1990).

★ 129 ★

Family Characteristics

Families, by type, labor force status of husbands, wives, and persons maintaining families, and presence and age of youngest child, March 1988.

Family type	Total	With no own children under age 18	With own children under age 18		
			Total	Age 6 to 17, no younger	Under age 6
Total families, in thousands	65,670	33,323	32,347	17,486	14,860
All families	100.0%	50.7%	49.3%	26.6%	22.6%
Married-couple families	79.0%	41.5%	37.5%	19.3%	18.2%
Husband only in labor force	20.9%	8.7%	12.2%	4.8%	7.4%
Husband and wife in labor force	41.2%	17.6%	23.6%	13.5%	10.1%
Wife only in labor force	3.6%	2.8%	.8%	.5%	.3%
Neither husband nor wife in labor force	13.3%	12.4%	.8%	.5%	.3%
Families maintained by women (no spouse present)	16.8%	6.7%	10.2%	6.2%	3.9%
Householder in labor force	10.4%	3.6%	6.8%	4.7%	2.1%
Householder not in labor force	6.4%	3.1%	3.3%	1.5%	1.8%
Families maintained by men (no spouse present)	4.2%	2.6%	1.6%	1.1%	.5%
Householder in labor force	3.2%	1.7%	1.5%	1.0%	.5%
Householder not in labor force	1.0%	.9%	.2%	.1%	[1]

Source: Howard V. Hayghe, "Family members in the work force," *Monthly Labor Review* 113:3 (March 1990), Table 4, p. 14+. Children are "born" children and include sons, daughters, stepchildren, and adopted children. Not included are other related children, such as nieces, nephews, and grandchildren and unrelated children. *Note:* 1. Less than 0.05%.

★ 130 ★

Family Characteristics of "Other Families": 1940-1988

Trends in the composition of "other families," by type, March of selected years, 1940-88. In "other families," the person who maintains the household is not in the labor force.

Other families type	1940[1]	1950[1]	1960	1980	1988
Total "other families" (in thousands)	4,788	5,584	6,883	13,314	15,974
Married-couple families	46.2%	51.2%	62.5%	69.3%	69.3%
Wife in labor force, not husband	4.5%	9.3%	11.8%	14.6%	14.8%
Neither wife nor husband in labor force	42.2%	41.9%	50.7%	54.7%	54.5%
Families maintained by women not in labor force (no spouse present)	45.5%	40.9%	32.8%	27.3%	26.5%
Families maintained by men not in labor force (no spouse present)	8.3%	7.8%	4.7%	3.4%	4.3%

Source: Howard V. Hayghe, "Family members in the work force," *Monthly Labor Review* 113:3 (March 1990), p. 14+. *Notes:* 1. Data are from *Historical Statistics of the United States, Colonial Times to 1970*, Series A 288-319 (Bureau of the Census, 1975), p. 41; and *Current Population Reports*, Series P-50, Nos. 5 and 29, and Series P-S, No. 20 (Bureau of the Census, May 1948, May 1951, and March 1947, respectively).

★ 131 ★

Labor Force Activity of Families with Children: 1975-1988

Trends in labor force activity of families with children under age 18, by type of family, March of selected years, 1975-1988.

Family type	1975	1980	1985	1988
	(Numbers in thousands)			
Total families with children	30,375	31,325	31,496	32,347
Married-couple families:				
Number	25,400	24,974	24,225	24,611
Percent of total families with children	84%	79.7%	76.9%	76.1%
Percent with--				
Father in labor force	96.0%	95.7%	95.7%	95.6%
Father only	52.6%	43.2%	36.6%	32.7%
Father and mother	43.4%	52.5%	59.1%	63.0%
Mother only in labor force	1.6%	1.8%	1.9%	2.2%
Neither parent in labor force	2.4%	2.5%	2.4%	2.2%
Families maintained by women (no spouse present):				
Number	4,461	5,718	6,345	6,666
Percent of total families with children	14.6%	18.3%	20.1%	20.6%
Percent with--				
Mother in labor force	59.9%	67.4%	67.8%	67.2%
Mother not in labor force	40.1%	32.6%	32.2%	32.8%
Families maintained by men (no spouse present):				
Number	454	633	926	1,070
Percent of total families with children	1.4%	2.0%	2.9%	3.3%
Percent with--				
Father in labor force	87.0%	88.6%	90.0%	90.2%
Father not in labor force	13.0%	11.5%	9.9%	9.8%

Source: Howard V. Hayghe, "Family members in the work force," *Monthly Labor Review* 113:3 (March 1990), p. 14+. Children are "born" children and include sons, daughters, stepchildren, and adopted children. Not included are other related children, such as nieces, nephews, and grandchildren and other unrelated children.

★ 132 ★

Mother-Only Families: 1950-1983

Characteristics of mothers in families headed by mothers, by race, 1950-1980.

Proportion of growth in families headed by mothers due to a change in:	1950s	1960s	1970s
White families			
Proportion of formerly married women	45.1%	45.5%	56.5%
Marriage rate	6.2%	-7.4%	-9.4%
Marital birth rate	24.6%	-7.4%	-18.8%
Marital disruption and remarriage rate	14.3%	60.3%	84.7%
Proportion of never-married women	1.7%	7.3%	8.2%

[Continued]

★ 132 ★

Mother-Only Families: 1950-1983
[Continued]

Proportion of growth in families headed by mothers due to a change in:	1950s	1960s	1970s
Marriage rate	0.4%	0.7%	2.1%
Out-of-wedlock birth rate	1.3%	6.6%	6.1%
Proportion of single mothers who head independent households	29.8%	14.2%	9.9%
Size of population	12.5%	24.3%	29.4%
Interaction (simultaneous change in two or more components)	11.9%	8.7%	-4.0%
Black families			
Proportion of formerly married women	45.4%	28.4%	2.9%
Marriage rate	-2.2%	-6.6%	-17.1%
Marital birth rate	28.8%	11.4%	-2.1%
Marital disruption and remarriage rate	18.8%	23.7%	22.1%
Proportion of never-married women	9.2%	20.0%	23.2%
Marriage rate	1.1%	4.5%	12.7%
Out-of-wedlock birth rate	8.1%	15.5%	10.5%
Proportion of single mothers who head independent households	14.9%	13.6%	7.1%
Size of population	11.9%	20.2%	44.0%
Interaction (simultaneous change in two or more components)	18.6%	17.8%	23.1%

Source: "Decomposition of Growth of White Families Headed by Mothers Aged Eighteen to Fifty-Nine, 1950-80," and "Decomposition of Growth of Black Families Headed by Mothers Aged Eighteen to Fifty-Nine, 1950-80," *Single Mothers and Their Children: A New American Dilemma,* 1986, p. 53-54 (Washington, D.C.: The Urban Institute Press, 1986).

★ 133 ★

Poverty Levels of Married Couples and Female Householders

Characteristic	1989			1988		
	Total	Below poverty level		Total	Below poverty level	
		Number	Percent		Number	Percent
			Numbers in thousands			
White	56,590	4,409	7.8%	56,492	4,471	7.9%
Married-couple	46,981	2,329	5.0%	46,877	2,294	4.9%
Female householder, no spouse present	7,306	1,858	25.4%	7,342	1,945	26.5%
Black	7,470	2,077	27.8%	7,409	2,089	28.2%
Married-couple	3,750	443	11.8%	3,722	421	11.3%
Female householder, no spouse present	3,275	1,524	46.5%	3,223	1,579	49.0%
Other races	2,030	297	14.6%	1,935	315	16.3%
Married-couple	1,586	160	10.1%	1,501	181	12.1%
Female householder, no spouse present	309	122	39.6%	325	117	36.0%
Asian or Pacific Islander	1,531	182	11.9%	1,481	201	13.6%
Married-couple	1,256	119	9.4%	1,179	118	10.0%
Female householder, no spouse present	188	57	30.2%	222	71	32.0%
Hispanic origin[1]	4,840	1,133	23.4%	4,823	1,141	23.7%
Married-couple	3,395	549	16.2%	3,398	547	16.1%
Female householder, no spouse present	1,116	530	47.5%	1,112	546	49.1%

Source: Selected from "Persons and Families Below Poverty Level, by Detailed Race: 1988-89," *Current Population Reports*, Series P-60, Table C, No. 168, "Money Income and Poverty Status in the United States 1989 (Advance Data from the March 1990 Current Population Survey), September 1990, p. 9. Also in source: persons below poverty level; 1989-1988 difference. *Note:* 1. Persons of Hispanic origin may be of any race.

★ 134 ★

Single-Parent Families Worldwide

Percentage of children in single-parent families, selected countries, 1960 to 1986.

Country	1960	1970	1975	1980	1983-86
Canada	-	-	10.5%	12.8%	-
Norway	-	-	8.1%	10.9%	13.9%
Sweden	7.8%	12.0%	11.4%	13.5%	-
United Kingdom	-	8.0%	10.0%	12.0%	14.0%
United States	9.1%	11.9%	-	19.7%	23.4%

Source: "Percentage of Children in Single-Parent Families, Selected Countries: 1960 to 1986," *Children's Well-Being: An International Comparison*, A Report of the Select Committee on Children, Youth, and Families, 101st Cong., 2d sess., March 1990, p. 104. Primary source: Jencks, Christopher and Barbara Boyle Torrey, 1988, "Beyond Income and Poverty: Trends in Social Welfare Among Children and the Elderly Since 1960," in Palmer, John L., Timothy Smeeding, and Barbara Boyle Torrey (eds.), *The Vulnerable*, Washington, D.C., figure 10.1, p. 257. All data for the United Kingdom refer to Great Britain. 1983-86 data for the United Kingdom refer to 1986, to 1983 for Norway, and to 1985 for the United States. Children are defined as follows: Canada—age 0 to 24 years; Norway—under age 20; Sweden—18 years and under for 1960, 1970, and 1975, and 15 years and under for 1980; United Kingdom—under age 16 or aged 16-18 and in full-time education; United States—under age 18.

Households and Other Living Arrangements

★ 135 ★

Elderly Home Alone: Selected Countries

Elderly population living alone in selected developed countries as a percentage of the total elderly population, latest available year.

Country, year	Proportion of the population 65 years old and over living alone		
	Total	Female	Male
Australia, 1970	-	34.2%	14.8%
Canada, 1976	-	28.9%	11.9%
Japan, 1985	9.5%	-	-
United Kingdom, 1980-81	-	45.0%	17.0%
United States, 1981	28.7%	38.8%	-

Source: "Elderly population living alone in selected developed countries," *1989 Report on the World Social Situation*, 1989, p. 6 (New York: United Nations, 1989). Primary source: *Consequences of Mortality Trends and Differentials* (United Nations publication, Sales No. E.85.XIII.3), table X.5, and S. Kono, "The social consequences of changing family and household structure associated with an aging population" in *Economic and Social Implications of Population Aging,* Proceedings of the International Symposium on Population Structure and Development, Tokyo, 10-12 September 1987 (New York, 1988), p. 288.

★ 136 ★

Guns in the House

Q. All respondents were asked if they had any guns in the house. Those respondiing affirmatively were then asked what type. Number of interviews: women = 201; men = 272.

Characteristic of respondent	Type of gun owned				
	Pistol	Shotgun	Rifle	Assault weapon	Other
U.S. Total	52%	60%	65%	2%	3%
Sex					
Female	50%	54%	58%	1%	2%
Male	54%	64%	70%	3%	2%

Source: George Gallup, Jr., *The Gallup Report,* Report Nos. 282-283 (Princeton, NJ: The Gallup Poll, March/April 1989).

★ 137 ★

Homeowners and Renters

Number and percent distribution of homeowners and renters by type of household, 1985.

Household type	Number (thousands)	Percent Distribution			Percent Who	
		All	Owners	Renters	Own	Rent
All households						
Married couples	49,972	57%	69%	34%	78%	22%
Female-headed families	11,806	13%	9%	21%	42%	58%
Single females	12,845	15%	12%	19%	52%	48%
Male-headed families	5,661	6%	5%	10%	45%	55%
Single males	8,142	9%	5%	16%	37%	63%
Black households						
Married couples	3,528	36%	53%	22%	65%	35%
Female-headed families	3,071	31%	20%	39%	29%	71%
Single females	1,393	14%	13%	15%	29%	61%
Male-headed families	684	7%	6%	8%	37%	63%
Single males	1,226	12%	8%	16%	27%	73%
Households of Hispanic origin						
Married couples	2,718	54%	72%	41%	53%	47%
Female-headed families	1,058	21%	11%	27%	21%	79%
Single females	431	8%	7%	10%	32%	68%
Male-headed families	436	9%	6%	11%	25%	75%
Single males	435	9%	4%	11%	20%	80%

Source: Selected from "Tenure of Households in Occupied Housing Units by Type of Household, Race, and Hispanic Origin, 1985 (numbers in thousands)," *The American Woman 1990-91*, 1990, p. 99 (New York: W.W. Norton & Company, 1990). Primary source: U.S. Department of Housing and Urban Development and U.S. Bureau of the Census, December 1988, Tables 2-9, 5-9, and 6-9. Also in source: data for other household types. People of Hispanic origin may be of any race.

★ 138 ★

Household Composition

Non-family Household 29.2%

Female Householder 11.7%

Male Householder 3.1%

Married Families 56.0%

1990 composition of U.S. households, estimate, March 1990.

Type of household	Total
Total households, 1990	93.3 million
Married-couple families	56.0%
Non-family households	29.2%
Female householder (no husband present)	11.7%
Male householder (no wife present)	3.1%

Source: "Number of Two-Parent Family Households Still Decreasing," *Census and You,* Vol. 26, No. 2, February 1991, p. 3. Primary source: *Household and Family Characteristics: 1990 and 1989,* Current Population Reports P-20, No. 447.

★ 139 ★

Household Size

Total and female and male adult households, by number of persons, 1990.

Characteristic	Number (thousands)		
	Total	Female	Male
Total adults	180,974	94,667	86,307
Household Size			
1 person	22,006	13,337	8,669
2 persons	56,768	29,035	27,732
3 or more persons	102,201	52,295	49,905

Source: Selected from *Mediamark Research Multimedia Audiences Report, Spring 1990* (New York: Mediamark Research Inc., 1990).

★ 140 ★

Household Size Worldwide: 1970-1985

Estimates of average household size by region, 1970-1985.

Region	Number of persons per household			
	1970	1975	1980	1985
Developed countries	3.36	3.18	3.03	2.90
Northern America	3.23	3.04	2.88	2.73
Japan	3.90	3.60	3.39	3.22
Oceania	3.65	3.52	3.40	3.25
Northern Europe	3.00	2.87	2.75	2.67
Western Europe	2.98	2.86	2.73	2.64
Southern Europe	3.67	3.53	3.40	3.28
Eastern Europe	3.10	2.97	2.84	2.73
USSR	3.57	3.32	3.14	2.98
Developing Countries	5.07	5.00	4,89	4.76
Eastern Africa	4.99	4.97	4.95	4.93
Northern Africa	5.44	5.41	5.31	5.15
Middle Africa	4.58	4.60	4.62	4.66
Southern Africa	5.00	5.05	5.09	5.09
Western Africa	4.90	4.93	4.97	5.00
Caribbean	4.67	4.64	4.56	4.44
Middle America	5.01	4.99	4.90	4.80
Temperate South America	4.02	3.85	3.69	3.53
Tropical South America	5.19	5.10	4.96	4.81
China	4.58	4.42	4.21	4.01
East Asia[1]	5.63	5.33	5.02	4.64
South Asia	5.46	5.44	5.39	5.28

Source: 1989 Report on the World Social Situation, 1989 (New York: United Nations, 1989), p. 2. Primary source: United Nations, Department of International Economic and Social Affairs, "Estimates and projections of households" (provisional report, 22 January 1979), table 5. *Note:* 1. Excluding China and Japan.

★ 141 ★

Household Types by Income Level

Households by total money income in 1989, by type of households, by female householder, by race, and by Hispanic origin of householder.

Total money income	Total	Family households			Nonfamily households	
		Total	Female householder no husband present	Total	Female householder	Living alone
Numbers in thousands						
Total	93,347	66,090	10,890	27,257	15,651	13,950
Under $5,000	4,970	2,236	1,423	2,734	1,882	1,839
$5,000 to $9,999	9,622	4,022	1,826	5,601	4,038	3,963
$10,000 to $14,999	9,057	5,252	1,557	3,805	2,417	2,298

[Continued]

★ 141 ★

Household Types by Income Level
[Continued]

Total money income	Total	Family households			Nonfamily households	
		Total	Female householder no husband present	Total	Female householder	Living alone
$15,000 to $19,999	8,620	5,502	1,263	3,118	1,825	1,677
$20,000 to $24,999	8,134	5,465	1,051	2,669	1,428	1,224
$25,000 to $29,999	7,778	5,583	879	2,195	1,160	978
$30,000 to $34,999	7,062	5,340	706	1,722	800	637
$35,000 to $39,999	6,154	4,940	546	1,214	535	410
$40,000 to $44,999	5,556	4,506	414	1,050	439	302
$45,000 to $49,999	4,472	3,745	258	727	265	160
$50,000 to $54,999	4,090	3,580	240	510	200	132
$55,000 to $59,999	2,972	2,617	150	354	143	79
$60,000 to $64,999	2,630	2,317	149	313	94	52
$65,000 to $69,999	2,148	1,892	88	255	114	46
$70,000 to $74,999	1,684	1,486	69	198	69	32
$75,000 to $79,999	1,403	1,289	60	114	50	25
$80,000 to $84,999	1,178	1,048	41	130	37	22
$85,000 to $89,999	857	788	29	69	26	13
$90,000 to $94,999	759	705	21	53	18	8
$95,000 to $99,999	570	541	27	29	6	3
$100,000 and over	3,631	3,236	94	396	104	51
White						
Total	80,163	56,590	7,306	23,573	13,622	12,161
Under $5,000	3,354	1,367	716	1,987	1,402	1,372
$5,000 to $9,999	7,532	2,785	1,039	4,747	3,519	3,463
$10,000 to $14,999	7,564	4,173	1,012	3,391	2,186	2,092
$15,000 to $19,999	7,288	4,529	857	2,759	1,667	1,534
$20,000 to $24,999	6,994	4,659	802	2,335	1,248	1,070
$25,000 to $29,999	6,792	4,861	646	1,931	1,029	870
$30,000 to $34,999	6,202	4,690	519	1,512	701	563
$35,000 to $39,999	5,413	4,334	406	1,078	464	368
$40,000 to $44,999	5,017	4,061	332	957	398	263
$45,000 to $49,999	4,055	3,376	206	679	250	149
$50,000 to $54,999	3,696	3,259	197	437	159	104
$55,000 to $59,999	2,669	2,342	106	327	130	76
$60,000 to $64,999	2,355	2,068	122	288	89	49
$65,000 to $69,999	1,934	1,700	64	235	101	46
$70,000 to $74,999	1,531	1,353	54	178	62	29
$75,000 to $79,999	1,281	1,181	52	100	39	21
$80,000 to $84,999	1,098	976	33	123	33	22
$85,000 to $89,999	785	720	28	65	26	13
$90,000 to $94,999	702	653	16	49	16	8

[Continued]

★ 141 ★

Household Types by Income Level
[Continued]

Total money income	Total	Family households			Nonfamily households	
		Total	Female householder no husband present	Total	Female householder	Living alone
$95,000 to $99,999	499	472	19	27	4	1
$100,000 and over	3,402	3,031	78	371	99	47
Black						
Total	10,486	7,470	3,275	3,015	1,702	1,525
Under $5,000	1,479	793	673	686	453	441
$5,000 to $9,999	1,802	1,075	712	727	453	433
$10,000 to $14,999	1,250	910	498	339	184	162
$15,000 to $19,999	1,111	820	378	291	127	113
$20,000 to $24,999	941	661	240	279	150	131
$25,000 to $29,999	786	573	206	213	104	87
$30,000 to $34,999	661	515	170	146	79	63
$35,000 to $39,999	552	461	118	91	54	31
$40,000 to $44,999	418	350	81	68	27	26
$45,000 to $49,999	284	253	43	31	11	7
$50,000 to $54,999	264	218	35	47	22	17
$55,000 to $59,999	198	174	38	25	12	2
$60,000 to $64,999	190	169	22	21	2	2
$65,000 to $69,999	148	136	17	13	9	-
$70,000 to $74,999	92	85	14	7	2	-
$75,000 to $79,999	65	61	6	4	4	4
$80,000 to $84,999	47	46	5	1	1	-
$85,000 to $89,999	43	39	-	4	-	-
$90,000 to $94,999	31	27	2	5	3	-
$95,000 to $99,999	43	41	6	2	2	2
$100,000 and over	81	65	12	16	5	3
Hispanic Origin[1]						
Total	5,933	4,840	1,116	1,093	506	442
Under $5,000	480	303	207	178	100	97
$5,000 to $9,999	793	549	253	244	143	143
$10,000 to $14,999	727	575	159	151	62	56
$15,000 to $19,999	705	586	130	120	55	42
$20,000 to $24,999	594	484	91	110	45	37
$25,000 to $29,999	515	441	78	74	31	23
$30,000 to $34,999	425	359	41	66	22	17
$35,000 to $39,999	341	303	31	38	12	11
$40,000 to $44,999	298	270	37	28	7	2
$45,000 to $49,999	234	214	18	20	8	4

[Continued]

★ 141 ★

Household Types by Income Level
[Continued]

Total money income	Total	Family households			Nonfamily households	
		Total	Female householder no husband present	Total	Female householder	Living alone
$50,000 to $54,999	203	189	21	15	7	3
$55,000 to $59,999	124	114	13	10	4	2
$60,000 to $64,999	114	105	6	9	3	2
$65,000 to $69,999	76	67	5	9	1	-
$70,000 to $74,999	55	51	7	4	1	-
$75,000 to $79,999	39	36	-	3	1	1
$80,000 to $84,999	39	38	6	1	-	-
$85,000 to $89,999	26	26	6	-	-	-
$90,000 to $94,999	31	30	1	1	1	-
$95,000 to $99,999	20	20	4	-	-	-
$100,000 and over	95	82	2	14	3	2

Source: Selected from "Type of Household—Households, by Total Money Income in 1989, Race, and Hispanic Origin of Householder," *Current Population Reports*, "Money Income and Poverty Status in the United States 1989 (Advance Data from the March 1990 Current Population Survey), September 1990, p. 23-24. Also in source: data for married-couple families, male householders, male nonfamily households. Households as of March 1990. *Note:* 1. Persons of Hispanic origin may be of any race.

★ 142 ★

Household Types in Selected Countries, 1960-1980

Types of households as a percentage of total households, developed countries, 1960-1980.

Country	Percentage of total households								
	One person			Couple with children			Single parent w/ children		
	1960	1970[1]	1980	1960	1970[1]	1980	1960	1970[1]	1980
Canada	9%	13%	20%	-	50%	37%	-	2%	3%
England and Wales	12%	18%	22%	49%	44%	39%	7%	7%	8%
France	20%	22%	24%	45%	41%	39%	4%	5%	5%
Germany, Federal Republic	21%	26%	31%	55%	47%	42%	2%	2%	3%
Netherlands	12%	17%	22%	56%	53%	43%	6%	7%	6%
Sweden	20%	25%	33%	37%	30%	25%	3%	3%	4%
Switzerland	15%	20%	27%	48%	45%	41%	5%	5%	4%
United States	13%	17%	23%	44%	40%	29%	4%	5%	8%

Source: "Changes in the size of households in selected developed countries (percentage of total households)," *1989 Report on the World Social Situation*, 1990, p. 5 (New York: United Nations, 1989). Primary source: L. Roussel, "Evolution recente de la structure des menage dans quelques pays industriels," *Population*, No. 6, 1986, p. 933. *Note:* 1. Circa 1970.

★ 143 ★

Household Types: 1990-2000

Households by type: Series A projections 1990-2000.

Year	Total	Family				Nonfamily		
		Total	Married couple	Female house-holder[1]	Male house-holder[1]	Total	Female house-holder	Male house-holder
				Numbers in thousands				
1990	95,243	65,964	51,704	11,538	2,723	29,279	16,270	13,008
1995	102,785	68,219	52,178	12,765	3,276	34,565	18,463	16,102
2000	110,217	70,024	52,263	13,916	3,845	40,193	20,722	19,471

Source: Selected from "Households, by Type—Projections: 1990 to 2000," *Statistical Abstract of the United States 1990,* 1990, p. 45. Primary source: U.S. Bureau of the Census, *Current Population Reports,* Series P-25, No. 986. Also in source: Series B and Series C projections. As of July. Series A figures reflect the assumption that the recent moderation in marriage and divorce trends will continue, but that historical changes spanning the last 25 years must be taken into consideration. Series A assumes a continuation of past trends in householder proportions but changes in recent years are given more weight. *Note:* 1. With no spouse present.

★ 144 ★

Households With and Without Children, Worldwide

Percent of households by number of children, circa 1980.

Country	Year	No children	Households with children		
			1 child	2 children	3 or more children
Canada	1981	57.5%	16.0%	16.6%	9.9%
Germany, Federal Republic	1981	57.1%	20.4%	16.6%	5.9%
Israel	1979	40.8%	15.0%	21.2%	23.1%
Norway	1979	56.6%	15.6%	16.0%	11.8%
Sweden	1981	52.6%	21.4%	18.7%	7.4%
United Kingdom	1979	61.1%	14.1%	16.6%	8.2%
United States	1979	60.5%	15.8%	14.0%	9.6%

Source: "Percent of Households by Number of Children, Selected Countries: Circa 1980," *Children's Well-Being: An International Comparison,* A Report of the Select Committee on Children, Youth, and Families, 101st Cong., 2d sess., March 1990, p. 104. Primary source: U.S. Bureau of the Census, Center for International Research, Youth Data Base. The percentages shown are based on sample data from the Luxembourg Income Study. The sample has not been inflated to national levels.

★ 145 ★

Households by Family Type, Selected Countries: 1960-1988

Percent distribution of households by type, 9 countries, selected years, 1960-1988.

Country and year	Types of households					
	Married-couple[1]			Single-parent	One-person	Other[3]
	Total	With children[2]	Without children			
United States:						
1960	74.3%	44.2%	30.1%	4.4%	13.1%	8.2%
1970	70.5%	40.3%	30.3%	5.0%	17.1%	7.4%
1980	60.8%	30.9%	29.9%	7.5%	22.7%	9.0%
1987	57.6%	27.5%	30.0%	8.1%	23.6%	10.7%
1988	56.9%	27.0%	29.9%	8.0%	24.0%	11.1%
Canada:						
1961	78.0%[4]	50.8%[4]	26.7%[4]	3.8%[4]	9.3%	8.9%[4]
1971	74.0%	46.5%	27.5%	4.5%	13.4%	8.1%
1981	66.8%	36.3%	30.5%	5.3%	20.3%	7.6%
1986	64.5%	32.3%	32.2%	5.6%	21.5%	8.4%
Japan:						
1960	65.3%	49.4%	15.9%	3.1%	17.2%	14.4%
1970	64.3%	44.6%	19.7%	2.3%	20.3%	13.1%
1980	68.4%	42.9%	25.6%	2.2%	19.8%	9.6%
1985	67.4%	39.2%	28.2%	2.5%	20.8%	9.3%
Denmark:[5]						
1976	44.5%	23.5%	21.0%	4.9%	[6]	[6]
1983	43.7%	22.6%	21.1%	5.4%	[6]	[6]
1988	41.0%	19.9%	21.1%	5.1%	[6]	[6]
France:						
1968	70.1%	43.6%	26.5%	4.2%	20.3%	5.4%
1975	68.8%	42.1%	26.8%	4.1%	22.1%	5.0%
1982	67.0%	39.7%	27.2%	4.3%	24.6%	4.1%
1988	63.4%	36.2%	27.3%	5.1%	27.1%	4.4%
Germany:						
1961	66.7%	44.3%	22.4%	10.8%	20.6%	1.9%
1970	64.8%	41.7%	23.1%	6.2%	26.5%	2.5%
1980	60.5%	37.0%	23.5%	6.6%	30.2%	2.7%
1988	54.3%	31.4%	22.9%	6.7%	34.9%	4.1%
Netherlands:						
1961	77.6%	55.4%	22.3%	5.7%	11.9%	4.8%
1971	74.1%	51.8%	22.3%	5.1%	17.1%	3.7%
1981	66.5%	43.7%	22.9%	6.1%	21.4%	6.0%
1985	60.0%	38.5%	21.5%	6.7%	27.8%	5.5%
Sweden:						
1960	66.4%	35.7%	30.6%	3.5%	20.2%	9.9%
1970	64.3%	30.2%	34.1%	3.2%	25.3%	7.2%

[Continued]

★ 145 ★

Households by Family Type, Selected Countries: 1960-1988
[Continued]

| Country and year | Types of households | | | | | |
| | Married-couple[1] | | | Single-parent | One-person | Other[3] |
	Total	With children[2]	Without children			
1980	57.9%	24.8%	33.1%	3.1%	32.8%	6.2%
1985	54.8%	21.7%	33.1%	3.2%	36.1%	5.9%
United Kingdom:[7]						
1961	73.7%	37.8%	36.0%	2.3%	11.9%	12.1%
1971	69.7%	34.4%	35.2%	2.8%	18.1%	9.4%
1981	64.3%	30.5%	33.7%	4.7%	21.8%	9.2%
1987	64.0%	28.0%	36.0%	4.0%	25.0%	7.0%

Source: "Percent distribution of households by type, nine countries, selected years, 1960-88," *Monthly Labor Review*, March 1990, p. 47. Primary source: Compiled by the Bureau of Labor Statistics from national population censuses, household surveys, and other sources. *Notes:* 1. May include unmarried cohabiting couples. 2. Children are defined as unmarried children living at home; ages vary by country. 3. Includes both family and nonfamily households not elsewhere classified. 4. Estimated by the U.S. Bureau of Labor Statistics, based on ratios of adjusted to unadjusted series in 1971. 5. From family-based statistics. However, one person living alone constitutes a family in Denmark. 6. Not available. 7. Great Britain only (excludes Northern Ireland).

★ 146 ★

Households with Children

Total and female and male adult households with children, by age of children, 1990.

| Characteristic of children | Number (thousands) | | |
	Total	Female	Male
Households with Children	73,586	39,949	33,637
Children Under 2 Years	14,151	8,079	6,072
Children 2-5 Years	27,156	15,220	11,936
Children 6-11 Years	34,115	18,608	15,507
Children 12-17 Years	33,599	17,385	16,214

Source: Selected from *Mediamark Research Multimedia Audiences Report, Spring 1990* (New York: Mediamark Research Inc., 1990).

★ 147 ★

Households, Worldwide

Households with children as percent of all households and family households with children, selected countries, selected years, 1982 to 1988.

| Country | Year | Total households (thousands) | Family households w/ children | | | % of all households | | | % of family households with children | |
			Total (thousands)	Married (thousands)	Single-parent (thousands)	Family households w/ children	Married w/ children	Single-parent w/ children	Married	Single-parent
Australia	1982	5,214	1,770	1,569	201	33.9%	30.1%	3.9%	88.6%	11.4%
Canada	1986	8,992	3,406	2,903	503	37.9%	32.3%	5.6%	85.2%	14.8%
Germany, Federal Republic	1988	27,403	6,918	5,984	934	25.2%	21.8%	3.4%	86.5%	13.5%
France	1988	20,853	7,070	6,301	769	33.9%	30.2%	3.7%	89.1%	10.9%

[Continued]

★ 147 ★

Households, Worldwide
[Continued]

Country	Year	Total households (thousands)	Family households w/ children			% of all households			% of family households with children	
			Total (thousands)	Married (thousands)	Single-parent (thousands)	Family households w/ children	Married w/ children	Single-parent w/ children	Married	Single-parent
Japan	1985	37,980	15,836	14,896	940	41.7%	39.2%	2.5%	94.1%	5.9%
Sweden	1985	3,670	1,051	873	178	28.6%	23.8%	4.9%	83.1%	16.9%
United Kingdom	1987	-	-	-	-	32.0%	28.0%	4.0%	87.3%	12.7%
United States	1988	91,066	31,920	24,601	7,319	35.1%	27.0%	8.0%	77.1%	22.9%

Source: "Households with Children as Percent of all Households and Family Households with Children, Selected Countries: Selected Years, 1982 to 1988," *Children's Well-Being: An International Comparison*, A Report of the Select Committee on Children, Youth, and Families, 101st Cong., 2d sess., March 1990, p. 103. Primary source: Australian Bureau of Statistics; Statistics Canada, unpublished tabulations, Ottawa; France Institut National de la Statistique et des Etudes Economiques, Paris; Germany, Federal Republic of, Statistisches Bundesamt, Statisches Jahrboch; unpublished tabulations, Wiesbaden; Japan Bureau of Statistics, Japan Statistical Yearbook, Tokyo; Statistics Sweden, Statistical Abstract of Sweden, Stockholm; United Kingdom Central Statistical Office, General Household Survey, Social Trends No. 19, London, and U.S. Bureau of the Census, 1989, Household and Family Characteristics: March 1988, *Current Population Reports*, Series P-20, No. 437 (see source for more detailed source listing). Children are defined as under 18 years old with the following exceptions: Australia includes all children under 15 and full-time students ages 15 to 20 years. The United Kingdom includes all children under 16 and full-time students ages 16 and 17 years; data refer only to Great Britain (excludes Northern Ireland), and are based on a household survey that has not been inflated to national levels. The definitions of households, children, and the treatment of unmarried cohabiting couples may differ across countries so comparisons should be made with caution. Households may include related or unrelated individuals. A small proportion of other household types may contain children. Households of unmarried cohabiting couples may be classified as single-parent households, married couple households, or "other" households, depending on responses to surveys, in all countries except Canada, Sweden, and France where they are explicitly included under married couples. Single-parent sub-families living in larger household are excluded from the data on single-parent households.

★ 148 ★

Living Arrangements of the Elderly

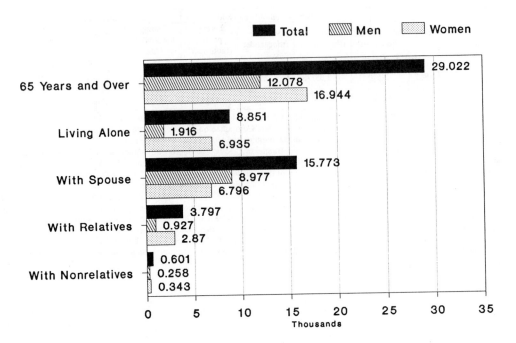

Living arrangements of elderly women, by age.

Living arrangement and age	1989		Percent distribution	
	Total	Women	Total	Women
	Numbers in thousands			
65 years and over	29,022	16,944	100%	100%
Living--				
Alone	8,851	6,935	30.5%	40.9%
With spouse	15,773	6,796	54.3%	40.1%
With other relatives	3,797	2,870	13.1%	16.9%
With nonrelatives only	601	343	2.1%	2.0%
65 to 74 years	17,747	9,867	100%	100%
Living--				
Alone	4,355	3,310	24.5%	33.5%
With spouse	11,252	5,075	63.4%	51.4%
With other relatives	1,832	1,331	10.3%	13.5%
With nonrelatives only	308	151	1.7%	1.5%
75 to 84 years	9,175	5,669	100%	100%
Living--				
Alone	3,509	2,864	38.2%	50.5%
With spouse	4,060	1,593	44.3%	28.1%
With other relatives	1,386	1080	15.1%	19.1%
With nonrelatives only	220	132	2.4%	2.3%

[Continued]

★ 148 ★

Living Arrangements of the Elderly
[Continued]

Living arrangement and age	1989		Percent distribution	
	Total	Women	Total	Women
85 years and over	2,101	1,408	100%	100%
Living--				
Alone	987	760	47.0%	54.0%
With spouse	462	128	22.0%	9.1%
With other relatives	579	459	27.6%	32.6%
With nonrelatives only	73	61	3.5%	4.3%

Source: Selected from *Current Population Reports*, Series P-20, No. 445, "Marital Status and Living Arrangements: March 1989," 1990, p. 5. Also in source: Living arrangements of men. Noninstitutional population.

★ 149 ★

Persons Living in Institutions and Group Quarters

Total and female population in institutions and other group quarters, by type of quarters, 1970 to 1980.

Type of Quarters	1970		1980	
	Total	Female	Total	Female
	Numbers in thousands			
Total	5,786	2,349	5,738	2,586
Institutional inmates	2,127	1,000	2,492	1,261
Homes for the aged and dependent	928	629	1,426	1,004
Mental hospitals and residential treatment centers	434	189	255	99
Correctional institutions	328	15	466	27
Tuberculosis hospitals	17	5	8	1
Chronic disease hospitals (excl. TB and mental)	67	29	61	25
Homes and schools for the mentally handicapped	202	88	149	65
Homes and schools for the physically handicapped	23	6	27	12
Homes for dependent and neglected children	48	19	38	14
Homes for unwed mothers	4	4	2	2
Training schools for juvenile delinquents	66	14	42	8
Detention homes	10	4	17	3
College dormitories	1,765	874	1,994	1,006
Military quarters	1,025	20	671	58
Rooming and boarding houses	330	139	176	69
Other	539	315	404	192

Source: Selected from "Population in Institutions and Other Group Quarters, by Sex and Type of Quarters: 1960 to 1980," *Statistical Abstract of the United States 1990*, 1990, p. 55. Primary source: U.S. Bureau of the Census, *Census of Population: 1970*, Vols. I and II; and *1980 Census of Population*, Vol. 2 (PC80-2-4D). Also in source: data for 1960 (not by gender); data for males. As of April 1. Based on sample data and subject to sampling variability.

★ 150 ★

Poverty Status of Female-Headed Households: 1970-1989

Poverty status of families headed by female householders, no husband present, 1970 to 1989.

Year	Female householders With & without childrren under 18		With children under 18	
	Total families (thousands)	Percent below poverty	Total families (thousands)	Percent below poverty
All Races				
1989	10,890	32.2%	7,445	42.8%
1988[1]	10,890	33.4%	7,361	44.7%
1987[1]	10,696	34.2%	7,216	45.5%
1986	10,445	34.6%	7,094	46.0%
1985	10,211	34.0%	6,892	45.4%
1984	10,129	34.5%	6,832	45.7%
1983	9,896	36.0%	6,622	47.1%
1982	9,469	36.3%	6,397	47.8%
1981	9,403	34.6%	6,488	44.3%
1980	9,082	32.7%	6,299	42.9%
1979	8,705	30.4%	4,917	43.7%
1978	8,458	31.4%	4,597	43.2%
1977	8,236	31.7%	4,321	44.5%
1976	7,713	33.0%	4,077	44.9%
1975	7,482	32.5%	3,837	43.8%
1974	7,230	32.1%	4,917	43.7%
1973	6,804	32.2%	4,597	43.2%
1972	6,607	32.7%	4,321	44.5%
1971	6,191	33.9%	4,077	44.9%
1970	6,001	32.5%	3,837	43.8%
White				
1989	7,306	25.4%	4,627	36.1%
1988[1]	7,342	26.5%	4,553	38.2%
1987[1]	7,297	26.9%	4,548	38.3%
1986	7,227	28.2%	4,552	39.8%
1985	7,111	27.4%	4,470	38.7%
1984	6,941	27.1%	4,337	38.8%
1983	6,796	28.3%	4,210	39.8%
1982	6,507	27.9%	4,037	39.3%
1981	6,620	27.4%	4,237	36.9%
1980	6,266	25.7%	3,995	35.9%
1979	6,052	22.3%	3,866	31.3%
1978	5,918	23.5%	3,780	33.5%
1977	5,828	24.0%	3,735	33.8%

[Continued]

★ 150 ★

Poverty Status of Female-Headed Households: 1970-1989
[Continued]

Year	Female householders With & without childrren under 18		With children under 18	
	Total families (thousands)	Percent below poverty	Total families (thousands)	Percent below poverty
1976	5,467	25.2%	3,456	36.4%
1975	5,380	25.9%	3,406	37.3%
1974	5,208	24.8%	3,244	36.4%
1973	4,853	24.5%	2,988	35.2%
1972	4,672	24.3%	2,748	35.3%
1971	4,489	26.5%	2,664	36.9%
1970	4,408	25.0%	NA	NA
Black				
1989	3,275	46.5%	2,624	53.9%
1988[1]	3,223	49.0%	2,583	56.2%
1987[1]	3,089	51.1%	2,453	58.6%
1986	2,967	61.1%	2,386	58.0%
1985	2,874	61.5%	2,269	58.9%
1984	2,964	51.7%	2,335	58.4%
1983	2,871	53.7%	2,244	60.7%
1982	2,734	56.2%	2,199	63.7%
1981	2,605	52.9%	2,118	59.5%
1980	2,634	49.4%	2,171	56.0%
1979	2,495	49.4%	2,063	54.7%
1978	2,390	61.6%	1,946	58.4%
1977	2,277	51.0%	1,878	57.5%
1976	2,151	52.2%	1,781	58.6%
1975	2,634	49.4%	1,651	57.5%
1974	1,934	52.2%	1,623	58.5%
1973	1,849	52.7%	1,538	58.8%
1972	1,822	53.3%	1,494	61.0%
1971	1,642	53.5%	1,369	60.0%
1970	1,535	54.3%	NA	NA
Hispanic Origin[2]				
1989	1,116	47.5%	848	57.9%
1988	1,112	49.1%	861	59.2%
1987	1,082	52.2%	865	60.9%
1986	1,032	51.2%	822	59.5%
1985	980	53.1%	771	64.0%
1984	905	53.4%	711	62.8%
1983	860	52.8%	660	63.4%
1982	767	55.4%	613	63.8%

[Continued]

★ 150 ★

Poverty Status of Female-Headed Households: 1970-1989
[Continued]

Year	Female householders With & without childrren under 18		With children under 18	
	Total families (thousands)	Percent below poverty	Total families (thousands)	Percent below poverty
1981	750	53.2%	622	60.0%
1980	706	51.3%	NA	NA
1979	610	49.2%	502	57.3%
1978	542	53.1%	NA	NA
1977	561	53.6%	NA	NA
1976	517	53.1%	NA	NA
1975	622	53.6%	NA	NA
1974	462	49.6%	NA	NA
1973	411	51.4%	NA	NA
1972	NA	NA	NA	NA

Source: "Poverty status of famillies, by type of family, presence of related children, race, and Hispanic origin: 1959 to 1989," *Current Population Reports,* "Money Income and Poverty Status in the United States 1989 (Advance Data from the March 1990 Current Population Survey)," Series P-60, Table 21, No. 168, September,1990, p. 61. Also in source: data for families, for male householders, for years 1959-1989. *Notes:* 1. Figures based on new processing procedures. The 1987 and 1988 figures are also revised to reflect corrections to the files after publication of the 1988 advance report, Money Income and Poverty Status in the United States, P-60, No. 166. 2. Persons of Hispanic origin may be of any race.

★ 151 ★

Women Living Alone: 1970-1988

Women living alone, by age, 1970-1988.

Age	Number of persons, in thousands						Percent Distribution				
	1970	1975	1980	1985	1987	1988	1970	1975	1980	1985	1988
Both sexes	10,851	13,939	18,296	20,602	21,128	21,889	100%	100%	100%	100%	100%
Female	7,319	9,021	11,330	12,680	12,881	13,101	67.5%	64.7%	61.9%	61.5%	59.9%

Source: Selected from "Persons Living Alone, by Sex and Age: 1970 to 1988," *Statistical Abstract of the United States 1990,* 1990, p. 54. Primary source: U.S. Bureau of the Census, *Current Population Reports,* series P-20, No. 433 and earlier reports; and unpublished data. As of March. *Note:* 1. 1970 and 1975, persons 14-24 years old.

Mothers

★ 152 ★

Family Life Cycle Stages, Divorced Mothers

Once-married, currently divorced mothers at stages of the family life cycle, by year of birth, as of 1985.

Stage of family life cycle	All mothers born 1920-54	Birth cohort						
		1920-24	1925-29	1930-34	1935-39	1940-44	1945-49	1950-54
Total once-married, currently divorced mothers (at time of survey)(in thousands)	3,590	287	334	370	449	656	776	720
Median age at--								
First marriage	20.4	21.9	21.5	21.2	20.2	20.1	20.0	19.8
Birth of first child	22.0	23.7	23.2	22.8	22.1	21.5	21.7	20.8
Birth of last child	27.2	31.0	30.4	29.1	28.5	27.0	26.3	24.0
Separation before divorce	32.7	44.0	43.7	40.2	37.5	34.4	31.2	27.3
Divorce	34.2	46.3	46.3	41.5	39.5	36.1	32.5	28.7
Years between age at--								
First marriage and first birth	1.6	1.8	1.7	1.6	1.9	1.4	1.7	1.0
First birth and last birth	5.2	7.3	7.2	6.3	6.4	5.5	4.6	3.2
Average number of children per woman	2.65	3.04	3.23	3.17	3.14	2.72	2.33	1.93

Source: Arthur J. Norton and Louisa F. Miller, "The Family Life Cycle: 1985," *Work and Family Patterns of American Women*, Current Population Reports Special Studies Series P-23, No. 165, 1990, p. 4 (Washington, DC, 1990).

★ 153 ★

Family Life Cycle Stages, Ever-Married Mothers

Ever-married mothers at stages of the family life cycle, by year of birth, as of 1985.

Stage of family life cycle	All mothers born 1920-54	Birth cohort						
		1920-24	1925-29	1930-34	1935-39	1940-44	1945-49	1950-54
Total (in thousands)	40,581	4,819	5,181	4,930	5,199	6,212	7,118	7,122
Median age at--								
First marriage	20.4	21.0	20.7	20.2	19.9	20.3	20.5	20.3
Birth of first child	22.3	23.3	22.7	22.0	21.5	21.9	22.4	22.4
Birth of last child	28.8	31.5	31.1	30.1	28.7	28.0	27.9	27.3
Years between age at--								
First marriage and first birth	1.9	2.3	2.0	1.8	1.6	1.6	1.9	2.1
First birth and last birth	6.5	8.2	8.4	8.1	7.2	6.1	5.5	4.9
Average number of children per woman	2.89	3.18	3.38	3.45	3.27	2.82	2.44	2.20

Source: Arthur J. Norton and Louisa F. Miller, "The Family Life Cycle: 1985," *Work and Family Patterns of American Women*, Current Population Reports Special Studies Series P-23, No. 165, 1990, Table A, p. 2 (Washington, DC, 1990).

★ 154 ★

Family Life Cycle Stages, Once-Married Mothers

Once-married, currently married mothers at stages of the family life cycle, by year of birth, as of 1985.

Stage of family life cycle	All mothers born 1920-54	Birth cohort						
		1920-24	1925-29	1930-34	1935-39	1940-44	1945-49	1950-54
Total once-married, currently married mothers (at time of survey)(in thousands)	25,194	2,645	3,203	3,118	3,262	3,795	4,497	4,674
Median age at--								
First marriage	20.9	21.5	21.0	20.5	20.3	20.9	21.2	21.0
Birth of first child	22.9	23.9	23.2	22.4	21.9	22.6	23.2	23.4
Birth of last child	29.2	32.1	31.3	30.2	28.9	28.6	28.6	28.0
Years between age at--								
First marriage and first birth	2.0	2.4	2.2	1.9	1.6	1.7	2.0	2.4
First birth and last birth	6.3	8.2	8.1	7.8	7.0	6.0	5.4	4.6
Average number of children per woman	2.85	3.19	3.29	3.40	3.20	2.77	2.46	2.21

Source: Arthur J. Norton and Louisa F. Miller, "The Family Life Cycle: 1985," *Work and Family Patterns of American Women,* Current Population Reports Special Studies Series P-23, Table B, No. 165, 1990, p. 3 (Washington, DC, 1990).

★ 155 ★

Family Life Cycle Stages, Twice-Married Mothers

Twice-married, currently married mothers at stages of the family life cycle, by year of birth, as of 1985.

Stage of family life cycle 1	All mothers born 920-54	Birth cohort						
		1920-24	1925-29	1930-34	1935-39	1940-44	1945-49	1950-54
Total twice-married, currently married mothers (at time of survey)(in thousands)	4,485	311	374	512	588	787	957	957
Median age at--								
First marriage	19.0	19.1	18.9	18.6	18.8	19.2	19.3	19.0
Birth of first child	20.8	21.9	21.7	20.4	20.4	20.6	20.8	21.0
Birth of last child	27.6	28.8	29.9	28.7	27.5	26.9	26.8	26.8
Separation before divorce	26.1	27.8	27.1	28.9	28.9	27.6	25.7	23.9
Divorce	27.3	28.9	29.2	30.5	30.2	28.8	26.7	25.0
Remarriage	30.9	35.4	34.5	35.1	34.9	33.3	30.1	28.1
Years between age at--								
First marriage and first birth	1.8	2.8	2.8	1.8	1.6	1.4	1.5	2.0
First birth and last birth	6.8	6.9	8.2	8.3	7.1	6.3	6.0	5.8
Average number of children per woman	2.76	2.78	3.23	3.47	3.28	2.82	2.39	2.19

Source: Arthur J. Norton and Louisa F. Miller, "The Family Life Cycle: 1985," *Work and Family Patterns of American Women,* Current Population Reports Special Studies Series P-23, No. 165, 1990, p. 4 (Washington, DC, 1990). Excludes separated women and women whose first marriage ended in widowhood.

Time Allocation

★ 156 ★

Household Labor and Child Care Time Allocation

Adjusted mean time spent in hours per week in household labor and child care, by gender, wife's employment status, and presence of children.

Wife's Employment Status	Women			Men		
	Homemaker	Part-time	Full-time	Homemaker	Part-time	Full-time
Preschool-age children in household						
Household labor	33.4	30.3	15.0	9.4	13.1	8.2
Child care	19.1	10.2	5.2	4.8	5.2	2.8
Number of respondents	16	16	9	12	8	13
School-age children in household						
Household labor	35.6	28.7	18.9	12.5	12.3	11.7
Child care	3.5	3.3	2.7	1.7	1.9	1.1
Number of respondents	12	23	14	14	18	26
No children in household						
Household labor	31.0	32.9	14.6	14.7	13.3	13.6
Number of respondents	36	11	10	25	11	27
All households						
Household labor	35.6	28.7	18.9	11.6	14.0	12.1
Child care	7.0	3.7	2.1	2.1	1.8	1.0
Total households	64	50	33	51	37	66

Source: Beth Anne Shelton, "The Distribution of Household Tasks," *Journal of Family Issues* 11:2 (June 1990, Table 2, p. 115-135. Primary source: data made available by the Inter-University Consortium for Political and Social Research, State University of New York at Buffalo. Data collected from 620 respondents and 376 of their spouses.

★ 157 ★

Housework and Child Care: Selected Countries

Amount of time spent on housework and other household obligations and on child care per workday for employed women and men (minutes per working day).

Country	Housework and other household obligations		Child care	
	Employed women	Employed men	Employed women	Employed men
	Minutes per working day			
Belgium	163	34	14	6
Bulgaria	149	66	21	13
Czechoslovakia	255	78	30	18
France	173	58	24	8
Germany, Federal Republic[1]	216	48	26	7
German, Democratic Republic	220	80	33	15
Hungary	217	78	26	17
Poland	200	60	27	20
United States[1]	162	46	17	8
USSR	197	67	30	30
Yugoslavia[1]	231	76	25	13

Source: "Average daily time budget of employed men, employed women, and housewifes (sic) in 12 countries (in hours)," *The Economic Role of Women in the ECE Region: Developments 1975,* 1985, p. 110 (New York: United Nations, 1985). Primary source: A. Szalai (ed.). *The Use of Time; Daily Activities of Urban and Suburban Populations in Twelve Countries. Report on the Multinational Comparative Time-Budget Resarch Project.* The Hague, 1972; A. Szalai, "Women's Time. Women in the Light of Contemporary Time-Budget Research" in *Futures,* vol. 7, No. 5, pp. 385-399, October 1977. *Notes:* 1. Unweighted average of results of two investigations carried out under the multinational project on time use in these countries.

★ 158 ★

Time Allocation in Agricultural Societies

Time allocation in hours per week.

Activity	Women		Men	
	Rural Botswana 1975	Nepalese Villages 1981	Rural Botswana 1975	Nepalese Villages 1981
Total work	59.4	75.6	47.8	52.6
Marketable work	23.2	32.3	38.8	40.7
Housework	36.2	43.3	9.0	11.9
Leisure	42.0	27.8	55.5	46.3

Source: F. Thomas Juster and Frank P. Stafford, "Time Allocation in Agricultural Societies," *The Allocation of Time: Empirical Findings, Behavioral Models, and Problems of Measurement,* Table 2, p. 96 (contact Peter Seidman, Information Officer, News and Information Serivces, The University of Michigan, 412 Maynard, Ann Arbor, MI 48109-1399; 313-747-4416).

★ 159 ★

Time Allocation per Day in Selected Countries

Time allocation in twelve countries, in hours per day.

Activities	Employed Women	Employed Men	Housewives
	Hours per day		
On workdays (employed people) and weekdays (housewives)			
Paid work and ancillary tasks (work brought home, journey to work, workplace chores, etc.)	7.9	9.4	0.2
Housework and household obligations (not including child care)	3.3	1.0	7.5
Child care	0.4	0.2	1.1
Sleep, meals, personal hygiene, and other personal needs	9.9	9.9	11.2
Free time (remaining disposable time)	2.5	3.5	4.0
Total	24.0	24.0	24.0
	Hours per day		
On days off (employed people) and Sundays (housewives)			
Paid work and ancillary tasks (work brought home, journey to work, workplace chores, etc.)	0.4	0.9	0.1
Housework and household obligations (not including child care)	5.1	2.3	5.2
Child care	0.6	0.3	0.7
Sleep, meals, personal hygiene, and other personal needs	11.9	12.2	11.7

[Continued]

★ 159 ★

Time Allocation per Day in Selected Countries
[Continued]

Activities	Employed Women	Employed Men	Housewives
Free time (remaining disposable time)	6.0	8.3	6.3
Total	24.0	24.0	24.0

Source: "Average daily time budget of employed men, employed women, and housewives in 12 countries (in hours)," *The Economic Role of Women in the ECE Region: Developments 1975*, 1985, p. 106 (New York: United Nations, 1985). Primary source: A. Szalai (ed.). *The Use of Time; Daily Activities of Urban and Suburban Populations in Twelve Countries. Report on the Multinational Comparative Time-Budget Resarch Project.* The Hague, 1972; A. Szalai, "Women's Time. Women in the Light of Contemporary Time-Budget Research" in *Futures*, vol. 7, No. 5, pp. 385-399, October 1977. Eleven countries were included in the project: Belgium, Bulgaria, Czechoslovakia, France, the German Democratic Republic, the Federal Republic of Germany, Hungary, Poland, the United States, the Soviet Union and Yugoslavia, and also Peru.

★ 160 ★

Time Allocation per Week in Selected Countries

Time allocation (hours per week), selected countries, various years.

Activity	Country, year, hours per week					
	U.S. 1981	Japan 1985	USSR 1985	Finland 1979	Hungary 1977	Sweden 1984
Total work						
Women	54.4	55.6	66.3	61.1	68.9	55.5
Men	57.8	55.5	65.7	57.8	63.7	57.9
Market work						
Women	23.9	24.6	39.3	32.5	35.1	23.7
Men	44.0	52.0	53.8	44.0	50.8	39.8
Commuting						
Women	2.0	1.2	3.4	2.5	2.6	2.1
Men	3.5	4.5	5.2	3.0	4.0	3.8
Housework						
Women	30.5	31.0	27.0	28.6	33.8	31.8
Men	13.8	3.5	11.9	13.8	12.9	18.1
Personal care (including sleep)						
Women	71.6	72.1	69.8	72.7	73.6	73.8
Men	68.2	72.4	67.8	72.5	74.0	70.9
Sleep						
Women	59.9	57.0	58.2	60.9	60.4	56.9
Men	57.9	60.0	56.9	6.2	59.4	55.3
Leisure (including activities listed below)						

[Continued]

★ 160 ★

Time Allocation per Week in Selected Countries
[Continued]

| Activity | Country, year, hours per week | | | | | |
	U.S. 1981	Japan 1985	USSR 1985	Finland 1979	Hungary 1977	Sweden 1984
Women	41.9	40.3	32.0	33.6	25.3	38.5
Men	41.8	40.3	34.6	38.1	30.4	39.0
Adult Education						
Women	0.4	2.2	2.6	1.2	1.3	1.0
Men	0.6	1.2	1.0	0.9	1.9	1.0
Socializing						
Women	17.6	7.0	9.6	10.2	4.6	11.2
Men	14.9	8.0	7.8	12.1	7.1	9.6
Active Leisure						
Women	4.2	3.6	3.0	2.7	1.8	8.4
Men	5.6	5.3	4.1	4.3	2.4	7.2
Passive Leisure						
Women	19.8	27.5	16.8	19.5	17.6	17.9
Men	20.8	25.5	21.7	20.8	19.0	21.2
Television						
Female	11.5	21.4	11.2	7.7	9.2	10.8
Male	12.7	17.3	14.5	9.7	10.2	13.4

Source: F. Thomas Juster and Frank P. Stafford, "Time Allocation Across Countries", *The Allocation of Time: Empirical Findings, Behavioral Models, and Problems of Measurement,* Table 1, p. 95 (contact Peter Seidman, Information Officer, News and Information Serivces, The University of Michigan, 412 Maynard, Ann Arbor, MI 48109-1399; 313-747-4416).

★ 161 ★

Time Spent in Gathering Fuel: Developing Countries

Country	Hours per day
Burkina Faso	4-6
Ghana	3-1/2 to 4[1]
India (Gujarat State)	3[2]
Kenya	3-1/2[3]
Nepal	1-5[4]
Niger	4-6[5]
Peru	2-1/2[6]

[Continued]

★ 161 ★

Time Spent in Gathering Fuel: Developing Countries
[Continued]

Country	Hours per day
Senegal	4-5[7]
United Republic of Tanzania	8[8]

Source: "Time spent in gathering fuel," *World Survey on the Role of Women in Development*, 1986, p. 192 (New York: United Nations, 1986). Primary source: Mangalam Srinivasan, "The role of women in the use, conservation and development of energy resources," working paper, United Nations, 1984. "In most parts of the developing world rural women and children spend a considerable amount of time collecting fuel-wood; owing to constantly receding forests, they are obliged to walk longer distances to find it" (source). *Notes:* 1. One full day's search provides wood for 3 days. 2. Often one member of a family of five devotes all of her/his time in searching for and collecting fuel. 3. Women do 75% of wood fuel collection. 4. Time depends on the terrain. 5. Women sometimes walk 25 km in search of fuel. 6. Women are also involved in the cutting of wood. 7. Firewood often has to be carried about 45 km. 8. Often one member of the family has to spend every day gathering fuel.

Violence

★ 162 ★

Violence Toward Spouse

Answers to questions about spouse/partner abuse.

Questions/Responses	Total		Females		Males	
	Number	Percent	Number	Percent	Number	Percent
Did you ever walk out on your (husband/wife/ partner with whom you were living as married) either permanently or for at least several weeks? (For those who have been married or lived as though married)						
No	847	87.2%	526	85.4%	321	90.4%
Yes	124	12.8%	90	14.6%	34	9.6%
Did you ever hit or throw things at your (husband/wife/partner)?						
No	780	80.3%	477	77.4%	303	85.4%
Yes	191	19.7%	139	22.6%	52	14.6%
Were you ever the one who hit or threw things first, regardless of who started the argument?						
No	59	30.9%	37	26.6%	22	42.3%
Yes	132	69.1%	102	73.4%	30	57.7%
Did you hit or throw things first on more than one occasion?						

[Continued]

★ 162 ★

Violence Toward Spouse
[Continued]

Questions/Responses	Total		Females		Males	
	Number	Percent	Number	Percent	Number	Percent
No	58	43.9%	50	49.0%	8	26.7%
Yes	74	56.1%	52	51.0%	22	73.3%

Source: Roger Bland, M.B., F.R.C.P.(C), and Helene Orn, B.Ed., "Family Violence and Psychiatric Disorder," *Canadian Journal of Psychiatry*, Vol. 31 (March 1986), p. 131. Based on interviews with 1,200 non-institutionalized residents of the City of Edmonton.

★ 163 ★

Violence to Children

Answers to a question about violence to children.

Question	Total		Females		Males	
	Number	Percent	Number	Percent	Number	Percent
Have you ever spanked or hit a child (your's or anyone else's) hard enough so that he or she had bruises or had to stay in bed or see a doctor? (For those who have looked after children)						
No	978	98.0%	620	97.5%	358	98.9%
Yes	20	2.0%	16	2.5%	4	1.1%
Note: this question does not require the respondent to have been the parent or acting as the parent of the child, but all 20 of the affirmative respondents had children. Thus, for those who had children and had looked after them, the results are:						
No	752	97.4%	507	96.9%	245	98.4%
Yes	20	2.6%	16	3.1%	4	1.6%

Source: Roger Bland, M.B., F.R.C.P.(C), and Helene Orn, B.Ed., "Family Violence and Psychiatric Disorder," *Canadian Journal of Psychiatry*, Vol. 31 (March 1986), p. 131. Based on interviews with 1,200 noninstitutionalized residents of the City of Edmonton.

★ 164 ★

Wife Beating in Five Societies

Frequency and ubiquty of wife beating, wife battering, and mutual violence in 5 societies.

Society	Wife Beating	Wife Battering	Mutual Violence
Iran	3	3	0
India	3	3	0
Taiwan	3	2	0
Ecuadorian Village	2	1	0
Marshall Islanders	2	1	0

Source: Selected from "Frequency and Ubiquity of Wife Beating, Wife Battering, and Mutual Violence in 14 Societies," *Sanctions and Sanctuary: Cultural Perspectives on the Beating of Wives*, Chapter 17, Table 1 (to be published 1991, Westview Press, Boulder, CO). Also in source: data for other societies. 3 = High Frequency and ubiquity; 2 = Medium frequency and ubiquity; 1 = Low frequency and ubiquity; 0 = Essentially none. "It is proposed...that individual psychological factors within a context of cultural tolerance...may be most predictive of the occurrence of wife beating (a particular man hitting a woman occasionally and not seriously throughout the course of a relationship), while societal level cultural, political, and economic factors can control or facilitate that individual's acts of violence toward his spouse becoming and remaining frequently repeated and severe" (source).

EDUCATION

Degrees

★ 165 ★

Bachelors' Degrees Conferred by Field

Numbers conferred in 1988.

Field	Total	Women
Agriculture and natural resources	14,222	4,478
Allied health and health sciences	60,095	51,308
Architecture and environmental design	8,606	3,329
Area and ethnic studies	3,463	2,070
Business and management	243,344	113,580
Communications and communications technologies	46,705	28,117
Computer and information sciences	34,548	11,201
Education	91,013	70,008
Engineering and engineering technologies	88,791	12,184
Foreign languages	10,028	7,301
Home economics and vocational home economics	14,825	13,600
Law	1,303	890
Letters	39,503	26,351
Liberal/general studies	21,796	12,298
Library and archival sciences	123	106
Life sciences	36,761	18,500
Mathematics	15,888	7,375
Military sciences and military technologies	349	18
Multi-interdisciplinary studies	17,366	9,173
Parks and recreation	4,081	2,401
Philosophy and religion	5,959	2,101
Physical sciences and science technologies	17,776	5,401
Protective services	13,369	5,020
Psychology	44,961	31,477
Public affairs and social work	14,232	9,699
Social sciences	100,270	43,973
Theology	5,584	1,397
Visual and performing arts	36,600	22,494

[Continued]

131

★ 165 ★

Bachelors' Degrees Conferred by Field

[Continued]

Field	Total	Women
Not classified by field of study	1,801	670
All fields	993,362	516,520

Source: Chronicle of Higher Education Almanac, September 5, 1990, p. 19. Primary source: U.S. Department of Education. Also in source: Master's degrees and doctoral degrees conferred.

★ 166 ★

Bachelors' Degrees, 1975-2000

Bachelors' degrees conferred 1975-1987; estimates 1988 and 1989; projections 1990-2000.

Year ending	Total	Women	Men
1975	922,933	418,092	504,841
1976	925,746	420,821	504,925
1977	919,549	424,004	495,545
1978	921,204	433,857	487,347
1979	921,390	444,046	477,344
1980	929,417	455,806	473,611
1981	935,140	465,257	469,883
1982	952,998	479,634	473,364
1983	969,510	490,370	479,140
1984	974,309	491,990	482,319
1985	979,477	496,949	482,528
1986	987,823	501,900	485,923
1987	991,339	510,485	480,854
1988	989,000	517,000	472,000
1989	994,000	521,000	473,000
1990	1,005,000	530,000	475,000
1991	995,000	532,000	463,000
1992	1,011,000	543,000	468,000
1993	1,016,000	548,000	468,000
1994	1,006,000	542,000	464,000
1995	990,000	534,000	456,000
1996	973,000	522,000	451,000
1997	962,000	512,000	450,000
1998	961,000	509,000	452,000
1999	968,000	507,000	461,000
2000	976,000	509,000	467,000

Source: Selected from "Bachelor's degrees, by sex of recipient, with projections: 50 States and D.C., 1974-75 to 1999-2000," *Projections of Education Statistics to 2000,* p. 67 (Washington, D.C.: National Center for Education Statistics, 1989). Primary source: U.S. Department of Education, National Center for Education Statistics, "Degrees and Other Formal Awards Conferred" survey, Integrated Postsecondary Education Data System (IPEDS), and Early National Estimates survey, 1987 and 1988. (This table was prepared April 1989.). Because of rounding, details may not add to totals.

★ 167 ★

Doctorates Awarded to Minority Women: 1978 and 1988

Number of minority women doctorates by race/ethnicity, 1978 and 1988.

Race/ethnicity	1978	1988
Black	457	519
Asian	214	363
Hispanic	169	307
American Indian	10	42

Source: "Number of Minority Women Doctorates, by Race/Ethnicity, 1978 and 1988," *A Decade of Change: The Status of U.S. Women Doctorates, 1978-88,* p. 3 (Washington, D.C.: American Council on Education, 1990). Primary source: National Research Council, 1990. Data is for U.S. citizens and permanent residents.

★ 168 ★

Doctorates Awarded to Women: 1978 and 1988

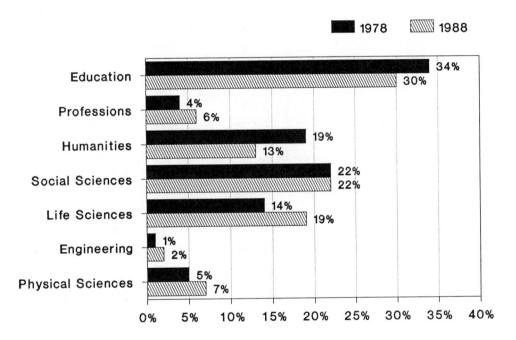

Percent of doctorates awarded to women, by field, 1978 and 1988.

Field	1978	1988
Education	34%	30%
Professions	4%	6%
Humanities	19%	13%
Social Sciences	22%	22%
Life Sciences	14%	19%

[Continued]

★ 168 ★

Doctorates Awarded to Women: 1978 and 1988
[Continued]

Field	1978	1988
Engineering	1%	2%
Physical Sciences	5%	7%

Source: "Percent of Doctorates Awarded to Women, by Field, 1978 and 1988," *A Decade of Change: The Status of U.S. Women Doctorates, 1978-88,* p. 2 (Washington, D.C.: American Council on Education, 1990). Primary source: National Research Council, 1990. Data is for all women U.S. citizens and non-U.S. citizens.

★ 169 ★

Doctors' Degrees Conferred by Field
Percentage of doctors' degrees received, by field, 1988.

Field	Total	Women	Men
Arts/humanities	3,553	44.3%	55.7%
Business and management	1,039	23.8%	76.2%
Education	6,349	55.2%	44.8%
Engineering	4,190	6.8%	93.2%
Life sciences	6,143	36.8%	63.2%
Physical sciences	5,309	16.6%	83.4%
Social sciences	5,769	45.0%	55.0%
Other professional fields[1]	1,053	40.4%	59.6%
All fields[2]	33,456	35.2%	64.8%

Source: Chronicle of Higher Education Almanac, September 5, 1990, p. 18. Primary source: National Research Council. Also in source: recipients of doctorates by citizenship; planned postdoctoral study/ employment; primary postdoctoral employment activity. *Notes:* 1. Excludes business and management, which is listed separately. 2. Includes degree categories not listed separately.

★ 170 ★

Doctors' Degrees, 1975-2000
Doctors' degrees conferred, 1975-1987; estimates 1988-1989; projections 1990-2000.

Year ending	Total	Women	Men
1975	34,083	7,266	26,817
1976	34,064	7,797	26,267
1977	33,232	8,090	25,142
1978	32,131	8,473	23,658
1979	32,730	9,189	23,541
1980	32,615	9,672	22,943
1981	32,958	10,247	22,711
1982	32,707	10,483	22,224
1983	32,775	10,873	21,902
1984	33,209	11,145	22,064
1985	32,943	11,243	21,700
1986	33,653	11,834	21,819

[Continued]

★ 170 ★

Doctors' Degrees, 1975-2000
[Continued]

Year ending	Total	Women	Men
1987	34,120	12,021	22,099
1988	34,000	12,000	22,000
1989	34,200	12,600	21,600
1990	34,400	12,900	21,500
1991	34,500	13,200	21,300
1992	34,600	13,700	20,900
1993	34,700	14,200	20,500
1994	34,800	14,700	20,100
1995	34,900	15,200	19,700
1996	34,900	15,700	19,200
1997	35,000	16,300	18,700
1998	35,000	16,900	18,100
1999	35,000	17,600	17,400
2000	35,100	18,400	16,700

Source: "Doctor's degrees, by sex of recipient, with projections: 50 States and D.C., 1974-75 to 1999-2000," *Projections of Education Statistics to 2000,* p. 69 (Washington, D.C.: National Center for Education Statistics, 1989). Primary source: U.S. Department of Education, National Center for Education Statistics, "Degrees and Other Formal Awards Conferred" survey, Integrated Postsecondary Education Data System (IPEDS), and Early Natijonal Estimates survey, 1987 and 1988. (This table was prepared April 1989.). Because of rounding, details may not add to totals.

★ 171 ★

Masters' Degrees Conferred by Field

Numbers conferred in 1988.

Field	Total	Women
Agriculture and natural resources	3,479	1,052
Allied health and health sciences	18,523	14,495
Architecture and environmental design	3,159	1,117
Area and ethnic studies	905	410
Business and management	69,630	23,348
Communications and communications technologies	3,932	2,358
Computer and information sciences	9,166	2,464
Education	77,704	58,321
Engineering and engineering technologies	23,426	2,923
Foreign languages	1,847	1,258
Home economics and vocational home economics	2,059	1,813
Law	1,880	494
Letters	6,171	4,061
Liberal/general studies	1,342	831
Library and archival sciences	3,713	2,923
Life sciences	4,769	2,352
Mathematics	3,423	1,371
Military sciences and military technologies	49	1

[Continued]

★ 171 ★

Masters' Degrees Conferred by Field
[Continued]

Field	Total	Women
Multi-interdisciplinary studies	3,097	1,298
Parks and recreation	461	256
Philosophy and religion	1,098	423
Physical sciences and science technologies	5,727	1,412
Protective services	1,024	297
Psychology	7,862	5,273
Public affairs and social work	17,150	10,826
Social sciences	10,293	4,058
Theology	4,775	1,616
Visual and performing arts	7,925	4,488
Not classified by field of study	4,144	2,271
All fields	298,733	153,810

Source: Chronicle of Higher Education Almanac, September 5, 1990, p. 19. Primary source: U.S. Department of Education. Also in source: Bachelor's, doctoral, and professional degrees conferred.

★ 172 ★

Masters' Degrees, 1975-2000

Masters' degrees conferred 1975-1987; estimates 1988 and 1989; projections 1990-2000.

Year ending	Total	Women	Men
1975	292,450	130,880	161,570
1976	311,771	144,523	167,248
1977	317,164	149,381	167,783
1978	311,620	150,408	161,212
1979	301,079	147,709	153,370
1980	298,081	147,332	150,749
1981	295,739	148,696	147,043
1982	295,546	150,014	145,532
1983	289,921	145,224	144,697
1984	284,263	140,668	143,595
1985	286,251	142,861	143,390
1986	288,567	145,059	143,508
1987	289,557	148,194	141,363
1988	292,000	150,000	142,000
1989	293,000	156,000	137,000
1990	301,000	158,000	143,000
1991	300,000	158,000	142,000
1992	302,000	159,000	143,000
1993	301,000	158,000	143,000
1994	299,000	157,000	142,000
1995	295,000	155,000	140,000
1996	292,000	153,000	139,000

[Continued]

★ 172 ★

Masters' Degrees, 1975-2000
[Continued]

Year ending	Total	Women	Men
1997	290,000	152,000	138,000
1998	289,000	151,000	138,000
1999	287,000	150,000	137,000
2000	286,000	150,000	137,000

Source: Selected from "Master's degrees, by sex of recipient, with projections: 50 States and D.C., 1974-75 to 1999-2000," *Projections of Education Statistics to 2000*, p. 68 (Washington, D.C.: National Center for Education Statistics, 1989). Primary source: U.S. Department of Education, National Center for Education Statistics, "Degrees and Other Formal Awards Conferred" survey, Integrated Postsecondary Education Data System (IPEDS), and Early Natijonal Estimates survey, 1987 and 1988. (This table was prepared April 1989.). Because of rounding, details may not add to totals.

★ 173 ★

Professional Degrees Conferred by Field

Field	Total	Women
Chiropractic	2,632	669
Dentistry	4,351	1,135
Law	35,469	14,345
Medicine	15,091	4,984
Optometry	1,023	351
Osteopathic medicine	1,544	421
Pharmacy	951	568
Podiatry and podiatric medicine	645	150
Theological professions	6,474	1,386
Veterinary medicine	2,235	1,118
All fields	70,415	25,127

Source: Chronicle of Higher Education Almanac, September 5, 1990, p. 19. Primary source: U.S. Department of Education. Also in source: Bachelor's, master's, and doctoral degrees conferred.

★ 174 ★

Professional Degrees, 1975-2000

First-professional degrees conferred 1975-1987; estimates 1988 and 1989; projections 1990-2000.

Year ending	Total	Women	Men
1975	55,916	6,960	48,956
1976	62,649	9,757	52,892
1977	64,359	11,985	52,374
1978	66,581	14,311	52,270
1979	68,848	16,196	52,652
1980	70,131	17,415	52,716
1981	71,956	19,164	52,792
1982	72,032	19,809	52,223

[Continued]

★ 174 ★

Professional Degrees, 1975-2000
[Continued]

Year ending	Total	Women	Men
1983	73,136	21,826	51,310
1984	74,407	23,073	51,334
1985	75,063	24,608	50,455
1986	73,910	24,649	49,261
1987	72,750	25,290	47,460
1988	72,000	25,000	46,000
1989	72,200	25,800	46,400
1990	72,400	26,400	46,000
1991	72,300	26,000	45,700
1992	72,100	26,600	45,500
1993	72,700	27,100	45,600
1994	72,200	27,800	44,400
1995	70,600	27,600	43,000
1996	69,200	27,000	42,200
1997	68,300	26,800	41,500
1998	67,800	26,800	41,000
1999	67,600	26,800	40,800
2000	67,100	26,800	40,400

Source: "First-professional degrees, by sex of recipient, with projections: 50 States and D.C., 1974-75 to 1999-2000," *Projections of Education Statistics to 2000,* p. 70 (Washington, D.C.: National Center for Education Statistics, 1989). Primary source: U.S. Department of Education, National Center for Education Statistics, "Degrees and Other Formal Awards Conferred" survey, Integrated Postsecondary Education Data System (IPEDS), and Early Natijonal Estimates survey, 1987 and 1988. (This table was prepared April 1989.). Because of rounding, details may not add to totals.

Educational Attainment

★ 175 ★

Educational Attainment

Educational attainment of U.S. adult population, 1990.

Educational Attainment	Number (thousands)		
	Total	Women	Men
Total, all adults	180,974	94,667	86,307
Graduated College	32,229	14,333	17,896
Attended College	33,285	17,363	15,922
Graduated High School	71,202	39,830	31,372
Did Not Graduate High School	44,259	23,142	21,117

Source: Selected from *Mediamark Research Multimedia Audiences Report, Spring 1990* (New York: Mediamark Research Inc., 1990).

★ 176 ★

Educational Attainment of Women at the Time of First Birth

Educational attainment of women at the time of their first birth: 1970 and 1985.

Educational Attainment	Time of first birth	
	1970	1985
High school graduates	73.1%	80.1%
1 or more years of college	26.0%	38.6%
4 or more years of college	9.9%	18.1%

Source: Martin O'Connell, "Maternity Leave Arrangements: 1961-85," *Work and Family Patterns of American Women,* Current Population Reports Special Studies Series P-23, No. 165, 1990, p. 11+.

★ 177 ★

Elementary Student Progress, 1970-1985

The percentage of students *below* the grade in which most children their age are enrolled.

Year	8-year-olds		13-year-olds	
	Female	Male	Female	Male
1970	13.1%	18.7%	18.3%	27.7%
1971	13.1%	17.7%	18.0%	27.3%
1972	12.7%	18.0%	18.3%	27.3%
1973	12.1%	17.9%	18.3%	27.4%
1974	12.3%	18.0%	18.1%	27.1%
1975	12.7%	17.6%	17.3%	25.2%
1976	12.6%	16.7%	16.8%	24.1%
1977	12.9%	17.2%	16.2%	23.5%
1978	13.2%	18.9%	16.8%	23.8%
1979	14.4%	20.2%	17.1%	24.9%
1980	15.2%	21.1%	18.6%	26.0%
1981	16.5%	21.7%	19.8%	28.0%
1982	16.7%	23.2%	21.2%	30.5%
1983	17.0%	23.9%	21.9%	32.0%
1984	17.7%	24.4%	22.5%	32.6%
1985	18.4%	24.9%	23.3%	31.5%

Source: "Enrollment in Modal Grade for 8-and 13-Year-Olds, by Sex and Race: 1970-1985," *The Condition of Education 1990, Volume 1: Elementary and Secondary Education,* p. 18, 98 (Washington, D.C.: National Center for Education Statistics, 1990). Primary source: U.S. Department of Commerce, Bureau of the Census, *Current Population Reports,* Series P-20, "School Enrollment...," various years, and unpublished tabulations. Also in source: percentages by age and race. *Notes:* 1. Percentages given are three-year averages. For example, the 3-year average for 1985 is the average of the percentages for 1984, 1985, and 1986.

★ 178 ★

Worldwide Female Education and Quality of Life

Estimates and projections. The worldwide education of females would result in the following improvements in the quality of life, according to the Research Triangle Institute.

An increase in the female gross primary enrollment rate from **20%** to **70%**, accompanied by proportional growth in the female secondary enrollment rate, can be expected to result in a reduction of the infant mortality rate, 20 years later, of nearly **38%**.

An increase in the female gross primary enrollment rate from **20%** to **70%**, accompanied by proportional growth in the female secondary enrollment rate and a moderate level of governmental support for family planning, can be expected to result in a reduction in the total fertility rate, 20 years later, by about **0.5** births per woman.

An increase in the female primary enrollment rate from **20%** to **70%** will produce an increase of **7.3** percentage points in the labor force participation of women 20 years later, even with other relevant factors controlled. Increasing the female secondary rate from **4%** to **16%** would produce an increase in labor force participation of over **12** percentage points after 20 years.

An increase in the female gross primary enrollment rate from **20%** to **70%** may result in a 6-year increase in the life expectancy of children born 20 years later.

Source: Selected from "Female Education and Infant Mortality," "Female Education and Fertility," "Female Education and Labor Force Participation," and "Female Education and Life Expectancy," Summary of Research Findings of BRIDGES and ABEL Projects, (North Carolina: Research Triangle Institute, February 1990).

★ 179 ★

Years of School Completed

Years of school completed by persons (civilian noninstitutional population) age 18 and over, by sex and age, 1988.

Age	Total	Elementary level		High school		College		
		<8 years	8 years	1-3 years	4 years	1-3 years	4 years	5+ years
				Numbers in thousands				
	177,677	10,876	8,403	22,464	70,194	32,932	19,622	13,188
Women								
18 and over	92,902	5,444	4,579	11,743	39,051	17,494	9,308	5,284
18 and 19 years old	3,640	34	53	1,171	1,832	549	1	---
20 to 24 years old	9,586	194	167	974	3,953	3,213	963	119
25 years old and over	79,676	5,216	4,359	9,597	33,266	13,731	8,345	5,165
25 to 29 years old	10,854	216	176	1,015	4,718	2,348	1,750	633
30 to 34 years old	10,795	286	173	849	4,577	2,442	1,607	860
35 to 39 years old	9,533	325	138	818	3,896	2,119	1,275	962
40 to 49 years old	14,645	585	358	1,567	6,399	2,745	1,654	1,338
50 to 59 years old	11,385	792	597	1,762	5,186	1,586	869	594
60 to 69 years old	11,117	1,089	1,008	1,758	4,880	1,376	590	415
70 years old and over	11,347	1,921	1,909	1,828	3,610	1,115	600	363

[Continued]

★ 179 ★

Years of School Completed
[Continued]

Age	Total	Elementary level		High school		College		
		<8 years	8 years	1-3 years	4 years	1-3 years	4 years	5+ years
Men								
18 and over	84,776	5,429	3,824	10,724	31,143	15,439	10,311	7,905
18 and 19 years old	3,581	54	79	1,439	1,621	387	1	-
20 to 24 years old	9,254	250	145	1,067	3,848	2,999	786	159
25 years old and over	71,941	5,125	3,600	8,217	25,674	12,053	9,525	7,746
25 to 29 years old	10,669	286	154	1,190	4,375	2,166	1,733	764
30 to 34 years old	10,651	349	115	1,028	4,219	2,112	1,738	1,091
35 to 39 years old	9,321	372	147	705	3,266	2,045	1,497	1,289
40 to 49 years old	13,959	618	377	1,287	4,946	2,516	1,982	2,233
50 to 59 years old	10,485	881	688	1,318	3,757	1,461	1,180	1,199
60 to 69 years old	9,478	1,123	880	1,551	3,159	1,099	909	759
70 years old and over	7,377	1,496	1,239	1,139	1,952	654	486	410

Source: Selected from "Years of school completed by persons[1] age 18 and over, by age, sex, and race/ethnicity: 1988," *Digest of Education Statistics,* Table 9, p. 16 (Washington, D.C.: National Center for Education Statistics, 1989). Primary source: U.S. Department of Commerce, Bureau of the Census, Current Population Survey, unpublished data. Also in source: data by race/ethnicity. Data are based on sample surveys of the noninstitutional population. Although cells with fewer than 75,000 people are subject to relatively wide sampling variation, they are included in the table to permit various types of aggregations. Because of rounding, details may not add to totals.

Enrollment

★ 180 ★

College and University Enrollment

College and university enrollment by level, fall 1987.

Student characteristics	Undergraduate		First-professional		Graduate		All levels	
	Total	Women	Total	Women	Total	Women	Total	Women
Full-time students	6,463,066	3,299,312	241,804	88,143	526,636	233,133	7,231,506	3,620,588
Part-time students	4,584,836	2,679,906	26,663	10,191	925,302	525,491	5,536,801	3,215,588
All students	11,047,902	5,979,218	268,467	98,334	1,451,938	758,624	12,768,307	6,836,176

Source: Chronicle of Higher Education Almanac, September 5, 1990, p. 18. Primary source: U.S. Department of Education. Also in source: Enrollment by age of student.

★ 181 ★

College and University Enrollment, 1980-2000

College and university enrollment by age, in thousands, 1980-2000.

Age	1980[1]	1985[1]	1988[1]	1995[2]	2000[2]
			Numbers in thousands		
Total	12,097	12,247	12,849	12,935	13,378
Women	6,223	6,429	6,904	7,042	7,254
14 to 17 years	148	113	137	126	138
18 to 19 years	1,526	1,370	1,532	1,502	1,687
20 to 21 years	1,165	1,166	1,222	1,253	1,379
22 to 24 years	925	885	977	958	925
25 to 29 years	878	962	949	840	795
30 to 34 years	667	687	736	743	656
35 years and over	914	1,246	1,354	1,620	1,676
Men	5,874	5,818	5,946	5,893	6,124

Source: Selected from "Enrollment in all institutions of higher education, by age, sex, and attendance status, with middle alternative projections: 50 States and D.C., fall 1980, 1985, 1988, 1995, and 2000, *Projections of Higher Education Statistics to 2000,* Table 6, p. 31 (Washington, D.C.: National Center for Education Statistics, 1989). Primary source: U.S. Department of Education, National Center for Education Statistics, "Fall Enrollment in Colleges and Universities" surveys, Integrated Postsecondary Education Data System (IPEDS) surveys, "National Estimates of Higher Education: School Year 1988-89," *Early Estimates;* and U.S. Department of Commerce, Bureau of the Census, *Current Population Reports,* Series P-25, No. 1018. Also in source: breakdown for full-time and part-time students; data for men by age. Because of rounding, details may not add to totals. *Notes:* 1. Estimated 2. Projected.

★ 182 ★

Early Childhood Education Worldwide

Average increase in female enrollment from 1975 to 1980 and 1980 to 1987, education preceding the first level.

Major areas	Total		Female	
	1975-1980	1980-1987	1975-1980	1975-1980
World Total (Including China)	5.8%	4.3%	-	-
World Total (Excluding China)	4.3%	3.7%	4.2%	3.7%
Africa	19.0%	4.0%	20.3%	5.4%
America	4.3%	6.9%	4.2%	7.0%
Asia	8.1%	6.1%	8.6%	5.7%
Europe (Including USSR)	2.3%	1.0%	2.3%	1.0%
Oceania	-0.8%	1.0%	-0.6%	1.0%
Developed Countries	1.7%	1.2%	1.7%	1.2%
Developing Countries	12.5%	8.4%	12.9%	8.5%
Africa (Excluding Arab States)	25.2%	3.1%	25.0%	4.5%
Asia (Excluding Arab States)	8.2%	6.1%	8.7%	5.7%
Arab States	9.6%	5.6%	9.4%	7.0%

[Continued]

★ 182 ★

Early Childhood Education Worldwide
[Continued]

Major areas	Total		Female	
	1975-1980	1980-1987	1975-1980	1975-1980
Northern America	0.1%	3.6%	-0.3%	3.8%
Latin America and the Caribbean	11.2%	10.1%	11.1%	10.1%

Source: Selected from "Estimated Teaching Staff and Enrolment by Sex for Education Preceding the First Level," *Statistical Yearbook,* Table 2.8, p. 2-26/2-28 (Paris: UNESCO, 1989). See introduction to this book for an explanation of levels of education. Also in source: estimated teaching staff and enrollment figures (see separate tables).

★ 183 ★

Female Engineering Enrollment in Europe
Female representation in engineering educational enrollment, 1960 and 1980.

Country	1960	1980
Austria	3.5%	7.7%
Belgium	5.3%	7.0%
Bulgaria	26.4%	38.9%
Czechoslovakia	11.8%	21.5%
Denmark	4.9%	7.2%
Finland	2.3%	9.0%
German Democratic Republic	---	28.8%
Germany, Federal Republic	1.5%	5.1%
Greece	2.8%	13.3%
Hungary	12.2%	13.3%
Ireland	---	5.8%
Italy	0.6%	4.1%
Netherlands	1.3%	9.3%
Norway	2.0%	11.6%
Poland	17.0%	26.0%
Portugal	7.4%	15.4%
Romania	14.5%	34.9%
Spain	0.5%	7.3%
Switzerland	0.5%	2.2%
Turkey	5.8%	13.6%
United Kingdom	1.4%	---
Yugoslavia	13.9%	18.0%
All countries in Europe	8.0%	15.2%

Source: Selected from "Female representation in engineering enrolment in twenty-three European countries and Canada, 1960 and 1980," *Women in Engineering Education,* p. 79 (Paris: UNESCO, 1988).

★ 184 ★

High School Graduates Enrolled in College: 1973-1988

Percent of high school graduates 16-24 and 25-34 years old enrolled in 2-year and 4-year colleges: 1973-1988.

Year	16- to 24-year-olds			25- to 34-year-olds		
	Total	2-year	4-year	Total	2-year	4-year
Female						
1973	24.5%	5.6%	18.1%	3.3%	1.7%	1.5%
1974	25.9%	6.2%	18.6%	4.0%	1.9%	1.9%
1975	28.2%	7.9%	19.0%	5.4%	2.2%	2.3%
1976	29.8%	7.6%	21.2%	4.5%	2.4%	2.0%
1977	28.4%	7.7%	19.3%	5.6%	2.7%	2.5%
1978	27.9%	7.9%	18.9%	5.1%	2.2%	2.6%
1979	28.8%	7.9%	20.0%	5.4%	2.6%	2.6%
1980	29.3%	8.6%	19.5%	5.8%	2.9%	2.5%
1981	29.7%	9.1%	19.4%	6.0%	2.7%	2.9%
1982	30.7%	9.7%	20.1%	5.6%	2.8%	2.5%
1983	29.6%	9.0%	19.5%	5.7%	2.8%	2.7%
1984	29.9%	8.3%	20.3%	5.7%	2.5%	2.9%
1985	31.4%	9.0%	21.2%	6.0%	3.1%	2.7%
1986	31.5%	9.0%	21.6%	5.8%	2.9%	2.8%
1987	33.4%	10.7%	22.7%	5.5%	2.7%	2.8%
1988	35.4%	11.2%	24.3%	5.6%	3.1%	2.5%
Male						
1973	32.7%	7.9%	23.8%	6.4%	2.5%	3.7%
1974	33.1%	8.5%	23.3%	7.3%	3.1%	3.8%
1975	33.2%	9.4%	23.8%	8.2%	4.2%	3.9%
1976	32.9%	8.6%	24.4%	7.4%	3.5%	3.8%
1977	32.9%	8.6%	24.2%	6.9%	3.1%	3.8%
1978	31.6%	8.3%	23.4%	5.9%	2.8%	3.2%
1979	31.1%	7.8%	23.3%	5.4%	2.2%	3.3%
1980	32.1%	8.7%	22.4%	5.2%	2.0%	2.8%
1981	33.4%	9.3%	23.1%	5.7%	2.2%	3.2%
1982	33.4%	9.2%	23.0%	5.4%	2.3%	2.8%
1983	33.8%	9.2%	23.3%	5.8%	2.6%	3.0%
1984	34.6%	9.2%	24.2%	5.3%	2.2%	2.8%
1985	34.4%	8.5%	24.5%	5.1%	1.9%	3.1%
1986	34.2%	9.3%	24.1%	5.3%	2.2%	3.0%
1987	37.3%	10.2%	27.2%	5.0%	2.1%	2.9%
1988	36.9%	11.0%	25.9%	4.9%	1.9%	3.1%

Source: Selected from "Percent of High School Graduates 16-24 and 25-34 years old enrolled in 2-year and 4-year colleges: 1973-1988," *The Condition of Education 1990: Volume 2: Postsecondary Education,* Table 2:2-1, p. 18,104. Primary source: U.S. Department of Commerce, Bureau of the Census, *Current Population Reports,* Series P-20, "School Enrollment...," various years, based on the October supplement to the Current Population Survey.

★ 185 ★

Nursing School Enrollment

Trends in nursing school enrollment: 1970-1990.

	Number
Number of students enrolled in registered nursing programs:	
Fall 1990	230,000[1]
Fall 1989	201,458
Fall 1983	250,000
Average age of new nurses:	
1990	31
Early eighties	24-25
Projected new jobs for registered nurses by 2000[2]	350,000

Source: "Big Gain in Nursing Students Lifts Hopes Amid a Shortage," *New York Times,* December 28, 1990, p. 1+. Primary source: National League for Nursing. *Notes:* 1. Number is approximate. 2. As projected by Bureau of Labor Statistics.

★ 186 ★

Percent of Population 3 to 34 Years Old Enrolled in School

Percent of the population 3 to 34 years old enrolled in school, October 1987.

Age	All races	White	Black	Hispanic[2]
Both sexes				
Total, 3 to 34 years	48.6%	47.7%	51.7%	45.3%
Female				
Total, 3 to 34 years	47.4%	46.7%	49.6%	45.4%
3 and 4 years	36.5%	36.4%	34.4%	28.9%
5 and 6 years	94.5%	94.4%	94.1%	91.2%
7 to 9 years	99.5%	99.5%	99.3%	98.7%
10 to 13 years	99.2%	99.1%	99.7%	98.6%
14 and 15 years	98.4%	98.3%	98.6%	95.2%
16 and 17 years	91.1%	91.1%	91.2%	81.8%
18 and 19 years	53.4%	53.3%	48.2%	38.6%
20 and 21 years	36.4%	37.3%	27.4%	25.6%
22 to 24 years	16.4%	16.2%	14.6%	14.7%
25 to 29 years	9.0%	8.7%	10.0%	7.9%
30 to 34 years	6.7%	6.4%	8.1%	5.1%
Male				
Total, 3 to 34 years	49.8%	48.8%	54.0%	45.2%
3 and 4 years	40.0%	39.8%	39.0%	27.7%
5 and 6 years	95.7%	95.2%	97.4%	93.6%

[Continued]

★ 186 ★

Percent of Population 3 to 34 Years Old Enrolled in School
[Continued]

Age	All races	White	Black	Hispanic[2]
7 to 9 years	99.7%	99.6%	100.0%	99.4%
10 to 13 years	99.7%	99.75	99.8%	100.0%
14 and 15 years	98.7%	98.8%	98.1%	99.4%
16 and 17 years	92.3%	92.5%	91.8%	91.0%
18 and 19 years	57.9%	57.3%	58.7%	44.4%
20 and 21 years	41.2%	42.1%	30.3%	30.1%
22 to 24 years	18.7%	18.4%	15.5%	10.6%
25 to 29 years	9.1%	8.6%	8.4%	8.3%
30 to 34 years	5.0%	5.0%	3.4%	3.7%

Source: Selected from "Percent of the population 3 to 34 years old enrolled in school,[1] by race/ethnicity, sex, and age: October 1987," *Digest of Education Statistics,* Table 7, p. 14 (Washington, D.C.: National Center for Education Statistics, 1989). Primary source: U.S. Department of Commerce, Bureau of the Census, Current Population Survey, unpublished data. (This table was prepared March 1989.) Also in source: total, both sexes, by age. Data are based upon a sample survey of the civilian noninstitutional population. *Notes:* 1. Includes enrollment in any type of graded public, parochial, or other private school in regular school systems. Attendance may be on either a full-time or part-time basis and during the day or night. Enrollments in "special" schools, such as trade schools, business colleges, or correspondence schools, are not included. 2. Persons of Hispanic origin may be of any race.

★ 187 ★

Preschool Enrollment by Level and Labor Force Status of Mother

Preschool enrollment of children by level of enrollment and labor force status of mother: 1978 and 1988.

Labor Force Status	All Children (1,000)		Percent Enrolled In-			
			Nursery school		Kindergarten	
	1978	1988	1978	1988	1978	1988
All children 3 to 5 years old	9,110	10,994	20.0%	23.8%	30.3%	30.5%
Living with mother	8,883	10,403	19.8%	24.1%	30.4%	30.4%
Mother in labor force	4,097	6,061	22.1%	25.3%	31.0%	32.1%
Employed	3,737	5,641	22.5%	25.9%	31.0%	31.9%
Full-time	2,446	3,717	22.3%	24.3%	31.2%	33.3%
Part-time	1,291	1.932	23.0%	28.8%	30.5%	29.1%
Unemployed	360	419	17.4%	18.1%	30.6%	34.4%
Mother not in labor force	4,786	4,342	17.9%	22.5%	29.9%	28.1%

Source: Selected from "Preprimary School Enrollment, By Level of Enrollment and Labor Force Status of Mother: 1978 and 1988," *Statistical Abstract,* 1990, p. 136. Primary source: U.S. Bureau of the Census, *Current Population Reports,* series P-20, No. 318; and unpublished data.

★ 188 ★

Professional School Enrollment, 1975-2000

First-professional enrollment in all institutions, in thousands, 1975 to 2000. Data for 1988 are estimates. Data for 1989 through 2000 are middle alternative projections.

Year	Total	Women	
		Full-time	Part-time
Numbers in thousands			
1975	242	43	7
1976	244	48	6
1977	251	53	7
1978	257	58	7
1979	263	63	7
1980	278	70	9
1981	275	73	9
1982	278	78	9
1983	279	81	10
1984	279	83	10
1985	274	84	10
1986	270	86	10
1987	268	88	10
1988	268	90	10
1989	279	92	10
1990	281	93	11
1991	282	93	12
1992	282	93	12
1993	283	94	12
1994	280	93	12
1995	276	91	12
1996	274	90	12
1997	272	90	12
1998	271	90	11
1999	271	90	11
2000	269	89	10

Source: Selected from "First-professional enrollment in all institutions, by sex and attendance status, with alternative projections: 50 States and D.C., fall 1975 to fall 2000," *Projections of Education Statistics to 2000,* Table 20, p. 45 (Washington, D.C.: National Center for Education Statistics, 1989). Primary source: U.S. Department of Education, National Center for Education Statistics, "Fall Enrollment in Colleges and Universities" surveys, Integrated Postsecondary Education Data System (IPEDS) surveys, and "National Estimates of Higher Education: School Year 1988-89," *Early Estimates.* Also in source: data for men and by full-and part-time attendance status; low and high alternative projections. Projections are based on data through 1987. Because of rounding, details may not add to totals.

★ 189 ★

Projections of College Enrollment, 1990-2000

Enrollment	1990	1991	1992	1993	1994	1995	1996	1997	1998	1999	2000
Total	13,213,000	13,233,000	13,126,000	13,026,000	12,955,000	12,935,000	12,973,000	13,048,000	13,162,000	13,282,000	13,378,0
Women	7,203,000	7,231,000	7,174,000	7,106,000	7,054,000	7,042,000	7,049,000	7,089,000	7,148,000	7,207,000	7,254,0

Source: Chronicle of Higher Education Almanac, September 5, 1990, p. 19. Primary source: U.S. Department of Education. Also in source: Projections by various criteria.

★ 190 ★

Worldwide Enrollment Ratios: 1970-1987

Percentage of the population in the age group enrolled at any level of education, by sex, 1970-1987.

Continent or Major Area	Year	Age groups								
		6 - 11			12 - 17			18 - 23		
		MF	M	F	MF	M	F	MF	M	F
World Total	1970	65.4%	70.6%	60.0%	45.7%	50.6%	40.5%	14.8%	17.5%	12.0%
	1975	70.7%	76.2%	64.9%	51.3%	56.0%	46.3%	17.7%	20.9%	14.4%
	1980	73.5%	79.1%	67.7%	50.6%	55.2%	45.7%	19.2%	22.1%	16.2%
	1985	77.1%	82.4%	71.6%	51.3%	56.1%	46.2%	18.2%	20.6%	15.6%
	1986	78.5%	83.3%	73.5%	51.5%	56.5%	46.2%	18.6%	21.0%	16.0%
	1987	78.8%	83.6%	73.8%	52.2%	57.2%	46.8%	19.0%	21.6%	16.3%
Africa	1970	40.6%	47.8%	33.3%	25.6%	32.7%	18.4%	4.2%	6.2%	2.1%
	1975	48.6%	55.6%	41.5%	31.8%	39.2%	24.3%	6.1%	8.8%	3.4%
	1980	60.0%	66.9%	53.0%	42.3%	50.8%	33.9%	8.8%	12.4%	5.3%
	1985	57.9%	63.6%	52.1%	44.7%	53.2%	36.0%	10.6%	14.7%	6.5%
	1986	58.2%	63.6%	52.8%	45.2%	53.4%	36.9%	11.4%	16.0%	6.9%
	1987	59.1%	64.6%	53.7%	46.4%	54.8%	38.0%	11.8%	16.5%	7.1%
America	1970	80.7%	80.7%	80.7%	64.6%	66.8%	62.3%	27.0%	30.1%	23.8%
	1975	83.2%	83.5%	82.9%	71.0%	72.4%	69.4%	30.9%	34.5%	27.3%
	1980	85.9%	86.2%	85.65	71.1%	71.8%	70.4%	33.0%	33.6%	32.4%
	1985	87.5%	87.9%	87.2%	74.7%	75.6%	73.7%	33.2%	33.2%	33.2%
	1986	88.6%	89.1%	88.1%	74.6%	75.6%	73.7%	34.2%	33.9%	34.5%
	1987	88.9%	89.4%	88.4%	75.7%	76.7%	74.7%	35.1%	35.0%	35.2%
Asia	1970	60.4%	67.7%	52.7%	37.5%	43.6%	31.0%	11.1%	13.9%	8.1%
	1975	68.2%	75.6%	60.4%	43.8%	50.1%	37.1%	14.3%	18.0%	10.3%
	1980	70.6%	77.9%	62.8%	41.9%	47.9%	35.6%	15.8%	19.7%	11.6%
	1985	77.2%	84.4%	69.6%	42.3%	48.1%	36.2%	13.8%	17.1%	10.3%
	1986	79.3%	85.7%	72.5%	42.4%	48.6%	35.8%	14.2%	17.5%	10.7%
	1987	79.7%	86.1%	72.9%	43.0%	49.1%	36.4%	14.5%	17.8%	11.0%
Europe (Incl. USSR)	1970	89.2%	89.0%	89.4%	70.1%	71.6%	68.5%	22.9%	25.1%	20.6%
	1975	89.7%	89.6%	89.7%	74.8%	75.3%	74.3%	25.3%	26.6%	24.0%
	1980	90.3%	90.3%	90.3%	76.5%	75.95	77.3%	25.8%	26.4%	25.3%
	1985	89.3%	89.2%	89.4%	80.1%	80.7%	79.5%	27.8%	27.8%	27.9%
	1986	89.4%	89.4%	89.5%	81.3%	81.9%	80.85	28.2%	28.3%	28.1%
	1987	89.4%	89.4%	89.5%	81.85	82.3%	81.3%	29.5%	29.8%	29.3%

[Continued]

★ 190 ★

Worldwide Enrollment Ratios: 1970-1987

[Continued]

Continent or Major Area	Year	Age groups								
		6 - 11			12 - 17			18 - 23		
		MF	M	F	MF	M	F	MF	M	F
Oceania	1970	94.7%	96.1%	93.2%	71.2%	73.6%	68.6%	12.4%	16.0%	8.6%
	1975	95.1%	96.8%	93.2%	74.4%	75.4%	73.4%	17.7%	21.3%	13.9%
	1980	97.8%	99.0%	96.6%	71.5%	71.1%	71.8%	19.0%	21.0%	17.0%
	1985	96.4%	97.5%	95.3%	75.6%	75.5%	75.8%	20.9%	21.9%	19.9%
	1986	96.7%	97.8%	95.6%	76.3%	76.1%	76.5%	21.7%	22.2%	21.1%
	1987	97.3%	98.5%	96.0%	75.7%	75.6%	75.8%	23.3%	23.7%	22.9%
Developed Countries	1970	92.4%	92.2%	92.6%	76.1%	77.4%	74.9%	27.2%	30.5%	23.8%
	1975	92.6%	92.5%	92.8%	80.7%	80.9%	80.6%	30.0%	32.95	27.0%
	1980	92.2%	92.0%	92.4%	81.0%	80.3%	81.8%	30.8%	31.6%	29.9%
	1985	91.2%	91.0%	91.5%	85.6%	85.9%	85.4%	32.8%	32.9%	32.7%
	1986	91.8%	91.6%	91.9%	86.3%	86.4%	86.1%	33.5%	33.6%	33.5%
	1987	91.7%	91.5%	91.9%	86.8%	87.0%	86.5%	34.9%	35.2%	34.6%
Developing Countries	1970	57.8%	64.5%	50.8%	35.7%	41.9%	29.3%	10.1k%	12.6%	7.5%
	1975	65.5%	72.3%	58.4%	42.5%	48.6%	36.0%	13.6%	16.9%	10.0%
	1980	69.6%	76.3%	62.5%	43.0%	48.9%	36.8%	15.6%	19.1%	11.9%
	1985	74.2%	80.7%	67.4%	43.8%	49.6%	37.7%	14.3%	17.4%	11.1%
	1986	75.8%	81.5%	69.7%	44.0%	50.1%	37.6%	14.8%	17.9%	11.5%
	1987	76.2%	82.0%	70.1%	44.8%	50.9%	38.4%	15.1%	18.2%	11.8%
Africa	1970	37.0%	43.0%	31.1%	25.1%	31.3%	18.9%	2.9%	4.4%	1.5%
	1975	45.1%	50.7%	39.6%	31.4%	38.2%	24.6%	4.0%	5.9%	2.1%
	1980	58.5%	64.5%	52.5%	42.9%	51.1%	34.9%	6.4%	9.2%	3.6%
	1985	54.6%	59.6%	49.5%	44.0%	52.5%	35.5%	7.6%	11.2%	4.1%
	1986	54.9%	59.5%	50.2%	44.3%	52.5%	36.2%	8.5%	12.7%	4.5%
	1987	55.8%	60.4%	51.1%	45.8%	54.2%	37.3%	9.2%	13.7%	4.7%
Asia (Excluding Arab States)	1970	60.6%	67.8%	53.0%	37.6%	43.6%	31.2%	11.1%	13.9%	8.2%
	1975	68.3%	75.5%	60.6%	43.9%	50.0%	37.3%	14.2%	18.0%	10.3%
	1980	70.5%	77.7%	62.8%	41.8%	47.7%	35.5%	15.8%	19.7%	11.6%
	1985	77.2%	84.4%	69.6%	42.1%	47.7%	36.0%	13.7%	17.0%	10.2%
	1986	79.3%	85.6%	72.6%	42.2%	48.3%	35.6%	14.1%	17.4%	10.6%
	1987	79.7%	86.0%	73.0%	42.7%	48.8%	36.25	14.4%	17.7%	10.9%
Arab States	1970	51.1%	62.5%	39.1%	28.4%	38.7%	17.7%	8.6%	12.8%	4.3%
	1975	61.3%	73.6%	48.4%	35.0%	44.7%	24.7%	13.0%	18.0%	7.8%
	1980	68.1%	78.0%	57.9%	42.9%	52.5%	33.0%	16.6%	21.8%	11.1%
	1985	71.5%	79.9%	62.8%	49.1%	58.1%	39.7%	19.6%	24.9%	14.0%
	1986	72.4%	80.4%	64.0%	50.1%	58.8%	41.1%	20.0%	25.2%	14.5%
	1987	73.4%	81.5%	65.0%	50.8%	59.3%	42.0%	20.2%	25.1%	15.0%

[Continued]

★ 190 ★

Worldwide Enrollment Ratios: 1970-1987

[Continued]

Continent or Major Area	Year	Age groups								
		6 - 11			12 - 17			18 - 23		
		MF	M	F	MF	M	F	MF	M	F
Northern America	1970	100%	100%	100%	89.8%	91.4%	88.1%	48.2%	53.1%	43.3%
	1975	100%	100%	100%	100%	100%	100%	48.9%	54.5%	43.2%
	1980	100%	100%	100%	100%	100%	100%	48.5%	47.4%	49.6%
	1985	100%	100%	100%	100%	100%	100%	53.1%	50.8%	55.4%
	1986	100%	100%	100%	100%	100%	100%	55.7%	52.9%	58.5%
	1987	100%	100%	100%	100%	100%	100%	57.6%	55.4%	59.9%
Latin America and the Caribbean	1970	71.0%	70.7%	71.3%	49.8%	52.1%	47.5%	11.6%	13.6%	9.7%
	1975	76.3%	76.4%	76.1%	58.0%	59.8%	56.1%	18.9%	21.0%	16.8%
	1980	82.4%	82.8%	81.9%	62.6%	63.6%	61.6%	23.6%	25.1%	22.0%
	1985	85.2%	85.8%	84.7%	66.2%	67.3%	65.1%	23.8%	24.8%	22.8%
	1986	85.9%	86.6%	85.3%	66.7%	67.8%	65.6%	24.2%	24.9%	23.5%
	1987	86.3%	86.9%	85.7%	68.2%	69.2%	67.2%	25.1%	25.8%	24.4%

Source: Selected from "Enrolment ratios by age-group and sex," *Statistical Yearbook 1989,* Table 2.11, p. 2-33/2-34. Also in source: data for 1960.

★ 191 ★

Worldwide Enrollment at the Third Level

Enrollment at the third level, number and percent female, latest available year.

Country	Year	Students enrolled		
		Total	Female	% Female
Africa				
Algeria	1986	201,982	50,685	-
Benin	1986	8,870	1,397	16%
Botswana	1984	1,693	560	42%
Burkino Faso	1986	4,498	1,057	23%
Burundi	1987	3,266	814	25%
Central African Republic	1987	2,754	371	13%
Chad	1984	1,643	142	9%
Congo	1985	10,684	1,665	16%
Cote D'Ivoire	1975	7,174	1,218	17%
Egypt	1987	790,399	264,301	33%
Ethiopia	1987	29,253	5,029	17%
Gabon	1986	4,089	1,173	29%
Ghana	1981	16,350	3,398	21%
Guinea	1987	5,923	693	12%
Kenya	1985	21,756	5,710	26%
Lesotho	1984	2,339	1,479	63%

[Continued]

★ 191 ★

Worldwide Enrollment at the Third Level
[Continued]

Country	Year	Students enrolled		
		Total	Female	% Female
Liberia	1987	5,095	1,177	23%
Libyan Arab Jamahiriya	1982	27,535	7,010	25%
Madagascar	1986	35,106	14,329	41%
Malawi	1986	3,979	1,111	28%
Mali	1986	5,536	728	13%
Mauritania	1987	5,407	695	13%
Mauritius	1987	1,589	576	36%
Morocco	1987	212,151	70,636	33%
Mozambique	1987	2,335	516	22%
Niger	1986	3,317	590	18%
Rwanda	1986	2,029	323	16%
St. Helena	1981	37	5	14%
Senegal	1980	13,626	2,507	18%
Seychelles	1980	144	128	89%
Sierra Leone	1975	1,642	266	16%
Somalia	1986	15,672	3,093	20%
Sudan	1985	37,367	13,742	37%
Swaziland	1980	1,875	751	40%
Togo	1980	4,750	703	15%
Tunisia	1987	43,797	16,305	37%
Uganda	1986	11,037	3,098	28%
United Republic of Tanzania	1987	5,070	641	13%
Zambia	1975	8,403	1,170	14%
Zimbabwe	1986	17,915	5,932	33%
North America				
Bahamas	1987	4,880	3,416	70%
Barbados	1984	5,227	2,565	49%
Bermuda	1980	608	312	51%
Canada	1987	1,277,624	589,831	-
Cuba	1987	262,225	145,892	56%
Dominica	1984	60	40	67%
El Salvador	1986	74,024	31,921	43%
Grenada	1983	535	295	55%
Guatemala	1975	22,881	5,277	23%
Haiti	1983	6,289	2,119	34%
Honduras	1980	25,825	9,736	38%
Mexico	1983	1,105,469	394,802	36%
Nicaragua	1987	26,878	14,579	55%

[Continued]

★ 191 ★

Worldwide Enrollment at the Third Level
[Continued]

Country	Year	Students enrolled		
		Total	Female	% Female
Panama	1985	55,303	31,856	58%
Puerto Rico	1981	137,171	82,975	60%
St. Kitts and Nevis	1985	167	84	50%
St. Lucia	1986	367	202	55%
St. Vincent and the Grenadines	1986	795	505	64%
Trinidad and Tobago	1982	5,470	2,343	43%
United States	1986	12,398,000	6,558,000	53%
U.S. Virgin Islands	1986	2,545	1,861	73%
South America				
Argentina	1986	902,882	479,172	53%
Brazil	1983	1,479,397	740,327	50%
Chile	1987	224,338	99,669	44%
Colombia	1987	434,623	213,998	49%
Ecuador	1983	266,222	103,371	39%
Guyana	1985	2,328	1,113	48%
Peru	1980	306,353	107,980	35%
Suriname	1986	3,402	1,732	51%
Uruguay	1975	32,627	14,313	44%
Venezuela	1987	467,371	221,896	47%
Asia				
Afghanistan	1986	22,306	3,124	14%
Bahrain	1985	4,180	2,490	60%
Bangladesh	1986	462,265	88,889	19%
Bhutan	1983	288	49	17%
Brunei Darussalam	1987	945	479	51%
Burma	1978	121,609	61,206	50%
China	1986	1,976,950	613,981	31%
Cyprus	1987	4,247	2,096	49%
Democratic Yemen	1981	3,645	1,907	52%
Hong Kong	1984	76,844	26,542	35%
India	1979	5,345,580	1,396,466	26%
Indonesia	1984	980,162	316,273	32%
Iran, Islamic Republic	1986	219,332	61,288	28%
Iraq	1987	183,608	72,665	40%
Israel	1986	118,608	54,824	46%
Japan	1987	2,398,261	887,132	37%

[Continued]

★ 191 ★

Worldwide Enrollment at the Third Level
[Continued]

Country	Year	Students enrolled		
		Total	Female	% Female
Jordan	1986	60,553	29,015	48%
Korea, Republic of	1987	1,548,772	458,602	30%
Kuwait	1987	25,521	13,970	55%
Lao People's Democratic Republic	1987	5,322	1,753	33%
Lebanon	1984	70,510	27,473	39%
Malaysia	1987	105,964	50,766	48%
Mongolia	1986	39,072	23,409	60%
Nepal	1983	48,229	9,549	20%
Oman	1986	2,159	795	37%
Pakistan	1986	99,309	17,475	18%
Philippines	1985	1,973,182	1,074,045	54%
Qatar	1987	5,347	3,691	69%
Saudi Arabia	1986	130,924	50,434	39%
Singapore	1983	35,192	14,759	42%
Sri Lanka	1986	61,628	25,122	41%
Syrian Arab Republic	1986	182,933	64,925	35%
Thailand	1975	130,965	52,112	40%
Turkey	1987	534,459	178,272	33%
United Arab Emirates	1984	6,856	3,975	58%
Viet-Nam	1980	114,701	27,090	24%
Yemen	1980	4,519	508	11%
Europe				
Albania	1987	23,784	11,746	49%
Austria	1987	188,192	86,179	46%
Belgium	1987	254,329	120,401	47%
Bulgaria	1987	135,852	75,565	56%
Czechoslovakia	1987	170,550	72,219	42%
Denmark	1986	118,641	59,082	50%
Finland	1987	139,375	70,241	50%
France	1987	1,327,771	679,548	51%
German Democratic Republic	1987	437,919	229,229	52%
Germany, Federal Republic	1986	1,579,085	654,207	41%
Greece	1986	197,808	97,767	49%
Holy See	1987	9,882	3,358	34%
Hungary	1987	99,025	52,785	53%
Iceland	1986	4,744	2,572	54%
Ireland	1985	70,301	30,385	43%

[Continued]

★ 191 ★

Worldwide Enrollment at the Third Level
[Continued]

Country	Year	Students enrolled		
		Total	Female	% Female
Italy	1986	1,141,127	533,511	47%
Luxembourg	1984	843	289	34%
Malta	1987	1,447	527	36%
Netherlands	1986	399,786	167,131	42%
Norway	1986	104,246	53,457	51%
Poland	1987	458,585	257,519	56%
Portugal	1985	103,585	55,599	54%
Romania	1985	159,798	71,658	45%
Spain	1986	954,005	477,494	50%
Sweden	1987	184,324	96,962	53%
Switzerland	1987	121,693	38,622	32%
United Kingdom	1986	1,068,386	493,368	46%
Yugoslavia	1987	348,068	165,210	47%
Oceania				
American Samoa	1982	1,007	516	51%
Australia	1986	389,734	190,163	49%
Cook Islands	1980	360	163	45%
Fiji	1986	2,211	766	35%
French Polynesia	1982	68	33	49%
Guam	1986	7,052	3,754	53%
New Caledonia	1985	761	336	44%
New Zealand	1987	105,598	50,670	48%
Pacific Islands	1980	2,129	514	24%
Samoa	1983	562	264	47%
Tonga	1985	705	397	56%
USSR				
USSR	1987	5,025,700	2,752,400	55%
Ukrainian SSR	1975	831,300	408,800	49%

Source: Selected from "Education at the third level: teachers and students by type of institution," *Statistical Yearbook,* 1989, p. 3-233/3-269 (Paris: UNESCO, 1989). Also in source: data for various years and by type of institution; teaching staff; extensive footnotes. See Introduction to this book for an explanation of levels of education.

★ 192 ★

Worldwide Enrollment at the Third Level by Field - Part I

Total and female students enrolled at the third level, by field of study.

Country, Year, and Field of Study	All 3rd Level[1]	
	MF	F
Africa		
Algeria, 1986		
Total	201,982	50,685
Education Science & Teacher Training	27,456	2,015
Humanities, Religion & Theology	12,455	6,208
Fine and Applied Arts	221	6
Law	12,174	3,320
Social and Behavioral Science	15,329	4,484
Commercial & Business Administration	2,569	607
Mass Communication & Document.	1,267	495
Service Trades	278	-
Natural Science	6,325	2,337
Mathematics & Computer Science	5,273	1,107
Medical Science & Health-Related	36,466	10,790
Engineering	18,238	1,141
Architecture & Town Planning	5,751	1,166
Trade, Craft & Industrial Programs	1,058	114
Transport & Communications	1,717	41
Agriculture, Forestry and Fishery	8,173	1,512
Benin, 1986		
Total	8,870	1,397
Education Science & Teacher Training	430	51
Humanities, Religion & Theology	2,074	413
Law	2,417	441
Social and Behavioral Science	1,467	186
Commercial & Business Administration	176	9
Home Economics (Domestic Science)	78	44
Natural Science	884	135
Mathematics & Computer Science	459	28
Medical Science & Health-Related	373	56
Trade, Craft & Industrial Programs	290	21
Agriculture, Forestry and Fishery	222	13
Botswana, 1987		
Total	2,255	-
Education Science & Teacher Training	452	-
Humanities, Religion & Theology	443	-
Law	123	-
Social and Behavioral Science	437	-
Commercial & Business Administration	544	
Natural Science	244	-
Burkina Faso, 1986		
Total	4,405	1,055
Education Science & Teacher Training	34	5

[Continued]

★ 192 ★

Worldwide Enrollment at the Third Level by Field - Part I
[Continued]

Country, Year, and Field of Study	All 3rd Level[1]	
	MF	F
Humanities, Religion & Theology	798	296
Fine and Applied Arts	24	4
Law	547	168
Social and Behavioral Science	840	217
Commercial & Business Administration	688	180
Natural Science	290	61
Mathematics & Computer Science	293	16
Medical Science & Health-Related	324	61
Agriculture, Forestry and Fishery	567	47
Burundi, 1987		
Total	3,266	814
Education Science & Teacher Training	522	119
Humanities, Religion & Theology	543	153
Law	263	64
Social and Behavioral Science	340	95
Commercial & Business Administration	309	171
Mass Communication & Document.	39	16
Natural Science	196	32
Mathematics & Computer Science	57	2
Medical Science & Health-Related	322	77
Engineering	190	24
Architecture & Town Planning	83	17
Trade, Craft & Industrial Programs	73	3
Agriculture, Forestry and Fishery	258	36
Cameroon, 1980		
Total	10,631	-
Education Science & Teacher Training	823	112
Humanities, Religion & Theology	765	-
Law	2,217	518
Social and Behavioral Science	858	140
Commercial & Business Administration	2,609	465
Mass Communication & Document.	73	4
Service Trades	117	-
Natural Science	1,237	182
Mathematics & Computer Science	373	14
Medical Science & Health-Related	319	67
Engineering	373	-
Agriculture, Forestry and Fishery	825	-
Chad, 1984		
Total	1,643	142
Education Science & Teacher Training	173	3
Humanities, Religion & Theology	316	31
Law	460	46
Social and Behavioral Science	499	52

[Continued]

★ 192 ★

Worldwide Enrollment at the Third Level by Field - Part I
[Continued]

Country, Year, and Field of Study	All 3rd Level[1]	
	MF	F
Natural Science	195	10
Cote D'Ivoire, 1984		
Total	19,660	-
Education Science & Teacher Training	5,046	-
Humanities, Religion & Theology	2,911	873
Fine and Applied Arts	255	43
Law	3,644	427
Social and Behavioral Science	735	241
Commercial & Business Administration	725	326
Natural Science	1,939	206
Mathematics & Computer Science	270	8
Medical Science & Health-Related	2,510	808
Engineering	365	13
Architecture & Town Planning	461	14
Trade, Craft & Industrial Programs	306	6
Transport & Communications	172	9
Agriculture, Forestry and Fishery	321	23
Egypt, 1986		
Total	592,256	203,115
Education Science & Teacher Training	85,196	40,951
Humanities, Religion & Theology	83,581	39,794
Fine and Applied Arts	7,904	3,607
Law	88,282	18,397
Social and Behavioral Science	5,830	2,373
Commercial & Business Administration	137,782	42,532
Mass Communication & Document.	1,,692	912
Home Economics (Domestic Science)	2,024	1,566
Service Trades	1,192	759
Natural Science	25,371	9,387
Mathematics & Computer Science	2,536	580
Medical Science & Health-Related	50,245	19,780
Engineering	52,363	6,772
Agriculture, Forestry and Fishery	39,565	12,555
Ethiopia, 1987		
Total	29,253	5,029
Education Science & Teacher Training	5,680	679
Humanities, Religion & Theology	1,211	264
Fine and Applied Arts	46	7
Law	633	62
Social and Behavioral Science	2,833	466
Commercial & Business Administration	7,471	2,464
Mass Communication & Document.	257	81
Home Economics (Domestic Science)	34	21
Natural Science	2,486	212

[Continued]

★ 192 ★

Worldwide Enrollment at the Third Level by Field - Part I
[Continued]

Country, Year, and Field of Study	All 3rd Level[1]	
	MF	F
Mathematics & Computer Science	950	151
Medical Science & Health-Related	1,438	180
Engineering	2,417	180
Architecture & Town Planning	103	10
Trade, Craft & Industrial Programs	501	24
Agriculture, Forestry and Fishery	3,193	228
Gabon, 1986		
Total	4,089	1,173
Education Science & Teacher Training	293	54
Humanities, Religion & Theology	389	114
Law	461	140
Social and Behavioral Science	900	280
Commercial & Business Administration	585	231
Mass Communication & Document.	234	80
Service Trades	44	-
Natural Science	91	15
Mathematics & Computer Science	278	50
Medical Science & Health-Related	366	164
Engineering	188	17
Architecture & Town Planning	50	6
Trade, Craft & Industrial Programs	75	3
Transport & Communications	39	11
Agriculture, Forestry and Fishery	70	7
Guinea, 1987		
Total	5,923	693
Education Science & Teacher Training	279	36
Law	145	7
Social and Behavioral Science	893	90
Natural Science	1,138	170
Mathematics & Computer Science	285	13
Medical Science & Health-Related	418	68
Engineering	1,396	140
Architecture & Town Planning	298	11
Trade, Craft & Industrial Programs	784	126
Transport & Communications	59	5
Agriculture, Forestry and Fishery	228	27
Kenya, 1985		
Total	21,756	5,710
Education Science & Teacher Training	5,595	2,069
Fine and Applied Arts	19	10
Law	390	154
Social and Behavioral Science	1,453	414
Commercial & Business Administration	1,770	678
Mass Communication & Document.	118	56

[Continued]

★ 192 ★

Worldwide Enrollment at the Third Level by Field - Part I
[Continued]

Country, Year, and Field of Study	All 3rd Level[1]	
	MF	F
Home Economics (Domestic Science)	185	165
Natural Science	1,306	181
Mathematics & Computer Science	131	36
Medical Science & Health-Related	1,132	280
Engineering	3,325	55
Architecture & Town Planning	392	69
Trade, Craft & Industrial Programs	4,765	1,310
Agriculture, Forestry and Fishery	1,175	233
Lesotho, 1984		
Total	2,339	1,479
Education Science & Teacher Training	1,594	1,149
Humanities, Religion & Theology	94	54
Law	168	65
Social and Behavioral Science	34	19
Commercial & Business Administration	229	119
Natural Science	198	59
Mathematics & Computer Science	9	5
Medical Science & Health-Related	13	9
Liberia, 1987		
Total	5,095	1,177
Education Science & Teacher Training	388	156
Humanities, Religion & Theology	22	5
Fine and Applied Arts	497	143
Law	108	27
Social and Behavioral Science	45	28
Commercial & Business Administration	2,006	586
Mass Communication & Document.	33	20
Natural Science	479	159
Mathematics & Computer Science	36	7
Medical Science & Health-Related	58	11
Engineering	355	5
Architecture & Town Planning	569	2
Trade, Craft & Industrial Programs	240	20
Agriculture, Forestry and Fishery	253	7
Madagascar, 1987		
Total	36,269	-
Education Science & Teacher Training	1,089	355
Humanities, Religion & Theology	7,519	4,683
Natural Science	7,250	-
Mathematics & Computer Science	179	29
Medical Science & Health-Related	5,648	2,453
Engineering	2,464	319
Agriculture, Forestry and Fishery	186	55

[Continued]

Worldwide Enrollment at the Third Level by Field - Part I
[Continued]

Country, Year, and Field of Study	All 3rd Level[1]	
	MF	F
Mauritius, 1987		
Total	1,589	576
Education Science & Teacher Training	711	336
Law	37	15
Social and Behavioral Science	52	11
Commercial & Business Administration	184	54
Natural Science	26	7
Mathematics & Computer Science	237	91
Medical Science & Health-Related	81	15
Engineering	113	6
Trade, Craft & Industrial Programs	56	15
Agriculture, Forestry and Fishery	67	25
Morocco, 1987		
Total	212,151	70,636
Education Science & Teacher Training	9,853	2,747
Humanities, Religion & Theology	71,777	30,214
Fine and Applied Arts	309	10
Law	22,496	6,032
Social and Behavioral Science	13,808	4,289
Commercial & Business Administration	9,533	4,881
Mass Communication & Document.	607	295
Service Trades	1,533	587
Natural Science	54,315	15,236
Medical Science & Health-Related	6,953	2,305
Engineering	2,489	294
Architecture & Town Planning	352	6
Trade, Craft & Industrial Programs	10,448	1,527
Transport & Communications	834	91
Agriculture, Forestry and Fishery	3,311	728
Niger, 1986		
Total	3,317	590
Education Science & Teacher Training	292	51
Humanities, Religion & Theology	943	246
Law	386	65
Social and Behavioral Science	714	119
Natural Science	245	19
Mathematics & Computer Science	238	8
Medical Science & Health-Related	311	71
Agriculture, Forestry and Fishery	188	11
Rwanda, 1986		
Total	2,029	323
Education Science & Teacher Training	192	57
Humanities, Religion & Theology	527	52
Law	152	42

[Continued]

★ 192 ★

Worldwide Enrollment at the Third Level by Field - Part I
[Continued]

Country, Year, and Field of Study	All 3rd Level[1]	
	MF	F
Social and Behavioral Science	146	39
Commercial & Business Administration	272	69
Natural Science	175	12
Mathematics & Computer Science	176	9
Medical Science & Health-Related	195	41
Engineering	79	-
Agriculture, Forestry and Fishery	115	2
Sudan, 1985		
Total	33,432	13,480
Education Science & Teacher Training	1,365	471
Humanities, Religion & Theology	9,295	3,946
Fine and Applied Arts	257	37
Law	5,866	2,144
Social and Behavioral Science	7,031	4,065
Home Economics (Domestic Science)	706	705
Natural Science	1,184	389
Mathematics & Computer Science	87	19
Medical Science & Health-Related	2,011	723
Engineering	2,448	212
Architecture & Town Planning	132	25
Agriculture, Forestry and Fishery	3,050	744
Swaziland, 1986		
Total	1,289	538
Education Science & Teacher Training	53	24
Humanities, Religion & Theology	173	105
Law	148	49
Social and Behavioral Science	161	88
Commercial & Business Administration	244	106
Home Economics (Domestic Science)	53	53
Natural Science	260	74
Agriculture, Forestry and Fishery	197	39
Tunisia, 1987		
Total	43,797	16,305
Education Science & Teacher Training	2,670	809
Humanities, Religion & Theology	11,273	4,904
Fine and Applied Arts	432	233
Law	4,458	1,510
Social and Behavioral Science	2,450	821
Commercial & Business Administration	3,697	1,503
Mass Communication & Document.	481	304
Home Economics (Domestic Science)	306	132
Service Trades	350	88
Natural Science	2,935	1,116
Mathematics & Computer Science	2,301	586

[Continued]

★ 192 ★

Worldwide Enrollment at the Third Level by Field - Part I
[Continued]

Country, Year, and Field of Study	All 3rd Level[1]	
	MF	F
Medical Science & Health-Related	6,330	3,404
Engineering	3,705	453
Architecture & Town Planning	387	98
Transport & Communications	387	49
Agriculture, Forestry and Fishery	1,635	295
Uganda, 1986		
Total	11,037	3,098
Education Science & Teacher Training	2,689	662
Humanities, Religion & Theology	554	193
Fine and Applied Arts	145	60
Law	209	69
Social and Behavioral Science	887	201
Commercial & Business Administration	2,402	1,287
Mass Communication & Document.	82	45
Service Trades	59	39
Natural Science	1,062	153
Mathematics & Computer Science	178	10
Medical Science & Health-Related	468	110
Engineering	1,359	61
Agriculture, Forestry and Fishery	555	104
United Republic of Tanzania, 1987		
Total	5,070	641
Education Science & Teacher Training	643	131
Humanities, Religion & Theology	674	127
Law	194	51
Commercial & Business Administration	397	63
Natural Science	47	2
Medical Science & Health-Related	267	45
Engineering	585	31
Trade, Craft & Industrial Programs	1,531	84
Transport & Communications	144	41
Agriculture, Forestry and Fishery	547	62
Zambia, 1985		
Total	4,680	810
Education Science & Teacher Training	1,246	239
Law	153	41
Social and Behavioral Science	909	262
Commercial & Business Administration	356	75
Natural Science	690	63
Medical Science & Health-Related	302	94

[Continued]

★ 192 ★

Worldwide Enrollment at the Third Level by Field - Part I
[Continued]

Country, Year, and Field of Study	All 3rd Level[1]	
	MF	F
Engineering	544	-
Agriculture, Forestry and Fishery	291	14

Source: Selected from "Education at the third level: enrollment by ISCED level of programme and field of study," *Statistical Yearbook 1989*, Table 3.13, p. 3-320/3-358. Also in source: data at level 5, level 6, and level 7. Level 5 programs lead to an award not equivalent to a first university degree. Level 6 programs lead to a first university degree or equivalent qualification. Level 7 programs lead to a post-graduate university degree or equivalent qualification. *Notes:* 1. Education at the third level requires as a minimum condition of admission the successful completion of education at the second level or evidence of the attainment of an equivalent level of knowledge (e.g., at university, teacher's college, or higher professional school).

★ 193 ★

Worldwide Enrollment at the Third Level by Field - Part II

Total and female students enrolled at the third level, by field of study.

Country, Year, and Field of Study	All 3rd Level[1]	
	MF	F
North America		
Barbados, 1984		
Total	5,227	2,565
Education Science & Teacher Training	373	234
Humanities, Religion & Theology	706	472
Fine and Applied Arts	66	43
Law	297	165
Social and Behavioral Science	1,344	898
Home Economics (Domestic Science)	47	47
Service Trades	265	174
Natural Science	773	312
Medical Science & Health-Related	142	89
Engineering	117	4
Trade, Craft & Industrial Programs	1,003	78
Agriculture, Forestry and Fishery	40	12
Canada, 1987		
Total	1,160,525	627,329
Education Science & Teacher Training	76,858	56,907
Humanities, Religion & Theology	58,696	35,937
Fine and Applied Arts	39,446	24,500
Law	12,794	6,151
Social and Behavioral Science	118,709	69,836
Commercial & Business Administration	174,931	91,469
Mass Communication & Document.	15,108	8,931
Home Economics (Domestic Science)	5,574	5,092
Service Trades	2,907	1,654

[Continued]

★ 193 ★

Worldwide Enrollment at the Third Level by Field - Part II
[Continued]

Country, Year, and Field of Study	All 3rd Level[1]	
	MF	F
Natural Science	39,134	15,814
Mathematics & Computer Science	39,302	11,419
Medical Science & Health-Related	82,203	59,912
Engineering	79,827	8,414
Architecture & Town Planning	9,810	2,256
Transport & Communications	991	114
Agriculture, Forestry and Fishery	16,020	5,688
Cuba, 1987		
Total	262,225	145,892
Education Science & Teacher Training	131,032	80,852
Humanities, Religion & Theology	2,524	1,702
Fine and Applied Arts	1,613	893
Law	2,950	1,963
Social and Behavioral Science	16,092	8,239
Commercial & Business Administration	7,531	5,108
Mass Communication & Document.	1,829	1,022
Natural Science	3,152	2,160
Mathematics & Computer Science	1,743	900
Medical Science & Health-Related	33,779	21,270
Engineering	25,288	8,684
Architecture & Town Planning	6,652	3,413
Trade, Craft & Industrial Programs	287	219
Transport & Communications	2,700	252
Agriculture, Forestry and Fishery	13,598	6,373
El Salvador, 1986		
Total	74,024	19,878
Education Science & Teacher Training	12,120	5,316
Humanities, Religion & Theology	1,847	396
Fine and Applied Arts	169	146
Law	5,256	703
Social and Behavioral Science	5,905	1,545
Commercial & Business Administration	17,472	5,873
Mass Communication & Document.	1,350	644
Service Trades	246	142
Natural Science	2,219	155
Mathematics & Computer Science	313	3
Medical Science & Health-Related	8,307	1,628
Engineering	11,311	1,024
Architecture & Town Planning	2,679	1,028
Trade, Craft & Industrial Programs	174	10
Agriculture, Forestry and Fishery	2,710	111
Haiti, 1984		
Total	4,513	1,432
Education Science & Teacher Training	230	71

[Continued]

★ 193 ★

Worldwide Enrollment at the Third Level by Field - Part II
[Continued]

Country, Year, and Field of Study	All 3rd Level[1]	
	MF	F
Humanities, Religion & Theology	165	47
Law	1,077	279
Social and Behavioral Science	709	191
Commercial & Business Administration	1,020	420
Medical Science & Health-Related	768	342
Engineering	357	55
Agriculture, Forestry and Fishery	187	27
Mexico, 1987		
Total	1,244,888	499,778
Education Science & Teacher Training	149,958	89,658
Humanities, Religion & Theology	11,325	5,465
Fine and Applied Arts	7,005	4,430
Law	118,289	43,567
Social and Behavioral Science	90,377	51,717
Commercial & Business Administration	253,202	121,690
Mass Communication & Document.	27,107	17,206
Natural Science	48,274	26,092
Mathematics & Computer Science	30,620	12,920
Medical Science & Health-Related	114,546	55,381
Engineering	296,800	40,538
Architecture & Town Planning	52,646	16,501
Agriculture, Forestry and Fishery	31,898	6,028
Nicaragua, 1987		
Total	26,878	14,759
Education Science & Teacher Training	4,617	3,010
Humanities, Religion & Theology	168	137
Fine and Applied Arts	152	109
Law	948	461
Social and Behavioral Science	2,443	1,263
Commercial & Business Administration	3,242	1,869
Mass Communication & Document.	388	343
Home Economics (Domestic Science)	360	329
Natural Science	415	297
Mathematics & Computer Science	1,005	702
Medical Science & Health-Related	3,634	2,388
Engineering	3,432	911
Architecture & Town Planning	332	209
Trade, Craft & Industrial Programs	241	165
Agriculture, Forestry and Fishery	4,065	2,245
St. Lucia, 1986		
Total	367	202
Education Science & Teacher Training	163	124
Commercial & Business Administration	50	47
Service Trades	23	20

[Continued]

★ 193 ★

Worldwide Enrollment at the Third Level by Field - Part II
[Continued]

Country, Year, and Field of Study	All 3rd Level[1]	
	MF	F
Architecture & Town Planning	31	6
Trade, Craft & Industrial Programs	100	5
Trinidad and Tobago, 1985		
Total	3,164	1,589
Education Science & Teacher Training	210	134
Fine and Applied Arts	652	460
Law	34	16
Social and Behavioral Science	707	419
Natural Science	697	327
Engineering	529	74
Agriculture, Forestry and Fishery	335	159
South America		
Chile, 1987		
Total	224,338	99,669
Education Science & Teacher Training	41,837	28,873
Humanities, Religion & Theology	3,056	1,607
Fine and Applied Arts	6,672	4,352
Law	5,789	1,705
Social and Behavioral Science	5,090	2,986
Commercial & Business Administration	38,822	13,887
Mass Communication & Document.	4,058	2,690
Home Economics (Domestic Science)	107	105
Service Trades	11,412	10,459
Natural Science	2,846	2,317
Mathematics & Computer Science	19,891	5,606
Medical Science & Health-Related	16,629	9,809
Engineering	42,461	8,290
Architecture & Town Planning	3,368	1,140
Trade, Craft & Industrial Programs	10,248	1,140
Transport & Communications	1,552	541
Agriculture, Forestry and Fishery	9,608	3,449
Colombia, 1987		
Total	434,623	213,998
Education Science & Teacher Training	89,866	60,493
Humanities, Religion & Theology	3,267	1,689
Fine and Applied Arts	10,719	6,550
Law	50,541	28,584
Commercial & Business Administration	109,940	56,456
Natural Science	6,653	2,587
Medical Science & Health-Related	42,497	25,029
Engineering	109,141	29,418
Agriculture, Forestry and Fishery	11,999	3,192

[Continued]

★ 193 ★

Worldwide Enrollment at the Third Level by Field - Part II
[Continued]

Country, Year, and Field of Study	All 3rd Level[1]	
	MF	F
Guyana, 1985		
Total	2,328	1,113
Education Science & Teacher Training	769	546
Humanities, Religion & Theology	125	76
Law	25	13
Social and Behavioral Science	195	92
Commercial & Business Administration	242	107
Mass Communication & Document.	21	7
Service Trades	1	-
Natural Science	137	45
Mathematics & Computer Science	30	8
Medical Science & Health-Related	98	41
Engineering	224	17
Architecture & Town Planning	13	-
Agriculture, Forestry and Fishery	280	77
Suriname, 1985		
Total	2,751	1,475
Education Science & Teacher Training	1,583	963
Fine and Applied Arts	21	7
Law	64	42
Social and Behavioral Science	74	49
Commercial & Business Administration	120	62
Mass Communication & Document.	18	8
Home Economics (Domestic Science)	54	25
Natural Science	27	1
Medical Science & Health-Related	110	47
Architecture & Town Planning	23	1
Agriculture, Forestry and Fishery	19	9
Uruguay, 1986		
Total	91,580	-
Education Science & Teacher Training	1,561	-
Humanities, Religion & Theology	3,675	-
Fine and Applied Arts	3,008	-
Law	17,805	-
Social and Behavioral Science	10,014	-
Commercial & Business Administration	14,078	
Mass Communication & Document.	1,217	-
Home Economics (Domestic Science)	160	146
Natural Science	1,937	-
Mathematics & Computer Science	5,190	-
Medical Science & Health-Related	18,613	11,816
Engineering	4,367	-
Architecture & Town Planning	3,714	-

[Continued]

★ 193 ★

Worldwide Enrollment at the Third Level by Field - Part II
[Continued]

Country, Year, and Field of Study	All 3rd Level[1]	
	MF	F
Trade, Craft & Industrial Programs	480	-
Agriculture, Forestry and Fishery	4,849	1,583

Source: Selected from "Education at the third level: enrollment by ISCED level of programme and field of study," *Statistical Yearbook 1989*, Table 3.13, p. 3-320/3-358. Also in source: data at level 5, level 6, and level 7. Level 5 programs lead to an award not equivalent to a first university degree. Level 6 programs lead to a first university degree or equivalent qualification. Level 7 programs lead to a post-graduate university degree or equivalent qualification. *Notes:* 1. Education at the third level requires as a minimum condition of admission the successful completion of education at the second level or evidence of the attainment of an equivalent level of knowledge (e.g., at university, teacher's college, or higher professional school).

★ 194 ★

Worldwide Enrollment at the Third Level by Field - Part III
Total and female students enrolled at the third level, by field of study.

Country, Year, and Field of Study	All 3rd Level[1]	
	MF	F
Asia		
Bangladesh, 1986		
Total	462,265	88,889
Education Science & Teacher Training	3,624	1,009
Humanities, Religion & Theology	151,572	34,067
Law	6,953	302
Social and Behavioral Science	116,030	21,315
Commercial & Business Administration	59,955	9,778
Home Economics (Domestic Science)	632	632
Natural Science	94,947	16,889
Mathematics & Computer Science	9,233	2,067
Medical Science & Health-Related	9,020	2,334
Engineering	4,825	167
Architecture & Town Planning	350	40
Agriculture, Forestry and Fishery	5,124	289
Brunei Darussalam, 1987		
Total	945	479
Education Science & Teacher Training	623	343
Commercial & Business Administration	175	90
Mathematics & Computer Science	65	32
Engineering	82	14
Cyprus, 1987		
Total	4,247	2,096
Education Science & Teacher Training	600	483
Fine and Applied Arts	64	45

[Continued]

★ 194 ★

Worldwide Enrollment at the Third Level by Field - Part III
[Continued]

Country, Year, and Field of Study	All 3rd Level[1]	
	MF	F
Law	9	5
Social and Behavioral Science	3	-
Commercial & Business Administration	1,551	842
Mass Communication & Document.	5	2
Home Economics (Domestic Science)	7	7
Service Trades	334	208
Mathematics & Computer Science	475	173
Medical Science & Health-Related	164	128
Engineering	595	102
Architecture & Town Planning	57	3
Trade, Craft & Industrial Programs	180	3
Transport & Communications	43	40
Agriculture, Forestry and Fishery	36	-
Hong Kong, 1984		
Total	76,844	26,542
Education Science & Teacher Training	6,007	3,808
Humanities, Religion & Theology	4,657	2,854
Fine and Applied Arts	1,546	718
Law	373	197
Social and Behavioral Science	3,882	1,913
Commercial & Business Administration	19,194	10,177
Mass Communication & Document.	1,007	614
Service Trades	1,787	552
Natural Science	2,863	618
Mathematics & Computer Science	2,508	648
Medical Science & Health-Related	2,459	792
Engineering	22,146	547
Architecture & Town Planning	1,589	186
Trade, Craft & Industrial Programs	3,911	1,411
Indonesia, 1984		
Total	980,162	316,273
Education Science & Teacher Training	236,324	89,907
Humanities, Religion & Theology	28,098	10,274
Fine and Applied Arts	4,152	1,421
Law	109,989	30,055
Social and Behavioral Science	218,173	72,709
Commercial & Business Administration	136,425	54,728
Mass Communication & Document.	5,281	1,999
Home Economics (Domestic Science)	1,982	1,602
Service Trades	2,215	974
Natural Science	21,411	8,337
Mathematics & Computer Science	6,441	791
Medical Science & Health-Related	24,855	7,978
Engineering	109,472	18,008
Architecture & Town Planning	12,410	2,430

[Continued]

★ 194 ★

Worldwide Enrollment at the Third Level by Field - Part III
[Continued]

Country, Year, and Field of Study	All 3rd Level[1]	
	MF	F
Trade, Craft & Industrial Programs	3,694	935
Transport & Communications	474	108
Agriculture, Forestry and Fishery	54,643	13,587
Iran, Islamic Republic, 1986		
Total	219,332	61,288
Education Science & Teacher Training	76,215	22,472
Humanities, Religion & Theology	13,551	5,886
Fine and Applied Arts	2,540	1,253
Law	3,087	402
Social and Behavioral Science	11,109	4,209
Commercial & Business Administration	5,270	1,656
Mass Communication & Document.	971	445
Natural Science	9,921	3,648
Mathematics & Computer Science	5,251	1,518
Medical Science & Health-Related	37,910	16,904
Engineering	43,095	1,565
Architecture & Town Planning	2,030	426
Trade, Craft & Industrial Programs	679	171
Agriculture, Forestry and Fishery	100	-
Israel, 1986		
Total	105,102	48,078
Education Science & Teacher Training	41,331	23,907
Law	2,360	977
Social and Behavioral Science	20,282	9,407
Natural Science	5,861	2,909
Mathematics & Computer Science	4,353	1,473
Medical Science & Health-Related	6,573	4,181
Engineering	21,966	4,015
Agriculture, Forestry and Fishery	1,123	413
Japan, 1986		
Total	2,409,687	865,094
Education Science & Teacher Training	218,824	156,054
Humanities, Religion & Theology	380,911	262,585
Fine and Applied Arts	67,197	48,084
Social and Behavioral Science	772,640	110,261
Home Economics (Domestic Science)	140,622	140,156
Natural Science	50,534	7,803
Mathematics & Computer Science	17,566	3,976
Medical Science & Health-Related	152,300	61,036
Engineering	418,939	14,977
Transport & Communications	2,720	58
Agriculture, Forestry and Fishery	64,770	10,990
Jordan, 1986		

[Continued]

★ 194 ★

Worldwide Enrollment at the Third Level by Field - Part III
[Continued]

Country, Year, and Field of Study	All 3rd Level[1]	
	MF	F
Total	60,553	29,015
Education Science & Teacher Training	15,113	12,151
Humanities, Religion & Theology	7,765	3,934
Law	1,661	580
Social and Behavioral Science	879	498
Commercial & Business Administration	12,910	4,362
Service Trades	110	5
Natural Science	4,836	1,918
Mathematics & Computer Science	2,027	711
Medical Science & Health-Related	6,389	3,298
Engineering	7,383	1,121
Transport & Communications	324	6
Agriculture, Forestry and Fishery	1,156	431
Korea, Republic of, 1987		
Total	1,508,939	454,260
Education Science & Teacher Training	155,676	90,882
Humanities, Religion & Theology	213,124	96,075
Fine and Applied Arts	70,660	45,324
Law	50,976	5,151
Social and Behavioral Science	79,921	16,704
Commercial & Business Administration	269,586	44,465
Mass Communication & Document.	9,422	6,039
Home Economics (Domestic Science)	45,162	42,909
Service Trades	8,741	4,430
Natural Science	56,036	14,608
Mathematics & Computer Science	36,990	9,780
Medical Science & Health-Related	82,339	40,081
Engineering	227,640	13,566
Architecture & Town Planning	69,150	2,759
Trade, Craft & Industrial Programs	22,770	2,717
Transport & Communications	5,771	511
Agriculture, Forestry and Fishery	84,678	12,031
Kuwait, 1987		
Total	25,521	13,970
Education Science & Teacher Training	5,485	4,193
Humanities, Religion & Theology	2,651	1,663
Fine and Applied Arts	1,107	410
Law	2,414	1,393
Social and Behavioral Science	1,549	825
Commercial & Business Administration	2,893	1,748
Natural Science	1,943	1,045
Mathematics & Computer Science	997	632
Medical Science & Health-Related	1,618	1,062
Engineering	1,694	529
Trade, Craft & Industrial Programs	2,698	284

[Continued]

★ 194 ★

Worldwide Enrollment at the Third Level by Field - Part III
[Continued]

Country, Year, and Field of Study	All 3rd Level[1]	
	MF	F
Transport & Communications	472	186
Lao People's Democratic Republic, 1985		
Total	5,382	1,918
Education Science & Teacher Training	2,722	1,130
Medical Science & Health-Related	981	521
Engineering	212	31
Architecture & Town Planning	575	102
Transport & Communications	703	111
Lebanon, 1984		
Total	70,510	27,473
Education Science & Teacher Training	425	150
Humanities, Religion & Theology	16,996	9,120
Fine and Applied Arts	1,250	780
Law	12,620	3,050
Social and Behavioral Science	10,130	4,515
Commercial & Business Administration	12,480	3,275
Mass Communication & Document.	590	450
Service Trades	230	130
Natural Science	4,789	2,350
Mathematics & Computer Science	2,032	640
Medical Science & Health-Related	2,560	1,250
Engineering	4,130	505
Architecture & Town Planning	1,502	390
Malaysia, 1987		
Total	105,964	50,766
Education Science & Teacher Training	34,364	21,161
Humanities, Religion & Theology	5,787	2,584
Fine and Applied Arts	905	389
Law	1,206	600
Social and Behavioral Science	4,465	2,209
Commercial & Business Administration	21,263	10,214
Mass Communication & Document.	1,036	575
Home Economics (Domestic Science)	287	130
Service Trades	90	56
Natural Science	283	124
Mathematics & Computer Science	3,293	1,473
Medical Science & Health-Related	3,143	1,561
Engineering	10,195	1,283
Architecture & Town Planning	2,229	611
Agriculture, Forestry and Fishery	2,066	579
Mongolia, 1986		
Total	39,072	23,409
Education Science & Teacher Training	5,723	4,202

[Continued]

★ 194 ★

Worldwide Enrollment at the Third Level by Field - Part III
[Continued]

Country, Year, and Field of Study	All 3rd Level[1]	
	MF	F
Humanities, Religion & Theology	764	561
Fine and Applied Arts	1,579	878
Law	491	262
Social and Behavioral Science	2,292	1,533
Mass Communication & Document.	30	13
Service Trades	1,954	1,492
Natural Science	583	415
Mathematics & Computer Science	519	300
Medical Science & Health-Related	5,899	5,190
Engineering	9,589	4,123
Architecture & Town Planning	62	9
Transport & Communications	3,152	1,333
Agriculture, Forestry and Fishery	5,788	2,744
Pakistan, 1986		
Total	60,716	8,740
Education Science & Teacher Training	2,125	718
Humanities, Religion & Theology	10,355	3,106
Law	4,531	186
Commercial & Business Administration	4,492	451
Natural Science	12,884	2,932
Medical Science & Health-Related	1,737	479
Engineering	15,612	489
Agriculture, Forestry and Fishery	6,853	65
Philippines, 1985		
Total	1,973,182	1,074,045
Education Science & Teacher Training	292,545	215,499
Humanities, Religion & Theology	8,975	3,035
Fine and Applied Arts	6,233	3,272
Law	23,701	6,436
Social and Behavioral Science	16,834	12,510
Commercial & Business Administration	636,349	477,467
Mass Communication & Document.	4,916	2,515
Home Economics (Domestic Science)	10,540	10,174
Service Trades	22,268	15,864
Natural Science	15,854	10,545
Mathematics & Computer Science	55,051	31,321
Medical Science & Health-Related	125,406	96,795
Engineering	315,179	45,717
Architecture & Town Planning	23,449	4,102
Trade, Craft & Industrial Programs	292,056	103,063
Transport & Communications	43,706	2,739
Agriculture, Forestry and Fishery	57,629	25,059
Qatar, 1987		
Total	5,347	3,691

[Continued]

173

★ 194 ★

Worldwide Enrollment at the Third Level by Field - Part III
[Continued]

Country, Year, and Field of Study	All 3rd Level[1]	
	MF	F
Education Science & Teacher Training	3,523	2,557
Humanities, Religion & Theology	1,061	749
Commercial & Business Administration	245	130
Natural Science	369	255
Engineering	149	-
Saudi Arabia, 1985		
Total	113,529	44,697
Education Science & Teacher Training	29,059	15,275
Humanities, Religion & Theology	42,380	17,698
Commercial & Business Administration	310	-
Social and Behavioral Science	14,471	4,247
Natural Science	11,345	4,230
Medical Science & Health-Related	5,989	2,497
Engineering	7,152	124
Trade, Craft & Industrial Programs	266	-
Agriculture, Forestry and Fishery	2,557	626
Singapore, 1983		
Total	35,192	14,759
Education Science & Teacher Training	5,188	3,754
Humanities, Religion & Theology	2,828	2,123
Law	602	321
Commercial & Business Administration	4,170	2,772
Natural Science	2,375	1,522
Mathematics & Computer Science	350	218
Medical Science & Health-Related	1,121	370
Engineering	15,374	2,574
Architecture & Town Planning	1,725	825
Transport & Communications	107	-
Sri Lanka, 1986		
Total	61,628	25,122
Education Science & Teacher Training	8,741	5,622
Fine and Applied Arts	775	587
Law	684	301
Social and Behavioral Science	7,385	3,542
Commercial & Business Administration	12,724	7,068
Home Economics (Domestic Science)	124	124
Natural Science	4,468	1,932
Medical Science & Health-Related	3,123	1,388
Engineering	9,343	1,775
Architecture & Town Planning	226	81
Trade, Craft & Industrial Programs	7,130	172
Agriculture, Forestry and Fishery	1,455	480
Syrian Arab Republic, 1986		

[Continued]

★ 194 ★

Worldwide Enrollment at the Third Level by Field - Part III
[Continued]

Country, Year, and Field of Study	All 3rd Level[1]	
	MF	F
Total	182,933	64,925
Education Science & Teacher Training	23,121	14,537
Humanities, Religion & Theology	31,556	17,488
Fine and Applied Arts	625	225
Law	22,601	3,625
Social and Behavioral Science	3,201	946
Commercial & Business Administration	16,549	5,349
Mass Communication & Document.	298	125
Service Trades	86	63
Natural Science	10,632	4,278
Mathematics & Computer Science	6,532	2,253
Medical Science & Health-Related	18,945	6,936
Engineering	30,377	6,141
Architecture & Town Planning	2,433	832
Trade, Craft & Industrial Programs	8,227	538
Agriculture, Forestry and Fishery	7,750	1,589
Turkey, 1987		
Total	534,459	178,272
Education Science & Teacher Training	60,829	27,233
Humanities, Religion & Theology	27,189	11,300
Fine and Applied Arts	6,447	3,376
Law	16,181	5,898
Social and Behavioral Science	158,290	49,752
Commercial & Business Administration	47,651	16,744
Mass Communication & Document.	5,347	2,913
Home Economics (Domestic Science)	567	548
Service Trades	4,648	1,178
Natural Science	18,590	8,373
Mathematics & Computer Science	10,413	4,248
Medical Science & Health-Related	55,322	21,861
Engineering	85,082	14,275
Architecture & Town Planning	8,815	4,581
Trade, Craft & Industrial Programs	1,696	714
Transport & Communications	93	1
Agriculture, Forestry and Fishery	20,582	5,277
United Arab Emirates, 1987		
Total	7,428	4,538
Education Science & Teacher Training	2,280	1,877
Humanities, Religion & Theology	890	623
Law	455	99
Social and Behavioral Science	903	527
Commercial & Business Administration	1,224	626
Mass Communication & Document.	186	66
Home Economics (Domestic Science)	21	21
Natural Science	516	351

[Continued]

★ 194 ★

Worldwide Enrollment at the Third Level by Field - Part III
[Continued]

Country, Year, and Field of Study	All 3rd Level[1]	
	MF	F
Mathematics & Computer Science	199	128
Medical Science & Health-Related	33	21
Engineering	295	39
Architecture & Town Planning	122	86
Agriculture, Forestry and Fishery	120	-
Viet-Nam, 1980		
Total	114,701	27,090
Education Science & Teacher Training	42,363	12,169
Humanities, Religion & Theology	4,247	1,310
Fine and Applied Arts	1,022	148
Law	1,005	48
Social and Behavioral Science	818	169
Commercial & Business Administration	14,030	3,527
Mass Communication & Document.	621	68
Natural Science	2,487	505
Mathematics & Computer Science	1,961	499
Medical Science & Health-Related	11,462	1,839
Engineering	11,231	1,806
Architecture & Town Planning	2,432	653
Trade, Craft & Industrial Programs	8,374	1,724
Transport & Communications	1,809	251
Agriculture, Forestry and Fishery	10,839	2,374

Source: Selected from "Education at the third level: enrollment by ISCED level of programme and field of study," *Statistical Yearbook 1989*, Table 3.13, p. 3-320/3-358. Also in source: data at level 5, level 6, and level 7. Level 5 programs lead to an award not equivalent to a first university degree. Level 6 programs lead to a first university degree or equivalent qualification. Level 7 programs lead to a post-graduate university degree or equivalent qualification. *Notes:* 1. Education at the third level requires as a minimum condition of admission the successful completion of education at the second level or evidence of the attainment of an equivalent level of knowledge (e.g., at university, teacher's college, or higher professional school).

★ 195 ★

Worldwide Enrollment at the Third Level by Field - Part IV

Total and female students enrolled at the third level, by field of study.

Country, Year, and Field of Study	All 3rd Level[1]	
	MF	F
Europe		
Albania, 1987		
Total	23,784	11,746
Education Science & Teacher Training	4,401	2,643
Humanities, Religion & Theology	1,361	845
Fine and Applied Arts	629	224

[Continued]

★ 195 ★

Worldwide Enrollment at the Third Level by Field - Part IV
[Continued]

Country, Year, and Field of Study	All 3rd Level[1]	
	MF	F
Law	500	208
Social and Behavioral Science	2,877	2,024
Natural Science	1,496	905
Medical Science & Health-Related	1,517	788
Engineering	4,619	1,312
Agriculture, Forestry and Fishery	5,826	2,633
Austria, 1987		
Total	209,254	93,706
Education Science & Teacher Training	13,117	9,457
Humanities, Religion & Theology	29,650	18,634
Fine and Applied Arts	11,114	6,278
Law	18,875	6,801
Social and Behavioral Science	18,879	10,260
Commercial & Business Administration	35,236	13,710
Mass Communication & Document.	3,513	1,880
Home Economics (Domestic Science)	300	269
Service Trades	815	633
Natural Science	12,506	4,746
Mathematics & Computer Science	7,680	1,965
Medical Science & Health-Related	22,002	11,788
Engineering	17,330	1,369
Architecture & Town Planning	5,458	1,708
Trade, Craft & Industrial Programs	32	30
Agriculture, Forestry and Fishery	6,767	2,303
Belgium, 1987		
Total	254,329	120,401
Education Science & Teacher Training	26,502	18,708
Humanities, Religion & Theology	14,845	9,139
Fine and Applied Arts	2,650	1,246
Law	14,366	6,832
Social and Behavioral Science	29,863	12,835
Commercial & Business Administration	52,712	27,592
Mass Communication & Document.	809	459
Service Trades	3,313	1,837
Natural Science	16,279	5,469
Mathematics & Computer Science	10,227	2,648
Medical Science & Health-Related	35,195	22,517
Engineering	22,943	3,716
Architecture & Town Planning	2,918	1,037
Trade, Craft & Industrial Programs	11,144	1,878
Transport & Communications	224	79
Agriculture, Forestry and Fishery	5,211	1,546
Bulgaria, 1987		
Total	135,852	75,565

[Continued]

★ 195 ★

Worldwide Enrollment at the Third Level by Field - Part IV
[Continued]

Country, Year, and Field of Study	All 3rd Level[1]	
	MF	F
Education Science & Teacher Training	24,976	18,788
Humanities, Religion & Theology	10,354	7,745
Fine and Applied Arts	2,239	970
Law	2,554	1,172
Social and Behavioral Science	3,311	1,934
Commercial & Business Administration	16,698	3,499
Mass Communication & Document.	799	463
Service Trades	1,113	783
Natural Science	4,065	2,636
Mathematics & Computer Science	1,776	1,015
Medical Science & Health-Related	11,923	5,770
Engineering	47,097	27,204
Architecture & Town Planning	998	310
Transport & Communications	1,471	680
Agriculture, Forestry and Fishery	6,478	2,596
Denmark, 1986		
Total	118,641	59,082
Education Science & Teacher Training	16,656	12,041
Humanities, Religion & Theology	16,871	11,559
Fine and Applied Arts	4,032	2,380
Law	4,720	2,311
Social and Behavioral Science	11,543	5,019
Commercial & Business Administration	10,988	3,253
Mass Communication & Document.	1,432	787
Service Trades	177	176
Natural Science	4,081	1,368
Mathematics & Computer Science	4,456	1,057
Medical Science & Health-Related	17,116	13,605
Engineering	16,628	2,376
Architecture & Town Planning	1,808	742
Trade, Craft & Industrial Programs	1,130	113
Transport & Communications	1,196	12
Agriculture, Forestry and Fishery	2,872	1,163
Finland, 1987		
Total	139,375	70,241
Education Science & Teacher Training	14,250	10,617
Humanities, Religion & Theology	19,317	14,052
Fine and Applied Arts	3,156	1,946
Law	4,022	1,753
Social and Behavioral Science	8,807	5,785
Commercial & Business Administration	12,836	6,297
Mass Communication & Document.	297	160
Home Economics (Domestic Science)	951	919
Service Trades	1,006	787
Natural Science	8,716	4,192

[Continued]

★ 195 ★

Worldwide Enrollment at the Third Level by Field - Part IV
[Continued]

Country, Year, and Field of Study	All 3rd Level[1]	
	MF	F
Mathematics & Computer Science	9,149	2,513
Medical Science & Health-Related	18,121	14,836
Engineering	31,298	3,840
Architecture & Town Planning	1,457	605
Transport & Communications	58	3
Agriculture, Forestry and Fishery	4,752	1,856
German Democratic Republic, 1987		
Total	437,919	229,229
Education Science & Teacher Training	58,339	44,189
Humanities, Religion & Theology	9,302	3,734
Fine and Applied Arts	4,741	2,212
Law	4,364	1,074
Social and Behavioral Science	22,789	15,603
Commercial & Business Administration	37,745	28,160
Mass Communication & Document.	2,671	1,862
Service Trades	3,824	2,718
Natural Science	7,322	2,823
Mathematics & Computer Science	6,053	2,696
Medical Science & Health-Related	59,017	50,703
Engineering	87,789	22,276
Architecture & Town Planning	1,243	560
Trade, Craft & Industrial Programs	49,516	10,152
Transport & Communications	3,934	1,234
Agriculture, Forestry and Fishery	24,570	10,895
Germany, Federal Republic, 1986		
Total	1,579,085	654,207
Education Science & Teacher Training	89,366	65,866
Humanities, Religion & Theology	200,078	121,403
Fine and Applied Arts	49,036	25,630
Law	85,401	33,871
Social and Behavioral Science	301,837	119,076
Commercial & Business Administration	31,080	12,102
Mass Communication & Document.	8,045	4,286
Home Economics (Domestic Science)	15,485	14,442
Service Trades	758	410
Natural Science	119,657	36,775
Mathematics & Computer Science	64,231	14,625
Medical Science & Health-Related	220,845	144,363
Engineering	271,710	18,424
Architecture & Town Planning	45,312	17,177
Trade, Craft & Industrial Programs	5,697	394
Agriculture, Forestry and Fishery	45,731	13,829
Greece, 1985		
Total	181,901	88,963

[Continued]

★ 195 ★

Worldwide Enrollment at the Third Level by Field - Part IV
[Continued]

Country, Year, and Field of Study	All 3rd Level[1]	
	MF	F
Education Science & Teacher Training	13,844	10,391
Humanities, Religion & Theology	29,580	19,438
Fine and Applied Arts	1,793	1,040
Law	13,564	7,478
Social and Behavioral Science	12,096	5,966
Commercial & Business Administration	21,810	10,909
Mass Communication & Document.	688	494
Home Economics (Domestic Science)	466	195
Service Trades	3,403	1,873
Natural Science	8,461	3,483
Mathematics & Computer Science	7,963	2,853
Medical Science & Health-Related	24,549	14,450
Engineering	29,991	5,270
Architecture & Town Planning	1,472	748
Trade, Craft & Industrial Programs	796	397
Transport & Communications	1,038	31
Agriculture, Forestry and Fishery	10,387	3,947
Holy See, 1987		
Total	9,882	3,358
Education Science & Teacher Training	552	331
Humanities, Religion & Theology	8,426	2,876
Fine and Applied Arts	54	21
Law	701	86
Social and Behavioral Science	149	44
Hungary, 1987		
Total	99,025	52,785
Education Science & Teacher Training	40,016	29,948
Humanities, Religion & Theology	2,442	1,543
Fine and Applied Arts	1,101	508
Law	5,757	3,050
Social and Behavioral Science	2,928	1,258
Commercial & Business Administration	7,117	4,743
Service Trades	929	548
Natural Science	1,076	357
Mathematics & Computer Science	1,263	353
Medical Science & Health-Related	8,939	5,364
Engineering	9,212	1,008
Architecture & Town Planning	4,115	964
Trade, Craft & Industrial Programs	6,562	1,260
Transport & Communications	1,346	279
Agriculture, Forestry and Fishery	5,632	1,470
Italy, 1986		
Total	1,141,127	533,511
Education Science & Teacher Training	35,922	31,155

[Continued]

★ 195 ★

Worldwide Enrollment at the Third Level by Field - Part IV
[Continued]

Country, Year, and Field of Study	All 3rd Level[1]	
	MF	F
Humanities, Religion & Theology	159,094	127,241
Fine and Applied Arts	14,490	9,028
Law	172,240	81,437
Social and Behavioral Science	229,593	98,489
Commercial & Business Administration	18,504	5,603
Mass Communication & Document.	226	101
Natural Science	74,257	38,172
Mathematics & Computer Science	37,888	16,402
Medical Science & Health-Related	183,072	75,389
Engineering	96,409	6,258
Architecture & Town Planning	66,692	25,432
Agriculture, Forestry and Fishery	33,935	9,264
Luxembourg, 1984		
Total	843	289
Education Science & Teacher Training	103	66
Humanities, Religion & Theology	100	57
Law	34	9
Social and Behavioral Science	221	92
Natural Science	73	28
Medical Science & Health-Related	55	29
Engineering	256	8
Malta, 1987		
Total	1,447	527
Education Science & Teacher Training	376	223
Law	74	28
Commercial & Business Administration	323	102
Medical Science & Health-Related	345	156
Engineering	237	12
Architecture & Town Planning	92	6
Netherlands, 1986		
Total	381,686	161,428
Education Science & Teacher Training	52,614	30,027
Humanities, Religion & Theology	30,981	17,906
Fine and Applied Arts	20,949	11,393
Law	28,288	11,948
Social and Behavioral Science	63,589	29,377
Commercial & Business Administration	30,008	8,572
Mass Communication & Document.	3,547	2,186
Home Economics (Domestic Science)	2,555	1,838
Service Trades	1,943	1,026
Natural Science	10,905	2,717
Mathematics & Computer Science	2,789	431
Medical Science & Health-Related	40,144	24,522
Engineering	23,848	2,160

[Continued]

★ 195 ★

Worldwide Enrollment at the Third Level by Field - Part IV
[Continued]

Country, Year, and Field of Study	All 3rd Level[1]	
	MF	F
Trade, Craft & Industrial Programs	38,754	4,596
Transport & Communications	3,255	118
Agriculture, Forestry and Fishery	15,510	4,561
Norway, 1986		
Total	104,246	53,457
Education Science & Teacher Training	13,244	9,921
Humanities, Religion & Theology	8,365	5,244
Fine and Applied Arts	1,012	602
Law	4,713	2,328
Social and Behavioral Science	7,872	4,538
Commercial & Business Administration	26,107	10,968
Mass Communication & Document.	618	443
Home Economics (Domestic Science)	49	46
Service Trades	54	35
Natural Science	6,970	2,433
Mathematics & Computer Science	1,481	411
Medical Science & Health-Related	10,746	8,482
Engineering	12,367	2,814
Architecture & Town Planning	656	320
Trade, Craft & Industrial Programs	205	130
Transport & Communications	877	213
Agriculture, Forestry and Fishery	1,326	545
Poland, 1987		
Total	458,585	257,519
Education Science & Teacher Training	95,844	75,376
Humanities, Religion & Theology	40,525	26,787
Fine and Applied Arts	8,374	4,442
Law	15,038	7,505
Social and Behavioral Science	13,988	7,817
Commercial & Business Administration	66,382	41,221
Mass Communication & Document.	3,078	2,387
Home Economics (Domestic Science)	551	463
Natural Science	15,170	9,942
Mathematics & Computer Science	5,461	3,536
Medical Science & Health-Related	60,156	43,988
Engineering	65,297	9,596
Architecture & Town Planning	3,730	1,771
Trade, Craft & Industrial Programs	13,011	3,963
Transport & Communications	3,247	149
Agriculture, Forestry and Fishery	32,674	12,752
Portugal, 1984		
Total	112,851	59,763
Education Science & Teacher Training	13,828	11,515
Humanities, Religion & Theology	16,137	12,012

[Continued]

★ 195 ★

Worldwide Enrollment at the Third Level by Field - Part IV
[Continued]

Country, Year, and Field of Study	All 3rd Level[1]	
	MF	F
Fine and Applied Arts	1,592	904
Law	12,119	5,395
Social and Behavioral Science	12,240	6,708
Commercial & Business Administration	8,860	3,777
Mass Communication & Document.	965	707
Home Economics (Domestic Science)	126	83
Natural Science	2,749	1,754
Mathematics & Computer Science	2,619	1,416
Medical Science & Health-Related	11,125	6,851
Engineering	20,294	4,482
Architecture & Town Planning	1,907	695
Trade, Craft & Industrial Programs	227	124
Agriculture, Forestry and Fishery	3,591	1,592
Spain, 1986		
Total	954,005	477,494
Education Science & Teacher Training	107,373	79,750
Humanities, Religion & Theology	113,437	75,665
Fine and Applied Arts	11,731	6,415
Law	146,483	69,241
Social and Behavioral Science	124,333	60,775
Commercial & Business Administration	52,621	23,731
Mass Communication & Document.	19,902	11,311
Service Trades	13,272	9,603
Natural Science	59,931	27,466
Mathematics & Computer Science	33,427	12,488
Medical Science & Health-Related	89,602	57,257
Engineering	98,266	11,239
Architecture & Town Planning	26,288	5,726
Agriculture, Forestry and Fishery	13,524	5,561
Sweden, 1987		
Total	184,324	96,962
Education Science & Teacher Training	20,034	15,809
Humanities, Religion & Theology	27,464	17,133
Law	9,222	4,469
Social and Behavioral Science	44,209	23,060
Service Trades	134	113
Natural Science	17,353	5,535
Medical Science & Health-Related	26,042	19,048
Engineering	33,420	6,896
Trade, Craft & Industrial Programs	1,448	69
Transport & Communications	620	42
Agriculture, Forestry and Fishery	2,694	1,069
Switzerland, 1987		
Total	121,693	38,622

[Continued]

Worldwide Enrollment at the Third Level by Field - Part IV
[Continued]

Country, Year, and Field of Study	All 3rd Level[1]	
	MF	F
Education Science & Teacher Training	5,277	3,379
Humanities, Religion & Theology	15,709	8,387
Fine and Applied Arts	3,490	2,313
Law	9,195	3,240
Social and Behavioral Science	21,122	7,883
Commercial & Business Administration	14,045	2,749
Mass Communication & Document.	75	50
Home Economics (Domestic Science)	2,258	1,105
Natural Science	9,551	2,299
Mathematics & Computer Science	2,721	379
Medical Science & Health-Related	10,431	4,489
Engineering	19,567	748
Architecture & Town Planning	2,370	752
Trade, Craft & Industrial Programs	3,433	42
Transport & Communications	22	-
Agriculture, Forestry and Fishery	2,427	807
United Kingdom, 1985		
Total	1,032,491	469,945
Education Science & Teacher Training	83,715	54,471
Humanities, Religion & Theology	83,251	50,007
Fine and Applied Arts	46,339	26,584
Social and Behavioral Science	247,695	106,949
Mass Communication & Document.	35,369	14,719
Natural Science	134,697	44,901
Medical Science & Health-Related	151,637	117,946
Engineering	159,041	12,261
Agriculture, Forestry and Fishery	8,856	3,213
Yugoslavia, 1987		
Total	348,068	165,210
Education Science & Teacher Training	26,586	16,062
Humanities, Religion & Theology	28,477	20,140
Fine and Applied Arts	4,551	2,518
Law	30,818	16,853
Social & Behavioral Science	51,079	29,727
Commercial & Business Administration	3,882	1,601
Service Trades	3,476	1,744
Natural Science	19,121	11,684
Medical Science & Health-Related	29,658	18,373
Engineering	98,442	27,676
Architecture & Town Planning	4,735	2,504
Trade, Craft & Industrial Programs	1,784	1,126
Transport & Communications	9,208	1,813
Agriculture, Forestry and Fishery	31,342	11,990

[Continued]

★ 195 ★

Worldwide Enrollment at the Third Level by Field - Part IV
[Continued]

Country, Year, and Field of Study	All 3rd Level[1]	
	MF	F
Oceania		
Australia, 1985		
Total	370,048	176,178
Education Science & Teacher Training	75,162	49,256
Humanities, Religion & Theology	92,910	60,119
Law	9,945	4,217
Commercial & Business Administration	68,411	21,974
Natural Science	52,547	19,089
Medical Science & Health-Related	23,431	13,876
Engineering	28,285	1,466
Architecture & Town Planning	7,988	1,845
Agriculture, Forestry and Fishery	8,068	2,729
Guam, 1986		
Total	7,052	3,754
Education Science & Teacher Training	1,229	883
Humanities, Religion & Theology	16	7
Fine and Applied Arts	64	39
Law	1,975	971
Social and Behavioral Science	393	169
Commercial & Business Administration	2,000	1,051
Mass Communication & Document.	93	53
Service Trades	81	46
Natural Science	182	91
Mathematics & Computer Science	292	113
Medical Science & Health-Related	359	312
Engineering	173	9
Trade, Craft & Industrial Programs	139	7
Agriculture, Forestry and Fishery	56	3
New Caledonia, 1985		
Total	761	336
Education Science & Teacher Training	117	87
Law	152	83
Commercial & Business Administration	38	25
Service Trades	15	13
Mathematics & Computer Science	371	126
Engineering	68	2
New Zealand, 1987		
Total	108,733	52,075
Education Science & Teacher Training	8,050	6,211
Humanities, Religion & Theology	19,044	12,964
Fine and Applied Arts	1,316	758
Law	5,580	2,994
Social and Behavioral Science	3,768	2,553

[Continued]

★ 195 ★

Worldwide Enrollment at the Third Level by Field - Part IV

[Continued]

Country, Year, and Field of Study	All 3rd Level[1]	
	MF	F
Commercial & Business Administration	27,803	10,949
Mass Communication & Document.	347	215
Home Economics (Domestic Science)	319	282
Service Trades	3,016	430
Natural Science	9,652	3,905
Mathematics & Computer Science	560	157
Medical Science & Health-Related	7,843	6,017
Engineering	8,625	615
Architecture & Town Planning	5,827	1,575
Trade, Craft & Industrial Programs	303	122
Transport & Communications	381	20
Agriculture, Forestry and Fishery	4,127	1,400
Papua New Guinea, 1986		
Total	6,397	1,565
Education Science & Teacher Training	596	183
Humanities, Religion & Theology	1,387	230
Fine and Applied Arts	69	6
Law	260	36
Commercial & Business Administration	803	176
Mass Communication & Document.	100	62
Natural Science	383	53
Mathematics & Computer Science	2	-
Medical Science & Health-Related	1,089	639
Engineering	479	20
Architecture & Town Planning	62	3
Transport & Communications	79	11
Agriculture, Forestry and Fishery	584	48
Tonga, 1985		
Total	705	397
Education Science & Teacher Training	211	106
Humanities, Religion & Theology	100	45
Law	25	4
Commercial & Business Administration	62	62
Home Economics (Domestic Science)	105	105
Medical Science & Health-Related	75	75
Engineering	22	-
Agriculture, Forestry and Fishery	105	-

Source: Selected from "Education at the third level: enrollment by ISCED level of programme and field of study," *Statistical Yearbook 1989*, Table 3.13, p. 3-320/3-358. Also in source: data at level 5, level 6, and level 7. Level 5 programs lead to an award not equivalent to a first university degree. Level 6 programs lead to a first university degree or equivalent qualification. Level 7 programs lead to a post-graduate university degree or equivalent qualification. *Notes:* 1. Education at the third level requires as a minimum condition of admission the successful completion of education at the second level or evidence of the attainment of an equivalent level of knowledge (e.g., at university, teacher's college, or higher professional school).

★ 196 ★

Worldwide First Level Enrollment

Pupils enrolled at the first level, number and percent female, and pupil/teacher ratio, by country, latest available year.

Country and year	Pupils Enrolled			Pupil/Teacher Ratio
	Total	Female	% Female	
Africa				
Algeria-1988	3,911,388	1,741,376	45%	28
Angola-1982	1,178,430	536,105	45%	46
Benin-1987	470,277	158,587	34%	33
Botswana-1986	235,941	122,248	52%	32
Burkina Faso-1986	411,907	153,253	37%	65
Burundi-1986	452,424	193,446	43%	62
Cameroon-1986	1,795,254	821,781	46%	50
Cape Verde-1986	60,226	29,588	49%	34
Central African Republic-1987	286,422	109,228	38%	63
Chad-1987	419,406	119,885	29%	-
Comoros-1986	62,404	27,410	44%	35
Congo-1986	498,588	235,915	47%	64
Cote D-Ivoire-1985	1,214,511	502,672	41%	36
Djibouti-1986	27,136	11,177	41%	-
Egypt-1987	7,034,617	3,008,721	43%	30
Equatorial Guinea-1983	61,532	-	-	-
Ethiopia-1987	2,884,000	1,097,000	38%	49
Gabon-1986	191,280	95,093	50%	47
Gambia-1988	73,673	28,540	39%	28
Ghana-1987	1,581,870	702,270	44%	24
Guinea-1987	288,914	89,398	31%	40
Guinea-Bissau-1986	77,004	27,171	35%	25
Kenya-1987	5,031,340	2,427,354	48%	34
Lesotho-1985	314,003	174,687	56%	-
Liberia-1984	132,889	46,510	35%	-
Libyan Arab Jamahiriya-1982	721,710	341,979	47%	17
Madagascar-1988	1,487,728	721,628	49%	40
Malawi-1987	1,066,642	473,338	44%	-
Mali-1987	307,587	114,394	37%	38
Mauritania-1987	157,216	64,464	41%	50
Mauritius-1987	144,130	71,210	49%	22
Morocco-1987	2,176,847	840,824	39%	26
Mozambique-1987	1,287,681	564,787	44%	-
Niger-1986	293,512	105,178	36%	38
Nigeria-1983	14,383,487	6,331,658	44%	40
Reunion-1986	73,526	35,362	48%	19

[Continued]

★ 196 ★

Worldwide First Level Enrollment
[Continued]

Country and year	Pupils Enrolled			Pupil/Teacher Ratio
	Total	Female	% Female	
Rwanda-1987	969,908	478,702	49%	57
St. Helena-1985	582	318	55%	18
Sao Tome and Principe-1987	18,095	8,759	48%	35
Senegal-1987	642,063	262,844	41%	54
Seychelles-1988	14,451	7,165	50%	21
Sierra Leone-1982	350,160	143,397	41%	34
Somalia-1985	194,335	66,189	34%	20
Sudan-1985	1,738,341	702,987	40%	35
Swaziland-1987	146,229	72,498	50%	34
Togo-1987	527,853	203,745	39%	52
Tunisia-1987	1,345,921	601,997	45%	31
Uganda-1986	2,203,824	996,184	45%	30
United Republic of Tanzania-1987	3,159,726	1,574,618	50%	33
Zaire-1986	4,156,029	1,822,656	44%	37
Zimbabwe-1986	1,357,714	641,567	47%	47
	2,262,071	1,103,638	49%	39
North America				
Antigua and Barbuda-1983	11,394	5,276	46%	-
Bahamas-1986	29,518	14,568	49%	28
Barbados-1984	30,161	14,605	48%	21
Belize-1986	40,729	19,666	48%	25
Bermuda-1984	5,398	2,692	50%	17
British Virgin Islands-1984	2,069	987	48%	-
Canada-1987	2,290,535	1,104,550	48%	17
Cayman Islands-1980	2,123	1,045	49%	19
Costa Rica-1987	393,305	190,416	48%	31
Cuba-1987	936,914	441,967	47%	13
Dominica-1987	12,600	6,145	49%	24
Dominican Republic-1986	1,296,366	649,201	50%	41
El Salvador-1987	995,890	502,536	50%	45
Grenada-1986	21,095	10,050	48%	26
Guadeloupe-1984	44,978	21,394	48%	20
Guatemala-1986	1,040,781	469,980	45%	36
Haiti-1985	872,500	407,002	47%	38
Honduras-1986	810,412	405,532	50%	39
Jamaica-1986	323,609	159,350	49%	34
Martinique-1986	33,492	15,986	48%	-
Mexico-1987	14,768,008	7,172,380	49%	32
Montserrat-1981	1,725	865	50%	20

[Continued]

★ 196 ★

Worldwide First Level Enrollment
[Continued]

Country and year	Pupils Enrolled			Pupil/Teacher Ratio
	Total	Female	% Female	
Netherlands Antilles-1982	32,380	15,902	49%	-
Nicaragua-1987	583,725	302,123	52%	32
Panama-1986	343,616	164,242	48%	22
Puerto Rico-1981	492,908	-	-	-
St. Kitts and Nevis-1986	7,796	3,867	50%	25
St. Lucia-1986	32,798	15,928	49%	29
St. Pierre and Miquelon-1986	556	260	47%	15
St. Vincent and the Grenadines-1987	25,702	12,507	49%	19
Trinidad and Tobabo-1987	182,764	90,492	50%	24
Turks and Caicos Islands-1984	1,429	697	49%	21
United States-1986	27,117,000	13,127,000	48%	-
U.S. Virgin Islands-1985	20,548	-	-	15
South America				
Argentina-1987	4,906,907	2,421,237	49%	19
Bolivia-1987	1,299,664	606,360	47%	27
Brazil-1987	26,208,051	-	-	24
Chile-1988	2,004,710	979,309	49%	-
Colombia-1986	4,002,543	2,000,871	50%	29
Ecuador-1987	1,822,252	892,100	49%	31
Falkland Islands (Malvinas)-1980	223	130	58%	15
French Guiana-1983	9,780	-	-	23
Guyana-1983	121,869	-	-	37
Paraguay-1986	579,687	277,858	48%	25
Peru-1985	3,711,592	1,787,244	48%	35
Suriname-1986	62,633	30,370	48%	-
Uruguay-1986	354,883	173,188	49%	22
Venezuela-1986	2,880,333	1,409,171	49%	26
Asia				
Afghanistan-1986	611,106	203,877	33%	37
Bahrain-1987	60,605	29,871	49%	21
Bangladesh-1987	11,075,476	4,829,714	44%	59
Bhutan-1986	49,485	17,312	35%	37
Brunei Darussalam-1987	36,861	17,540	48%	23
Burma-1983	4,696,300	-	-	45
China-1987	128,358,500	58,217,600	45%	24
Cyprus-1987	56,530	27,140	48%	22

[Continued]

★ 196 ★

Worldwide First Level Enrollment
[Continued]

Country and year	Pupils Enrolled			Pupil/Teacher Ratio
	Total	Female	% Female	
Democratic Yemen-1983	294,028	77,390	26%	26
Hong Kong-1984	534,309	255,799	48%	27
India-1986	89,993,046	36,143,018	40%	46
Indonesia-1986	29,882,556	14,371,220	48%	28
Iran, Islamic Republic-1987	7,757,707	3,450,374	44%	26
Iraq-1987	2,996,953	1,352,580	45%	25
Israel-1987	705,756	349,709	50%	16
Japan-1987	10,226,323	4,988,708	49%	23
Jordan-1987	570,795	279,018	49%	30
Korea, Democratic People's Republic-1976	2,561,674	1,242,980	49%	-
Korea, Republic of-1988	4,819,857	2,339,499	49%	36
Kuwait-1987	181,607	88,656	49%	18
Lao People's Democratic Republic-1985	523,347	234,790	45%	25
Lebanon-1984	329,340	154,320	47%	-
Malaysia-1987	2,274,453	1,105,964	49%	22
Maldives-1986	39,775	-	-	-
Mongolia-1986	155,740	77,859	50%	31
Nepal-1984	1,818,668	-	-	35
Oman-1987	215,416	99,025	46%	26
Pakistan-1987	7,609,069	2,498,135	33%	41
Philippines-1988	9,601,322	4,731,531	49%	32
Qatar-1987	45,367	21,501	47%	12
Saudi Arabia-1986	1,460,283	649,509	44%	16
Singapore-1984	288,623	135,556	47%	27
Sri Lanka-1986	2,304,499	1,112,403	48%	32
Syrian Arab Republic-1987	2,217,993	1,028,872	46%	26
Thailand-1987	7,392,563	3,562,975	48%	23
Turkey-1987	6,880,304	3,244,250	47%	31
United Arab Emirates-1987	180,270	87,276	48%	18
Viet-Nam-1985	8,125,836	3,864,348	48%	34
Yemen-1987	1,078,673	244,312	23%	-
Europe				
Albania-1987	543,143	260,424	48%	20
Andorra-1982	3,435	1,639	47%	10
Austria-1987	350,734	169,810	48%	11
Belgium-1987	728,718	357,616	49%	15
Bulgaria-1987	1,093,540	529,800	48%	18

[Continued]

★ 196 ★

Worldwide First Level Enrollment
[Continued]

Country and year	Pupils Enrolled			Pupil/Teacher Ratio
	Total	Female	% Female	
Czechoslovakia-1987	2,062,215	1,013,531	49%	21
Denmark-1986	391,895	191,697	49%	11
Finland-1987	390,469	190,556	49%	-
France-1987	4,151,664	2,013,341	48%	19
German Democratic Republic-1987	945,720	457,043	48%	17
Germany, Federal Republic-1986	2,287,622	1,120,226	49%	17
Gibraltar-1984	2,830	1,362	48%	15
Greece-1985	887,735	429,906	48%	23
Hungary-1987	1,277,257	623,752	49%	14
Iceland-1986	24,560	11,973	49%	-
Ireland-1985	420,236	205,236	49%	27
Italy-1984	3,904,143	1,898,984	49%	14
Luxembourg-1986	21,959	10,756	49%	12
Malta-1987	36,564	17,392	48%	22
Monaco-1982	1,354	-	-	-
Netherlands-1986	1,447,776	714,396	49%	17
Norway-1986	325,577	159,327	49%	16
Poland-1987	5,036,114	2,450,682	49%	16
Portugal-1985	1,235,312	588,646	48%	17
Romania-1985	3,030,666	1,476,503	49%	21
San Marino-1987	1,288	631	49%	7
Spain-1986	3,412,939	1,657,761	49%	26
Sweden-1984	630,505	309,934	49%	-
Switzerland-1987	375,302	184,393	49%	-
United Kingdom-1986	4,322,000	2,110,000	49%	-
Yugoslavia-1987	1,432,452	694,183	48%	23
Oceania				
American Samoa-1987	8,042	3,783	47%	16
Australia-1987	1,514,575	735,947	49%	17
Cook Islands-1987	2,808	1,335	48%	20
Fiji-1986	131,201	63,775	49%	30
French Polynesia-1984	27,401	13,173	48%	20
Guam-1983	15,676	7,519	48%	23
Kiribati-1988	13,551	6,686	49%	30
Nauru-1985	1,451	679	47%	20
New Caledonia-1987	22,821	11,160	49%	19
New Zealand-1987	317,470	154,657	49%	21
Niue-1988	378	191	51%	14

[Continued]

★ 196 ★

Worldwide First Level Enrollment
[Continued]

Country and year	Pupils Enrolled			Pupil/Teacher Ratio
	Total	Female	% Female	
Pacific Islands				
1975	30,285	14,544	48%	20
1981	31,099	-	-	23
Papua New Guinea-1987	384,367	169,904	44%	31
Samoa-1983	31,412	15,218	48%	27
Solomon Islands-1986	39,563	17,219	44%	21
Tokelau-1985	411	196	48%	12
Tonga-1986	16,912	8,064	48%	-
Tuvalu-1987	1,364	633	46%	21
Vanuatu-1981	22,969	10,474	46%	21
USSR				
USSR-1987	24,423,000	-	-	17
Byelorussian SSR-1987	846,400	-	-	15
Ukrainian SSR-1987	3,945,800	-	-	15

Source: Selected from "Education at the first level: institutions, teachers and pupils," *Statistical Yearbook*, p. 3-85/3-100 (Paris: UNESCO, 1989). Also in source: data for various years; number of schools and teaching staff (see *Labor and Employment: Teachers*). See *Introduction* for an explanation of levels of education. In general, data in this table cover both public and private schools at the first level of education, including primary classes attached to secondary schools. *Notes:* 1. Data comparability may be affected, particulary as regards the pupil-teacher ratios presented, as the proportion of part-time teachers varies greatly from one country to another. Data exclude other instructional personnel without teaching function; however, it has not been possible to ascertain whether for certain countries such other personnel are included.

★ 197 ★

Worldwide School Enrollment
Estimated enrollment in thousands by level of education and percent female in total enrollment, major world areas, 1987.

Continent, major area or group of countries, year	Total	Female Enrollment				% Female of Total Enrollment			
		Total	1st Level	2nd Level	3rd Level	Total	1st Level	2nd Level	3rd Level
World Total	932,066	415,953	264,800	125,063	26,091	45%	45%	43%	44%
Africa	91,034	38,298	30,149	7,560	589	42%	44%	37%	29%
America	161,726	79,449	49,405	19,588	10,456	49%	48%	50%	51%
Asia	531,623	255,170	152,252	65,629	7,289	42%	44%	40%	35%
Europe(incl. USSR)	142,694	70,622	31,753	31,372	7,498	49%	49%	50%	50%
Oceania	4,989	2,414	1,241	915	258	48%	48%	49%	48%
Developed Countries	227,998	112,568	51,947	44,771	15,850	49%	49%	50%	50%
Developing Countries	704,068	303,385	212,853	80,292	10,241	43%	45%	40%	37%
Africa(excluding Arab States)	63,036	26,660	22,761	3,784	116	42%	45%	33%	18%

[Continued]

★ 197 ★

Worldwide School Enrollment
[Continued]

Continent, major area or group of countries, year	Total	Female Enrollment				% Female of Total Enrollment			
		Total	1st Level	2nd Level	3rd Level	Total	1st Level	2nd Level	3rd Level
Asia(excluding Arab States)	516,733	219,003	148,042	63,960	7,001	42%	44%	40%	35%
Arab States	42,888	17,805	11,598	5,445	761	42%	43%	40%	35%
Northern America	60,283	29,922	14,662	7,936	7,324	50%	48%	49%	53%
Latin America and the Caribbean	101,443	49,527	34,743	11,652	3,132	49%	48%	51%	46%

Source: Selected from "Estimated School Enrolment and Teaching Staff, by Level of Education" and "Estimated Female School Enrolment by Level of Education," *Statistical Yearbook 1989*, Table 2.4, p. 2-12/2-13, 2-17/2-18 (Paris: UNESCO, 1989). Also in source: data for various years; percent change 1975-80 and 1980-87. Figures do not include data relating to adult education and to special education provided outside regular schools. Second level education includes general, teacher training and vocational education. Third level education includes universities and other institutions of higher education.

★ 198 ★

Worldwide School Enrollment Preceding First Level
Total enrollment in thousands for education preceding the first level, number and percent female, world summaries, 1987.

Major areas	In Thousands		% Female
	Total	Female	
World Total (Including China)	77,423	37,117	48
World Total (Excluding China)	59,344	28,650	48
Africa	2,904	1,271	44
America	16,453	8,049	49
Asia	13,554	6,356	47
Europe (Including USSR)	26,156	12,839	49
Oceania	278	135	49
Developed Countries	35,450	17,320	49
Developing Countries	23,894	11,330	47
Africa (Excluding Arab States)	1,687	829	49
Asia (Excluding Arab States)	13,028	6,107	47
Arab States	1,743	691	40
Northern America	7,142	3,424	48
Latin American and the Caribbean	9,311	4,625	50

Source: Selected from "Estimated Teaching Staff and Enrolment by Sex for Education Preceding the First Level," *Statistical Yearbook*, p. 2-26/2-28 (Paris: UNESCO, 1989). Also in source: data for various years; data on private school attendance.

★ 199 ★

Worldwide Science Enrollment by Area

The enrollment of women in various fields of science by area.

Area	Educational science and teacher training	Social and behavioral sciences	Natural sciences	Mathematics and computer science	Medicine and health	Engineering	Agriculture	Total in scientific fields
				Percent female enrollment				
Africa	30	25	20	20[1]	30	5	15	25
Latin America and the Caribbean	60	55	50	45[1]	50	10	20	45
Asia and Oceania	55	35	30	30	40	10	20	25
Western Europe	65	40	35	30	50	5	25	40
Eastern Europe	70	60	50	45	70	25	35	45

Source: "The enrolment of women in various fields of science by area," *World Survey on the Role of Women in Development,* 1986, p. 143 (New York: United Nations, 1986). Primary source: Figures compiled from national data in Shirley M. Malcom, "The participation of women in policy and decision-making regarding the use and development of technologies," *Science and Technology and Women— Proceedings of the Joint Panel of Experts on Science Technology and Women (12-16 September 1983),* Shirley M. Malcom, ed. (Washington, American Associaiton for the Advancement of Science, 1984). Malcom has based her own figures on the *UNESCO Yearbook 1982* (Paris, UNESCO, 1982). *Notes:* 1. Mathematics and computer sciences are separately listed only for about half of the countries involved.

★ 200 ★

Worldwide Science and Engineering Enrollment

Total and female enrollment in science and engineering, by country, 1986.

Country	Total	Female Enrollment				
		Total	Nat. Science Computer	Math./ Health	Med. Sci./	Engineering
AFRICA						
Algeria	201,982	50,685	2,337	1,107	10,790	1,141
Benin	8,870	1,397	135	28	56	---
Burkina Faso	4,405	1,055	61	16	61	---
Burundi	2,731	738	62	---	49	2
Central African Republic	2,651	287	9	---	113	4
Chad	1,643	142	10	---	---	---
Egypt	592,256	203,115	9,387	580	19,780	6,772
Ethiopia	30,210	5,003	131	110	348	144
Gabon	4,089	1,173	15	50	164	17
Guinea	6,753	923	425	1	59	16
Ivory Coast	19,660	NA	206	8	808	13
Kenya	21,756	5,710	181	36	280	55
Lesotho	2,339	1,479	59	5	9	---
Madagascar	35,106	14,329	2,250	269	2,337	338
Malawi	3,979	1,111	27	---	199	---
Mali	5,536	728	---	---	124	24
Mauritius	1,106	367	---	16	6	5
Morocco	143,023	47,952	10,075	1	2,075	66
Mozambique	1,442	332	21	---	82	42

[Continued]

★ 200 ★

Worldwide Science and Engineering Enrollment
[Continued]

Country	Total	Female Enrollment				
		Total	Nat. Science Computer	Math./ Health	Med. Sci./	Engineering
Niger	3,137	590	19	8	71	---
Rwanda	2,029	323	12	9	41	---
Senegal	14,789	3,149	328	1	985	41
Somalia	15,672	3,093	105	---	228	17
Sudan	33,432	13,480	389	19	723	212
Swaziland	1,289	538	74	1	---	---
Tunisia	40,830	14,967	1,592	392	3,066	350
Uganda	11,037	3,098	153	10	110	61
United Rep. of Tanzania	4,987	689	2	---	38	31
Zambia	4,680	810	63	---	94	---
NORTH AMERICA						
Barbados	5,227	2,565	312	1	89	4
Canada	1,141,816	606,331	15,229	12,348	59,131	8,526
Cuba	256,619	141,697	1,999	1,001	18,400	8,176
El Salvador	74,024	19,878	155	3	1,628	1,024
Haiti	4,513	1,432	---	---	342	55
Honduras	36,620	NA	148	79	3,413	1,641
Mexico	1,191,997	473,074	12,695	10,198	68,990	36,696
Nicaragua	26,775	15,252	675	244	2,917	880
St. Lucia	367	202	---	---	---	---
St. Vincent and the Grenadines	736	509	---	---	---	6
Trinidad and Tobago	3,164	1,589	327	1	---	74
SOUTH AMERICA						
Argentina	902,882	479,172	25,157	26,464	49,663	14,375
Colombia	417,654	203,384	2,465	1	24,198	27,018
Guyana	2,328	1,113	45	8	41	17
Suriname	2,751	1,475	1	---	47	---
ASIA						
Afghanistan	22,306	3,124	960	---	748	50
Bahrain	4,180	2,490	---	252	545	88
Bangladesh	462,265	88,889	16,889	2,067	2,334	167
Brunei Darussalam	601	302	---	5	18	10
Cyprus	3,419	1,612	---	132	143	117
Hong Kong	76,844	26,542	618	648	792	547
Indonesia	980,162	316,273	8,337	791	7,978	18,008
Iran, Islamic Rep.	219,332	61,288	3,648	1,518	16,904	1,565

[Continued]

★ 200 ★

Worldwide Science and Engineering Enrollment
[Continued]

Country	Total	Female Enrollment				
		Total	Nat. Science Computer	Math./ Health	Med. Sci./	Engineering
Israel	105,102	48,078	2,909	1,473	4,181	4,015
Japan	2,409,687	865,094	7,803	3,976	61,036	14,977
Jordan	60,553	29,015	1,918	711	3,298	1,121
Korea, Republic of	1,481,311	445,180	13,742	13,668	38,812	9,440
Kuwait	24,384	13,325	1,120	668	800	578
Lao People's Democ. Rep.	5,382	1,918	---	---	521	31
Lebanon	70,510	27,473	2,350	640	1,250	505
Mongolia	39,072	23,409	415	300	5,190	4,123
Pakistan	60,716	8,740	2,932	[1]	479	489
Philippines	1,973,182	1,074,045	10,545	31,321	96,795	45,717
Qatar	5,281	3,532	194	[1]	---	---
Saudi Arabia	113,529	44,697	4,230	[1]	2,497	124
Singapore	35,192	14,759	1,522	218	370	2,574
Sri Lanka	61,628	25,122	1,932	[1]	1,388	1,775
Syrian Arab Republic	182,933	64,925	4,278	2,253	6,936	6,141
Turkey	505,091	168,920	7,811	3,981	19,168	14,151
United Arab Emirates	7,640	4,438	456	72	---	65
EUROPE						
Albania	22,403	10,644	756	[1]	638	1,357
Austria	199,898	88,860	4,404	1,868	12,177	1,199
Belgium	252,236	118,491	4,412	3,039	23,083	3,476
Bulgaria	125,576	69,498	2,483	1,801	5,762	15,964
Czechoslovakia	169,723	71,664	1,304	799	7,642	14,991
Denmark	118,641	59,082	1,368	1,057	13,605	2,376
Finland	133,933	66,630	3,995	2,325	13,980	3,537
German Democratic Rep.	436,720	232,383	2,935	2,475	51,817	23,217
Germany, Federal Rep.	1,579,085	654,207	36,775	14,625	144,363	18,424
Greece	197,808	97,767	3,658	3,031	24,512	5,688
Holy See	10,440	3,434	---	---	---	---
Hungary	98,505	52,771	358	386	5,705	1,084
Iceland	4,949	2,621	103	60	715	38
Ireland	67,378	29,088	4,256	[1]	1,736	1,110
Italy	1,141,127	533,511	38,172	16,402	75,389	6,258
Luxembourg	843	289	28	[1]	29	8
Malta	1,449	500	---	---	152	12
Netherlands	381,686	161,428	2,717	431	24,522	2,160
Norway	104,246	53,457	2,433	411	8,482	2,814
Poland	450,205	251,737	9,063	3,539	44,890	10,388
Portugal	103,585	55,599	1,990	1,777	5,845	4,312
Spain	954,005	477,494	27,466	12,488	57,257	11,239
Sweden	183,645	95,922	2,752	18,786	18,801	6,575

[Continued]

★ 200 ★

Worldwide Science and Engineering Enrollment
[Continued]

Country	Total	Female Enrollment				
		Total	Nat. Science Computer	Math./ Health	Med. Sci./	Engineering
Switzerland	117,017	37,590	2,182	379	4,563	679
United Kingdom	1,068,386	493,368	46,739	[1]	119,052	13,970
Yugoslavia	350,876	164,574	11,145	[1]	18,113	24,891
OCEANIA						
Australia	370,048	176,178	19,089	[1]	13,876	1,466
Fiji	2,211	766	134	34	103	---
Guam	7,052	3,754	91	113	312	9
New Caledonia	761	336	[1]	126	---	2
New Zealand	105,569	49,652	3,745	142	5,528	706
Papua New Guinea	6,397	1,565	53	---	639	20
Tonga	705	397	---	---	75	---
USSR						
USSR	5,088,400	NA	NA	NA	NA	NA
Byelorussian SSR	180,200	NA	NA	NA	NA	NA
Ukrainian SSR	850,700	NA	NA	NA	NA	NA

Source: Selected from "Education at the Third Level: Enrolment by Sex and Field of Study (1980,1986 and 1987), *Statistical Yearbook 1989*, Table 3.12, p. 3-270/3-319 (Paris: UNESCO, 1989). Also in source: data for the following fields: education science & teacher training; humanities; fine & applied arts; law; social & behavioral science; commercial & business administration; mass communication & documentation; home economics; service trades; architecture & town planning; trade, craft & industrial programs; transport & communications; agriculture , forestry & fishery; other; 1980 and 1987. *Note:* 1. Data included elsewhere in source under another category.

★ 201 ★

Worldwide Second Level Enrollment - Part I

Pupils enrolled at the second level of education, number and percent female, by type of education, by country, latest available year.

Country	Type of Education[1]	Year	Pupils Enrolled		
			Total	Female	%Female
Africa					
Algeria	Second	1986	1,999,091	827,808	41%
	General	1988	1,954,869	841,183	43%
	Teacher	1986	23,238	9,446	41%
	Vocational	1988	156,423	48,352	31%
Angola	Second	1984	151,759	-	-
	General	1984	144,612	-	-

[Continued]

★ 201 ★

Worldwide Second Level Enrollment - Part I
[Continued]

Country	Type of Education[1]	Year	Pupils Enrolled		
			Total	Female	%Female
	Teacher	1984	3,586	-	-
	Vocational	1984	3,561	-	-
Benin	Second	1986	102,171	29,471	29%
	General	1986	95,121	26,707	28%
	Teacher	1986	935	323	35%
	Vocational	1986	6,115	2,441	40%
Botswana	Second	1986	39,713	20,749	52%
	General	1986	35,966	18,900	53%
	Teacher	1986	1,317	1,100	84%
	Vocational	1986	2,430	749	31%
Burkino Faso	Second	1987	72,207	-	-
	General	1987	67,271	21,288	32%
	Teacher	1987	350	-	-
	Vocational	1987	4,586	2,158	47%
Burundi	Second	1986	29,027	10,397	36%
	General	1986	16,798	5,739	34%
	Teacher	1986	6,678	3,131	47%
	Vocational	1986	5,551	1,527	28%
Cameroon	Second	1986	386,610	151,327	39%
	General	1986	291,842	111,527	38%
	Teacher	1986	4,002	1,746	44%
	Vocational	1986	90,766	38,054	42%
Cape Verde	Second	1986	5,675	2,599	46%
	General	1986	5,026	2,362	47%
	Teacher	1986	118	54	46%
	Vocational	1986	531	183	34%
Central Africal Republic	Second	1987	46,258	12,870	28%
	General	1987	44,250	11,983	27%
	Teacher	1987	45	1	2%
	Vocational	1987	1,963	886	45%
Chad	Second	1986	44,379	-	-
	General	1987	41,073	6,277	15%
	Teacher	1986	1,030	162	16%
	Vocational	1987	2,646	719	27%
Comoros	Second	1986	21,168	8,432	40%
	General	1986	20,834	8,347	40%

[Continued]

★ 201 ★

Worldwide Second Level Enrollment - Part I
[Continued]

Country	Type of Education[1]	Year	Pupils Enrolled		
			Total	Female	%Female
	Teacher	1986	32	5	16%
	Vocational	1986	302	80	26%
Congo	Second	1986	235,050	104,145	44%
	General	1986	201,228	86,047	43%
	Teacher	1986	1,591	570	36%
	Vocational	1986	32,231	17,528	54%
Cote D'Ivoire	Second	1980	221,940	66,624	30%
	General	1987	272,911	83,177	30%
	Teacher	1980	2,454	423	17%
	Vocational	1986	25,328	9,767	39%
Djibouti	Second	1986	8,003	3,285	41%
	General	1986	5,537	1,931	35%
	Teacher	1986	108	21	19%
	Vocational	1986	2,358	1,333	57%
Egypt	Second	1987	4,130,812	1,685,449	41%
	General	1987	3,123,233	1,260,530	40%
	Teacher	1987	106,308	62,530	59%
	Vocational	1987	901,271	362,389	40%
Equatorial Guinea	Second	1975	4,523	751	17%
	General	1975	3,984	709	18%
	Teacher	1975	169	42	25%
	Vocational	1975	370	-	-
Ethiopia	General	1987	842,700	326,700	39%
	Vocational	1986	5,859	-	-
Gabon	Second	1987	47,948	20,764	43%
	General	1987	32,731	14,625	45%
	Teacher	1987	5,260	2,885	55%
	Vocational	1987	9,957	3,254	33%
Gambia	Second	1984	15,913	4,802	30%
	General	1987	15,520	4,512	29%
	Teacher	1985	367	127	35%
	Vocational	1984	1,107	423	38%
Ghana	Second	1987	862,914	337,834	39%
	General	1987	810,651	321,541	40%
	Teacher	1987	16,974	7,538	44%
	Vocational	1987	35,289	8,755	25%

[Continued]

★ 201 ★

Worldwide Second Level Enrollment - Part I
[Continued]

Country	Type of Education[1]	Year	Pupils Enrolled		
			Total	Female	%Female
Guinea	Second	1986	83,024	21,068	25%
	General	1987	74,633	17,520	23%
	Teacher	1986	936	380	41%
	Vocational	1986	5,550	1,850	33%
Guinea-Bissau	Second	1986	6,450	1,621	25%
	General	1986	5,665	1,549	27%
	Teacher	1986	434	49	11%
	Vocational	1986	351	23	7%
Kenya	Second	1987	544,745	222,104	41%
	General	1987	522,261	214,217	41%
	Teacher	1987	16,883	6,810	40%
	Vocational	1987	5,601	1,079	19%
Lesotho	Second	1984	34,732	20,753	60%
	General	1984	33,564	20,142	60%
	Teacher	1975	304	221	73%
	Vocational	1984	1,168	611	52%
Liberia	Second	1980	54,623	15,343	28%
	General	1980	51,666	14,632	28%
	Teacher	1980	635	84	13%
	Vocational	1980	2,322	627	27%
Libyan Arab Jamahiriya	Second	1982	340,703	141,077	41%
	General	1982	280,208	113,522	41%
	Teacher	1982	32,132	21,303	66%
	Vocational	1982	28,363	6,252	22%
Madagascar	Second	1987	366,455	167,290	46%
	General	1987	350,929	161,718	46%
	Teacher	1987	1,008	341	34%
	Vocational	1987	14,518	5,231	36%
Malawi	Second	1987	27,589	10,045	36%
	General	1987	26,645	9,953	37%
	Vocational	1987	944	92	10%
Mali	Second	1987	66,431	19,238	29%
	General	1987	56,618	16,725	30%
	Teacher	1987	2,177	454	21%
	Vocational	1987	7,636	2,059	27%
Mauritania	Second	1987	39,837	11,706	29%
	General	1987	37,308	11,145	30%

[Continued]

★ 201 ★

Worldwide Second Level Enrollment - Part I

[Continued]

Country	Type of Education[1]	Year	Pupils Enrolled		
			Total	Female	%Female
	Teacher	1987	729	191	26%
	Vocational	1987	1,800	370	21%
Mauritius	Second	1987	71,922	34,281	48%
	General	1987	71,059	33,970	48%
	Teacher	1975	589	245	42%
	Vocational	1987	863	311	36%
Morocco	Second	1987	1,347,202	534,843	40%
	General	1987	1,329,960	529,409	40%
	Teacher	1975	3,953	1,716	43%
	Vocational	1987	17,242	5,434	32%
Mozambique	Second	1987	116,928	38,690	33%
	General	1987	103,322	36,150	35%
	Teacher	1987	4,288	878	20%
	Vocational	1987	9,318	1,662	18%
Niger	Second	1980	38,861	11,334	29%
	General	1985	51,448	14,398	28%
	Teacher	1981	1,062	373	35%
	Vocational	1985	615	72	12%
Nigeria	Second	1982	3,393,186	867,142	26%
	General	1982	3,009,751	798,447	27%
	Teacher	1982	296,439	60,973	21%
	Vocational	1982	86,996	7,722	9%
Reunion	Second	1986	69,585	37,164	53%
	General	1986	51,826	29,478	57%
	Vocational	1986	17,759	7,686	43%
Rwanda	Second	1987	50,631	20,613	41%
	General	1987	9,978	2,560	26%
	Teacher	1987	7,190	3,216	45%
	Vocational	1987	33,463	14,837	44%
St. Helena	Second	1985	513	252	49%
	General	1985	470	245	52%
	Teacher	1985	11	7	64%
	Vocational	1983	31	1	3%
Sao Tome and Principe	Second	1987	6,452	3,055	47%
	General	1987	6,171	2,922	47%
	Teacher	1987	188	114	61%
	Vocational	1987	93	19	20%

[Continued]

★ 201 ★

Worldwide Second Level Enrollment - Part I
[Continued]

Country	Type of Education[1]	Year	Total	Female	%Female
			Pupils Enrolled		
Senegal	Second	1987	146,310	48,865	33%
	General	1987	140,950	47,332	34%
	Teacher	1987	576	102	18%
	Vocational	1987	4,784	1,431	30%
Seychelles	Second	1988	4,048	1,856	46%
	General	1988	2,643	1,254	47%
	Teacher	1987	235	143	61%
	Vocational	1987	1,177	472	40%
Sierra Leone	Second	1975	50,478	15,991	32%
	General	1982	81,759	26,048	32%
	Teacher	1982	2,130	840	39%
	Vocational	1975	799	47	6%
Somalia	Second	1985	44,335	15,300	35%
	General	1985	37,181	13,602	37%
	Teacher	1984	613	266	43%
	Vocational	1985	7,154	1,698	24%
Sudan	Second	1985	556,587	235,400	42%
	General	1985	525,533	226,445	43%
	Teacher	1985	5,444	2,851	52%
	Vocational	1985	25,610	6,104	24%
Swaziland	Second	1987	33,981	16,732	49%
	General	1987	32,945	16,419	50%
	Teacher	1987	569	205	36%
	Vocational	1987	467	108	23%
Togo	Second	1987	115,295	28,383	25%
	General	1987	108,557	26,414	24%
	Teacher	1984	58	58	100%
	Vocational	1987	6,738	1,969	29%
Tunisia	Second	1987	480,245	199,461	42%
	General	1987	385,680	165,592	43%
	Teacher	1987	3,839	2,710	71%
	Vocational	1987	90,726	31,159	34%
Uganda	Second	1986	213,733	73,611	34%
	General	1986	196,012	68,500	35%
	Teacher	1986	11,229	4,379	39%
	Vocational	1986	6,492	732	11%
United Republic of Tanzania	Second	1987	113,546	44,724	39%

[Continued]

★ 201 ★

Worldwide Second Level Enrollment - Part I
[Continued]

Country	Type of Education[1]	Year	Pupils Enrolled		
			Total	Female	%Female
	General	1988	127,703	45,000	35%
	Teacher	1987	9,500	3,529	37%
Zaire	Second	1986	983,334	296,747	30%
	General	1983	1,570,887	445,573	28%
	Teacher	1983	365,823	109,867	30%
	Vocational	1986	227,007	71,062	31%
Zambia	Second	1982	110,416	39,085	35%
	General	1985	131,502	48,366	37%
	Teacher	1984	3,770	1,517	40%
	Vocational	1982	2,316	592	26%
Zimbabwe	Second	1986	537,348	216,494	40%
	General	1988	572,892	267,700	47%
	Vocational	1986	256	32	13%
North America					
Antigua and Barbuda	Second	1975	6,827	-	-
	General	1983	4,104	2,328	57%
	Teacher	1975	96	77	80%
	Vocational	1975	102	-	-
Bahamas	Second	1986	29,765	15,257	51%
	General	1986	29,765	15,257	51%
	Teacher	1975	731	-	-
	Vocational	1975	1,823	-	-
Barbados	Second	1984	28,695	14,445	50%
	General	1984	28,695	14,445	50%
Belize	Second	1986	7,560	4,004	53%
	General	1986	7,233	3,816	53%
	Teacher	1986	234	173	74%
	Vocational	1986	93	15	16%
Bermuda	General	1984	4,741	2,391	50%
British Virgin Islands	Second	1983	1,323	762	58%
	General	1984	1,078	593	55%
	Vocational	1983	309	203	66%
Canada	Second	1987	2,242,938	1,095,187	49%
	General	1987	2,242,938	1,095,187	49%

[Continued]

★ 201 ★

Worldwide Second Level Enrollment - Part I
[Continued]

Country	Type of Education[1]	Year	Pupils Enrolled		
			Total	Female	%Female
Cayman Islands	Second	1980	2,075	1,001	48%
	General	1980	2,075	1,001	48%
Costa Rica	Second	1987	116,928	59,219	51%
	General	1987	90,093	46,090	51%
	Vocational	1987	26,835	13,129	49%
Cuba	Second	1987	1,143,137	582,508	51%
	General	1987	775,345	403,989	52%
	Teacher	1987	33,004	25,487	77%
	Vocational	1987	334,788	153,032	46%
Dominica	Second	1986	6,308	3,400	54%
	General	1987	6,150	3,221	52%
	Teacher	1975	43	32	74%
	Vocational	1986	70	65	93%
Dominican Republic	Second	1985	463,511	-	-
	General	1985	438,922	240,898	55%
	Teacher	1986	3,602	2,536	70%
	Vocational	1985	21,156	-	-
El Salvador	Second	1987	99,311	52,072	52%
	General	1987	30,716	14,729	48%
	Teacher	1987	477	472	99%
	Vocational	1987	68,118	36,871	54%
Grenada	Second	1986	6,437	3,729	58%
	General	1986	6,437	3,729	58%
Guadeloupe	Second	1986	52,040	27,638	53%
	General	1986	39,897	21,448	54%
	Vocational	1986	12,143	6,190	51%
Guatemala	Second	1980	171,903	76,918	45%
	General	1980	119,879	51,299	43%
	Teacher	1980	22,256	13,880	62%
	Vocational	1980	29,768	11,739	39%
Haiti	Second	1985	143,758	-	-
	General	1985	139,422	65,367	47%
	Teacher	1985	867	588	68%
	Vocational	1985	3,469	-	-
Honduras	Second	1984	164,453	88,374	54%
	General	1984	112,956	57,065	51%
	Teacher	1984	10,032	6,882	69%

[Continued]

★ 201 ★

Worldwide Second Level Enrollment - Part I
[Continued]

Country	Type of Education[1]	Year	Pupils Enrolled		
			Total	Female	%Female
	Vocational	1984	41,465	24,427	59%
Jamaica	Second	1983	233,354	119,724	51%
	General	1986	235,928	120,677	51%
	Vocational	1983	8,508	4,228	50%
Martinique	Second	1983	46,709	25,460	55%
	General	1983	31,912	18,001	56%
	Vocational	1983	14m797	7,459	50%
Mexico	Second	1987	6,806,073	3,324,400	49%
	General	1987	5,933,355	2,785,217	47%
	Teacher	1986	27,110	20,794	77%
	Vocational	1987	872,718	539,183	62%
Montserrat	Second	1980	887	-	-
	General	1981	871	453	52%
	Vocational	1975	53	24	45%
Netherlands Antilles	Second	1981	21,249	11,197	53%
	General	1982	11,032	6,881	62%
	Teacher	1981	34	34	100%
	Vocational	1982	10,088	4,249	42%
Nicaragua	Second	1987	177,202	116,743	66%
	General	1987	132,733	83,273	63%
	Teacher	1987	11,228	9,451	84%
	Vocational	1987	33,241	24,019	72%
Panama	Second	1986	187,312	97,514	52%
	General	1986	135,886	69,448	51%
	Teacher	1986	1,160	787	68%
	Vocational	1986	50,266	27,279	54%
Puerto Rico	Second	1981	191,015	-	-
St. Kitts and Nevis	Second	1984	4,197	2,028	48%
	General	1986	4,153	2,102	51%
	Vocational	1984	159	43	27%
St. Lucia	Second	1986	7,013	4,269	61%
	General	1986	6,423	3,679	57%
	Teacher	1975	156	-	-
	Vocational	1986	590	590	100%
St. Pierre and Miquelon	Second	1986	800	421	53%

[Continued]

★ 201 ★

Worldwide Second Level Enrollment - Part I
[Continued]

Country	Type of Education[1]	Year	Pupils Enrolled		
			Total	Female	%Female
	General	1986	548	293	53%
	Vocational	1986	252	128	51%
St. Vincent and the Grenadines	Second	1987	7,237	4,352	60%
	General	1987	6,857	4,116	60%
	Teacher	1987	110	68	62%
	Vocational	1987	270	168	62%
Trinidad and Tobago	Second	1984	92,752	46,497	50%
	General	1987	98,884	49,349	50%
	Vocational	1986	755	228	30%
Turks and Caicos Islands	Second	1984	707	-	-
	General	1984	707	-	-
U.S. Virgin Islands	Second	1985	7,948	-	-
South America					
Argentina	Second	1987	1,980,815	1,037,248	52%
	General	1987	773,615	489,348	65%
	Vocational	1987	1,207,200	547,900	45%
Bolivia	Second	1987	218,268	101,258	46%
Brazil	Second	1980	2,819,182	1,515,859	54%
	General	1975	882,059	563,427	64%
	Teacher	1975	271,337	246,838	91%
	Vocational	1975	782,507	222,831	28%
Chile	Second	1988	735,701	374,631	51%
	General	1988	601,760	310,138	52%
	Vocational	1988	133,941	64,493	48%
Colombia	Second	1986	2,136,239	1,067,794	50%
	General	1986	1,617,388	806,384	50%
	Teacher	1986	74,287	39,819	54%
	Vocational	1986	444,564	221,591	50%
Ecuador	Second	1987	771,928	389,074	50%
	General	1987	504,481	240,774	48%
	Teacher	1987	6,597	4,622	70%
	Vocational	1987	260,850	143,678	55%

[Continued]

★ 201 ★

Worldwide Second Level Enrollment - Part I
[Continued]

Country	Type of Education[1]	Year	Pupils Enrolled		
			Total	Female	%Female
Falkland Islands (Malvinas)	Second	1980	90	50	56%
	General	1980	90	50	56%
French Guiana	Second	1983	8,485	4,435	52%
	General	1983	5,862	3,164	54%
	Vocational	1983	2,623	1,271	48%
Guyana	Second	1975	71,327	36,021	51%
	General	1981	73,762	37,664	51%
	Vocational	1975	5,001	2,491	50%
Paraguay	Second	1975	75,424	37,363	50%
	General	1986	140,656	69,613	49%
	Vocational	1975	5,376	1,256	23%
Peru	Second	1980	1,203,116	547,393	45%
	General	1985	1,427,261	667,399	47%
	Vocational	1980	51,368	20,613	40%
Suriname	Second	1986	35,878	19,381	54%
	General	1986	24,411	13,816	57%
	Teacher	1986	1,943	1,831	94%
	Vocational	1986	9,524	3,734	39%
Uruguay	Second	1980	148,294	78,487	53%
	General	1980	125,438	72,390	58%
	Vocational	1986	41,251	15,786	38%
Venezuela	Second	1986	1,058,058	575,362	54%
	General	1986	1,003,977	546,459	54%
	Teacher	1975	16,445	14,708	89%
	Vocational	1986	54,081	28,903	53%

Source: Selected from "Education at the second level (general, teacher-training and vocational): teachers and pupils," *Statistical Yearbook*, p. 3-146/3-202 (Paris: UNESCO, 1989). Also in source: data for various years; teaching staff (see *Labor and Employment: Teachers*). See *Introduction* for explanation of levels of education. *Notes:* 1. Second=Total Second Level; General=General; Teacher=Teacher Training; Vocational=Vocational Training.

★ 202 ★

Worldwide Second Level Enrollment - Part II

Pupils enrolled at the second level of education, number and percent female, by type of education, by country, latest available year.

Country	Type of Education[1]	Year	Total	Female	%Female
			Pupils Enrolled		
Asia					
Afghanistan	Second	1975	93,497	10,505	11%
	General	1986	89,448	29,605	33%
	Vocational	1975	5,960	651	11%
Bahrain	Second	1987	40,540	19,637	48%
	General	1987	33,246	17,369	52%
	Vocational	1987	7,294	2,268	31%
Bangladesh	Second	1985	3,125,219	875,353	28%
	General	1988	3,308,347	1,046,377	32%
	Teacher	1988	6,893	4,122	60%
	Vocational	1985	19,045	995	5%
Bhutan	Second	1984	5,872	1,026	17%
	General	1988	3,456	997	29%
	Teacher	1984	94	47	50%
	Vocational	1984	2,170	105	5%
Brunei Darussalam	Second	1987	17,527	8,837	50%
	General	1987	16,252	8,426	52%
	Teacher	1987	260	160	62%
	Vocational	1987	1,015	251	25%
Burma	Second	1983	1,234,000	-	-
	General	1975	917,896	406,237	44%
	Teacher	1975	4,890	2,827	58%
China	Second	1987	54,031,100	22,198,800	41%
	General	1987	49,481,100	20,186,200	41%
	Teacher	1987	651,300	327,500	50%
	Vocational	1987	3,898,700	1,685,100	43%
Cyprus	Second	1987	42,191	20,866	49%
	General	1987	38,709	20,397	53%
	Vocational	1987	3,482	469	13%
Democratic Yemen	Second	1983	34,803	10,327	30%
	General	1983	29,201	9,592	33%
	Teacher	1983	1,261	229	18%
	Vocational	1983	4,341	506	12%

[Continued]

★ 202 ★

Worldwide Second Level Enrollment - Part II
[Continued]

Country	Type of Education[1]	Year	Pupils Enrolled		
			Total	Female	%Female
Hong Kong	Second	1987	458,444	222,251	49%
	General	1987	412,501	210,766	51%
	Vocational	1987	45,943	14,485	31%
India	Second	1980	30,531,881	10,006,469	33%
	General	1986	46,348,795	15,589,970	34%
	Teacher	1980	15,349	8,300	54%
	Vocational	1983	585,579	172,635	29%
Indonesia	Second	1984	8,722,310	3,708,670	43%
	General	1984	7,673,278	3,267,776	43%
	Teacher	1984	280,313	167,214	60%
	Vocational	1984	768,719	273,680	36%
Iran, Islamic Republic	Second	1987	3,843,177	1,518,895	40%
	General	1987	3,640,541	1,472,871	40%
	Teacher	1985	1,477	68	5%
	Vocational	1987	202,636	46,024	23%
Iraq	Second	1987	1,161,578	433,884	37%
	General	1987	985,123	376,123	38%
	Teacher	1987	27,965	16,711	60%
	Vocational	1987	148,490	41,050	28%
Israel	Second	1987	279,130	142,650	51%
	General	1987	173,617	95,196	55%
	Vocational	1987	105,513	47,454	45%
Japan	Second	1987	11,456,437	5,634,924	49%
	General	1986	9,834,831	4,884,020	50%
	Vocational	1986	1,415,421	657,843	46%
Jordan	Second	1987	357,475	172,135	48%
	General	1987	323,942	158,086	49%
	Vocational	1987	33,533	14,049	42%
Korea, Republic of	Second	1988	4,822,097	2,284,403	47%
	General	1988	3,967,207	1,843,510	46%
	Vocational	1988	854,890	440,893	52%
Kuwait	Second	1986	245,697	116,114	47%
	General	1986	244,843	116,022	47%
	Vocational	1987	836	80	10%
Lao People's Democratic Republic	Second	1985	113,630	46,490	41%
	General	1985	97,197	41,033	42%
	Teacher	1985	9,634	3,796	39%

[Continued]

★ 202 ★
Worldwide Second Level Enrollment - Part II
[Continued]

Country	Type of Education[1]	Year	Pupils Enrolled		
			Total	Female	%Female
	Vocational	1985	6,799	1,661	24%
Lebanon	General	1984	230,934	115,526	50%
	Teacher	1980	1,663	1,316	79%
	Vocational	1984	37,036	14,058	38%
Malaysia	Second	1987	1,490,637	731,379	49%
	General	1987	1,470,796	726,248	49%
	Vocational	1987	19,841	5,131	26%
Maldives	General	1975	459	255	56%
	Vocational	1983	412	-	-
Mongolia	Second	1982	256,700	135,100	53%
	General	1986	267,805	138,185	52%
	Teacher	1982	2,300	1,900	83%
	Vocational	1986	25,036	11,835	47%
Nepal	Second	1984	455,401	104,509	23%
Oman	Second	1987	58,527	22,815	39%
	General	1987	57,777	22,745	39%
	Teacher	1985	161	63	39%
	Vocational	1987	750	70	9%
Pakistan	Second	1987	3,190,654	884,985	28%
	General	1987	3,127,668	872,871	28%
	Teacher	1986	10,735	2,204	21%
	Vocational	1986	52,410	7,226	14%
Philippines	Second	1988	3,494,460	1,702,850	49%
Qatar	Second	1987	24,712	12,702	51%
	General	1987	23,181	12,702	53%
	Teacher	1975	324	269	83%
Saudi Arabia	Second	1986	654,202	255,766	39%
	General	1986	630,251	249,655	40%
	Teacher	1986	11,649	6,111	52%
	Vocational	1985	11,905	1,228	10%
Singapore	Second	1984	197,183	97,799	50%
	General	1984	187,764	94,968	51%
	Vocational	1984	9,419	2,831	30%
Sri Lanka	Second	1976	1,088,089	554,442	51%

[Continued]

★ 202 ★

Worldwide Second Level Enrollment - Part II
[Continued]

Country	Type of Education[1]	Year	Pupils Enrolled		
			Total	Female	%Female
	General	1986	1,526,086	792,829	52%
	Teacher	1976	6,809	3,946	58%
	Vocational	1976	4,778	1,598	33%
Syrian Arab Republic	Second	1987	925,381	374,736	40%
	General	1987	868,779	358,286	41%
	Teacher	1980	174	88	60%
	Vocational	1987	56,602	16,450	29%
Thailand	Second	1975	1,193,741	523,203	44%
	General	1980	1,617,465	740,077	46%
	Teacher	1980	5,388	2,746	51%
	Vocational	1975	191,066	85,798	45%
Turkey	Second	1987	3,288,309	1,182,819	36%
	General	1987	2,556,630	959,253	38%
	Teacher	1987	10,841	4,001	37%
	Vocational	1987	720,838	219,565	30%
United Arab Emirates	Second	1987	76,404	37,643	49%
	General	1987	75,813	37,643	50%
Viet-Nam	Second	1976	3,200,912	1,563,012	49%
	General	1985	4,022,858	1,902,929	47%
	Teacher	1980	20,397	4,601	23%
	Vocational	1976	66,553	22,992	35%
Yemen	Second	1986	194,982	23,357	12%
	General	1987	222,025	23,930	11%
	Teacher	1986	12,806	3,238	25%
	Vocational	1986	2,748	214	8%
Europe					
Albania	Second	1987	188,465	84,807	45%
	General	1987	53,414	29,757	56%
	Teacher	1987	2,254	1,511	67%
	Vocational	1987	132,797	56,539	40%
Andorra	Second	1982	2,516	1,271	51%
	General	1982	2,516	1,271	51%
Austria	Second	1987	626,757	311,316	50%
	General	1987	454,848	219,720	48%

[Continued]

★ 202 ★

Worldwide Second Level Enrollment - Part II

[Continued]

Country	Type of Education[1]	Year	Pupils Enrolled		
			Total	Female	%Female
	Teacher	1987	8,451	5,447	64%
	Vocational	1987	163,458	86,149	53%
Belgium	Second	1987	805,647	395,084	49%
	General	1987	433,264	220,326	51%
	Vocational	1987	372,383	174,758	47%
Bulgaria	Second	1987	389,445	190,538	49%
	General	1987	167,845	106,750	64%
	Vocational	1987	221,600	83,788	38%
Czechoslovakia	Second	1987	351,199	220,741	63%
	General	1987	136,243	83,700	61%
	Teacher	1987	8,006	7,848	98%
	Vocational	1987	206,950	129,193	62%
Denmark	Second	1986	488,775	238,451	49%
	General	1986	332,264	170,165	51%
	Vocational	1986	156,511	68,286	44%
Finland	Second	1987	398,904	210,613	53%
	General	1987	287,490	151,732	53%
	Teacher	1987	1,061	758	71%
	Vocational	1987	110,353	58,123	53%
France	Second	1987	5,383,946	2,724,198	51%
	General	1987	4,141,825	2,152,570	52%
	Vocational	1987	1,242,121	571,628	46%
German Democratic Republic	Second	1987	1,425,385	682,956	48%
	General	19087	1,061,015	526,111	50%
	Vocational	1987	364,370	156,845	43%
Germany, Federal Republic	Second	1986	6,777,614	3,247,841	48%
	General	1986	4,304,207	2,125,103	49%
	Vocational	1986	2,473,407	1,122,738	45%
Gibraltar	Second	1984	1,806	885	49%
	General	1984	1,749	881	50%
	Vocational	1984	57	4	7%
Greece	Second	1985	813,534	387,134	48%
	General	1985	704,119	355,389	50%
	Vocational	1985	109,415	31,745	29%

[Continued]

★ 202 ★

Worldwide Second Level Enrollment - Part II
[Continued]

Country	Type of Education[1]	Year	Pupils Enrolled		
			Total	Female	%Female
Hungary	Second	1987	426,932	209,265	49%
	General	1987	105,976	69,461	66%
	Teacher	1987	5,045	5,045	100%
	Vocational	1987	315,911	134,759	43%
Iceland	Second	1985	27,856	13,210	47%
	General	1985	20,097	10,180	51%
	Teacher	1985	297	249	84%
	Vocational	1985	7,462	2,781	37%
Ireland	Second	1985	338,256	173,158	51%
	General	1985	315,584	158,583	50%
	Vocational	1985	22,672	14,575	64%
Italy	Second	1984	5,338,731	2,594,545	49%
	General	1984	3,395,935	16,52,985	49%
	Teacher	1984	208,750	196,071	94%
	Vocational	1984	1,734,046	745,489	43%
Luxembourg	Second	1985	25,656	12,438	48%
	General	1986	7,772	4,224	54%
	Teacher	1985	86	67	78%
	Vocational	1986	17,099	7,854	46%
Malta	Second	1987	28,806	13,733	48%
	General	1987	22,341	11,842	53%
	Vocational	1987	6,465	1,891	29%
Monaco	Vocational	1981	753	380	50%
Netherlands	Second	1986	1,393,574	672,065	48%
	General	1986	775,826	409,394	53%
	Teacher	1986	85	83	98%
	Vocational	1986	617,663	262,588	43%
Norway	Second	1986	378,871	189,629	50%
	General	1986	273,925	138,696	51%
	Teacher	1986	668	610	91%
	Vocational	1986	104,278	50,323	48%
Poland	Second	1987	1,688,997	849,340	50%
	General	1987	372,604	269,901	72%
	Teacher	1987	26,352	23,946	91%
	Vocational	1987	1,290,041	555,493	43%
Portugal	Second	1983	489,696	261,224	53%
	General	1984	529,855	284,259	54%

[Continued]

★ 202 ★

Worldwide Second Level Enrollment - Part II
[Continued]

Country	Type of Education[1]	Year	Pupils Enrolled		
			Total	Female	%Female
	Teacher	1975	9,166	7,841	86%
	Vocational	1975	127,317	47,068	37%
Romania	Second	1985	1,537,548	711,018	46%
	General	1987	102,553	71,724	70%
	Teacher	1987	4,851	4,588	95%
	Vocational	1985	1,429,994	634,916	44%
San Marino	Second	1987	1,207	585	48%
	General	1987	1,093	567	52%
	Vocational	1987	114	18	16%
Spain	Second	1986	4,660,801	2,360,611	51%
	General	1986	3,440,786	1,739,950	51%
	Vocational	1986	1,220,015	620,661	51%
Sweden	Second	1987	619,860	306,488	49%
	General	1987	399,891	203,915	51%
	Teacher	1984	115	49	43%
	Vocational	1987	219,969	102,573	47%
Switzerland	Second	1987	388,326	198,265	51%
	General	1987	352,627	175,024	50%
	Teacher	1987	8,108	6,594	81%
	Vocational	1987	27,591	16,647	60%
United Kingdom	Second	1986	4,688,000	2,319,000	49%
	General	1986	4,270,000	2,092,000	49%
	Vocational	1986	418,000	227,000	54%
Yugoslavia	Second	1987	2,358,064	1,123,658	48%
	General	1987	1,653,929	801,573	48%
	Teacher	1987	25,330	21,832	86%
	Vocational	1987	678,805	300,253	44%
Oceania					
American Samoa	Second	1987	3,210	1,557	49%
	General	1987	3,053	1,549	51%
	Vocational	1987	157	8	5%
Australia	Second	1987	1,295,337	642,528	50%
	General	1987	1,295,337	642,528	50%
Cook Islands	General	1985	1,595	847	53%

[Continued]

★ 202 ★

Worldwide Second Level Enrollment - Part II
[Continued]

Country	Type of Education[1]	Year	Pupils Enrolled		
			Total	Female	%Female
	Teacher	1988	22	20	91%
Fiji	Second	1986	46,457	23,203	50%
	General	1986	42,216	21,029	50%
	Teacher	1983	256	119	46%
	Vocational	1986	4,241	2,174	51%
French Polynesia	Second	1986	17,878	9,822	55%
	General	1986	13,765	7,819	57%
	Teacher	1975	111	85	77%
	Vocational	1986	4,113	2,003	49%
Guam	Second	1983	13,375	6,457	48%
	General	1983	12,507	6,063	48%
	Vocational	1983	868	394	45%
Kiribati	Second	1988	2,601	1,283	49%
	General	1988	2,191	1,132	52%
	Teacher	1988	60	24	40%
	Vocational	1988	350	127	36%
Nauru	Second	1985	482	242	50%
	General	1985	465	234	50%
	Vocational	1985	17	8	47%
New Caledonia	Second	1987	19,417	10,139	52%
	General	1987	13,540	7,361	54%
	Teacher	1975	135	85	63%
	Vocational	1987	5,877	2,778	47%
New Zealand	Second	1987	343,830	170,674	50%
	General	1987	340,908	168,412	49%
	Vocational	1987	2,922	2,262	77%
Niue	Second	1988	281	130	46%
	General	1988	281	130	46%
Pacific Islands	Second	1975	7,951	3,500	44%
	General	1975	7,951	3,500	44%
Papua New Guinea	Second	1975	41,391	11,731	28%
	General	1987	53,752	19,564	36%
	Teacher	1987	53,752	19,564	36%
	Vocational	1975	9,639	1,637	17%
Samoa	Second	1980	19,785	9,691	49%

[Continued]

★ 202 ★

Worldwide Second Level Enrollment - Part II
[Continued]

Country	Type of Education[1]	Year	Pupils Enrolled Total	Pupils Enrolled Female	Pupils Enrolled %Female
	General	1986	20,168	10,108	50%
	Teacher	1983	314	186	59%
	Vocational	1980	264	108	41%
Solomon Islands	Second	1986	6,615	2,483	38%
	General	1986	5,336	2,016	38%
	Teacher	1986	135	46	34%
	Vocational	1986	1,144	421	37%
Tokelau	Second	1983	488	245	50%
	General	1983	108	56	52%
	Vocational	1983	380	189	50%
Tonga	Second	1986	13,527	6,679	49%
	General	1986	13,120	6,469	49%
	Teacher	1986	113	44	39%
	Vocational	1986	294	166	56%
Tuvalu	General	1987	293	168	57%
Vanuatu	Second	1983	2,904	1,093	38%
	General	1983	2,186	920	42%
	Teacher	1983	85	35	41%
	Vocational	1983	633	138	22%
USSR					
USSR	Second	1987	21,138,900	-	-
Byelorussian SSR	Second	1987	720,700	-	-
Ukrainian SSR	Second	1987	3,466,800	-	-

Source: Selected from "Education at the second level (general, teacher-training and vocational): teachers and pupils," *Statistical Yearbook,* p. 3-146/3-202 (Paris: UNESCO, 1989). Also in source: data for various years; teaching staff (see *Labor and Employment: Teachers*). See *Introduction* for explanation of levels of education. *Notes:* 1. Second=Total Second Level; General=General; Teacher=Teacher Training; Vocational=Vocational Training.

Head Start

★ 203 ★

Head Start

Growth of the Head Start program, inception to 1994. Legislation enacted by the 101st Congress in 1990 resulted in the changes shown in the Head Start program.

Number of eligible children admitted to Head Start program, 1964-1990	25% (approx)
Number of eligible children who can be enrolled immediately following passage of legislation:	40%
Number of eligible children who can be enrolled by 1994	100%

Source: "A Huge Gain in the Poverty War," *New York Times,* October 31, 1990, p. A18. Primary sources: Children's Defense Fund; House Education and Labor Committee. Also in source: a discussion of new medical and child-care legislation enacted by Congress; details of funding for Head Start.

High School

★ 204 ★

High School Completion at Ages 25-29

Percentage of 25-to 29-year-olds who have completed 12 years of school or more, 1971-1987 (selected years).

Year	Female	Male	Both
	Percentage		
1971	76.4	78.1	77.2
1973	79.8	80.6	80.2
1974	80.8	88.8	84.6
1975	81.8	84.5	83.1
1976	83.5	86.0	84.7
1977	84.2	86.6	85.4
1978	84.6	86.0	85.3
1979	84.9	86.3	85.6
1980	85.5	85.4	85.4
1981	86.1	86.5	86.3
1982	86.1	86.4	86.2
1983	86.0	86.0	86.0
1984	86.3	85.6	85.9
1985	86.4	85.9	86.2

[Continued]

★ 204 ★

High School Completion at Ages 25-29
[Continued]

Year	Female	Male	Both
1986	86.4	85.9	86.1
1987	86.4	85.5	86.0

Source: Selected from "High School Completion at Ages 25-29," *The Condition of Education 1990, Volume 1: Elementary and Secondary Education,* p. 22 (Washington, D.C.: National Center for Education Statistics, 1990). Primary source: U.S. Department of Commerce, Bureau of the Census, *Current Population Reports,* Series P-20, "Educational Attainment in the United States: March...," various years. Also in source: percentage White, Black, and Hispanic.

★ 205 ★

High School Courses Taken

High school courses taken by persons age 16 and over who have completed at least 12 years of school, by sex and race: Spring 1984.

Courses taken	Total	Sex		Race	
		Women	Men	White	Black
Persons[1]	129,856	67,522	62,334	114,366	12,180
Courses[2]					
Algebra	79.1%	76.8%	81.6%	79.3%	76.1%
Trigonometry or geometry	55.0%	50.3%	60.1%	55.6%	46.5%
Chemistry or physics	48.0%	42.3%	54.2%	47.5%	48.6%
English, 3 years or more	93.5%	94.1%	92.8%	93.6%	94.3%
Foreign language, 2 years or more	43.8%	48.1%	39.1%	44.2%	36.6%
Industrial arts, shop, or home economics, 2 years or more	56.9%	55.7%	58.1%	55.7%	67.6%
Business courses, 2 years or more	41.8%	56.7%	25.7%	41.9%	42.6%

Source: Selected from "High school courses taken by persons age 16 and over, by sex, race, and age: Spring 1984," *Digest of Education Statistics,* Table 118, p. 129 (Washington, D.C.: National Center for Education Statistics, 1989). Primary source: U.S. Department of Commerce, Bureau of the Census, *Current Population Reports,* Series P-70, No. 11, "Educational Background and Economic Status: Spring 1984." (This table was prepared October 1987.) Also in source: courses taken by age; number of persons completing courses. Data are based on sample surveys of the civilian noninstitutional population. *Notes:* 1. Number of people, in thousands. 2. Percentage of persons completing courses.

★ 206 ★

High School Dropouts

Percentage of high school dropouts among persons 14 to 34 years old, race/ethnicity: 1970, 1975, 1980, and 1986.

Year, race/ethnicity	Total 14-34	Female 14-34	Male 14-34
October 1970			
All races	17.0%	17.7%	16.2%
White[1]	15.2%	16.0%	14.4%
Black[1]	30.0%	29.5%	30.4%
October 1975			
All races	14.1%	15.0%	13.2%
White[1]	12.8%	13.5%	12.1%

[Continued]

★ 206 ★

High School Dropouts
[Continued]

Year, race/ethnicity	Total 14-34	Female 14-34	Male 14-34
Black[1]	23.4%	24.7%	21.9%
Hispanic origin[2]	33.0%	35.7%	29.9%
October 1980			
All races	13.0%	12.8%	13.2%
White[1]	12.1%	11.8%	12.4%
Black[1]	18.8%	18.7%	19.0%
Hispanic origin[2]	35.2%	34.9%	35.6%
October 1986			
All races	11.9%	11.4%	12.4%
White[1]	11.3%	10.6%	12.1%
Black[1]	15.5%	15.5%	15.5%
Hispanic origin[2]	32.2%	30.4%	33.9%

Source: Selected from "Percentage of high school dropouts among persons 14 to 34 years old, by age, race/ethnicity, and sex: October 1970, 1975, 1980, and 1986," *Digest of Education Statistics*, p. 106 (Washington, D.C.: National Center for Education Statistics, 1989). Primary source: U.S. Bureau of the Census, *Current Population Reports*, Series P-20, Nos. 222,303,362,392,409, and 429; and unpublished data. Also in source: data by age. Dropouts are persons who are not enrolled in school and who are not high school graduates. Data are based upon sample surveys of the civilian noninstitutional population. *Notes:* 1. Includes persons of Hispanic origin. 2. Persons of Hispanic origin may be of any race.

★ 207 ★

High School Mathematics Achievement

Advanced mathematics credits for high school seniors, by race and sex (in percent), 1982.

Number of credits	Black		White	
	Female	Male	Female	Male
0	33.1%	30.0%	14.2%	16.9%
1	20.1%	23.0%	19.3%	16.3%
2	20.3%	17.7%	24.6%	18.9%
3	15.5%	16.5%	22.9%	21.9%
4	8.4%	11.4%	15.7%	21.6%
5	2.6%	1.4%	3.3%	4.4%
Sample size	616	538	3,277	3,030

Source: "Advanced Mathematics Credits for High School Seniors, by Race and Sex (in percent), 1982," *A Common Destiny: Blacks and American Society*, 1989, p. 351 (Washington, D.C.: National Academy Press, 1989). Primary source: Lyle V. Jones, "The influence on mathematics test scores, by ethnicity and sex, of prior achievement and high school mathematics courses," *Journal for Research in Mathematics Education* 18:180-186 (1987).

★ 208 ★

High School Students Who Work

Percent of high school students 16-24 years old who were employed: 1970-1989.

Year	Female employed		Male employed	
	Total	Full time	Total	Full time
1970	27.3%	1.7%	30.9%	3.7%
1971	26.1%	1.3%	29.8%	2.9%
1972	27.5%	1.7%	32.0%	4.1%
1973	31.5%	1.8%	35.0%	5.0%
1974	30.9%	2.0%	33.6%	4.6%
1975	30.2%	2.1%	30.0%	3.5%
1976	30.4%	1.6%	31.1%	3.5%
1977	31.2%	2.1%	35.4%	4.1%
1978	35.4%	2.3%	35.6%	4.0%
1979	35.5%	2.3%	35.4%	3.6%
1980	33.2%	1.7%	32.5%	2.9%
1981	29.5%	1.5%	31.2%	2.5%
1982	29.0%	1.3%	25.7%	1.7%
1983	28.2%	1.6%	26.1%	2.4%
1984	30.1%	0.9%	29.4%	2.3%
1985	30.6%	1.0%	29.8%	2.1%
1986	34.6%	1.3%	30.9%	2.4%
1987	35.4%	1.6%	33.6%	2.5%
1988	35.7%	1.5%	34.6%	2.9%
1989	37.2%	1.8%	33.2%	3.5%

Source: Selected from "Working While in High School," *The Condition of Education 1990: Volume 1: Elementary and Secondary Education*, p. 66 (Washington, D.C.: National Center for Education Statistics, 1990). Primary source: U.S. Department of Labor, Bureau of Labor Statistics, *Labor Force Statistics Derived from the Current Population Survey: 1940-1987*, and unpublished tabulations. Also in source: percent employed by race. Full-time is 35 or more hours per week.

★ 209 ★

High School Test Scores, Geography

Average geographic proficiency of seniors in high school: 1988.

Sex	Scale Score
All Students	293.1
Female	285.7
Male	301.2

Source: Selected from "Geography Learning of High School Seniors: 1988," *The Condition of Education 1990, Volume 1: Elementary and Secondary Education*, Table 1:8-1, p. 34,116 (Washington, D.C.: National Center for Education Statistics, 1990). Primary source: The National Assessment of Education Progress, *The Geography Learning of High School Seniors, 1990*. Also in source: scores by race, ethnicity, and parental education.

Higher Education

★ 210 ★

Age of Women College Students: 1980-2000

Percentage distribution of women enrolled in institutions of higher education, by age group: Fall 1980, 1988, and 2000.

Age	1980	1988	2000
Under 25	60.5%	56.1%	56.9%
25-29	14.1%	13.7%	11.0%
30-34	10.7%	10.6%	9.0%
35+	14.7%	19.6%	23.1%

Source: "Percentage Distribution of Women Enrolled in Institutions of Higher Education, by Age Group: Fall 1980, 1988, and 2000," *Projections of Education Statistics to 2000,* Figure 19, p. 25 (Washington, D.C.: National Center for Education Statistics, 1989). Primary source: data collected from many sources, including Federal and State agencies, private research organizations, and professional organizations. The age distribution for the year 2000 is based on the middle alternative projections.

★ 211 ★

All-Male State-Supported Colleges

As reported in the *New York Times*.

The last single-sex, four-year state-supported colleges in the United States in March 1991:

The Citadel, Charleston, SC
Virginia Military Institute, Lexington, VA

Source: Ronald Smothers, "In a Coed Age, the Citadel Stands Fast," *New York Times,* March 15, 1991, p. A12.

★ 212 ★

Astronomy and Physics Graduates

Characteristics of astronomy and physics graduates, 1988-1989.

Characteristics of graduate students	All graduate students	First-year graduate	Doctorate recipients
Physics			
Total Population	13,361	3,132	1,112
Number of respondents	7,391	1,329	708
Respondents' sex:			
Female	14%	15%	8%
Male	86%	85%	92%

[Continued]

★ 212 ★

Astronomy and Physics Graduates
[Continued]

Characteristics of graduate students	All graduate students	First-year graduate	Doctorate recipients
Astronomy			
Total population	169	780	94
Number of respondents	107	547	56
Respondents' sex:			
Female	20%	19%	17%[1]
Male	80%	81%	83%

Source: "Characteristics of the graduate astronomy student population, 1988-89," *AIP Report*, September 1990, p. 2, 11 (New York: American Institute of Physics, 1990). Also in source: other survey results. *Notes:* 1. These data were reported by astronomy department chairpersons as part of the survey of Enrollments and Degrees.

★ 213 ★

Astronomy and Physics Graduates - Minorities
Minority group physics students, by sex, 1988-89.

Sex	Black		Native Amer. Indian	Hispanic				Asian Indian		Oriental		Arab	
						Other							
	U.S.	Foreign		Puerto Rican	Mexican Amer.	U.S.	Foreign	U.S.	Foreign	U.S.	Foreign	U.S.	Foreign
Total number	68	35	15	16	17	52	100	32	340	146	1,721	16	119
Sex:													
Female	13	5	-	2	2	6	9	7	75	23	289	-	13
Male	55	30	15	14	15	46	91	25	265	123	1,432	16	106

Source: "Characteristics of minority group physics students, 1988-89," *AIP Report*, September 1990, p. 3 (New York: American Institute of Physics, 1990). Also in source: other survey results. *Notes:* 1. These data were reported by astronomy department chairpersons as part of the survey of Enrollments and Degrees.

★ 214 ★

College Freshmen Plans and Objectives
Survey responses of over 200,000 freshmen, fall 1989.

	Women	Men	Total
Highest degree planned			
None	0.9%	1.2%	1.1%
Vocational certificate	0.9%	0.6%	1.3%
Associate or equivalent	4.5%	5.0%	3.9%
Bachelor's	31.6%	33.3%	32.3%
Master's	37.6%	36.3%	37.0%
Ph.D. or Ed.D.	11.5%	12.0%	11.7%
M.D.,D.O.,D.D.S., or D.V.M.	5.7%	6.0%	5.4%
LL.B. or J.D.	4.9%	4.9%	4.9%
B.D. or M.Div.	0.2%	0.4%	0.3%
Other	1.7%	1.5%	1.6%

[Continued]

★ 214 ★

College Freshmen Plans and Objectives
[Continued]

	Women	Men	Total
Reasons noted as very important in deciding to go to college:			
Could not find job	7.0%	7.5%	6.3%
To get away from home	15.5%	14.5%	15.0%
To be able to get a better job	76.3%	75.4%	75.9%
To gain a general education and appreciation of ideas	68.9%	55.0%	62.5%
To improve reading and study skills	44.4%	35.8%	40.5%
Parent wanted me to go	36.2%	32.4%	34.3%
Nothing better to do	2.4%	1.9%	3.0%
To become a more cultured person	40.8%	29.5%	35.6%
To be able to make more money	69.3%	75.6%	72.2%
To learn more about things that interest me	76.2%	67.9%	72.4%
To prepare for graduate or professional school	55.1%	47.3%	51.5%
Objectives considered essential or very important:			
Becoming accomplished in a performing art	11.5%	10.7%	11.1%
Becoming an authority in own field	64.1%	67.8%	65.8%
Obtaining recognition from colleagues for contributions to field	54.0%	56.1%	55.0%
Influencing the political structure	17.7%	22.4%	19.9%
Influencing social values	46.1%	35.2%	41.1%
Raising a family	69.0%	68.5%	68.8%
Having administrative responsibility for the work of others	42.6%	44.9%	43.6%
Being very well-off financially	71.9%	79.5%	75.4%
Helping others who are in difficulty	68.7%	49.0%	59.7%
Making a theoretical contribution to science	14.1%	20.7%	17.1%
Writing original works	12.7%	12.2%	12.5%
Creating artistic work	12.6%	12.4%	12.5%
Becoming successful in own business	40.8%	50.1%	45.1%
Becoming involved in programs to clean up environment	24.3%	28.3%	26.1%
Developing a meaningful philosophy of life	41.6%	40.0%	40.8%
Participating in a community-action program	25.9%	20.2%	23.3%
Helping to promote racial understanding	37.6%	32.5%	35.2%
Keeping up to date with political affairs	36.0%	43.4%	39.4%

Source: Chronicle of Higher Education Almanac, September 5, 1990, p. 14. Primary source: *The American Freshman: National Norms for Fall 1989*, by Alexander W. Astin, published by American Council on Education and University of California at Los Angeles. Also in source: a number of other tables reporting results from the survey. Statistics are based on a survey of 216,362 freshmen entering 403 two-year and four-year institutions in the fall of 1989. The figures were statistically adjusted to represent the total population of 1.6 million first-time, full-time freshmen. Because of rounding of multiple responses, figures may add to more than 100%.

★ 215 ★

Colleges with Most Female Students

Co-ed liberal arts colleges with most female students.

Institution	% Female
Marywood College	90%
Groucher College	89%
Mercy College	86%
Lourdes College	85%
Spalding University	84%
Marygrove College	84%
Marymount University	84%
Molloy College	83%
Barat College	82%
St. Joseph's College (NY)	82%

Source: Gilbert, Jersey, "The *Money* College Value Exam," *Money* 18: 78-79 (September 1989).

★ 216 ★

Female Medical School Entrants

Top 10 institutions with largest percentage of female medical school entrants, 1975-1978.

Institution	% Female in Med. School
Massachusetts Institute of Technology	13.2%
Cornell University	11.9%
University of Chicago	11.7%
Harvard University	11.6%
Johns Hopkins University	11.0%
Barnard College	10.8%
Yale University	10.7%
Bryn Mawr College	9.9%
Stanford University	9.6%
Swarthmore College	9.0%

Source: Tidball, M. Elizabeth, "Baccalaureate Origins of Entrants into American Medical Schools," *Journal of Higher Education* 56: 385-402 (July/August 1985).

★ 217 ★

High School Graduates Immediately Entering College

Percent of high school graduates enrolling in college in the October following graduation: 1976-1987 (selected 3-year averages).

Year	Total[2]	Female			Male		
		Total	2-year	4-year	Total	2-year	4-year
1976	50.1%	49.5%	16.7%	31.0%	50.8%	16.4%	32.7%
1977	49.9%	49.6%	17.0%	30.8%	50.3%	15.3%	33.3%
1978	50.0%	49.0%	17.5%	29.8%	51.3%	16.1%	33.5%
1979	49.6%	49.7%	18.7%	29.4%	49.5%	16.0%	31.7%

[Continued]

★ 217 ★

High School Graduates Immediately Entering College

[Continued]

Year	Total[2]	Female			Male		
		Total	2-year	4-year	Total	2-year	4-year
1980	50.9%	51.0%	19.3%	30.0%	50.7%	17.9%	31.5%
1981	51.3%	52.3%	20.4%	30.7%	50.2%	18.1%	30.9%
1982	52.4%	52.9%	19.4%	32.2%	51.9%	19.1%	31.6%
1983	52.8%	53.3%	20.0%	32.2%	52.2%	18.5%	31.8%
1984	55.1%	54.8%	19.6%	33.8%	55.4%	19.3%	34.0%
1985	55.5%	54.4%	19.2%	33.8%	56.8%	19.8%	35.1%
1986	56.1%	54.6%	18.8%	34.9%	57.6%	19.3%	37.5%
1987	56.5%	55.9%	19.8%	35.6%	57.1%	19.9%	36.9%

Source: Selected from "Percent enrolling in college in October following high school graduation: 1968-1987 (3-year averages), *The Condition of Education 1990: Volume 2: Postsecondary Education*, Table 2:1-1, p. 16,100 (Washington, D.C.: National Center for Education Statistics, 1990). Primary source: U.S. Department of Commerce, Bureau of the Census, *Current Population Reports*, Series P-20, "School Enrollment...," various years and unpublished tabulations of the Bureau of Labor Statistics. Also in source: data for 1968-1974; percent by race/ethnicity. *Notes:* 1. Three-year averages. For example, the 3-year average percentage for 1987 reported in this table is the average of the percentages for 1986, 1987, and 1988. 2. Total equals the sum of those enrolled in 2-year, 4-year, and those not reporting the type of college.

★ 218 ★

Higher Education Attainment in Selected Countries

Total population age 24 and percentages of the total that are graduates from higher education institutions.

Sex and country	Year	Population age 24	Higher Education Graduates		
			All fields	Sciences	Engineering
Females					
Japan	1988	817,000	12.4%	0.6%	0.3%
USA	1986	2,092,000	24.0%	2.2%	0.6%
Canada	1987	234,275	23.3%	2.1%	0.4%
England	1986	466,700	13.0%	2.4%	0.3%
West Germany	1985	504,700	10.0%	0.7%	0.2%
France	1987	425,061	14.5%	2.1%	0.6%
Males					
Japan	1988	849,000	33.4%	2.5%	8.8%
USA	1986	1,947,000	25.0%	3.7%	4.3%
Canada	1987	234,525	20.6%	3.5%	2.9%
England	1986	477,000	16.0%	3.6%	3.3%
West Germany	1985	534,100	15.3%	1.9%	3.9%
France	1987	426,554	14.3%	3.6%	2.8%

Source: Selected from "International Comparisons of Higher Education Attainment" and "Number of Graduates from Higher Education Institutions, by Sex, Field of Study, and Country," *The Condition of Education 1990: Volume 2: Postsecondary Education*, Table 2:8, p. 34,117 (Washington, D.C.: National Center for Educational Statistics, 1990). Primary source: Data collected for the Organization for Economic Cooperation and Development Indicators Project on Higher Education. Also in source: Total numbers of higher education graduates.

★ 219 ★

Institutional Origins of Natural Science Doctorates

Baccalaureate institutions graduating 40 or more women who later earned life sciences doctorates.

Univ. of California, Berkeley	Mount Holyoke College
Univ. of California, Davis	Ohio State University
Univ. of California, Los Angeles	Pennsylvania State Univ.
Univ. of California, San Diego	Univ. of Pennsylvania
Univ. of California, Santa Barbara	Purdue University
City Univ. of NY, Brooklyn	Univ. of Rochester
Cornell University	Rutgers University
Univ. of Delaware	Smith College
Duke University	Stanford University
Harvard University	State Univ. of NY, Buffalo
Univ. of Illinois	State Univ. of NY, Stony Brook
Indiana University	Univ. of Texas, Austin
Univ. of Maryland	Univ. of Washington
Michigan State Univ.	Wellesley College
Univ. of Michigan	Univ. of Wisconsin
Univ. of Minnesota	

Source: M. Elizabeth Tidball, "Baccalaureate Origins of Recent Natural Science Doctorates," *Journal of Higher Education* 57: 606-620 (November/December 1986). Institutions are listed alphabetically, not ranked. Study employs the universe of baccalaureate institutions that graduated at least 20 women or 40 men from 1970-1979 who later received science doctorates. The Doctorate Records File of the National Research Council provided a listing of the number of natural science doctorates by baccalaureate institution, by sex, and by field. **Number listed: 31.**

★ 220 ★

Nursing Programs

Number of nursing programs, students, and graduates, 1970-1987.

	1970	1975	1980	1981	1982	1983	1984	1985	1986	1987
Nursing programs, number	1,340	1,362	1,385	1,401	1,432	1,466	1,477	1,473	1,469	1,465

Numbers in thousands

Students[1]	163	248	231	235	242	251	237	218	194	183
Graduates[1]	46	77	76	74	74	77	80	82	77	71

Source: Selected from "Physicians, Dentists, and Nurses: 1970 to 1987," *Statistical Abstract of the United States 1990*, 1990, p. 101. Primary source: National League for Nursing, *NLN Data Book*, annual issues. *Notes:* 1. Number of programs and students are as of October 15 and number of graduates are for academic year ending in year shown.

★ 221 ★

Persons with Degrees

Number of persons (in thousands) age 18 and over who hold a bachelor's or higher degree, by field of study, sex, and race: Spring 1984.

Field of study	Total	Sex		Race	
		Women	Men	White	Black
		Number in thousands			
Total population, 18 and over	170,232	89,398	80,834	147,147	18,475
Total with bachelor's or higher degree	26,381	11,670	14,711	24,036	1,334
Percent of population	15.5%	13.1%	18.2%	16.3%	7.2%
Fields:					
Agriculture and forestry	427	38	389	419	---
Biology	620	298	322	556	21
Business and management	4,462	1,116	3,346	4,058	238
Economics	462	71	391	403	23
Education	5,297	3,783	1,514	4,890	347
Engineering	2,176	176	2,000	1.952	72
English and journalism	1,029	623	406	975	35
Home economics	366	345	21	330	23
Law	928	151	777	860	45
Liberal arts and humanities	2,371	1,392	979	2,215	73
Mathematics and statistics	541	190	351	488	33
Medicine and dentistry	872	165	707	776	32
Nursing, pharmacy, and health technologies	1,151	957	194	997	57
Physical and earth sciences	741	188	553	669	17
Police science and law enforcement	154	41	113	140	14
Psychology	749	455	294	707	27
Religion and theology	467	65	402	445	18
Social Sciences	1,764	924	840	1,560	156
Vocational and technical studies	157	15	142	138	15
Other fields	1,647	677	970	1,458	88

Source: Selected from "Number of persons age 18 and over who hold a bachelor's or higher degree, by field of study, race, and age: Spring 1984," *Digest of Education Statistics,* Table 10, p. 17 (Washington, D.C.: National Center for Education Statistics, 1989). Primary source: U.S. Department of Commerce, Bureau of the Census, *Current Population Reports,* Series P-70, No. 11, "Educational Background and Economic Status: Spring 1984." (This table was prepared October 1987.) Also in source: Data by age; percentage distribution of degree holders by field. Data are based on sample surveys of the civilian noninstitutional population. Because of rounding, details may not add to totals.

★ 222 ★

Science and Engineering Graduate Students, 1980-1988

Science and engineering graduate students in doctorate-granting institutions: 1980-1988.

Field	1980	1981	1982	1983	1984	1985	1986	1987	1988
Total science and engineering	297,264	302,390	309,547	317,865	320,506	328,256	339,349	343,228	347,533
Female	86,469	91,026	95,070	98,207	99,332	102,206	105,980	108,747	112,811
Total science	227,121	228,017	231,369	232,541	233,391	238,017	242,555	246,226	250,555

[Continued]

227

Science and Engineering Graduate Students, 1980-1988
[Continued]

Field	1980	1981	1982	1983	1984	1985	1986	1987	1988
Female	80,332	83,695	86,752	88,930	89,572	91,767	94,276	96,691	100,397
Physical sciences	25,393	25,780	26,499	27,747	28,410	29,312	30,543	30,967	31,266
Female	4,217	4,555	4,920	5,381	5,674	5,994	6,344	6,593	6,958
Environmental sciences	12,795	13,063	13,757	14,281	14,286	14,217	13,989	13,368	12,967
Female	2,905	3,099	3,401	3,610	3,546	3,616	3,645	3,490	3,494
Mathematical sciences	13,625	14,004	14,758	14,885	15,067	15,268	15,663	16,221	16,795
Female	3,457	3,730	4,108	4,230	4,234	4,445	4,591	4,775	4,925
Computer science	11,384	13,141	15,576	18,306	20,366	23,823	25,204	26,083	26,950
Female	2,485	3,235	4,134	4,981	5,301	5,889	5,932	6,216	6,614
Life sciences[1]	54,325	53,330	53,454	53,147	53,290	53,170	54,044	53,987	55,032
Female	19,016	19,113	20,026	20,246	20,466	20,781	21,418	21,565	22,560
Psychology	29,384	29,052	29,082	30,011	30,126	30,581	30,739	31,584	32,680
Female	15,166	15,558	16,122	17,012	17,459	18,274	18,721	19,528	20,465
Social Sciences	80,285	79,647	78,243	74,164	71,846	71,646	72,373	74,016	74,865
Female	33,156	34,405	34,041	33,470	32,892	32,768	33,625	34,524	35,381
Total engineering	70,143	74,373	78,178	85,324	87,115	90,239	96,794	97,002	96,978
Female	6,137	7,331	8,318	9,277	9,760	10,439	11,704	12,056	12,414

Source: Selected from "S/E graduate students in doctorate-granting institutions, by gender: 1980-1988," *Science and Engineering Indicators - 1989,* p. 215 (Washington, D.C.: National Science Board, 1989). Primary source: NSF, Division of Science Resources Studies. Also in source: data for men. *Notes:* 1. Includes biological and agricultural sciences and excludes health fields.

Literacy

Growth in Literacy in Developed and Developing Countries: 1970-1985
Population in developed and developing countries, number of literates, and percent change, 1970-1985.

Region	Number (millions)			Percent change	
	1970	1980	1985	1970-80	1980-85
Developed countries					
Population:					
Female	414.4	465.9	485.3	12.4%	4.2%
Male	370.1	423.8	445.6	14.5%	5.1%

[Continued]

★ 223 ★

Growth in Literacy in Developed and Developing Countries: 1970-1985
[Continued]

Region	Number (millions)			Percent change	
	1970	1980	1985	1970-80	1980-85
Literates:					
Female	396.6	451.8	473.0	13.9%	4.7%
Percent of female population	(95.7%)	(97.0%)	(97.4%)		
Male	359.2	415.5	438.2	15.7%	5.5%
Percent of male population	(97.1%)	(98.0%)	(98.3%)		
Developing countries					
Population:					
Female	750.1	981.4	1,121.5	30.8%	14.3%
Male	775.2	1,008.0	1,150.6	30.0%	14.2%
Literates:					
Female	325.3	504.9	619.1	55.2%	22.6%
Percent of female population	(43.4%)	(51.4%)	(55.2%)		
Male	468.5	683.1	815.6	45.8%	19.4%
Percent of male population	(60.4%)	(67.8%)	(70.9%)		

Source: "Comparative growth in literacy among males and females: developed and developing countries (estimates for 1970 and 1980, and projections for 1985), *World Labour Report 1-2*, 1987, p. 261 (New York: Oxford University Press, 1987). Primary source: UNESCO data on computer printout (1983). Data cover population at age 15 and above. The figures in parentheses show literacy levels among males and females expressed as percentages of their respective populations.

★ 224 ★

Population and Literacy by Residence in Selected Countries

Urban and rural population and literate population over 10 years of age, latest available year.

Country or area, year	Urban		Urban Literate		Rural		Rural Literate	
	Total	Female	Total	Female	Total	Female	Total	Female
AFRICA								
Egypt-1986	15,878,449	7,677,292	10,298,688	4,267,899	18,894,946	9,089,850	7,314,083	2,141,788
Morocco-1982	6,414,160	3,265,398	3,576,034	1,385,152	7,805,656	3,970,055	1,429,289	213,132
Mozambique-1980	1,049,023	484,143	649,902	214,350	6,680,587	3,511,559	1,645,212	420,420
NORTH AMERICA								
Panama-1980	698,034	365,968	668,064	349,177	560,329	256,680	453,253	206,602
SOUTH AMERICA								
Argentina-1980	18,389,508	9,603,377	17,642,275	9,171,359	3,533,341	1,610,707	3,015,924	1,366,931

[Continued]

★ 224 ★

Population and Literacy by Residence in Selected Countries
[Continued]

Country or area, year	Urban		Urban Literate		Rural		Rural Literate	
	Total	Female	Total	Female	Total	Female	Total	Female
Brazil-1980	61,058,968	31,628,100	50,987,319	25,826,320	26,746,297	12,840,107	14,381,095	6,816,895
Uruguay-1985	2,114,937	1,129,918	2,031,906	1,086,907	307,822	124,963	280,204	116,674
Venezuela-1985[1]	8,542,264	4,372,094	7,725,184	3,885,962	1,554,576	712,366	991,431	440,066
ASIA								
Bangladesh-1981	9,499,021	4,018,802	4,423,952	1,405,768	48,669,848	23,862,440	12,106,393	3,883,629
India-1981	119,442,086	55,118,686	80,318,790	30,590,408	368,455,989	179,505,915	132,093,066	37,451,395
Malaysia								
Sarawak-1980	164,527	84,284	125,773	58,131	714,896	356,023	356,012	145,516
Pakistan-1981	16,710,747	7,595,662	7,874,274	2,831,407	41,109,465	19,329,595	6,965,580	1,374,561
Philippines-1980	13,057,945	6,817,381	12,078,345	6,272,285	20,623,479	10,171,478	15,782,846	7,765,959
Sri Lanka-1981	2,541,945	1,202,527	2,375,376	1,098,779	8,767,540	4,338,923	7,490,131	3,509,495
EUROPE								
Greece-1981[1]	4,754,913	2,476,725	4,478,121	2,267,867	2,514,795	1,269,967	2,139,390	968,599

Source: Selected from "Population by Literacy, Sex, Age and Urban/Rural Residence: Each Census, 1975-1988," *1988 Demographic Yearbook*, p. 750-770 (New York: United Nations, 1990). Literacy is defined as ability both to read and write; semi-literates (persons able to read but not write) are included with illiterate population. *Note:* 1. See source for semi-urban data.

★ 225 ★

Reading Disability

Comparison of two groups of reading-disabled children in a longitudinal study: those identified by research and those identified by schools. "Results of previous investigations indicating an increased prevalence of reading disability in boys compared with girls reflected a bias in subject selection" (source).

Characteristic of reading-disabled child:	Total children	Girls	Reading disabled	
			Girls	Boys
Research-identified				
Second grade	312	216	15	17
Third grade	314	215	13	18
School-identified				
Second grade	314	216	7	27
Third grade	314	215	9	20

Source: Sally E. Shaywitz et. al., "Prevalence of Reading Disability in Boys and Girls: Results of the Connecticut Longitudinal Study," *JAMA* 264:8 (August 22/29, 1990), p. 998+. Reprint requests: Department of Pediatrics, Yale University School of Medicine, PO Box 3333, New Haven, CT 06510-8064 (Dr. S.E. Shaywitz). Related reading: Gina Kolata, "Studies Dispute View of Dyslexia, Finding Girls as Afflicted as Boys," *New York Times*, August 22, 1990, p. 1-B8.

★ 226 ★

Worldwide Educational Attainment

Total population over 25 years of age, number of females, and percentage distribution of the female population over 25 years of age by educational attainment.

Country or area, year	Total Population >25 years	Female >25 years	Highest Level Attained			
			No Schooling	First Level Completed	Entered Second Level	Post-Secondary
Africa						
Algeria-1971	4,173,435	2,256,695	95.9%	---	2.2%[1]	0.1%
Benin-1979	1,191,179	651,159	94.3%	---	0.9%[1]	0.1%
Botswana-1981	310,303	172,274	51.4%	8.7%	3.3%	0.2%
Cameroon-1976	2,780,576	1,462,952	84.3%	---	1.6%[1]	0.1%
Egypt-1976	14,641,740	7,326,340	92.9%	---	3.1%[1]	1.3%
Gambia-1973	203,986	97,345	97.1%	0.2%	2.0%	0.1%
Ghana-1970	3,227,660	1,689,000	88.0%	---	7.1%[1]	0.1%
Kenya-1979	4,818,310	2,442,417	73.0%	---	4.0%[1]	---
Lesotho-1976	483,002	255,898	24.8%	10.2%	3.6%	0.1%
Liberia-1974	607,806	296,114	94.3%	0.5%	0.3%	0.1%
Libyan Arab Jamahiriya-1973						
Libyan Population	691,054	331,711	95.3%	0.9%	0.7%	0.1%
Malawi-1977	2,064,965	1,086,793	68.8%	1.6%	0.9%	0.1%
Mali-1976	2,445,774	1,273,821	98.1%	0.4%	0.2%	0.1%
Mauritius-1983	440,134	230,126	32.4%	---	17.5%[1]	1.9%
Morocco-1971	5,750,690	2,953,936	96.3%	0.7%	2.1%	---
Rwanda-1978	1,568,661	839,613	88.2%	1.5%	1.3%	0.1%
Sao Tome and Principe-1981	33,308	17,330	74.6%	9.7%	3.7%	0.1%
Seychelles-1971	21,193	11,089	25.6%	22.7%	13.2%	1.7%
South Africa-1970	8,685,224	4,448,424	43.7%	5.6%	26.9%	3.1%
Swaziland-1976	168,168	91,516	56.3%	8.3%	9.0%	---
Togo-1981	1,084,488	604,296	87.3%	---	4.2%[1]	0.5%
Tunisia-1984	2,714,100	1,347,700	79.0%	---	6.9%[1]	1.3%
Zambia-1980	1,880,124	961,086	64.2%	---	6.0%[1]	0.2%
North America						
Antigua and Barbuda-1970	64,316[2]	34,004[2]	14.4%	---	4.1%[1]	0.9%
Barbados-1980	116,874	68,807	0.9%	---	32.0%	1.9%
Belize-1980	45,596	22,632	10.5%	---	11.7%[1]	1.2%
Bermuda-1970	28,015	14,050	1.3%	---	51.0%[1]	6.2%
British Virgin Islands-1980	5,136	2,437	2.4%	---	25.4%[1]	7.4%
Canada-1981	13,971,280	7,161,655	2.2%	9.4%	39.6%	34.7%
Cayman Islands-1970	4,533	2,571	2.7%	---	14.0%[1]	1.3%
Costa Rica-1973	657,543	331,240	16.0%	17.7%	11.0%	5.4%
Cuba-1981	3,013,315[3]	1,511,380[3]	4.1%	28.4%	35.9%	4.5%

[Continued]

★ 226 ★

Worldwide Educational Attainment
[Continued]

Country or area, year	Total Population >25 years	Female >25 years	Highest Level Attained			
			No Schooling	First Level Completed	Entered Second Level	Post-Secondary
Dominica-1981	27,508	14,581	6.8%	--	10.6%[1]	1.0%
Dominican Republic-1970	1,145,090	563,150	42.8%	3.9%	11.1%	1.3%
El Salvador-1980	3,132,400[4]	1,635,100[4]	33.1%	---	6.6%[1]	1.9%
Grenada-1981	33,401	18,362	2.3%	---	8.5%[1]	0.8%
Guadeloupe-1982	150,253	79,984	10.3%	---	31.8%	4.2%
Guatemala-1973	1,785,720	897,960	94.7%	---	4.8%[1]	0.5%
Haiti-1982	2,103,124	1,093,992	81.3%	---	5.9%	0.4%
Honduras-1983	---	---	34.1%	---	12.7%[1]	2.2%
Jamaica-1982	703,714	365,612	3.0%	---	15.8%[1]	1.8%
Mexico-1980	24,309,593	12,455,708	37.1%	18.0%	11.5%	2.7%
Montserrat-1980	5,544	3,023	1.7%	---	9.9%[1]	4.0%
Netherlands-1981	115,087	62,076	67.3%	---	27.8%[1]	4.9%
Nicaragua-1971[5]	593,100	NA	53.9%	---	4.4%[1]	---
Panama-1980	725,878	358,714	19.1%	23.1%	23.8%	7.8%
Puerto Rico-1980	1,577,686	839,399	9.1%	11.9%	42.9%	18.3%
St. Kitts and Nevis-1980	16,695	9,233	1.0%	---	67.5%[1]	1.2%
St. Lucia-1980	39,599	21,756	16.8%	---	6.8%[1]	0.7%
St. Vincent and the Grenadines-1980	32,444	17,893	2.5%	---	8.0%	0.9%
Trinidad and Tobago-1980	408,215	201,148	1.3%	42.4%	24.5%	1.9%
Turks and Caicos Islands-1980	2,859	1,545	1.0%		16.4%[1]	5.1%
United States-1981	132,899,000	70,390,000	3.1%	68.8%	---	28.0%[1]
South America						
Argentina-1980	14,913,575	7,711,356	6.7%	35.2%	20.1%	5.8%
Bolivia-1976	1,759,432	918,709	62.2%	---	13.8%	3.3%
Brazil-1980	48,310,722	24,576,023	35.2%	4.6%	7.2%	4.1%[1]
Chile-1982	5,204,698	2,724,739	10.0%	---	26.9%[1]	7.2%
Colombia-1973	8,478,100[6]	4,483,086[6]	23.7%	---	18.5%[1]	1.8%
Ecuador-1982	2,887,330	1,457,435	29.6%	31.1%	17.0%	5.6%
French Guiana-1982	34,145[5]	NA	20.8%	---	32.4%[1]	6.4%
Guyana-1980	270,849	138,083	10.6%	---	15.5%[1]	0.9%
Paraguay-1982	1,141,841	573,256	17.9%	15.3%	14.8%	2.5%
Peru-1981	6,526,328	3,308,370	34.2%	15.5%	18.3%	7.7%
Uruguay-1975	1,590,200	824,700	10.4%	31.2%	16.6%	6.8%
Venezuela-1981	5,542,852	2,802,602	26.4%	---	21.9%[1]	5.5%

[Continued]

★ 226 ★

Worldwide Educational Attainment
[Continued]

Country or area, year	Total Population >25 years	Female >25 years	Highest Level Attained			
			No Schooling	First Level Completed	Entered Second Level	Post-Secondary
ASIA						
Afghanistan-1979	4,891,473	2,405,187	97.6%	0.1%	0.3%	0.6%
Bahrain-1971	81,520	34,633	86.2%	2.4%	5.6%	2.2%
Bangladesh-1981	31,593,122	14,904,705	84.0%	---	4.1%[1]	0.3%
Brunei Darussalam-1981	75,283	33,701	45.8%	---	25.6%[1]	6.9%
Burma-1973	11,118,272	5,559,102	82.0%	---	5.1%[1]	0.0%
China-1982	466,915,380	227,191,450	62.3%	23.6%	13.5%	6.3%
Cyprus-1976[4]	NA	NA	0.7%	---	34.0%[1]	6.3%
Hong Kong-1981	2,601,296	1,239,697	35.9%	19.5%	24.3%	5.0%
India-1981	280,599,720	135,517,843	85.2%	---	6.6%[1]	1.1%
Indonesia-1980	58,441,240	29,764,530	53.9%	12.9%	6.3%	0.4%
Israel-1982	2,003,500	1,030,200	14.1%	---	34.8%[1]	20.9%
Jewish Population	1,785,400	918,500	10.5%	---	37.7%[1]	23.0%
Non Jewish Population	218,100	111,700	43.5%	---	11.2%[1]	4.2%
Japan-1980	73,368,684	38,110,839	0.6%	47.6%	39.7%	14.3%
Korea, Republic of-1980	16,457,362	8,503,065	26.9%	---	29.6%[1]	4.0%
Kuwait-1985	565,330	178,989	49.9%	---	31.6%[1]	11.6%
Lebanon-1970	836,060	412,010	59.5%	9.9%	10.7%	1.1%
Macau-1970	93,557	47,800	33.7%	---	10.2%[1]	0.9%
Malaysia-1970[2]	10,319,324	5,120,906	51.0%	10.6%	10.8%	---
Peninsular Malaysia-1980[5]	4,395,441	NA	34.3%	23.0%	19.9%	1.4%
Sabah-1980	338,303	154,964	69.9%	---	11.6%[1]	0.7%
Sarawak-1980	473,144	237,108	69.3%	12.1%	9.6%	0.5%
Pakistan-1981	30,707,279	14,400,805	90.4%	---	4.2%[1]	0.7%
Philippines-1980	17,865,290	8,980,215	13.3%	23.7%	16.6%	15.1%
Qatar-1986	211,485	50,673	56.0%	---	22.1%[1]	15.3%
Singapore-1980	1,176,282	583,726	54.3%	---	12.5%	2.0%
Sri Lanka-1981	6,490,502	3,163,187	22.7%	---	31.3%[1]	0.8%
Syrian Arab Republic-1970	2,061,729	1,028,918	87.5%	---	2.0%	0.4%
Thailand-1980	17,491,470	9,000,623	26.3%	1.6%	4.3%	2.4%
Turkey-1980	18,277,340	9,207,179	68.3%	---	5.7%[1]	1.5%
United Arab Emirates-1975	285,947	65,743	79.3%	---	14.1%[1]	4.1%
Europe						
Austria-1981	4,558,681	2,508,936	---	---	36.6%[1]	1.6%
Belgium-1977[7]	6,995,797	3,630,767	---	---	11.9%	5.3%
Czechoslovakia-1980	9,274,694	4,899,960	0.5%	---	37.2%[1]	4.0%

[Continued]

★ 226 ★

Worldwide Educational Attainment
[Continued]

Country or area, year	Total Population >25 years	Female >25 years	Highest Level Attained			
			No Schooling	First Level Completed	Entered Second Level	Post-Secondary
Finland-1985	3,235,017	1,713,747	---	---	30.3%[1]	11.7%
German Democratic Rep.-1981	10,714,841	5,935,267	---	---	43.9%[1]	14.1%
Germany, Federal Rep.-1970	38,558,900	21,103,700	81.2%	---	16.9%[1]	1.9%
Greece-1981	5,966,511	3,113,632	17.7%	41.7%	17.3%	4.9%
Hungary-1980	6,903,881	3,670,474	1.7%	3.4%	81.1%	5.0%
Ireland-1981	1,793,855	909,047	50.2%	---	43.2%	6.5%
Italy-1981	35,596,616	18,790,372	23.2%	---	25.1%[1]	2.9%
Liechtenstein-1970	11,483	5,814	0.4%	---	16.2%[1]	0.8%
Netherlands-1971	5,679,695	2,851,945	---	---	42.7%[1]	4.8%
Norway-1980	2,574,641	1,324,409	1.6%	---	89.5%[1]	8.8%
Poland-1978	20,271,991	10,752,794	3.7%	47.5%	29.6%	4.4%
Portugal-1970	4,800,335	2,710,085	52.4%	23.2%	5.1%	0.9%
Romania-1977[5]	12,622,808	---	55.6%	---	39.8%[1]	4.6%
San Marino-1976[8]	14,473	7,263	5.4%	---	26.8%[1]	1.9%
Spain-1981	21,758,498	11,411,664	38.9%	32.5%	11.3%	5.5%
Sweden-1979[9]	4,998,000	2,540,000	43.6%	---	42.3%[1]	14.1%
Switzerland-1970	3,196,376	1,730,620	5.6%	---	19.3%[1]	---
Yugoslavia-1981	13,083,762	6,786,385	23.3%	---	15.8%[1]	4.8%
Oceania						
American Samoa-1974	10,157	4,943	---	17.7%	55.8%	9.3%
Australia-1971	6,878,445	3,472,417	0.9%	---	59.0%[1]	10.0%
Cook Islands-1971	7,702	3,627	4.3%	58.4%	9.0%	0.7%
Fiji-1986	287,175	147,154	14.8%	24.9%	21.9%	3.4%
Guam-1980	46,906	22,366	2.1%	3.5%	44.2%	30.8%
New Caledonia-1976[7]	76,774	36,291	10.5%	---	12.2%[1]	1.4%
New Zealand-1981	1,720,383	884,310	1.2%	---	28.9%[1]	27.6%
Niue-1976	1,337	734	---	5.4%	36.5%	0.5%
Pacific Islands-1970	32,155	15,374	38.5%	24.4$	8.7%	3.2%
Papua New Guinea-1980 Nationals Only	1,135,783	551,886	87.3%	3.6%	1.8%	---
Samoa-1976	47,031	23,665	62.1%	--	36.6%	1.3%
Solomon Islands-1976 Indigenous Population	68,102	31,714	64.8%	---	1.7%	1.0%
Vanuatu-1979	38,488	17,612	43.5%	5.8%	17.0%	---

[Continued]

★ 226 ★

Worldwide Educational Attainment
[Continued]

Country or area, year	Total Population >25 years	Female >25 years	Highest Level Attained			
			No Schooling	First Level Completed	Entered Second Level	Post-Secondary
USSR						
USSR-1979[4]	NA	NA	40.3%	---	52.1%[1]	7.6%
Byelorussian SSR[4]	NA	NA	45.1%	---	47.9%	7.0%
Ukrainian SSR-1970[6]	31,482,631	18,157,359	54.5%	---	40.2%[1]	5.3%

Source: Selected and condensed from "Percentage Distribution of Population by Educational Attainment and by Sex," *Statistical Yearbook 1989*, p. 1-26-1-57 (Paris: UNESCO, 1989). Also in source: data by urban/rural residence; number of persons who entered but did not complete first level; number who entered second level S-1 and S-2. See Introduction to this for explanation of levels of education. *Notes:* 1. Data from preceding blank column totalled here. 2. All ages. 3. Ages 25-49. 4. Ages >10. 5. Figures are for both sexes. 6. Ages >20. 7. Ages >14. 8. Ages >15. 9. Ages 25-74.

★ 227 ★

Worldwide Illiterate Population

Total and female numbers of illiterates. Illiterate population as percentage of total. Persons 15 years of age and over unless otherwise noted. Latest available year.

Country, year	Illiterate Population		Percentage Illiterate		
	Total	Female	Total	Female	Male
Africa					
Algeria-1982	5,880,350	3,583,003	55.3%	68.3%	42.7%
Benin-1979	1,418,051	854,700	83.5%	90.5%	74.8%
Botswana-1971	182,944	99,933	59.0%	56.0%	63.1%
Burkino Faso-1975	2,803,440	1,530,847	91.2%	96.7%	85.3%
Burundi-1982[1]	-	-	66.2%	74.3%	57.2%
Cameroon-1976	2,360,088	1,496,204	58.8%	70.9%	45.4%
Cape Verde-1980 [2]	-	-	52.6%	61.4%	38.6%
Central African Republic-1975	-	-	73.0%	85.0%	67.0%
Comoros-1980	88,780	52,351	52.1%	60.0%	44.0%
Congo-1985	365,632	233,462	37.1%	44.6%	28.6%
Egypt-1976	13,317,501	8,265,999	61.8%	77.6%	46.4%
Equatorial Guinea-1980	105,100	-	63.0%	-	-
Ethiopia-1970	9,120,600	4,761,600	95.8%	99.8%	91.7%
Ghana-1970	3,293,320	2,008,000	69.8%	81.6%	56.9%
Guinea-Bissau-1979	342,393	211,471	80.0%	91.4%	66.7%
Liberia-1974	714,502	400,844	80.4%	89.7%	71.0%
Libyan Arab Jamahiriya-1973 (Libyan Population)	608,050	407,237	61.0%	85.2%	38.7%
Mali-1976	3,236,240	1,766,608	90.6%	94.3%	86.5%
Morocco-1971	6,407,137	3,753,096	78.6%	90.2%	66.4%
Mozambique-1980	4,557,751	2,906,799	72.8%	87.8%	56.0%

[Continued]

★ 227 ★

Worldwide Illiterate Population
[Continued]

Country, year	Illiterate Population		Percentage Illiterate		
	Total	Female	Total	Female	Male
Reunion-1982	73,220	34,359	21.4%	19.5%	23.5%
Rwanda-1978	1,619,117	998,265	61.8%	73.4%	49.2%
St. Helena-1976[3]	92	42	2.9%	2.5%	3.2%
Sao Tome and Principe-1981	22,080	15,325	42.6%	57.6%	26.8%
Seychelles-1971	12,494	6,029	42.3%	40.2%	44.4%
Somalia-1975[2]	-	-	45.2%	52.1%	39.1%
Swaziland-1976	115,836	66,555	44.8%	46.5%	42.7%
Togo-1981	927,712	599,215	68.6%	81.5%	53.3%
Tunisia-1984	2,076,900	1,236,500	49.3%	59.4%	39.5%
United Republic of Tanzania-1978	5,058,986	3,330,961	53.7%	68.6%	37.8%
North America					
Barbados-1970	1,093	600	0.7%	0.7%	0.7%
Belize-1970	5,353	2,699	8.8%	8.8%	8.8%
Bermuda-1970	586	195	1.6%	1.1%	2.1%
British Virgin Islands-1970	100	39	1.7%	1.5%	1.9%
Cayman Islands-1970	152	82	2.5%	2.4%	2.5%
Costa Rica-1984	112,946	57,515	7.4%	7.4%	7.3%
Cuba-1979[4]	218,358	117,239	4.6%	4.9%	4.3%
Dominica-1970	2,083	1,139	5.9%	5.8%	6.0%
Dominican Republic-1981[5]	1,519,198	748,440	31.4%	30.9%	31.8%
El Salvador-1980[2]	946,000	542,700	30.2%	33.2%	26.9%
Grenada-1970	1,070	646	2.2%	2.4%	2.0%
Guadeloupe-1982	22,359	11,128	10.0%	9.6%	10.4%
Guatemala-1973	1,528,732	876,817	54.0%	61.5%	46.4%
Haiti-1982	2,004,791	1,078,040	65.2%	67.5%	62.7%
Honduras-1974	594,194	319,379	43.1%	44.9%	41.1%
Jamaica-1970	38,063	17,689	3.9%	3.5%	4.4%
Martinique-1982	16,814	7,990	7.2%	6.6%	8.0%
Mexico-1985	4,400,000	2,700,000	9.7%	11.7%	7.7%
Montserrat-1970	231	131	3.4%	3.4%	3.2%
Netherlands Antilles-1981	10,236	5,739	6.2%	6.6%	5.8%
Nicaragua-1971	410,755	217,277	42.5%	42.9%	42.0%
Panama-1980	156,531	81,794	14.4%	15.1%	13.7%
Puerto Rico-1980	239,095	131,723	10.9%	11.5%	10.3%
St. Kitts and Nevis-1970	546	299	2.4%	2.3%	2.4%
St. Lucia-1970	9,195	4,944	18.3%	17.6%	19.2%
St. Vincent and the Grenadines-1970	1,839	1,060	4.4%	4.5%	4.2%
Trinidad and Tobago-1980	34,800	22,910	5.1%	6.6%	3.5%
Turks and Caicos Islands-1970	56	38	1.9%	2.3%	1.4%

[Continued]

★ 227 ★

Worldwide Illiterate Population
[Continued]

Country, year	Illiterate Population		Percentage Illiterate		
	Total	Female	Total	Female	Male
South America					
Argentina-1980	1,184,964	641,790	6.1%	6.4%	5.7%
Bolivia-1976	993,437	677,977	36.8%	48.6%	24.2%
Brazil-1980	18,716,847	10,156,671	25.5%	27.2%	23.7%
Chile-1982	681,039	365,501	8.9%	9.2%	8.5%
Colombia-1981	2,407,458	1,316,051	14.8%	16.1%	13.6%
Ecuador-1982	758,272	460,254	19.8%	23.8%	15.8%
French Guiana-1982	8,372	4,051	17.0%	17.7%	16.4%
Guyana-1970	31,042	20,588	8.4%	11.0%	5.7%
Paraguay-1982	219,120	134,780	12.5%	15.2%	9.7%
Peru-1981	1,799,458	1,313,972	18.1%	26.1%	9.9%
Suriname-1985	-	-	10.0%	10.0%	10.0%
Uruguay-1985	108,400	51,100	5.0%	4.5%	5.6%
Venezuela-1981	1,319,265	740,085	15.3%	17.0%	13.5%
Asia					
Afghanistan-1979	5,832,988	3,249,407	81.8%	95.0%	69.7%
Bahrain-1981	71,160	36,762	30.2%	41.4%	23.5%
Bangladesh-1981	32,923,083	18,421,500	70.8%	82.0%	60.3%
Brunei Darussalam-1981	26,224	16,650	22.2%	31.0%	14.8%
Burma-1973	4,761,785	3,475,471	29.0%	41.7%	15.9%
China-1982	230,146,750	159,036,130	34.5%	48.9%	10.8%
Cyprus-1976[2]	-	-	9.5%	3.5%	15.2%
Democratic Yemen-1973[2]	7,736,224	482,047	72.9%	92.1%	52.3%
Hong Kong-1971	571,840	445,688	22.7%	35.9%	9.9%
India-1981	238,097,747	144,197,913	59.2%	74.3%	45.2%
Indonesia-1980	28,325,026	18,834,111	32.7%	42.3%	22.5%
Iran, Islamic Republic-1976	11,733,299	6,857,922	63.5%	75.6%	51.8%
Iraq-1985[6]	-	-	10.7%	12.5%	9.8%
Israel-1983	224,080	157,140	8.2%	11.3%	5.0%
Jordan-1979	-	-	34.6%	49.5%	19.9%
Korea, Republic-1970	2,263,783	1,763,587	12.4%	19.0%	5.6%
Kuwait-1985	273,513	132,431	25.5%	31.2%	21.8%
Lao People's Democratic Republic-1985[6]	-	-	16.1%	24.2%	8.0%
Lebanon-1970[2]	-	-	-	42.1%	21.5%
Macau-1970	31,917	20,023	20.6%	26.1%	15.2%
Malaysia-1980	2,399,790	1,608,790	30.4%	40.3%	20.4%
Peninsular Malaysia-1980[2]	1,962,250	1,334,500	24.0%	33.0%	16.0%
Sabah-1980	244,254	141,950	45.0%	55.4%	35.8%
Sarawak-1980	351,847	216,046	48.9%	59.2%	38.4%

[Continued]

★ 227 ★

Worldwide Illiterate Population

[Continued]

Country, year	Illiterate Population		Percentage Illiterate		
	Total	Female	Total	Female	Male
Maldives-1985	8,568	4,003	8.7%	8.5%	8.8%
Nepal-1981	6,998,148	3,945,065	79.4%	90.8%	68.3%
Pakistan-1981	33,597,018	18,085,034	73.85	84.8%	64.0%
Philippines-1980	4,626,922	2,426,437	16.7%	17.2%	16.1%
Qatar-1986	64,891	19,638	24.3%	27.5%	23.2%
Saudi Arabia-1982	-	-	48.9%	69.2%	28.9%
Singapore-1980	300,994	225,572	17.1%	26.0%	8.4%
Sri Lanka-1981	1,271,984	847,560	13.2%	18.0%	8.7%
Syrian Arab Republic-1970	1,851,949	1,222,045	60.0%	80.0%	40.4%
Thailand-1980	3,296,606	2,246,942	12.0%	16.0%	7.7%
Turkey-1984	-	-	25.8%	37.5%	14.1%
United Arab Emirates-1975	186,058	59,472	46.5%	61.9%	41.6%
Viet-Nam-1979	4,846,849	3,506,404	16.0%	21.7%	9.5%
Europe					
Greece-1981	701,056	560,512	9.5%	14.7%	3.9%
Hungary-1980	95,542	67,786	1.1%	1.5%	0.7%
Italy-1985	-	-	3.0%	3.7%	2.1%
Malta-1985	43,800	25,700	15.9%	17.7%	14.0%
Poland-1978	334,586	241,977	1.2%	1.7%	0.7%
Portugal-1985	-	-	16.0%	20.3%	11.2%
San Marino 1976[2]	640	380	3.9%	4.7%	3.2%
Spain-1981	1,971,695	1,430,215	7.1%	9.9%	4.0%
Yugoslavia-1981	1,764,042	1,393,484	10.4%	16.1%	4.5%
Oceania					
Fiji-1976	65,957	41,652	21.0%	26.0%	16.0%
New Caledonia-1976	7,133	3,763	8.7%	9.7%	7.8%
Papua New Guinea-1971[2]	1,106,880	594,167	67.9%	75.6%	60.7%
Tonga-1976	193	112	0.4%	0.5%	0.3%
Samoa-1971	1,581	762	2.2%	2.1%	2.2%
Vanuatu-1979	28,647	14,824	47.1%	52.2%	42.7%
USSR					
USSR-1979[7]	-	-	0.3%	0.3%	0.2%

Source: Selected from "Illiterate population 15 years of age and over and percentage illiteracy by sex," *Statistical Yearbook*, p. 1-15/1-23 (Paris: UNESCO, 1989). Also in source: breakdown by urban/rural residence; data for various years. *Notes:* 1. Age group 10+. 2. Age group 14+ 3. Age group 16+ 4. Age group 15-49 5. Age group 5+ 6. Age group 15-45 7. Age group 9-49.

Test Scores

★ 228 ★

ACT Test Scores, 1990

Average ACT test scores, 1990.

	English	Math	Social Sciences	Natural Sciences	Average
Female	3.11	2.73	3.09	2.91	2.95
Male	2.83	2.68	3.03	2.84	1.84
Total	2.98	2.71	3.06	2.88	2.90

Source: "Averages of the Four HS Grades," *ACT High School Profile Report,* p. 7 (Iowa City: American College Testing Program, 1990).

★ 229 ★

Advanced Placement Test Scores: Science and Mathematics

Advanced placement examination scores in science and mathematics, 1988.

Exam	Female	Male
Biology	2.87	3.23
Chemistry	2.64	3.09
Physics B[1]	2.50	2.96
Physics C-mechanics[2]	2.70	3.42
Physics C-electricity and magnetism[2]	2.86	3.37
Mathematics/calculus AB[3]	2.95	3.21
Mathematics/calculus BC[4]	3.30	3.63
Computer science AB[4]	2.01	2.65
Computer science A[4]	2.24	2.99

Source: "AP examination scores for female and male test-takers: 1988," *Women and Minorities in Science and Engineering,* 1990, p. 17 (Washington, D.C.: National Science Foundation, January 1990). *Notes:* 1. Physics B exam covers all aspects of physics; a student who scores well on this exam may earn as much as a semester's course credit in this field. 2. The physics C-electricity/ magnetism AP exam and the physics C-mechanics exam allow a student the opportunity to earn placement or credit in only one of these respective areas of physics. 3. Two advanced placement exams are offered in mathematics/calculus. The calculus AB exam is not as rigorous as the calculus BC exam. 4. In 1988 the examination for computer science placement was divided into two tests, A and AB.

★ 230 ★

GRE Test Scores

Graduate Record Examination scores by undergraduate major, 1987.

Component and field	Women	Men
Verbal		
Physical science	509	504
Mathematical science	474	488
Biological science	506	502
Behavioral science	504	513
Social science	456	461
Engineering	492	461
Quantitative		
Physical science	615	648
Mathematical science	635	670
Biological science	558	585
Behavioral science	494	539
Social science	454	511
Engineering	663	675
Analytical		
Physical science	580	568
Mathematical science	585	590
Biological science	563	551
Behavioral science	530	530
Social science	493	495
Engineering	601	557

Source: "GRE scores for women and men test-takers, by undergraduate major: 1987," *Women and Minorities in Science and Engineering,* 1990, p. 19-20 (Washington, D.C.: National Science Foundation, January 1990). Primary source: Graduate Record Examination Board, *A Summary of Data Collected from Graduate Record Examination Test-Takers During 1986-87,* Data Summary Report #12 (Princeton: Educational Testing Service, 1988), p. 68.

★ 231 ★

High School Test Scores, Literature and History

National Assessment of Educational Progress in literature and U.S. history for 11th graders by sex and race: Spring 1986.

Student characteristics	% Distribut.	Average score	
		History	Literature
All Students	100.0%	285.0	285.0
Sex			
Female	48.9%	279.0	287.3
Male	51.1%	290.7	282.8
Race			
White	76.9%	290.8	289.9

[Continued]

★ 231 ★

High School Test Scores, Literature and History
[Continued]

Student characteristics	% Distribut.	Average score	
		History	Literature
Black	12.9%	263.1	267.5
Hispanic	7.1%	262.5	264.8

Source: Selected from "National Assessment of Educational Progress in literature and U.S. history for 11th graders by student characteristics: Spring 1986," *Digest of Education Statistics,* Table 102, p. 114 (Washington, D.C.: National Center for Education Statistics, 1989). Primary source: U.S. Department of Education, National Assessment of Educational Progress, "Literature and U.S. History." (This table was prepared in August 1988.) Also in source: other student characteristics. As with the NAEP reading scale, these scales range from 0 to 550. For the literature and U.S. history scales, the mean and standard deviation were sset to 285 and 40, respectively. These values were chosen to be similar to the mean and standard deviation for 11th graders on the 1983-84 reading scale.

★ 232 ★

Profile of SAT Takers, 1990: Part 1

SAT test takers, 1990, by ethnic group and mean scores.

Characteristic	# SAT takers	Percent	%Female/Male	Verbal Mean	Math Mean
All Students	1,025,523	100%	52/48	424	476
Females	535,103	52%	100/0	419	455
Males	490,420	48%	100/0	429	499
Ethnic Group					
American Indian/Alaskan Native	10,466	1%	53/47	388	437
Asian/Asian Amer/Pacific Islander	71,792	8%	50/50	410	528
Black/African American	94,311	10%	58/42	352	385
Hispanic: Mexican Amer/Chicano	26,073	3%	54/46	380	429
Puerto Rican	11,400	1%	55/45	359	405
Other Hispanic	23,608	2%	55/45	383	434
White	694,976	73%	52/48	442	491
Other	14,632	2%	53/47	410	467
Citizenship					
U.S. Citizen	883,419	93%	53/47	430	477
Permanent Resident	40,954	4%	53/47	356	465
Citizen of Another Country	25,777	3%	44/56	392	532

Source: Selected from "1990 Profiles," *College-Bound Seniors: 1990 Profile of SAT and Achievement Test Takers,* p. 6 (New York: College Board, 1990). Also in source: other characteristics of test takers.

★ 233 ★

Profile of SAT Takers, 1990: Part 2

Academic preparation in high school, 1990 SAT test takers.

Percentage of students taking at least...	Female	Male
4 years English	87%	85%
4 years Mathematics	62%	68%
3 years Social Sciences and History	85%	84%
2 years Foreign Language	89%	84%
3 years Natural Sciences	76%	81%
1 year Arts or Music	77%	69%

Source: "Academic Preparation in High School," *College-Bound Seniors: 1990 Profile of SAT and Achievement Test Takers, p. v* (New York: College Board, 1990).

★ 234 ★

Profile of SAT Takers, 1990: Part 3

Most frequently planned areas of study, 1990 SAT test takers.

Total	Female	Male
Business & Commerce (21%)	Business & Commerce (20%)	Business & Commerce (22%)
Social Sciences & History (13%)	Social Sciences & History (16%)	Engineering (18%)
Health & Allied Services (12%)	Health & Allied Services (15%)	Social Sciences & History (9%)
Engineering (10%)	Education (11%)	Health & Allied Services (8%)
Education (7%)	Visual & Performing Arts (7%)	Undecided (6%);

Source: "Most frequently planned areas of study," *College-Bound Seniors: 1990 Profile of SAT and Achievement Test Takers*, p. vi (New York: College Board, 1990).

★ 235 ★

Reading Test Scores: 1975-1984

Proficiency in reading for ages 9, 13, and 17 for the years 1975, 1980, and 1984.

Selected characteristics of participants School year ending...	Reading proficiency score								
	Age 9			Age 13			Age 17[1]		
	1975	1980	1984	1975	1980	1984	1975	1980	1984
All participants	209.6	213.5	213.2	254.8	257.4	257.8	284.5	284.5	288.2
Sex									
Female	215.1	218.5	216.3	261.2	261.8	262.3	289.6	287.9	293.1
Male	204.2	208.5	210.0	248.4	252.8	253.5	279.2	281.1	283.4
Race									
White	215.9	219.7	220.1	260.9	263.1	263.4	290.7	291.0	294.6

[Continued]

★ 235 ★

Reading Test Scores: 1975-1984
[Continued]

Selected characteristics of participants School year ending...	Reading proficiency score								
	Age 9			Age 13			Age 17[1]		
	1975	1980	1984	1975	1980	1984	1975	1980	1984
Black	181.9	188.9	188.4	224.4	231.9	236.8	244.0	246.1	263.5
Hispanic	182.9	189.1	193.0	231.1	236.0	239.2	254.7	261.7	268.7

Source: Selected from "National Assessment of Educational Progress in reading for ages 9, 13, and 17, by selected characteristics of participants: 1974-75, 1979-80, and 1983-84," *Digest of Education Statistics,* p. 108 (Washington, D.C.: National Center for Education Statistics, 1989). Primary source: U.S. Department of Education, National Institute of Education, National Assessment of Educational Progress, *The Reading Report Card.* (This table was prepared May 1986.) Also in source: other characteristics of participants. The NAEP scores have been evaluated at certain performance levels. A score of 300 (adept) implies an ability to find, understand, summarize, and explain relatively complicated literary and informational material. A score of 250 (intermediate) implies an ability to search for specific information, interrelate ideas, and make generalizations about literature, science, and social studies materials. A score of 200 (basic) implies an ability to understand, combines ideas, and make inferences based on short uncomplicated passages about specific or sequentially related information. A score of 150 implies an ability to follow written directions and select phrases to describe pictures. *Note:* 1. All participants of this age were in school.

★ 236 ★

SAT Scores for College-Bound Seniors

Mean SAT scores for college-bound seniors, 1980-1990.

Year	Verbal			Math		
	Females	Males	Total	Females	Males	Total
1980	420	428	424	443	491	466
1981	418	430	424	443	492	466
1982	421	431	426	443	493	467
1983	420	430	425	445	493	468
1984	420	433	426	449	495	471
1985	425	437	431	452	499	475
1986	426	437	431	451	501	475
1987	425	435	430	453	500	476
1988	422	435	428	455	498	476
1989	421	434	427	454	500	476
1990	419	429	424	455	499	476

Source: Selected from "Mean SAT scores for College-Bound Seniors 1967-1990," *College-Bound Seniors: 1990 Profile of SAT and Achievement Test Takers, p. iii* (New York: College Board, 1990). Also in source: scores for 1967-1979. Related Reading: "Scholastic Test Scores Show Drop in Verbal Skills," *New York Times,* Tuesday, August 28, 1990, p. A14.

★ 237 ★

Student Mathematics Proficiency

Mathematics proficiency scores for 9-, 13-, and 17-year-olds, 1981-82 and 1985-86.

Characteristics of students	9-year-olds		13-year-olds		17-year-olds	
	1981-82	1985-86	1981-82	1985-86	1981-82	1985-86
All Students	219	222	269	269	299	302
Female	221	222	268	268	296	299
Male	217	222	269	270	302	305

Source: Selected from "Mathematics proficiency scores for 9-, 13-, and 17-year-olds, by selected characteristics of students: 1977-78, 1981-82, and 1985-86," *Digest of Education Statistics,* p. 116 (Washington, D.C.: National Center for Education Statistics, 1989). Primary source: U.S. Department of Education, National Center for Educational Statistics, National Assessment of Educational Progress, *The Mathematics Report Card,* prepared by Educational Testing Service. (This table was prepared January 1989.) Also in source: other characteristics of students. Performers at the 150 level know some basic addition and subtraction facts, and most can add two-digit numbers without regrouping. They recognize simple situations in which addition and subtraction apply. Performers at the 200 level have considerable understanding of two-digit numbers and know some basic multiplication and division facts. Performers at the 250 level have an initial understanding of the four basic operations. Performers at the 300 level can compute decimals, simple fractions, and percents. Performers at the 350 level can apply a range of reasoning skills to solve multi-step problems.

★ 238 ★

Student Science Proficiency

Science proficiency scores for 9-, 13-, and 17-year-olds: 1981-82 and 1985-86.

Characteristics of students	9-year-olds		13-year-olds		17-year-olds	
All students	220.9	224.3	250.2	251.4	283.3	288.5
Female	220.7	221.3	245.0	246.9	275.2	282.3
Male	221.0	227.3	255.7	256.1	291.9	294.9

Source: Selected from "Science proficiency scores for 9-, 13-, and 17-year-olds, by selected characteristics of students: 1976-77, 1981-82, and 1985-86," *Digest of Education Statistics,* p. 119 (Washington, D.C.: National Center for Education Statistics, 1989). Primary source: U.S. Department of Education, National Center for Educational Statistics, National Assessment of Educational Progress, *The Science Report Card, 1988,* prepared by Educational Testing Service. (This table was prepared January 1989.) Also in source: other characteristics of students. Performers at the 150 level know some general scientific facts of the type that could be learned from everyday experriences. Performers at the 200 level are developing some understanding of simple scientific principles, particularly in the life sciences. Performers at the 250 level can interpret data from simple tables and make inferences about the outcomes of experimental procedures. Performers at the 300 level can evaluate the appropriateness of the design of an experiment and have the skill to apply their scientific knowledge in interpreting information from text and graphs.

★ 239 ★

Student Writing Proficiency

Scale scores of writing performance of 4th, 8th, and 11th graders: 1984.

Characteristics of students	Grade 4	Grade 8	Grade 11
All students	158	205	219
Female	166	214	229
Male	150	196	209

Source: "Writing performance of 4th, 8th, and 11th graders, by selected characteristics of students: 1984," *Digest of Education Statistics,* p. 112 (Washington, D.C.: National Center for Education Statistics, 1989). Primary source: U.S. Department of Education, Office of Educational Research and Improvement, National Assessment of Educational Progress, *The Writing Report Card.* (This table was prepared June 1987.) Also in source: other characteristics of students. The writing scale score ranges from 0 to 400 and is defined as the average of a respondent's estimated scores on 10 specific writing tasks. The average response method is used to estimate average writing achievement for each participant as if each had performed all 10 writing tasks.

★ 240 ★

Student Writing Progress

Percentage of students writing at a minimal level or better, 1979 and 1984.

Age, writing task, and year	All students	Female	Male
	Percentage		
Informative writing			
1979	53.4	59.4	47.1
1984	55.7	60.7	50.9
Persuasive writing			
1979	63.7	68.7	58.8
1984	58.2	65.8	51.1
Imaginative writing			
1979	41.4	46.1	36.8
1984	54.6	58.2	50.7
Age 13			
Informative writing			
1979	74.4	80.6	68.5
1984	81.4	84.2	78.6
Persuasive writing			
1979	60.7	65.9	55.8
1984	66.7	73.1	61.1
Imaginative writing			
1979	60.7	65.9	55.8
1984	66.7	73.1	61.1
Age 17[2]			
Informative writing			
1979	87.1	91.8	81.6
1984	89.0	90.7	87.4
Persuasive writing			
1979	60.6	62.4	58.7
1984	63.8	65.4	62.3
Imaginative writing			

[Continued]

★ 240 ★

Student Writing Progress
[Continued]

Age, writing task, and year	All students	Female	Male
1979	71.3	78.7	66.0
1984	75.1	79.5	70.6

Source: Selected from "Percentage of students writing at a minimal level or better,[1] by sex and race/ethnicity, by age: 1974, 1979, 1984," *Digest of Education Statistics,* p. 113 (Washington, D.C.: National Center for Education Statistics, 1989). Primary source: U.S. Department of Education, Office of Educational Research and Improvement, National Assessment of Educational Progress, *Writing: Trends Across the Decade, 1974-1984.* (This table was prepared June 1987.) Also in source: data for 1974 and by race/ethnicity. Informative writing is used to share knowledge and convey messages, instructions, and ideas. Persuasive writing attempts to bring about some action or change. Imaginative writing provides a special way of sharing our experiences and understanding the world. *Notes:* 1. Standards for minimal performance level differ by grade level. 2. All participants of this age group were in school.

HEALTH AND MEDICAL CARE

Alcohol and Controlled Substances

★ 241 ★

Alcohol Consumption in the Past Month-Young Adults: 1979-1988

Alcohol use in the past month by females 12-17 and 18-25 years of age, 1979, 1982, 1985, and 1988.

Age	1979	1982	1985	1988
	Percent of population over 12 years			
Both sexes:				
12-17 years	37	27	31	25
18-25 years	76	68	71	65
Female:				
12-17 years	36	27	28	23
18-25 years	68	61	64	57

Source: Selected from "Use of selected substances in the past month by youths 12-17 years of age and young adults 18-25 years of age, according to age and sex: United States, selected years 1974-88," *Health United States—1989*, p. 167. Primary source: National Institute on Drug Abuse: National Household Survey on Drug Abuse: Main Findings, 1979, by P.M. Fisburne, H.I. Abelson, and I. Cisin. DHHS Pub. No. (ADM)80-976. Alcohol, Drug Abuse, and Mental Health Administration. Washington, D.C. U.S. Government Printing Office, 1980; National Household Survey on Drug abuse: Main Findings, 1982, by J.D. Miller et al. DHHS Pub. No. (ADM)83-1263. Alcohol, Drug Abuse, and Mental Health Administration. Washington, D.C. U.S. Government Printing Office, 1983; National Household Survey on Drug Abuse: Main Findings, 1985. DHHS Pub. No. (ADM)88-1586. National Household Survey on Drug Abuse: Main Findings, 1988; unpublished data. Also in source: data for males and for 1974, 1976, 1977. Data are based on household interviews of a sample of the population 12 years of age and over in the coterminous United States. *Notes:* 1. In 1979, 1982, 1985, and 1988, private answer sheets were used for alcohol questions; in earlier years, respondents answered questions aloud.

★ 242 ★

Use of Marijuana and Cocaine: Young Adults: 1979-1988

Use of marijuana and cocaine in the past month by females 12-17 and 18-25 years of age, 1979, 1982, 1985, and 1988.

Age	1979	1982	1985	1986
Percent of population over 12 years				
Marijuana				
Both sexes:				
12-17 years	17	12	12	6
18-25 years	35	27	22	15
Female:				
12-17 years	14	10	11	7
18-25 years	26	19	17	11
Cocaine[2]				
Both sexes:				
12-17 years	1.4	1.6	1.5	1.1
18-25 years	9.3	6.8	7.6	4.5
Female:				
12-17 years	-	1.5[1]	1.0[1]	1.4
18-25 years	-	4.7	6.3	3.0

Source: Selected from "Use of selected substances in the past month by youths 12-17 years of age and young adults 18-25 years of age, according to age and sex: United States, selected years 1974-88," *Health United States—1989*, p. 167. Primary source: National Institute on Drug Abuse: National Household Survey on Drug Abuse: Main Findings, 1979, by P.M. Fisburne, H.I. Abelson, and I. Cisin. DHHS Pub. No. (ADM)80-976. Alcohol, Drug Abuse, and Mental Health Administration. Washington, D.C. U.S. Government Printing Office, 1980; National Household Survey on Drug Abuse: Main Findings, 1982, by J.D. Miller et al. DHHS Pub. No. (ADM)83-1263. Alcohol, Drug Abuse, and Mental Health Administration. Washington, D.C. U.S. Government Printing Office, 1983; National Household Survey on Drug Abuse: Main Findings, 1985. DHHS Pub. No. (ADM)88-1586. National Household Survey on Drug Aubse: Main Findings, 1988; unpublished data. Also in source: data for males and for 1974, 1976, 1977. Data are based on household interviews of a sample of the population 12 years of age and over in the coterminous United States. *Notes:* 1. Relative standard error greater than 30%. 2. The Drug Abuse Warning Network provides data on the number of people admitted to emergency rooms following cocaine use. See source for further explanation.

★ 243 ★

Women and Alcohol: Numbers and Effects

A summary of some of what is known about problem drinking in women, reported in *National Business Woman.*

Some numbers and effects of problem drinking on women, according to the author:

1. Of the estimated 14 million alcoholics and problem drinkers in the United States, from **3.5 million to 6 million are women.**

2. The average duration of problem drinking before the first recorded incidence of fatty liver disease, hypertension, obesity, anemia, malnutrition, and gastrointestinal hemorrhage is **14.2 years for women** compared to 20.2 years for men.

3. In a follow-up of 103 women treated for alcohol abuse after 11 years, **31% of the women were dead.**

Source: C. Lynne Beauregard, "Women and Alcohol: Caution is Advised," *National Business Woman,* Winter 1989, p. 18+. Also in source: a discussion of the physiological effects of prolonged heavy drinking.

Cancer

★ 244 ★

Breast Cancer Mortality Rates for Cities of the U.S.

Cities with the highest and lowest breast cancer mortality rates (deaths per 100,000 women) for white women, in 87 areas evaluated.

City	Mortality rate (per 100,000 women)
Honolulu	20.5
Phoenix	21.0
Tampa	21.0
Fort Worth	21.3
Las Vegas	21.7
Albuquerque	22.3
Boston	30.2
Cleveland	30.7
Chicago	30.8
New York	32.9

Source: Frank C. Garland, Ph.D., Cedric F. Garland, Dr.P.H., Edward D. Gorham, M.P.H., and Jeffrey F. Young, B.A., "Geographic Variation in Breast Cancer Mortality in the United States: A Hypothesis Involving Exposure to Solar Radiation," *Preventive Medicine* 19, 614-622 (1990). Reprint requests to Frank C. Garland, Ph.D., Dept. of Community and Family Medicine, M-007, University of California San Diego, La Jolla, CA 92093. Related reading: Natalie Angier, "Sunlight and Breast Cancer: Danger in Darkness?," *New York Times,* December 6, 1990, p. B8. The authors evaluated the association between total average annual sunlight energy striking the ground and age-adjusted breast cancer mortality rates in 87 regions of the country.

★ 245 ★

Breast Cancer Risk

Summary of statistics on breast cancer reported in the *New York Times*.

The article summarizes a statement on January 24, 1991, by Dr. Clark Heath of the American Cancer Society:

1. The average American woman runs a **1-in-9** risk of developing breast cancer, an increase over the previous estimate of 1 in 10, making the risk **11%**.

2. Approximately **175,000 women** will get breast cancer in 1991 and **44,500 women** will die from breast cancer.

3. Women who have not produced a live birth before age 30 are at increased risk for breast cancer.

Source: "Rise Seen in Risk of Breast Cancer," *New York Times,* January 25, 1991, p. A11.

★ 246 ★

Breast Cancer Risks

Characteristics of a selection of breast cancer victims[1] and a randomly selected control group.[2] "Cases [victims] were more likely to be of low parity, to be older at first term pregnancy, to be premenopausal, to have a history of biopsy for benign breast disease and to have a first-degree family history of breast cancer" (source).

Characteristics	Cases (n=4711)	Controls (n=4676)
Age(years)		
20-29	3.0%	5.9%
30-39	22.9%	21.8%
40-44	18.3%	16.5%
45-54	55.8%	55.8%
Race		
White	83.3%	83.3%
Black	10.4%	10.3%
Other	6.3%	6.4%
Parity		
0	16.4%	13.0%
1-2	39.5%	35.4%
3-4	32.6%	36.1%
>4	10.8%	14.9%
unknown	0.7%	0.6%
Age at first-term pregnancy (years)		
<20	21.2%	25.4%
20-24	45.6%	46.3%
>24	30.7%	25.5%
unknown	2.5%	2.8%

[Continued]

★ 246 ★

Breast Cancer Risks
[Continued]

Characteristics	Cases (n=4711)	Controls (n=4676)
Menopausal status		
premenopausal	45.1%	38.5%
perimenopausal	17.2%	18.1%
natural menopause	13.0%	14.7%
surgical menopause	21.6%	25.9%
other or unknown	3.1%	2.8%
Age at menarche (years)		
<12	23.7%	21.5%
12-14	65.8%	66.7%
>14	10.2%	11.4%
unknown	0.3%	0.4%
History of benign brease disease	16.7%	11.3%
First-degree family history of breast cancer	11.3%	5.8%

Source: "Cancer and Steroid Hormone Study, 1980-82: Characteristics of cases and controls," *Oral Contraceptives and Breast Cancer: The implications of the present findings for informed consent and informed choice,* 1990, p. 69 (Park Ridge, NJ: Parthenon Publishing Group, 1990). *Notes:* 1. "Cases were women aged 20-54 years with histologically confirmed, primary breast cancer, newly diagnosed between December 1, 1980 and December 31, 1982, and who resided in one of eight geographical locations in the United States." 2. "Controls were women aged 20-54 years selected by telephoning randomly selected households located in the same geographical locations where cases resided."

★ 247 ★

Breast Cancer and Oral Contraceptives
"We did not find that oral contraceptive use increased the risk of breast cancer for women otherwise at higher risk for disease" (source).

Oral contraceptive use/ Time since first use	Cases (n=4711)	Controls (n=4676)	Relative risk[1]
Oral contraceptive use (years)			
Never-use	1756	1699	1.0
Ever-use	2264	2367	1.0
<1	381	431	0.9
1-2	560	614	0.9
3-5	534	560	1.0
6-9	441	429	1.0
10-14	305	265	1.1
>14	43	68	0.6
Time since first use (years)			
Never-use	1756	1699	1.0
<5	39	71	0.8
5-9	242	268	1.1

[Continued]

★ 247 ★

Breast Cancer and Oral Contraceptives

[Continued]

Oral contraceptive use/ Time since first use	Cases (n = 4711)	Controls (n = 4676)	Relative risk[1]
10-14	720	695	1.0
15-19	1,013	1,009	1.0
>19	250	324	0.8

Source: "Cancer and Steroid Hormone Study, 1980-82: Relative Risk of Breast Cancer by Duration of Oral Contraceptive Use," (Table 2), and "Cancer and Steroid Hormone Study, 1980-82: Relative Risk of Breast Cancer by Time Since First Use," (Table 3), *Oral Contraceptives and Breast Cancer: The implications of the present findings for informed consent and informed choice,* 1990, p. 70 (Park Ridge, NJ: Parthenon Publishing Group, 1990). Adjusted for age, parity, menopausal status, age at first term pregnancy, family history of breast cancer, area of residence and history of benign breast disease before first oral contraceptive use. Excludes cases and controls with unknown covariates in the model and unknown time since first use. *Notes:* 1. Relative risk of breat cancer by duration of oral constraceptive use and time since first use, according to the "Cancer and Steroid Hormone Study, 1980-1982."

★ 248 ★

Breast Cancer and Sunlight

Some results of a study done to explore the relationship between sunlight and mortality from breast cancer in the United States.

The team evaluated the association between total average annual sunlight striking the ground and age-adjusted breast cancer mortaility rates in 87 regions of the United States. Risk of fatal breast cancer in major urban areas was inversely proportional to intensity of local sunlight. Age-adjusted mortality rates of breast cancer were found to vary from **17-19 per 100,000 women** in the south and southwest to **33 per 100,000 women** in New York City and environs. The overall U.S. rate was **27.3 per 100,000 women**. The highest mortality rates were in the northern and northeastern states.

Source: Frank C. Garland, Ph.D., Cedric F. Garland, Dr.P.H., Edward D. Gorham, M.P.H., and Jeffrey F. Young, B.A., "Geographic Variation in Breast Cancer Mortality in the United States: A Hypothesis Involving Exposure to Solar Radiation," *Preventive Medicine* 19, 614-622 (1990). Reprint requests to Frank C. Garland, Ph.D., Dept. of Community and Family Medicine, M-007, University of California San Diego, La Jolla, CA 92093. Related reading: Natalie Angier, "Sunlight and Breast Cancer: Danger in Darkness?," *New York Times*, December 6, 1990, p. B8.

★ 249 ★

Estimated New Cancer Cases and Deaths: 1990

Estimated new cancer cases and deaths, total and female, for selected sites, 1990.

Site	Estimated new cases		Estimated deaths	
	Total	Female	Total	Female
All Sites	1,040,000	520,000[1]	502,000	236,000
Oral	30,500	10,100	8,350	2,775
Colon-Rectum	110,000	58,000	53,300	27,300
Lung	157,000	55,000	142,000	50,000
Skin	27,600[2]	12,800[2]	8,800[3]	3,100

[Continued]

★ 249 ★

Estimated New Cancer Cases and Deaths: 1990
[Continued]

Site	Estimated new cases		Estimated deaths	
	Total	Female	Total	Female
Breast	150,900[4]	150,000[4]	44,300	44,000
Uterus	13,500[4]	13,500[4]	6,000	6,000

Source: "Estimated New Cancer Cases and Deaths by Sex for Selected Sites, 1990," *The World Almanac and Book of Facts 1991*, p. 197 (New York: Pharos Books, 1991). Primary source: American Cancer Society. The estimates of new cancer cases are offered as a rough guide and should not be regarded as definitive. *Notes:* 1. Carcinoma in situ and non-melanoma skin cancers are not included in totals. Carcinoma in situ of the uterine cervix accounts for more than 50,000 new cases annually, and carcinoma in situ of the female breast accounts for about 15,000 new cases annually. Non-melanoma skin cancer accounts for more than 600,000 new cases annually. 2. Melanoma only. 3. Melanoma 6,300; other skin 2,500. 4. Invasive cancer only.

★ 250 ★

Female Cancer Incidence Rates: 1980-1987

Cancer incidence rates for selected cancer sites, by race, 1980-1987.

Race and site	1980	1983	1984	1985	1986	1987
	Number of new cases per 100,000 population					
White female						
All sites	308.5	321.8	330.1	339.7	336.8	344.0
Colon and rectum	44.5	43.9	44.5	45.7	42.8	40.5
Colon	32.7	32.5	32.1	33.8	31.9	29.7
Rectum	11.7	11.4	12.3	11.9	10.8	10.9
Pancreas	7.3	8.1	8.4	8.2	7.8	7.3
Lung and bronchus	28.3	34.4	34.9	35.9	37.5	38.7
Melanoma of skin	8.9	9.0	8.8	9.7	9.8	10.1
Breast	86.7	95.2	99.5	105.7	108.4	115.9
Cervix uteri	9.0	8.0	8.3	7.5	7.9	7.3
Corpus uteri	25.2	24.6	23.9	23.2	22.3	22.5
Ovary	14.0	14.0	14.7	15.0	13.4	14.5
Non-Hodgkin's lymphoma	9.1	10.0	10.9	11.1	11.1	10.9
Black female						
All sites	302.6	317.0	321.3	323.5	328.6	321.8
Colon and rectum	49.3	49.1	47.4	45.9	47.2	46.7
Colon	40.8	36.1	37.6	36.1	36.6	36.1
Rectum	8.5	13.0	9.8	9.8	10.6	10.5
Pancreas	12.9	12.3	13.3	11.5	13.2	14.5
Lung and bronchus	33.9	34.6	39.8	40.8	43.2	37.5
Breast	73.3	85.7	83.6	92.9	94.6	90.9
Cervix uteri	19.0	15.0	17.5	16.1	15.5	15.1

[Continued]

★ 250 ★

Female Cancer Incidence Rates: 1980-1987
[Continued]

Race and site	1980	1983	1984	1985	1986	1987
Corpus uteri	14.0	15.8	14.8	14.9	14.0	13.0
Ovary	9.9	11.6	9.3	10.2	8.8	10.1
Non-Hodgkin's lymphoma	5.9	7.9	6.1	6.8	6.6	8.0

Source: Selected from "Age-adjusted cancer incidence rates for selected cancer sites, according to sex and race: Selected years 1973-87," *Health United States—1989*, p. 35. Primary source: National Cancer Institute, National Institutes of Health, 1988 Annual Cancer Statistics Review, including a Report on the Status of Cancer Control. NIH Pub. No. 89-2789. U.S. Department of Health and Human Services. Public Health Service. Bethesda, MD., 1989. Also in source: data for 1973 and 1975 and for males.

★ 251 ★

Female Cancer Survival Rates

Five-year relative cancer survival rates for females for selected sites, according to race: 1977-80 and 1981-86.

Site	All races		White		Black	
	1977-80	1981-86	1977-80	1981-86	1977-80	1981-86
Percent of patients						
All sites	55.4	55.9	56.2	57.0	45.7	44.4
Colon	53.1	55.9	53.3	56.5	49.2	48.7
Rectum	50.6	54.9	51.4	55.6	36.9	44.9
Pancreas	2.7	3.4	2.2	3.1	6.7	3.8
Lung and bronchus	16.2	16.0	16.2	16.2	16.9	13.7
Melanoma of skin	86.1	86.5	86.3	86.6	-	67.5[1]
Breast	74.3	76.6	75.0	77.5	62.9	64.3
Cervix uteri	67.3	65.8	68.2	67.3	61.9	57.1
Corpus uteri	84.3	82.6	85.6	84.0	56.0	55.0
Ovary	38.0	38.9	37.4	38.7	39.4	37.6
Non-Hodgkin's lymphoma	50.4	51.9	50.4	52.2	56.6	49.4

Source: Selected from "Five-year relative cancer survival rates for selected sites, according to race and sex: 1974-76, 1977-80, and 1981-86," *Health United States—1989*, p. 161. Primary source: National Cancer Institute, National Institutes of Health, 1988 Annual Cancer Statistics Review, Including a Report on the Status of Cancer Control, NIH Pub. No. 89-2789. U.S. Department of Health and Human Services. Public Health Service, Bethesda, MD., 1989; National Cancer Institute, Division of Cancer Prevention and Control; unpublished data. Also in source: data for 1974-76. Rates are based on followup of patients through 1986. The rate is the ratio of the observed survival rate for the patient group to the expected survival rate for persons in the general population similar to the patient group with respect to age, sex, race, and calendar year of observation. It estimates the chance of surviving the effects of cancer. *Note:* 1. Standard error is greater than 10 percentage points.

★ 252 ★

Tamoxifen Treatment for Prevention of Breast Cancer

A cancer drug is found to protect women against heart disease.

The author discusses a study conducted by a team led by Dr. Richard R. Love at the University of Wisconsin Clinical Center in Madison of **140 post-menopausal women** who were taking the hormonal drug tamoxifen to help prevent recurrence of breast cancer. It was found that the drug may also protect women against heart disease. The team demonstrated that a standard regimen of tamoxifen reduces total blood cholesterol by about **12%** and harmful LDL cholesterol by **20%**, with a presumed corresponding reduction in risk of coronary heart disease.

Source: Ross L. Prentice, "Tamoxifen as a Potential Preventive Agent in Healthy Postmenopausal Women," *Journal of the National Cancer Institute* 82:16 (August 15, 1990), p. 1310+. Correspondence to: R.L. Prentice, M.D., Division of Health Sciences, Fred Hutchinson Cancer Research Center, 1124 Columbia St., Seattle, WA 98104.

Cigarette Smoking

★ 253 ★

Cancer Deaths and Smoking

Further evidence is offered on the link between smoking and cancer deaths in women.

The authors discuss a long-term study of 1.2 million people signed up in 1982. Over **676,000 women, mostly over age 45**, were enrolled. Of these women, **42.4%** had smoked at some time. In the period 1982-1986, **1,527** of the women died of smoking-related cancer sites. **85.5%** of current smokers' deaths and **69.3%** of former smokers' deaths were attributed to smoking. Cigarette smoking is responsible for over **50%** of the deaths from six types of cancer in women: oral cavity, esophagus, pancreas, larynx, lung, and bladder.

Source: Steven D. Stellman, PhD, and Lawrence Garfinkel, MA, "Proportions of Cancer Deaths Attributable to Cigarette Smoking in Women," *Women and Health* 15:2 (1989), p. 19+.

★ 254 ★

Current Cigarette Smoking, Females

Current cigarette smoking by women 18 years of age and over, by race and age: 1979, 1983, 1985, and 1987.

Race and age	1979	1983	1985	1987
	Percent of women 18 years of age and over			
All Females				
18 years and over, age adjusted	30.3	29.9	28.2	26.7
18-24 years	33.8	35.5	30.4	26.1
25-34 years	33.7	32.6	32.0	31.8
35-44 years	37.0	33.8	31.5	29.6
45-64 years	30.7	31.0	29.9	28.6

[Continued]

★ 254 ★

Current Cigarette Smoking, Females
[Continued]

Race and age	1979	1983	1985	1987
65 years and over	13.2	13.1	13.5	13.7
White females				
18 years and over, age adjusted	30.6	30.1	28.3	27.2
18-24 years	34.5	36.5	31.8	27.8
25-34 years	34.1	32.2	32.0	31.9
35-44 years	37.2	34.8	31.0	29.2
45-64 years	30.6	30.6	29.7	29.0
65 years and over	13.8	13.2	13.3	13.9
Black females				
18 years and over, age adjusted	30.8	31.8	30.7	27.2
18-24 years	31.8	32.0	23.7	20.4
25-34 years	35.2	38.0	36.2	35.8
35-44 years	37.7	32.7	40.2	35.3
45-64 years	34.2	36.3	33.4	28.4
65 years and over	8.5	13.1	14.5	11.7

Source: Selected from "Current cigarette smoking by persons 18 years of age and over, according to sex, race, and age: United States, selected years 1965-87," *Health United States—1989*, p. 165. Primary source: Division of Health Interview Statistics, National Center for Health Statistics: Data from the National Health Interview Survey; Data computed by the Division of Epidemiology and Health Promotion from data compiled by the Division of Health Interview Statistics. Also in source: data for 1965 and 1974. A current smoker is a person who has smoked at least 100 cigarettes and who now smokes; includes occasional smokers. Excludes unknown smoking status.

★ 255 ★

Smokers' Chances of Dying

Estimated probability of dying in the next 16.5 years for smokers 55 to 59 years old, for those who had quit smoking and for those who never smoked.

Smoking History, Persons 55 to 59 Years Old	Chances of dying	
	Women	Men
Smokers	27%	46%
Quitters	15%	33%
Nonsmokers	11%	18%

Source: Philip J. Hilts, "Report Cites Health Gains for the Smokers Who Quit," *New York Times*, September 26, 1990, p. A12. Primary source: Office on Smoking and Health. Related reading: ""Depression Cases Linked to Smoking: Data Lend Support to Theory that the Depressed Turn to the Habit for Relief," *New York Times*, September 26, 1990, p. A12.

★ 256 ★

Smoking and Cervical Cancer

Summary of findings on cervical cancer, reported in the *New York Times*.

The author summarizes the results of a study at the Montefiore Medical Center in the Bronx of **60 women with advanced cervical cancer** and notes:

1. **85%** were smokers and the remainder had significant exposure to passive smoking.

2. There are **13,500 cases of cervical cancer and 6,000 deaths each year** from the disease;

3. Each year **1.2 million women have abnormal Pap tests**; "they might not if they didn't smoke."

Source: Elisabeth Rosenthal, "Cervical Cancer Linked to Smoking in a Study," *New York Times*, October 18, 1990, p. B7.

★ 257 ★

Smoking in Adolescence

Grades in which students first smoked a cigarette, based on recollections of 10th graders in a 1987 national survey.

Grade when first smoked	Girls	Boys
Never smoked	35.9%	38.1%
Grade 10	4.6%	2.1%
Grade 9	10.9%	6.9%
Grades 7 or 8	26.1%	24.1%
Grades 5 or 6	14.0%	17.9%
Grade 4	8.5%	11.0%

Source: Anthony Ramirez, "Tobacco Campaign Set to Warn off Teen-Agers," *New York Times*, December 11, 1990, p. C1. Primary source: National Adolescent Student Health Survey, Department of Health and Human Services.

Clitoridectomy

★ 258 ★

Female Circumcision - Reasons

Results of a survey of 300 women in western Sierra Leone.

Rank and reason	No. of respondents	% of sample
1. Tradition	257	85.6%
2. Social identity (to belong to the group)	105	35%
3. Religion	51	17%
4. Marriage (to increase matrimonial chances)	12	4%

[Continued]

★ 258 ★

Female Circumcision - Reasons
[Continued]

Rank and reason	No. of respondents	% of sample
5. Chastity (preservation of virginity)	11	3.7%
6. Female hygiene	10	3.3%
7. Prevention of promiscuity	6	2%
8. Fertility enhancement	3	1%
9. To please husband	2	0.7%
10. To maintain good health	1	0.3%

Source: "Reasons why female circumcision is performed," *The Circumcision of Women: A Strategy for Eradication*, 1987, p. 46 (Atlantic Highlands, New Jersey: Zed Books, 1987).

★ 259 ★

Health Problems of Circumcised Women

Health problems of girls who have undergone female circumcision.

Type and symptoms	Number Affected	Number Hospitalized	Deaths
Emergencies:			
Vaginal bleeding	10	-	-
Pain	8-10	12	1
Acute urine retention	8	-	-
Tetanus	5	-	-
Ordinary:			
Vaginal discharge	50		
Dysuria	15		
No obvious clinical symptoms	17		

Source: "Health problems," *The Circumcision of Women: A Strategy for Eradication*, 1987, p. 30. (Atlantic Highlands, New Jersey: Zed Books, 1987). Results of a study of 100 circumcised girls between the ages of 8 and 12 in Sierra Leone.

★ 260 ★

Instruments Used and Types of Female Circumcision

Type of female circumcision performed and instrument used. Results of a survey of 300 women in western Sierra Leone.

Type	Razor blade	Traditional knife	Surgical scalpel	Broken bottle	Others	Total
Type I[1]	32	62	2	1	8	105
Type II[2]	48	102	4	3	4	161
Type III[3]	1	2	-	-	-	3
Total	81	1'66	6	4	12	269

Source: "Type of FC with instrument used (absolute numbers)," *The Circumcision of Women: A Strategy for Eradication*, 1987, p. 52 (Atlantic Highlands, New Jersey: Zed Books, 1987). Results of a survey of 300 women in western Sierra Leone. "As members climb the educational ladder, so surgical instruments are introduced" (source). *Notes:* 1. Clitoridectomy - the removal of the prepuce of the clitoris. 2. Excision - the removal of the prepuce, the clitoris, and all or part of the labia minora, leaving the labia majora intact and the rest of the vulva unsutured. 3. Infibulation - the removal of the prepuce, the whole of labiae minora and majora, and the suturing of the two sides of the vulva, leaving a very small orifice to permit the flow of urine and menstrual discharge.

★ 261 ★

Physical Effects of Female Circumcision

Types of genital malformations resulting from female circumcision, by type of circumcision.

Type	Keloid scar	Fistula	Prolapse	Cysts	Abscesses	None
Type I[1]	62	0	32	0	0	22
Type II[2]	104	1	49	8	4	63
Type III[3]	2	0	1	0	0	1
Total for all types	168	1	82	8	4	86

Source: "Visual malformations present by type of circumcision (Total sample 269)," *The Circumcision of Women: A Strategy for Eradication*, 1987, p. 55 (Atlantic Highlands, New Jersey: Zed Books, 1987). *Notes:* 1. Clitoridectomy - the removal of the prepuce of the clitoris. 2. Excision - the removal of the prepuce, the clitoris, and all or part of the labia minora, leaving the labia majora intact and the rest of the vulva unsutured. 3. Infibulation - the removal of the prepuce, the whole of labiae minora and majora, and the suturing of the two sides of the vulva, leaving a very small orifice to permit the flow of urine and menstrual discharge.

Conditions

★ 262 ★

AIDS

Some trends in reported AIDS cases.

Cases of AIDS among women reported to the Centers for Disease Control since 1981, totaled **10,611** as of December 31, 1989, amounting to **9.2%** of all reported AIDS cases. The proportion of AIDS among women increased from **6.4%** in 1984 to **10.4%** in 1988.

Source: David M. Allen, MD, MPH, Nancy C. Lee, MD, Susan Lloyd Schulz, PA-C, MPH, Marguerite Pappaioanou, CVM,PhD, Timothy J. Dondero, Jr., MD, MPH, and Ida M. Onorato, MD, "Determining HIV Seroprevalence Among Women in Women's Health Clinics," *Public Health Reports* 105:2 (March-April 1990, p. 130+. Tearsheet requests to CDC, Technical Information Activity, Mail Stop G29, Atlanta, GA 30333. Also in source: a discussion of surveys being done at women's health clinics to determine the prevalence of HIV infection by race, ethnicity, age, and geographic location.

★ 263 ★

AIDS - Methods of Transmission

Total and female AIDS cases according to transmission category for persons 13 years of age and over, 1983-1989.

Transmission category	Number, by year of report							Percent distribution		
	1983	1984	1985	1986	1987	1988	1989[2]	1984	1988	1989[2]
Total[3]	2,032	4,395	8,076	12,981	20,821	30,377	24,995	-	-	-
Female	141	277	525	970	1,684	3,064	2,553	100%	100%	100%
Intravenous drug use	80	171	283	476	837	1,615	1,316	61.7%	52.7%	51.5%
Hemophilia/coagulation disorder	-	2	3	4	5	5	7	0.7%	0.2%	0.3%
Born in Caribbean/African countries	12	17	30	56	75	109	95	6.1%	3.6%	3.7%
Heterosexual[4]	21	46	114	273	458	804	673	16.6%	26.2%	26.4%
Sexual contact with intravenous drug user	15	32	80	187	310	589	471	11.6%	19.2%	18.4%
Transfusion	10	22	59	104	215	330	221	7.9%	10.8%	8.7%
Undetermined[5]	18	19	36	57	94	201	241	6.9%	6.6%	9.4%

Source: Selected from "Acquired immunodeficiency syndrome (AIDS) cases, according to race/ethnicity, sex, and transmission category for persons 13 years of age and over: United States, 1983-89," *Health United States—1989*, p. 152-53. Primary source: Centers for Disease Control, Center for Infectious Diseases, AIDS Programs. Also in source: total for all years; data for males. Statistics, National Center for Health Statistics: Data from the National Health Interview Survey. Also in source: data by age, race, family income, geographic region, and location of residence. Data are based on reporting by State health departments. The AIDS case definition was changed in September 1987 to allow for the presumptive diagnosis of AIDS-associated diseases and conditions and to expand the spectrum of HIV-associated diseases reportable as AIDS. Excludes residents of U.S. territories. *Notes:* 1. Includes cases prior to 1983. 2. Data are as of September 30, 1989, and reflect reporting delays. 3. Includes all other races not shown separately. 4. Includes persons who have had heterosexual contact with a person with HIV infection or at risk of HIV infection. 5. Includes persons for whom risk information is incomplete (because of death, refusal to be interviewed, or loss to followup), persons still under investigation, men reported only to have had heterosexual contact with prostitutes, and interviewed persons for whom no specific risk is identified.

★ 264 ★

AIDS Cases by Age at Diagnosis

Female AIDS cases according to age at diagnosis and race/ethnicity, 1983-1989.

Age at diagnosis and race/ethnicity	1983	1984	1985	1986	1987	1988	1989[2]	Distribution All years[1,2]
	Number, by year of report							
Total[3]	2,066	4,445	8,205	13,167	21,140	30,947	25,467	
Female								
All females, 13 years and over[3]	141	277	525	970	1,684	3,064	2,553	100%
White, not Hispanic	34	79	143	272	544	864	723	28.8%
Black, not Hispanic	67	141	284	523	896	1,663	1,438	54.4%
Hispanic	38	57	94	162	230	502	357	15.6%
13-19 years	3	4	4	12	11	24	18	0.8%
20-29 years	57	94	175	279	477	784	665	27.6%
30-39 years	51	130	233	447	751	1,512	1,231	47.2%
40-49 years	14	25	49	129	233	419	383	13.6%
50-59 years	11	8	27	47	90	146	132	5.0%
60 years and over	5	16	37	56	122	179	124	5.8%

Source: Selected from "Acquired immunodeficiency syndrome (AIDS) cases, according to diagnosis, sex, and race-ethnicity: United States, 1983-89," *Health United States—1989*, p. 150. Primary source: Centers for Disease Control, Center for Infectious Diseases, AIDS Program. Also in source: data for males and children; totals for "All years." Data are based on reporting by State health departments. *Notes:* 1. Includes cases prior to 1983. 2. Data are as of September 30, 1989, and reflect reporting delays. 3. Includes all other races not shown separately.

★ 265 ★

Acute Conditions

Average annual number of acute conditions, total and female, by age, race, and family income, 1985-87.

Characteristic	All ages			Under 18 years		18-44 years		45-64 years		65 years and over	
	All races	White	Black	White	Black	White	Black	White	Black	White	Black
	Numbers in thousands										
Total[1]	423,359	372,334	39,252	150,584	17,268	150,156	15,410	44,819	4,520	26,775	2,053
Female	239,008	209,690	22,381	77,237	8,567	87,916	9,709	26,762	2,663	17,775	1,442
Family income less than $20,000											
Total[1]	144,051	117,436	22,212	40,875	10,368	49,485	8,199	12,786	2,141	14,290	1,504
Female	86,232	70,257	13,366	20,864	5,036	30,472	5,791	8,806	1,441	10,115	1,097
Family income $20,000 or more											
Total[1]	233,954	216,492	11,593	95,632	4,944	87,566	5,027	25,494	1,463	7,801	160
Female	126,496	117,089	6,097	48,889	2,518	49,992	2,856	13,698	634	4,510	90

Source: Selected from "Average annual number of acute conditions by age, race, family income, and other sociodemographic characteristics: United States, 1985-87," National Center for Health Statistics, "Health of Black and White Americans, 1985-87, *Vital and Health Statistics*, Series 10, No. 171, January 1990, Table 2. Also in source: datat by other characteristics. Data are based on household interviews of the civilian noninstitutionalized population. *Notes:* 1. Unknowns for any characteristic are included in total. Excludes data for "Other." 2. Persons 18 years of age and over.

★ 266 ★

Cardiovascular Disease and Oral Contraceptives

Some results of a World Health Organization study on the relation between cardiovascular disease and the use of oral contraceptives.

A hospital-based case-control study of **women aged 20-44 years** was conducted in Hong Kong, Mexico, and the German Democratic Republic. Use of oral contraceptives was connected with the development of venous thrombo-embolic disease (VTE), thrombotic stroke (PE) and myocardial infarction; the links with haemorrhagic stroke were less clear. An overall relative risk of 2.9 (95% confidence limits, 1.4-6.1) for VTE/PE was found among recent or current users of oral contraceptives.

Source: "Cardiovascular Disease and Use of Oral Contraceptives: WHO Collaborative Study," *Bulletin of the World Health Organization* 67(4): 417-423 (1989). Also in source: a discussion of the significance of findings of ischaemic heart disease and stroke among current or recent users of oral contraceptives. See source for list of collaborating centers and names of investigators.

★ 267 ★

Elevated Blood Pressure

Females aged 20-74 years with systolic blood pressure at least 140 mmHg or diastolic pressure at least 90 mmHg, by race and age: 1971-74 and 1976-80.

Age	All races		White		Black	
	1971-74	1976-80	1971-74	1976-80	1971-74	1976-80
	Percent of population					
20-74 years, age adjusted	38.4	38.0	37.3	37.0	49.6	46.6
Female[1]						
20-74 years, age adjusted	34.3	32.6	32.6	31.0	48.5	45.2
20-24 years	7.1	7.8	6.9	6.5	9.3	12.2
25-34 years	12.7	11.7	11.2	11.0	24.0	15.6
35-44 years	26.9	27.1	23.8	24.6	49.9	43.7
45-54 years	41.5	42.4	39.1	40.1	61.0	65.6
55-64 years	59.5	54.9	57.9	53.0	75.3	69.4
65-74 years	74.1	63.9	73.4	62.9	80.6	74.0

Source: Selected from "Elevated blood pressure among persons 20-74 years of age, according to race, sex, and age: United States, 1960-62, 1971-74, and 1976-80," *Health United States—1989*, p. 169. Primary source: Division of Health Examination Statistics, National Center for Health Statistics; unpublished data. Also in source: data for 1960-62, 1971-74, and for males; data for percent of population with systolic pressure at least 160 mmHg or diastolic pressure at least 95 mmHg. *Note:* 1. Excludes pregnant women.

★ 268 ★

Health Problems of VDT Operators

Health problems reported by secretaries after the introduction of new technology into the office. N = 158.

Health Problem	% reporting problem
Eye strain	32.7%
Headaches	17.9%
Colds/sore throats	3.1%
Nausea	3.1%
Insomnia	5.6%
Muscle strain	20.9%
Exhaustion	19.1%
Stomach pains	3.1%
Menstrual problems	1.2%
Skin rashes	7.4%
Shortness of breath	1.9%
Pressure in chest	1.9%
"Nerves"	17.3%
Unstable feelings/anger	10.5%
Loss of sex drive	2.5%
Depression	9.3%

Source: Ann Statham and Ellen Bravo, "The Introduction of New Technology: Health Implications for Workers," *Women and Health* 16(2) 1990, p. 105+. Data from surveys of 75 workers in 3 settings revealed planning deficiences (among other issues) that seemed to cause difficulty for the workers involved. Surveys of 162 secretaries were used to explore the resulting hypothesis that the planning deficiences would result in symptoms of stress.

★ 269 ★

Health Problems of the Homeless

Health problems diagnosed among homeless health care clients, with percentage of alcohol abusers and nonabusers and abuser/nonabuser ratio for each diagnosis.

Diagnosis	Women			Men		
	Abusers	Nonabusers	Abuser/ nonabuser ratio	Abusers	Nonabusers	Abuser/ nonabuser ratio
Mental illness	52.8%	35.2%	1.5	27.7%	21.3%	1.3
Peripheral vascular disorder	14.1%	10.7%	1.3	15.5%	13.2%	1.2
Hypertension	14.1%	10.3%	1.4	21.9%	12.3%	1.8
Gastrointestinal disorder	20.0%	14.9%	1.3	17.1%	11.2%	1.5
Trauma						
Lacerations	8.5%	3.7%	2.3	13.5%	8.8%	1.5
Fractures	5.4%	2.1%	2.6	7.0%	4.5%	1.6
Contusions	10.6%	4.5%	2.4	8.0%	4.4%	1.8
Drug abuse	26.1%	5.3%	4.0	18.1%	7.3%	2.5(sic)
Eye Disorder	9.6%	6.9%	1.4	18.1%	7.3%	2.5(sic)
Neurological disorder	11.7%	9.6%	1.2	9.7%	6.7%	1.4
Cardiac disease	6.3%	5.6%	1.1	8.5%	6.1%	1.4
Tuberculosis	3.1%	2.7%	1.1	6.9%	5.5%	1.3

[Continued]

★ 269 ★

Health Problems of the Homeless
[Continued]

Diagnosis	Women			Men		
	Abusers	Nonabusers	Abuser/ nonabuser ratio	Abusers	Nonabusers	Abuser/ nonabuser ratio
Chronic obstructive pulmonary disease	8.9%	3.7%	2.4	6.0%	4.2%	1.4
Arterial disease	6.8%	4.0%	1.7	5.4%	3.5%	1.5
Diabetes mellitus	3.1%	2.8%	1.1	2.2%	2.2%	1.0
Seizures	5.6%	2.5%	2.2	6.8%	2.2%	3.1
Anemia	3.1%	3.6%	0.9	2.2%	1.4%	1.6
Nutritional disorder	4.5%	2.1%	2.1	2.4%	1.3%	1.8
Liver disease	4.2%	0.6%	7.0	3.0%	0.7%	4.3
Pregnancy	7.0%	12.0%	0.6	-	-	-

Source: Selected from "Health problems diagnosed among homeless health care clients, by sex, with percentage of alcohol abusers and nonabusers and abuser/nonabuser ratio for each diagnosis," *Seventh Special Report to the U.S. Congress on Alcohol and Health from the Secretary of Health and Human Services,* January 1990, p. 32. Primary source: Wright, J.D.; Knight, J.W.; et al., Ailments and alcohol: Health status among the drinking homeless. *Alcohol Health and Research World* 11(3):22-27, 1987. "...it has been estimated that at least 250,000 Americans are homeless on any given night and that as many as 3 million may experience some type of homelessness each year. Estimates of the prevalence of current alcohol abuse or dependence among the homeless generally range from 20 to 45 percent..." (source, p. 30).

★ 270 ★

Heart Problems

Summary of the American Heart Association's annual update on heart disease reported in the *Chicago Tribune*.

Among the statistics released by the American Heart Association cited in the article:

1. American women suffer **244,000 heart attacks** each year; the figure for men is 268,000.

2. In 1988, **83,000 heart bypass operations** were done in women; the figure for men is 270,000.

3. In 1988, angioplasty was performed on women **67,000 times**; the figure for men is 160,000.

4. women who smoke and use birth control pills are **39 times** as likely as other women to have a heart attack and **22 times** as likely to have strokes.

Source: "Study: Heart ills kill more in South," *Chicago Tribune,* January 14, 1991, p. 4. Also in source: a discussion of other findings of the American Heart Association from its annual update on heart disease.

★ 271 ★

Hypertension

Hypertension among persons 20-74 years of age, by race and age, 1971-74 and 1976-80.

Age	All races		White		Black	
	1971-74	1976-80	1971-74	1976-80	1971-74	1976-80
Percent of population						
20-74 years, age adjusted	40.0	40.6	38.7	39.4	53.5	50.5
Female[1]						
20-74 years, age adjusted	36.1	36.0	34.1	34.2	52.9	50.6
20-24 years	7.2	8.3	6.9	6.8	9.5	14.6
25-34 years	13.7	12.8	11.7	12.0	29.6	17.7
35-44 years	28.2	28.8	24.9	26.2	52.8	46.0
45-54 years	43.6	47.1	40.9	44.5	65.6	73.9
55-64 years	62.5	61.1	60.5	59.0	82.5	77.9
65-74 years	78.3	71.8	77.5	70.6	85.6	85.0
Male						
20-74 years, age adjusted	44.0	45.3	43.3	44.8	54.2	50.5
20-24 years	20.4	24.7	20.9	25.6	18.4	22.2
25-34 years	27.6	31.4	27.3	31.7	33.6	32.1
35-44 years	39.1	40.5	36.6	38.6	64.7	54.3
45-54 years	55.0	53.6	54.6	53.5	61.1	53.3
55-64 years	62.5	61.8	62.1	60.8	72.0	73.8
65-74 years	67.2	67.1	65.8	65.8	81.5	75.1

Source: Selected from "Hypertension among persons 20-74 years of age, according to race, sex, and age: United States, 1960-62, 1971-74, and 1976-80," *Health United States—1989*, p. 171. Primary source: Division of Health Examination Statistics, National Center for Health Statistics; unpublished data. Also in source: data for males and for 1960-62. See source for the definition of a person with hypertension. Data are based on physical examinations of a sample of the civilian noninstitutionalized population. *Note:* 1. Excludes pregnant women.

★ 272 ★

Hypertension Treatment

Prevalence rates of hypertension for persons aged 25-74 by treatment history and race, 1960-1980.

Hypertension Prevalence	Percent who have been treated				
	All People[1]	White Women	White Men	Black Women	Black Men
In the population					
1960-1962	20.3%	20.4%	16.3%	39.8%	31.8%
1974-1976	22.1%	19.6%	21.4%	35.5%	37.1%
1976-1980	22.0%	20.0%	21.2%	39.8%	28.3%
Never diagnosed[2]					
1960-1962	51.1%	43.9%	57.6%	35.1%	70.5%
1974-1976	36.4%	29.7%	42.3%	28.9%	41.0%
1976-1980	26.6%	25.2%	40.6%	14.5%	35.7%
On medication					
1960-1962	31.3%	38.2%	22.4%	48.1%	18.5%

[Continued]

★ 272 ★

Hypertension Treatment
[Continued]

Hypertension Prevalence	Percent who have been treated				
	All People[1]	White Women	White Men	Black Women	Black Men
1974-1976	34.2%	48.5%	25.9%	36.4%	24.0%
1976-1980	56.2%	58.6%	38.3%	60.6%	40.9%
On medication/controlled[3]					
1960-1962	16.0%	21.9%	11.8%	20.2%	5.0%
1974-1976	19.6%	28.1%	15.1%	22.3%	12.7%
1976-1980	36.1%	40.3%	20.9%	30.9%	16.1%

Source: "Prevalence Rates of Hypertension for Persons Aged 25-74 (in percent) by Treatment History, Race, and Sex, 1960-1980," *A Common Destiny: Blacks and American Society,* 1989, p. 423. Primary source: Data from the U.S. Department of Health and Human Services. Hypertension is defined as elevated blood pressure, that is, a systolic measurement of at least 160 mm Hg or a diastolic measurement of at least 95 mm Hg, or as taking antihypertensive medication. *Notes:* 1. Includes all other races not shown separately. 2. Reported that was never told by physician that he or she had high blood pressure or hypertension. 3. Subset of "on medication" group; those taking antihypertensive medication whose blood pressure was not elevated at the time of the examination.

★ 273 ★

Infertility Among Married Couples

Number of currently married women 15-44 years of age and percent distribution by infertility status, according to parity, 1965, 1982, and 1988.

Parity	All married women (thousands)			Surgically sterile			Infertile		
	1988	1982	1965	1988	1982	1965	1988	1982	1965
All parities	29,147	28,231	26,454	42.4%	38.9%	15.8%	7.9%	8.5%	11.2%
Parity 0	5,533	5,098	3,492	11.5%	9.9%	7.3%	18.5%	19.6%	14.5%
Parity 1 or more	23,614	23,134	22,962	49.7%	45.3%	16.9%	5.4%	6.0%	10.8%

Source: William D. Mosher, Ph.D., and William F. Pratt, Ph.D., "Fecundity and Infertility in the United States, 1965-88," *Advance Data from Vital and Health Statistics of the National Center for Health Statistics,* No. 192, December 4, 1990, Table 3, p. 5. Statistics are based on samples of the female population. Because of rounding of estimates, figures may not add to totals.

★ 274 ★

Menstrual Dysfunction in Athletes

Frequency distribution of menstrual characteristics of 130 habitual women runners by mileage group. High mileage = 30+ miles per week.

Menstrual characteristic	Mileage group			
	High	Number	Low	Number
Before starting to run				
Started menstruating	100%	32	96%	98
Periods were regular	69%	32	86%	93
Menstrual cramps interfered with daily activity	31.3%	32	31.2%	93
Irregularity	33.3%	30	11.5%	87
Oral contraceptive use	51.6%	31	44.1%	93
After starting to run				

[Continued]

★ 274 ★

Menstrual Dysfunction in Athletes
[Continued]

Menstrual characteristic	Mileage group			
	High	Number	Low	Number
Missed more than one period	50%	30	24.7%	89
Spotting between periods	30%	30	25.8%	89
Lighter periods	53.3%	30	46.6%	88
Less regular periods	24.1%	29	15.7%	89
Periods have stopped	20.0%	30	7.9%	89
Menstrual cramps interfered with running	14.8%	27	13.6%	88
Irregularity	30.0%	30	7.9%	89
Oral contraceptive use	28.1%	32	32.9%	97
Oral contraceptive use/current	18.8%	32	21.1%	95

Source: Vilma E. Cokkinades, MS, MSPH, C.A. Macera, PhD, and R.R. Pate, PhD, "Menstrual Dysfunction Among Habitual Runners," *Women & Health* 16(2); 1990, p. 59+. Of 1,576 questionnaires mailed, 966 were completed.

★ 275 ★

Mother-Child AIDS Transmission Worldwide

Total and pediatric AIDS cases and percent of pediatric cases transmitted by parent-child, 1989.

Country	Total AIDS cases	Pediatric AIDS Cases	
		Total	Mother-child
Germany, Federal Republic	3,497	37	26
France	7,149	193	154
Israel	85	1	1
Italy	4,158	118	103
Norway	119	1	1
Soviet Union	7	1	1
Sweden	309	4	3
United Kingdom	2,372	34	22
United States	104,210	1,780	1,422

Source: "Total and Pediatric AIDS Cases, and Pediatric Cases by Transmission Group, Selected Countries: 1989," *Children's Well-Being: An International Comparison*, A Report of the Select Committee on Children, Youth, and Families, 101st Cong., 2d sess., March 1990, p. 110. Primary source: U.S. Center for Disease Control, 1989, telephone communication; and World Health Organization Collaborating Centre on AIDS, 1989, "AIDS Surveillance in Europe," Quarterly Report No. 22, 30 June, Paris, tables 7 and 10. Data for United States are through August 1989, data for all other countries are through June 1989. Percent of pediatric AIDS cases due to parent-child transmission based on total pediatric cases, excluding unknown.

★ 276 ★

Osteoporosis

Discussion of a new option for treating osteoporosis.

The author summarizes the results of a study appearing in the same *Journal*, in which **429 women** with postmenopausal osteoporosis and vertebral fractures were treated with cyclical etidronate for 14 days followed by 500 mg of calcium daily for 73 days. The two groups receiving etidronate had significant increases in bone mass of the lumbar spine of **4.2%** and **5.2%** and smaller increases in the bone mass of the proximal femur.

Source: B. Lawrence Riggs, M.D., "A New Option for Treating Osteoporosis," *New England Journal of Medicine,* 323:2, July 12, 1990, p. 124; N.B. Watts, S.T. Harris, H.K. Genant, et al. "Intermittent cyclical etidronate treatment of postmenopausal osteoporosis, *New England Journal of Medicine*, 323:2, July 12, 1990, p. 73-9. Related reading: Lawrence K. Altman, "New Therapy Shown to Fight Bone Loss in Elderly," *New York Times*, July 12, 1990, p. 1+.

★ 277 ★

Overweight

Overweight women 20-74 years of age by race and age, 1971-74 and 1976-80.

Age	All races		White		Black	
	1971-74	1976-80	1971-74	1976-80	1971-74	1976-80
Percent of population						
20-74 years, age adjusted	25.7	26.2	24.8	25.1	35.7	37.7
Female						
20-74 years, age adjusted	26.9	27.4	25.0	25.2	44.5	46.1
20-24 years	10.5	11.4	9.1	9.6	22.5	23.7
25-34 years	17.6	20.0	15.9	17.9	31.5	33.5
35-44 years	27.3	27.0	24.5	24.8	49.9	40.8
45-54 years	30.0	31.7	29.1	30.2	39.4	52.1
55-64 years	32.0	32.8	31.0	31.9	43.9	44.2
65-74 years	38.0	38.5	37.0	36.5	49.2	60.8
Men						
20-74 years, age adjusted	24.1	24.8	24.3	24.9	25.0	27.5
20-24 years	12.1	12.1	12.8	12.7	8.2	5.5
25-34 years	23.6	20.4	23.6	20.9	26.1	17.5
35-44 years	29.4	28.9	28.9	28.2	39.3	40.9
45-54 years	27.6	31.0	28.2	30.5	22.4	41.4
55-64 years	24.8	28.1	24.9	28.6	25.6	26.0
65-74 years	23.0	25.2	23.1	25.8	21.6	26.4

Source: Selected from "Overweight persons 20-74 years of age, according to race, sex, and age: United States, 1960-62, 1971-74, and 1976-80," *Health United States—1989*, p. 174. Primary source: Division of Health Examination Statistics, National Center for Health Statistics; unpublished data. Also in source: data for both sexes and males broken down by age; data for 1960-62. Data are based on physical examinations of a sample of the civilian noninstitutionalized population. See source for a definition of overweight.

★ 278 ★

Overweight and Severely Overweight Adults by Race/Ethnicity

Percentage of persons aged 20-74 years who are overweight or severely overweight, by race/ethnicity and sex, 1982-1984. .

Ethnic group or race	Percent overweight		Percent severely overweight	
	Female	Male	Female	Male
Mexican American	41.6%	30.9%	16.9%	10.8%
Cuban	31.6%	27.6%	6.6%	10.7%
Puerto Rican	40.2%	25.6%	15.7%	8.0%
Non-Hispanic White	23.9%	24.2%	9.4%	7.7%
Non-Hispanic Black	44.4%	26.0%	19.8%	10.0%

Source: "Age-Adjusted Percent of Overweight and Severely Overweight Persons Aged 20-74 Years, by Sex and Ethnic Group or Race: Hispanic Health and Nutrition Examination Survey, 1982-84, and Second National Health and Nutrition Examination Sruvey, 1976-80," *Nutrition Monitoring in the United States,* September 1989, p. 49. Primary source: U.S. Department of Health and Human Services and U.S. Department of Agriculture. .

★ 279 ★

Pelvic Inflammatory Disease

Some statistics on the current understanding of PID.

Pelvic inflammatory disease is an often-serious consequence of gonococcal and chlamydial infection. It is estimated that **1 million women** in the United States are treated annually for the condition, and at least **one fourth** of these women will suffer one or more serious sequelae. It is estimated that the cost of these sequelae will reach $3.5 billion per year by 1990.

Source: Herbert B. Peterson, Edward I. Galaid, and Jonathan M. Zenilman, "Pelvic Inflammatory Disease: Review of Treatment Options," *Reviews of Infectious Diseases* 12:Supplement 6 (July-August 1990), p. S656+. Address reprint requests to Technical Information Services (E06), Center for Prevention Services, Centers for Disease Control, Atlanta, GA 30333. Also in source: a discussion of treatment options and costs. Related reading: Philip J. Hilts, "Growing Concern Over Pelvic Infection in Women," *New York Times*, October 11, 1990, p. B7.

★ 280 ★

Persons with Diabetes

Total persons with known diabetes and rate per 1,000 population, by sex, 1986.

Sex	Number, in thousands				Rate per 1,000 population			
	Total	Under 45	45-64 years	65+ years	Total	Under 45	45-64 years	65+ years
Total persons with known diabetes	6,641	1,340	2,535	2,766	27.8	8.1	56.4	98.2
Female	3,437	676	1,257	1,504	27.9	8.1	53.5	91.1
Male	3,205	665	1,278	1,262	27.8	8.1	59.5	108.3

Source: Selected from "Persons with Known Case of Diabetes, by Selected Characteristics: 1986," *Statistical Abstract of the United States 1990*, 1990, p. 120. Primary source: U.S. National Center for Health Statistics, unpublished data. Also in source: data by race. Covers civilian noninstitutional population 18 years old and over. Annual average. Based on subsampes of households in the National Health Interview Survey.

★ 281 ★

Premenstrual Syndrome and the Media

Some physical conditions and behavior of premenstrual women, according to the popular press.

Symptom/Behavior	% of Articles
Water retention	
swelling/bloating	71%
painful/tender breasts	55%
weight gain	33%
skin blemishes/acne	29%
Negative affect	
depression/despair/sadness	72%
mood swings	51%
anxiety	42%
tension	35%
crying	31%
suicidal ideation/attempt	26%
Pain	
headache	58%
fatigue/lassitude	40%
Change in eating habits	
cravings for sugar/salt	44%
Impaired concentration	
poor motor coordination/clumsiness	13%
insomnia/sleep irregularities	12%
Behavior change	
violence	26%
lethargy	19%
Automonic reactions	
constipation	18%
dizziness/faintness	15%

Source: Joan C. Chrisler, PhD, and Karen B. Levy, BA, "The Media Construct a Menstrual Monster: A Content Analysis of PMS Articles in the Popular Press," *Women & Health* 16(2): 1990, p. 89+. Also in source: a discussion of the implications of negative coverage of menstrual cycle changes and recommendations to improve media reports. The authors' search of *Reader's Guide to Periodical Literature* from 1980 to 1987 turned up 81 articles on premenstrual syndrome.

★ 282 ★

Restricted-Activity Days Due to Medical Conditions

Average annual number of restricted-activity days, total and per female, due to acute and chronic conditions, by age, race, and family income, 1985-87.

Characteristic	All ages			Under 18 years		18-44 years		45-64 years		65 years and over	
	All races	White	Black	White	Black	White	Black	White	Black	White	Black
	Number per person per year										
Total[1]	14.8	14.7	16.8	9.4	7.5	11.1	13.9	19.1	30.3	30.8	44.4
Female	16.6	16.5	19.0	10.0	7.7	12.8	16.2	20.5	32.7	33.1	47.7
Family income less than $20,000											
Total[1]	20.4	20.8	20.1	10.2	8.2	14.8	16.9	32.9	40.7	34.8	47.3
Female	22.3	22.8	22.1	11.0	7.9	16.6	18.8	31.9	41.9	36.6	49.4
Family income $20,000 or more											
Total[1]	11.3	11.4	11.4	9.4	6.5	9.7	11.5	13.9	18.6	24.6	21.8
Female	12.6	12.7	12.6	9.8	7.1	11.2	13.4	15.4	18.3	27.8	23.6

Source: Selected from "Average annual number of restricted-activity days due to acute and chronic conditions by age, race, family income, and other sociodemographic characteristics: United States, 1985-87," National Center for Health Statistics, "Health of Black and White Americans, 1985-87, *Vital and Health Statistics*, Series 10, No. 171, January 1990, Table 13. Also in source: data by other characteristics; number of days in thousands (Table 14, p. 51). Data are based on household interviews of the civilian noninstitutionalized population. *Notes:* 1. Unknowns for any characteristic are included in total. Data for "Other" are not included here.

★ 283 ★

Serum Cholesterol Levels

High serum cholesterol levels among persons 20-74 years of age, by race and age, 1971-74 and 1976-80.

Age	All races		White		Black	
	1971-74	1976-80	1971-74	1976-80	1971-74	1976-80
	Percent of population with high serum cholesterol					
20-74 years, age adjusted	28.7	28.0	28.7	28.0	28.9	26.2
Female						
20-74 years, age adjusted	29.7	29.2	29.6	29.6	30.8	26.6
20-24 years	9.8	6.6	9.4	6.5	10.6	7.0
25-34 years	11.7	11.8	11.5	12.4	12.7	8.7
35-44 years	19.3	20.7	18.9	21.1	22.0	16.9
45-54 years	38.7	40.5	38.2	40.6	44.6	40.7
55-64 years	53.1	52.9	53.7	53.7	49.4	46.5
65-74 years	57.7	51.6	57.9	52.1	54.8	48.4
Male						
20-74 years, age adjusted	33.7	31.6	34.1	31.9	29.2	27.5
20-24 years	19.6	20.4	19.6	20.7	19.8	18.9
25-34 years	30.8	28.0	31.6	28.3	25.2	22.6
35-44 years	36.0	33.0	37.0	33.7	25.4	28.1
45-54 years	38.0	35.2	38.0	35.5	38.6	31.8

[Continued]

★ 283 ★

Serum Cholesterol Levels
[Continued]

Age	All races		White		Black	
	1971-74	1976-80	1971-74	1976-80	1971-74	1976-80
55-64 years	39.9	37.3	40.0	37.6	33.6	29.7
65-74 years	35.8	34.8	36.3	34.6	32.0	35.7

Source: Selected from "Borderline high and high serum cholesterol levels among persons 20-74 years of age, according to race, sex, and age: United States, 1960-62, 1971-74, and 1976-80," *Health United States—1989*, p. 172-3. Primary source: Division of Health Examination Statistics, National Center for Health Statistics; unpublished data. Also in source: data for 1960-62 and for males; data for population with borderline high serum cholesterol. See source of a discussion of serum cholesterol levels. Data are based on physical examinations of a sample of the civilian noninstitutionalized population.

★ 284 ★

Signs of Morbidity Among the Elderly
Selected morbidity indicators, all ages and 65 and over, by race.

Selected Morbidity Indicator	White				Black			
	All Ages		65 and Over		All Ages		65 and Over	
	Female	Male	Female	Male	Female	Male	Female	Male
Limitation in major activity due to chronic condition	10.5%	11.2%	34.2%	42.5%	12.2%	12.7%	46.5%	56.5%
Restricted activity (days per year)	20.6	16.6	41.4	34.1	20.5	19.0	58.7	54.3
Bed disability (days per year)	7.6	5.5	13.9	11.4	10.7	8.0	21.5	24.8
Days lost from work	5.1	4.6	4.9	3.5	8.3	7.1	6.5	3.5

Source: "Selected Morbidity Indicators for Elderly People, by Race, 1978-1980," *A Common Destiny: Blacks and American Society*, 1989, p. 429. Primary source: Data from National Center for Health Statistics (1984).

★ 285 ★

Syphilis

A discussion of trends in the epidemiology of syphilis, 1981 through 1989, reported in *JAMA*.

According to the authors, the incidence of primary and secondary syphilis in the United States increased 34% from 13.7 to 18.4 cases per 100,000 persons in the period 1981-1989. This was the greatest increase since 1949. From 1982 to 1985, the incidence among black men decreased from 101.9 to 71.5 cases per 100,000 and in black women **decreased from 45.8 to 35.8 cases per 100,000.** In 1986 this trend reversed for blacks and the incidence more than doubled from 1985 to 1989 (**from 35.8 to 98.7 cases per 100,000 persons** for black women, and from 71.5 to 147.4 cases per 100,000 persons for black men), indicating a profound change in sexual behavior. At the same time, incidence remained low and changed little for white and Asian/Pacific Islander women. Rates for American Indian/Alaskan native women were based on less than 100 cases per year; no trend was apparent. Rates for Hispanic women increased from **8.1 to 13.7 cases per 100,000** from 1981 to 1988 and then decreased in 1989 to **10.0 cases per 100,000.** From 1981 to 1989, the male-to-female ratio decreased to 7.9/**1.6** for whites, 6.4/**2.7** for Asian/Pacific Islanders, 4.4/**2.5** for Hispanics, 2.2 to **1.3** for American Indians/Alaskan natives, and 2.3 to **1.5** for blacks. Incidence rates are highest for women between the ages of **15 to 34** and for men between the ages of 20 and 39.

Source: Robert T. Rolfs, MD, and Allyn K. Nakashima, MD, "Epidemiology of Primary and Secondary Syphilis in the United States, 1981 Through 1989," *JAMA* 264(11), September 19, 1990, p. 1432+. Reprint requests: Technical Information Services, Center for Prevention Services, Centers for Disease Control (E06), Atlanta, GA 30333. Also in source: known reasons and speculation about the rise or decline of incidences of syphilis; a discussion of drug-related high-risk sexual behaviors.

★ 286 ★

Urinary Incontinence

Summary of a series of new studies on urinary incontinence reported in the *New York Times*.

The author states that the National Institutes of Health estimate that at least 10 million Americans suffer from urinary incontinence. Women are more prone to the problem, in part because of the toll exacted on the bladder by childbirth. The author cites a study by Dr. John O.L. DeLancey, assistant professor of obstetrics and gynecology at the University of Michigan Medical School, in which **47%** of a group of 326 gynecology patients were found to leak minor amounts of urine on a regular basis. "So pervasive is the problem, he said, that **50 percent** of all sanitary products are sold not for menstruation, but for incontinence." It is estimated that from **10 to 15%** of women aged 35 to 50 suffer from severe incontinence. Among people over 60, **almost 40%** of women and 20% of men are incontinent.

Source: Natalie Angier, "New Focus on Urinary Incontinence," *New York Times*, October 25, 1990, p. B7. Also in source: methods of controlling the problem; where to go for help.

Dietary and Health Practices

★ 287 ★

Dieting

Responses of 739 women to the question: "How often do you diet?"

Response	Percent
Constantly	18%
Several times a year	21%
Once a year	25%

Source: Family Circle 103:2 (February 1, 1990), p. 41-46. The survey covered 900 women on the *Family Circle* consumer panel; 739 responses were received.

★ 288 ★

Dieting Among Adolescent Girls

Summary of testimony before a House subcommittee on the topic of the safety of nonprescription diet pills, reported in the *New York Times*.

The author cites a study conducted at the University of California at San Francisco of 500 9-, 10-, and 11-year-old girls which found that almost **half** of the 9-year-olds were dieting although few were overweight. Only **17%** of all the girls were overweight. The author also cites a statement by a spokesperson for the Centers for Disease Control that "nearly **7%** of 8th-and 10th-grade girls in the United States used diet pills or diet candies" in 1986.

Source: Marian Burros, "Children are the focus of new inquiries into the effects of weight-loss pills," *New York Times,* October 3, 1990, p. B5. Also in source: a discussion of the use of diet aids by young people.

★ 289 ★

Personal Health Practices

Personal health practices of persons 18 years of age and over, 1985.

Characteristic	Sleeps 6 hours or less	Never eats breakfast	Snacks every day	Less physi-cally active[1]	Had 5 or more drinks on any day[2]	Current smoker	30% or more above weight[3]
All persons[4]	22.0%	24.3%	39.0%	16.4%	37.5%	30.1%	13.0%
Female	21.4%	23.6%	37.5%	16.3%	23.3%	27.8%	13.7%
Male	22.7%	25.2%	40.7%	16.5%	49.3%	32.6%	12.1%

Source: Selected from "Personal Health Practices, by Selected Characteristic: 1985," *Statistical Abstract of the United States 1990,* 1990, p. 122. Primary source: U.S. National Center for Health Statistics, *Health Promotion and Disease Prevention, United States 1985, Vital and Health Statistics,* series 10, No. 163, and unpublished data. Also in source: other characteristics of persons. For persons 18 years of age and over. Based on National Health Interview Survey. *Notes:* 1. Than contemporaries. 2. Percent of drinkers who had 5 or more drinks on any one day in the past year. 3. Above desirable weight. Based on 1960 Metropolitan Life Insurance Company standards. Data are self-reported. 4. Excludes persons whose health practices are unknown.

★ 290 ★

Persons Taking Vitamins

Total number of persons, by age group, in thousands, and percent using vitamin-mineral products, 1986.

Characteristic	Persons, in thousands					Percent using vitamin-mineral products				
	Adults 18 years old and over				Children	Adults 18 years old and over				Children
	Total	18-44	45-64	65+	2-6 years	Total	18-44	45-64	65+	2-6 years
Total	169,587	97,541	44,660	27,386	18,162	36.4%	34.4%	39.8%	38.2%	43.3%
Female	87,783	48,316	23,371	16,096	8,910	41.3%	38.6%	46.2%	42.4%	42.2%
Male	81,804	49,225	21,289	11,290	9,252	31.2%	30.2%	32.7%	33.2%	44.4%

Source: Selected from "Persons Using Vitamin-Mineral Products, by Selected Characteristic: 1986," *Statistical Abstract of the United States 1990*, 1990, p. 126. Primary source: U.S. National Center for Health Statistics, *Advance Data from Vital and Health Statistics*, No. 174. Also in source: data by other characteristics. Based on the National Health Interview Survey and subject to sampling error.

Elder Care

★ 291 ★

Nursing Home Discharges

Nursing home discharges and median duration of stay, 1976 and 1985.

Characteristic	Discharges				Median duration of stay (days)	
	Total (thousands)		% distribution			
	1976	1985	1976	1985	1976	1985
All discharges[1]	1,117.5	1,223.5	100%	100%	75	82
Female	709.8	768.0	63.5%	62.8%	88	93
Male	407.7	455.5	36.5%	37.2%	60	66

Source: Selected from "Nursing Home Discharges, by Selected Characteristics: 1976 and 1985," *Statistical Abstract of the United States 1990*, p. 113. Primary source: U.S. National Center for Health Statistics, *The National Nursing Home Survey, 1985 Summary for the United States, Vital and Health Statistics*, Series 13, No. 97, January 1989, and unpublished data. Also in source: data by other characteristics. *Note:* 1. Total includes small number of unknown by discharge status.

★ 292 ★

Nursing Home Residents

Nursing home residents 65 years of age and over and rate per 1,000 population by age and sex, 1977 and 1985.

Age and sex	Residents		Residents per 1,000 population	
	1977[1]	1985	1977[1]	1985
All ages	1,126,000	1,318,300	47.1	46.2
Female	832,000	983,900	58.6	57.9
65-74 years	131,200	131,500	15.8	13.8
75-84 years	342,600	367,700	75.4	66.4
85 years and over	358,200	484,700	262.4	250.1

[Continued]

★ 292 ★

Nursing Home Residents
[Continued]

Age and sex	Residents		Residents per 1,000 population	
	1977[1]	1985	1977[1]	1985
Male	294,000	334,400	30.3	29.0
65-74 years	80,200	80,600	12.6	10.8
75-84 years	122,100	141,300	44.9	43.0
85 years and over	91,700	112,600	146.3	145.7

Source: Selected from "Nursing home and personal care home residents 65 years of age and over and rate per 1,000 population, according to age, sex, and race: United States, 1963, 1973-74, 1977, and 1985," *Health United States—1989,* p. 196. Primary source: See source for detailed breakdown. Also in source: data by age and race; data for 1963 and 1973-74. Data are based on a sample of nursing homes. *Note:* 1. Includes residents in personal care or domiciliary care homes.

Health Care Coverage

★ 293 ★

Coverage for Persons Over 65

Health care coverage for persons 65 years of age and over according to type of coverage, 1980, 1982, and 1986.

Characteristic	Medicare and private insurance			Medicare and Medicaid[1]			Medicare[2]		
	1980	1982	1986	1980	1982	1986	1980	1982	1986
Total[3,4]	64.4%	65.5%	71.6%	8.1%	6.1%	5.8%	22.7%	23.1%	17.9%
Sex[3]									
Female	63.6%	65.0%	70.8%	9.6%	7.3%	7.3%	22.4%	23.0%	17.5%
Male	65.6%	66.2%	72.8%	5.7%	4.3%	3.7%	23.1%	23.4%	18.4%

Source: Selected from "Health care coverage for persons 65 years of age and over, according to type of coverage and selected characteristics: United States, 1980, 1982, and 1986," *Health United States—1989,* p. 251. Primary source: Division of Health Interview Statistics, National Center for Health Statistics: Data from the National Health Interview Survey. Also in source: data by age, race, family income, geographic region, and location of residence. Data are based on household interviews of the civilian noninstitutionalized population. *Notes:* 1. Includes persons receiving AFDC or SSI or those with current Medicaid cards. 2. Includes persons not covered by private insurance or Medicaid. 3. Age adjusted. 4. Includes all other races not shown separately.

★ 294 ★

Coverage for Persons Under 65

Health care coverage for persons under 65 according to type of coverage, 1980, 1982, and 1986.

Characteristic	Private insurance			Medicaid			Not covered[2]		
	1980	1982	1986	1980	1982	1986	1980	1982	1986
Total[3,4]	78.8%	77.3%	75.9%	5.9%	5.6%	5.9%	12.5%	14.7%	15.3%
Sex[3]									
Female	78.2%	76.7%	75.4%	7.1%	6.6%	6.8%	12.2%	14.5%	14.9%
Male	79.5%	78.0%	76.4%	4.7%	4.5%	4.8%	12.7%	14.8%	15.8%

Source: Selected from "Health care coverage for persons under 65 years of age, according to type of coverage and selected characteristics: United States, 1980, 1982, and 1986," *Health United States—1989*, p. 250. Primary source: Division of Health Interview Statistics, National Center for Health Statistics: Data from the National Health Interview Survey. Also in source: data by age, race, family income, geographic region, and location of residence. Data are based on household interviews of the civilian noninstitutionalized population. Denominators include persons with unknown health insurance (1.7% in 1986). Percents do not add to 100 because the percent with other types of health insurance (e.g., Medicare, military) and unknown health insurance are not shown, and because persons with both private insurance and Medicaid appear in both columns. *Notes:* 1. Includes persons receiving AFDC or SSI or those with current Medicaid cards. 2. Includes persons not covered by private insurance, Medicaid, Medicare, and military plans. 3. Age adjusted. 4. Includes all other races not shown separately.

Health Care Personnel/Institution Contacts

★ 295 ★

Hospital Stays and Discharges

Discharges, days of care, and average length of stay in short-stay hospitals, 1984 and 1988.

Characteristic	Number per 1,000 population				Number of days	
	Discharges		Days of care		Average stay	
	1984	1988	1984	1988	1984	1988
Total[1,2]	114.7	93.4	871.9	622.7	7.6	6.7
Sex[1]						
Female	115.8	92.9	829.2	605.8	7.2	6.5
Male	114.2	94.8	926.6	647.4	8.1	6.8

Source: Selected from "Discharges, days of care, and average length of stay in short-stay hospitals, according to selected characteristics: United States, 1964, 1984, and 1988," *Health United States—1989*, Table 69, p. 183. Primary source: Division of Health Interview Statistics, National Center for Health Statistics: Data from the National Health Interview Survey. Also in source: data by age, race, family income, geographic region, and location of residence; data for 1964. Data are based on household interviews of a sample of the civilian noninstitutionalized population. *Notes:* 1. Age adjusted. 2. Includes all other races not shown separately.

★ 296 ★

Interval Since Last Physician Contact

Interval since last physician contact, 1983 and 1988.

Characteristic	Less than 1 year		1 year-less than 2 years		2 years or more[1]	
	1983	1988	1983	1988	1983	1988
Total[2,3]	75.2%	77.1%	10.9%	10.5%	13.9%	12.4%
Sex[2]						
Female	79.4%	81.7%	9.9%	9.3%	10.7%	9.0%
Male	70.6%	72.3%	12.0%	11.8%	17.3%	15.9%

Source: Selected from "Interval since last physician contact, according to selected patient characteristics: United States, 1964, 1983, and 1988," *Health United States—1989*, p. 179. Primary source: Division of Health Interview Statistics, National Center for Health Statistics: Data from the National Health Interview Survey. Also in source: data by age, race, family income, geographic region, and location of residence; data for 1964. Data are based on household interviews of a sample of the civilian noninstitutionalized population. *Notes:* 1. Includes persons who never visited a physician. 2. Age adjusted.

★ 297 ★

Office Visits to Physicians

Office visits to physicians, 1980 and 1985.

Characteristic	Patient's first visit		Visit lasted 10 minutes or less[1]		Return visit scheduled	
	1980	1985	1980	1985	1980	1985
Total[2]	15.3%	17.7%	47.3%	42.6%	58.0%	58.8%
Sex[2]						
Female	14.4%	16.9%	47.7%	42.2%	58.9%	59.8%
Male	17.3%	19.5%	46.4%	43.3%	55.9%	56.7%

Source: Selected from "Office visits to physicians, according to selected patient characteristics: United States, 1980 and 1985," *Health United States—1989*, p. 181. Primary source: Division of Health Care Interview Statistics, National Center for Health Statistics: Data from the National Ambulatory Medical Care Survey. Also in source: data by age, race, location of physician's office; office visits to dentists (p. 182). Data are based on reporting by a sample of office-based physicians. Rates are based on the civilian noninstitutionalized population, excluding Alaska and Hawaii. *Notes:* 1. Time spent in face-to-face contact between physician and patient. 2. Age adjusted.

★ 298 ★

Physician Contacts by Place of Contact

Physician contacts according to place of contact, 1983 and 1988.

	Physician contacts		Place of contact							
			Doctor's office		Hospital out-patient dept.[1]		Telephone		Home	
	1983	1988	1983	1988	1983	1988	1983	1988	1983	1988
Total[2]	5.1	5.3	56.1%	59.3%	14.9%	12.8%	15.5%	13.7%	1.5%	1.4%
Sex[2]										
Female	5.7	6.0	56.8%	60.1%	13.6%	11.8%	16.8%	14.4%	1.5%	1.4%
Male	4.4	4.6	54.8%	58.2%	17.1%	14.7%	13.5%	12.3%	1.5%	1.4%

Source: Selected from "Physician contacts, according to place of contact and selected patient characteristics: United States, 1983 and 1988," *Health United States—1989*, p. 178. Primary source: Division of Health Interview Statistics, National Center for Health Statistics: Data from the National Health Interview Survey. Also in source: data by age, race, family income, geographic region, and location of residence. Data are based on household interviews of a sample of the civilian noninstitutionalized population. *Notes:* 1. Includes hospital outpatient clinic, emergency room, and other hospital contacts. 2. Age adjusted.

★ 299 ★

Treatment for Infertility

Number (in thousands) and percent of women who had 1 visit or more to a doctor or clinic for advice or treatment to help them become pregnant or carry a pregnancy to term, by when the most recent visit occurred, 1982 and 1988.

Date of most recent infertility visit	1988	1982	Increase	1988	1982
In the last year	1,346	1,082	264	2.3%	2.0%
In the last 3 years	2,392	2,056	336	4.1%	3.8%
In the last 5 years	3,123	2,867	256	5.4%	5.3%

Source: William D. Mosher, Ph.D., and William F. Pratt, Ph.D., "Fecundity and Infertility in the United States, 1965-88," *Advance Data from Vital and Health Statistics of the National Center for Health Statistics*, No. 192, December 4, 1990, Table 5, p. 6. Because of rounding of estimates, figures may not add to totals.

★ 300 ★

Visits to the Dentist

Total visits to the dentist, in millions, and visits per person, by sex, 1970-1986.

Year	Total visits (millions)		Visits per person	
	Female	Male	Female	Male
1970	171	133	1.7	1.4
1980	207	158	1.8	1.5
1983	239	183	2.0	1.6
1986	256	210	2.2	1.9

Source: Selected from "Physician and Dental Visits by Patient Characteristics: 1970 to 1987," *Statistical Abstract of the United States 1990*, 1990, p. 103. Primary source: U.S. National Center for Health Statistics, *Vital and Health Statistics*, series 10, and unpublished data. Also in source: physician visits; data by race and age (not by gender).

Health Worldwide

★ 301 ★

Indicators of Health and Development Worldwide

Global Health-For-All and other indicators relating to women, health, and development, by UN geographical region, about 1982. WHO = World Health Organization.

Region	WHO Global Indicators				Others			
	% adults literate f/m (1)	% births attended by trained personnel (2)	% infants low birth weight (3)	Infant mortality rate f/m (4)	% enrolled in school		% women aged 15-19 married (7)	Average no. of children per woman (8)
					Aged 6-11 f/m (5)	Aged 12-17 f/m (6)		
World	54/67	56	16	92/103	64/76	46/55	30	3.8
Developed countries	97/98	98	7	18/24	94/94	85/84	8	2.0
Developing countries	32/52	49	18	104/116	53/70	28/42	39	4.4
Africa	15/33	33	14	129/151	43/59	24/39	44	6.4
Northern Africa	18/44	30	10	114/128	45/70	43/42	34	6.2
Western Africa	6/20	39	17	145/171	30/44	16/29	70	6.8
Eastern Africa	14/29	26	13	121/142	41/55	20/33	32	6.6
Middle Africa	9/35	24	16	153/181	54/78	26/52	49	6.0
Southern Africa	56/55	66	12	92/109	86/82	74/70	2	5.2
North America	99/99	100	7	12/16	99/99	95/95	11	1.8
Latin America	70/76	65	10	80/90	78/78	54/58	16	4.5
Middle Latin America	67/75	49	12	67/76	83/84	46/58	21	5.3
Caribbean	66/67	60	12	68/78	87/85	59/60	19	3.8
Tropical South Latin America	67/74	70	9	92/104	72/70	54/56	15	4.6
Temperate South Latin America	91/93	88	7	41/47	98/98	73/70	10	2.9
Asia	34/56	51	20	99/108	54/73	28/43	42	3.9
South-West Asia	31/58	51	7	99/123	57/78	32/54	25	5.8
Middle South Asia	17/44	24	31	135/138	44/70	35/17	54	5.5
South-East Asia	53/75	52	17	87/105	65/71	35/43	24	4.7
East Asia	92/97	94	6	45/57	99/99	80/85	2	2.3
Europe	93/96	97	7	19/25	96/95	80/81	7	2.0
Northern Europe	99/99	100	6	11/15	98/98	83/82	9	1.8
Western Europe	98/98	100	5	13/17	96/95	89/87	5	1.6
Eastern Europe	92/97	99	8	21/30	91/92	81/80	9	2.3
Southern Europe	85/93	93	7	25/31	97/97	66/73	7	2.3
USSR	100/100	-	8	27/35	99/99	82/72	10	2.4
Oceania	88/90	-	12	39/48	87/88	71/75	10	2.8

Source: "Global Health-for-All and Other Indicators Relating to Women, Health and Development," *Women, Health and Development*, Annex 1, page 40 (1985). Primary source: Columns 1,5, and 6 - UNESCO; Columns 2 AND 3 - WHO estimates; columns 4, 7, and 8 - Population Reference Bureau and United Nations Population Division.

Injuries/Accidents

★ 302 ★

Automobile Accidents

Number of automobile accidents per 1,000 drivers in California, by age of driver, 1981-1987.

Age	Accident rate per 1,000 drivers	
	Females	Males
16	76.7	85.3
17	77.0	106.9
18	80.2	127.1
19-24	58.9	87.9
25-34	43.9	66.3
35-49	37.6	53.5
50-64	29.9	48.1
65+	29.5	43.8

Source: Los Angeles Times, June 18, 1990, p. 3.

★ 303 ★

Injured Persons

Total and female persons injured, in millions, rate per 100 population, 1970 to 1986, and by age and place, 1987.

Year/Age and Place	Persons injured (millions)		Rate per 100 population		
	Total	Female	Total	Female	Male
1970	56.0	24.2	28.0	23.3	33.0
1975	71.9	32.5	34.4	30.0	39.1
1979	69.1	28.9	32.0	25.9	
1978	67.5	29.4	31.6	26.6	36.9
1980	68.1	29.1	31.2	25.8	37.1
1981	70.3	30.2	31.2	25.9	36.9
1982	60.0	27.6	26.4	23.4	29.6
1983	61.1	28.1	26.6	23.7	29.8
1984	61.1	27.4	26.4	22.9	30.1
1985	62.6	28.0	26.8	23.1	30.6
1986	62.4	28.4	26.4	23.3	29.8
Age and Place					
1987, total[1]	62.1	28.4	26.0	23.1	29.1
Under 5 years	4.8	2.1	26.1	23.2	28.9
5-17 years	14.4	6.0	31.9	27.3	36.4
18-44 years	29.0	12.2	28.3	23.5	33.5
45-64 yers	8.0	4.0	17.9	17.2	18.7
65 years and over	6.0	4.1	21.1	24.8	15.9

[Continued]

★ 303 ★

Injured Persons
[Continued]

Year/Age and Place	Persons injured (millions)		Rate per 100 population		
	Total	Female	Total	Female	Male
Home	21.0	9.9	8.8	8.1	9.6
Street or highway	7.7	3.5	3.2	2.9	3.6
Industrial	7.4	1.9	3.1	1.5	4.7
Other	15.8	7.1	6.6	5.8	7.6

Source: Selected from "Persons Injured, by Sex, 1970 to 1987, and by Age and Place, 1987," *Statistical Abstract of the United States 1990*, 1990, p. 115. Primary source: U.S. National Center for Health Statistics, *Vital and Health Statistics*, series 10, and unpublished data. Covers civilian noninstitutional population and comprises incidents leading to restricted activity and/or medical attention. 1975 and beginning 1982, data not strictly comparable with other years. *Note:* 1. includes unknown place of accident, not shown separately.

Mental Health

★ 304 ★

Admissions for Psychiatric Care

Rate of admissions per 100,000 civilian population to selected inpatient psychiatric organizations by sex, race and age, 1975, 1980, and 1986.

Sex, age, and race	State and county mental hospitals			Private psychiatric hospitals			Non-Federal general hospitals[1]		
	1975	1980	1986	1975	1980	1986	1975	1980	1986
			Rate per 100,000 civilian population						
Female									
Total	124.7	111.1	98.1	67.8	63.3	81.5	278.1	265.1	335.5
Under 18 years	27.5	16.4	20.0	24.1	23.6	64.3	70.0	74.6	80.7
18-24 years	143.1	145.8	141.0	69.6	67.4	60.2	354.6	304.4	458.3
25-44 years	215.9	182.3	168.1	101.2	91.2	107.6	495.8	422.2	498.1
45-64 years	180.5	151.7	100.2	92.3	78.1	84.0	324.3	328.2	345.8
65 years and over	60.8	59.6	46.7	62.8	58.8	68.6	182.9	190.0	321.3
White	111.2	94.1	78.1	72.5	65.0	84.5	281.7	256.4	318.6
All other	212.0	212.6	207.2	37.7	52.8	65.5	254.9	316.7	428.0
Male									
Total	243.7	219.8	176.6	54.5	61.9	92.1	207.1	233.8	327.6
Under 18 years	48.3	35.4	30.1	22.5	28.9	69.8	59.1	62.6	63.7
18-24 years	409.0	387.9	292.6	78.0	92.2	103.2	350.8	365.3	428.5

[Continued]

★ 304 ★

Admissions for Psychiatric Care
[Continued]

Sex, age, and race	State and county mental hospitals			Private psychiatric hospitals			Non-Federal general hospitals[1]		
	1975	1980	1986	1975	1980	1986	1975	1980	1986
25-44 years	418.4	388.1	338.4	76.6	86.8	136.1	332.8	374.7	584.2
45-64 years	291.5	202.3	114.4	66.8	63.2	65.5	228.6	219.1	281.1
65 years and over	136.4	105.3	57.1	50.3	47.3	52.1	152.0	203.4	223.1
White	214.2	182.2	137.1	57.0	61.7	90.3	206.9	226.3	278.3
All other	444.5	457.8	403.0	38.1	62.7	102.8	209.1	281.1	610.3

Source: Selected from "Admissions to selected inpatient psychiatric organizations and rate per 100,000 civilian population, according to sex, age, and race: United States, 1975, 1980, and 1986," *Health United States—1989*, p. 200-201. Primary source: Survey and Reports Branch, Division of Biometry and Applied Sciences, National Institute of Mental Health; C.A. Taube and S.A. Barrett: Mental Health, United States, 1985. DHHS Pub. No. (ADM)85-1378. U.S. Government Printing Office, 1985; unpublished data. Also in source: numbers in thousands for both sexes; admissions according to selected primary diagnoses and age (p. 202+). Data are based on a survey of patients. *Note:* 1. Non-Federal general hospitals include public and nonpublic facilities.

★ 305 ★

Depression by Marital Status

Sex differences in depression across marital groups.

Marital status	Mean depression scores	
	Female (n=958)	Male (n=679)
Married	9.26	7.33
Divorced/separated	14.19	8.51
Never married	10.20	10.05
Widowed	10.46	11.28

Source: "Sex Differences in Depression Across Marital Groups," *Sex Differences in Depression*, 1990, p. 27 (Stanford, CT: Stanford University Press, 1990). Primary source: Adoped by the author from L.S. Radloff, "Sex differences in depression: The effects of occupation and marital status," *Sex Roles* 1 (1975), p. 249-267. Subjects completed the Center for Epidemiological Studies Depression Scale.

★ 306 ★

Depressive Disorders

Rates of persons treated for depressive disorders per 100,000 people, by age.

Age group	Females	Males
18-24 years	151	123
25-44 years	266	178
45-64 years	251	141
65+ years	154	110

Source: "Rates of Persons Treated for Depressive Disorders, per 100,000 People," *Sex Differences in Depression*, 1990, p. 33 (Stanford, CT: Stanford University Press, 1990). Primary source: National Institute of Mental Health (1987), unpublished data on numbers of persons treated for affective disorders in psychiatric disorders in psychiatric facilities in the United States; data gathered in 1980, made available to the author in 1987.

★ 307 ★

Effects of Menopause on Mental Health

Percentage of menopausal women reporting selected symptoms at *neither* baseline (premenopausal) *nor* follow-up (postmenopausal) examination. The authors concluded that natural menopaus did not have negative mental health consequences for most middle-aged healthy women.

Symptom	Percent
Body worry	
Natural menopause	67%
Hormone users	44%
Excitable	
Natural menopause	57%
Hormone users	78%
Aches in neck and skull	
Natural menopause	57%
Hormone users	41%
Depression	
Natural menopause	45%
Hormone users	44%
Nervous	
Natural menopause	33%
Hormone users	31%
Trouble sleeping	
Natural menopause	55%
Hormone users	41%

Source: Karen A. Matthews, Rena R. Wing, Lewis H. Kuller, Elaine N. Meilahn, Sheryl F. Kelsey, E. Jane Costello, and Arlene W. Caggiula, "Influences of natural Menopause on Psychological Characteristics and Symptoms of Middle-Aged Healthy Women," *Journal of Consulting and Clinical Psychology* 58:3, 1990, p. 345-351. Address correspondence to Karen A. Matthews, Dept. of Psychiatry, University of Pittsburgh, 3811 O'Hara Street, Pittsburgh, PA 15213. Related reading: "Study Suggests Menopause Doesn't Affect Mental Health," *New York Times,* July 26, 1990, p. B7. The study began with 541 initially premenopausal healthy women given an extensive evaluation at baseline. After 3 years, 69 women ceased cycling for 12 months; another 32 had ceased cycling and had taken hormone replacement therapy for 12 months. These women were reevaluated in a clinic examination identical to the baseline examination, as were 101 age-matched premenopausal control women.

★ 308 ★

Rates of Depressive Disorders

Rates of depressive disorders in the general population diagnosed through structured clinical interviews.

Age group and number	% Females	% Males
Elementary school children (n=792)	0.5%	2.5%
Adolescents (n=150)	13.3%	2.7%
Adults (n=9,543)		
18-24 years	6.9%	3.8%
25-44 years	10.8%	4.8%
45-64 years	7.8%	3.3%
65+ years	3.2%	1.2%

Source: "Rates of Depressive Disorders in the General Population Diagnosed Through Structured Clinical Interviews," *Sex Differences in Depression*, 1990, p. 32 (Stanford, CT: Stanford University Press, 1990). Primary sources: J.C. Anderson et al., "DSM-III Disorders in Preadolescent Children," *Archives of General Psychiatry*, 44 (1987), 69-76; J.H. Kashani et al., "Seriously depressed preschoolers," *American Journal of Psychiatry*, 144 (1987), 3; J.K. Myers et al., "Six-month prevalence of psychiatric disorders in three communities: 1980 to 1982," *Archives of General Psychiatry*, 41 (1984), 959-967.

★ 309 ★

Self-Esteem in Adolescent Girls

Some results of a study of loss of self-esteem in girls on the way to adolescence, as reported in the *New York Times*.

The author, reporting on a survey of 3,000 children commissioned by the American Association of University Women, states that at the age of 9, most girls are confident, assertive, and feel positive about themselves. By the time they reach high school, less than a third feel that way. Among the findings:

1. In answer to a question about how often they feel "happy the way I am," 67% of elementary school boys answered "always"; by high school, 47% of boys still felt that way. With girls, the figures dropped from **60%** to **29%**.

2. Significantly more black girls surveyed still felt self-confident in high school compared to white and Hispanic girls.

Source: Suzanne Daley, "Girls' Self-Esteem Is Lost on Way to Adolescence, New Study Finds, *New York Times*, January 9, 1991, p. B1+. Also in source: a discussion of racial differences among respondents; a discussion of other aspects of the survey. The study was conducted by Greenberg-Lake Analysis Group and included 2,400 girls and 600 boys at 36 public schools in 12 communities throughout the country during the fall of 1989.

Operations and Other Procedures

★ 310 ★

Abortions by Income Level

Family income of women having an abortion, 1987.

Income	Percentage
Less than $11,000	33%
$11,000-$24,999	34%
$25,000-$34,999	12%
$35,000-$49,000	10%
More than $50,000	11%

Source: Scholastic Update 122:16 (April 20, 1990), p. 4-5. Primary source: Alan Guttmacher Institute.

★ 311 ★

Abortions-Reasons

The top six reasons for having an abortion given by 1,900 women seeking abortions in clinics or hospitals in a 1988 nationwide survey.

Reason	Percent
Not ready for how a baby could change her life.	76
Cannot afford a baby now.	68
Has problems with relationship or wants to avoid single parenthood.	51
Not ready for responsibility.	31
Does not want others to know she has had sex or is pregnant.	31
Is not mature enough or is too young to raise a child.	30

Source: Scholastic Update 122 (16), April 20, 1990, p. 4-5. Primary source: Alan Guttmacher Institute. Respondents could choose up to four different reasons.

★ 312 ★

Breast Examination

Women who have had a mammogram, breast physical exam, or who perform breast self exams (BSE), 1987, by age and race.

Age and race	Total women (thousands)	Percent Having A						Percent Perfoming BSE		
		Mammogram			Breast physical exam			At least once a week	Once a month to less than once a week	Less than once a mont
		Ever	In the past-		Ever	In the past-				
			11 months	36 months		11 months	36 months			
Total[1]	47,676	38.1	14.8	14.3	81.3	33.2	30.4	14.5	32.8	20.0
40-54 years old	19,597	42.2	16.8	16.1	86.7	39.0	32.3	13.4	37.4	24.5
55-64 years old	11,749	41.1	16.9	13.6	83.1	31.9	32.4	14.8	35.0	18.6
65-74 years old	9,665	35.2	12.9	14.3	76.8	30.7	26.3	15.7	30.4	17.2
75 years old and over	6,665	24.8	8.0	9.9	68.2	21.8	26.7	15.3	18.8	13.1

[Continued]

★ 312 ★

Breast Examination
[Continued]

ge and race	Total women (thousands)	Percent Having A						Percent Perfoming BSE		
		Mammogram			Breast physical exam			At least once a week	Once a month to less than once a week	Less than once a month
		Ever	In the past-		Ever	In the past-				
			11 months	36 months		11 months	36 months			
White	41,877	39.2	15.3	14.8	82.8	33.6	30.9	13.5	33.5	20.9
Black	4,830	31.2	12.9	10.4	73.7	33.4	25.8	21.9	30.1	14.5

ource: Selected from "Women Who Have Had a Mammogram, Breast Physical Exam or Who Perform Breast Self Exams (BSE): 1987," *Statistical Abstract of the United tates 1990,* 1990, p. 121. Primary source: U.S. National Center for Health Statistics, *Vital and Health Statistics,* series 10, No. 172. Also in source: data by five-year intervals. 'or women 40 years old and over. Based on the National Health Interview Survey and subject to sampling error. *Note:* 1. Includes other races, not shown separately.

★ 313 ★

Breast Reconstruction
Summary of the advantages of flap surgery reported in the *New York Times*.

Among the points made by the author in her discussion of women opting for flap surgery over other reconstruction methods:

1. In 1988, **33,000 women** had silicon (sic) implants after cancer; **1,300 women** had flap surgery.

2. The implant procedure takes about 45 minutes; when reconstruction by flap surgery follows a mastectomy of **4 to 6 hours**, the patient could be in the operating room for a total of **9 to 12 hours**.

3. The cost of the procedure varies from **$4,000 to $12,000.**

4. Only about 20 surgeons were performing the operation in 1990.

Source: Sandra Blakeslee, "Latest in Breast Reconstruction: Take Wedges of the Patient's Fat," *New York Times,* August 23, 1990, p. B7. Also in source: a discussion of the mechanics of the procedure.

★ 314 ★

Diagnostic Procedures
Diagnostic and other nonsurgical procedures for female inpatients discharged from non-Federal short-stay hospitals according to procedure category, 1980, 1985, 1987, and 1988.

Procedure Category	Procedures in thousands				Procedures per 1,000 population			
	1980	1985	1987	1988[1]	1980	1985	1987	1988[1]
All ages[2,3]	3,532	6,072	6,820	6,902	27.5	43.3	47.3	47.3
Diagnostic ultrasound	204	756	981	963	1.6	5.4	6.7	6.6
Computerized axial tomography (CAT scan)	154	707	833	838	1.2	4.9	5.6	5.6
Radioisotope scan	289	463	409	390	2.1	3.2	2.8	2.6
Endoscopy of small intestine	164	281	341	279	1.3	2.0	2.3	1.8
Angiocardiography using contrast material	84	219	375	439	0.7	1.6	2.7	3.1
Laparoscopy (excl. that for ligation and								

[Continued]

★ 314 ★

Diagnostic Procedures
[Continued]

Procedure Category	Procedures in thousands				Procedures per 1,000 population			
	1980	1985	1987	1988[1]	1980	1985	1987	1988[1]
division of fallopian tubes)	235	209	176	133	1.8	1.5	1.2	0.9
Cystoscopy	324	184	149	143	2.6	1.3	1.0	1.0

Source: Selected from "Diagnostic and other nonsurgical procedures for inpatients discharged from non-Federal short-stay hospitals, according to sex, age, and procedure category: United States, 1980, 1985, 1987, and 1988," *Health United States—1989*, p. 193-94. Primary source: Division of Health Care Statistics, National Center for Health Statistics: Data from the National Hospital Discharge Survey. Also in source: detailed data broken down by age; data for males. Data are based on a sample of hospital records. See Source for description of data. *Notes:* 1. Comparisons of 1988 data with data for earlier years should be made with caution as estimates of change between 1987 and 1988 may reflect improvements in the 1988 design rather than true changes in hospital use. 2. Rates are age adjusted. 3. Includes nonsurgical procedures not shown.

★ 315 ★

Hysterectomy

A discussion of expert opinions on the necessity for hysterectomy, reported in the *New York Times*.

According to the author, by the age of 60, **1 woman in 3** has undergone a hysterectomy, making it the second-most common operation after Cesarean sections for American women. In 1991 it is expected that **650,000 women between the ages of 35 and 45** will have the operation. It is estimated that **1 to 3 patients in 1,000** die as a result of this procedure.

Source: Jane B. Brody, "Hysterectomies, the second-most frequent operation, need not be so common, some say," *New York Times*, January 3, 1991, p. B7. Also in source: a discussion of the reasons for and the mechanics of the procedure; a discussion of alternatives; list of sources to consult for further information.

★ 316 ★

Inpatient Operations
Operations for inpatient females discharged from non-Federal short-stay hospitals, according to surgical category: 1980, 1985, 1987, and 1988.

Surgical Category	Operations in thousands				Operations per 1,000 population			
	1980	1985	1987	1988[1]	1980	1985	1987	1988[1]
All ages[2,3]	15,989	15,994	16,583	16,555	126.1	117.2	118.3	116.9
Procedures to assist delivery	2,391	2,494	2,938	3,131	18.4	18.0	20.7	22.0
Cesarean section[4]	619	877	953	933	4.8	6.3	6.7	6.5
Hysterectomy	649	670	655	578	5.2	5.0	4.8	4.3
Oophorectomy and salpingo-oophorectomy	483	525	490	451	3.9	4.0	3.7	3.4
Repair of current obstetrical laceration	355	548	660	690	2.8	3.9	4.7	4.9
Bilateral destruction or occlusion of fallopian tubes	641	466	415	406	4.9	3.3	2.9	2.9
Diagnostic dilation (sic) and curettage of uterus	923	349	206	143	7.3	2.6	1.5	1.1

Source: Selected from "Operations for inpatients discharged from non-Federal short-stay hospitals, according to sex, age, and surgical category: United States, 1980, 1985, 1987, and 1988," *Health United States—1989*, p. 191-2. Primary source: Division of Health Care Statistics, National Center for Health Statistics; data from the National Hospital Discharge Survey. Also in source; detailed breakdown by age; data for men. Data are based on a sample of hospital records. *Notes:* 1. Comparisons of 1988 data with data for earlier years should be made with caution as estimates of change between 1987 and 1988 may reflect improvements in the 1988 design rather than true changes in hospital use. 2. Rates are age-adjusted. 3. Includes operations not listed in table. 4. Cesarean sections accounted for 16.5% of all deliveries in 1980, 22.7% in 1985, 24.4% in 1987, and 24.7% in 1988.

★ 317 ★

Mammography

Summary of the National Cancer Institute's Breast Cancer Screening Consortium report on mammography, reported in the *New York Times*.

Studies show that the incidence of breast cancer, the second leading cause of cancer deaths in American women, is rising. Highlights of the report include:

1. Mammograms, properly performed and interpreted, can detect tiny cancers not detectable by touch. For early cancers detectable by mammography, the cure rate is greater than **90%**.

2. If women followed current mammography guidelines, discussed in the article and said to be endorsed by 11 major health organizations, breast cancer deaths could be cut at least **30%**.

3. Fewer than **40%** of women over the age of 40 have ever had a mammogram.

4. **94%** of women whose doctors recommended mammograms over a two-year period had one; **36%** of women whose doctors said nothing about a mammogram had one.

5. **95%** of women who have a mammogram performed do so with negative results; follow-up tests on the remaining **5%** usually show no cancer.

6. About **10%** of breast cancers occur in women in their forties.

7. About **10%** of breast cancers do not show up on mammograms.

Source: Jane E. Brody, "In Fight Against Breast Cancer, Mammograms Are a Crucial Tool, but not Foolproof," *New York Times*, Vol. 139, August 2, 1990, p. B7. Primary source: The NCI Breast Cancer Screeing Consortium, "Screening Mammography: A Missed Clinical Opportunity? Results of the NCI Breast Cancer Screeing Consortium and National Health Interview Survey Studies," *JAMA*, 264:1 (July 4, 1990), p. 54-58. Address reprint requests to Chief, Health Promotion Sciences Branch, Division of Cancer Prevention and Control, Executive Plaza North, Room 241, 900 Rockville Pike, Bethesda, MD 20892 (Dr. Haynes).

Pregnancy and Infant Health

★ 318 ★

Amniocentesis

Percent of women 35 years and over who had amniocentesis, 1980.

Year	All races	White	Black
1980	29.0%	30.0%	16.7%

Source: "Percent of women 35 years and over who had amniocentesis," *Health United States—1989*, p. 35. Primary source: National Center for Health Statistics, Division of Vital Statistics.

★ 319 ★

Awareness of Risks During Pregnancy

The proportion of women 18-44 years of age who were aware of the effects on the fetus of various activities during pregnancy, 1985.

Activity/effect	% of women who were aware of effect
Heavy drinking during pregnancy increases the chance	
of birth defects	54%
of low birth weight	52%
of mental retardation	52%
of miscarriage	51%
Smoking during pregnancy increases the chance	
of low birth weight	52%
of stillbirth	30%
of premature birth	38%
of miscarriage	36%
Number who had ever heard of fetal alcohol syndrome	62%

Source: Health United States—1989, p. 35 Primary source: National Center for Health Statistics, Division of Health Interview Statistics. Also in source: a discussion of drinking and smoking levels of interviewees (p. 31-2).

★ 320 ★

Battering During Pregnancy

Some results of research into battering during pregnancy.

The author discusses a 1987 study of 290 healthy pregnant women in a large metropolitan area done to establish the prevalence of battering during pregnancy in a normal obstetric population. Among the findings:

- **8%** of the women (**1 out of 12**) reported battering during the current pregnancy.

- An additional **15%** reported battering before the pregnancy.

- **29%** of the battered women reported that the abuse increased during the pregnancy.

The author discusses another study done to determine the pregnancy outcomes of battered women. **12.5%** of battered women delivering at public hospitals delivered low-birthweight infants, compared to **6.6%** of non-battered women. When women delivering at private hospitals were considered as a separate sample, **17.5%** of battered women delivered low-birthweight infants, compared to **4.2%** of non-battered women.

Source: Judith McFarlane, RN, C, DrPH, "Battering During Pregnancy: Tip of an Iceberg Revealed," *Women & Health*, Vol 15(3)1989, p. 69+. Also in source: mention of (and sources given for) several other studies on violence against women; a discussion of the implications of battering during pregnancy and suggestions for its prevention.

★ 321 ★

Childbirth, Worldwide

Proportion of births attended by trained personnel and proportion occurring in institutions, by country, latest available year.

Country	Year	Trained Attendant	Institutional Deliveries
Northern Africa			
Algeria	1979	40%[1]	40%
Egypt			
Cairo	1983	22%	-
Libyan Arab Jamahiriya	1983	-	68%
Morocco	1980	29%	-
Sudan			
Khartoum City	1983	-	25%
Tunisia	1983	50%	-
Western Africa			
Benin	1982	-	19%
Burkino Faso	1979	5%	-
Gambia	1978	-	25%
Ghana	1974	-	25%
Accra	1974	-	95%
Guinea	1980	-	90%
Guinea-Bissau	1972	31%	-
Liberia	1983	10%	-
Mali	1981	14%	-
Niger	1980	25%	-
Senegal	1978	50%	-
Sierra Leone	1976	30%	-
Togo	1978	-	50%
Eastern Africa			
Burundi	1978	-	15%
Comoros	1982	-	35%
Djibouti			
urban	1970	-	40%
rural	1970	-	20%
Ethiopia	1980	10-15%	-
Kenya	1974	10%	-
Madagascar	1979	-	52%
Malawi	1979	40%	-
Mauritius	1978	90%	-

[Continued]

★ 321 ★

Childbirth, Worldwide
[Continued]

Country	Year	Trained Attendant	Institu-tional Deliveries
Rwanda	1979	25%	-
Seychelles	1969	-	94%
Somalia	1983	2%	-
Uganda	1975	-	32%
United Republic of Tanzania	1983	50%	-
Zambia	1980	37%	-
Middle Africa			
Angola			
Luanda	1983	20%	-
Central African Republic	1971	71%	-
Chad	1978	45%	-
Congo	1970	-	47%
Sao Tome and Principe	1983	88%	-
Cameroon	1975	52%	-
Southern Africa			
Botswana	1984	52%	-
Lesotho	1972	26%	25%
Cape Town	1981	98%	73%
Swaziland	1977-8	-	25%
Northern America			
Canada	1983	100%	-
United States	1976	-	100%
Middle America			
Belize	1972-4	73%	-
Costa Rica	1980	-	98%
El Salvador	1978	-	34%
Guatemala	1977	16%	20%
Honduras	1977	34%	18%
Mexico	1970	-	35%
Nicaragua	1976	-	32%
Panama	1978	77%	76%

[Continued]

★ 321 ★

Childbirth, Worldwide
[Continued]

Country	Year	Trained Attendant	Institu-tional Deliveries
Caribbean			
Antigua and Barbuda	1972	-	80%
Bahamas	1977	-	87%
Barbados	1978	100%	-
Cuba	1978	-	96%
Dominican Republic	1972	-	49%
Grenada	1972	-	28%
Haiti	1984	-	15%
Jamaica	1981	86%	73%
Puerto Rico	1981	-	99%
Saint Lucia	1979	90%	-
Trinidad and Tobago	1977	94%	90%
Tropical South America			
Bolivia	1972	-	14%
Brazil			
rural	1983	-	59%
urban	1983	-	96%
Colombia	1977	-	40%
Ecuador	1978	36%	-
Guyana	1973	-	60%
Paraguay	1977	65%	-
Peru	1981	30%	-
Venezuela	1979	87%	-
Western South Asia			
Bahrain	1981	98%	90%
Cyprus	1973	100%	90%
Democratic Yemen			
Aden	1973	33%	-
Iraq	1974	79%	24%
Israel	1980	-	100%
Jordan	1983	65%	-
Kuwait	1977	-	95%
Lebanon	1976	30-60%	-
Oman	1983	-	74%
Saudi Arabia			
Riyadh	1983	-	70%

[Continued]

★ 321 ★

Childbirth, Worldwide
[Continued]

Country	Year	Trained Attendant	Institu- tional Deliveries
Syrian Arab Republic			
urban	1979	63%	17%
rural	1979	12%	3%
Turkey	1979-81	70%	-
United Arab Emirates	1980	-	85%
Yemen	1978	-	3%
Middle South Asia			
Afghanistan	1978	5%	-
Bangladesh	1984	-	1%
Bhutan	1982	-	1%
India	1982	25%	-
Nepal	1982	-	4%
Pakistan	1979	5%	-
Sri Lanka	1980	85%	76%
Eastern South Asia			
Brunei Darussalam	1972	60%	-
Burma	1974	50-60%	-
Democratic Kampuchea	1971	20%	-
Indonesia	1984	-	20%
Lao People's Democratic Republic	1974	15%	-
Malaysia			
Peninsular	1980	85%	52%
Philippines	1975	86%[2]	22%
Singapore	1981	100%	98%
Thailand	1977	-	36%
Viet Nam	1982	-	99%
East Asia			
China			
People's Republic of			
Shanghai	1980	-	100%
Shangdong Province	1980	-	40%
Democratic People's Republic of Korea	f1980	60%	57%
Hong Kong	1974	100%	-
Japan	1977	100%	99%
Mongolia	1977	-	90%

[Continued]

★ 321 ★

Childbirth, Worldwide
[Continued]

Country	Year	Trained Attendant	Institutional Deliveries
Republic of Korea	1980	60%	57%
Northern Europe			
Denmark	1979	100%	99%
Finland	1979	100%	100%
Iceland	1974	-	98%
Norway	1974	100%	99%
Sweden	1976	100%	-
United Kingdom			
England and Wales	1978	100%	98%
Scotland	1978	100%	98%
Western Europe			
Austria	1976	-	85%
Belgium	1973	98%	98%
France	1976	-	99%
Germany, Federal Republic of	1979	100%	-
Luxembourg	1976	-	100%
Netherlands	1978	100%	64%
Switzerland	1976	99%	-
Eastern Europe			
Bulgaria	1973	99%	-
Czechoslovakia	1972	100%	100%
German Democratic Republic	-	99%	-
Hungary	1982	99%	99%
Poland	1980	100%	92%
Romania	1979	100%	100%
Southern Europe			
Greece	1978	97%	94%
Italy	1979	100%	95%
Portugal	1979	88%	64%
Spain	1975	-	90%
Yugoslavia	1979	86%	83%

[Continued]

★ 321 ★

Childbirth, Worldwide
[Continued]

Country	Year	Trained Attendant	Institutional Deliveries
Oceania			
Fiji	1981	-	92%
New Zealand	1971	100%	100%
Papua New Guinea	1976	24%	-
Solomon Islands	1981	50%	-

Source: Selected from "The Coverage of Maternity Care: A Critical Review of Available Information," Erica Royston et al., *World Health Statistics Quarterly*, 38:3 (1985), p. 267-288. Also in source: Some data on pre-and postnatal care; data for other years. *Notes:* 1. Midwives, assumed to be trained. 2. "Traditional birth attendant" assumed to be trained.

★ 322 ★

Death from Pregnancy-Related Causes Worldwide

Estimated lifetime chance of dying from pregnancy-related causes, by region, 1975-1984.

Region	Lifetime chance of maternal death
Africa	1 in 21
Asia	1 in 54
South America	1 in 73
Caribbean	1 in 140
North America	1 in 6366
Northern Europe	1 in 9850

Source: Population Today 18:5 (May 1990), Table 2. Primary Source: Calculated by Dr. Roger Rochat, Emory University School of Medicine, Master in Public Health Program, using maternal-mortality rates from the World Health Organization and total fertility rates from Population Reference Bureau; in Barbara herz and Anthony R. Measham, *The Safe Motherhood Initiative: Proposals for Action*, Washington, D.C., World Bank, 1987.

★ 323 ★

Drug Use Among Pregnant Women: Part 1

Characteristics of black and white women testing positive for alcohol and drug use during pregnancy.

Characteristic	White (n=499)[1]	Black (n=199)	Total (n=699)
Socioeconomic status[2]			
Low (<$12,000)	135	126	261
Middle ($12,000-$25,000)	325	59	384
High (>$25,000)	39	14	53
Drugs identified in urine			
Alcohol	3	4	7
Cannabinoids	72	12	84
Cocaine	9	15	24
Opiates	2	0	2
Any of the above	77	28	105

Source: Ira J. Chasnoff, M.D, Harvey J. Landress, A.C.S.W., and Mark E. Barrett, Ph.D., "The Prevalence of Illicit-Drug or Alcohol Use During Pregnancy and Discrepancies in Mandatory Reporting in Pinellas County, Florida," *New England Journal of Medicine* 332:17 (April 26, 1990, p. 1202-1206. Related reading: Dorothy Roberts, "The Bias in Drug Arrests of Pregnant Women," *New York Times*, August 11, 1990, p. 17. *Notes:* 1. Includes only non-Hispanic white women. 2. The median annual family income in the ZIP Code where the woman lived was used as an indicator of socioeconomic status.

★ 324 ★

Drug Use Among Pregnant Women: Part 2

Characteristics of 715 pregnant women screened for alcohol and drugs at public health clinics and private obstetrical offices in Pinellas County, Florida.

Characteristic	Percent
Positive response on toxicologic test of urine	14.8%
on women at public clinics (n=380)	16.3%
on women at private offices (n=335)	13.1%
on white women	15.4%
on black women	14.1%
Positive response for cocaine	
white women	1.8%
black women	7.5%
Positive response for cannabinoids	
white women	14.4%
black women	6.0%

Source: Ira J. Chasnoff, M.D, Harvey J. Landress, A.C.S.W., and Mark E. Barrett, Ph.D., "The Prevalence of Illicit-Drug or Alcohol Use During Pregnancy and Discrepancies in Mandatory Reproting in Pinellas County, Florida," *New England Journal of Medicine* 332:17 (April 26, 1990, p. 1202-1206. Related reading: Dorothy Roberts, "The Bias in Drug Arrests of Pregnant Women," *New York Times*, August 11, 1990, p. 17. "Florida is one of several states that have sought to protect newborns by requiring that mothers known to have used alcohol or illicit drugs during pregnancy be reported to health authorities" (source).

★ 325 ★

Effects of Maternal Diet on Infants

Summary of a study on the link between allergies in infants and maternal diet reported in the *New York Times*.

"Research suggests that babies are least likely to develop allergies when mothers avoid certain foods or smoking while pregnant or nursing." Dr. Ranjit K. Chandra, a pediatric immunologist at the Memorial University of New-foundland, tested a restricted diet on **121 pregnant women** who already had at least one child with allergies. Half the women were placed on a diet that eliminated some dairy products, eggs, fish, beef, and peanuts, for the duration of the pregnancy and until they completed nursing. The remaining women ate their usual foods. Fifty-five women on the restricted diet and 54 women on the unrestricted diet completed the study. Among the findings:

1. 17 infants of mothers on restricted diets developed eczema, 5 out of 35 who were breast-fed and 12 out of 20 who were formula-fed;

2. 24 infants of mothers on unrestricted diets developed eczema, 11 out of 36 who were breast-fed and 13 out of 18 who were formula-fed.

Source: Jane E. Brody, "Allergies in Infants are Linked to Mothers' Diets," *New York Times*, August 30, 1990, p. B8. Primary source: R.K. Chandra et al., "Influence of maternal food antigen avoidance during pregnancy and lactation on incidence of atopic eczema in infants," *Clinical Allergy* 16 (1986), p. 563-569; "Predictive value of cord blood IgE in the development of atopic disease and role of breast-feeding in its prevention," *Clinical Allergy*, 1985 (15), p. 517-522; "Influence of maternal diet during lactation and use of formula feeds on develop-ment of atopic eczema in high risk infants," *British Medical Journal* 299 (July 22, 1989), p. 228-230. Also in source: discussion of relationship of smoking to allergies and asthma.

★ 326 ★

Iron Deficiency in Pregnant Women

Number and percent of women with low hematocrit at initial [prenatal] visit, by race or ethnic group and trimester of pregnancy.

Race or ethnic group	Total		First trimester		Second trimester		Third trimester	
	n[1]	% low	n[1]	% low	n[1]	% low	n[1]	% low
Total women	77,771	14.7%	15,261	5.6%	36,367	9.9%	26,143	26.8%
White	43,908	9.4%	10,575	3.2%	19,885	5.8%	13,448	19.4%
Black	25,702	24.2%	3,609	12.2%	12,584	16.8%	9,509	38.6%
Hispanic	7,130	13.6%	902	7.5%	3,450	7.9%	2,778	22.8%
Native American	263	9.1%	48	0%	111	4.5%	104	18.2%
Asian	592	15.2%	99	9.1%	265	12.1%	228	21.5%

Source: "Prevalence of Low Hematocrit at Initial Visit, by Race or Ethnic Group and Trimester of Pregnancy: CDC Pregnancy Nutrition Surveillance System, 1987," *Nutrition Monitoring in the United States*, September 1989, p. 87. Primary source: Centers for Disease Control. n is the number of persons in the sample; for n < 100, interpret data with caution.

★ 327 ★

Maternal Drug Abuse

Number of drug-exposed infants and infant mortality rates among drug-exposed infants, New York City, 1978-1986. Rate is per 1,000 drug-exposed live births.

Year	Number of Drug-Exposed Infants	Infant Mortality Among Drug-Exposed Infants	
		Number	Rate
1978	781	35	44.8
1979	766	33	43.1
1980	794	41	51.6
1981	730	33	45.2
1982	803	35	43.6
1983	884	42	47.5
1984	1,084	54	49.8
1985	1,229	42	34.2
1986	2,066	64	31.0

Source: Leo Habel, BS, Katherine Kaye, MD, MPH, and Jean Lee, MS, "Trends in Reporting of Maternal Drug Abuse and Infant Mortality Among Drug-Exposed Infants in New York City," *Women and Health*, Vol. 16(2), 1990, p. 41+. Also in source: a discussion of causes of death among drug-exposed infants and the association between maternal drug abuse and other factors contributing to infant mortality.

★ 328 ★

Pregnancy Problems and Hormones

A study links pregnancy problems to a surge in a hormone.

In a study of **193 women** with regular menstrual cycles, it was found that a hormone called LH (luteinising hormone), which is normally secreted on the 14th day of the menstrual cycle, when secreted in large amounts on the eighth day was linked with a higher rate of miscarriage. In the normal LH group were **147 women; 88% conceived** as compared to **67%** of women with high amounts of LH. **65%** of the pregnancies in the high LH group ended in miscarriage compared with **12%** of the pregnacies in the normal LH group. The findings offer the possibility of a simple predictive test of fertility/potential for miscarriage before pregnancy and the identification of women with endocrine abnormalities that can be remedied.

Source: Lesley Regan, Elisabeth J. Owen, Howard S. Jacobs, "Hypersecretion of luteinising hormone, infertility, and miscarriage," *Lancet*: 336(8724): November 10, 1990, p. 1141+. Correspondence to Miss L. Regan, Dept. of Obstetrics and Gynaecology, St. Mary's Hospital Medical School, London W21PG, UK. Related reading: Lawrence K. Altman, "Pregnancy Problems, Hormone Linked," *New York Times*, November 13, 1990, p. B7.

★ 329 ★

Prenatal Alcohol Exposure

One result of a study of the effects of moderate prenatal alcohol exposure on child IQ and learning problems at age 7-1/2 years.

The authors examined the long-term effects of moderate prenatal alcohol exposure on 482 school-aged children. Consumption of two drinks per day or more on the average was related to a 7-point decrement in IQ in 7-year-old children.

Source: Ann P. Streissguth, PhD, Helen M. Barr, MS, and Paul D. Sampson, PhD, "Moderate Prenatal Alcohol Exposure: Effects on Child IQ and Learning Problems at Age 7-1/2 Years," *Alcoholism: Clinical and Experimental Research*, Vol. 14, No. 5 (September/October 1990). Reprint requests: Dr. Ann P. Streissguth, Department of Psychiatry and Behavioral Sciences, GG-20, University of Washington, Seattle, WA 98195. This study began with prenatal interviews of 1,529 pregnant women, all receiving prenatal care by the fifth month of pregnancy. The mothers were primarily white, married, middle class, and at low risk for adverse pregnancy outcome.

★ 330 ★

Prenatal Care and Live Births

Percentage of live births by trimester prenatal care began, by race and Hispanic origin, 1970-1987.

	Percentage of live births					
	1970	1975	1980	1985	1986	1987
Prenatal Care Began First Trimester						
All races and origins	68%	72%	76%	76%	76%	76%
White	72%	76%	79%	79%	79%	79%
Black	44%	56%	63%	62%	62%	61%
All Hispanic women	-	-	60%	61%	60%	61%
Cuban	-	-	83%	83%	82%	83%
Mexican	-	-	60%	60%	59%	60%
Puerto Rican	-	-	58%	58%	57%	57%
Non-Hispanic women	-	-	77%	77%	77%	77%
Prenatal Care Began Third Trimester or No Prenatal Care						
All races and origins	8%	6%	5%	6%	6%	6%
White	6%	5%	4%	5%	5%	5%
Black	17%	10%	9%	10%	11%	11%
All Hispanic Women	-	-	12%	12%	13%	13%
Cuban	-	-	4%	4%	4%	4%
Mexican	-	-	12%	13%	13%	13%
Puerto Rican	-	-	16%	16%	17%	17%
Non-Hispanic women	-	-	5%	5%	6%	6%

Source: "Percentage of Live Births by Trimester Prenatal Care Began, by Race and Hispanic Origin, 1970-1987," *U.S. Children and Their Families*, 1989, p. 163. Primary Source: National Center for Health Statistics, *Health, United States, 1982*, Table 24; *Vital Statistics of the United States*, 1985, Vol. 1 - Natality, Table 1-84. *Monthly Vital Statistics Report*, Vol 31, No. 8, Supplement, November 1982, Tables 13,20; Vol. 35, No. 4, Supplement, July 1986, Table 25; Vol. 36, No. 4, Supplement, July 1987, Table 25; Vol. 37, No. 3, Supplement, June 1989, Tables 27 and 30. Birth figures for Hispanic women in 1985-87 are based on data for 23 states and the District of Columbia which report Hispanic origin of the mother on the birth certificate. These states accounted for 90% of the Hispanic population in 1980. Hispanic data for 1980 from *Monthly Vital Statistics Report*, Vol. 32, No. 6, Supplement, September 1983, Table 13 (based on 22 states). Non-Hispanic women are white, black, and other women not of Hispanic origin, in the same 23 states that report data on origin.

★ 331 ★

Unattended Births: 1980-1987

Percent of births out-of-hospital and unattended.

Year	% of births out-of-hospital and unattended
1980	0.3%
1981	0.3%
1982	0.3%
1983	0.3%
1984	0.3%
1985	0.3%
1986	0.3%
1987	0.3%

Source: "Percent of births out-of-hospital and unattended," *Health United States— 1989*, p. 35. Primary source: National Center for Health Statistics, Division of Vital Statistics. Also in source: data for 1977-1979 and goal of 0% for 1990.

★ 332 ★

Vaginal Birth After Cesarean

Responses of Fellows of the American College of Obstetricians and Gynecologists to the question: "Do you encourage VBAC with your patients?"

Base and responses	Total	Females
Physicians who currently practice obstetrics		
Unweighted	1755	260
Weighted	1769	267
Yes	1620	257
No	126	8
No response	22	1

Source: "Vaginal Birth After Cesarean Section: Report of a 1990 Survey of ACOG's Membership," Table 6 and Table 9, August 1990. Prepared by: The American College of Obstetricians and Gynecologists, Washington, D.C. Results of a survey of Fellows of the American College of Obstetricians and Gynecologists conducted in March 1990 to determine the attitudes and practices of ACOG Fellows concerning vaginal birth after a previous cesarean section (VBAC).

★ 333 ★

Vaginal Delivery After Cesarean

Summary of a survey of obstetricians and gynecologists reported in the *New York Times*.

The author summarizes a survey of 2,213 obstetricians and gynecologists conducted for the American College of Obstetricians and Gynecologists (ACOG), which found:

1. **6 out of 10 women** who tried vaginal delivery (which tends to pose less of a health risk to the mother) after a Cesarean were successful.

2. Doctors under the age of 55 were more likely to encourage vaginal delivery, and their patients were more likely to succeed at it.

Summarizing the remarks of Dr. Mary Jo O'Sullivan, secretary of ACOG, the author states that:

3. The rate of Cesarean deliveries rose to **24.7%** of all American births in 1988 from **5.5%** in 1970.

4. The rate of vaginal deliveries after Cesareans rose to **12.6%** in 1988 from **2.2%** in 1970; the rate in 1990 could be as high as **18%**.

Source: Warren E. Leary, "Alternative to Caesarean Grows More Popular," *New York Times,* August 29, 1990, p. A12. Primary source: "Vaginal Birth After Cesarean Section: Report of a 1990 Survey of ACOG's Membership," August 1990, Prepared by: The American College of Obstetricians and Gynecologists, Washington, D.C.

★ 334 ★

Women with No Prenatal Care by Race/Origin: 1980-1987

Percent of women with no prenatal care during the first trimester, by race/origin, 1980-1987.

Year	% with no prenatal care during first trimester			
	White	Black	Amer.Indian	Hispanic
1980	20.7%	37.3%	41.3%	39.8%
1981	20.6%	37.6%	40.7%	39.4%
1982	20.7%	38.5%	39.5%	39.0%
1983	20.6%	38.5%	40.3%	39.0%
1984	20.4%	37.8%	40.0%	38.5%
1985	20.6%	38.2%	39.7%	38.8%
1986	20.8%	38.4%	39.3%	39.7%
1987	20.6%	38.9%	39.8%	39.0%

Source: "Percent with no prenatal care during 1st trimester," *Health United States - 1989,* p. 35. Primary source: Data from National Center for Health Statistics, Division of Vital Statistics. Also in source: goal for 1990 (proportion of women obtaining no prenatal care during first trimester should not exceed 10%); data for 1978-1979. A discussion of the effects of prenatal care during the first trimester appears on p. 31.

★ 335 ★
Working During Pregnancy
Some results of a study of demanding, highly stressful work during pregnancy, designed to separate the effects of work from those of socioeconomic status.

The authors studied the outcomes of pregnancy of **4,412 women** who became pregnant during medical school residency and **4,236 wives** of their medical school classmates to determine the effects of physically demanding, stressful work during pregnancy. During each trimester of pregnancy, the residents worked many more hours than the wives of male residents. The results of the authors' survey "suggest that working long hours in a stressful occupation has little effect on the outcome of pregnancy in an otherwise health population of high socioeconomic status." Among the results:

13.8% of residents' pregnancies ended in miscarriage compared to **11.8%** of classmates' wives;

6.5% of residents delivered pre-term (less than 37 weeks' gestation) compared to **6.0%** of classmates' wives;

0.5% of residents' pregnancies ended in ectopic gestations and **0.2%** in stillbirths, compared to **0.8%** and **0.5%** of classmates' wives, respectively;

infants who were small for gestational age were born to **5.4%** of residents and **5.8%** of classmates' wives.

residents more often reported preterm labor (**11%** vs. **6%**) but not preterm delivery (**11%** vs. **6%**);

8.8% of residents experienced preeclampsia compared to **3.5%** of classmates' wives.

Source: Mark A. Klebanoff, M.D., M.P.H., Patricia H. Shiono, Ph.D., and George G.Rhoads, M.D., M.P.H., "Outcomes of Pregnancy in a National Sample of Resident Physicians," *New England Journal of Medicine*, Vol 323, No. 15, October 15, 1990, p. 1040+. Related reading: Natalie Angier, "Hard Work Found Not to Harm Pregnancy," *New York Times*, October 11, 1990, p. B7.

INCOME, SPENDING, AND WEALTH

★ 336 ★

Earnings by Level of Education

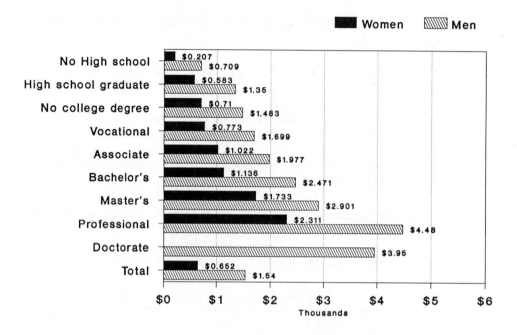

Mean monthly earnings for adults aged 18 and over, by degree level: Spring 1987.

Degree level	Mean monthly earnings	
	Female	Male
U.S. Total	$ 652.00	$1,540.00
Doctorate	-	3,950.00
Professional	2,311.00	4,480.00
Master's	1,733.00	2,901.00
Bachelor's	1,136.00	2,471.00
Associate	1,022.00	1,977.00
Vocational	773.00	1,699.00
Some college, no degree	710.00	1,483.00

[Continued]

304

★ 336 ★

Earnings by Level of Education
[Continued]

Degree level	Mean monthly earnings	
	Female	Male
High school graduate only	583.00	1,350.00
Not a high school graduate	207.00	709.00

Source: "Does Education Really Pay Off?," *Census and You* 26:1 (January 1991), p. 8. Primary source: *What's It Worth? Educational Background and Economic Status: Spring 1987*, Current Population Reports, Series P-70, No. 21. Also in source: a discussion of other aspects of the report, including mean monthly earnings by field.

★ 337 ★

Managers' Median Earnings
Median annual earnings of persons employed as executives, administrators, and managers who worked year-round, full-time, 1987.

Sex	Earnings
Female	$21,874
Male	$36,155

Source: Facts on Working Women, No.89-4, December 1989, p. 7.

Benefits

★ 338 ★

Maternity/Parental Leave Benefits by State
States with maternity/parental leave laws, type, and duration, 1990. See below for an explanation of abbreviations.

State	Type	Pub/Priv	Duration
Arizona	MD[2]	state	12 weeks
California[1]	MD	all	4 months
California	P[2]	state	1 year
Colorado	MD	all	reasonable
Colorado	A	all	biological
Connecticut	P[2]	state[4]	24 weeks
Connecticut	P[2]	private[4]	12 weeks
Delaware	A	state	6 weeks
Florida	MD	state	6 months
Hawaii[1]	MD	all	reasonable
Illinois	P[2]	state[4]	1 year
Iowa	MD	all	8 weeks
Kansas	MD	all	reasonable

[Continued]

★ 338 ★

Maternity/Parental Leave Benefits by State
[Continued]

State	Type	Pub/Priv	Duration
Kentucky	A	all	6 weeks
Louisiana	MD	all	4 months
Maine	P[2]	all[4]	8 weeks
Maryland	P[2]	state[4]	12 weeks
Massachusetts	M[2]	all	8 weeks
Minnesota	P[2]	all	6 weeks
Missouri	A	state	biological
Montana	MD	all	reasonable
New Jersey[1]	P[2]	all[4]	12 weeks
New York[1]	A	all	biological
North Dakota	P[2]	state[4]	4 months
Oklahoma	P[2]	state[4]	not specified
Oregon	P[2]	all	12 weeks
Pennsylvania	P[2]	state[4]	6 months
Pennsylvania	A	private	biological
Puerto Rico[1]	M	all	8 weeks[3]
Rhode Island[1]	P[2]	all[4]	13 weeks
Tennessee	M	all	4 months
Vermont	M	all	12 weeks
Washington	P[2]	all[4]	12 weeks
West Virginia	P[2]	state[4]	12 weeks
Wisconsin	P[2]	all[4]	6 weeks

Source: "State Maternity/Parental Leave Laws," *Facts on Working Women*, No. 90-1, June 1990, p. 2. Also in source: State Maternity/Parental Family Illness Laws; TDI Laws by Jurisdiction. Type Codes: A = adoption; M = maternity; MD = maternity disability; P = parental. Duration abbreviations: reasonable = reasonable period; biological = same as for biological. *Notes:* 1. States offering "temporary disability insurance" with partial salary replacements. 2. Adoption included. 3. Partial payment for leave prior to and after child's arrival. 4. Includes family illness.

★ 339 ★

Maternity/Paternity Leave Benefits

Percentage of workers receiving paid and unpaid maternity and paternity leave in private nonagricultural establishments with 100 or more employees.

Employee Benefit Program	Covered employees, in percent			
	All employees	Profes- sional & Adminis- trative	Technical & Clerical	Production & Service
Number of workers covered in survey: 31 million				
Paid:				
Maternity leave	2%	3%	2%	2%
Paternity leave	1%	2%	1%	1%

[Continued]

★ 339 ★

Maternity/Paternity Leave Benefits
[Continued]

Employee Benefit Program	Covered employees, in percent			
	All employees	Profes-sional & Adminis-trative	Technical & Clerical	Production & Service
Unpaid:				
Maternity leave	33%	37%	34%	31%
Paternity leave	16%	19%	17%	13%

Source: Selected from "Full-time employees participating in selected employee benefit programs, medium and large private firms, United States, 1988 (in percent)," *The Dow Jones-Irwin Business and Investment Almanac 1990*, p. 626 (Homewood, Ill.: Dow Jones-Irwin, 1990). Survey coverage excludes executives and employees in constant travel status, such as airline pilots, as well as data for Alaska and Hawaii. Tabulations provide representative data for 31 million workers in private nonagricultural establishments with 100 or more employees.

Financial Support

★ 340 ★

Financial Support Provided to Others

Annual financial support provided and annualized family income of provider, by type of person supported and selected characteristics of the provider.

Characteristic of provider	Number of providers (thousands)	Amount of support		Annual family income	
		Mean	Std. error	Mean	Std. error
Total	6,275	$3,006	$170	$37,830	$1,656
Sex:					
Female	995	1,987	352	36,327	3,151
Male	5,280	3,198	189	38,113	1,877
Total supporting children	4,326	2,607	113	34,260	1,808
Sex:					
Women	324	1,545	271	39,148	7,395
Men	4,001	2,694	117	33,863	1,858
Total supporting adults	2,316	3,276	375	45,399	3,064
Child(ren) also supported	366	3,977	794	43,518	6,196
Adults only supported	1,949	3,144	419	45,753	3,452
Sex:					
Female	700	2,109	467	36,100	3,259
Male	1,616	3,781	492	49,424	4,124

Source: Martin O'Connell et al., *Who's Helping Out? Support Networks Among American Families*, Current Population Reports Household Economic Studies, Series P-70, No. 13, October 1988, p. 15-17. Also in source: numerous other characteristics of providers.

★ 341 ★

Odds of Providing Financial Support for Nonhousehold Member

Odds of providing financial support for a person living outside the provider's household.

Category	All persons	Type of person supported			
		Children	All adults	Parents	Spouse or ex-spouse[1]
Overall odds of providing support[2]	1:26	1:39	1:73	1:208	1:42
Relative odds of providing support:[3]					
Male vs. Female	6:1	11:1	3:1	2:1	10:1
Separated/divorced vs.--					
Single/widowed	6:1	9:1	4:1	1:1	[4]
Married, spouse present	5:1	6:1	4:1	1:1	[4]
Married, spouse absent vs.--					
Separated	[4]	[4]	[4]	[4]	5:1
Divorced	[4]	[4]	[4]	[4]	11:1
Interaction term (Marital*Sex):					
Male--sep/div. vs. male--single/wid	3:1	4:1	2:1	[4]	[4]
25 to 44 years vs. 65 years and over	2:1	31:1	1:2	2:1	1:2
College, 1 or more years vs. less than high school	1:1	1:1	1:1	1:1	1:1
Family income $45,000+ vs. <$15,000	2:1	2:1	4:1	3:1	8:1

Source: Martin O'Connell et al., *Who's Helping Out? Support Networks Among American Families,* Current Population Reports Household Economic Studies, Series P-70, No. 13, October 1988, p. 11. Primary source: Relative odds derived from log-linear regression in table E-1. *Notes:* 1. Universe limited to persons separated, divorced, or married spouse absent, at time of the interview. 2. Observed odds based on frequency of reporting on being a provider for the total population 18 years and over. 3. Relative odds derived from log-linear regression including all of the above variables plus the marital status*sex interaction term. Odds terms refer to relative odds of one category in a variable being more likely to be a provider than another category. 4. Term not included in model.

★ 342 ★

Persons Receiving Financial Support From Nonhousehold Member

Amount of annual financial support received by adults and annualized family income of the provider, by relationship of the supported adult to the provider.

Relationship and sex of provider	Adults supported[1] (thousands)	Support received per person		Family income of provider	
		Mean	Std. error	Mean	Std. error
Total	2,726	$2,728	$311	$44,973	$2,686
Female	824	1,744	391	35,396	2,919
Male	1,902	3,156	409	49,140	3,597
Parent of provider	918	1,484	301	41,605	3,623
Supported by son	590	1,561	239	45,607	2,762
Supported by daughter	328	1,347	725	34,406	4,200

[Continued]

★ 342 ★

Persons Receiving Financial Support From Nonhousehold Member
[Continued]

Relationship and sex of provider	Adults supported[1] (thousands)	Support received per person		Family income of provider	
		Mean	Std. error	Mean	Std. error
Spouse or ex-spouse of provider	614	5,712	925	50,763	7,694
Supported by ex-husband	553	5,999	994	54,033	8,413
Child 21 and over of provider	495	3,755	966	49,246	5,223
Supported by mother	217	2,878	692	47,591	7,434
Supported by father	280	4,408	1,608	50,177	7,162
All other persons	697	1,017	120	41,402	5,200
Supported by women	219	821	177	28,450	3,475
Supported by men	480	1,103	154	47,138	7,206

Source: Martin O'Connell et al., *Who's Helping Out? Support Networks Among American Families*, Current Population Reports Household Economic Studies, Series P-70, No. 13, October 1988, p. 9. *Note:* 1. Excludes 138,000 persons for whom relationship was not ascertained.

★ 343 ★

Persons Supporting Nonhousehold Members
Selected characteristics of persons supporting nonhousehold members, by type of person supported.

Characteristic of person providing support	Total persons 18 and over	Total number of providers	Providing support for--		
			Adults and children	Adults only	Children only
			Numbers in thousands		
Total	171,290	6,275	366	1,949	3,959
Sex:					
Female	89,979	995	29	670	295
Male	81,310	5,280	337	1,279	3,664

Source: Martin O'Connell et al., *Who's Helping Out? Support Networks Among American Families*, Current Population Reports Household Economic Studies, Series P-70, No. 13, October 1988, p. 3. Also in source: data by numerous other characteristics of persons providing support.

★ 344 ★

Women Receiving Child Support Payments

Selected characteristics of women receiving child support payments, 1985.

Characteristic	Number of women (thousands)	Annual child support payments		Annualized family income	
		Mean	Std. error	Mean	Std. error
Women, 18 to 64 years old	89,602	[3]	[3]	$29,925	$376
Supposed to receive child support	5,179	[3]	[3]	23,020	918
Actually received child support	4,017	$2,506	$117	23,545	1,111
Race and Hispanic origin:					
White	3,406	$2,682	$134	$24,948	$1,277
Black	563	1,429	144	15,254	1,430
Hispanic origin[1]	208	2,088	435	21,224	4,991
Age:					
18 to 24 years old	301	$1,450	$162	$13,457	$2,399
25 to 44 years old	3,402	2,474	109	23,712	1,222
45 to 64 years old	314	3,872	868	31,388	4,189
Marital status:					
Married, spouse present	1,161	$2,034	$140	$37,479	$3,089
Separated[2]	675	2,977	427	16,467	1,402
Widowed	10	[4]	[4]	[4]	[4]
Divorced	1,901	2,860	167	18,974	958
Never married	268	908	137	13,659	2,441
Years of school completed:					
Less than high school	726	$1,737	$150	$15,942	$1,594
High school	1,817	2,266	124	21,080	1,004
College:					
1 to 3 years	1,045	2,865	320	28,090	3,364
4 or more years	428	3,957	441	35,812	3,175
Employment status:					
In labor force	3,177	$2,530	$136	$25,535	$1,320
With a job	2,904	2,558	145	26,908	1,412
Worked all weeks last month	2,764	2,608	150	27,356	1,469
Worked part of last month	140	[4]	[4]	[4]	[4]
Without a job, looking for work, on layoff	273	2,222	371	10,920	1,937
Not in labor force	840	2,419	223	16,015	1,640
Frequency of payments:					
Regular	3,126	$2,891	$141	$23,963	$1,317
Occasional	457	1,409	187	22,841	2,524

[Continued]

★ 344 ★

Women Receiving Child Support Payments
[Continued]

Characteristic	Number of women (thousands)	Annual child support payments		Annualized family income	
		Mean	Std. error	Mean	Std. error
Seldom	387	946	182	20,707	3,148
Never	46	4	4	4	4

Source: Martin O'Connell et al., "Who's Helping Out? Support Networks Among American Familie"s, *Current Population Reports Household Economic Studies,* Series P-70, No. 13, October 1988, p. 19. Primary source: SIPP Wave 5, 1984 panel topical module on child support. Also in source: type of agreement and method of receiving payments. *Notes:* 1. Persons of Hispanic origin may be of any race. 2. Includes married, spouse absent. 3. Not applicable. 4. Base too small to show derived measures.

Government Spending

★ 345 ★

Government Spending on Social Programs: 5 Countries: 1980-2025

Government spending on social programs as a percentage of gross domestic product.

Country	Spending as % of GDP			
	1980	2000	2010	2025
United States	18%	16%	17%	19%
Canada	20%	17%	17%	21%
Japan	15%	21%	26%	27%
United Kingdom	23%	23%	24%	27%
France	31%	32%	33%	35%
West Germany	31%	33%	35%	39%

Source: "Government Spending on Social Programs as a Percentage of Gross Domestic Product," *America in the 21st Century: A Demographic Overview*, 1989, p. 20 (Washington, D.C.: Population Reference Bureau, 1989). Primary source: International Monetary Fund, *Aging and Social Expenditure in the Major Industrial Countries, 1980-2025*, Occasional paper No. 47, 1986. Social programs include pensions, medical care, education, unemployment insurance and other welfare payments.

★ 346 ★

Income and Program Characteristics of Persons Needing Assistance

Women and men 15 years and older who need assistance with everyday activities, compared to all women and men at all income levels and to women and men participating in aid programs, 1986.

Characteristic of person needing assistance	Total	Needed assistance with--						Did not need assistance
		One or more activities	Personal care	Gettiing around outside	Preparing meals	Doing housework	Keeping track of bills and/ or money	
Females 15 years and over, in thousands	97,064	5,655	1,953	3,607	3,417	4,508	1,916	91,409
Monthly household income								
Under $600	10,544	1,549	529	1,037	814	1,131	595	8,996
$600 to $1,199	14,423	1,313	415	854	707	1,041	497	13,111
$1,200 to $1,999	19,670	1,110	396	693	744	908	334	18,560
$2,000 to $2,999	19,915	795	277	463	534	689	258	19,121
$3,000 and over	32,512	889	336	559	618	740	231	31,623
Program participation								
Received:								
Means-tested cash assistance[1]	6,500	1,150	443	734	663	862	453	5,350
Food Stamps	6,484	715	243	407	417	551	248	5,769
Public or subsidized housing	3,957	553	152	380	238	420	187	3,404
Medicaid coverage	7,469	1,314	510	829	793	996	520	6,155
Social Security	19,555	3,671	1,371	2,554	2,171	2,861	1,547	15,884
Veteran's payments	697	149	60	102	85	123	58	549
Males 15 years and over, in thousands	88,958	2,551	1,258	1,606	1,413	1,418	1,123	86,407
Monthly household income								
Under $600	5,682	368	140	181	216	248	117	5,315
$600 to $1,199	10,643	743	357	469	384	424	385	9,900
$1,200 to $1,999	17,813	621	316	409	328	288	240	17,192
$2,000 to $2,999	19,821	410	215	265	243	207	200	19,411
$3,000 and over	34,997	408	229	282	241	251	182	34,589
Program participation								
Received:								
Means-tested cash assistance[1]	2,831	469	188	264	276	296	233	2,362
Food Stamps	3,093	222	78	119	121	122	91	2,871
Public or subsidized housing	2,038	127	63	71	85	87	43	1,912
Medicaid coverage	2,931	496	231	268	307	304	295	2,435
Social Security	14,158	1,753	858	1,157	997	989	828	12,406
Veteran's payments	2,539	278	111	177	127	161	93	2,261

Source: The need for Personal Assistance with Everyday Activities: Recipients and Caregivers, *Current Population Reports*, Series P-70, No. 19, 1990, p. 27. Also in source: characteristics of persons needing assistance. *Notes:* 1. Means-tested cash assistance programs include: Federal or State Supplemental Security Income (SSI), Veteran's pensions, Aid to Families with Dependent Children (AFDC), General Assistance, Indian, Cuban, or Refugee Assistance, and other welfare.

★ 347 ★

Reagan Administration Expenditures for Mother-Only Families

Federal expenditures for mother-only families with children in 1985 with and without Reagan Administration program changes.

	Estimated 1985 Expenditures under 1981 Law	Projected 1985 Expenditures under 1983 Law	Estimated Reduction in Budget	
			Total	Percentage
	Billions of Dollars			
Total	38.2	33.8	4.4	12%
Income-tested welfare programs				
Cash				
Total	9.6	8.5	1.1	* 12%
AFDC[1]	8.9	7.7	1.2	10%
Supplemental Security Income	0.7	0.8	0.1	9%
In-kind benefits				
Total	19.5	17.9	1.6	11%
Food stamps	6.0	5.4	0.6	12%
Energy assistance	0.5	0.5	0.0	10%
Medicaid[1]	8.0	7.8	0.2	3%
Housing assistance	3.5	3.1	0.4	12%
Child Nutrition	1.5	1.1	0.4	29%
Work-related programs,				
total	3.0	1.7	1.3	46%
Employment and training	1.4	0.4	1.0	71%
Day care and Head Start	1.6	1.3	0.3	19%
Nonincome-tested programs				
Cash				
Total	6.1	5.7	0.4	5%
Survivors Insurance	4.4	4.2	0.2	5%
Unemployment Insurance	1.0	0.8	0.2	18%
Veterans' benefits	0.7	0.7	0.0	1%

Source: "Federal expenditures for mother-only families with children in 1985, with and without Reagan Administration program changes (billions of dollars unless otherwise indicated)," *Single Mothers and Their Children: A New American Dilemma*, p. 140 (Washington, D.C.: Urban Institute Press,). Primary source: The estimated expenditures under 1981 law were calculated using expenditure data from U.S. Congressional Budget Office, "Major Legislative Changes in Human Resources Program Since January 1981," staff memorandum, August 1983. Consult source for further explanation of calculation. *Note:* 1. Includes state and local as well as federal expenditures.

Household Income

★ 348 ★

Economic Condition of Mother-Only Families: 1975-1983

Trends in the economic well-being, prevalence, and welfare dependence of mother-only families with children, 1975-1983.

Year	Economic Well-Being[1] (% poor)	Prevalence[2] (% of all families with children	Welfare dependence[3] (% on welfare)
1975	47.9%	14.7%	0.57%
1976	47.3%	15.3%	0.56%
1977	45.8%	15.9%	0.54%
1978	45.8%	17.1%	0.49%
1979	43.8%	17.4%	0.48%
1980	46.7%	17.5%	0.50%
1981	48.1%	18.0%	0.46%
1982	51.6%	18.9%	0.44%
1983	51.2%	18.6%	0.47%

Source: "Short-term trends in the economic well-being, prevalence, and welfare dependence of mother-only families with children, 1975-83," *Single Mothers and Their Children: A New American Dilemma*, 1986, p. 138 (Washington, D.C.: Urban Institute Press, 1986). Primary source: Economic well-being is from Christine Ross, "The Trend in Poverty, 1965-1983," paper prepared for the conference entitled Poverty and Policy: Retrospect and Prospects (sponsored by the Institute for Research on Poverty, held at Williamsburg, Virginia, December 6-8, 1984), table 8A. Prevalence is from U.S. Bureau of the Census, *Current Population Reports,* "Household and Family Characteristics," series P-20, nos. 291, 311, 326, 340, 352, 366, 371, 381, 388. Welfare dependence data for 1975-82 are from U.S. Department of Health and Human Services, *Social Security Bulletin,* Vol 47, no. 12, p. 51. Because these data pertain to all families receiving AFDC, the authors multiplied by 0.72, that is, the proportion of families headed by women receiving AFDC in 1979. The denominator (total number of female-headed families each year) was derived from U.S. Bureau of the Census, *Current Population Reports,* "Household and Family Characteristics, series P-20. *Notes:* 1. Proportion poor of families headed by single women with children under age 18. 2. Proportion of all families headed by single women with children under age 18. 3. Proportion of households receiving AFDC.

★ 349 ★

Economic Status of Children Worldwide

Indicators of the economic status of children, circa 1980.

Country	Year	Earnings of poor families with children (before taxes and transfers) as % of U.S. poverty line		Government transfers to families with children (before taxes and transfers) in 1979 U.S. dollars thousands		Poverty rate for children		Poverty rate for families with children		% of pre-tax and transfer poor who receive transfers
		All families	Single parent	Means tested	Social insurance	All families	Single parent	All families	Single parent	All families
Australia	1981	21%	11%	$2,397	$369	16.9%	65.0%	15.0%	61.4%	99%
Canada	1981	36%	16%	$1,383	$1,498	9.6%	38.7%	8.6%	35.3%	99%
Germany, Federal Republic	1981	45%	15%	$328	$2,726	8.2%	35.1%	6.9%	31.9%	100%
Sweden	1981	48%	39%	$2,357	$4,028	5.1%	8.6%	4.4%	7.5%	100%

[Continued]

★ 349 ★

Economic Status of Children Worldwide
[Continued]

Country	Year	Earnings of poor families with children (before taxes and transfers) as % of U.S. poverty line		Government transfers to families with children (before taxes and transfers) in 1979 U.S. dollars thousands		Poverty rate for children		Poverty rate for families with children		% of pre-tax and transfer poor who receive transfers All families
		All families	Single parent	Means tested	Social insurance	All families	Single parent	All families	Single parent	All families
United Kingdom	1979	48%	17%	$1,239	$1,971	10.7%	38.6%	8.5%	36.8%	99%
United States	1979	33%	21%	$1,660	$692	17.1%	51.0%	13.8%	42.9%	73%

Source: "Indicators of the Economic Status of Children, Selected Countries: Circa 1980," *Children's Well-Being: An International Comparison*, A Report of the Select Committee on Children, Youth, and Families, 101st Cong., 2d sess., March 1990, p. 106. Primary source: The source of the estimates of earnings, government transfers, and poverty rates is the Luxembourg Income Study (LIS). See source for a listing of publications that discuss the LIS. Poverty is defined as the percentage of people who have adjusted disposable income below the U.S. poverty line ($5,763 for a family of 3 in 1979) converted into national currencies using the purchasing power parities developed by the Organization for Economic Co-operation and Development. The definition of adjustable disposable income includes all forms of cash income (earnings, property income, and all cash transfers including the value of food stamps in the United States and housing allowances in the United Kingdom and Sweden) and it subtracts income and payroll taxes. This definition differs slightly from the definition of income used in the official U.S. calculation of poverty rates. In 1979, the U.S. Bureau of the Census estimated that 16% of U.S. children were in families with income below the poverty line.

★ 350 ★

Homeowners and Renters: Income and Poverty

Median income and poverty rates of households by household type and tenure, 1985.

Household type	Owners		Renters	
	Median Income	Poverty Rate	Median Income	Poverty Rate
All households	$27,816	9.1%	$14,460	25.3%
Married couples	33,315	5.4%	21,160	16.6%
Female headed families	19,076	17.2%	9,302	44.9%
Under age 45	19,837	17.2%	8,921	47.3%
Age 65 and over	14,178	20.2%	9,137	35.4%
Single females	9,808	24.1%	9,091	30.6%
Age 65 and over	8,254	28.5%	6,446	40.2%

Source: Selected from "Median Income and Poverty Rates of Households by Household Type and Tenure, 1985 (income in dollars)," *The American Woman 1990-91*, 1990, p. 101 (New York: W.W. Norton & Company, 1990). Primary source: U.S. Department of Housing and Urban Development and U.S. Bureau of the Census, December 1988, Tables 3-1, 3-20, 4-1, and 4-20.

★ 351 ★

Household Income by Female Age

Female adults, in thousands, by age group and annual household income.

Household Income	Total	Age 18-24	Age 25-34	Age 35-44	Age 45-54	Age 55-64	Age 65+
$75,000 or more	7,136	1,036	1,155	2,050	1,664	991	240
$60,000-74,999	6,633	872	1,460	2,002	1,456	475	367
$50,000-59,999	7,430	630	2,081	2,126	1,245	966	383
$40,000-49,999	10,943	1,232	3,204	2,908	1,911	1,076	612
$30,000-39,999	14,473	1,793	4,301	3,060	2,094	1,715	1,510

[Continued]

★ 351 ★

Household Income by Female Age
[Continued]

Household Income	Total	Age 18-24	Age 25-34	Age 35-44	Age 45-54	Age 55-64	Age 65+
$20,000-29,999	15,927	2,395	4,140	3,057	1,763	1,915	2,656
$10,000-19,999	18,041	2,459	3,222	1,950	1,626	3,031	5,753
Less than $10,000	14,083	2,263	2,493	1,023	974	1,602	5,727

Source: Selected from *Mediamark Research Multimedia Audiences Report, Spring 1990,* p. 116-118 (New York: Mediamark Research Inc., 1990).

★ 352 ★

Household Income by Female Educational Attainment

Number of women in thousands, by educational attainment and annual household income, 1990.

Household Income	Total	Graduated College	Attended College	Graduated High School	Did Not Graduate HS
Total Women	94,667	14,333	17,363	39,830	23,142
$75,000 or more	7,136	3,054	1,852	1,959	272
$60,000-74,999	6,633	2,214	1,520	2,469	430
$50,000-59,999	7,430	1,941	1,811	2,978	701
$40,000-49,999	10,043	2,185	2,398	5,189	1,172
$30,000-39,999	14,473	2,117	3,171	6,922	2,264
$20,000-29,999	15,927	1,596	1,751	8,285	3,295
$10,000-19,999	18,041	866	2,407	7,843	6,926
Less than $10,000	14,083	361	1,454	4,185	8,082

Source: Selected from *Mediamark Research Multimedia Audiences Report, Spring 1990,* p. 114 (New York: Mediamark Research Inc., 1990).

★ 353 ★

Household Income by Female Household Status

Female adults, in thousands, by household status and income.

Household Income	Total	Heads of Households	Working Mothers	Mothers	Female Homemakers
$75,000 or more	7,136	753	1,894	2,503	5,950
$60,000-74,999	6,633	821	2,166	2,702	5,600
$50,000-59,999	7,430	1,210	2,373	3,220	6,353
$40,000-49,999	10,943	1,486	3,451	4,831	9,623
$30,000-39,999	14,473	2,984	4,240	6,167	12,677
$20,000-29,999	15,927	4,646	3,679	6,136	13,762
$10,000-19,999	18,041	8,185	2,474	5,041	16,448
Less than $10,000	14,083	9,844	1,267	3,660	12,953

Source: Selected from *Mediamark Research Multimedia Audiences Report, Spring 1990,* p. 112, 204, 206 (New York: Mediamark Research Inc., 1990).

★ 354 ★

Household Income by Female Marital Status

Female adults, in thousands, by marital status and annual household income.

Household Income	Total	Single	Married	All Others	Engaged
All Women	94,667	16,895	55,273	22,500	3,026
Household Income					
$75,000 or more	7,136	1,431	5,371	334	131
$60,000-74,999	6,633	1,096	4,960	577	346
$50,000-59,999	7,430	1,125	5,445	860	206
$40,000-49,999	10,943	1,645	8,210	1,089	380
$30,000-39,999	14,473	1,997	10,006	2,470	327
$20,000-29,999	15,927	2,855	9,511	3,561	575
$10,000-19,999	18,041	3,086	8,536	6,419	572
Less than $10,000	14,083	3,660	3,234	7,189	487

Source: Selected from *Mediamark Research Multimedia Audiences Report, Spring 1990*, p. 142 (New York: Mediamark Research Inc., 1990).

★ 355 ★

Ratio of Family Income to National Mean, Worldwide

Ratio of adjusted disposable income to national mean for families with children, by age of family head, circa 1980.

Country	Year	24 years	25-34 years	35-44 years	45-54 years	55-64 years	Total
Australia	1981	.68	.80	.89	1.07	1.05	.90
Canada	1981	.65	.84	.93	1.02	.96	.91
Germany, Federal Republic	1981	.62	.79	.89	.86	.96	.86
Norway	1979	.80	.93	.99	1.03	1.15	.99
Sweden	1981	.91	.98	1.01	1.09	1.01	1.01
United Kingdom	1979	.80	.87	.95	1.10	1.14	.95
United States	1979	.62	.82	.93	1.02	.94	.90
Overall mean		.71	.85	.94	1.02	1.05	.93

Source: "Ratio of adjusted disposable income to national mean for families with children, by age of family head, selected countries: circa 1980," *Children's Well-Being: An International Comparison*, A Report of the Select Committee on Children, Youth, and Families, 101st Cong., 2d sess., March 1990, p. 105. Primary source: Smeeding, Timothy, Barbara Boyle Torrey, and Martin Rein, 1988, "Patterns of income and Poverty: The Economic Status of Children and the Elderly in Eight Countries," in Palmer, John L., Timothy Smeeding, and Barbara Boyle Torrey (eds.), *The Vulnerable*, Washington, D.C., table 5.1. Adjusted disposable income is post tax and transfer income. It includes all forms of cash income (earnings, property income, and all cash transfers including the value of food stamps in the United States and housing allowance in the United Kingdom and Sweden) and it subtracts income and payroll taxes. It is adjusted for family size. The national mean adjusted income equals 1.00 for each country. Families with children are those that include at least one child under age 18.

Income

★ 356 ★

Budgets of Women's Groups

Annual budgets of feminist groups, 1984.

Group	1984 Budget
ACLU-WRP	$280,000
ACLU-RFP	547,000
CWPS	171,810
NARAL	2,600,000
NOW	5,637,000
NOW-LDEF	2,143,449
CLASP-WRP (NWLC)	700,000
NWPC	1,000,000
WLDF	583,326

Source: "Change in Annual Budgets (1978-1984) and Major Sources of Revenue (1984)," *Women and Public Policies,* 1987, p. 42-43 (Princeton, NJ: Princeton University Press, 1987). Primary source: All data derive from available annual reports and telephone interviews; *National NOW Times,* Aug.- Sept. 1985, 11. Also in source: funding sources and amounts. ACLU = American Civil Liberties Union; WRP = Women's Rights Project; RFP = Reproductive Freedom Project; CWPS = Center for Women Policy Studies; NARAL = National Abortion Rights Action League; NOW = National Organization for Women; LDEF = Legal Defense Education and Fund; NWLC = National Women's Law Center (formerly Women's Rights Project of the Center for Law and Social Policy); NWPC = National Women's Political Caucus; WLDF = Women's Legal Defense Fund.

★ 357 ★

Changes in Income, Families with Children: 1973-1986

Annual rates of change in adjusted family income for families with children (1987 dollars), 1973-1986.

Year	All Families w/children	Married Couples w/children	Married Couples Childless[1]	Single Mothers
		Annual rates of change		
1973-79	0.2%	0.7%	0.5%	2.0%
1979-86	-0.6%	0.1%	0.0%	-2.7%

Source: "Growth rate of adjusted family income for families with children (1987 dollars)," *The State of Working America,* 1990, p. 5 (Washington, D.C.: Economic Policy Institute, 1990). *Note:* 1. Non-elderly.

★ 358 ★

Consulting Income for Faculty Members

Consulting income for full-time faculty: Fall 1987.

Full-time faculty	Number	Consulting income				
		None	$1 to 749	$750 to 2,499	$2,500 to 9,999	$10,000 or more
All institutions[1]	488,922	58%	13%	10%	10%	9%
Females	133,405	65%	16%	9%	6%	4%
Males	355,517	56%	12%	10%	12%	11%

Source: Selected from "Consulting income for full-and part-time regular faculty, by gender and academic rank: Fall 1987," *Faculty in Higher Education Institutions, 1988,* p. 37 (Washington, D.C.: National Center for Educational Statistics, March 1990). Primary source: U.S. Department of Education, National Center for Educational Statistics, "1988 National Survey of Postsecondary Faculty." Also iin source: data for part-time faculty and by academic rank. *Notes:* 1. All accredited, nonproprietary U.S. postsecondary institutions that grant a two-year (A.A.) or higher degree and whose accreditation at the higher education level is recognized by the U.S. Department of Education.

★ 359 ★

Distribution of Income in Families

Distribution of income in families and numbers of persons per family, 1989.

Total money income	Number (thousands)	Mean family income (dollars)	Income per family member (dollars)	Average number of-		
				Persons per family	Related children per family	Earners per family
Total	66,090	$41,506	$13,093	3.17	.96	1.66
Under $5,000	2,398	2,501	835	3.00	1.46	.52
$5,000 to $9,999	4,141	7,582	2,584	2.93	1.16	.76
$10,000 to $14,999	5,354	12,465	4,301	2.90	.94	.95
$15,000 to $19,999	5,565	17,392	5,830	2.98	.94	1.22
$20,000 to $24,999	5,461	22,343	7,411	3.01	.92	1.38
$25,000 to $29,999	5,576	27,328	8,834	3.09	.93	1.57
$30,000 to $34,999	5,294	32,296	10,281	3.14	.95	1.71
$35,000 to $39,999	4,959	37,312	11,640	3.21	.98	1.83
$40,000 to $44,999	4,464	42,274	12,890	3.28	.99	1.92
$45,000 to $49,999	3,689	47,323	14,471	3.27	.92	2.00
$50,000 to $54,999	3,545	52,214	15,566	3.35	.98	2.06
$55,000 to $59,999	2,595	57,292	17,030	3.36	.94	2.14
$60,000 to $64,999	2,278	62,163	18,220	3.41	.94	2.19
$65,000 to $69,999	1,839	67,210	19,543	3.44	.88	2.33
$70,000 to $74,999	1,463	72,317	21,514	3.36	.83	2.29
$75,000 to $79,999	1,251	77,252	22,851	3.38	.81	2.34
$80,000 to $84,999	1,036	82,180	23,971	3.43	.84	2.39
$85,000 to $89,999	774	87,356	24,974	3.50	.85	2.37
$90,000 to $94,999	695	92,331	27,459	3.36	.79	2.36

[Continued]

★ 359 ★

Distribution of Income in Families
[Continued]

Total money income	Number (thousands)	Mean family income (dollars)	Income per family member (dollars)	Average number of-		
				Persons per family	Related children per family	Earners per family
$95,000 to $99,999	518	97,435	28,230	3.45	.72	2.45
$100,000 and over	3,197	150,091	44,094	3.40	.75	2.29

Source: Selected from"Summary Measures—Families, by Total Money Income in 1989, Race and Hispanic Origin of Householder," *Current Population Reports*, "Money Income and Poverty Status in the United States 1989 (Advance Data from the March 1990 Current Population Survey), Series P-60, No. 168, September 1990, p. 40. Also in source; data by race and Hispanic origin of householder. Families as of March 1990.

★ 360 ★

Effect of Working Wives on Family Income
Change in family income controlling for increase in wives' hours of work, 1986.

	Lowest Fifth	Lower Middle Fifth	Middle Fifth	Upper Middle Fifth	Highest Fifth	Average
(1)Actual Income Growth, 1979 to 1986	-10.9%	-2.1%	3.0%	6.9%	13.8%	7.3%
(2)If Wives Had Maintained 1979 Annual Hours	-11.5%	-5.7%	-1.0%	2.9%	9.5%	4.9%
(3)Effect of Increased Work of Wives[1]	0.6%	3.6%	4.0%	4.0%	4.3%	2.4%

Source: "Change in family income controlling for increase (in) wives' hours of work," *Family Incomes in the 1980s: New Pressure on Wives, Husbands, and Young Adults*, 1988, Table 5, p. 8 (Washington, D.C.: Economic Policy Institute, 1988). *Note:* 1. Calculated as row (1) less row (2).

★ 361 ★

Family Income Distribution by Education: 1979 and 1986
Percent of individuals at a given education level falling into one of three family income levels.

Income level	High School or Less		1 to 3 Years College		4 Years College or More	
	Female	Male	Female	Male	Female	Male
1979						
Bottom 40%	49.6%	40.3%	32.0%	27.0%	17.5%	16.8%
Middle 20%	22.6%	24.2%	23.3%	22.4%	18.4%	18.7%
Top 40%	27.8%	35.4%	44.7%	50.7%	64.1%	64.5%
1986						
Bottom 40%	55.4%	45.3%	33.4%	29.8%	15.3%	15.6%

[Continued]

★ 361 ★

Family Income Distribution by Education: 1979 and 1986

[Continued]

Income level	High School or Less		1 to 3 Years College		4 Years College or More	
	Female	Male	Female	Male	Female	Male
Middle 20%	21.4%	24.7%	24.3%	23.7%	19.5%	16.3%
Top 40%	23.3%	30.3%	42.4%	46.5%	65.1%	68.2%

Source: "Family Income Distribution by Sex and Education, 25 to 34-year-olds," *Family Incomes in the 1980s: New Pressure on Wives, Husbands, and Young Adults*, 1988, p. 22 (Washington, D.C.: Economic Policy Institute, 1988).

★ 362 ★

Income of Families

Families with wage and salary earners by race, Hispanic origin, type of family, and median usualy weekly wage and salary earnings, third quarter averages, 1990, not seasonally adjusted.

Characteristic	Number of families (thousands) 1989	1990	Median weekly earnings 1989	1990
Total				
Families with wage or salary earners[1]	43,748	43,950	$633	$659
Married-couple families	34,394	34,176	710	742
Families maintained by women	7,209	7,476	360	371
Families maintained by men	2,145	2,298	521	511
White				
Families with wage or salary earners[1]	37,159	37,266	660	690
Married-couple families	30,397	30,252	722	758
Families maintained by women	5,043	5,215	374	386
Families maintained by men	1,719	1,800	558	535
Black				
Families with wage or salary earners[1]	5,149	5,195	462	454
Married-couple families	2,838	2,771	591	586
Families maintained by women	1,986	2,029	317	324
Families maintained by men	325	395	414	389
Hispanic origin				
Families with wage or salary earners[1]	3,625	3,732	510	509
Married-couple families	2,787	2,622	541	584

[Continued]

★ 362 ★

Income of Families
[Continued]

Characteristic	Number of families (thousands)		Median weekly earnings	
	1989	1990	1989	1990
Families maintained by women	539	725	342	332
Families maintained by men	299	385	514	486

Source: Selected from "Families with wage and salary earners by race, Hispanic origin, type of family, and median usual weekly wage and salary earnings, quarterly averages, not seasonally adjusted," *United States Department of Labor News*, No. 90-545, Table 6, October 22, 1990. Also in source: detailed breakdown of types of families; percent distribution. Data exclude families in which there is no wage or salary earner or in which the husband, wife, or other person maintaining the family is either self-employed or in the Armed Forces. *Notes:* 1. Number and type of families and median weekly earnings, third quarter, 1989 and 1990.

★ 363 ★

Median Income by Education: 1987-1989
Median income by years of school completed, 1987-1989.

Years of school completed	1989			1988			1987[1]		
	Number with income (thousands)	Median income		Number with income (thousands)	Median income		Number with income (thousands)	Median Income	
		Value (dollars)	Std. error (dollars)		Value (dollars)	Std. error (dollars)		Value (dollars)	Std. error (dollars)
Total females, age 25 years and over	77,284	$10,814	$79	76,083	$10,082	$80	74,802	$9,435	$72
8 years or less	8,006	5,627	85	8,206	5,205	95	8,460	5,056	82
High school:									
Total	40,188	9,428	90	40,016	8,697	99	39,834	8,264	87
1 to 3 years	8,526	6,752	107	8,601	6,295	111	8,554	6,292	103
4 years	31,662	10,439	101	31,415	9,748	117	31,280	9,143	102
College:									
Total	29,090	17,536	172	27,861	16,649	166	26,507	15,430	139
1 to 3 years	14,269	14,244	225	13,459	13,367	245	13,276	12,487	182
4 years or more	14,821	21,659	226	14,402	20,465	199	13,231	18,872	247
4 years	9,195	19,454	318	8,843	18,415	341	8,133	16,893	249
5 years or more	5,626	26,076	384	5,559	23,477	460	5,099	22,382	392
Total males, age 25 years and over	73,237	$22,860	$160	71,988	$22,038	$112	70,737	$21,221	$98
8 years or less	8,298	10,033	172	8,342	9,922	162	8,420	9,742	142
High school:									
Total	33,747	20,106	131	33,264	19,491	159	33,238	18,609	151
1 to 3 years	7,737	14,439	248	7,826	14,067	232	7,985	14,141	229
4 years	26,010	21,650	138	25,438	21,186	147	25,254	20,262	139
College:									
Total	31,192	32,180	175	30,382	30,821	172	29,079	30,152	155
1 to 3 years	13,143	26,402	220	12,584	25,397	237	11,928	24,687	302
4 years or more	18,049	37,553	338	17,799	35,697	273	17,150	34,148	355
4 years	9,979	34,680	462	9,785	32,328	356	9,445	31,406	273
5 years or more	8,070	41,827	409	8,014	40,047	533	7,705	37,857	547

Source: Selected from "Median Income of Persons, by Selected Characteristics: 1989, 1988, and 1987," *Current Population Reports*, "Money Income and Poverty Status in the United States 1989 (Advance Data from the March 1990 Current Population Survey)," Series P-60, No. 168, p. 42. Also in source: data by other characteristics. Persons 15 years old and over as of March of the following year. *Note:* 1. Revised (new processing system).

★ 364 ★

Median Income by Occupation Group: 1987-1989

Median income by occupation group of longest job, 1987-1989.

Occupation group of longest job	1989 Number with income (thousands)	1989 Median income Value (dollars)	1989 Median income Std. error (dollars)	1988 Number with income (thousands)	1988 Median income Value (dollars)	1988 Median income Std. error (dollars)	1987[1] Number with income (thousands)	1987[1] Median income Value (dollars)	1987[1] Median income Std. error (dollars)
Total females with earnings[3]	61,338	$11,736	$79	60,700	$11,101	$79	59,356	$10,620	$70
Executive, administrators, and managerial	6,370	21,551	232	6,411	20,688	257	5,878	19,270	278
Professional specialty	8,703	22,089	284	8,498	20,261	234	8,010	19,429	302
Technical and related support	2,056	18,484	437	1,914	17,173	414	1,826	16,066	318
Sales	8,653	6,990	158	8,569	6,569	168	8,205	6,436	140
Administrative support, incl. clerical	16,539	13,542	157	16,116	12,595	145	16,398	12,243	100
Precision production, craft, and repair	1,311	14,121	644	1,343	12,384	517	1,414	11,826	379
Machine operators, assemblers, and inspectors	3,788	10,845	200	4,058	10,269	193	3,867	10,090	184
Transportation and material moving	511	9,114	595	532	7,130	414	464	8,079	561
Handlers, equipment cleaners, helpers, laborers	1,061	6,654	385	1,039	6,694	577	1,045	6,064	402
Service workers	11,611	5,487	116	11,477	5,181	115	11,553	4,758	100
Private household	1,047	2,042	96	1,262	2,170	96	1,215	1,830	76
Service workers, except private household	10,564	5,940	118	10,215	5,649	120	10,338	5,302	106
Farming, forestry, and fishing	656	3,977	628	691	2,439	240	676	2,660	355
Total males with earnings[3]	72,045	$21,376	$105	71,328	$20,591	$112	69,545	$19,818	$145
Executive, administrators, and managerial	9,221	36,696	317	9,165	34,204	636	8,851	32,553	544
Professional specialty	8,053	35,548	359	8,206	33,731	587	7,819	32,435	375
Technical and related support	2,105	27,453	643	1,913	27,726	849	2,020	25,668	508
Sales	7,929	22,777	526	7,612	21,805	300	7,621	21,504	292
Administrative support, incl. clerical	4,152	19,991	429	3,984	18,617	509	3,908	18,226	481
Precision production, craft, and repair	13,661	22,146	182	13,828	21,506	209	13,441	20,503	175
Machine operators, assemblers, and inspectors	5,080	19,200	358	5,221	18,115	391	5,161	17,474	320
Transportation and material moving	4,858	19,474	396	4,727	19,485	496	4,845	18,004	452
Handlers, equipment cleaners, helpers, laborers	5,045	9,264	338	5,034	8,583	326	4,967	7,956	325
Service workers	7,465	10,558	255	7,205	9,601	289	7,155	8,801	257
Private household	51	-	-	38	-	-	67	-	-
Service workers, exc. private household	7,413	10,599	255	7,167	9,650	291	7,088	8,931	256
Farming, forestry, and fishing	3,531	7,668	449	3,467	7,290	348	3,559	6,407	271

Source: Selected from "Median Income of Persons, by Selected Characteristics: 1989, 1988, and 1987," *Current Population Reports,* "Money Income and Poverty Status in the United States 1989 (Advance Data from the March 1990 Current Population Survey)," Series P-60, No. 168, p. 42. Also in source: data by other characteristics. Persons 15 years old and over as of March of the following year. *Notes:* 1. Revised (new processing system). 2. Amounts shown are median earnings. 3. Includes persons whose longest job was in the Armed Forces.

★ 365 ★

Median Income by Race and Age: 1987-1989

Characteristic	1989 Number with income (thousands)	1989 Median income Value (dollars)	1989 Median income Std. error (dollars)	1988 Number with income (thousands)	1988 Median income Value (dollars)	1988 Median income Std. error (dollars)	1987[1] Number with income (thousands)	1987[1] Median income Value (dollars)	1987[1] Median income Std. error (dollars)
Total Females	91,399	$9,624	$70	90,593	$8,884	$76	89,661	$8,295	$66
Race and Hispanic Origin									
White	77,933	9,812	74	77,493	9,103	82	76,940	8,507	71
Black	10,577	7,875	241	10,380	7,349	145	10,164	6,949	135
Hispanic origin[2]	5,677	7,647	237	5,532	6,990	227	5,357	6,630	167

[Continued]

★ 365 ★

Median Income by Race and Age: 1987-1989
[Continued]

Characteristic	1989			1988			1987[1]		
	Number with income (thousands)	Median income		Number with income (thousands)	Median income		Number with income (thousands)	Median income	
		Value (dollars)	Std. error (dollars)		Value (dollars)	Std. error (dollars)		Value (dollars)	Std. error (dollars)
Age									
Under 65 years	74,338	10,470	83	73,865	9,704	96	73,195	8,965	81
15 to 24 years	14,115	4,739	83	14,510	4,485	88	14,859	4,408	77
25 to 34 years	20,209	12,231	144	20,228	11,565	149	20,188	10,979	124
35 to 44 years	17,692	13,805	228	17,044	12,546	211	16,465	11,995	166
45 to 54 years	12,007	13,143	257	11,687	12,020	209	11,180	11,263	195
55 to 64 years	10,315	9,163	227	10,397	8,377	229	10,502	7,541	180
65 years and over	17,060	7,655	96	16,728	7,103	66	16,466	6,896	61
65 to 74 years	9,850	7,948	134	9,744	7,256	99	9,629	6,986	89
75 years and over	7,211	7,377	84	6,983	6,944	87	6,837	6,798	82
Total Males									
Race and Hispanic Origin									
White	75,858	$20,863	$113	75,247	$19,959	$130	74,647	$18,905	$128
Black	8,806	12,609	308	8,610	12,044	272	8,488	11,215	206
Hispanic origin[2]	6,592	13,400	335	6,342	13,030	361	6,102	12,230	208
Age									
Under 65 years	75,194	21,275	107	74,564	20,537	115	73,983	19,480	133
15 to 24 years	14,217	6,313	137	14,595	5,843	135	14,976	5,457	116
25 to 34 years	20,998	21,367	146	20,912	20,782	157	20,783	19,927	172
35 to 44 years	18,073	29,437	341	17,400	28,545	377	16,803	27,042	199
45 to 54 years	12,088	30,962	290	11,702	29,578	446	11,398	28,487	398
55 to 64 years	9,818	24,427	541	9,955	22,647	388	10,023	21,883	275
65 years and over	12,260	13,107	164	12,019	12,471	160	11,730	11,927	131
65 to 74 years	7,966	14,465	199	7,837	13,941	211	7,690	13,412	193
75 years and over	4,294	10,847	229	4,182	10,228	234	4,040	9,698	168

Source: Selected from "Median Income of Persons, by Selected Characteristics: 1989, 1988, and 1987," *Current Population Reports,* "Money Income and Poverty Status in the United States 1989 (Advance Data from the March 1990 Current Population Survey)," Series P-60, No. 168, p. 42. Also in source: data by other characteristics. Persons 15 years old and over as of March of the following year. *Notes:* 1. Revised (new processing system). 2. Persons of Hispanic origin may be of any race.

★ 366 ★

Median Income of Full-Time Workers by Education: 1987-1989

Years of School Completed	1989			1988			1987[1]		
	Number with income (thousands)	Median income		Number with income (thousands)	Median income		Number with income (thousands)	Median income	
		Value (dollars)	Std. error (dollars)		Value (dollars)	Std. error (dollars)		Value (dollars)	Std. error (dollars)
Year-round, full-time female workers									
Total, age 25 years and over	28,056	$20,570	$112	28,021	$19,497	$133	26,486	$18,608	$119
8 years or less	906	12,188	310	942	11,358	261	945	11,018	305
High school:									
Total	13,614	17,067	113	13,737	16,334	118	13,254	16,048	105
1 to 3 years	1,830	13,923	310	1,881	13,104	315	1,868	12,939	289
4 years	11,785	17,528	151	11,857	16,810	125	11,386	16,549	113
College:									
Total	13,535	25,278	175	13,341	24,023	215	12,286	22,538	180

[Continued]

★ 366 ★

Median Income of Full-Time Workers by Education: 1987-1989
[Continued]

Years of School Completed	1989			1988			1987[1]		
	Number with income (thousands)	Median income		Number with income (thousands)	Median income		Number with income (thousands)	Median income	
		Value (dollars)	Std. error (dollars)		Value (dollars)	Std. error (dollars)		Value (dollars)	Std. error (dollars)
1 to 3 years	6,217	21,631	212	6,018	20,845	223	5,714	19,946	224
4 years or more	7,318	28,799	344	7,323	26,804	229	6,573	25,735	203
4 years	4,465	26,709	280	4,363	25,187	308	3,998	23,399	348
5 years or more	2,854	32,050	411	2,960	30,136	513	2,575	30,060	488
Year-round, full-time male workers	48,831	$28,605	$204	48,290	$27,342	$121	47,023	$26,681	$111
Total, age 25 years and over	44,596	30,465	121	44,003	29,331	197	42,730	28,232	163
8 years or less	2,425	17,555	391	2,493	17,190	359	2,561	16,691	313
High school:									
Total	19,704	25,685	154	19,529	25,298	156	19,267	24,650	203
1 to 3 years	3,312	21,065	302	3,512	20,777	365	3,649	20,863	269
4 years	16,392	26,609	170	16,017	26,045	175	15,618	25,490	151
College:									
Total	22,467	36,967	200	21,982	35,291	203	20,902	34,435	278
1 to 3 years	9,028	31,308	227	8,545	30,129	259	8,054	29,820	310
4 years or more	13,439	41,892	273	13,437	39,967	365	12,847	38,416	406
4 years	7,473	38,565	563	7,398	36,434	353	7,090	35,527	349
5 years or more	5,966	46,842	539	6,039	43,938	674	5,758	41,973	362

Source: Selected from "Median Income of Persons, by Selected Characteristics: 1989, 1988, and 1987," *Current Population Reports*, "Money Income and Poverty Status in the United States 1989 (Advance Data from the March 1990 Current Population Survey)," Series P-60, No. 168, p. 44. Also in source: data by other characteristics. Persons 15 years old and over as of March of the following year. *Note:* 1. Revised (new processing system).

★ 367 ★

Median Income of Full-Time Workers by Occupation Group: 1987-1989
Median income of year-round, full-time workers by occupation group of longest job, 1987-1989.

Occupation group of longest job	1989			1988			1987[1]		
	Number with income (thousands)	Median income		Number with income (thousands)	Median income		Number with income (thousands)	Median income	
		Value (dollars)	Std. error (dollars)		Value (dollars)	Std. error (dollars)		Value (dollars)	Std. error (dollars)
Total females with earnings[3]	31,290	$18,778	$127	31,237	$17,606	$125	29,912	$16,911	$78
Executive, administrators, and managerial	4,765	24,589	359	4,880	23,356	374	4,337	21,815	219
Professional specialty	4,701	27,933	403	4,882	25,789	243	4,546	24,523	283
Technical and related support	1,337	21,768	371	1,208	21,039	452	1,133	19,532	398
Sales	3,384	16,057	264	3,273	15,474	290	3,066	14,462	371
Administrative support, incl. clerical	9,619	17,517	139	9,452	16,676	116	9,507	16,350	96
Precision production, craft, and repair	835	17,457	549	799	16,869	539	802	17,190	584
Machine operators, assemblers, and inspectors	2,142	14,463	324	2,329	13,289	308	2,226	12,919	290
Transportation and material moving	184	16,288	2,396	169	13,021	1,261	145	13,315	1,121
Handlers, equipment cleaners, helpers, laborers	342	14,095	846	372	13,397	1,020	377	13,486	645
Service workers	3,763	11,669	154	3,665	11,032	152	3,566	10,965	149
Private household	201	6,882	611	224	7,299	522	189	6,814	741
Service workers, except private household	3,563	11,868	155	3,441	11,232	155	3,377	11,206	149
Farming, forestry, and fishing	205	11,305	942	194	9,926	1,355	196	6,350	1,098
Total males with earnings[3]									
Executive, administrators, and managerial	48,825	27,430	135	48,285	26,656	117	47,013	25,946	107
Professional specialty	7,940	40,103	456	7,860	36,759	374	7,567	36,198	321

[Continued]

★ 367 ★

Median Income of Full-Time Workers by Occupation Group: 1987-1989

[Continued]

Occupation group of longest job	1989 Number with income (thousands)	1989 Median income Value (dollars)	1989 Median income Std. error (dollars)	1988 Number with income (thousands)	1988 Median income Value (dollars)	1988 Median income Std. error (dollars)	1987[1] Number with income (thousands)	1987[1] Median income Value (dollars)	1987[1] Median income Std. error (dollars)
Technical and related support	6,316	39,449	607	6,458	37,490	434	6,237	36,242	315
Sales	1,583	31,371	543	1,563	30,369	422	1,509	29,435	670
Administrative support, incl. clerical	2,912	25,138	445	2,706	24,399	606	2,665	23,715	620
Precision production, craft, and repair	9,622	26,449	219	9,759	25,746	218	9,407	24,607	308
Machine operators, assemblers, and inspectors	3,608	22,343	313	3,741	21,382	309	3,701	20,929	248
Transportation and material moving	3,172	23,612	548	3,205	23,453	537	3,054	22,517	361
Handlers, equipment cleaners, helpers, laborers	2,129	18,046	424	2,071	17,042	372	2,075	16,806	316
Service workers	3,939	18,903	366	3,655	18,648	385	3,556	17,459	343
Private household	17	-	-	13	-	-	6	-	-
Service workers, except private household	3,921	18,970	365	3,642	18,670	384	3,550	17,480	346
Farming, forestry, and fishing	1,769	13,885	526	1,687	14,300	605	1,655	12,416	418

Source: Selected from "Median Income of Persons, by Selected Characteristics: 1989, 1988, and 1987," *Current Population Reports*, "Money Income and Poverty Status in the United States 1989 (Advance Data from the March 1990 Current Population Survey)," Series P-60, No. 168, p. 44. Also in source: data by other characteristics. Persons 15 years old and over as of March of the following year. *Notes:* 1. Revised (new processing system). 2. Amounts shown are median earnings. 3. Includes persons whose longest job was in the Armed Forces.

★ 368 ★

Median Income of Full-Time Workers by Race and Age

Median income of year-round, full-time female workers, by race and age, 1987-1989.

Year-round, full-time workers, race and age	1989 Number with income (thousands)	1989 Median income Value (dollars)	1989 Median income Std. error (dollars)	1988 Number with income (thousands)	1988 Median income Value (dollars)	1988 Median income Std. error (dollars)	1987[1] Number with income (thousands)	1987[1] Median income Value (dollars)	1987[1] Median income Std. error (dollars)
Total Females	31,336	$19,643	$121	31,306	18,545	$126	29,945	$17,564	$108
Race and Hispanic Origin									
White	26,246	19,873	133	26,272	18,823	138	25,352	17,889	123
Black	3,960	17,908	366	3,985	16,867	273	3,640	15,978	223
Hispanic origin[2]	2,076	16,006	403	1,971	15,201	477	1,883	14,802	404
Age									
Under 65 years	30,805	19,612	122	30,780	18,521	129	29,431	17,523	103
15 to 24 years	3,280	13,653	246	3,285	13,183	232	3,459	12,329	140
25 to 34 years	9,551	19,706	203	9,880	18,486	225	9,504	17,552	160
35 to 44 years	8,983	21,498	209	8,706	20,635	231	8,136	19,934	233
45 to 54 years	6,008	20,905	247	5,796	20,174	258	5,372	19,299	265
55 to 64 years	2,982	19,895	369	3,113	18,347	361	2,960	18,047	358
65 years and over	531	21,505	872	526	19,493	711	514	19,502	768
65 to 74 years	464	21,463	909	468	19,454	708	453	19,282	724
75 years and over	67	3	3	58	3	3	61	3	3
Total Males	48,831	$28,605	$204	48,290	$27,342	$121	47,023	$26,681	$111
Race and Hispanic Origin									
White	43,054	29,846	200	42,721	28,262	209	41,742	27,303	117
Black	4,206	20,706	284	4,108	20,716	348	3,948	19,522	435
Hispanic origin[2]	3,656	18,570	418	3,608	18,190	516	3,459	17,680	468
Age									
Under 65 years	47,883	28,511	206	47,341	27,316	121	46,100	26,649	113
15 to 24 years	4,235	15,501	205	4,287	14,863	249	4,294	14,170	236
25 to 34 years	14,987	24,991	199	15,148	24,284	252	14,729	23,554	244

[Continued]

★ 368 ★

Median Income of Full-Time Workers by Race and Age
[Continued]

Year-round, full-time workers, race and age	1989 Number with income (thousands)	1989 Median income Value (dollars)	1989 Median income Std. error (dollars)	1988 Number with income (thousands)	1988 Median income Value (dollars)	1988 Median income Std. error (dollars)	1987[1] Number with income (thousands)	1987[1] Median income Value (dollars)	1987[1] Median income Std. error (dollars)
35 to 44 years	14,009	32,370	225	13,425	31,847	194	12,905	30,802	192
45 to 54 years	9,323	35,356	321	9,080	32,701	408	8,770	32,170	248
55 to 64 years	5,329	34,505	575	5,401	31,645	340	5,402	30,869	356
65 years and over	948	34,110	1,932	949	29,070	1,149	924	28,593	1,244
65 to 74 years	831	34,034	2,179	810	28,696	1,289	801	28,122	1,235
75 years and over	117	34,316	3,866	139	30,840	5,727	122	33,036	3,557

Source: Selected from "Median Income of Persons, by Selected Characteristics: 1989, 1988, and 1987," *Current Population Reports,* "Money Income and Poverty Status in the United States 1989 (Advance Data from the March 1990 Current Population Survey)," Series P-60, No. 168, p. 44. Also in source: data by other characteristics. Persons 15 years old and over as of March of the following year. *Notes:* 1. Revised (new processing system). 2. Persons of Hispanic origin may be of any race. 3. Base less than 75,000.

★ 369 ★

Pension Receipt Rates

Pension receipt rates for women and men by single years of age, ages 50-70, in 1983, as percentage of total population.

Age	Women	Men
50	2%	5%
51	3%	7%
52	2%	8%
53	3%	8%
54	4%	7%
55	6%	10%
56	5%	14%
57	7%	14%
58	6%	16%
59	7%	19%
60	10%	22%
61	12%	24%
62	14%	29%
63	16%	34%
64	16%	36%
65	23%	47%
66	22%	51%
67	20%	48%
68	22%	46%
69	22%	40%
70	24%	40%

Source: "Pension Receipt Rates for Men and Women by Single Years of Age, 1983 (Percentages of Total Population)," *Issues in Contemporary Retirement,* 1988, p. 249 (Stanford: Hoover Institution Press, 1988). Primary source: U.S. Government Accounting Office (1986).

★ 370 ★

Persons Receiving Work Disability Payments

Persons with work disability who received disability payments, 1988.

Participation status in assistance programs	Total	Female	Male
Persons with work disability, in thousands	13,420	6,714	6,706
Percent of work disabled--			
Receiving Social Security income	29.5%	27.2%	31.9%
Receiving food stamps	18.8%	22.0%	15.7%
Covered by Medicaid	21.6%	25.2%	18.1%

Source: "Persons with Work Disability, by Selected Characteristics: 1988," *Statistical Abstract of the United States 1990*, 1990, p. 364. Primary source: U.S. Bureau of the Census, *Current Population Report*, series P-23, No. 160. As of March. Covers civilian noninstitutional population and members of Armed Forces living off post or with their families on post. Persons are classified as having a work disability if they (1) have a health problem or disability which prevents them from working or which limits the kind or amount of work they can do; (2) have a service-connected disability or ever retired or left a job for health reasons; (3) did not work in survey reference week or previous year because of long-term illness or disability; or (4) are under age 65 and are covered by Medicare or receive Supplemental Security Income. Based on Current Population Survey.

★ 371 ★

Social Security Beneficiaries: 1940-1988

Year	Retired workers		Disabled workers	
	Total (thousands)	Women	Total (thousands)	Women
1940	112	12%	-	-
1950	1,771	17%	-	-
1960	8,061	35%	455	22%
1970	13,349	42%	1,493	28%
1980	19,562	47%	2,859	33%
1988	23,858	48%	2,830	34%

Source: "Women-worker beneficiaries, 1940-88," *Fast Facts & Figures About Social Security*, p. 21 (Washington, D.C.: U.S. Department of Health and Human Services, 1989). Primary source: *Annual Statistical Supplement, 1988*, tables 5.A4, 5.B5, 5.D4, and Office of Research and Statistics, Social Security Administration.

★ 372 ★

Sports Winnings

Leading money winners, 1988.

Sport and player	Winnings
Tennis	
Steffi Graf	$1,378,128
Mats Wilander	1,726,731
Bowling	

[Continued]

★ 372 ★

Sports Winnings
[Continued]

Sport and player	Winnings
Lisa Wagner	105,500
Brian Voss	225,485

Source: The Universal Almanac 1990, p. 577-578 (Kansas City: Andrews and McMeel, 1990). Also in source: data for other players; male data for other years.

★ 373 ★

Support for Doctorate Recipients
Primary sources of graduate support reported by 1988 science and engineering doctorate recipients by source.

Field	Total known support	Family support	University Total	Federal support	Student loan
Total, all fields	$16,846	$4,008	$8,181	$2,792	$603
Women	4,544	1,406	1,937	709	285
Men	12,302	2,602	6,244	2,083	318
Sciences, total	13,389	3,490	6,286	2,230	574
Women	4,302	1,386	1,800	656	282
Men	9,087	2,104	4,486	1,574	292
Engineering, total	3,457	518	1,895	562	29
Women	242	20	137	53	3
Men	3,215	498	1,758	509	26

Source: Selected from "Primary sources of graduate support reported by 1988 science and engineering doctorate recipients, by source, field, gender, and racial/ethnic group," *Women and Minorities in Science and Engineering*, 1990, p. 157-58 (Washington, D.C.: National Science Foundation, January 1990). Also in source: sources of support by teaching and research assistantships, fellowships, other; detailed breakdown by field.

★ 374 ★

Types of Income, Elderly Women
Types of income for women aged 65 and over, 1984.

Type of income	Women aged 65 and over with income	Median	Mean
Total money income		$6,020	$8,800
Wage or salary income	9.4%	10,640	13,082
Property income, total[1]	67.5%	7,698	10,724
Social Security or railroad retirement income	93.4%	6,072	8,769
Retirement income, total[2]	20.8%	10,601	13,739

[Continued]

★ 374 ★

Types of Income, Elderly Women

[Continued]

Type of income	Women aged 65 and over with income	Median	Mean
Private pensions or annuities only	11.3%	9,344	12,319
Federal employee pensions only	2.5%	13,353	15,846
State or local employee pensions only	5.6%	11,869	14,441
Combinations of income types:			
Earnings	10.6%	10,458	13,713
Earnings and property income	8.1%	11,855	15,288

Source: "Type of income for women aged 65 and over, 1984," *Issues in Contemporary Retirement*, 1988, p. 86 (Stanford: Hoover Institution Press, 1988). Primary source: U.S. Bureau of the Census (1986). Excludes approximately 220,000 women who receive no income (1.4% of sample of women aged 65 and over). *Notes:* 1. Includes interest, dividends, net rent, and estates or trusts. 2. Includes private pensions, annuities, military retirement pensions, and federal, state, and local pensions.

Spending

★ 375 ★

Artists' Commissions, Grants, and Fellowships

Commissions, grants, and fellowships awarded to artists, 1980-1989.

Type of award	Year	Females	Males
J.S. Guggenheim Fellowships	1980	33%	67%
NEA Artists Grants	1980	29%	71%
NEA Artists Grants	1981	28%	72%
J.S. Guggenheim Fellowships	1981	30%	70%
NEA Photography Fellowships	1981	14%	86%
NEA Visual Artists Fellowships	1981-2	33%	67%
NEA Grants to womens' organizations	1982-88	35% cut	
NEA Artists Grants	1982	34%	66%
J.S. Guggenheim Fellowships	1982	36%	64%
NEA Artists Grants	1983	34%	66%
J.S. Guggenheim Fellowships	1983	24%	76%
NEA Grants, Fellowships	1983	37%	63%
J.S. Guggenheim Fellowships	1984	30%	70%
NEA Artist Grants	1984	37%	63%
NEA Artist Grants	1985	36%	64%
J.S. Guggenheim Fellowships	1985	28%	72%
Mass. Artists Foundation	1985	65%	35%
"Young Talents Awards," L.A. County Museum	1963-86	23%	77%
J.S. Guggenheim Grants	1986	19%	81%
J.S. Guggenheim Fellowships in Photography	1987	25%	75%
NEA Grants	1987	40%	60%

[Continued]

★ 375 ★

Artists' Commissions, Grants, and Fellowships
[Continued]

Type of award	Year	Females	Males
NEA Grants	1988	43%	57%
NEA Grants	1989	43%	57%

Source: Eleanor Dickinson, "Gender Discrimination in the Art Field: Incomplete and random statistics of number of artists, art faculty, art criticism, art exhibitions, etc. which may be useful in indicating patterns and trends," 1990, p. 4-5 (Washington, D.C.: Artists Equity Association, 1990). Also in source: data for 1962-1979.

★ 376 ★

Charitable Giving

Question: During the past 12 months have you contributed money to any charitable organization? ... church...? Number surveyed: women = 616; men = 614.

Characteristic of Respondent	Gave money for non-church activities	Gave money for church activities
U.S. Total	70%	60%
Sex:		
Female	73%	63%
Male	66%	57%
Age:		
18-29 years	62%	49%
30-49 years	73%	60%
50 and older	72%	67%

Source: George Gallup, Jr., *The Gallup Report,* Report No. 290 (Princeton, NJ: The Gallup Poll, November 1989), p. 20. Also in source: other characteristics of respondents; contributions of food, clothing, etc.

★ 377 ★

Corporate Support of Women's Groups

Companies that gave to at least two women's organizations in 1989 or have demonstrated interest in women's organizations, according to Catalyst, National Foundation for Women Business Owners, and Women and Foundations/Corporate Philanthropy.

Organization	Grant amount in 1989
AT & T Foundation	$36 million
Deloitte and Touche	NA
Equitable Life Assurance Society of the U.S./ Equitable Foundation	$4.5 million

[Continued]

★ 377 ★

Corporate Support of Women's Groups
[Continued]

Organization	Grant amount in 1989
Exxon Corp./Exxon Education Foundation	$51 million
IBM Corp.	$135 million
Sara Lee Corp./Sara Lee Foundation	$7.4 million

Source: "Women's Organizations Predict Future Needs," *Corporate Giving Watch*, X(7)(October 1990): p. 1+. Also in source: A discussion of a study by *Women and Foundations/Corporate Philanthropy* entitled: "Far from Done: Status of Women and Girls in America"; profiles of the companies named by *Business Week* (8/6/90) as "The Best Companies for Women"; a discussion of funding needs.

★ 378 ★

Government Spending on Disease Research

Federal allotment for disease research, fiscal year 1990.

Disease and number of deaths in 1990	Spending
AIDS, 23,000 deaths	$1.1 billion
Breast cancer, 43,000 deaths	$77 million

Source: Jane Gross, "Turning Disease Into a Cause: Breast Cancer Follows AIDS," *New York Times*, January 7, 1991, p. 1+.

★ 379 ★

Grants for Women and Girls

Ford Foundation Grants to women's groups, 1983-1984. See below for explanation of acronyms.

Group	Grant
ACLU-RPF	$50,000
ACLU-WRP	300,000
CWPS	24,650
NOW-LDEF	150,000
NWLC	440,000
WEAL	200,000
WLDF	155,000

Source: "Ford Foundation Grants (1983-1984)," *Women and Public Policies*, 1987, p. 44 (Princeton, NJ: Princeton University Press, 1987). Primary source: *Grants for Women and Girls* (New York: Foundation Center, 1984), 131-39. ACLU = American Civil Liberties Union; WRP = Women's Rights Project; RFP = Reproductive Freedom Project; CWPS = Center for Women Policy Studies; NOW = National Organization for Women; LDEF = Legal Defense Education and Fund; NWLC = National Women's Law Center (formerly Women's Rights Project of the Center for Law and Social Policy); WEAL = Women's Equity Action League; WLDF = Women's Legal Defense Fund. .

★ 380 ★

Housing Costs

Monthly housing costs for renters and owners as a percent of income, by household income, 1985.

Costs as Percent of Income	Annual Household Income				
	Total	Under $10,000	$10,000 to $19,999	$20,000 to $39,999	$40,000 or more
Renters					
Less than 15%	13.1%	1.8%	6.9%	21.9%	59.4%
15 to 24%	27.0%	7.8%	28.8%	49.0%	31.1%
25 to 34%	19.6%	14.0%	31.5%	18.5%	3.8%
35 to 49%	13.0%	17.1%	18.8%	4.7%	0.5%
50 to 69%	7.9%	16.7%	5.9%	0.7%	0.2%
70% or more	11.1%	29.4%	1.7%	0.1%	0.0%
Total number (in thousands)	32,280	11,574	9,422	8,859	2,424
Percent female-maintained	**40.4%**	**61.1%**	**38.5%**	**23.1%**	**12.4%**
Owners					
Less than 15%	36.7%	6.0%	27.5%	39.9%	54.4%
15 to 24%	26.6%	19.1%	31.5%	28.4%	25.0%
25 to 34%	14.0%	19.5%	16.3%	15.2%	8.3%
35 to 49%	7.3%	16.7%	10.8%	6.0%	1.9%
50 to 69%	3.1%	10.1%	4.8%	1.5%	0.2%
70% or more	3.5%	17.8%	2.7%	0.8%	0.1%
Total number (in thousands)	56,145	8,514	10,812	20,205	16,614
Percent female-maintained	**20.7%**	**53.1%**	**29.7%**	**15.1%**	**5.0%**

Source: Selected from "Monthly Housing Costs for Renters and Owners as a Percent of Income, by Household Income, 1985," *The American Woman 1990-91,* 1990, p. 109 (New York: W.W. Norton & Company, 1990). Primary source: U.S. Department of Housing and Urban Development and U.S. Bureau of the Census, December 1988, Tables 3-20 and 4-20. Also in source: other costs data.

★ 381 ★

Monthly Family Income Spent on Child Care

Monthly family income spent on child care, by income and poverty status, Fall 1987.

	% spent on child care
Total at all income levels	6.6%
Monthly family income:	
Less than $1,250	20.7%
$1,250-$2,499	9.2%
2,500-$3,749	6.6%
$3,750 or more	4.9%
Poverty status:	
In poverty	25.0%

[Continued]

★ 381 ★

Monthly Family Income Spent on Child Care
[Continued]

	% spent on child care
Near poverty	16.3%
Not poor	6.3%

Source: Martin O'Connell and Amara Bachu, *Who's Minding the Kids? Child Care Arrangements: Winter, 1986-87,* Current Population Reports Household Economic Studies, Series P-70, No. 20, 1990, p. 11.

★ 382 ★

Purchases of Sporting Goods

Consumer purchases of sporting goods, 1988.

Characteristic	Total households	Footwear				Equipment					
		Aerobic shoes	Gym shoes/ sneakers	Jogging/ running shoes	Walking shoes	Bicycles[1]	Camping equipment	Exercise equipment	Rifles	Shotguns	Golf equipment
Female	51.2%	83.4%	42.0%	33.9%	61.4%	30.0%	24.0%	39.0%	6.6%	1.3%	18.0%
Male	48.8%	16.6%	58.0%	66.1%	38.6%	59.1%	63.0%	50.0%	90.0%	96.5%	77.0%
Both[2]	-	-	-	-	-	10.9%	13.0%	11.0%	3.4%	2.2%	5.0%

Source: Selected from "Consumer Purchases of Sporting Goods, by Consumer Characteristics: 1988," *Statistical Abstract of the United States 1990,* 1990, p. 232. Primary source: National Sporting Goods Association, Mt. Prospect, IL, *The Sporting Goods Market in 1989,* and prior issues. Also in source: data by age, education, and household income. Based on sample survey of consumer purchases of 80,000 households. Excludes Alaska and Hawaii. *Notes:* 1. 10-12-15-18+ speed. 2. Equipment used by both sexes.

★ 383 ★

Spending by Young Adults

Some statistics on the young consumer.

The author cites a Rand Youth Poll of girls and boys aged 16 to 19 years old. The findings include:

1. The leading purchase of both boys and girls is clothes.

2. Average amount that girls have to spend per week: **$73.95.**

Source: Trish Hall, "The Young are Getting and Spending, Too," *New York Times,* August 23, 1990, p. B6. Also in source: interviews with children around the country on their spending habits.

★ 384 ★

Spending of High School Seniors

Spending patterns of employed high school seniors, 1985.

Expense and spending pattern	Female	Male
Savings for education		
None or only a little	70.9%	70.6%
Some	11.8%	11.1%
About half	6.8%	8.6%
Most	5.9%	6.3%
All or almost all	4.5%	3.4%
Car expenses		
None or only a little	73.0%	57.1%
Some	11.6%	15.4%
About half	7.0%	11.6%
Most	4.3%	9.1%
All or almost all	3.9%	6.8%
Long-term savings		
None or only a little	72.0%	69.9%
Some	12.6%	13.1%
About half	5.7%	7.5%
Most	5.2%	4.6%
All or almost all	4.5%	4.8%
Personal items		
None or only a little	22.1%	25.1%
Some	17.1%	19.1%
About half	14.7%	17.5%
Most	19.1%	17.6%
All or almost all	27.0%	20.8%
Family expenses		
None or only a little	82.3%	82.1%
Some	10.0%	8.7%
About half	2.7%	3.6%
Most	2.2%	2.5%
All or almost all	2.8%	3.0%

Source: "Spending of High School Seniors: Spending patterns of employed high school seniors: 1981 and 1985," *Youth Indicators 1988: Trends in the Well-Being of American Youth,* Volume 1, August 1988, p. 86. Primary source: University of Michigan, Institute for Social Research, *Monitoring the Future,* 1981 and 1985. Also in source: data by race and college plans.

★ 385 ★

Weekly Cost of Child Care

Weekly cost of child care, selected periods, 1984-87.

Period	Current dollars		Constant 1987 dollars	
	Mean	Std. error	Mean	Std. error
Fall 1987	$48.50	1.8	$48.50	1.8
Fall 1986	$44.30	1.4	$46.30	1.5
Winter 1984-85	$40.30	1.1	$43.90	1.2

Source: Martin O'Connell and Amara Bachu, *Who's Minding the Kids? Child Care Arrangements: Winter, 1986-87,* Current Population Reports Household Economic Studies, Series P-70, No. 20, 1990, p. 11. Constant dollars were derived using the consumer price index for all urban consumers for the specified periods.

Wages and Salaries

★ 386 ★

Accountants' Salaries

Compensation of members of National Association of Accountants, 1989.

Compensation	Women	Men
Average salaries	$35,661	$51,664
Compensation (salary plus additional compensation)	$38,075	$58,997

Source: Karl E. Reichardt, CMA, David L. Schroeder, "NAA Salaries: CMAs earn more than those without a professional designation," *Management Accounting*, May 1990, p. 18+. Results derived from a survey of 2,400 National Association of Accountants members during September 1989.

★ 387 ★

Administrative/Clerical Support Earnings

Number in thousands and median weekly earnings of full-time wage and salary workers, administrative support, including clerical, 1988.

Occupation	Both sexes		Women		Men	
	Number of workers (thousands)	Median weekly earnings	Number of workers (thousands)	Median weekly earnings	Number of workers (thousands)	Median weekly earnings
Administrative support, including clerical	14,230	$318	11,129	$305	3,101	$418
Supervisors	751	457	424	402	326	564
General office	442	436	290	392	152	567
Computer equipment operators	51	572	19	[1]	31	[1]
Financial records processing	93	488	65	440	28	[1]
Supervisors, distribution, scheduling, and adjusting clerks	161	475	48	[1]	113	512
Computer equipment operators	759	342	497	311	262	415
Computer operators	754	342	494	312	260	414
Secretaries, stenographers, and typists	3,842	310	3,779	310	63	315
Secretaries	3,206	312	3,179	312	26	[1]
Typists	603	299	570	298	34	[1]
Information clerks	1,012	270	888	264	124	376
Interviewers	116	288	104	278	12	[1]

[Continued]

Administrative/Clerical Support Earnings
[Continued]

Occupation	Both sexes		Women		Men	
	Number of workers (thousands)	Median weekly earnings	Number of workers (thousands)	Median weekly earnings	Number of workers (thousands)	Median weekly earnings
Hotel clerks	73	214	48	[1]	25	[1]
Transportation ticket and reservation agents	110	423	62	355	48	[1]
Receptionists	572	256	556	255	16	[1]
Records processing, except financial	577	311	493	305	84	370
Order clerks	155	387	127	372	27	[1]
Personnel clerks, except payroll and timekeeping	54	322	47	[1]	6	[1]
Library clerks	66	294	57	286	9	[1]
File clerks	177	278	154	276	23	[1]
Records clerks	110	315	95	315	15	[1]
Financial records processing	1,681	310	1,503	305	178	408
Bookkeepers, accounting, and auditing clerks	1,322	308	1,199	304	123	385
Payroll and timekeeping clerks	149	333	135	321	15	[1]
Billing clerks	123	301	109	297	14	[1]
Cost and rate clerks	59	341	41	[1]	19	[1]
Duplicating, mail and other office machine operators	57	287	34	[1]	24	[1]
Communications equipment operators	170	301	149	298	21	[1]
Telephone operators	166	300	147	298	19	[1]
Mail and message distributing	776	463	261	404	515	485
Postal clerks, exc. mail carriers	281	489	129	462	151	502
Mail carriers, postal service	296	495	54	440	242	505
Mail clerks, exc. postal service	123	278	62	264	61	290
Messengers	76	264	16	[1]	60	267
Material recording, scheduling, and distributing clerks[2]	1,455	342	521	303	933	374
Dispatchers	142	364	59	304	83	431
Production coordinators	179	439	74	349	106	505
Traffic, shipping, and receiving clerks	476	306	124	270	352	320
Stock and inventory clerks	456	332	175	300	281	371
Weighers, measurers, and checkers	64	347	27	[1]	37	[1]
Expediters	76	370	42	[1]	34	[1]
Adjusters and investigators	854	344	633	319	221	472
Insurance adjusters, examiners, and investigators	259	375	188	342	71	537
Investigators and adjusters, except insurance	424	331	321	311	103	491
Eligibility clerks, social welfare	67	339	59	321	8	[1]
Bill and account collectors	104	319	66	311	38	[1]
Miscellaneous administrative support occupations	2,296	296	1,945	287	352	380
General office clerks	580	297	476	288	104	374
Bank tellers	346	247	315	246	31	[1]
Data-entry keyers	301	303	275	298	26	[1]
Statistical clerks	71	347	48	[1]	23	[1]
Teachers' aides	181	224	174	222	7	[1]

Source: Selected from "Median weekly earnings of full-time wage and salary workers by detailed occupation and sex, 1983-88," *Handbook of Labor Statistics,* 1989, p. 194-198 (Washington, D.C.: U.S. Department of Labor, August 1989). Also in source: detailed data by other occupations, 1983-1988. *Notes:* 1. Data not shown where base less than 50,000. 2. Not elsewhere classified; designates broad categories of occupations which cannot be more specifically identified.

★ 388 ★

Art School Faculty Earnings

Distribution of faculty salaries in art school: 1975-1988.

Type of institution and level	Year	Females	Males
College faculty salaries-All Fields			
Professor	1975	$24,500	$27,600
Associate professor	1975	18,400	19,500
Assistant professor	1975	15,500	16,400
Instructor	1975	11,900	12,900
College faculty salaries:			
Doctoral level, prof.	1988	47,740	53,390
Four-year colleges; compehensive	1988	42,090	44,230
Four-year colleges; general	1988	35,650	38,280
Two-year colleges	1988	36,270	38,370

Source: Eleanor Dickinson, "Gender Discrimination in the Art Field: Incomplete and random statistics of number of artists, art faculty, art criticism, art exhibitions, etc. which may be useful in indicating patterns and trends," 1990, p. 4 (Washington, D.C.: Artists Equity Association, 1990).

★ 389 ★

Average Hourly Pay: Female-Dominated Occupations

Hourly pay for selected occupations and U.S. averages, 1986.

Occupation	Percent Female	Average Hourly Pay
Registered Nurse	93%	$11.79
Office Clerk	80%	8.11
Nursing Aide	88%	6.05
Cashier	80%	5.37
Waiter/Waitress	79%	5.05
Retail Sales	69%	4.82
Food-Counter Worker	79%	3.80
U.S. Average Hourly Female Wage		7.80
U.S. Average Male Hourly Wage		11.24

Source: "So You Think You've Come a Long Way, Baby?," *Business Week* (February 29, 1988):48+. Primary source: Bureau of Labor Statistics, Census Bureau, and *Business Week* estimates.

★ 390 ★

Changes in Real Hourly Wages: 1973-1987

Changes in real hourly wages, hourly and salaried workers, 1973-1987.

Year	Hourly workers		Salaried workers	
	Women	Men	Women	Men
Annual rates of change				
1973-79	-0.5%	-1.2%	-0.7%	-0.5%
1979-87	-0.1%	-1.5%	1.6%	0.4%

Source: "Changes in real hourly wages, hourly and salaried workers, 1973-87," *The State of Working America*, 1990, p. 13 (Washington, D.C.: Economic Policy Institute, 1990).

★ 391 ★

Chemical Engineering Salaries

Median salary of chemical engineers earning their BS in 1989.

Year	Women		Men	
	Median	Mean	Median	Mean
1989	$32,500	$31,700	$34,100	$66,994

Source: "Salary by Year of BS, Women Versus Men," *AIChE 1990 Salary Survey Report*, 1990, p. 7 (New York: American Institute of Chemical Engineers, 1990). Also in source: data back to 1939.

★ 392 ★

Chemists' Salaries

Median annual salaries of chemists by type of employer and degree level, 1987.

Type of employer	Bachelor's Degree		Master's Degree		Ph.D.	
	Women	Men	Women	Men	Women	Men
Private industry	$34,300	$39,400	$39,700	$45,400	$49,200	$56,400
Government	30,600	36,500	33,700	36,800	41,800	50,900
Academic	22,300	26,600	27,400	31,900	36,100	42,300

Source: "Median annual salaries of chemists by type of employer, degree level, and sex, 1987," *The Changing Role of Women in Research and Development*, 1988, p. 68 (Philadelphia: Wharton School of the University of Pennsylvania, 1988). Primary source: *Salaries of Scientists, Engineers, and Technicians* (Washington, D.C.: Commission on Professionals in Science and Technology, 1987), p. 75. Data from American Mathematical Society.

★ 393 ★

Dislocated Workers - Earnings Reductions: 1979-1984

Earnings reductions experienced by dislocated workers in new jobs, 1979-1984.

Earnings Reductions	Earnings reductions experienced by dislocated workers in new jobs			
	Blue-Collar		White-Collar/Service	
	Female	Male	Female	Male
A. Workers Dislocated 1981-84				
Total	100%	100%	100%	100%
No Loss	36.5%	37.0%	45.1%	42.1%
1-25 percent	22.9%	28.4%	23.8%	29.0%
25-50 percent	19.9%	20.9%	18.2%	17.9%
More than 50 percent	20.7%	13.8%	12.8%	11.0%
Percent Reemployed	63.8%	79.2%	72.0%	89.4%
B. Workers Dislocated 1979-82				
Total	100%	100%	100%	100%
No loss	34.3%	31.3%	37.4%	48.0%
1-25 percent	29.3%	30.3%	29.7%	29.2%
25-50 percent	19.9%	20.9%	16.6%	17.3%
More than 50 percent	16.5%	17.6%	19.5%	10.4%
Percent Reemployed	56.5%	71.3%	66.8%	82.7%

Source: "Earnings reductions of dislocated workers," *The State of Working America*, 1990, p. 29 (Washington, D.C.: Economic Policy Institute, 1990). *Notes:* 1. The percentage by which the weekly wage in the current job is less than the wage in the job which was lost.

★ 394 ★

Earning Levels of Workers Who Have Been to College

Ratio of mean annual earnings of all workers with 1-3 and 4 or more years of college to those with 4 years of high school, by age: 1975-1987 (selected years).

Year	Females				Males			
	1-3 years college		4+ years college		1-3 years college		4+ years college	
	Age 25-29	Age 30-34	Age 25-29	Age 30-34	Age 25-29	Age 30-34	Age 25-29	Age 30-34
1975	1.219	1.377	1.560	1.707	1.030	1.156	1.163	1.439
1977	1.192	1.251	1.480	1.448	1.024	1.079	1.170	1.333
1979	1.192	1.283	1.471	1.619	1.030	1.066	1.161	1.321
1980	1.268	1.272	1.491	1.607	1.019	1.062	1.185	1.336
1982	1.166	1.353	1.517	1.622	1.097	1.089	1.328	1.506
1984	1.256	1.306	1.580	1.607	1.065	1.125	1.321	1.439
1985	1.237	1.356	1.698	1.623	1.060	1.212	1.406	1.616
1986	1.286	1.431	1.724	1.841	1.119	1.176	1.455	1.616
1987	1.259	1.415	1.676	1.827	1.089	1.134	1.425	1.570

Source: "Annual earnings of Young Adults," *The Condition of Education 1990: Volume 2: Postsecondary Education*, p. 52 (Washington, D.C.: National Center for Education Statistics, 1990). Primary source: U.S. Department of Commerce, Bureau of the Census, Series P-60, *Current Population Reports*, "Money Income of Families and Persons...," various years.

★ 395 ★

Earning Levels of Workers with 12 and Fewer Years of Education

Ratio of mean annual earnings of all workers with 8 or fewer and 9 to 11 years of schooling to those with 12 years of schooling, by age and sex: 1975-1987.

	Female				Male			
	8 years or less		9-11 years		8 years or less		9-11 years	
	Age 25-29	Age 30-34	Age 25-29	Age 30-34	Age 25-29	Age 30-34	Age 25-29	Age 30-34
1975	0.557	0.598	0.741	0.852	0.586	0.671	0.809	0.802
1976	0.645	0.629	0.710	0.895	0.616	0.718	0.793	0.823
1977	0.648	0.588	0.713	0.854	0.675	0.672	0.807	0.780
1978	0.647	0.625	0.732	0.866	0.687	0.648	0.819	0.803
1979	0.627	0.635	0.801	0.835	0.637	0.627	0.858	0.792
1980	0.655	0.579	0.770	0.823	0.650	0.579	0.799	0.727
1981	0.642	0.550	0.626	0.829	0.669	0.611	0.834	0.726
1982	0.641	0.612	0.742	0.862	0.641	0.615	0.739	0.788
1983	0.617	0.556	0.687	0.816	0.601	0.611	0.746	0.762
1984	0.637	0.553	0.718	0.819	0.618	0.550	0.714	0.699
1985	0.537	0.587	0.773	0.817	0.571	0.613	0.719	0.816
1986	0.617	0.554	0.718	0.801	0.578	0.552	0.756	0.743
1987	0.583	0.574	0.738	0.807	0.603	0.596	0.727	0.764

Source: "Earnings of Young Adults," *The Condition of Education 1990, Volume 1: Elementary and Secondary Education,* p. 42 (Washington, D.C.: National Center for Education Statistics, 1990). Primary source: U.S. Department of Commerce, Bureau of the Census, *Current Population Reports,* Series P-60, "Money Incomes of Families and Persons: March...," various years.

★ 396 ★

Earnings Changes in Manufacturing Worldwide

Average annual rates of growth of female real earnings in manufacturing in selected developing and developed countries, 1971-1982.

Country	1971-1975	1976-1980	1981-1982
Developing countries			
Burma	-12.2%	0.6%	17.9%[1]
Cyprus	-	11.1%	9.6%
Egypt	1.7%	3.8%[3]	-
El Salvador	-2.5%	3.6%	-2.5%[5]
Jordan	-	1.4%[4]	4.9%[5]
Kenya	-	-2.0%	1.6%
Korea, Republic of	-	10.6%	2.3%
Syrian Arab Republic	0.8%	3.2%[3]	-
United Republic of Tanzania	-7.3%[2]	-4.8%	-
Developed countries			
Australia	10.0%	0.2%	4.0%
Finland	5.9%	1.0%	1.6%
Germany, Federal Republic	4.4%	2.3%	-0.3%
Greece	4.6%	6.7%	8.7%
Netherlands	7.1%	0.8%	-0.8%

[Continued]

341

★ 396 ★

Earnings Changes in Manufacturing Worldwide
[Continued]

Country	1971-1975	1976-1980	1981-1982
Sweden	4.8%	0.9%	-2.5%
Switzerland	3.9%	1.5%	1.3%
United Kingdom	6.3%	0.2%	-0.6%

Source: Selected from "Average annual rates of growth of female real earnings in manufacturing in selected developing and developed countries, 1960-1982," *World Survey on the Role of Women in Development,* 1986, p. 89 (New York: United Nations, 1986). Primary source: *Yearbook of Labour Statistics* (Geneva, International Labour Office), various issues. *Notes:* 1. 1967-1970. 2. 1973-1975. 3. 1975-1977. 4. 1978-1980. 5. 1981.

★ 397 ★

Earnings Ratios Worldwide
Average earnings of women as a percentage of men's in selected countries.

Country	Year	Period	All non-agricultural activities	Manufacturing
Developing countries				
Cyprus	1982	weekly	58.2%	56.3%
Egypt	1977	weekly	62.8%	63.1%
Jordan	1981	daily	87.9%	63.6%
Kenya	1982	monthly	83.7%	75.8%
Korea, Republic of	1982	monthly	45.1%	45.1%
Singapore	1982	hourly	63.6%[1]	63.2%
Sri Lanka	1982	hourly	80.1%	81.9%
United Republic of Tanzania	1980	monthly	85.1%	78.5%
Developed countries				
Australia	1982	hourly	82.9%	78.2%
Belgium	1982	hourly	73.6%	73.5%
France	1981	hourly	80.4%	78.1%
Germany, Federal Republic	1982	hourly	72.7%	73.0%
Japan	1982	monthly	52.8%	43.1%
Netherlands	1982	hourly	76.9%	74.0%
Switzerland	1982	hourly	67.3%	67.0%
United Kingdom	1982	hourly	69.1%	68.8%

Source: "Average earnings of women workers in all non-agricultural activities and in manufacturing industries as a percentage of men's in selected countries," *World Survey on the Role of Women in Development,* 1986, p. 91 (New York: United Nations, 1986). Primary source: *Yearbook of Labour Statistics, 1984* (Geneva, International Labour Office).

★ 398 ★

Earnings as a Percentage of Men's: 1970-1988

Changes in women's earnings as a percentage of men's among full-time workers, 1970-1988.

Year	Median annual earnings	Median weekly earnings
1970	59.4%	62.3%
1975	58.8%	62.0%
1976	60.2%	62.2%
1977	58.9%	61.9%
1978	59.4%	61.3%
1979	59.7%	62.5%
1980	60.2%	64.4%
1981	59.2%	64.6%
1982	61.7%	65.4%
1983	63.6%	66.7%
1984	63.7%	67.8%
1985	64.6%	68.2%
1986	64.3%	69.2%
1987	65.0%	70.0%
1988	-	70.2%

Source: Selected from "Changes in Women's Earnings as a Percentage of Men's Among Full-Time Workers," *Briefing Paper #1: The Wage Gap,* National Committee on Pay Equity, Washington, D.C. Primary source: Data through 1983 are from Francine D. Blau and Marianne A. Ferber, *The Economics of Women, Men and Work* (Prentice-Hall, 1986). Annual data for 1984, 1985, and 1986 and 1987 are from the Census Bureau, U.S. Department of Commerce, *Current Population Reports,* Consumer Income, Series P-60, nos. 150, 154, 157 and 162. Weekly data for 1984 and 1985 are from *Statistical Abstract of the United States 1987,* Table 680; 1986, 1987, and 1988 data are from the Bureau of Labor Statistics, unpublished. Also in source: data for 1955 to 1970.

★ 399 ★

Earnings in Selected Professions

Number of workers in thousands and median weekly earnings, full-time wage and salary workers, by profession, 1988.

Profession	Both sexes		Women		Men	
	Number of workers (thousands)	Median weekly earnings	Number of workers (thousands)	Median weekly earnings	Number of workers (thousands)	Median weekly earnings
Professional speciality	11,045	$555	5,315	$485	5,730	$651
Engineers, architects, surveyors	1,833	717	137	624	1,696	727
Architects	97	616	16	[1]	80	634
Engineers	1,719	723	120	639	1,599	734
Aerospace engineers	110	805	6	[1]	104	820
Chemical engineers	58	781	8	[1]	50	[1]
Civil engineers	192	717	10	[1]	182	724
Electrical and electronic engineers	557	741	37	[1]	520	749
Industrial engineers	224	664	29	[1]	195	676
Mechanical engineers	284	709	11	[1]	273	717
Mathematical and computer scientists	675	667	227	575	448	733
Computer systems analysts and scientists	421	674	126	594	295	730
Operations and systems researchers and analysts	208	675	78	578	130	740
Natural scientists	356	635	81	540	275	677

[Continued]

★ 399 ★

Earnings in Selected Professions
[Continued]

Profession	Both sexes		Women		Men	
	Number of workers (thousands)	Median weekly earnings	Number of workers (thousands)	Median weekly earnings	Number of workers (thousands)	Median weekly earnings
Chemists, except biochemists	123	666	26	1	97	668
Biological and life scientists	67	554	27	1	40	1
Lawyers and judges	396	909	100	765	296	930
Lawyers	366	914	94	774	272	930
Writers, artists, entertainers, and athletes	1,053	482	453	388	600	559
Technical writers	58	523	24	1	33	1
Designers	308	507	133	354	175	597
Actors and directors	69	488	31	1	38	1
Painters, sculptors, craft artists, and artist printmakers	92	393	43	1	50	1
Photographers	60	424	16	1	44	1
Editors and reporters	198	494	93	412	105	588
Public relations specialists	133	501	77	443	56	713

Source: Selected from "Median weekly earnings of full-time wage and salary workers by detailed occupation and sex, 1983-88," *Handbook of Labor Statistics,* 1989, p. 194-198 (Washington, D.C.: U.S. Department of Labor, August 1989). Also in source: detailed data by other occupations, 1983-1988. *Note:* 1. Data not shown where base less than 50,000.

★ 400 ★

Engineers' Salaries

Number and median income of Institute of Electrical and Electronic Engineers members employed full-time by years of experience, 1986.

Years of experience	Number		Median income	
	Female	Male	Female	Male
Less than 2 years	48	383	$40,300	$30,200
3-4 years	65	678	33,000	34,500
5-7 years	67	875	40,000	39,500
8-10 years	40	774	42,300	45,800
11-15 years	26	1,155	46,900	50,600

Source: "Number, Median, and Mean Annual Income of IEEE Engineers Employed Full-Time by Sex and Years of Experience, 1986," *The Changing Role of Women in Research and Development,* 1988, p. 72 (Philadelphia: Wharton School of the University of Pennsylvania, 1988). Primary source: *Salaries of Scientists, Engineers and Technicians* (Washington, D.C.: Commission on Professionals in Science and Technolgy, p. 144. Data from American Institute of Electrical and Electronic Engineers, Inc.

★ 401 ★

Equivalent Annual Salaries for Husbands and Wives: 1979 and 1986

Equivalent annual salaries for husbands and wives and percentage change, 1979 and 1986..

	Lowest Fifth	Lower Middle Fifth	Upper Middle Fifth	Middle Fifth	Highest Fifth	Average
Wives						
1979	$6,990	$9,759	$12,162	$14,917	$20,216	$14,064
1986	6,858	10,063	13,208	16,803	23,988	15,768
Percentage change	-1.9%	3.1%	8.6%	12.6%	18.7%	12.1%
Husbands						
1979	7,615	14,318	19,931	24,535	35,663	23,204
1986	5,902	12,459	17,861	23,826	36,756	22,240
Percentage change	-22.5%	-13.0%	-10.4%	-2.9%	3.1%	-4.2%

Source: "Equivalent annual salaries for husbands and wives," *Family Incomes in the 1980s: New Pressure on Wives, Husbands, and Young Adults*, 1988, p. 7 (Washington, D.C.: Economic Policy Institute, 1988). *Note:* 1. Annual salary measured as hourly wage times 2,080 hours.

★ 402 ★

Faculty Salaries in Higher Education

Faculty salaries by rank and type of institution, 1990.

Rank	All colleges[1]		Public	Private indep.	Church-related
	Women	Men			
Professor	$50,530	$57,080	$55,830	$61,620	$47,240
Associate	$39,600	$42,600	$42,210	$43,280	$37,540
Assistant	$32,890	$35,840	$35,200	$35,540	$31,050
Lecturer	$27,830	$32,370	$29,310	$33,190	$27,690
Instructor	$25,310	$27,120	$26,330	$26,240	$24,800

Source: Anthony DePalma, "Pressed Private Colleges Reining in Tuition," *New York Times*, April 3, 1991, p. B7. Primary source: American Association of University Professors. *Notes:* 1. Including two-and four-year colleges and universities, but excluding a small number of two-year colleges that do not use academic ranks.

★ 403 ★

Faculty Salaries in Higher Education: 1980-1995

Weighted average salaries of faculty in higher education by rank and sex, 1980-1985.

Year and Sex	Salaries (in dollars)				
	Professor	Assoc.Prof.	Asst.Prof.	Instructor	Lecturer
1980-1981					
Women	$28,250	$22,290	$18,300	$14,780	NA
Men	$31,140	$23,530	$19,340	$15,550	NA
1982-1983					
Women	$32,010	$25,470	$20,940	$17,030	$18,260
Men	$35,960	$27,270	$22,550	$18,340	$20,970
1983-1984					
Women	$33,730	$26,870	$22,050	$17,960	$19,150
Men	$37,860	$28,610	$23,870	$19,410	$22,050
1984-1985					
Women	$35,590	$28,240	$23,320	$18,500	$20,450
Men	$40,390	$30,410	$25,370	$19,880	$23,430

Source: Selected from "Weighted Average Salaries of Faculty in Higher Education, by Rank and Sex, Selected Years, 1975-1985," *Working Women: Past, Present, and Future*, 1987, Table 6, p. 251. Primary source: *AAUP Bulletin: Academe.* "Annual Report on the Economic Status of the Profession," Vols. 62-65, 67, 69-71 (1976-1985). Also in source: Data for 1975-1979; women's salary as a percent of men's. "Weighted" refers to weighting average salary by number in each group. Samples include between 1,278 and 2,598 institutions providing data by sex. Figures have been rounded to the nearest $10.

★ 404 ★

Faculty Salaries in Institutions of Higher Education: 1980-1988

Average salary of full-time instructional faculty in institutions of higher education, by academic rank and sex: 1980-81 to 1987-88.

Academic year and sex	Current dollars					
	All ranks	Professor	Assoc.Prof.	Asst.Prof.	Instructor	Lecturer
1980-81						
Total	23,302	30,753	23,214	18,901	15,178	17,301
Female	19,996	27,959	22,295	18,302	14,854	16,168
Male	24,499	31,082	23,451	19,227	15,545	18,281
1981-82						
Total	25,449	33,437	25,278	20,608	16,450	18,756
Female	21,802	30,438	24,271	19,866	16,054	17,676
Male	26,796	33,799	25,553	21,025	16,906	19,721
1982-83						
Total	27,196	35,540	26,921	22,056	17,601	20,072
Female	23,261	32,221	25,738	21,130	17,102	18,830
Male	28,664	35,956	27,262	22,586	18,160	21,225

[Continued]

★ 404 ★

Faculty Salaries in Institutions of Higher Education: 1980-1988
[Continued]

Academic year and sex	Current dollars					
	All ranks	Professor	Assoc.Prof.	Asst.Prof.	Instructor	Lecturer
1984-85						
Total	30,447	39,743	29,945	24,668	20,230	22,334
Female	25,941	35,824	28,517	23,575	19,362	21,004
Male	32,182	40,269	30,392	25,330	21,159	23,557
1985-86						
Total	32,392	42,268	31,787	26,277	20,918	23,770
Female	27,576	38,252	30,300	24,966	20,237	22,273
Male	34,294	42,833	32,273	27,094	21,693	25,238
1987-88						
Total	36,011	47,285	35,308	29,219	22,542	26,069
Female	30,364	42,655	33,625	27,680	21,812	24,448
Male	38,295	47,967	35,892	30,209	23,434	27,771

Source: Selected from "Average salary of full-time instructional faculty in institutions of higher education, by academic rank and sex: 1972-73 to 1987-88," *Digest of Education Statistics,* Table 192, p. 213 (Washington, D.C.: National Center for Education Statistics, 1989). Primary source: U.S. Department of Education, National Center for Educational Statistics, *Faculty Salaries, Tenure, and Benefits;* and Integrated Postsecondary Education Data System (IPEDS), "Salaries, Tenure, and Fringe Benefits of Full-Time Instructional Faculty" survey. Also in source: date for males; data for 1972-1980; data in constant (1987-88) dollars. Data for 1972-73, 1975-76, and 1987-88 are for faculty on 9-to 10-month contracts; data for 1979-80 to 1985-86 are for faculty on 9-month contracts. Data exclude imputations for nonrespondent institutions.

★ 405 ★

Female Earnings as Percentage of Male Earnings: Selected Countries

Female earnings as a percentage of male earnings in selected industrialized countries, 1981.

Country	Percentage
Australia	80.4%
Canada	63.6%
New Zealand	71.6%
Sweden	90.1%
United Kingdom	68.8%
United States	59.2%

Source: "Female Earnings as a Percentage of Male Earnings in Selected Industrialized Countries, 1981," *A Comparable Worth Primer,* 1986, p. 78 (Lexington: Lexington Books, 1986). Primary source: Adapted from International Labour Office, *Women at Work,* no. 1 (Geneva: International Labour Office, 1983), 5; Statistics Canada, Social and Economic Studies Division, *Women in Canada A Statistical Report* (Ottawa: Minister of Supply & Services, Canada, 1985), 61; U.S. Department of Labor, *Time of Change: 1983 Handbook on Women Workers* (Washington, D.C.: U.S. Government Printing Office, 1983), 82. Because of differences in methodologies and data bases, strict comparisons between countries should not be made on the basis of these statistics.

★ 406 ★

Gerontologist Salaries and Placements

Salaries and agencies of placement, holders of master's degrees in gerontology, 1983.

Salaries/Agencies	Women	Men	Average
Mean annual salary, administrators	$22,485	$31,368	$25,446
Mean annual salary, non-administrators	19,180	23,850	20,350
Agencies where graduates are employed:			
Home for the Aged			17%
Government Agency			14%
Nursing Home			13%
Educational Institution			12%
Proprietary Business			12%
Non-profit Organization			9%
Health Organization			8%
Senior/Community Center			5%
Other			10%

Source: David A. Peterson, PhD, "Job Placement and Career Advancement of Gerontology Master's Degree Graduates," *Gerontologist* 27:1 (1987), p. 34+. Also in source: a discussion of the field of gerontology in general. Data drawn from a 1983 survey of 17 colleges and universities identified as having graduated persons with master's degrees in gerontology. Of 389 respondents, 73% were female.

★ 407 ★

Health Care Workers' Earnings

Median weekly earnings of full-time wage and salary workers in the health care field, 1988.

Occupation	Median weekly earnings		
	Both sexes	Women	Men
Health diagnosing occupations	$710	$553	$807
Physicians	716	572	815
Health assessment and treating occupations	518	511	591
Registered nurses	516	515	561
Pharmacists	718	[1]	720
Therapists	497	489	517
Inhalation therapists	473	[1]	[1]
Physical therapists	528	[1]	[1]
Speech therapists	522	[1]	[1]

Source: Selected from "Median weekly earnings of full-time wage and salary workers by detailed occupation and sex, 1983-88," *Handbook of Labor Statistics,* 1989, p. 194 (Washington, D.C.: U.S. Department of Labor, August 1989). Also in source: detailed data by sex and other occupations for 1983-88, including numbers of workers in each occupation. *Note:* 1. Data not shown where base is less than 50,000.

★ 408 ★

Hourly Earnings for Persons with No Work Interruptions

Hourly earnings for those with no work interruptions by age and years of school; ratio of women's earnings to men's, 1984.

Age and school years completed	Women	Men	Women/Men ratio
Workers 21 to 64 years of age	$7.44	$10.76	69.1%
21 to 29 years of age	6.64	7.98	83.2%
Less than 12 years of school	5.30	6.59	80.4%
12 to 15 years of school	6.15	7.70	79.9%
16 years or more of school	8.54	9.91	86.2%
30 to 44 years of age	8.40	11.60	72.4%
Less than 12 years of school	5.56	8.09	68.7%
12 to 15 years of school	7.60	10.71	71.0%
16 years or more of school	10.85	14.68	73.9%
45 to 64 years of age	7.57	12.60	60.1%
Less than 12 years of school	5.54	9.01	61.5%
12 to 15 years of school	7.62	12.07	63.1%
16 years or more of school	11.10	18.03	61.6%

Source: "Hourly earnings for those with no work interruptions by sex, age, and years of school, 1984," *Facts on Working Women*, No. 90-3, October 1990, p. 5.

★ 409 ★

Hourly Earnings: 1980-1988

Median hourly earnings of workers paid hourly rates, by age and race, 1980-1988.

Age	1980	1981	1982	1983	1984	1985	1986	1987	1988
Women, 16 years and over	$3.95	$4.28	$4.61	$4.80	$4.97	$5.13	$5.33	$5.60	$5.84
Men, 16 years and over	6.10	6.57	6.85	6.92	7.12	7.33	7.59	7.77	7.91
Women, 16 to 24 years	3.45	3.71	3.78	3.82	3.93	4.01	4.11	4.22	4.48
Men, 16 to 24 years	4.10	4.31	4.38	4.38	4.57	4.68	4.79	4.91	5.03
Women, 25 years and over	4.24	4.69	5.02	5.23	5.48	5.73	5.95	6.16	6.44
Men, 25 years and over	7.22	7.78	8.08	8.31	8.60	8.85	9.02	9.16	9.38
White Women, 16 years and over	3.96	4.28	4.61	4.81	4.98	5.14	5.35	5.62	5.86
White Men, 16 years and over	6.23	6.71	6.98	7.07	7.26	7.58	7.78	7.93	8.06
Black Women, 16 years and over	3.88	4.19	4.49	4.72	4.87	5.04	5.17	5.40	5.61
Black Men, 16 years and over	5.18	5.81	5.97	5.96	6.16	6.15	6.57	6.74	6.94

Source: Selected from "Median hourly earnings of workers paid hourly rates by sex, age, and race, 1979-88," *Handbook of Labor Statistics*, 1989, p. 160 (Washington, D.C.: U.S. Department of Labor, August 1989). Also in source: detailed data for men by age and race; data for 1979; number of workers.

★ 410 ★

Individual Employment Income

Total, female, and male adults, and average annual employment income, 1990.

Base:	Total	Income			
		$50,000 or more	$40,000-49,999	$30,000-39,999	$25,000-29,999
All Adults	180,974	8,389	7,617	16,425	12,357
Women	94,667	2,046	1,466	4,622	4,391
Men	86,307	7,354	6,151	11,803	7,966

Source: Selected from *Mediamark Research Multimedia Audiences Report, Spring 1990*, p. 16, 198, 238 (New York: Mediamark Research Inc., 1990).

★ 411 ★

Industrial Physicists' Salaries

Number and median salary of industrial physicists by years since degree, 1985.

Years since degree	Number		Median salary	
	Female	Male	Female	Male
0-4 years	30	237	$39,500	$40,700
5-9 years	25	346	42,000	46,700
10+ years	25	977	45,000	57,000

Source: "Salaries of Industrial Physicists by Years Since Degree and Sex, 1985," *The Changing Role of Women in Research and Development*, 1988, p. 71 (Philadelphia: Wharton School of the University of Pennsylvania, 1988). Primary source: *Salaries of Scientists, Engineers and Technicians* (Washington, D.C.: Commission on Professionals in Science and Technology, 1987), p. 82. Data from American Institute of Physics.

★ 412 ★

Laboratory Assistants' Earnings Worldwide

Monthly salaries and the female/male salary ratio of laboratory assistants in the chemical industry in selected countries and areas, 1975-1982.

Country or area	Currency	1975			1980			1982		
		F	M	F/M	F	M	F/M	F	M	F/M
Bangladesh	Taka	-	500	-	-	889	-	438	953	46%
Bolivia	Peso	-	-	-	7060	5800	122%	7104[1]	5837	121%
Cyprus	Pound	39	66	59%	118	-	-	165	-	-
El Salvador	Colon	-	-	-	-	-	-	400	625	64%
Guatemala	Quetzal	-	-	-	95	135	70%	123	138	89%
Honduras	Lempira	-	196	-	330	350	94%	-	530	-
Hong Kong	Dollar	2160	1380	-	-	2334	-	1930	2535	76%
Jordan	Dinar	42	41	103%	60	60	100%	-	-	-
Mexico	Peso	2420	-	-	6540	-	100%	6300	8430[1]	75%
Pakistan	Rupee	630	838	75%	500	700	71%	700	700[1]	100%
Peru	Sol	8500	8800	97%	41821	46402	90%	88951	90455[1]	98%

[Continued]

★ 412 ★

Laboratory Assistants' Earnings Worldwide

[Continued]

Country or area	Currency	1975			1980			1982		
		F	M	F/M	F	M	F/M	F	M	F/M
Puerto Rico	Dollar	-	-	-	537	537	100%	580	580[1]	100%
Korea, Republic of	Won	-	-	-	173600	188128	92%	-	-	-
Syrian Arab Republic	Pound	505	508	99%	-	-	-	-	-	-
Venezuela	Bolivar	-	-	-	1625	1398	116%	3200	3200	100%
Australia	Dollar	-	630	-	987	987	100%	1242	1242	100%
Belgium	Franc	-	17326	-	24605	24605	100%	-	29405	-
Germany, Federal Republic	D.M.	-	-	-	-	-	-	3359	3882	87%
Norway	Crown	3972	5424	73%	6569	7826	84%	8973	9294	97%

Source: Selected from "Monthly salaries of male and female laboratory assistants in the chemical industry in selected countries and areas, 1965-1982," *World Survey on the Role of Women in Development*, 1986, p. 88 (New York: United Nations, 1986). Primary source: *Bulletin of Labour Statistics* (Geneva, International Labour Office), various years. Also in source: data for other years and other countries. Bangladesh: Chittagong and Dacca, 1982, Rajshahi; Chile: Valparaiso; Honduras: Teguicgalpa; Pakistan: in 1975, Lahore, in 1980 Peshawar and Sialkot; Peru: in 1970 Lima and Callao; Puerto Rico: in 1980 minimal salary; Syrian Arab Republic: Alep; Australia: Melbourne; Greece: Athens. *Note:* 1. 1981.

★ 413 ★

Librarian Salaries and Placements

Average salaries of graduates of American Library Association-accredited library school programs, 1989; placement status of 1989 graduates, spring 1990. spring, 1990.

Salary/number of graduates	Women	Men	Total
Average (mean) salary	$24,539	$24,669	$24,581
Median salary	23,832	23,500	23,768
Number of graduates	2,374	701	3,356
Not in library positions	213	80	293
Employment not known	463	145	876
Permanent professional placements	1,484	400	1,894
Temporary professional placements	149	47	198
Nonprofessional library placements	65	29	95
Total in library positions	1,698	476	2,187

Source: Carol Learmont and Stephen Van Houten, "Placements and Salaries 1989: Steady On," *Library Journal* (October 15, 1990), p. 46+. Also in source: other statistics on placements and salaries. Forty-three of 53 eligible schools responded to the 39th annual survey.

★ 414 ★

Librarians' Earnings

Median weekly earnings of full-time wage and salary workers, librarians, 1988.

Occupation	Median weekly earnings		
	Both sexes	Women	Men
Librarians, archivists, and curators	474	463	[1]
Librarians	476	465	[1]

Source: Selected from "Median weekly earnings of full-time wage and salary workers by detailed occupation and sex, 1983-88," *Handbook of Labor Statistics*, 1989, p. 194-198 (Washington, D.C.: U.S. Department of Labor, August 1989). Also in source: detailed data by other occupations, 1983-1988. *Note:* 1. Data not shown where base less than 50,000.

★ 415 ★

Lowest Faculty Salaries, by Field

Lowest faculty salaries in selected fields, 1988-1989.

Field	Salary
Nursing	$31,301
Library and archival sciences	$31,430
Secretarial and related programs	$32,415
Health services technologies	$32,739
Occupational therapy technology	$32,940
Home economics	$33,036
Visual and performing arts	$33,392
Communications	$33,812
Physical therapy	$33,874
Physical education	$33,887

Source: Blum, Debra E., "Fact File: Average Faculty Salaries by Rank in Selected Fields, 1988-1989," *Chronicle of Higher Education* 35:A14 (May 24, 1989). Also in source: Highest salaries in public institutions; highest and lowest salaries in private institutions. Rankings are based on reports from 281 public institutions that are members of the American Association of State College and Universities.

★ 416 ★

Management Earnings

Number of workers in thousands and median weekly earnings of full-time wage and salary workers in management, 1988.

Occupation	Both sexes		Women		Men	
	Number of workers (thousands)	Median weekly earnings	Number of workers (thousands)	Median weekly earnings	Number of workers (thousands)	Median weekly earnings
Managerial and professional speciality	21,770	$552	9,802	465	11,968	666
Executive, administrative, and managerial	10,725	547	4,487	430	6,238	682
Administrators and officials, public administration	436	550	179	476	257	617
Administrators, protective services	52	584	8	[1]	45	[1]
Financial managers	472	630	200	487	272	788
Personnel and labor relations managers	112	666	53	563	59	785
Purchasing managers	102	644	24	[1]	78	709
Managers, marketing, advertising, and public relations	453	702	140	503	313	814
Adminstrators, education and related fields	500	671	218	499	282	757
Managers, medicine and health	144	587	93	535	51	743
Managers, properties and real estate	241	424	123	355	117	516

[Continued]

352

★ 416 ★

Management Earnings
[Continued]

Occupation	Both sexes		Women		Men	
	Number of workers (thousands)	Median weekly earnings	Number of workers (thousands)	Median weekly earnings	Number of workers (thousands)	Median weekly earnings
Management-related occupations	3,204	501	1,664	426	1,540	610
Accountants and auditors	1,114	501	576	435	538	613
Underwriters and other financial officers	651	520	339	422	312	655
Management analysts	90	672	33	1	57	818
Personnel, training, and labor relations specialists	364	507	213	447	151	613
Buyers, wholesale and retail trade, except farm products	172	475	82	404	90	539
Construction inspectors	59	495	2	1	56	500
Inspectors and compliance officers, except construction	192	513	49	1	143	541

Source: Selected from "Median weekly earnings of full-time wage and salary workers by detailed occupation and sex, 1983-88," *Handbook of Labor Statistics,* 1989, p. 194-198 (Washington, D.C.: U.S. Department of Labor, August 1989). Also in source: detailed data by other occupations, 1983-1988. *Note:* 1. Data not shown where base less than 50,000.

★ 417 ★

Median Annual Earnings by Race/Ethnicity: 1986 and 1987

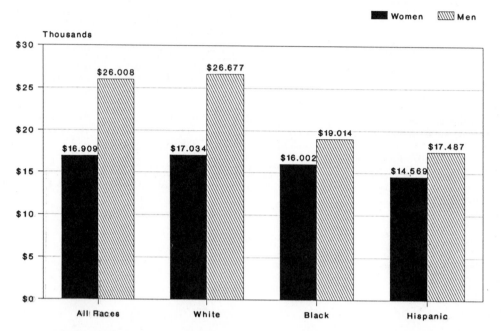

Median annual earnings for full-time, year-round workers aged 15 and over, by race/ethnicity, 1986 and 1987.

Race/Ethnicity	1987			1986		
	Women	Men	Ratio	Women	Men	Ratio
All races	$16,909	$26,008	65%	$16,232	$25,256	64.3%
White	17,034	26,677	63.8%	16,442	25,927	63.4%
Black	16,002	19,014	60%[1]	14,734	18,339	56.8%[1]
Hispanic[2]	14,569	17,487	54.6%[1]	13,386	16,815	53.4%[1]

Source: "Median Annual Earnings for Full-Time, Year Round Workers, Persons 15 and Over, Whites, Blacks, Hispanics," *Briefing Paper #1: The Wage Gap,* National Committee on Pay Equity, Washington, D.C. Primary source: *Current Population Reports,* Series P-60, Nos. 159 and 162, Table 41. *Notes:* 1. The base for this ratio is the earnings of white men. 2. Persons of Hispanic origin can be of any race.

★ 418 ★

Median Annual Earnings: 1980-1987

Median annual earnings of year-round full-time wage and salary workers by race, 1980-1987.

Race	1980	1981	1982	1983	1984	1985	1986	1987
Total, 16 years and over	$15,444	$16,563	$17,559	$18,232	$19,561	$20,468	$21,202	$21,823
Women, 16 years and over	11,287	12,345	13,352	14,111	15,006	15,728	16,336	17,047
Men, 16 years and over	18,910	20,593	21,542	22,296	23,816	24,839	25,676	26,312

[Continued]

★ 418 ★

Median Annual Earnings: 1980-1987
[Continued]

Race	1980	1981	1982	1983	1984	1985	1986	1987
White women, 16 years and over	11,413	12,476	13,520	14,288	15,110	15,901	16,571	17,209
White men, 16 years and over	19,570	21,087	22,149	22,917	24,683	25,592	26,441	27,073
Black women, 16 years and over	10,609	11,166	12,355	12,896	13,716	14,495	14,814	15,952
Black men, 16 years and over	13,737	14,988	15,596	16,193	16,687	17,456	18,148	19,147

Source: Selected from "Median annual earnings of year-round full-time wage and salary workers by age, sex, and race, 1979-87," *Handbook of Labor Statistics,* 1989, p. 231 (Washington, D.C.: U.S. Department of Labor, August 1989). Also in source: detailed data, including numbers of workers, by age, sex, and race, 1979-1987. Data relate to the earnings of wage and salary workers who usually worked 35 hours or more per week for 50 to 52 weeks during the year.

★ 419 ★

Nurses' Salaries
Average salaries of nurses, 1980-1990.

National average salary for starting nurses, 1980:	$14,000
National average salary for starting nurses, 1990:	$25,000
Salaries for experienced nurses, some large cities, 1990:	$60,000+

Source: "Big Gain in Nursing Students Lifts Hopes Amid a Shortage," *New York Times,* December 28, 1990, p. 1+. Also in source: a discussion of the nursing profession.

★ 420 ★

Occupations with Highest and Lowest Mean Earnings
Occupations with highest and lowest mean earnings, 1980, and percent female representation in occupation.

Ranking/Occupation	% Female	Mean earnings
Highest mean earnings		
1/Physicians	11%	$57,166
2/Dentists	5%	46,369
3/Lawyers	10%	39,132
4/Podiatrists	5%	38,402
5/Medical science teachers	17%	37,958
6/Law teachers	13%	36,411
7/Securities and financial services sales occupations	17%	35,448
8/Airline pilots and navigators	1%	34,488
9/Optometrists	6%	34,211
10/Medical scientists	35%	33,909
Lowest mean earnings		
1/Child care workers, private household	98%	$4,473
2/Private household cleaners and servants	92%	5,530
3/Housekeepers and butlers	95%	5,612
4/Child care workers, except private household	89%	6,617
5/Cooks, private household	83%	7,082

[Continued]

★ 420 ★

Occupations with Highest and Lowest Mean Earnings

[Continued]

Ranking/Occupation	% Female	Mean earnings
6/Waiters and waitresses	83%	7,095
7/Miscellaneous food preparation occupations	56%	7,548
8/Waiters' and waitresses' assistants	46%	7,623
9/Teachers' aides	88%	7,628
10/Textile sewing machine operators	93%	7,726

Source: "Occupations with Highest and Lowest Mean Earnings, 1980," *A Comparable Worth Primer*, 1986, p. 18 (Lexington: Lexington Books, 1986). Primary source: Adapted from Bureau of the Census, *1980 Census of Population, vol. 2, Subject Reports, Earnings by Occupation and Education* (Washington, D.C.: U.S. Government Printing Office, 1984), 1-252.

★ 421 ★

Pay Equity Legislation: Minnesota

Some findings of Elaine Sorenson, economist and pay equity expert at The Urban Institute in Washington, D.C., from her study of pay equity legislation in Minnesota, the first state to implement pay equity for state employees.

1. Pay equity adjustments required a $33.4 million appropriation from the legislature, totalling about 4% of the state's payroll over a four-year period. **Ninety-eight percent** of adjustments went to **female-dominated jobs.**

2. Prior to implementing adjustments, women employed by the State were paid **72 cents** for every dollar men were paid. After four years of pay equity implementation, in January, 1987, women were paid **81 cents**. Pay equity increased women's pay **10.7%** between 1983 and 1986; it increased the pay of men in female-dominated jobs by 16.5%.

3. If pay equity had not been implemented, total employment would have increased by another 90 jobs, or 0.3%. Considering that the State employs over 30,000 workers, the overall impact was minimal.

Source: "New Research: Pay Equity in Minnesota: Women's Wages Increased, State Economy Remained Sound," *National Committee on Pay Equity Newsnotes* 11:1 (October 1990), p. 1+.

★ 422 ★

Public School Teachers' Salaries

Average salary, in thousands, public elementary and secondary teachers, 1960-1988.

Year	Average salary ($1,000)		
	All teachers	Elementary	Secondary
1960	$5.0	$4.8	$5.3
1970	8.6	8.4	8.9
1975	11.7	11.3	12.0
1978	14.2	13.9	14.6
1979	15.0	14.7	15.4

[Continued]

★ 422 ★

Public School Teachers' Salaries
[Continued]

Year	Average salary ($1,000)		
	All teachers	Elementary	Secondary
1980	16.0	15.6	16.5
1981	17.6	17.2	18.1
1982	19.3	18.9	19.8
1983	20.7	20.2	21.3
1984	21.9	21.5	22.6
1985	23.6	23.2	24.2
1986	25.2	24.7	25.9
1987	26.6	26.0	27.3
1988	28.0	27.4	28.8

Source: Selected from "Public Elementary and Secondary Schools-Number and Average Salary of Classroom Teachers, 1960 to 1989, and by State, 1989," *Statistical Abstract of the United States 1990*, 1990, p. 141. Primary source: National Education Association, Washington, DC, *Estimates of School Statistics, 1988-89* and earlier issues. Also in source: data by state, 1989. Estimates for school year ending in June of year shown. Schools classified by type of organization rather than by grade-group; elementary includes kindergarten.

★ 423 ★

Ratio of Women's Earnings: 1989 and 1983

Ratio of median weekly earnings for women and men for selected occupations in 1989 and 1983.

Occupational class	Women to men earnings ratio	
	1989	1983
Total	70.1%	66.7%
Inspectors, compliance officers	80.6%	NA
Engineers	85.7%	82.8%
Computer scientists, analysts	83.0%	77.3%
Operations/systems analysts	83.7%	NA
Registered nurses	89.7%	99.5%
Therapists	87.8%	NA
Teachers, except college/university	85.6%	84.9%
Elementary teachers	90.3%	86.7%
Secondary teachers	96.1%	88.6%
Counselors, education/vocation	85.1%	80.3%
Psychologists	83.1%	NA
Social/religious workers	90.3%	86.5%
Social workers	85.1%	79.6%
Lab technicians/technologists	86.2%	83.7%
Engineering technicians	84.6%	73.0%
Drafting occupations	89.4%	NA

[Continued]

★ 423 ★

Ratio of Women's Earnings: 1989 and 1983

[Continued]

Occupational class	Women to men earnings ratio	
	1989	1983
Computer programmers	83.1%	82.7%
Advertising/related sales	85.2%	NA
Sales reps, except retail	84.5%	71.1%
Cashiers	94.8%	84.3%
Scheduling supervisors/clerks	91.3%	NA
Information clerks	80.6%	72.6%
Records clerks	85.5%	76.2%
Bookkeepers, accounting clerks	83.8%	79.1%
Postal clerks, except mail carriers	94.1%	93.4%
Mail carriers, postal service	88.9%	NA
Mail clerks, except postal service	94.8%	89.0%
Dispatchers	83.2%	77.6%
Shipping/receiving clerks	82.3%	77.4%
Stock/inventory clerks	85.2%	81.2%
Misc. admin. support occupations	80.7%	74.3%
General office clerks	91.6%	79.7%
Police and detectives	89.8%	77.5%
Public service police/detectives	92.1%	NA
Guards	86.4%	80.6%
Guards/police, except public service	95.5%	91.3%
Food preparation/service occupations	85.3%	86.2%
Bartenders	82.7%	84.4%
Cooks, except short order	84.7%	85.8%
Waiters'/waitresses' assistants	97.0%	NA
Misc. food preparation occupations	95.0%	102.5%
Health aides, except nursing	87.3%	NA
Nursing aides, orderlies	82.7%	81.0%
Maids/housemen	85.4%	79.0%
Janitors/cleaners	85.1%	81.0%
Mechanics/repairers	102.8%	89.4%
Electrical/electronic repairers	94.6%	NA
Textile sewing machine operators	82.4%	75.3%
Laundry/dry cleaning machine operators	89.9%	NA
Packaging/filling machine operators	88.5%	78.5%
Bus drivers	82.5%	71.0%
Handlers/helpers/laborers	81.1%	84.1%
Stock handlers/baggers	81.1%	91.9%
Freight/stock/material handlers	84.7%	NA
Laborers, except construction	87.5%	79.0%

[Continued]

★ 423 ★

Ratio of Women's Earnings: 1989 and 1983

[Continued]

Occupational class	Women to men earnings ratio	
	1989	1983
Farming/forestry/fishing occupations	83.7%	84.5%
Farm occupations, except managers	87.9%	86.7%
Farm workers	90.4%	88.5%
Related agricultural occupations	82.7%	NA

Source: "Ratio of median weekly earnings for women and men and ratio of women's employment to total employment for selected occupations in 1989 and 1983," *Facts on Working Women*, No. 90-3, October 1990, p. 3-4. Also in source: ratio of women's employment to total employment (see *Labor and Employment*).

★ 424 ★

Registered Nurses' Salaries

Wages and salaries of registered nursing personnel, 1988.

Characteristic	Dollars
Full-time head nurse:	
Lowest mean annual salary paid	$26,859
Highest mean annual salary paid	$30,557
Registered nurse, full-time:	
Lowest mean hourly wage paid	$10.51
Highest mean hourly wage paid	$14.02
Mean hourly wage paid	$12.17
Registered nurse, part-time:	
Lowest mean hourly wage paid	$10.55
Highest mean hourly wage paid	$13.77

Source: Selected from "Hospital Registered Nursing Personnel-Summary: 1988," *Statistical Abstract of the United States 1990*, 1990, p. 104. Primary source: American Hospital Association, Chicago, IL, *Report of the Hospital Nursing Personnel Survey, 1988*. Also in source: other characteristics of registered nurses. Based on a sample of 1,402 (20%) U.S. hospitals registered and unregistered by the American Hospital Association, with a response rate of 58%. See source for an explanation of "mean."

★ 425 ★

Salaries in Mathematics

Median salaries in mathematics for PhDs with one year of experience, by type of employer, 1986.

Type of employer	Women	Men
Teaching or teaching and research	$28,500	$30,500
Business and industry	36,000	42,000

Source: "Median salaries in mathematics for Ph.D.'s with one year of experience by type of employer and sex, 1986," *The Changing Role of Women in Research and Development*, 1988, p. 69 (Philadelphia: Wharton School of the University of Pennsylvania, 1988). Primary source: *Salaries of Scientists, Engineers, and Technicians* (Washington, D>C>: Commission on Professionals in Science and Technology, 1987), p. 75. Data from American Mathematical Society.

★ 426 ★

Salary Offers to Degree Candidates

Annual salary offered to candidates for degrees by field of study, 1989.

Field of study	Bachelor's	Master's
Accounting	$25,290	$28,874
Business, general	22,274	33,903
Marketing	22,523	34,462
Humanities	23,010	25,799
Social Sciences	20,205	23,814
Computer Science	28,557	35,823

Source: "Selected from "Salary Offers to Candidates for Degrees, by Field of Study: 1980 to 1989," *Statistical Abstract*, p. 161. Primary source: College Placement Council, Inc., Bethlehem, PA, *Salary Survey, A Study of Beginning Offers*, annual. In dollars. Data are average beginning salaries based on offers made by business, industrial, government, and nonprofit and educational employers to graduating students. Data from representative colleges throughout U.S.

★ 427 ★

Sales Occupations Earnings

Number of workers in thosuands and median weekly earnings of full-time wage and salary workers in sales occupations, 1988.

Occupation	Both sexes		Women		Men	
	Number of workers (thousands)	Median weekly earnings	Number of workers (thousands)	Median weekly earnings	Number of workers (thousands)	Median weekly earnings
Sales occupations	7,741	$385	3,222	$264	4,519	$488
Supervisors and proprietors	2,266	419	788	322	1,478	489
Sales representatives, finance and business services	1,476	493	616	395	860	595
Insurance sales	335	481	124	389	211	581
Real estate sales	351	512	170	446	181	613
Securities and financial services sales	250	614	73	408	177	768
Advertising and related sales	121	445	63	369	58	517
Sales occupations, other business services	419	456	186	351	233	522
Sales representatives, commodities, except retail	1,302	539	234	411	1,068	583
Sales workers, retail and personal services	2,683	229	1,578	199	1,105	315
Sales workers, motor vehicles and boats	234	439	16	1	218	448
Sales workers, apparel	166	207	131	199	35	1
Sales workers, furniture and home furnishings	104	354	39	1	64	366
Sales workers, radio, television, hi-fi, and appliances	104	322	31	1	73	379

[Continued]

★ 427 ★

Sales Occupations Earnings
[Continued]

Occupation	Both sexes		Women		Men	
	Number of workers (thousands)	Median weekly earnings	Number of workers (thousands)	Median weekly earnings	Number of workers (thousands)	Median weekly earnings
Sales workers, hardware and building supplies	139	300	25	[1]	114	315
Sales workers, parts	131	323	11	[1]	120	330
Sales workers, other commodities	652	217	456	204	196	280
Sales counter clerks	94	213	66	197	28	[1]
Cashiers	936	192	742	185	194	222
Street and door-to-door sales	68	302	36	[1]	32	[1]

Source: Selected from "Median weekly earnings of full-time wage and salary workers by detailed occupation and sex, 1983-88," *Handbook of Labor Statistics,* 1989, p. 194-198 (Washington, D.C.: U.S. Department of Labor, August 1989). Also in source: detailed data by other occupations, 1983-1988. *Note:* 1. Data not shown where base less than 50,000.

★ 428 ★

Scientists & Engineers-Average Salaries
Average annual salaries of scientists and engineers by race/ethnicity, 1986.

Field	Total[1]	White	Black	Asian	Native American	Hispanic[2]
Total, all fields	$38,400	$38,700	$31,500	$39,100	$41,000	$34,600
Women	29,900	30,200	26,200	30,100	29,800	25,200
Men	39,800	40,000	33,500	40,700	42,600	36,600
Scientists, total	35,700	35,900	29,000	37,000	40,500	30,600
Women	29,000	29,400	25,400	28,800	29,100	22,900
Men	38,000	38,100	31,400	40,500	44,100	33,900
Physical scientists	40,700	40,900	35,600	39,300	63,400	41,300
Women	31,300	31,800	24,300	31,400	[3]	33,900
Men	42,000	42,000	39,300	42,200	63,400	43,100
Mathematical scientists	39,800	40,000	37,000	38,500	22,500	38,700
Women	31,000	31,000	32,900	30,600	25,000	31,000
Men	42,500	42,800	38,400	39,300	19,900	42,100
Computer specialists	37,300	37,500	32,200	37,400	39,300	31,500
Women	33,200	33,700	29,300	30,800	20,500	25,800
Men	38,900	39,000	34,200	39,600	42,400	33,800
Environmental scientists	37,500	37,600	31,800	40,600	27,000	40,500
Women	30,100	30,100	36,100	35,100	28,000	21,200
Men	38,400	38,500	29,600	41,100	26,700	42,400
Life scientists	33,100	33,200	29,300	35,700	40,600	29,700
Women	25,200	25,100	21,600	28,400	32,500	18,700
Men	35,400	35,400	33,000	40,500	46,500	35,200
Psychologists	33,400	33,900	26,800	22,500	41,200	25,400

[Continued]

★ 428 ★

Scientists & Engineers-Average Salaries
[Continued]

Field	Total[1]	White	Black	Asian	Native American	Hispanic[2]
Women	29,000	29,700	26,600	19,300	37,400	24,000
Men	36,500	36,600	27,400	39,600	41,900	26,400
Social scientists	31,800	32,200	22,800	38,700	34,300	25,600
Women	25,000	25,200	21,400	31,700	21,500	18,700
Men	34,700	35,100	23,800	41,900	39,100	28,500
Engineers, total	40,800	41,000	35,700	40,500	41,300	38,000
Women	34,300	34,300	32,900	35,000	34,700	33,900
Men	41,100	41,200	35,900	40,800	41,500	38,300

Source: "Average annual salaries of scientists and engineers, by field, gender, and racial/ethnic group: 1986," *Women and Minorities in Science and Engineering*, 1990, p. 119 (Washington, D.C.: National Science Foundation, January 1990). Primary source: National Science Foundation, SRS. Also in source: salary breakdown by field. *Notes:* 1. Detail will not average to total because (a) racial and ethnic categories are not mutually exclusive and (b) total employed includes other and no report. 2. Includes members of all racial groups. 3. Too few cases to estimate.

★ 429 ★

Service Occupations Earnings

Number of workers in thousands and median weekly earnings of full-time wage and salary workers, service occupations, 1988.

Occupation	Both sexes Number of workers (thousands)	Both sexes Median weekly earnings	Women Number of workers (thousands)	Women Median weekly earnings	Men Number of workers (thousands)	Men Median weekly earnings
Service occupations	8,669	$245	4,352	$208	4,317	$299
Private household	328	140	320	139	8	[1]
Child care workers	154	119	153	119	1	[1]
Cleaners and servants	152	160	147	158	4	[1]
Protective services	1,747	417	204	347	1,543	424
Supervisors	180	583	14	[1]	167	589
Police and detectives	100	603	11	[1]	90	607
Firefighting and fire prevention	216	501	7	[1]	209	503
Firefighting	198	503	5	[1]	192	504
Police and detectives	750	476	99	430	650	484
Police and detectives, public service	425	522	42	[1]	384	523
Sheriffs, bailiffs, and other law enforcement officers	108	401	18	[1]	89	399
Correctional institution officers	217	409	39	[1]	178	411
Guards	601	267	84	250	517	269
Guards and police, except public services	560	273	68	283	491	272
Service occupations, exc. private household and protective	6,594	225	3,828	210	2,766	257
Food preparation and service occupations	2,404	205	1,328	192	1,077	225
Supervisors	216	267	119	222	97	323
Bartenders	160	240	78	208	82	288
Waiters and waitresses	561	189	432	179	129	230
Cooks, exc. short order	888	215	415	197	473	240
Food counter, fountain, and related occupations	65	161	46	[1]	19	[1]
Kitchen workers, food preparation	60	179	44	[1]	16	[1]
Waiters' and waitresses' assistants	121	191	43	[1]	79	183
Miscellaneous food preparation occupations	288	183	131	194	157	176
Health service occupations	1,438	236	1,259	230	179	277

[Continued]

★ 429 ★

Service Occupations Earnings
[Continued]

Occupation	Both sexes		Women		Men	
	Number of workers (thousands)	Median weekly earnings	Number of workers (thousands)	Median weekly earnings	Number of workers (thousands)	Median weekly earnings
Dental assistants	104	267	102	267	2	1
Health aides, exc. nursing	290	273	238	265	52	317
Nursing aides, orderlies, and attendants	1,044	221	920	217	125	263
Cleaning and building service occupations	1,999	250	686	207	1,313	279
Supervisors	151	352	49	1	102	425
Maids and housemen	398	201	324	196	74	234
Janitors and cleaners	1,397	259	308	213	1,089	272
Personal service occupations	752	232	555	222	198	267
Hairdressers and cosmetologists	268	237	241	229	27	1
Attendants, amusement and recreation facilities	62	282	23	1	40	1
Child care workers	157	187	139	179	17	1

Source: Selected from "Median weekly earnings of full-time wage and salary workers by detailed occupation and sex, 1983-88," *Handbook of Labor Statistics,* 1989, p. 194-198 (Washington, D.C.: U.S. Department of Labor, August 1989). Also in source: detailed data by other occupations, 1983-1988. *Note:* 1. Data not shown where base less than 50,000.

★ 430 ★

Sex-Based Wage Discrimination: An Overview

Some facts about wage discrimination, according to the National Committee on Pay Equity.

1. Of all women employed in 1986, **76%** were in non-professional occupations.

2. To achieve a fully sex-integrated workforce, **59%** of women would have to change jobs.

3. A 1986 study by the National Academy of Sciences found that each additional percentage point female in an occupation was associated with **$42** less in median annual earnings.

4. **59.5%** of black women work in only 2 of 12 major occupations; **53.3%** of white women are employed in those occupations (clerical and service work).

Source: "Sex-Based Wage Discrimination," mimeographed (Washington, D.C.: National Committee on Pay Equity). Also in source: other examples of sex-based wage discrimination; a discussion of race-based wage discrimination.

★ 431 ★

Social Scientists'/Social Workers' Earnings

Median weekly earnings of full-time wage and salary workers in the social sciences/social work, 1988.

Occupation	Median weekly earnings		
	Both sexes	Women	Men
Social scientists and urban planners	$596	$531	676
Economists	673	[1]	719
Psychologists	518	498	560
Social, recreation, and religious workers	405	395	414
Social workers	425	420	434
Recreation workers	275	[1]	[1]
Clergy	402	[1]	407

Source: Selected from "Median weekly earnings of full-time wage and salary workers by detailed occupation and sex, 1983-88," *Handbook of Labor Statistics,* 1989, p. 194-198 (Washington, D.C.: U.S. Department of Labor, August 1989). Also in source: detailed data by other occupations, 1983-1988. *Note:* 1. Data not shown where base less than 50,000.

★ 432 ★

Teacher Salaries

Average annual salary of instructional staff.

Year ending	Average Ann. Salary	Percent change from	
		1979-89	previous yr.
1980	$16,715	...	...
1981	18,404	10.1%	10.1%
1982	20,327	21.6%	10.4%
1983	21,641	29.5%	6.5%
1984	23,005	37.6%	6.3%
1985	24,666	47.6%	7.2%
1986	26,361	57.7%	6.9%
1987	27,707	65.8%	5.1%
1988	29,231	74.9%	5.5%
1989	31,003	85.5%	6.1%
1990	32,574	94.9%	5.1%

Source: Estimates of School Statistics 1989-1990, p. 16 (Washington, D.C.: National Education Association, 1990). Also in source: Estimated average annual salaries by state. In the computation of the national average, each state average is weighted by its number of instructional staff members. *Notes:* 1. Instructional staff is comprised of classroom teachers, principals, supervisors, and other instructional personnel.

★ 433 ★

Teachers' Salaries Compared to Salaries in Private Industry

Average starting salary of public school teachers compared with salaries in private industry, 1988.

Field	Salary
Teachers	$19,400
Engineering	$29,856
Accounting	$25,140
Economic-Finance	$23,928
Computer Science	$26,904

Source: Selected from "Average Starting Salary of Public School Teachers Compared with Salaries in Private Industry: 1975-1988," *The World Almanac and Book of Facts 1991*, p. 211 (New York: Pharos Books, 1991). Primary source: Northwestern Univ. Placement Center, *The Northwestern Lindquist-Endicott Report*. Salaries represent what corporations plan to offer graduates graduating in the year shown with bachelor's degrees. Based on survey of approximately 200 companies.

★ 434 ★

Teachers' and Counselors' Earnings

Median weekly earnings of full-time wage and salary workers in teaching and counseling, 1988.

Occupation	Median weekly earnings		
	Both sexes	Women	Men
Teachers, college and university	$676	$555	$752
Teachers, except college and university	487	463	560
Teachers, prekindergarten and kindergarten	321	320	[1]
Teachers, elementary school	481	476	522
Teachers, secondary school	521	491	580
Teachers, special education	489	485	[1]
Counselors, educational and vocational	562	522	599

Source: Selected from "Median weekly earnings of full-time wage and salary workers by detailed occupation and sex, 1983-88," *Handbook of Labor Statistics*, 1989, p. 194-98 (Washington, D.C.: U.S. Department of Labor, August 1989). Also in source: detailed data by occupation for 1983-88.

★ 435 ★

Technical Communicators: Part 1

Comparison of U.S. economic indicators to Society for Technical Communicators salaries, 1970-1988.

Year	GNP[1]	CPI[2]	STC salaries
1970	Parity	Parity	$13,000
1974	+45%	+127%	$15,000
1979	+154%	+189%	$20,000
1988	+292%	+280%	$30,500

Source: Russell B. Stoner, "Economic Consequences of Feminizing Technical Communications," *Proceedings, 35th ITCC, Philadelphia, 1988, Freedom to Communicate*, Society for Technical Communication, May 10, 1988, pp. MPD-109. *Notes:* 1. Gross National Product. 2. Consumer Price Index.

★ 436 ★

Technical Communicators: Part 2

Change in sexual profile, Society for Technical Communcations, 1970-1988, by percent of total membership.

Year	Women	Men
1970	20%	80%
1979	38%	59%
1983	48.5%	51.5%
1988	53%	47%

Source: Russell B. Stoner, "Economic Consequences of Feminizing Technical Communications," *Proceedings, 35th ITCC, Philadelphia, 1988, Freedom to Communicate,* Society for Technical Communication, May 10, 1988, pp. MPD-109.

★ 437 ★

Technical, Sales, Administrative Support Earnings

Number of workers in thousands and median weekly earnings of full-time wage and salary workers in technical, sales, and administrative support, 1988.

Occupation	Both sexes		Women		Men	
	Number of workers (thousands)	Median weekly earnings	Number of workers (thousands)	Median weekly earnings	Number of workers (thousands)	Median weekly earnings
Technical, sales, and administrative support	24,931	$347	15,664	$305	9,267	$472
Technicians and related support	2,960	448	1,313	384	1,647	510
Health technologists and technicians	909	367	718	355	191	413
Clinical laboratory technologists and technicians	216	417	160	399	57	484
Radiologic technicians	107	422	81	417	27	[1]
Licensed practical nurses	299	336	282	336	17	[1]
Engineering and related technologists and technicians	854	479	159	402	695	495
Electrical and electronic technicians	303	496	47	[1]	256	509
Drafting occupations	268	463	42	[1]	226	479
Surveying and mapping technicians	73	419	10	[1]	63	426
Science technicians	197	415	58	377	139	434
Chemical technicians	82	469	23	[1]	59	484
Technicians, except health, engineering, and space	1,000	529	378	451	622	605
Airplane pilots and navigators	60	811	1	[1]	59	823
Computer programmers	532	588	168	497	364	623
Legal assistants	174	421	138	413	36	[1]

Source: Selected from "Median weekly earnings of full-time wage and salary workers by detailed occupation and sex, 1983-88," *Handbook of Labor Statistics,* 1989, p. 194-198 (Washington, D.C.: U.S. Department of Labor, August 1989). Also in source: detailed data by other occupations, 1983-1988. *Note:* 1. Data not shown where base less than 50,000.

★ 438 ★

Union Status and Earnings

Median weekly earnings of full-time and salary workers by union status and sex, 1983-1988.

Year	Women		Men	
	Union member	Non-union	Union member	Non-union
1988	$403	$300	$506	$416
1987	388	288	494	406
1986	368	274	482	394
1985	350	262	465	383
1984	326	251	444	362
1983	307	238	411	353

Source: "Median weekly earnings of full-time and salary workers, by unions status and sex, 1983-1988," *Facts on Working Women,* No. 89-2, August 1989, p. 2. Data refer to members of a labor union or an employee association similar to a union.

★ 439 ★

Union Status and Earnings Ratios

Women's median weekly earnings as a percent of men's, by union membership status, 1983-1988.

Year	Earnings as % of men's	
	Union member	Nonunion
1988	79.6%	72.1%
1987	78.5%	70.9%
1986	76.3%	69.5%
1985	72.3%	68.4%
1984	73.4%	69.3%
1983	74.4%	67.4%

Source: "Women's Median Weekly Earnings as a Percent of Men's, by Membership Status, 1983-1988," *Facts on Working Women,* No. 89-2, August 1989, p. 3. Data refer to members of a labor union or an employee association similar to a union.

★ 440 ★

Wage Differentials: Selected Countries: 1973-1983

Women's wages as a percentage of men's, selected countries, 1973-1983.

Country	1973	1975	1977	1979	1981	1983
Austria	63.1%	64.4%	63.1%	-	-	77.5%
Australia	70.0%	-	82.0%	-	-	-
Denmark (hourly)	79.2%	83.2%	85.2%	84.7%	84.5%	-
Germany, Federal Republic of	70.3%	72.3%	72.7%	72.6%	72.5%	-
France						
Manual	75.8%	-	74.6%	-	-	-
Nonmanual	58.0%	-	66.2%	-	-	-
Italy						
Manual	75.5%	80.0%	83.1%	-	-	-

[Continued]

★ 440 ★

Wage Differentials: Selected Countries: 1973-1983
[Continued]

Country	1973	1975	1977	1979	1981	1983
Nonmanual	61.9%	-	68.8%	-	-	-
Sweden						
Manual	84.1%	85.2%	87.4%	89.3%	90.1%	-
United Kingdom	62.5%	67.6%	71.9%	70.7%	69.5%	-
Nonmanual	45.1%	-	54.6%	-	-	-
United States	56.6%	57.0%	58.9%	59.7%	59.2%	64.3%

Source: "Wage Differentials Between Women and Men (Nonagricultural; Percent Women/Men)," *Working Women: Past, Present, Future,* 1987, p. 344 (Washington, D.C.: Bureau of National Affairs, Inc., 1987). Primary source: Centre for Social Development and Humanitarian Affairs, Department of International Economic and Social Affairs, "Some Aspects of the Role of Women in Economic Development, Part II," unpublished paper prepared for the *Seminar on the Economic Role of Women in the ECE Region,* Vienna, October 1984, pp. 19,21; Ratner (1980); Cook, Lorwin, and Daniels (1984), p. 90; U.S. Department of Labor, Women's Bureau, *Time of Change: 1983 Handbook on Women Workers,* Bull. 298 (Washington, 1983); Eurostat (1981).

★ 441 ★

Wages in Agriculture: Selected Countries

Earnings or rates in agriculture per hour, day, week, or month, selected countries, latest available year.

Country, type, unit and year	Total	Women	Men
Africa			
Kenya (EG/m-Shillings), 1987	794.3	553.0	864.4
South America			
Netherlands Antilles (EG/m-Guilders), 1985	1213	992	1326
St. Lucia (RT/h-Dollars), 1985	-	1.05	1.20
Asia			
Cyprus (EG/w-Pounds), 1987	49.63	41.89	65.12
Japan (EG/d-Yen), 1987	-	4783	6245
Korea, Republic of (RT/d-Won), 1986	-	7254	10142
Philippines (RT/d-Pesos), 1985	23.74	22.93	24.55
Sri Lanka (EG/d-Rupees), 1987	-	23.45	25.23
Europe			
Austria (RT/m-Schillings), 1987	-	9866	10006
Belgium (EG/d-Francs), 1985	-	1076.7	1697.2
Finland (EG/h-Markkaa), 1987	-	23.71	26.52
Luxembourg (EG/h-Francs), 1984	151.40	155.89	151.17
Norway (EG/h-Kroner), 1987	-	51.81	54.15
Portugal (EG/d-Escudos), 1984	-	522.50	754.10
Switzerland (EG/h-Francs), 1987	-	12.36	15.63

[Continued]

★ 441 ★

Wages in Agriculture: Selected Countries
[Continued]

Country, type, unit and year	Total	Women	Men
Sweden (EG/h-Kronor), 1987	58.23	56.22	58.60
Turkey (EG/d-Liras), 1984	12774	11738	12834
United Kingdom (EG/w-Pounds), 1986	-	111.37	142.51
Oceania			
Australia (EG/w-Dollars), 1986	287	237	293
New Zealand (EG/h-Dollars), 1986	11.40	8.50	11.50

Source: "Wages in agriculture," *Year Book of Labour Statistics,* 1988, p. 891-898 (Geneva: International Labour Office, 1988). Also in source: data for other countries. Earnings (EG) or rates (RT) per hour (h), day (d), week (w) or month (m). See source for detailed explanation and extensive footnotes.

★ 442 ★

Wages in Manufacturing: Selected Countries

Earnings or rates per hour, day, week, or month, in manufacturing, latest available year, selected countries.

Country, type, unit and year	Total	Women	Men
Africa			
Kenya (EG/m-Shillings), 1987[1,2]	2293.8	1551.1	2376.7
Swaziland (EG/m-Emalangeni), 1986	-	572	946
Tanzania (EG/m-Shillings), 1981	973	773	993
South America			
El Salvador (EG/h-Colones), 1985	-	2.90	3.57
Netherlands Antilles (EG/m-Guilders), 1986	2,158	1,456	2,260
Asia			
Burma (EG/m-Kyats)	-	243.63	282.18
Korea, Republic of (EG/m-Won), 1987	328696	207906	413348
Singapore (EG/m-Dollars), 1987	772.69	611.78	1047.00
Sri Lanka (EG/h-Rupees), 1987	5.96	4.55	6.39
Europe			
Belgium (EG/m-Francs), 1986	73663	50207	81295
Czechoslovakia (EG/m-Koruny), 1987	2958	2297	3383
Denmark (EG/h-Kroner), 1987	86.76	75.92	90.18
Finland (EG/h-Markkaa),1987	36.48	30.28	39.18
France (EG/h-Francs), 1987	40.97	34.35	43.39
Germany, Federal Republic (EG/h-Mark)	17.53	13.60	18.62

[Continued]

★ 442 ★

Wages in Manufacturing: Selected Countries
[Continued]

Country, type, unit and year	Total	Women	Men
Gibraltar (EG/w-Pounds), 1987	152.74	118.63	158.66
Greece (EG/h-Drachmas), 1987	388.20	333.70	430.20
Ireland (EG/h-Pounds), 1987	4.70	3.59	5.33
Luxembourg (EG/h-Francs), 1987	345.30	358.10	217.60
Netherlands (EG/h-Guilders), 1986	19.42	15.35	20.53
Norway (EG/h-Kroner), 1987	78.64	67.83	81.00
Switzerland (EG/h-Francs), 1987	-	13.81	20.51
Sweden (EG/h-Kronor), 1987	67.04	61.67	68.48
United Kingdom (EG/h-Pounds),1987	4.227	3.095	4.551
Oceania			
Australia (EG/h-Dollars), 1986	9.95	8.34	10.43
New Zealand (EG/h-Dollars), 1986	10.01	7.80	10.87

Source: "Wages in manufacturing," *Year Book of Labour Statistics*, 1988, p. 811-820 (Geneva: International Labour Office, 1988). Also in source: data for other countries. Earnings (EG) or rates (RT) per hour (h), day (d), week (w) or month (m). See source for detailed explanation and extensive footnotes.

★ 443 ★

Wages in Non-Agricultural Activities: Selected Countries

Earnings or rates per hour, day, week, or month in non-agricultural activities, selected countries.

Country, type, unit, month, year	Total	Female	Male
Asia			
Hong Kong (RT/d, March 1990	178.40	152.30	217.40
Japan (EG/m-Yen), February 1990	245 574	153 624	301 105
Korea, Republic of (EG/m-Won), December 1987	540 611	234 071	467 286
Europe			
Belgium (EG/h-Francs), December 1988	310.35	245.25	327.07
Denmark (EG/h-Kroner), December 1989	-	92.81	112.17
France (EG/h-Francs), April 1988	41.25	35.17	42.98
Germany, Federal Republic (EG/h-Mark), January 1990	19.50	15.01	20.48
Luxembourg (EG/h-Francs), December 1988	339.10	219.70	348.10
Netherlands (EG/h-Guilders), December 1989	19.80	16.49	21.46
United Kingdom (Eg/h-Pounds), December 1984	-	2.549	3.667

[Continued]

★ 443 ★

Wages in Non-Agricultural Activities: Selected Countries
[Continued]

Country, type, unit, month, year	Total	Female	Male
Oceania			
New Zealand (EG/h-Dollars), May 1989	13.14	11.61	14.25

Source: "Wages in non-agricultural activities," *Bulletin of Labour Statistics*, 1990-3, p. 89-96. Earnings (EG) or rates (RT) per hour (h), day (d), week (w) or month (m).

★ 444 ★

Wages of Females as a Percentage of Wages of Males
Wages of females as a percentage of wages of males, 1977, 1980, and 1986.

Country or Area	1977	1980	1986
Developing countries or areas			
Cyprus	49.6%	50.2%	56.1%
El Salvador	80.8%	81.2%	81.5%[1]
Hong Kong	-	77.7%	77.9%
Kenya	55.6%	62.5%	75.6%[1]
Korea, Republic of	44.7%	45.1%	48.5%
Singapore	-	61.5%	63.4%[1]
Sri Lanka	-	75.4%	75.5%
Developed countries			
Belgium	70.7%	69.7%	74.1%
Czechoslovakia	67.4%	67.9%	67.9%
Denmark	86.5%	86.1%	84.9%
Finland	74.3%	75.4%	77.4%
France	75.8%	77.0%	79.5%
Germany, Federal Republic of	72.3%	72.7%	72.9%
Greece	68.8%	67.8%	76.9%
Ireland	61.2%	68.7%	68.7%
Japan	46.0%	43.6%	42.5%
Luxembourg	62.5%	61.2%	59.8%
Netherlands	75.5%	75.3%	74.3%
New Zealand	73.3%	71.4%	71.8%
Norway	79.8%	81.9%	83.8%
Switzerland	65.4%	66.4%	67.4%
Sweden	87.4%	89.9%	90.4%
United Kingdom	70.8%	68.8%	67.9%

Source: "Wages of Females as a Percentage of Wages of Males, *1989 Report on the World Social Situation, p. 13* (New York: United Nations, 1989). Primary source: ILO *Year Book of Labour Statistics,* 1987 (Geneva, 1987). *Note:* 1. Based on 1985.

★ 445 ★

Weekly Earnings by Occupation

Median weekly earnings of full-time wage and salary workers by occupation, 1988.

Occupation	Number of workers (thousands)	Median weekly earnings	
		Women	Men
Total, 16 years and over	82,692	$315	$449
Managerial and professional specialty	21,770	462	666
Executive, administrative, and managerial	10,725	430	682
Professional specialty	11,045	485	651
Technical, sales, and administrative support	24,931	305	472
Sales occupations	7,741	264	488
Administrative support, including clerical	14,230	305	418
Service occupations	8,669	208	299
Service occupations, exc. private household & protective	6,594	210	257
Precision production, craft, and repair	11,175	302	446
Operators, fabricators, and laborers	14,763	238	352
Transportation and material moving occupations	3,853	286	394
Handlers, equipment cleaners, helpers, and laborers	3,505	237	287
Farming, forestry, and fishing	1,383	201	234

Source: Selected from "Median weekly earnings of full-time wage and salary workers by detailed occupation and sex, 1983-88," *Handbook of Labor Statistics,* 1989, p. 194-198 (Washington, D.C.: U.S. Department of Labor, August 1989). Also in source: data for 1983-1987; data by detailed occupation and sex.

★ 446 ★

Weekly Earnings: 1980-1988

Median weekly earnings of full-time wage and salary workers by race, 1980-1988.

Race	1980	1981	1982	1983	1984	1985	1986	1987	1988
Total, 16 years and over	$261	$283	$302	$313	$326	$343	$358	$373	$385
Women, 16 years and over	201	219	238	252	265	277	290	303	315
Men, 16 years and over	312	339	364	378	391	406	419	433	449
White women, 16 years and over	202	220	241	254	268	281	294	307	318
White men, 16 years and over	319	349	375	387	400	417	433	450	465
Black women, 16 years and over	185	205	217	231	241	252	263	275	288
Black men, 16 years and over	244	268	278	293	302	304	318	326	347

Source: Selected from "Median weekly earnings of full-time wage and salary workers by age, race, and sex, 1979-88," *Handbook of Labor Statistics,* 1989, p. 161-62 (Washington, D.C.: U.S. Department of Labor, August 1989). Also in source: detailed data by age and sex; data for 1979. Data refer to the sole or principal job of full-time workers. Excluded are self-employed workers whose businesses are incorporated although they technically qualify as wage and salary workers.

★ 447 ★

Women's Earnings as Percent of Men's: 1979-1988

Women's earnings as percent of men's: 1979-1988.

Year	Hourly	Weekly	Annual
1979	64.1%	62.5%	60.0%
1980	64.8%	64.4%	59.7%
1981	65.1%	64.6%	59.9%
1982	67.3%	65.4%	62.0%
1983	69.4%	66.7%	63.3%
1984	69.8%	67.8%	63.0%
1985	70.0%	68.2%	63.3%
1986	70.2%	69.2%	63.6%
1987	72.1%	70.0%	64.8%
1988	73.8%	70.2%	66.0%

Source: "Women's earnings as percent of men's," *Facts on Working Women,* No. 90-3, October 1990, p. 2.

★ 448 ★

Worldwide Earnings Ratios in Manufacturing

Average earnings of women in manufacturing as a percentage of men's, 1960-1982.

Country, area	Time period	1960	1970	1975	1980	1982
Africa						
Egypt	week	51.6%	69.5%	67.8%	63.1%	-
Kenya	month	71.3%	-	66.1%	62.5%	75.8%
United Republic of Tanzania	month	-	78.6%	70.0%	78.5%	-
America						
Costa Rica	month	-	-	-	56.8%	-
El Salvador	hour	73.0%	81.9%	90.4%	81.2%	85.9%
United States	year	-	-	54.6%	57.3%	57.6%
Asia						
Burma	month	72.1%	83.65	88.5%	86.1%	88.8%
Cyprus	week	-	-	46.9%	50.2%	56.3%
Japan	month	-	44.5%	47.9%	43.4%	43.1%
Jordan	day	-	-	54.1%	57.5%	63.6%
Korea, Rubublic of	month	-	-	47.4%	45.1%	45.1%
Singapore	hour	-	-	-	61.5%	63.2%
Sri Lanka	hour	-	-	-	80.8%	81.9%
Syrian Arab Republic	week	-	59.9%	69.8%	68.8%	-
Europe						
Austria	hour	-	-	68.0%	72.0%	-
Belgium	hour	64.6%	67.7%	71.3%	69.7%	73.5%

[Continued]

★ 448 ★

Worldwide Earnings Ratios in Manufacturing
[Continued]

Country, area	Time period	1960	1970	1975	1980	1982
Denmark	hour	66.5%	74.4%	84.3%	86.1%	85.1%
Finland	hour	66.4%	70.4%	72.6%	75.4%	77.2%
France	hour	70.4%	76.7%	76.4%	77.0%	78.1%
Germany, Federal Republic	hour	65.6%	69.6%	72.1%	72.7%	73.0%
Greece	hour	64.7%	68.0%	69.5%	67.8%	73.1%
Ireland	hour	59.2%	56.2%	60.9%	68.7%	68.5%
Netherlands	hour	61.7%	71.8%	79.2%	80.2%	79.2%
Norway	hour	67.3%	75.1%	78.0%	81.9%	83.2%
Sweden	hour	68.8%	82.4%	85.2%	89.9%	90.3%
Switzerland	hour	63.3%	64.7%	66.0%	66.4%	67.0%
United Kingdom	hour	58.6%	57.6%	66.5%	68.8%	68.8%
Oceania						
Australia	hour	58.0%	63.7%	78.5%	78.6%	78.2%
New Zealand	hour	-	65.8%	65.6%	71.4%	71.1%

Source: Selected from "Average earnings of women workers in the manufacturing industry as a percentage of men's, 1960-1982," *World Survey on the Role of Women in Development,* 1986, p. 84-85 (New York: United Nations, 1986). Primary source: *Yearbook of Labour Statistics,* various issues (Geneva, International Labour Office); national statistics of Costa Rica and the United States; Caja Costarricense de seguro social, *Estadistica patronos, trabajadores y salarios, 1978,* San Jose; US Bureau of the Census, *Money Incomes of Families and Persons in the United States,* various editions. See source for extensive notes on sources. Data refer to manual workers, unless otherwise indicated.

Wealth and Poverty

★ 449 ★

Children in Poverty
Percent of children under 18 living in poverty: 1970-1987.

Year	Children in female-headed families				All children in families			
	Total	White	Black	Hispanic[1]	Total	White	Black	Hispanic[1]
1970	45.8%	36.6%	60.8%	---	14.9%	10.5%	41.5%	---
1975	51.4%	41.7%	70.1%	42.9%	16.8%	12.5%	41.4%	34.5%
1980	52.8%	41.3%	75.4%	47.1%	17.9%	13.4%	42.1%	33.0%
1981	52.2%	42.0%	74.3%	48.5%	19.5%	14.7%	44.2%	35.4%
1982	---	---	---	---	21.3%	16.5%	47.3%	38.9%
1983	50.0%	39.3%	74.5%	42.5%	21.8%	17.0%	46.2%	37.7%
1984	52.4%	41.8%	74.9%	47.2%	21.0%	16.1%	46.2%	38.7%
1985	53.8%	43.0%	78.4%	49.6%	20.1%	15.6%	43.1%	39.6%

[Continued]

★ 449 ★

Children in Poverty
[Continued]

Year	Children in female-headed families				All children in families			
	Total	White	Black	Hispanic[1]	Total	White	Black	Hispanic[1]
1986	56.6%	45.7%	80.5%	49.5%	19.8%	15.3%	42.6%	37.1%
1987	56.7%	46.0%	79.0%	47.2%	20.0%	15.0%	45.1%	39.3%

Source: Selected from "Children in Poverty," *The Condition of Education 1990, Volume 1: Elementary and Secondary Education,* p. 64 (Washington, D.C.: National Center for Education Statistics, 1990). Primary source: U.S. Department of Commerce, Bureau of the Census, *Current Population Reports,* Series P-60, "Poverty in the United States:...," various years. Also in source: data for 1960, 1965. *Note:* 1. Hispanics may be of any race.

★ 450 ★

Elderly Women and Economic Security: An Overview
Summary of an article by Representative Olympia J. Snowe on the economic aspects of old age, as reported in *National Business Woman.*

What women have to look forward to in retirement:

In 1987, **15%** of women aged 65 and older were poor, compared to 9% of men the same age.

A woman over 65 years of age has a **60% greater chance** of living in poverty than a man of the same age.

In 1988, **77%** of senior citizens who lived alone were women. This percentage is projected to rise to **85%** by the year 2020.

It is estimated that in 1987, Medicare paid for **33%** of the health costs of single older women, compared to 49% for single older men and 44% for older couples.

In 1987, the median income of women over 65 was **$6,425** compared to $11,500 for men.

As of 1984, **20%** of women 65 and over received any pension income, compared to 43% of men.

Source: Olympia J. Snowe, "Older Women and Economic Security," *National Business Woman,* Feb/Mar 1989, p. 27+. Also in source: A discussion of the provisions of the 1984 Retirement Equity Act.

★ 451 ★

Home Ownership and Value of Owned Home

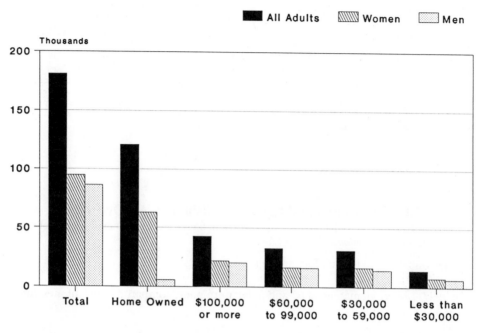

Number of persons and number who own homes, in thousands, and value of owned homes.

	Total	Home Owned	Value of Owned Home			
			$100,000 or more	$60,000- 99,000	$30,000- 59,000	Less than $30,000
All Adults	180,974	121,141	42,694	33,035	31,216	14,195
Women	94,667	63,081	22,133	16,599	16,647	7,703
Men	86,307	58,060	20,561	16,436	14,570	6,493

Source: Selected from *Mediamark Research Multimedia Audiences Report, Spring 1990*, p. 52-53 (New York: Mediamark Research Inc., 1990).

★ 452 ★

Shareholders in Public Corporations

Shareholders in public corporations, 1965-1985.

Characteristic	1985	1983	1981	1980	1975	1970	1965
Adult female shareowners (thousands)	22,509	20,385	14,154	13,696	11,750	14,290	9,430
Adult male shareowners (thousands)	22,484	19,226	15,785	14,196	11,630	14,340	9,060

Source: "Shareholders in Public Corporations," *Information Please Almanac*, 1990, p. 54 (Boston: Houghton Mifflin Company), 1990. Primary source: New York Stock Exchange.

★ 453 ★

The Elderly Poor: 1970-1987

Persons 65 years old and over below poverty level, 1970 to 1987.

Characteristic	Number, in thousands, below poverty level				
	1970	1979[1]	1985	1986	1987
Persons, 65 years and over[2]	4,793	3,682	3,456	3,477	3,491
In families	2,013	1,380	1,173	1,164	1,247
Householder	1,188	822	708	716	751
Female	209	193	210	196	218
Male	980	629	498	520	533
Unrelated individuals	2,779	2,299	2,281	2,311	2,241
Female	2,230	1,871	1,879	1,899	1,825
Male	549	482	402	412	416

Source: "Persons 65 years old and over below poverty level, by selected characteristics: 1970 to 1987," *Statistical Abstract of the United States 1990*, 1990, p. 460. Primary source: U.S. Bureau of the Census, *Current Population Reports*, series P-60, No. 161, and unpublished data. Also in source: data by other characteristics. Persons as of March of following year. Based on old processing procedures; therefore data will not agree with other tables. *Notes:* 1. Population controls based on 1980 census. 2. Beginning 1979, includes members of unrelated subfamilies not shown separately. For earlier years, unrelated subfamily members are included in the "In families" category.

★ 454 ★

Top U.S. Wealthholders

Top wealthholders with gross assets of $325,000 or more, by size of net worth, 1982.

Item	Unit	Total	Net Worth					
			Under $100,000[1]	$100,000 to $249,999	$250,000 to $499,999	$500,000 to $999,999	$1,000,000-$4,999,999	$5,000,000 or more
Top wealthholders, number	1,000	4,478.8	341.7	649.0	2,032.3	980.3	437.3	38.2
Total assets	Mil.dol.	3,218,225	93,776	200,942	868,468	734,872	874,391	445,755
Net worth	Mil.dol.	2,713,510	-14,193	116,863	749,472	661,212	786,989	413,167
Female								
Top wealthholders, number	1,000	1,715.3	37.0	121.0	896.2	450.5	193.8	16.8
Total assets	Mil.dol.	1,302,332	9,421	42,153	373,793	321,904	371,325	183,736
Net worth	Mil.dol.	1,178,010	-3,147	22,535	334,491	301,790	345,979	176,362

Source: "Top wealthholders with gross assets of $325,000 or more, by size of net worth and sex: 1982," *Statistical Abstract of the United States 1990*, p. 463. Primary source: U.S. Internal Revenue Service, *Statistics of Income Bulletin*, Spring 1988. All figures are estimates based on estate tax return samples. Net worth equals assets minus debits and mortgages. Minus sign indicates negative net worth. *Note:* 1. Includes those wealthholders with negative net worth.

LABOR, EMPLOYMENT, AND OCCUPATIONS

Labor and Laborers

★ 455 ★

Black Population: Employment Status: 1980-1988

Employment status of the Black civilian noninstitutional population by age, 1980-1988.

Employment status and age	1980	1981	1982	1983	1984	1985	1986	1987	1988
					Numbers in thousands				
Black Women, 16 Years and Over									
Civilian noninstitutional population	9,880	10,102	10,300	10,477	10,694	10,873	11,033	11,224	11,402
Civilian labor force	5,253	5,401	5,527	5,681	5,907	6,144	6,281	6,507	6,609
Percent of population	53.1%	53.5%	53.7%	54.2%	55.2%	56.5%	56.9%	58.0%	58.0%
Employed	4,515	4,561	4,552	4,622	4,995	5,231	5,386	5,648	5,834
Percent of population	45.7%	45.1%	44.2%	44.1%	46.7%	48.1%	48.8%	50.3%	51.2%
Agriculture	29	22	25	28	22	22	22	22	20
Nonagricultural industries	4,486	4,539	4,527	4,595	4,973	5,209	5,364	5,626	5,814
Unemployed	738	840	975	1,059	911	913	894	858	776
Unemployment rate	14.0%	15.6%	17.6%	18.6%	15.4%	14.9%	14.2%	13.2%	11.7%
Not in labor force	4,627	4,701	4,773	4,796	4,787	4,729	4,752	4,717	4,793
Black Women, 20 Years and Over									
Civilian noninstitutional population	8,700	8,924	9,146	9,340	9,588	9,773	9,945	10,126	10,298
Civilian labor force	4,841	5,001	5,140	5,306	5,520	5,727	5,855	6,071	6,190
Percent of population	55.6%	56.0%	56.2%	56.8%	57.6%	58.6%	58.9%	60.0%	60.1%
Employed	4,267	4,329	4,347	4,428	4,773	4,977	5,128	5,365	5,548
Percent of population	49.1%	48.5%	47.5%	47.4%	49.8%	50.9%	51.6%	53.0%	53.9%
Agriculture	26	19	21	25	21	19	22	20	18
Nonagricultural industries	4,241	4,310	4,326	4,403	4,752	4,959	5,106	5,345	5,530
Unemployed	574	671	793	878	747	750	728	706	642
Unemployment rate	11.9%	13.4%	15.4%	16.5%	13.5%	13.1%	12.4%	11.6%	10.4%
Not in labor force	3,859	3,923	4,006	4,034	4,069	4,046	4,090	4,054	4,108
Black Men, 16 Years and Over									
Civilian noninstitutional population	7,944	8,117	8,283	8,447	8,654	8,790	8,956	9,128	9,289
Civilian labor force	5,612	5,685	5,804	5,966	6,126	6,220	6,373	6,486	6,596
Percent of population	70.3%	70.0%	70.1%	70.6%	70.8%	70.8%	71.2%	71.1%	71.0%
Employed	4,798	4,794	4,637	4,753	5,124	5,270	5,428	5,661	5,824

[Continued]

★ 455 ★

Black Population: Employment Status: 1980-1988
[Continued]

Employment status and age	1980	1981	1982	1983	1984	1985	1986	1987	1988
Percent of population	60.4%	59.1%	56.0%	56.3%	59.2%	60.0%	60.6%	62.0%	62.7%
Agriculture	179	162	163	165	174	167	133	142	133
Nonagricultural industries	4,620	4,632	4,474	4,587	4,950	5,103	5,295	5,519	5,691
Unemployed	815	891	1,167	1,213	1,003	951	946	826	771
Unemployment rate	14.5%	15.7%	20.1%	20.3%	16.4%	15.3%	14.8%	12.7%	11.7%
Not in labor force	2,333	2,433	2,481	2,482	2,528	2,570	2,583	2,642	2,694
Black Men, 20 Years and Over									
Civilian noninstitutional population	6,834	7,007	7,186	7,360	7,599	7,731	7,907	8,063	8,215
Civilian labor force	5,134	5,223	5,368	5,533	5,686	5,749	5,915	6,023	6,127
Percent of population	75.1%	74.5%	74.7%	75.2%	74.8%	74.4%	74.8%	74.7%	74.6%
Employed	4,498	4,520	4,414	4,531	4,871	4,992	5,150	5,357	5,509
Percent of population	65.8%	64.5%	61.4%	61.6%	64.1%	64.6%	65.1%	66.4%	67.1%
Agriculture	162	148	150	152	161	154	125	135	129
Nonagricultural industries	4,336	4,372	4,264	4,379	4,710	4,837	5,025	5,222	5,381
Unemployed	636	703	954	1,002	815	757	765	666	617
Unemployment rate	12.4%	13.5%	17.8%	18.1%	14.3%	13.2%	12.9%	11.1%	10.1%
Not in labor force	1,701	1,785	1,819	1,828	1,913	1,982	1,991	2,040	2,089

Source: Selected from "Employment status of the black and Hispanic-origin civilian noninstitutional population by sex and age, 1980-1988," *Handbook of Labor Statistics,* 1989, p. 38 (Washington, D.C.: U.S. Department of Labor, August 1989). Also in source: data for Hispanic-origin population (see separate table).

★ 456 ★

Composition of the Labor Force: 1960-2000

Characteristics of workers	1960	1970	1980	1988	2000
Number of Workers (in millions)	72.1	82.8	106.9	121.7	141.1
Percentage of Workers:					
White females	28%	33%	36%	38%	39%
White males	61%	56%	51%	48%	45%
Blacks	11%	11%	10%	10%	12%
Hispanics	NA	NA	6%	7%	10%
Asians/others[1]	NA	NA	NA	3%	4%

Source: "Composition of the U.S. Labor Force: 1960-2000," *America in the 21st Century: Human Resource Development,* December 1989, p. 10 (Washington, D.C.: Population Reference Bureau, 1989). Primary source: U.S. Department of Labor. Figures may not add to 100% because persons of Hispanic origin may be of any race. *Note:* 1. Includes American Indians, Alaskan Natives, and Pacific Islanders.

★ 457 ★

Economically Active Female Population: 1970-1988

Employment status of the female noninstitutional population 16 years and over, including the resident Armed Forces: 1970-1988.

Year	Noninsti- tutional population	Labor force							
		Number	Percent of population	Employed					
				Total	Percent of population	Resident Armed Forces	Civilian		
							Total	Agriculture	Nonagricul- tural industr
Numbers in thousands									
1970	72,819	31,580	43.4%	29,725	40.8%	37	29,688	601	29,087
1971	74,313	32,241	43.4%	30,015	40.4%	39	29,976	599	29,377
1972[1]	76,331	33,520	43.9%	31,298	41.0%	41	31,257	635	30,622
1973[1]	77,853	34,853	44.8%	32,764	42.1%	49	32,715	622	32,093
1974	79,375	36,274	45.7%	33,832	42,6%	63	33,769	596	33,173
1975	80,938	37,553	46.4%	34,067	42.1%	78	33,989	584	33,404
1976	82,476	39,069	47.4%	35,701	43.3%	86	35,615	588	35,027
1977	83,932	40,705	48.5%	37,381	44.5%	92	37,289	612	36,677
1978[1]	85,434	42,731	50.0%	39,669	46.4%	100	39,569	669	38,900
1979	86,951	44,343	51.0%	41,325	47.5%	108	41,217	661	40,556
1980	88,472	45,611	51.6%	42,241	47.7%	124	42,117	656	41,461
1981	89,751	46,829	52.2%	43,133	48.1%	133	43,000	667	42,333
1982	90,887	47,894	52.7%	43,395	47.7%	139	43,256	665	42,591
1983	91,827	48,646	53.0%	44,190	48.1%	143	44,047	680	43,367
1984	92,924	49,855	53.7%	46,061	49.6%	146	45,915	653	45,262
1985	93,886	51,200	54.5%	47,409	50.5%	150	47,259	644	46,615
1986[1]	94,944	52,568	55.4%	48,861	51.5%	155	48,706	652	48,054
1987	96,013	53,818	56.1%	50,494	52.6%	160	50,334	666	49,668
1988	96,918	54,904	56.6%	51,858	53.5%	162	51,696	676	51,020

Source: Selected from "Employment status of the noninstitutional population 16 years and over, including the resident Armed Forces, by sex, 1950-1988," *Handbook of Labor Statistics,* 1989, p. 9 (Washington, D.C.: U.S. Department of Labor, August 1989). Also in source: data for men; data from 1950-1969.
Note: 1. Not strictly comparable with data for prior years.

★ 458 ★

Economically Active Male Population: 1970-1988

Employment status of the male noninstitutional population 16 years and over, including the resident Armed Forces: 1970-1988.

Year	Noninsti-tutional population	Labor force							
		Number	Percent of population	Employed					
				Total	Percent of population	Resident Armed Forces	Civilian		
							Total	Agriculture	Nonagricul-tural indus-tries

Numbers in thousands

Year	Noninsti-tutional population	Number	Percent of population	Total	Percent of population	Resident Armed Forces	Total	Agriculture	Nonagricul-tural industries
1970	66,385	53,309	80.3%	51,071	76.9%	2,081	48,990	2,862	46,128
1971	67,875	54,113	79.7%	51,323	75.6%	1,933	49,390	2,795	46,595
1972[1]	69,607	55,327	79.5%	52,668	75.7%	1,772	50,896	2,849	48,047
1973[1]	71,017	56,349	79.3%	54,074	76.1%	1,725	52,349	2,847	49,502
1974	72,466	57,397	79.2%	54,682	75.5%	1,658	53,024	2,919	50,105
1975	73,891	57,899	78.4%	53,457	72.3%	1,600	51,857	2,824	49,032
1976	75,341	58,756	78.0%	54,720	72.6%	1,582	53,138	2,744	50,394
1977	76,756	59,959	78.1%	56,291	73.3%	1,563	54,728	2,671	52,057
1978[1]	78,107	61,151	78.3%	58,010	74.3%	1,531	56,479	2,718	53,761
1979	79,509	62,215	78.2%	59,096	74.3%	1,489	57,607	2,686	54,921
1980	80,877	62,932	77.8%	58,665	72.5%	1,479	57,186	2,709	54,477
1981	82,023	63,486	77.4%	58,909	71.8%	1,512	57,397	2,700	54,697
1982	83,052	63,979	77.0%	57,800	69.6%	1,529	56,271	2,736	53,534
1983	84,064	64,580	76.8%	58,320	69.4%	1,533	56,787	2,704	54,083
1984	85,156	65,386	76.8%	60,642	71.2%	1,551	59,091	2,668	56,423
1985	86,025	65,967	76.7%	61,447	71.4%	1,556	59,891	2,535	57,356
1986[1]	87,349	66,973	76.7%	62,443	71.5%	1,551	60,892	2,511	58,381
1987	88,476	67,784	76.6%	63,684	72.0%	1,577	62,107	2,543	59,564
1988	89,404	68,474	76.6%	64,820	72.5%	1,547	63,273	2,493	60,780

Source: Selected from "Employment status of the noninstitutional population 16 years and over, including the resident Armed Forces, by sex, 1950-1988," *Handbook of Labor Statistics,* 1989, p. 9 (Washington, D.C.: U.S. Department of Labor, August 1989). Also in source: data for women; data from 1950-1969. *Note:* 1. Not strictly comparable with data for prior years.

★ 459 ★

Employment Status

Employment status of all adults and of homemakers and heads of households, in thousands.

	Total	Working Full Time	Working Part Time	Not Employed
Numbers in thousands				
All Adults	180,074	98,104	16,795	66,047
Female	94,667	40,087	11,616	42,965
Male	86,307	58,017	5,180	23,110
Heads of Household				
Female Heads of Households	28,345	12,412	2,293	13,640
Hale Heads of Households	19,493	12,363	1,039	6,091
Homemakers				
Female Homemakers	83,366	35,817	9,658	37,891
Male Homemakers	21,340	13,351	1,346	6,643

Source: Selected from *Mediamark Research Multimedia Audiences Report, Spring 1990,* p. 12, 172, 194 (New York: Mediamark Research Inc., 1990).

★ 460 ★

Employment Status of All Women by Presence of Children: 1980-1988

Employment status of all women with no children under 18, with children 6 to 17 years old, and with children under 6, 1980-1988.

Year	Female civilian labor force						
	Total (thousands)	Percent of population	Employed			Unemployed	
			Number (thousands)	Percent		Number (thousands)	Percent of labor force
				Full time[1]	Part time[2]		
With no children under 18 years old							
1980	27,144	48.1%	25,375	73.4%	26.6%	1,769	6.5%
1981	27,992	48.7%	25,934	72.8%	27.2%	2,059	7.4%
1982	28,351	48.6%	26,041	72.3%	27.7%	2,311	8.2%
1983	28,856	48.7%	26,373	71.6%	28.4%	2,483	8.6%
1984	29,684	49.3%	27,652	72.7%	27.3%	2,032	6.8%
1985	30,850	50.4%	28,814	73.6%	26.4%	2,036	6.6%
1986	31,112	50.5%	29,107	73.6%	26.4%	2,005	6.4%
1987	31,538	50.5%	29,688	74.1%	25.9%	1,850	5.9%
1988	32,459	51.2%	30,895	73.7%	26.3%	1,564	4.8%
With children 6 to 17 years old							
1980	11,252	64.3%	10,640	72.9%	27.1%	612	5.4%
1981	11,490	65.5%	10,725	72.1%	27.9%	765	6.7%

[Continued]

★ 460 ★

Employment Status of All Women by Presence of Children: 1980-1988
[Continued]

Year	Total (thousands)	Percent of population	Employed Number (thousands)	Full time[1]	Part time[2]	Unemployed Number (thousands)	Percent of labor force
1982	11,377	65.8%	10,440	71.2%	28.8%	936	8.2%
1983	11,340	66.3%	10,303	72.1%	27.9%	1,037	9.1%
1984	11,538	68.1%	10,739	73.0%	27.0%	799	6.9%
1985	11,826	69.9%	10,984	73.4%	26.6%	842	7.1%
1986	12,075	70.4%	11,320	73.3%	26.7%	756	6.3%
1987	12,438	72.0%	11,661	74.4%	25.5%	778	6.3%
1988	12,663	73.3%	12,028	75.3%	24.7%	636	5.0%
With children under 6 years old							
1980	6,538	46.8%	5,886	67.9%	32.1%	652	10.0%
1981	6,933	48.9%	6,227	67.4%	32.6%	706	10.2%
1982	7,367	49.9%	6,414	65.4%	34.6%	953	12.9%
1983	7,583	50.5%	6,489	65.9%	34.1%	1,094	14.4%
1984	8,017	52.1%	7,043	67.1%	32.9%	974	12.1%
1985	8,215	53.5%	7,322	68.2%	31.8%	893	10.9%
1986	8,545	54.4%	7,602	68.8%	31.2%	943	11.0%
1987	8,983	56.7%	8,137	66.7%	33.3%	846	9.4%
1988	8,865	56.1%	8,104	69.4%	30.6%	761	8.6%

Source: Selected from "Employment status of all women and single women by presence and age of children, March 1975-88," *Handbook of Labor Statistics,* 1989, p. 240-241 (Washington, D.C.: U.S. Department of Labor, August 1989). Also in source: data for single women (see separate table); data for 1975-1979; data by other ages of children. Data refers to married, spouse present, and widowed, divorced, and separated women. Children refer to own children of the husband, wife, or person maintaining the family and include sons and daughters, stepchildren, and adopted children. Excluded are other related children, such as grandchildren, nieces, nephews and cousins, and unrelated children. *Notes:* 1. Persons who worked 35 hours or more during the survey week and those who usually work full time but worked 1 to 34 hours. 2. Persons who usually work 1 to 34 hours.

★ 461 ★

Employment Status of Married Women by Presence of Children: 1980-1988
Employment status of married women, spouse present, with no children under 18, with children 6 to 17 years old, and with children under 6, 1980-1988.

Year	Total (thousands)	Percent of population	Employed Number (thousands)	Full time[1]	Part time[2]	Unemployed Number (thousands)	Percent of labor force
1980	11,246	46.0%	10,741	77.0%	23.0%	505	4.5%
1981	11,426	46.3%	10,871	76.4%	23.6%	554	4.9%
1982	11,789	46.2%	11,121	76.2%	23.8%	668	5.7%
1983	12,076	46.6%	11,383	75.6%	24.4%	693	5.7%
1984	12,315	47.2%	11,744	75.3%	24.7%	571	4.6%

[Continued]

★ 461 ★

Employment Status of Married Women by Presence of Children: 1980-1988
[Continued]

Year	Married women, spouse present Civilian labor force						
			Employed			Unemployed	
	Total (thousands)	Percent of population	Number (thousands)	Percent		Number (thousands)	Percent of labor force
				Full time[1]	Part time[2]		
1985	12,784	48.2%	12,184	77.6%	22.4%	600	4.7%
1986	12,874	48.2%	12,285	77.3%	22.7%	590	4.6%
1987	13,201	48.4%	12,732	77.7%	22.3%	468	3.5%
1988	13,526	48.9%	13,127	76.3%	23.7%	399	2.9%
With children 6 to 17 years old							
1980	8,428	61.7%	8,055	68.7%	31.3%	372	4.4%
1981	8,432	62.5%	7,983	67.5%	32.5%	449	5.3%
1982	8,277	63.2%	7,693	67.1%	32.9%	583	7.0%
1983	8,292	63.8%	7,733	68.0%	32.0%	560	6.7%
1984	8,322	65.4%	7,904	69.3%	30.7%	418	5.0%
1985	8,526	67.8%	8,054	69.7%	30.3%	472	5.5%
1986	8,750	68.4%	8,326	69.4%	30.6%	424	4.8%
1987	9,007	70.6%	8,563	71.4%	28.6%	444	4.9%
1988	9,269	72.5%	8,918	71.8%	28.2%	351	3.8%
With children under 6 years old							
1980	5,227	45.1%	4,794	64.9%	35.1%	433	8.3%
1981	5,603	47.8%	5,141	64.9%	35.0%	462	8.2%
1982	5,690	48.7%	5,113	61.9%	38.1%	577	10.1%
1983	5,859	49.9%	5,219	62.4%	37.6%	640	10.9%
1984	6,219	51.8%	5,668	64.7%	35.3%	551	8.9%
1985	6,406	53.4%	5,895	65.7%	34.3%	511	8.0%
1986	6,573	53.8%	6,072	66.8%	33.2%	501	7.6%
1987	6,952	56.8%	6,539	64.4%	35.6%	413	5.9%
1988	6,956	57.1%	6,535	66.5%	33.5%	421	6.1%

Source: Selected from "Employment status of all ever-married women and married women, spouse present, by presence and age of children, March 1960-88," *Handbook of Labor Statistics,* 1989, p. 242-243 (Washington, D.C.: U.S. Department of Labor, August 1989). Also in source: data for all ever-married women; data for 1960-1979; data by other ages of children. Children refer to own children of the husband, wife, or person maintaining the family and include sons and daughters, stepchildren, and adopted children. Excluded are other related children, such as grandchildren, nieces, nephews and cousins, and unrelated children. *Notes:* 1. Persons who worked 35 hours or more during the survey week and those who usually work full time but worked 1 to 34 hours. 2. Persons who usually work 1 to 34 hours.

★ 462 ★

Employment Status of Single Women by Presence of Children: 1980-1988

Employment status of single women with no children under 18, with children 6 to 17 years old, and with children under 6, 1980-1988.

Year	Single Female Civilian Labor Force						
	Total	Percent of population	Employed			Unemployed	
			Number (thousands)	Percent		Number (thousands)	Percent of labor force
				Full-time[1]	Part-time[2]		
With no children under 18 years old							
1980	10,690	62.1%	9,662	66.5%	33.5%	1,027	9.6%
1981	11,048	62.9%	9,867	65.8%	34.2%	1,182	10.7%
1982	10,912	63.4%	9,687	64.4%	35.6%	1,225	11.2%
1983	11,281	64.1%	9,926	63.7%	36.3%	1,355	12.0%
1984	11,519	64.5%	10,448	65.9%	34.1%	1,071	9.3%
1985	11,790	66.9%	10,736	66.2%	33.8%	1,054	8.9%
1986	11,925	66.8%	10,886	66.1%	33.9%	1,039	8.7%
1987	12,068	66.7%	11,051	66.5%	33.5%	1,017	8.4%
1988	12,232	67.3%	11,370	66.9%	33.1%	862	7.1%
With children 6 to 17 years old							
1980	243	67.6%	205	86.8%	13.2%	38	15.6%
1981	252	64.6%	197	80.2%	19.8%	55	21.8%
1982	316	64.0%	263	79.1%	20.9%	52	16.6%
1983	388	68.1%	294	84.4%	15.6%	93	24.0%
1984	393	70.2%	310	75.7%	24.3%	83	21.1%
1985	407	64.1%	345	84.1%	15.9%	63	15.4%
1986	439	65.9%	361	79.5%	20.5%	78	17.7%
1987	485	64.1%	399	81.0%	19.0%	85	17.6%
1988	557	67.1%	462	81.0%	19.0%	95	17.1%
With children under 6 years old							
1980	310	44.1%	219	81.7%	18.3%	91	29.2%
1981	328	45.7%	227	77.1%	22.9%	101	30.7%
1982	574	45.2%	376	79.5%	20.5%	198	34.4%
1983	613	42.5%	400	75.2%	24.8%	214	34.8%
1984	669	43.6%	451	71.0%	29.0%	218	32.6%
1985	727	46.5%	520	76.2%	23.8%	208	28.5%
1986	762	47.5%	498	74.9%	25.1%	264	34.6%
1987	901	49.9%	632	72.9%	27.1%	270	29.9%
1988	828	44.7%	616	78.2%	21.8%	211	25.5%

Source: Selected from "Employment status of all women and single women by presence and age of children, March 1975-88," *Handbook of Labor Statistics*, 1989, p. 240-241 (Washington, D.C.: U.S. Department of Labor, August 1989). Also in source: data for all women (see separate table); data for 1975-1979; data by other ages of children. Children refer to own children of the husband, wife, or person maintaining the family and include sons and daughters, stepchildren, and adopted children. Excluded are other related children, such as grandchildren, nieces, nephews and cousins, and unrelated children. *Notes:* 1. Persons who worked 35 hours or more during the survey week and those who usually work full time but worked 1 to 34 hours. 2. Persons who usually work 1 to 34 hours.

★ 463 ★

Employment Status of Women by Residence

Employment status of the civilian noninstitutional population in metropolitan, nonmetropolitan, urban, and rural areas, 1986-1988.

Employment status, year	Metropolitan areas			Nonmetropolitan areas			Urban areas	Rural areas
	Total	Central cities		Total	Farm	Nonfarm		
	Numbers in thousands							
Civilian noninstitutional population	67,980	28,229	39,751	19,595	1,321	18,274	65,398	22,177
Civilian labor force	38,438	15,602	22,835	10,158	708	9,449	36,698	11,897
Percent of population	56.5%	55.3%	57.4%	51.8%	53.6%	51.7%	56.1%	53.6%
Employed	36,188	14,498	21,690	9,375	683	8,691	34,433	11,129
Unemployed	2,250	1,105	1,145	783	25	758	2,265	768
Unemployment rate	5.9%	7.1%	5.0%	7.7%	3.5%	8.0%	6.2%	6.5%
Not in labor force	29,543	12,627	16,916	9,437	612	8,825	28,700	10,280
Women, 20 Years and Over, 1987								
Civilian noninstitutional population	69,087	28,302	40,785	19,506	1,269	18,237	66,109	22,485
Civilian labor force	39,553	15,798	23,755	10,236	704	9,532	37,591	12,198
Percent of population	57.3%	55.8%	58.2%	52.5%	55.5%	52.3%	56.9%	54.2%
Employed	37,490	14,783	22,706	9,591	686	8,905	35,544	11,536
Unemployed	2,063	1,015	1,048	645	18	627	2,047	662
Unemployment rate	5.2%	6.4%	4.4%	6.3%	2.6%	6.6%	5.4%	5.4%
Not in labor force	29,535	12,504	17,031	9,270	565	8,705	28,518	10,287
Women, 20 Years and Over, 1988								
Civilian noninstitutional population	69,878	28,347	41,530	19,662	1,239	18,424	66,697	22,843
Civilian labor force	40,444	16,030	24,414	10,432	711	9,720	38,343	12,532
Percent of population	57.9%	56.5%	58.8%	53.1%	57.4%	52.8%	57.5%	54.9%
Employed	38,535	15,086	23,450	9,852	697	9,155	36,468	11,920
Unemployed	1,909	944	964	579	14	566	1,876	612
Unemployment rate	4.7%	5.9%	4.0%	5.6%	1.9%	5.8%	4.9%	4.9%
Not in labor force	29,434	12,318	17,116	9,231	527	8,703	28,354	10,310

Source: Selected from "Employment status of the civilian noninstitutional population in metropolitan, nonmetropolitan, urban, and rural areas by sex, age, race, and Hispanic origin, 1986-88," *Handbook of Labor Statistics,* 1989, p.49 (Washington, D.C.: U.S. Department of Labor, August 1989). Also in source: data for men and by race/ethnicity.

★ 464 ★

Employment Status of the Adult Population

Employment characteristics, total, and female and male adult population, 1990.

Characteristic	Number (thousands)		
	Total	Female	Male
Total adults	180,974	94,667	86,307
Employed full time	98,104	40,087	58,017
Employed part time	16,795	11,616	5,180
Sole wage earner	32,480	11,803	20,677
Not employed	66,074	42,965	23,110

[Continued]

★ 464 ★

Employment Status of the Adult Population
[Continued]

Characteristic	Number (thousands)		
	Total	Female	Male
Professional	15,966	8,019	7,947
Executive/Admin./Managerial	14,845	5,871	8,974
Clerical/Sales/Technical	35,437	22,765	12,672
Precision/Crafts/Repair	13,595	1,207	12,388
Other employed	35,057	13,842	21,216

Source: Selected from *Mediamark Research Multimedia Audiences Report, Spring 1990* (New York: Mediamark Research Inc., 1990).

★ 465 ★

Facts on Women Workers
Some facts on women workers, according to the Department of Labor Women's Bureau.

The average woman worker 16 years of age between 1970-1980 could expect to spend **29.3 years** of her life in the labor force, compared to 39.1 years for a 16-year-old man. The figures for white and black women are **29.6 years** and **27.8 years**, respectively.

In 1989, women represented **80%** of all administrative support workers but only about **9%** of precision production, craft, and repair workers. Women were **68%** of retail and personal services sales workers but only **40%** of executives, managers, and administrators. At the end of 1989, women represented **7.2%** of apprentices.

The **33 million** women with children under the age of 18 had a labor force participation rate of **65%** in March 1988. **56%** of mothers with preschoolers were in the labor force in March 1988.

In 1988 women represented **62%** of all persons 16 years and over with poverty level incomes.

Source: Facts on Working Women, No. 90-2, September 1990.

★ 466 ★

Female Employees by Major Industry

Women employees on nonagricultural payrolls by major industry and manufacturing group, December 1989.

Industry	Female employees (thousands)
Total	52,234
Total private	42,704
Goods-producing	7,141
Mining	98
Construction	585
Manufacturing	
Service-producing	45,093
Transportation and public utilities	1,699
Wholesale trade	1,934
Retail trade	10,909
Finance, insurance, and real estate	4,330
Services	16,691
Government	9,530
Federal	1,060
State	2,091
Local	6,379

Source: Selected from "Women employees on nonagricultural payrolls by major industry and manufacturing group," *Employment and Earnings*, March 1990, p. 55. Not seasonally adjusted. Establishment survey estimates are currently projected from March 1988 benchmark levels. When more recent benchmark data are introduced, all unadjusted data from April 1988 forward are subject to revision.

★ 467 ★

Female Labor Force Participation Rates: 10 Countries: 1970-1988

Labor force participation rates of women, 10 countries, 1970-1988.

Year	United States	Canada	Australia	Japan	France	Germany, F.R.[1]	Italy	Netherlands	Sweden	United Kingdom
1970	43.3%	38.3%	40.4%	48.7%	39.8%	38.5%	26.4%	-	50.0%	42.2%
1971	43.4%	39.4%	41.0%	47.7%	40.2%	38.5%	26.3%	-	50.9%	42.0%
1972	43.9%	40.2%	41.2%	46.8%	40.6%	38.6%	25.6%	-	51.5%	42.8%
1973	44.7%	41.9%	42.4%	47.3%	41.0%	38.9%	26.1%	25.9%	51.7%	44.6%
1974	45.7%	43.0%	43.5%	45.7%	41.4%	38.8%	26.5%	26.1%	53.3%	45.7%
1975	46.3%	44.4%	44.5%	44.8%	41.7%	38.4%	26.8%	26.7%	55.2%	46.2%
1976	47.3%	45.2%	44.3%	44.9%	42.4%	38.1%	27.6%	27.1%	55.8%	46.5%
1977	48.4%	46.0%	44.8%	45.7%	43.2%	37.8%	28.9%	27.7%	56.7%	47.0%
1978	50.0%	47.9%	44.5%	46.4%	43.5%	37.8%	28.8%	28.2%	57.5%	47.6%
1979	50.9%	49.0%	44.3%	46.6%	44.0%	37.9%	29.5%	29.1%	58.5%	47.8%

[Continued]

★ 467 ★

Female Labor Force Participation Rates: 10 Countries: 1970-1988

[Continued]

Year	United States	Canada	Australia	Japan	France	Germany, F.R.[1]	Italy	Netherlands	Sweden	United Kingdom
1980	51.5%	50.4%	45.5%	46.6%	44.3%	38.1%	30.1%	31.2%	59.3%	47.8%
1981	52.1%	51.7%	45.5%	46.7%	44.5%	37.6%	30.4%	33.4%	60.1%	47.6%
1982	52.6%	51.7%	45.4%	47.0%	44.9%	38.4%	30.3%	34.3%	60.5%	48.2%[2]
1983	52.9%	52.6%	45.5%	48.0%	44.9%	38.4%[3]	30.5%	34.0%[3]	60.8%	48.4%[2]
1984	53.6%	53.6%	46.2%	47.8%	45.4%	38.8%	30.5%	34.5%	61.1%	49.3%[2]
1985	54.5%	54.6%	47.1%	47.6%	45.5%	39.1%	30.7%	34.8%	61.5%	49.7%[2]
1986	55.3%	55.3%	49.4%	47.6%	45.7%	39.5%[2]	31.9%[3]	38.5%[2]	61.7%	50.2%[2]
1987	56.0%	56.4%	50.0%	47.6%	45.9%	40.0%[2]	32.3%[2]	41.9%[2]	62.6%[3]	51.0%[2]
1988	56.6%	57.4%	50.7%	47.6%	-	-	32.9%[2]	-	63.2%[2]	51.4%[2]

Source: Selected from "Labor force participation rates by sex, 10 countries, 1960-1988," *Handbook of Labor Statistics,* 1989, p. 556 (Washington, D.C.: U.S. Department of Labor, August 1989). Primary source: Bureau of Labor Statistics. Based on data from national and international statistical publications. Also in source: data for 1960-1969 and for both sexes and men. Data relate to the civilian labor force as a percent of the civilian noninstitutionalized working age population. Working age is defined as 16-year-olds and over in the United States, France, and Sweden; 15-year-olds and over in Australia, Canada, Germany, and Japan; and 14-year-olds and over in Italy. For the United Kingdom, the lower age limit was raised from 15 to 16 in 1973. For the Netherlands, the lower age limit was raised from 14 to 15 in 1975. The institutionalized working age population is included in Japan and Germany. *Notes:* 1. Including West Berlin. 2. Preliminary. 3. Break in series.

★ 468 ★

Hispanic-Origin Population: Employment Status: 1980-1988

Employment status of the Hispanic-origin civilian noninstitutional population 16 years and over and 20 years and over, 1980-1988.

Employment status and age	1980	1981	1982	1983	1984	1985	1986	1987	1988
					Numbers in thousands				
Hispanic Women, 16 Years and Over									
Civilian noninstitutional population	4,909	5,151	5,377	5,597	5,816	6,029	6,238	6,496	6,721
Civilian labor force	2,328	2,486	2,586	2,671	2,888	2,970	3,128	3,377	3,573
Percent of population	47.4%	48.3%	48.1%	47.7%	49.6%	49.3%	50.1%	52.0%	53.2%
Employed	2,079	2,216	2,222	2,301	2,568	2,642	2,791	3,077	3,278
Percent of population	42.4%	43.0%	41.3%	41.1%	44.2%	43.8%	44.7%	47.4%	48.8%
Agriculture	41	44	42	44	46	38	42	47	51
Nonagricultural industries	2,038	2,172	2,180	2,257	2,522	2,604	2,749	3,030	3,227
Unemployed	249	269	364	369	320	327	337	300	296
Unemployment rate	10.7%	10.8%	14.1%	13.8%	11.1%	11.0%	10.8%	8.9%	8.3%
Not in labor force	2,580	2,665	2,792	2,927	2,929	3,059	3,110	3,119	3,147
Hispanic Women 20 Years and Over									
Civilian noninstitutional population	4,281	4,513	4,734	4,954	5,173	5,385	5,591	5,835	6,050
Civilian labor force	2,076	2,242	2,333	2,429	2,615	2,725	2,893	3,112	3,281
Percent of population	48.5%	49.7%	49.3%	49.0%	50.5%	50.6%	51.7%	53.3%	54.2%
Employed	1,886	2,029	2,040	2,127	2,357	2,456	2,615	2,872	3,047
Percent of population	44.1%	45.0%	43.1%	42.9%	45.6%	45.6%	46.8%	49.2%	50.4%
Agriculture	33	37	35	40	37	31	39	45	49
Nonagricultural industries	1,852	1,992	2,006	2,086	2,320	2,424	2,576	2,827	2,998

[Continued]

★ 468 ★

Hispanic-Origin Population: Employment Status: 1980-1988
[Continued]

Employment status and age	1980	1981	1982	1983	1984	1985	1986	1987	1988
Unemployed	190	212	293	302	258	269	278	241	234
Unemployment rate	9.2%	9.5%	12.5%	12.4%	9.9%	9.9%	9.6%	7.75	7.1%
Not in labor force	2,205	2,271	2,401	2,525	2,558	2,660	2,698	2,723	2,769
Hispanic men, 16 Years and Over									
Civilian noninstitutional population	4,689	4,968	5,203	5,432	5,661	5,885	6,106	6,371	6,604
Civilian labor force	3,818	4,005	4,148	4,362	4,563	4,729	4,948	5,163	5,409
Percent of population	81.4%	80.6%	79.7%	80.3%	80.6%	80.3%	81.0%	81.0%	81.9%
Employed	3,448	3,597	3,583	3,771	4,083	4,245	4,428	4,713	4,972
Percent of population	73.5%	72.4%	68.9%	69.4%	72.1%	72.1%	72.5%	74.0%	75.3%
Agriculture	224	229	243	271	296	264	287	351	356
Nonagricultural industries	3,224	3,369	3,340	3,499	3,787	3,981	4,140	4,361	4,616
Unemployed	370	408	565	591	480	483	520	451	437
Unemployment rate	9.7%	10.2%	13.6%	13.6%	10.5%	10.2%	10.5%	8.7%	8.1%
Not in labor force	871	963	1,055	1,070	1,098	1,157	1,158	1,208	1,195
Hispanic Men, 20 Years and Over									
Civilian noninstitutional population	4,036	4,306	4,539	4,771	5,005	5,232	5,451	5,700	5,921
Civilian labor force	3,426	3,647	3,815	4,014	4,218	4,395	4,612	4,818	5,031
Percent of population	84.9%	84.7%	84.0%	84.1%	84.3%	84.0%	84.6%	84.5%	85.0%
Employed	3,142	3,325	3,354	3,523	3,825	3,994	4,174	4,444	4,680
Percent of population	77.8%	77.2%	73.9%	73.8%	76.4%	76.3%	76.6%	78.0%	79.0%
Agriculture	200	205	222	246	271	239	263	327	327
Nonagricultural industries	2,942	3,120	3,132	3,276	3,554	3,754	3,911	4,118	4,353
Unemployed	284	321	461	491	393	401	438	374	351
Unemployment rate	8.3%	8.8%	12.1%	12.2%	9.3%	9.1%	9.5%	7.8%	7.0%
Not in labor force	610	659	724	758	787	837	839	882	890

Source: Selected from "Employment status of the black and Hispanic-origin civilian noninstitutional population by sex and age, 1980-88," *Handbook of Labor Statistics,* 1989, p.39 (Washington, D.C.: U.S. Department of Labor, August 1989). Also in source: data for men; data for Blacks (see separate table). Beginning in January, 1986, data for persons of Hispanic origin were revised to reflect new population estimates.

★ 469 ★

Hours of Work Per Week: Selected Countries
Hours of work per week in non-agricultural activities, latest available period.

Country, month, year	Total	Female	Male
Asia			
Israel, February 1990[1]	37.6	31.5	41.7
Japan, March 1990 (Incl. fishing)	47.2	40.4	51.7
Korea, Republic of, December 1987	51.9	52.6	51.5

[Continued]

★ 469 ★

Hours of Work Per Week: Selected Countries
[Continued]

Country, month, year	Total	Female	Male
Europe			
Spain, December 1986	37.6	35.5	38.5
Germany, Federal Republic of, January, 1990	39.4	38.4	39.6
Luxembourg, December 1988	41.5	41.1	41.5
Netherlands, December 1989	40.1	39.7	40.3
Switzerland, December 1988	42.4	40.9	42.7
United Kingdom, December 1984	-	38.2	43.4
Oceania			
Australia, December 1987	34.4	29.3	38.2
New Zealand, May, 1989	36.7	35.7	37.4

Source: Selected from "Hours of work per week in non-agricultural activities," *Bulletin of Labour Statistics*, 1990-3, Table 5, p. 73-78. Also in source: data for various years. *Note:* 1. Including forestry and logging, agriculture and fishing.

★ 470 ★

Labor Force Projections to 2000

Women in the labor force in 1986 and projected to year 2000, by race and Hispanic origin.

Group	1986	2000	Percent	Change
	\multicolumn{4}{c}{Numbers in thousands}			
Total	117,837	138,775	100%	20,938
Women	52,414	65,639	47.3%	13,225
White	44,585	54,449	39.2%	9,864
Black	6,311	8,408	6.1%	2,097
Asian, other[1]	1,518	2,782	2.0%	1,264
Hispanic[2]	3,128	5,783	4.2%	2,655

Source: "Women in the labor force in 1986 and projected to year 2000," *Facts on U.S. Working Women*, Fact Sheet No. 88-1, January 1988, p. 2. Primary source: U.S. Department of Labor, Bureau of Labor Statistics, *Monthly Labor Review*, September, 1987. *Notes:* 1. Includes American Indian, Alaskan Native, Asian, and Pacific Islanders. 2. Persons of Hispanic origin may be of any race.

★ 471 ★

Labor Force Status of High School Graduates and Dropouts

Labor force status of 1989 high school graduates and 1988-89 school dropouts, 16-24 years old, by school enrollment.

Characteristic	Civilian noninstitutional population (thousands)	Civilian labor force					
		Number (thousands)	Partici-pation rate	Employed		Unemployed	
				Number (thousands)	Percent of population	Number (thousands)	Percent of labor force
Total, 1989 high school graduates	2,454	1,495	61.0%	1,314	53.5%	182	12.2%
Women	1,245	733	58.8%	634	50.9%	99	13.5%
Men	1,208	763	63.1%	680	56.3%	83	10.9%
Enrolled in college	1,463	659	45.1%	600	41.0%	59	8.9%
Women	767	354	46.2%	319	41.6%	35	9.9%
Men	696	305	43.8%	281	40.4%	24	7.8%
Not enrolled in college	991	836	84.4%	713	72.0%	123	14.7%
Women	478	378	79.1%	314	65.8%	64	16.9%
Men	513	458	89.4%	399	77.8%	59	13.0%
Total, 1988-89 high school dropouts[1]	446	292	65.4%	210	47.1%	82	28.0%
Women	203	111	54.4%	83	40.6%	28	25.3%
Men	243	181	74.6%	127	52.5%	54	29.6%

Source: Selected from "Labor force status of 1989 high school graduates and 1988-89 school dropouts 16 to 24 years old by school enrollment, sex, race, and Hispanic origin, October 1989," *United States Department of Labor News*, USDL-326, June 26, 1990, p. 3-4. Also in source: data by race and Hispanic origin. *Notes:* 1. Data refer to persons who dropped out of school between October 1988 and October 1989.

★ 472 ★

Labor Force in Jerusalem by Religion and Origin

Percentage of population aged 15 and over in labor force in Jerusalem by religion, origin, and sex, 1983.

Religion and Origin	Women[1]	Men[1]
	Percent	
Total	40.5	64.0
Jews, total	50.7	64.7
Origin Israel	49.6	63.3
Origin Asia		
Born in Israel	48.1	65.7
Born abroad	44.9	65.3
Origin Africa		
Born in Israel	49.1	65.1
Born abroad	49.4	65.0
Origin Europe-America		
Born in Israel	57.0	66.1
Born abroad	56.2	65.8
Non-Jews, total	10.3	60.2

[Continued]

★ 472 ★

Labor Force in Jerusalem by Religion and Origin
[Continued]

Religion and Origin	Women[1]	Men[1]
Muslims	7.3	60.8
Christians	25.7	53.9

Source: "Percentage in Labor Force in Jerusalem, by Religion, Origin, and Sex, 1983," *American Jewish Year Book*, 1987, Table 17A, p. 101 (Scranton, PA: American Jewish Committee and Jewish Publication Society, 1987). *Notes:* 1. Age-standardized data according to age distribution of Jerusalem's total population (ages 15 and over); calculations by U.O. Schmelz, contributor.

★ 473 ★

Labor Market Characteristics by Education

Labor market characteristics by education, 25-to 34-year-olds, 1979 and 1986.

Year and Characteristic	Educational attainment					
	High School or Less		1 to 3 Years College		4+ Years College	
	Female	Male	Female	Male	Female	Male
1979						
Participation rate	58.9%	92.5%	70.0%	92.0%	78.0%	93.5%
Annual salary	$13,640	$21,630	$16,450	$23,780	$20,030	$26,780
1986						
Participation rate	64.0%	92.0%	76.2%	90.8%	84.0%	93.1%
Annual salary	$13,480	$18,500	$16,910	$22,080	$21,790	$27,840

Source: "Labor Market Characteristics by Sex and Education, 25 to 34-Year Olds," *Family Incomes in the 1980s: New Pressure on Wives, Husbands and Young Adults*, 1988, p. 12 (Washington, D.C.: Economic Policy Institute, November 1988).

★ 474 ★

Mexican, Puerto Rican, and Cuban Employment Status

Employment status of the civilian noninstitutional population 16 years and over and 20 years and over of Mexican, Puerto Rican, and Cuban origin, by age, 1986-1988.

Employment status and age	Mexican origin			Puerto Rican origin			Cuban origin		
	1986	1987	1988	1986	1987	1988	1986	1987	1988
	Numbers in thousands								
Women, 16 Years and Over									
Civilian noninstitutional population	3,605	3,722	3,880	829	871	894	420	412	432
Civilian labor force	1,821	1,952	2,090	316	343	370	239	230	237
Percent of population	50.5%	52.4%	53.9%	38.1%	39.3%	41.4%	56.9%	55.8%	54.9%
Employed	1,609	1,748	1,889	268	310	340	224	218	224
Unemployed	213	204	201	47	33	30	15	12	12
Unemployment rate	11.7%	10.4%	9.6%	15.0%	9.6%	8.1%	6.3%	5.3%	5.2%
Not in labor force	1,784	1,770	1,790	514	528	524	181	182	195

[Continued]

★ 474 ★

Mexican, Puerto Rican, and Cuban Employment Status
[Continued]

Employment status and age	Mexican origin			Puerto Rican origin			Cuban origin		
	1986	1987	1988	1986	1987	1988	1986	1987	1988
Women, 20 Years and Over									
Civilian noninstitutional population	3,182	3,299	3,438	736	783	801	403	393	409
Civilian labor force	1,663	1,779	1,886	287	319	342	231	220	226
Percent of population	52.3%	53.9%	54.9%	39.0%	40.7%	42.75	57.3%	56.0%	55.3%
Employed	1,491	1,617	1,730	249	293	319	218	210	215
Unemployed	172	162	156	38	26	23	13	10	11
Unemployment rate	10.3%	9.1%	8.3%	13.1%	8.3%	6.7%	5.7%	4.5%	5.0%
Not in labor force	1,519	1,520	1,553	449	464	459	171	173	183
Men, 16 Years and Over									
Civilian noninstitutional population	3,771	3,929	4,133	665	669	705	422	407	417
Civilian labor force	3,120	3,251	3,482	489	484	513	331	316	329
Percent of population	82.7%	82.7%	84.2%	73.5%	72.3%	72.8%	78.4%	77.6%	78.9%
Employed	2,778	2,941	3,177	423	433	467	310	300	313
Unemployed	342	310	304	65	50	46	21	16	16
Unemployment rate	11.0%	9.5%	8.7%	13.4%	10.4%	9.0%	6.5%	5.1%	4.8%
Not in labor force	652	678	652	176	185	192	91	90	88
Men, 20 Years and Over									
Civilian noninstitutional population	3,336	3,485	3,670	583	595	634	399	379	394
Civilian labor force	2,879	3,005	3,204	455	454	483	320	306	319
Percent of population	86.3%	86.2%	87.3%	78.0%	76.3%	76.2%	80.2%	80.7%	81.0%
Employed	2,596	2,755	2,966	399	411	443	301	291	304
Unemployed	283	251	237	57	44	40	19	15	15
Unemployment rate	9.8%	8.3%	7.4%	12.5%	9.6%	8.2%	5.9%	5.0%	4.7%
Not in labor force	457	479	466	128	141	152	79	73	75

Source: Selected from "Employment status of civilians of Mexican, Puerto Rican, and Cuban origin by sex and age, 1986-1988," *Handbook of Labor Statistics,* 1989, p. 40 (Washington, D.C.: U.S. Department of Labor, August 1989). Also in source: data for males. Data prior to 1986 are not available on a revised basis that reflects the adjustments to the population estimates introduced in January 1986.

★ 475 ★

New Technology in the Workplace
Problems reported by secretaries when new technology was introduced in the workplace. (N = 158.).

Problem	% Reporting Problem
Not enough training to use equipment	35.4%
Over-work during installation	4.3%
Deadlines for installation set by others	5.6%
Deadlines for installation unreasonable	2.5%
Amount of work expected unreasonable	13.6%
Deadlines for other projects conflicting	8.6%
Downtime of equipment	20.9%
Amount of time with equipment excessive	4.3%

[Continued]

★ 475 ★

New Technology in the Workplace
[Continued]

Problem	% Reporting Problem
Other supervisors requesting work with equipment	2.5%
Too little equipment, competition for access	24.1%

Source: Ann Statham and Ellen Bravo, "The Introduction of New Technology: Health Implications for Workers," *Women and Health* 16(2) 1990, p. 105+. Data from surveys of 75 workers in 3 settings revealed planning deficiencies (among other issues) that seemed to cause difficulty for the workers involved. Surveys of 162 secretaries were used to explore the resulting hypothesis that the planning deficiences would result in symptoms of stress.

★ 476 ★

On-Job Injuries Resulting in Death

Some statistics on on-job injuries.

According to the Centers for Disease Control's report of August 17, 1990:

1. From 1980 to 1985, **42%** of deaths of American women resulting from on-the-job injuries were homicides. The rate for men was 12%.

2. Vehicle accidents was the second most frequent cause of death, at about **39%**.

3. **Of the 950 killings identified over the years of the study,** 41% **involved women in the retail field.** Sixty-four percent **of the killings were shootings;** 19% **were stabbings.**

4. The workplace homicide rate for black women was almost double the rate for white women. Black women are nearly **four times** as likely to be murdered as white women.

Source: "Homicide is Top Cause of Death From On-Job Injury for Women," *New York Times*, August 18, 1990, p. 8.

★ 477 ★

Temporary Employment: Reasons

Why nurses and homemakers worked for a temporary help firm.

Reason	Total	Registered or Visiting Nurses	Licensed Practical	Nurses' Aides	Homemakers
Variety in work, that is, frequent changes in assignment	16.6%	8.6%	13.1%	21.5%	20.6%
A stopgap measure until I can obtain a permanent job	8.2%	9.2%	8.0%	7.2%	9.0%
Freedom to schedule my work in a flexible manner	60.2%	70.3%	65.3%	55.9%	50.8%

[Continued]

★ 477 ★

Temporary Employment: Reasons
[Continued]

Reason	Total	Registered or Visiting Nurses	Licensed Practical	Nurses' Aides	Homemakers
Employment during school vacation	1.0%	0.8%	0%	0.8%	2.6%
Other	14.1%	10.9%	13.6%	14.6%	16.9%

Source: "Survey Results: Nurses' and Homamakers' Most Important Reason for Working at a Particular Temporary Help Firm (percent)," *Computer Chips and Paper Clips: Technology and Women's Employment*, Vol. 2, 1987, p. 280 (Washington, D.C.: National Academy Press, 1987). Primary source: Gannon (1984). Related reading: Susan McHenry and Linda Lee Small, "Does Part-Time Pay Off?," *MS.*, March 1989, p. 88+. Sample = 1,101; registered or visiting nurses = 262; licensed practical nurses = 221; nurses' aides = 408; homemakers = 210.

★ 478 ★

Unemployed Female Population: 1970-1988

Noninstitutional female population, number in labor force, number and percent unemployed, number not in labor force, 1970-1988.

Year	Noninsti- tutional population	Number in labor force	Unemployed Number	Unemployed Percent of labor force	Not in labor force
		Numbers in thousands			
1970	72,819	31,580	1,855	5.9%	41,239
1971	74,313	32,241	2,227	6.9%	42,072
1972[1]	76,331	33,520	2,222	6.6%	42,811
1973[1]	77,853	34,853	2,089	6.0%	43,000
1974	79,375	36,274	2,441	6.7%	43,101
1975	80,938	37,553	3,486	9.3%	43,386
1976	82,476	39,069	3,369	8.6%	43,406
1977	83,932	40,705	3,324	8.2%	43,227
1978[1]	85,434	42,731	3,061	7.2%	42,703
1979	86,951	44,343	3,018	6.8%	42,608
1980	88,472	45,611	3,370	7.4%	42,861
1981	89,751	46,829	3,696	7.9%	42,922
1982	90,887	47,894	4,499	9.4%	42,993
1983	91,827	48,646	4,457	9.2%	43,181
1984	92,924	49,855	3,794	7.6%	43,068
1985	93,886	51,200	3,791	7.4%	42,686
1986[1]	94,944	52,568	3,707	7.1%	42,376
1987	96,013	53,818	3,324	6.2%	42,195
1988	96,918	54,904	3,046	5.5%	42,014

Source: Selected from "Employment status of the noninstitutional population 16 years and over, including the resident Armed Forces, by sex, 1950-1988," *Handbook of Labor Statistics*, 1989, p. 9 (Washington, D.C.: U.S. Department of Labor, 1989). Also in source: data for men; data from 1950-1969; data for employed population. *Notes:* 1. Not strictly comparable with data for prior years. See source for further explanation.

★ 479 ★

Unemployed Male Population: 1970-1988

Noninstitutional male population, number in labor force, number and percent unemployed, number not in labor force, 1970-1988.

Year	Noninsti- tutional population	Number in labor force	Unemployed		Not in labor force
			Number	Percent of labor force	
			Numbers in thousands		
1970	66,385	53,309	2,238	4.2%	13,076
1971	67,875	54,113	2,789	5.2%	13,762
1972[1]	69,607	55,327	2,659	4.8%	14,280
1973[1]	71,017	56,349	2,275	4.0%	14,667
1974	72,466	57,397	2,714	4.7%	15,069
1975	73,891	57,899	4,442	7.7%	15,993
1976	75,341	58,756	4,036	6.9%	16,585
1977	76,756	59,959	3,667	6.1%	16,797
1978[1]	78,107	61,151	3,142	5.1%	16,956
1979	79,509	62,215	3,120	5.0%	17,293
1980	80,877	62,932	4,267	6.8%	17,945
1981	82,023	63,486	4,577	7.2%	18,537
1982	83,052	63,979	6,179	9.7%	19,073
1983	84,064	64,580	6,260	9.7%	19,484
1984	85,156	65,386	4,744	7.3%	19,771
1985	86,025	65,967	4,521	6.9%	20,058
1986[1]	87,349	66,973	4,530	6.8%	20,376
1987	88,476	67,784	4,101	6.1%	20,692
1988	89,404	68,474	3,655	5.3%	20,930

Source: Selected from "Employment status of the noninstitutional population 16 years and over, including the resident Armed Forces, by sex, 1950-1988," *Handbook of Labor Statistics,* 1989, p. 9 (Washington, D.C.: U.S. Department of Labor, 1989). Also in source: data for women; data from 1950-1969; data for employed population. *Notes:* 1. Not strictly comparable with data for prior years. See source for further explanation.

★ 480 ★

Unemployment Levels: Selected Countries

Number of unemployed persons, in thousands, and/or percentages of unemployed persons, selected countries, latest available year.

Country, year	Number or rate (000's) (%)		
	Total	Women	Men
Africa			
Angola, 1986	69.40	25.76	43.64
Egypt, 1984	756.0	268.9	487.1
	6%	11.4%	4.8%
Ethiopia, 1987	58.24	20.33	37.91
Ghana, 1986	25.790	3.335	22.455
	0.5%	0.1%	0.8%

[Continued]

★ 480 ★

Unemployment Levels: Selected Countries
[Continued]

Country, year	Number or rate (000's) (%)		
	Total	Women	Men
Mauritius, 1987 (Excl. Rodrigues)	46.796	10.541	36.255
Niger, 1986	27.747	1.048	26.699
Reunion, 1986	51.639	24.506	26.821
Senegal, 1987	8.14	1.79	6.35
Seychelles, 1985	5.713	3.287	2.426
	22.5%	31.6%	16.2%
South Africa, 1986[1,2]	519	266	253
South Africa, 1986[3]	113	54	59
South Africa, 1986[4,5]	78	29	48
Sudan, 1986	63.720	14.459	48.613
	13.1%	8.0%	14.5%
Togo, 1985	4,076	0.484	3.592
Tunisia, 1987	83.708	16.355	67.353
America			
Argentina, 1987	230.5	103.7	126.8
Bahamas, 1986	13.500	7.800	5.700
	12.2%	15.0%	9.7%
Barbados, 1987	21.4	13.0	8.4
	17.9%	23.1%	13.3%
Bolivia, 1987	430.72	65.57	365.14
Brazil, 1986	1380	526	854
Canada, 1987	1167	533	634
	8.9%	9.4%	8.5%
Colombia, 1987	400.13	226.49	173.63
Costa Rica, 1987	54.537	21.410	33.127
	5.6%	7.9%	4.7%
Chile, 1987	343.6	120.9	222.4
Chile, 1986	8.8%	9.7%	8.4%
Greenland, 1985	2.360	1.173	1.187
Guadeloupe, 1987	27.814	16.119	11.695
Guatemala, 1985	0.221	0.079	0.142
Guiana, 1987	9209	4397	4812
French Guiana, 1987	3425	1787	1638
	11.0%	15.4%	8.4%
Honduras, 1983	254.2	42.0	212.2
Jamaica, 1986	250.4	165.2	85.3
	23.6%	33.8%	14.9%
Martinique, 1987	30.703	19.435	13.084

[Continued]

★ 480 ★

Unemployment Levels: Selected Countries
[Continued]

Country, year	Number or rate (000's) (%)		
	Total	Women	Men
Netherlands Antilles, 1985	17.161	9.876	7.285
	22.2%	31.3%	15.9%
Panama, 1987	89.33	41.96	47.37
	11.6%	16.5%	9.2%
Peru, 1987	103.5	54.9	48.6
Puerto Rico, 1987	171	46	125
	16.8%	12.4%	19.4%
St. Pierre and Miquelon, 1986	0.299	0.126	0.173
Suriname, 1986	13.405	6.100	7.305
Trinidad and Tobago, 1987	106.6	40.9	65.7
	22.3%	25.3%	20.7%
United States, 1987	7425	3324	4101
	6.1%	6.2%	6.1%
Uruguay, 1987	48.4	28.2	20.2
	9.3%	12.5%	6.8%
Uruguay, 1987[6]	102.1	56.9	45.2
	9.1%	12.6%	6.7%
Venezuela, 1987	573.44	124.51	448.92
	9.10%	7.20%	9.90%
Asia			
Brunei, 1983	2.081	1.537	0.544
China, 1987	2766	1398	953
	2.0%	1.0%	0.7%
Cyprus, 1987	8709	4342	4367
	3.4%	4.8%	2.6%
Hong Kong, 1987	47.5	17.7	29.8
	1.7%	1.8%	1.7%
India, 1987	30542	5291	25251
Israel, 1987	90.1	42.5	47.6
	6.1%	7.3%	5.2%
Japan, 1987	1730	690	1040
	2.8%	2.8%	2.8%
Korea, Republic of, 1987	519	122	397
	3.1%	1.8%	3.9%
Malaysia, 1987	78.55	29.61	49.64
Pakistan, 1985	1074	40	1034
Philippines, 1987	2085	922	1163
	9.1%	8.1%	10.9%
Singapore, 1987	58.80	19.14	39.67
	4.7%	4.0%	5.1%
Syrian Arab Republic, 1984	109.6	26.8	82.8

[Continued]

★ 480 ★

Unemployment Levels: Selected Countries
[Continued]

Country, year	Number or rate (000's) (%)		
	Total	Women	Men
Thailand	4.7%	8.2%	4.1%
	1337.0	741.1	595.8
	2.6%	2.9%	2.3%
Europe			
Austria, 1987	164.47	69.45	95.01
	5.6%	5.7%	5.5%
Belgium, 1987	500.8	292.0	208.9
	11.9%	8.3%	17.2%
Denmark, 1987	221.9	125.7	96.1
	8.0%	9.9%	6.5%
Spain, 1987	2924.1	1398.8	1525.4
	20.4%	29.7%	15.9%
Finland, 1987	130	78	53
	5.1%	4.3%	5.8%
France, 1987	2545.8	1403.1	1142.7
	10.6%	13.7%	8.3%
Germany, Federal Republic of, 1987	2228.8	1021.4	1207.4
	8.9%	10.2%	8.0%
Gibraltar, 1987	0.288	0.056	0.232
Greece, 1987	286.2	158.3	127.9
	7.4%	11.3%	5.1%
Iceland, 1987	0.588	0.348	0.240
Ireland, 1987	231.6	55.2	176.3
	17.6%	13.6%	19.4%
Isle of Man, 1987	1.624	0.554	1.070
	5.9%	5.3%	6.3%
Italy, 1987	2832	1604	1228
	11.9%	18.5%	8.1%
Luxembourg, 1987	2660	1150	1510
	2.7%	2.0%	1.5%
Malta, 1987	5.630	0.999	4.631
	4.4%	3.1%	4.8%
Netherlands, 1987	685.5	256.8	428.7
	11.5%	12.1%	11.1%
Norway, 1987	45	25	21
	2.1%	2.6%	1.7%
Portugal, 1987	329.0	185.6	143.4
	7.0%	9.3%	5.2%
St. Marin, 1986	0.742	0.538	0.204
	6.9%	12.0%	3.2%
Switzerland, 1987	24.673	12.141	12.532
	0.8%	1.1%	0.6%
Sweden, 1987	84	40	44

[Continued]

★ 480 ★

Unemployment Levels: Selected Countries
[Continued]

Country, year	Number or rate (000's) (%)		
	Total	Women	Men
	1.9%	1.9%	1.9%
Turkey, 1987	1124	194.95	929.07
United Kingdom, 1986	3289.1	1036.6	2252.5
Yugoslavia, 1987	1080.6	603.1	477.4
	13.6%	18.5% ·	10.2%
Oceania			
Australia, 1987	601.9	254.9	347.0
	7.8%	8.3%	7.5%
Guam, 1987	1.6	0.6	0.9
	4.4%	4.5%	4.3%
New Zealand, 1987	65.9	29.3	36.6
	4.1%	4.3%	3.9%
New Caledonia, 1987	4490	2103	2387

Source: Selected from "Unemployment," *Year Book of Labour Statistics*, 1988, p. 623-641 (Geneva: International Labour Office, 1990). Also in source: data for other countries. See source for explanation and extensive footnotes. *Notes:* 1. Excl. Transkei, Bophuthatswana, Venda, Ciskei; elsewhere persons enumerated at de facto dwelling place. 2. Blacks. 3. Coloreds. 4. Whites, coloreds, Asians; eligibility rules for registration not specified. 5. Excl. Transkei, Bophuthatswana, Venda, Ciskei, Kwazulu, KaNgwane, Qwa Qwa, Gazankulu, Lebowa, and KwaNdebele. 6. Urban areas.

★ 481 ★

Veteran Employment Status
Employment status of female war veterans age 18 and over, November 1987.

Veteran status and period of service	Civilian noninsti-tutional population (thousands)	Female Civilian Labor Force					
		Total (thousands)	Percent of population	Employed (thousands)	Unemployed		Not in labor force (thousands)
					Number (thousands)	Percent of	
Total veterans	1,052	576	54.8%	530	46	8.0%	476
War veterans	684	301	44.0%	284	17	5.7%	383
Vietnam era	247	188	76.1%	177	11	5.8%	59
Vietnam theater	33	19	[1]	17	1	[1]	15
Outside Vietnam theater	214	169	79.0%	160	10	5.6%	44
Other war veterans	437	113	25.9%	106	6	5.6%	324
Nonveterans	91,500	52,311	57.2%	49,521	2,790	5.3%	39,190

Source: "Employment status of women age 18 and over, by veteran status and period of service, November 1987, not seasonally adjusted," *Monthly Labor Review*, April 1990, p. 28. Because of the aging of the population, there were no longer any Vietnam-era veterans under 25 years of age or any other war veterans under 45 years of age. *Note:* 1. Data not shown where base is less than 75,000.

★ 482 ★

Women Employees by Major Industry: 1980-1988

Women employees on nonagricultural payrolls by major industry and manufacturing group, 1980-1988.

Industry	Female employees, in thousands								
	1980	1981	1982	1983	1984	1985	1986	1987	1988
Total	38,186	39,037	39,052	39,852	42,068	43,919	45,568	47,313	49,130
Mining	105	129	134	117	118	120	106	95	97
Construction	372	380	378	389	427	463	496	524	548
Manufacturing									
Total	6,317	6,341	5,990	5,965	6,297	6,234	6,187	6,251	6,389
Durable goods	3,009	3,034	2,827	2,793	3,037	3,029	2,981	2,996	3,070
Non-durable goods	3,308	3,306	3,163	3,172	3,261	3,205	3,206	3,255	3,319
Transportation and public utilities	1,292	1,340	1,339	1,314	1,387	1,450	1,482	1,535	1,593
Wholesale trade	1,362	1,395	1,415	1,454	1,548	1,623	1,676	1,729	1,804
Retail trade	7,489	7,595	7,664	7,926	8,537	9,059	9,431	9,798	10,142
Finance, insurance, and real estate	3,039	3,158	3,199	3,279	3,433	3,639	3,893	4,085	4,171
Services	10,452	10,971	11,339	11,773	12,443	13,172	13,877	14,625	15,464
Government									
Total	7,759	7,730	7,595	7,637	7,878	8,159	8,420	8,672	8,924
Federal	908	878	883	939	975	1,009	1,031	1,048	1,060
State	1,632	1,659	1,637	1,584	1,678	1,776	1,848	1,919	1,991
Local	5,219	5,193	5,075	5,114	5,224	5,374	5,541	5,705	5,873

Source: Selected from "Women employees on nonagricultural payrolls by industry, 1959-88," *Errata for Handbook of Labor Statistics*, March 1990, p. 2 (Washington, D.C.: U.S. Department of Labor, March 1990). Also in source: data for 1959-1979.

★ 483 ★

Women Labor Force Indicators

Characteristics of women in the labor force, second quarter, 1990.

Characteristic	Number or %
Population and labor force	
Women, 16 years and over, in thousands	
Civilian noninstitutional population[1]	98,289
Civilian labor force	56,682
Civilian labor force participation rates	
Women, 16 years and over	57.7%
16 to 19 years	52.2%
20 years and over	58.1%
20 to 24 years	71.8%
25 to 54 years	74.3%

[Continued]

★ 483 ★

Women Labor Force Indicators
[Continued]

Characteristic	Number or %
55 years and over	23.2%
White	57.6%
Black	58.5%
Employment status, in thousands	
Women, 16 years and over:	
Employed	53,730
Unemployed	2,952
Unemployment rates	
Women, 16 years and over	5.2%
16 to 19 years	13.9%
20 years and over	4.6%
White, 16 years and over	4.5%
White, 16 to 19 years	12.3%
Black, 16 years and over	10.0%
Black, 16 to 19 years	25.7%
Full-time workers	
Percent of employed women working full time	75.0%
Percent of unemployed women looking for full-time work	73.0%
Marital status	
Married women, husband present	
Civilian noninstitutional population, thousands[1]	53,048
Civilian labor force participation rate	58.4%
Unemployment rate	3.6%
Women who maintain families:	
Civilian noninstitutional population, thousands[1]	11,051
Civilian labor force participation rate	62.7%
Unemployment rate	7.6%

Source: Selected from "Summary indicators on women in the labor force, quarterly averages, 1989 and 1990," *Employment in Perspective: Women in the Labor Force,* Report 791, Second Quarter 1990, p. 2 (Washington, D.C.: U.S. Department of Labor, August 1990). Also in source: data for 1989 and first quarter 1990; data by other characteristics. Data are seasonally adjusted unless otherwise indicated. Due to rounding and independent seasonal adjustment, some components may not add to totals. *Note:* 1. Not seasonally adjusted.

★ 484 ★

Women Not in Labor Force, By Reason: 1980-1988

Women 16 years and over not in the labor force, by reason, 1980-1988.

Reason	1980	1981	1982	1983	1984	1984	1986[1]	1987	1988
					Numbers in thousands				
Total not in labor force	42,861	42,922	42,993	43,181	43,068	42,686	42,376	42,195	42,014
Do not want a job now	39,014	39,003	38,646	38,887	39,013	38,749	38,524	38,484	38,586
Current activity:									
Going to school	3,177	3,236	3,197	3,294	3,227	3,097	3,108	3,150	4,870
Ill, disabled	2,073	2,002	1,847	1,823	1,909	1,880	1,918	2,101	3,516
Keeping house	28,976	28,498	28,100	28,053	27,690	26,764	25,983	25,267	22,287
Retired	2,908	3,302	3,502	3,789	4,179	4,872	5,428	5,884	15,228
Other activity	1,879	1,965	2,000	1,928	2,008	2,136	2,087	2,082	3,675
Want a job now	3,847	3,919	4,347	4,293	4,055	3,937	3,851	3,711	3,429
Reason not looking:									
School attendance	754	778	809	751	762	751	718	702	670
Ill health, disability	424	409	444	427	426	435	435	436	430
Home responsibilities	1,267	1,280	1,391	1,413	1,378	1,317	1,304	1,266	1,168
Think cannot get a job	634	704	981	991	794	699	684	601	516
Other reasons[2]	768	748	722	711	695	735	710	706	645

Source: Selected from "Persons not in the labor force, by reason, sex, and race, 1970-88," *Handbook of Labor Statistics,* 1989, p. 59 (Washington, D.C.: U.S. Department of Labor, August 1989). Also in source: data for males and by race; data for 1970-1979. *Notes:* 1. Not strictly comparable with data for prior years. See source for explanation. 2. Includes a small number of men not looking for work because of "home responsibilities."

★ 485 ★

Women's Employment Ratios by Occupation, 1989 and 1983

Occupational class	Women to total employment ratio	
	1989	1983
Total	42.1%	40.4%
Inspectors, compliance officers	8.8%	22.4%
Engineers	8.0%	5.9%
Computer scientists, analysts	31.2%	29.6%
Operations/systems analysts	40.9%	30.1%
Registered nurses	92.9%	94.4%
Therapists	72.3%	75.1%
Teachers, except college/university	70.6%	68.0%
Elementary teachers	83.7%	82.5%
Secondary teachers	49.7%	49.1%
Counselors, education/vocation	55.1%	48.4%
Psychologists	51.9%	53.9%
Social/religious workers	46.9%	42.2%

[Continued]

★ 485 ★

Women's Employment Ratios by Occupation, 1989 and 1983
[Continued]

Occupational class	Women to total employment ratio	
	1989	1983
Social workers	66.8%	62.8%
Lab technicians/technologists	71.9%	73.3%
Engineering technicians	19.1%	17.6%
Drafting occupations	19.9%	16.8%
Computer programmers	35.7%	31.9%
Advertising/related sales	55.0%	46.5%
Sales reps, except retail	19.2%	14.5%
Cashiers	78.5%	80.9%
Scheduling supervisors/clerks	36.5%	20.1%
Information clerks	89.1%	88.6%
Records clerks	82.5%	82.0%
Bookkeepers, accounting clerks	91.4%	89.2%
Postal clerks, except mail carriers	39.5%	32.2%
Mail carriers, postal service	22.1%	14.3%
Mail clerks, except postal service	47.6%	48.9%
Dispatchers	50.6%	44.6%
Shipping/receiving clerks	26.8%	19.6%
Stock/inventory clerks	39.7%	38.4%
Misc. admin.support occupations	84.6%	85.2%
General office clerks	79.2%	80.7%
Police and detectives	12.3%	9.6%
Public service police/detectives	11.6%	6.0%
Guards	18.9%	13.7%
Guards/police, except public service	15.8%	11.1%
Food preparation/service occupations	52.9%	57.4%
Bartenders	48.3%	46.3%
Cooks, except short order	44.4%	47.8%
Waiters'/waitresses' assistants	37.5%	36.9%
Misc. food preparation occupations	40.7%	48.6%
Health aides, except nursing	81.9%	87.4%
Nursing aides, orderlies	88.4%	86.8%
Maids/housemen	77.1%	75.5%
Janitors/cleaners	24.0%	20.5%
Mechanics/repairers	3.5%	3.4%
Electrical/electronic repairers	8.1%	8.1%
Textile sewing machine operators	90.8%	81.7%
Laundry/dry cleaning machine operators	61.4%	63.0%
Packaging/filling machine operators	62.2%	64.2%
Bus drivers	40.1%	29.2%

[Continued]

★ 485 ★

Women's Employment Ratios by Occupation, 1989 and 1983
[Continued]

Occupational class	Women to total employment ratio	
	1989	1983
Handlers/helpers/laborers	16.1%	16.0%
Stock handlers/baggers	23.5%	19.0%
Freight/stock/material handlers	9.2%	5.9%
Laborers, except construction	19.5%	19.4%
Farming/forestry/fishing occupations	11.7%	11.2%
Farm occupations, except managers	13.5%	12.7%
Farm workers	13.0%	12.7%
Related agricultural occupations	10.6%	11.1%

Source: Selected from "Ratio of median weekly earnings for women and men and ratio of women's employment to total employment for selected occupations in 1989 and 1983," *Facts on Working Women*, No. 90-3, October 1990, p. 3-4. Also in source: ratio of median weekly earnings for women and men (See *Income* chapter in this book under subhead "Wages and Salaries").

★ 486 ★

World Labor Force: 1970-1980
Composition of world labor force by main sector of activity, 1970 and 1980.

Area	Agriculture		Industry		Services	
	1970	1980	1970	1980	1970	1980
Developing countries						
Female	73.6%	66.3%	12.5%	16.3%	13.9%	17.4%
Male	62.8%	55.7%	17.7%	21.6%	19.5%	22.7%
Industrialized market economies						
Female	11.4%	7.7%	25.4%	25.8%	63.2%	66.5%
Male	12.0%	8.5%	44.6%	45.9%	43.4%	45.6%
Industrialized centrally planned economies						
Female	31.7%	21.5%	29.6%	33.1%	38.6%	45.5%
Male	27.7%	19.4%	44.2%	50.3%	28.1%	30.3%
Total[1]						
Female	54.3%	47.8%	17.9%	20.8%	27.8%	31.4%
Male	49.2%	43.5%	25.7%	28.8%	25.1%	27.7%

Source: "Composition of world labour force, by sex and main sector of activity (1970 and 1980) (in percentages)," *World Labour Report 1-2*, 1987, p. 250 (New York: Oxford University Press, 1987). Primary source: ILO Bureau of Statistics. *Note:* 1. Including 124 countries having more than 1 million inhabitants.

★ 487 ★

Young Adults Not in School-Employment Status: 1980-1987

Employment status of the female civilian noninstitutional population 16 to 24 years of age not enrolled in school, by educational attainment, October 1980-1987.

Year	Civilian noninstitutional population	Female civilian noninstitutional population	Female civilian labor force					
			Total	Percent of population	Employed	Unemployed	
						Number	Percent of labor force
			Numbers in thousands				
Total not enrolled							
1980	21,389	11,145	8,059	72.3%	7,024	1,035	12.8%
1981	21,037	11,019	8,046	73.0%	6,863	1,183	14.7%
1982	20,828	10,881	7,826	71.9%	6,439	1,387	17.7%
1983	20,527	10,757	7,794	72.5%	6,605	1,189	15.3%
1984	20,029	10,562	7,756	73.4%	6,708	1,048	13.5%
1985	19,237	10,075	7,515	74.6%	6,514	1,001	13.3%
1986	18,534	9,684	7,281	75.2%	6,329	952	13.1%
1987	17,793	9,397	6,989	74.4%	6,210	779	11.2%
Less than 4 years of high school							
1980	5,254	2,481	1,221	49.2%	871	350	28.7%
1981	5,142	2,396	1,155	48.2%	794	361	31.3%
1982	5,055	2,455	1,159	47.2%	777	382	33.0%
1983	4,904	2,274	1,082	47.6%	764	318	29.4%
1984	4,625	2,187	1,053	48.1%	738	315	29.9%
1985	4,323	2,059	983	47.7%	690	293	29.8%
1986	4,087	1,936	957	49.4%	666	290	30.4%
1987	4,203	2,043	994	48.7%	768	226	22.8%
4 years of high school only							
1980	11,622	6,138	4,637	75.5%	4,105	523	11.5%
1981	11,451	6,091	4,671	76.7%	4,008	663	14.2%
1982	11,216	5,903	4,464	75.6%	3,695	769	17.2%
1983	11,035	5,803	4,342	74.8%	3,671	671	15.5%
1984	10,935	5,807	4,433	76.3%	3,850	583	13.2%
1985	10,381	5,487	4,255	77.5%	3,706	549	12.9%
1986	9,953	5,185	4,010	77.3%	3,500	510	12.7%
1987	9,352	4,916	3,807	77.4%	3,382	425	11.2%
1 to 3 years of college							
1980	3,044	1,730	1,461	84.5%	1,346	115	7.9%
1981	2,926	1,646	1,384	84.1%	1,259	125	9.0%
1982	3,024	1,691	1,428	84.4%	1,268	160	11.2%
1983	2,984	1,725	1,468	85.1%	1,337	131	8.9%
1984	2,975	1,705	1,453	85.2%	1,352	101	7.0%
1985	2,946	1,628	1,423	87.4%	1,301	122	8.6%

[Continued]

★ 487 ★

Young Adults Not in School-Employment Status: 1980-1987
[Continued]

Year	Civilian noninstitutional population	Female civilian noninstitutional population	Female civilian labor force				
			Total	Percent of population	Employed	Unemployed	
						Number	Percent of labor force
1986	2,956	1,647	1,432	86.9%	1,326	106	7.4%
1987	2,745	1,620	1,403	86.6%	1,315	88	6.3%
4 years of college or more							
1980	1,471	796	740	93.0%	700	40	5.4%
1981	1,517	885	835	94.4%	801	34	4.1%
1982	1,534	833	775	93.0%	699	76	9.8%
1983	1,603	955	904	94.7%	834	70	7.7%
1984	1,494	863	816	94.6%	768	48	5.9%
1985	1,584	899	853	94.9%	817	36	4.2%
1986	1,538	916	883	96.4%	837	46	5.2%
1987	1,492	818	785	95.9%	745	39	5.0%

Source: Selected from "Employment status of the civilian noninstitutional population 16 to 24 years of age not enrolled in school by educational attainment, sex, and race, October 1970-87," *Handbook of Labor Statistics,* 1989, p. 263 (Washington, D.C.: U.S. Department of Labor, August 1989). Also in source: data for 1970-1979; data for men and by race. Beginning with 1986, data are not strictly comparable with data for earlier years because of revisions in the weighting patterns used in aggregating these data. *Note:* 1. Data not shown where base is less than 75,000.

★ 488 ★

Young Adults' Employment by Educational Attainment
Percent of population 25-34 years old employed, by years of schooling completed: 1971-1988.

Year	Female			Male		
	<9 years of school	9 to 11 yrs of school	12 years of school	<9 years of school	9 to 11 yrs of school	12 years of school
1971	29.3%	35.2%	43.1%	82.2%	87.9%	93.6%
1972	33.5%	36.1%	44.9%	85.0%	88.5%	93.7%
1973	32.8%	38.4%	45.7%	83.9%	88.8%	93.1%
1974	33.3%	39.8%	47.6%	82.9%	90.2%	93.0%
1975	30.5%	34.5%	48.0%	73.3%	78.1%	88.4%
1976	33.7%	39.5%	49.8%	74.9%	79.6%	89.6%
1977	31.8%	41.0%	53.0%	74.2%	81.5%	89.5%
1978	35.6%	42.4%	55.9%	77.0%	82.4%	90.8%
1979	33.6%	43.2%	58.0%	78.6%	80.5%	91.3%
1980	35.0%	45.6%	59.5%	71.6%	77.7%	87.0%
1981	32.5%	42.7%	61.3%	75.0%	76.7%	86.9%
1982	32.8%	39.7%	59.6%	68.0%	73.2%	83.3%
1983	31.3%	37.1%	58.8%	64.2%	69.3%	78.6%
1984	31.7%	41.5%	61.0%	67.0%	72.2%	84.8%
1985	35.1%	40.3%	63.9%	73.0%	76.0%	86.1%
1986	35.2%	44.1%	63.8%	69.4%	73.3%	86.2%

[Continued]

★ 488 ★

Young Adults' Employment by Educational Attainment
[Continued]

Year	Female			Male		
	<9 years of school	9 to 11 yrs of school	12 years of school	<9 years of school	9 to 11 yrs of school	12 years of school
1987	34.3%	44.0%	65.6%	73.3%	75.0%	86.8%
1988	34.5%	46.9%	66.8%	71.4%	75.5%	87.2%

Source: "Employment of Young Adults," *The Condition of Education 1990, Volume 1: Elementary and Secondary Education,* p. 40 (Washington, D.C.: National Center for Education Statistics, 1990). Primary source: U.S. Department of Labor, Bureau of Labor Statistics, *Educational Attainment of Workers,* various years and unpublished tabulations.

★ 489 ★

Youth Labor Force Participation

Labor force participation of 16-and 17-year-olds enrolled in school, by sex and race, 1970-1985.

Year	Labor force participation rate[1]				Unemployment rate[2]			
	Women		Men		Women		Men	
	White	Black	White	Black	White	Black	White	Black
1970	35.5%	20.4%	41.1%	23.9%	14.8%	28.4%	15.1%	33.3%
1975	43.6%	20.8%	46.0%	16.9%	17.9%	32.4%	16.9%	25.1%
1980	48.1%	17.5%	47.5%	25.8%	15.3%	39.4%	17.4%	42.9%
1985	42.2%	23.9%	41.7%	22.7%	15.7%	50.9%	18.7%	41.3%

Source: "Labor force participation of 16-and 17-year-olds enrolled in school, by sex and race: 1955 to 1985," *Youth Indicators 1988: Trends in the Well-Being of American Youth,* Volume 1, August 1988, p. 76. Primary source: U.S. House of Representatives, Select Committee on Children, Youth, and Families, *U.S. Children and Their Families: Current Conditions and Recent Trends, 1987.* U.S. Department of labor, Bureau of Labor Statistics, *Handbook of Labor Statistics,* Bulletin 2217, June 1985. Also in source: data for 1955, 1960, 1965. *Notes:* 1. The labor force participation rate is the percentage of persons either employed or seeking employment. 2. The unemployment rate is the proportion of those in the labor force who are seeking employment.

Labor Unions

★ 490 ★

Union Membership Survey: 1974-1989

Persons responding "Yes" to the question: "Are you a member of any labor unions?"

Sex	Year										
	1974	1975	1977	1978	1980	1983	1984	1986	1987	1988	1989
Females	7%	8%	10%	8%	6%	8%	10%	7%	8%	9%	9%
Number surveyed	783	806	830	879	809	904	861	843	812	552	573
Males	28%	25%	26%	25%	22%	22%	21%	17%	20%	18%	21%
Number surveyed	682	653	689	640	637	686	589	617	636	432	433

Source: Selected from *An American Profile—Opinions and Behavior, 1972-1989*, p. 891 (Detroit: Gale Research Inc., 1990). Primary source: General Social Survey. Also in source: "No" responses.

★ 491 ★

Union Membership: 1983-1988

Number of female union members, and union women as percent of employed women and total union membership, 1983-1988.

Year	Number (thousands)	Union Women as % of	
		Employed Women	Total Union Membership
1988	5,982	12.6%	35.2%
1987	5,842	12.6%	34.5%
1986	5,802	12.9%	34.2%
1985	5,732	13.2%	33.7%
1984	5,829	13.8%	33.6%
1983	5,908	14.6%	33.3%

Source: "Women's Union Membership," *Facts on Working Women*, No. 89-2, August 1989, p. 2. Primary source: U.S. Department of Labor, Bureau of Labor Statistics.

★ 492 ★

Women on Trade Union Councils in Europe

Percentage of women on National Trade Union Councils in Europe (representing all major unions), 1981.

Country	Women as % of membership	Women as % of congress	Women as % of council members
Iceland	46.7%	27.0%	18.0%
Denmark	43.0%	14.9%	23.8%
Sweden	40.9%	25.0%	12.0%
United Kingdom	33.3%	9.8%	13.7%
Norway	33.0%	19.0%	12.0%

[Continued]

★ 492 ★

Women on Trade Union Councils in Europe
[Continued]

Country	Women as % of member-ship	Women as % of congress	Women as % of council members
Belgium	33.0%	6.4%	5.5%
Italy	33.0%	15.0%	15.0%
Austria	30.2%	NA	1.9%
France	30.0%	30.0%	24.0%
West Germany	21.0%	7.5%	7.9%
Switzerland	11.0%	6.0%	2.0%

Source: Eschel M. Rhoodie, *Discrimination Against Women: A Global Survey of the Economic, Educational, Social and Political Status of Women*, 1989, p. 183 (Jefferson, NC: McFarland & Company, 1989). Primary source: International Labour Organization, Geneva, 1983.

Lost Work Time

★ 493 ★

Lost Work Time

Absences from work of employed full-time wage and salary workers by age, sex, and marital status and by presence and age of children for females, 1990. The absence rate is the ratio of workers with absences to total full-time employment.

Age, sex, marital status, and presence and age of children	Total employed	Absence rate[1] Total	Absence rate[1] Illness	Lost worktime rate[2] Total	Lost worktime rate[2] Illness
		Numbers in thousands			
Total, 16 years and over	85,082	4.8	2.7	2.8%	1.7%
Women, 16 years and over	36,068	6.2	3.3	3.6%	2.0%
Men, 16 years and over	49,015	3.8	2.3	2.3%	1.5%
Married women, spouse present[3]	19,264	6.6	3.2	3.9%	2.0%
With no children under 18 years	9,639	5.4	3.3	3.0%	2.0%
Youngest child, 6 to 17 years	5,586	5.6	3.0	3.0%	1.8%
Youngest child, under 6 years	4,039	11.0	3.5	7.4%	2.2%
All other women[3]	16,803	5.8	3.4	3.1%	2.0%
With no children under 18 years	13,506	5.4	3.3	2.9%	1.9%
Youngest child, 6 to 17 years	2,295	6.4	3.7	3.6%	2.2%
Youngest child, under 6 years	1,002	8.6	4.4	5.3%	2.7%

[Continued]

★ 493 ★

Lost Work Time
[Continued]

Age, sex, marital status, and presence and age of children	Total employed	Absence rate[1]		Lost worktime rate[2]	
		Total	Illness	Total	Illness
Married men, spouse present[3]	31,933	3.7	2.3	2.3%	1.5%
All other men[3]	17,082	4.0	2.2	2.3%	1.4%

Source: "Absences from work of employed full-time wage and salary workers by age, sex, marital status, and presence and age of children," *Employment and Earnings*, 1991, Table 61, p. 232. Also in source: data for "other reasons"; data for other ages. *Notes:* 1. Absences refer to work missed due to illnesses or other personal reasons. Excluded is work missed due to vacation, holiday, labor-management dispute, or bad weather resulting in an employer temporarily curtailing business activity. The absence rate is the ratio of workers with absences to total full-time employment. To be counted as having had an absence, a person who usually works 35 hours or more per week must have been at work fewer than 35 hours or have not been at work at all during the survey reference week. 2. Hours absent as a percent of total hours usually worked. 3. Because of differences in definitions, estimates by marital status in this table are somewhat different from family relationship estimates shown in other tables for full-time wage and salary workers.

★ 494 ★

Lost Work Time Due to Caregiving Responsibilities

Relationship between caregiving responsibilities and lost productive time. (N = Percent of respondents who have missed work, left early, etc.).

Item	Type of caregiving responsibilities							
	Elder Care		Child Care		Dual Care		No care	
	Women	Men	Women	Men	Women	Men	Women	Men
Missed work	45%	28%	51%	30%	55%	28%	33%	25%
Arrived late	33%	25%	42%	32%	41%	27%	33%	25%
Left early	54%	46%	65%	53%	63%	47%	46%	42%
Dealt with family/work issues during work hours	81%	82%	86%	85%	87%	83%	74%	74%

Source: "Relationship between caregiving responsibilities and lost productive time," *The Politics and Reality of Family Care in Corporate America*, 1990, p. 181 (Lexington, Mass: Lexington Books, 1990). Data were collected through a self-administered questionnaire; N = 14,064 women and 12,140 men.

★ 495 ★

Lost Work Time Due to Failure in Child Care Arrangements

Employed women losing time from work during the last month because of failures in child care arrangements: Fall 1987.

Characteristic	All mothers		Mothers with 1 child	
	Number employed[1] (thousands)	% losing time	Number employed[1] (thousands)	% losing time
Total	8,957	7.0%	2,994	5.9%
Marital status:				
Married, spouse present	6,426	7.3%	2,097	6.1%
All other marital statuses[2]	2,531	6.2%	897	5.6%

[Continued]

★ 495 ★

Lost Work Time Due to Failure in Child Care Arrangements
[Continued]

Characteristic	All mothers		Mothers with 1 child	
	Number employed[1] (thousands)	% losing time	Number employed[1] (thousands)	% losing time
Age of youngest child:				
Less than 1 year	1,097	7.0%	410	7.4%
1 and 2 years	2,782	10.3%	1,227	8.4%
3 and 4 years	2,305	6.0%	910	4.2%
5 to 14 years	2,772	4.6%	446	1.3%
Employment status:				
Full time	6,578	6.5%	2,259	6.2%
Part time	2,379	8.4%	735	5.2%
Occupation:				
Managerial-professional	2,321	7.9%	694	7.0%
Technical, sales, administrative support	3,881	6.8%	1,437	5.9%
Service workers	1,479	5.7%	505	5.0%
Operators, fabricators, laborers	943	6.9%	260	7.0%
Educational attainment:				
Less than high school	1,098	4.1%	387	2.7%
High school	3,657	6.4%	1,154	5.5%
College, 1 or more years	4,202	8.3%	1,453	7.1%
Monthly family income:				
Less than $1,250	1,357	5.6%	481	4.6%
$1,250 to $2,499	2,835	6.2%	891	3.5%
$2,500 to $3,749	2,448	9.4%	853	8.3%
$3,750 and over	2,317	6.4%	768	6.9%

Source: Martin O'Connell and Amara Bachu, *Who's Minding the Kids? Child Care Arrangements: Winter, 1986-87,* Current Population Reports Household Economic Studies, Series P-70, No. 20, 1990, p. 10. *Notes:* 1. Universe consists of employed mothers who used any of the following arrangements for any of their three youngest children under 15 years of age: care by a grandparent or other relative (excluding their child's parents or siblings), a nonrelative, a day/group care center or nursery/preschool. Also in source: data by place of primary care and poverty level. 2. Includes married, husband absent (including separated), widowed, divorced, and never-married women.

★ 496 ★

Lost Work Time: Part I

Absences from work for female full-time wage and salary workers in families by marital status and presence and age of children, 1989 annual averages.

Marital status and presence and age of children	Total employed (thousands)	Absence rate		
		Total	Illness	Other reasons
Married women, spouse present				
With no children under 18 years old	9,465	5.8%	3.3%	2.4%
Youngest child 6 to 17 years old	5,698	6.0%	3.4%	2.6%
Youngest child under 6 years old	4,010	11.5%	4.0%	7.5%
Unmarried women				
With no children under 18 years old	13,160	5.7%	3.5%	2.2%
Youngest child 6 to 17 years old	2,193	6.8%	4.3%	2.5%
Youngest child under 6 years old	956	11.0%	5.0%	6.0%

Source: Selected from "Absences from work for full-time wage and salary workers in families by sex, marital status, and presence and age of children, 1989 annual averages," *Employment in Perspective: Women in the Labor Force*, Report 791, Second Quarter 1990, p. 1 (Washington, D.C.: U.S. Department of Labor, August, 1990).

★ 497 ★

Lost Work Time: Part II

Absences from work for male full-time wage and salary workers in families by marital status and presence and age of children, 1989 annual averages.

Marital status and presence and age of children	Total employed (thousands)	Absence rate		
		Total	Illness	Other reasons
Married men, spouse present				
With no children under 18 years old	12,839	4.1%	2.7%	1.5%
Youngest child 6 to 17 years old	9,429	3.7%	2.2%	1.5%
Youngest child under 6 years old	9,636	3.8%	2.3%	1.5%
Unmarried men				
With no children under 18 years old	15,990	4.3%	2.3%	2.0%
Youngest child 6 to 17 years old	471	4.2%	2.6%	1.6%
Youngest child under 6 years old	307	2.9%	1.4%	1.5%

Source: Selected from "Absences from work for full-time wage and salary workers in families by sex, marital status, and presence and age of children, 1989 annual averages," *Employment in Perspective: Women in the Labor Force*, Report 791, Second Quarter 1990, p. 1 (Washington, D.C.: U.S. Department of Labor, August 1990). Also in source: data for women.

★ 498 ★

Persons with Work Disability

Persons with work disability, by age, and percent of total population, 1988.

Age of work disabled	Total	Female	Male
	Numbers in thousands		
Persons with work disability	13,420	6,714	6,706
16-24 years old	1,285	610	674
25-34 years old	2,414	1,165	1,249
35-44 years old	2,455	1,147	1,308
45-54 years old	2,443	1,252	1,190
55-64 years old	4,825	2,540	2,285
Percent work disabled of total population	8.6%	8.4%	8.7%
16-24 years old	3.8%	3.6%	4.1%
25-34 years old	5.6%	5.4%	5.9%
35-44 years old	7.1%	6.5%	7.7%
45-54 years old	10.3%	10.2%	10.3%
55-64 years old	22.3%	22.2%	22.4%

Source: "Persons with Work Disability, by Selected Characteristics: 1988," *Statistical Abstract of the United States 1990*, 1990, p. 364. Also in source: persons receiving disability and other payments (see Income chapter in this book). As of March. Covers civilian noninstitutional population and members of Armed Forces living off post or with their families on post. Persons are classified as having a work disability if they (1) have a health problem or disability which prevents them from working or which limits the kind or amount of work they can do; (2) have a service-connected disability or ever retired or left a job for health reasons; (3) did not work in survey reference week or previous year because of long-term illness or disability; or (4) are under age 65 and are covered by Medicare or receive Supplemental Security Income. Based on Current Population Survey.

★ 499 ★

Potential Work Years Spent Away From Work

Percent of potential work years spent away from work by age and years of school, 1984.

Age and school years completed	Percent of potential work years			
	All workers		Full-time workers	
	Women	Men	Women	Men
Workers 21 to 64 years of age	14.7	1.6	11.5	1.3
21 to 29 years of age	5.3	2.3	3.7	1.8
Less than 12 years of school	8.8	3.3	6.5	2.2
12 to 15 years of school	5.7	2.2	3.8	1.8
16 years or more of school	2.6	2.0	2.3	1.6
30 to 44 years of age	16.6	1.6	12.3	1.2
Less than 12 years of school	20.2	2.6	16.3	1.8
12 to 15 years of school	17.6	1.5	12.8	1.3
16 years or more of school	12.1	1.2	9.5	1.0
45 to 64 years of age	22.7	0.9	19.5	0.7
Less than 12 years of school	19.2	1.0	16.9	0.7

[Continued]

★ 499 ★

Potential Work Years Spent Away From Work
[Continued]

Age and school years completed	Percent of potential work years			
	All workers		Full-time workers	
	Women	Men	Women	Men
12 to 15 years of school	24.1	0.8	20.3	0.6
16 years or more of school	23.0	0.9	20.4	0.9

Source: "Percent of potential work-years spent away from work by sex, age, and years of school, 1984," *Facts on Working Women,* No. 90-3, October 1990, p. 5.

Non-Traditional Occupations

★ 500 ★

Women in Construction
Summary of the results of a 10-year effort to recruit women for the construction trades in California, reported in the *New York Times.*

The author reports on California's success in meeting its 1978 goal of **20% female participation** in construction-industry apprenticeship programs. California is about the same as the rest of the nation, where women make up **2%** of the construction industry work force. The Coalition for Equality in the Trades contends that the representation of women in the programs overseen by the State Division of Apprenticeship Standards fell from **5.14% in 1988 to 4.9% in 1989.** The chief of the state agency, disputing that figure, stated that women hold **6,000 of 51,000 total apprenticeship slots**, an increase to **11% in 1989 from 8% in 1983.** The coalition contends that most of the gain was in training programs for jobs such as psychiatric technicians and correctional officers.

Source: Katherine Bishop, "Scant Success for California Efforts to Put Women in Construction Jobs," *New York Times,* February 15, 1991, p. A13.

★ 501 ★

Women in the Construction Trade
Women's representation in the construction industry, 1979.

Position in construction industry	% Female
Total experienced construction labor force (1978)	1.2%
Painters	4%
Machinists	3%
Electricians	2%

[Continued]

★ 501 ★

Women in the Construction Trade
[Continued]

Position in construction industry	% Female
Tool and die makers	2%
Plumbers	1%

Source: A Territorial Issue: A Study of Women in the Construction Trades, 1982, p. 2 (Washington, D.C.: Wider Opportunities for Women in conjunction with The Center for National Policy Review, 1982). Primary source: Newland, Kathleen: *The Sisterhood of Man* (New York: Norton & Co., 1979).

★ 502 ★

Women in the Steel Industry: Part 1
Total employment, number and percent female, in two selected Midwest Steel Mills, 1976-1979.

Year	Total	Female	% Female
1976	30,389	2,488	8.2%
1977	31,444	2,917	9.3%
1978	32,478	3,548	10.9%
1979	34,097	4,168	12.2%

Source: "Total, Male and Female Employment in Two Selected Midwest Steel Mills, 1976-79," *Women of Steel: Female Blue-Collar Workers in the Basic Steel Industry*, 1983, p. 85 (New York: Praeger Publishers, 1983). Based on a study of 2 plants with a total of 34,000 workers, 4,168 of whom were women.

★ 503 ★

Women in the Steel Industry: Part 2
Total, female and percent female employment in production and maintenance positions in two selected Midwest steel mills, 1976-79.

Year	Total	Female	% Female
1976	22,100	763	3.5%
1977	22,843	1,047	4.6%
1978	23,603	1,519	6.4%
1979	24,912	1,938	7.8%

Source: Selected from "Total, Male and Female Employment in Productin and Maintenance Positions in Two Selected Midwest Steel Mills, 1976-79," *Women of Steel: Female Blue-Collar Workers in the Basic Steel Industry*, 1983, p. 85 (New York: Praeger Publishers, 1983). Based on a study of 2 plants with a total of 34,000 workers, 4,168 of whom were women.

★ 504 ★

Women in the Steel Industry: Part 3

Total, female and percent female craft employment in two selected Midwest steel mills, 1976-1979.

Year	Total	Female	% Female
1976	7,332	27	0.4%
1977	7,826	66	0.8%
1978	8,170	154	1.7%
1979	8,780	197	2.2%

Source: Selected from "Total Male and Female Craft Employment in Two Selected Midwest Steel Mills, 1976-79," *Women of Steel: Female Blue-Collar Workers in the Basic Steel Industry,* 1983, p. 85 (New York: Praeger Publishers, 1983). Based on a study of 2 plants with a total of 34,000 workers, 4,168 of whom were women.

Occupations

★ 505 ★

Astronomers in Selected Countries

Some statistics on worldwide representation of women in astronomy, 1988, as reported in *New Scientist.*

United States—**1 in 12 members** of the American Astronomical Society is female

Argentina—of 165 astronomers, **42** are women

France—the proportion of women astronomers had long been **30%**; in the period 1986-1988, this proprotion fell to **10%**

Japan—of 600 astronomers, **14** are women

India—**1 in 20** astronomers is a woman

Chile—women represent **14%** of astronomers

Argentina and Mexico—women represent **25%** of astronomers

China—women represent **30%** of workers in observatories and universities but fill only **10%** of higher posts

Source: "A woman's place is in the dome: Why are most stargazers male, asks Nigel Henbest?", *New Scientist,* October 8, 1988, p. 62.

★ 506 ★

Black Women Managers

Black women in management executive, and administrative occupations, as a percent of all employed black women, 1983-1988.

Year	Percent
1988	7.0%
1987	6.4%
1986	6.0%
1985	5.8%
1984	5.2%
1983	4.9%

Source: Facts on Working Women, No. 89-4, December 1989, p. 6.

★ 507 ★

Clerical Occupations: 1984-1995

Clerical occupations with largest projected job growth, 1984-1995.

Occupation (and percent female)	Employment (thousands)		Change in female employment, 1984-1995	
	1984	1995	Number (thousands)	Percent
Secretaries (98.8%)	2,797	3,064	265	9.6%
General office clerks (82.1%)	2,398	2,629	190	9.6%
Bookkeeping, accounting, and auditing clerks (89.7%)	1,973	2,091	106	6.0%
Switchboard operators (91.0%)	347	447	91	28.7%
Teachers' aides and educational assistants (92.7%)	479	566	82	18.3%
Receptionists and information clerks (93.4%)	458	542	78	18.2%
Computer operators, excluding peripheral equipment operators (58.9%)	241	353	65	46.1%
Order clerks, material, merchandise, and services (67.4%)	297	355	38	19.2%
Billing, posting, and labeling machine operators (87.1%)	234	272	33	16.2%
Billing, cost, and rate clerks (80.7%)	216	254	31	17.5%

Source: "Clerical occupations with largest projected job growth for women, 1984-1995," *Computer Chips and Paper Clips: Technology and Women's Employment*, Vol. 1, 1986, p. 121 (Washington, D.C.: National Academy Press, 1986). Primary source: percent female from 1980 census data (Hunt and Hunt, 1985a; Table 2.4). Employment data from Silvestri and Lukasiewicz (1985: Table 2). Estimates of job growth for women are conservative; because the percentage female is likely to grow by 1995 in many of these occupations, these numbers underestimate job growth for women.

★ 508 ★

College and University Faculty Members

Faculty members at public and private institutions by state, and percent female, 1987-88.

State	Total at public instit.	% Female	Total at private instit.	% Female
United States	255,731	29.3%	100,553	28.5%
Alabama	4,500	33.8%	923	32.4%
Alaska	577	29.6%	45	37.8%
Arizona	4,206	26.0%	243	32.9%
Arkansas	2,210	34.0%	378	27.8%
California	31,296	27.9%	6,056	25.5%
Colorado	4,347	22.8%	610	29.0%
Connecticut	3,025	27.3%	2,537	25.7%
Delaware	1,056	34.0%	154	44.8%
District of Columbia	553	36.5%	2,616	30.7%
Florida	7,223	29.5%	2,363	25.1%
Georgia	5,136	32.3%	1,772	32.7%
Hawaii	1,494	29.5%	95	42.1%
Idaho	1,195	25.4%	117	21.4%
Illinois	11,788	29.3%	5,938	27.3%
Indiana	5,901	30.5%	2,581	25.1%
Iowa	3,123	28.6%	1.697	28.2%
Kansas	3,793	26.9%	682	32.3%
Kentucky	3,749	32.4%	1,058	36.2%
Louisiana	4,774	33.6%	980	30.3%
Maine	1,304	27.0%	557	33.4%
Maryland	4,561	35.1%	1,259	28.9%
Massachusetts	5,805	32.7%	9,195	27.7%
Michigan	10,597	26.6%	1,984	30.3%
Minnesota	4,786	26.8%	2,058	32.0%
Mississippi	3,287	41.9%	321	37.1%
Missouri	4,703	27.2%	2,225	32.3%
Montana	1,158	22.6%	145	33.1%
Nebraska	1,995	24.9%	605	29.3%
Nevada	877	27.3%	na	na
New Hampshire	1,023	27.3%	900	30.0%
New Jersey	5,873	33.7%	2,521	25.2%
New Mexico	2,045	27.7%	88	23.9%
New York	17,926	30.6%	15,351	28.9%
North Carolina	6,186	33.2%	2,856	30.4%
North Dakota	1,196	25.7%	116	44.8%
Ohio	10,389	27.7%	4,047	27.1%
Oklahoma	3,443	29.8%	843	31.2%
Oregon	3,735	31.1%	842	26.6%
Pennsylvania	10,403	27.3%	9,002	26.8%
Rhode island	1,143	32.5%	1,430	23.9%

[Continued]

★ 508 ★

College and University Faculty Members
[Continued]

State	Total at public instit.	% Female	Total at private instit.	% Female
South Carolina	3,747	32.0%	1,234	29.1%
South Dakota	862	26.9%	283	39.6%
Tennessee	4,701	30.7%	2,026	25.8%
Texas	16,463	31.4%	3,955	27.8%
Utah	2,096	22.5%	na	na
Vermont	660	25.8%	673	30.8%
Virginia	7,421	29.0%	2,069	33.6%
Washington	5,236	26.0%	1,214	28.4%
West Virginia	2,031	31.4%	381	39.4%
Wisconsin	7,960	26.9%	1,476	30.1%
Wyoming	933	26.5%	na	na

Source: Chronicle of Higher Education Almanac, September 5, 1990, p. 3, 29-88. Primary source: U.S. Department of Education, 1987-1988. Also in source: numerous other education-related statistics on a state-by-state basis. Figures cover full-time faculty members on nine-month contracts only. The figures are based on reports of those institutions that responded to the department's faculty-salary survey.

★ 509 ★

Criminal Justice Personal, Selected Countries

Number and percent women police and prosecutors, 1980.

Country or area	Number of police			Number of prosecutors		
	Female	Male	% Female	Female	Male	% Female
Asia						
Bahrain	-	-	-	0	11	-
Bangladesh	196	67,673	0.3%	0	218	-
Cyprus	69	3,299	2.0%	1	26	3.7%
India	389	23,164	1.7%	1	55	1.8%
Indonesia	-	-	-	497	4,156	10.7%
Israel	2,601	14,415	15.3%	-	-	-
Japan	-	-	-	30	2,008	1.5%
Korea, Republic of	399	55,104	0.7%	0	437	-
Philippines	2,150	-	-	106	1,006	9.5%
Singapore	931	6,083	13.3%	0	14	-

[Continued]

★ 509 ★

Criminal Justice Personal, Selected Countries
[Continued]

Country or area	Number of police			Number of prosecutors		
	Female	Male	% Female	Female	Male	% Female
Sri Lanka	197	16,695	1.2%	-	-	-
Thailand	-	-	-	26	963	2.6%
United Arab Emirates	-	-	-	0	23	-
Europe						
Czechoslovakia	-	-	-	60	51	54.1%
Denmark	119	8,494	1.4%	-	-	-
Finland	146	7,802	1.8%	15	355	4.1%
Germany, Federal Republic	-	-	-	432	3,893	10.0%
Greece	1,018	34,577	2.9%	2	310	0.6%
Italy	-	-	-	6	65	8.5%
Portugal	20	856	2.3%	-	-	-
Spain	-	-	-	5	282	1.7%
Sweden	-	-	-	89	519	14.6%
United Kingdom (England and Wales)	10,430	106,993	8.9%	-	-	-
Oceania						
New Zealand	-	-	-	2	83	2.4%
Tonga	45	255	15.0%	0	12	-

Source: Selected from "Selected series on criminal justice by sex, 1975 and 1980. Selected criminal justice occupations," *Compendium of Statistics and Indicators on the Situation of Women 1986,* p. 587-88 (New York: United Nations, 1989). Primary source: First and Second United Nations Surveys of Crime Trends, Operations of Criminal Justice systems and Crime Prevention Strategies, Centre for Social Development and Humanitarian Affairs of the United Nations Secretariat, unpublished data. Also in source: data for 1975; number per 1,000 population.

★ 510 ★

Doctoral Scientists and Engineers in Academic Institutions

Doctoral scientists and engineers in 4-year colleges and universities, by tenure status and academic rank, 1987.

Tenure status and academic rank	PhD Women	PhD Men
Tenure status		
Tenure track	58%	74%
Tenured	36%	60%
Not tenured	22%	14%
Non-tenure track	18%	7%
Academic rank		
Full professor	18%	46%
Associate professor	25%	24%
Assistant professor	29%	15%

Source: "Doctoral scientists and engineers in 4-year colleges and universities, by tenure status, academic rank, and gender: 1987," *Women and Minorities in Science and Engineering*, 1990, p. 7 (Washington, D.C.: National Science Foundation, January 1990).

★ 511 ★

Employed Persons by Occupation: 1985-1988

Total employed persons and percent distribution of female employed persons by occupation, 1985-1988.

Occupation	1985		1986		1987		1988	
	Total	Women	Total	Women	Total	Women	Total	Women
Total	107,150	47,259	109,597	48,706	112,440	50,334	114,968	51,696
Managerial and professional specialty	25,851	23.4%	26,554	23.7%	27,742	24.4%	29,190	25.2%
Executive, administrative, and managerial	12,221	9.2%	12,642	9.6%	13,316	10.0%	14,216	10.8%
Professional specialty	13,630	14.2%	13,911	14.1%	14,426	14.4%	14,974	14.4%
Technical, sales, and administrative support	33,231	45.5%	34,354	45.6%	35,082	45.1%	35,532	44.6%
Technicians and related support	3,255	3.3%	3,364	3.2%	3,346	3.2%	3,521	3.3%
Sales occupations	12,667	12.9%	13,245	13.1%	13,480	12.8%	13,747	13.0%
Administrative support, including clerical	17,309	29.4%	17,745	29.3%	18,256	29.0%	18,264	28.3%
Service Occupations	14,441	18.5%	14,680	18.3%	15,054	18.1%	15,332	17.9%
Private household	1,006	2.0%	981	1.9%	934	1.8%	909	1.7%
Protective service	1,718	.5%	7,787	.5%	1,907	.5%	1,944	.5%
Service, except private household and protective	11,718	16.0%	11,913	15.9%	12,213	15.8%	12,479	15.7%
Precision production, craft, and repair	13,340	2.4%	13,405	2.4%	13,568	2.3%	13,664	2.3%
Operators, fabricators, and laborers	16,816	9.1%	17,160	8.9%	17,486	9.0%	17,814	8.9%
Machine operators, assemblers, and inspectors	7,840	6.7%	7,911	6.5%	7,994	6.5%	8,117	6.4%
Transportation and material moving occupations	4,535	.8%	4,564	.8%	4,712	.8%	4,831	.8%
Handlers, equipment cleaners, helpers, and laborers	4,441	1.6%	4,685	1.6%	4,779	1.6%	4,866	1.6%
Farming, forestry, and fishing	3,470	1.2%	3,444	1.1%	3,507	1.1%	3,437	1.1%

Source: Selected from "Employed civilians by occupation, sex, race, and Hispanic origin, 1983-88," *Handbook of Labor Statistics*, 1989, p. 77-8 (Washington, D.C.: U.S. Department of Labor, August 1989). Also in source: numbers by occupation; data by race/ethnicity; data for 1983-84. These occupational data are based on the 1980 census classification system and are not comparable with the 1972-82 data based on the 1970 census classification system. See source for further explanation.

★ 512 ★

Expected Occupations of 8th Graders at Age 30

Expected occupations of 8th graders at age 30, 1988.

Expected occupation at age 30	All 8th graders	Female	Male
Craftsperson or operator	4.2%	0.9%	7.6%
Farmer or farm manager	1.0%	0.3%	1.7%
Housewife/homemaker	2.3%	4.4%	0.2%
Laborer or farm worker	0.6%	0.1%	1.0%
Military, police, or security officer	9.6%	4.3%	14.9%
Professional, business, or managerial	28.6%	37.6%	19.6%
Business owner	6.2%	5.6%	6.8%
Technical	6.2%	4.2%	8.3%
Salesperson, clerical, or office worker	2.8%	4.5%	1.2%
Science or engineering professional	5.9%	3.3%	8.5%
Service worker	4.9%	7.7%	2.1%
Other employment	17.0%	16.5%	17.6%
Don't know	10.5%	10.6%	10.4%

Source: Selected from "Expected occupations of 8th graders at age 30, by selected student and school characteristics: 1988," *Digest of Education Statistics*, p. 130 (Washington, D.C.: National Center for Education Statistics, 1989). Primary source: U.S. Department of Education, National Center for Education Statistics, "National Education Longitudinal Study of 1988" survey. (This table was prepared June 1989.) Also in source: other student and school characteristics. Data are preliminary.

★ 513 ★

Faculty in Institutions of Higher Education

Full-time instructional faculty in institutions of higher education by academic rank and race/ethnicity: Fall 1985.

Academic rank	Total	Race/ethnicity				
		White non-Hispanic	Black, non-Hispanic	Hispanic	Asian or PacIslander	Amer Indian/ Alaska Natv.
Women and men	464,072	417,036	19,227	7,704	18,370	1,735
Professors	129,269	119,868	2,859	1,455	4,788	299
Associate Professors	111,092	100,630	4,201	1,727	4,130	404
Assistant Professors	111,308	97,496	5,895	1,968	5,469	480
Instructors	75,411	66,799	4,572	1,798	1,806	436
Lecturers	9,766	8,477	631	251	360	47
Other faculty	27,226	23,766	1,069	505	1,817	69
Women	128,063	113,083	8,771	2,344	3,524	341
Professors	15,011	13,533	801	249	393	35
Associate professors	25,936	23,147	1,606	447	679	57
Assistant professors	39,845	34,914	2,972	652	1,229	78
Instructors	32,160	28,207	2,465	657	701	130

[Continued]

★ 513 ★

Faculty in Institutions of Higher Education
[Continued]

Academic rank	Total	Race/ethnicity				
		White non-Hispanic	Black, non-Hispanic	Hispanic	Asian or PacIslander	Amer Indian/ Alaska Natv.
Lecturers	4,668	4,041	327	134	148	18
Other faculty	10,443	9,241	600	205	374	23

Source: Selected from "Full-time instructional faculty in institutions of higher education, by race/ethnicity, academic rank, and sex: Fall 1985," *Digest of Education Statistics*, p. 212 (Washington, D.C.: National Center for Education Statistics, 1989). Primary source: U.S. Equal Employment Opportunity Commission, Higher Education Staff Information Report File, 1985, unpublished data. (This table was prepared June 1989.) Also in source: data for men. Data exclude faculty employed by system offices.

★ 514 ★

Federal Government Employment
Representation of women workers in the Federal government.

Level	% Female
Nonpostal Executive Branch Federal civilian jobs	42.2%
Professional	30.8%
Nonclerical administrative	37.1%
Executives	9.2%
Black	0.8%
Hispanic	0.3%
Asian or Pacific Islander	0.1%

Source: Facts on Working Women, No. 89-4, December 1989, p. 3. As of September 30, 1988.

★ 515 ★

Government Employment
Percentage distribution of women in Federal, and state and local positions, 1975-1985.

	1975 Positions		1985 Positions	
	Federal	State and Local	Federal	State and Local
Women	35.3%	37.5%	37.4%	41.2%

Source: "Percentage Distribution of Minorities and Women in Federal, and State and Local Positions, 1975-1985," *The Merit System and Municipal Civil Service: A Fostering of Social Inequality*, p. 64 (New York: Greenwood Press, 1988). Primary source: Robert D. Lee, Jr., *Public Personnel Systems* (Baltimore: University Park Press, 1979), p. 243; U.S. Equal Opportunity Commission, *Annual Report on the Employment of Minorities, Women and Handicapped Individuals in the Federal Government, Fiscal Year 1985* (Washington, D.C.: U.S. Government Printing Office, June 1987); and U.S. Equal Employment Opportunity Commission, "Minorities and Women in State and Local Government, 1985" (Washington, D.C.: U.S. Government Printing Office, 1987). Also in source: percent distribution of minorities.

★ 516 ★

Health Occupations Enrollment

Total and first-year enrollment of women in schools for selected health occupations, academic years 1977-78 and 1987-88.

Health occupation	All races, both sexes		Women	
	1977-78	1987-88	1977-78	1987-88[1]
Total enrollment				
Medicine:				
Allopathic	60,039	65,735	23.7%	34.3%
Osteopathic	3,926	6,586	14.5%	28.9%
Podiatry	2,388	2,790	9.3%	24.4%
Dentistry[2]	21,510	17,632	-	29.0%
Optometry	4,209	4,509	-	39.1%
Pharmacy[2,3]	23,373	27,292	38.1%	60.0%
Veterinary medicine	6,918	8,558	30.8%	55.0%
Registered nurses	245,390	182,947	95.2%	95.0%
First-year enrollment				
Medicine:				
Allopathic	16,136	16,713	25.6%	36.5%
Osteopathic	1,163	1,692	16.5%	29.0%
Podiatry	665	716	9.8%	24.2%
Dentistry[2]	5,890	4,316	14.8%	32.0%
Optometry	1,140	1,234	19.8%	43.8%
Pharmacy[2,3]	8,235	7,407	40.5%	59.2%
Veterinary medicine	1,973	2,207	35.8%	57.3%
Registered nurses	110,950	90,693	93.7%	92.8%

Source: Selected from "Total and first-year enrollment of minorities and women in schools for selected health occupations: United States, academic years 1977-78 and 1987-88," *Health United States—1989*, p. 213. Primary source: Association of American Medical Colleges, Section for Student Services: Unpublished data; American Association of Colleges of Osteopathic Medicine: Annual Statistical Report, 1988; National League for Nursing: Nursing Student Census, 1987 and 1988. American Association of Colleges of Podiatric Medicine: Podiatric Medical Education in the Eighties. American Dental Association; American Optometric Association; American Association of Colleges of Pharmacy; Association of American Veterinary Medical Colleges; unpublished data. Also in source: data for Blacks and other minorities. *Notes:* 1. Total and first-year enrollment percentages for registered nurses are based on 1986-87 data. 2. Excludes Puerto Rican schools. 3. Pharmacy enrollment data for 1977-78 are for students in the final 3 years of pharmacy education. 1987-88 data for all pharmacy students are shown.

★ 517 ★

Job Growth: 1984-1995

Female-dominated occupations with largest projected job growth, 1984-1995.

Occupation	Change in Total Employment (thousands)	Percent of Total Job Growth
Cashiers	556	3.6%
Nurses, registered	452	2.8%
Waiters and waitresses	424	2.7%
Nurses' aides and orderlies	348	2.2%

[Continued]

★ 517 ★

Job Growth: 1984-1995
[Continued]

Occupation	Change in Total Employment (thousands)	Percent of Total Job Growth
Salespersons, retail	343	2.2%
Teachers, kindergarten and elementary	281	1.9%
Secretaries	268	1.7%
General office clerks	231	1.4%

Source: "Female-Dominated Occupations with Largest Projected Job Growth, 1984-1995," *Computer Chips and Paper Clips: Technology and Women's Employment,* Vol. 1, 1986, p. 12 (Washington, D.C.: National Academy Press, 1986). Primary source: Silvestri and Lukasiewicz (1985: Table 3).

★ 518 ★

Job Growth: 1986-2000
Occupations with largest job growth, 1986-2000, and percent women, 1986.

Occupation	1986 Employment		New Jobs
	Number (thousands)	% Women	
Salespersons, retail	3,579	59.5%	1,201
Waiters and waitresses	1,702	85.1%	752
Registered nurses	1,406	94.3%	612
Janitors, cleaners (incl. maids and housekeeping cleaners)	2,676	42.7%	604
General managers and top executives	2,383	NA	582
Cashiers	2,165	82.9%	575
Truck drivers, light and heavy	2,211	4.3%	525
General office clerks	2,361	80.5%	462
Food counter, fountain and related workers	1,500	NA	449
Nursing aides, orderlies, and attendants	1,224	90.5%	433
Secretaries	3,234	99.0%	424

Source: "Occupations with largest job growth, 1986-2000," *Facts on U.S. Working Women,* Fact Sheet No. 88-1, January, 1988, p. 4. Primary source: U.S. Department of Labor, Bureau of Labor Statistics, *Monthly Labor Review,* September 1987.

★ 519 ★

Lawyers
Total lawyers and number female, 1970 to 1985.

Total	1970	1980	1985
All lawyers[1]	355,242	542,205	655,191
Female	9,103	44,185	85,542

Source: Selected from "Lawyers-Selected Characteristics: 1954 to 1985," *Statistical Abstract of the United States 1990*, 1990, p. 182. Primary source: American Bar Foundation, Chicago, IL, 1954-1970, *The 1971 Lawyer Statistical Report*, 1971; 1980, *The Lawyer Statistical Report: A Statistical Profile of the U.S. Legal Profession in the 1980s*, 1985; and 1985, *Supplement to the Lawyer Statistical Report: The U.S. Legal Profession in 1985*, 1986. Also in source: data for 1954-1966; data for status in practice, not by gender. Data based on 1971, 1980 and 1985 editions of *Martindale-Hubbell Law Directory*. Represents all persons who are members of the bar, including those in industries, educational institutions, etc., and those inactive or retired. *Notes:* 1. 1970 includes lawyers not reporting and an adjustment (subtraction) for duplications; 1980 and 1985 weighted to account for non-reporters and duplicate listings.

★ 520 ★

Librarians in Academic and Public Libraries
Librarians in academic and public libraries, by race/ethnicity.

Race/Ethnicity	Academic		Public	
	Number	Percent of work force	Number	Percent of work force
American Indian/Alaskan Native				
Female	10	0.1%	20	0.2%
Male	5	0.1%	7	0.1%
Asian/Pacific Islander				
Female	214	3.2%	283	2.3%
Male	91	1.3%	51	0.4%
Black				
Female	218	3.2%	756	6.2%
Male	56	0.8%	119	1.0%
White				
Female	3,943	58.4%	8,504	70.1%
Male	2,115	31.3%	2,153	17.7%
Total				
Female	4,446	65.9%	9,725	80.2%
Male	2,304	34.1%	2,407	19.8%

Source: Selected from "Distribution of Total Work Force by Racial/Ethnic/Sexual Group for Librarians in Academic and Public Libraries," *Academic and Public Librarians: Data by Race, Ethnicity and Sex*, 1986, p. 7 (Chicago: American Library Association, 1986). Based on responses from 1,098 libraries.

★ 521 ★

Major Occupation Groups: 1950-1980

Major occupation groups of employed women: 1950-1980.

Occupation	1950	1960	1970	1980
White-collar workers	52.5%	56.3%	61.3%	63.5%
Professional	12.2%	13.3%	15.5%	15.9%
Managers	4.3%	3.8%	3.6%	6.8%
Clerical	27.4%	30.9%	34.8%	33.8%
Sales	8.6%	8.3%	7.4%	7.0%
Blue-collar workers	43.9%	41.8%	37.9%	35.5%
Crafts	1.5%	1.3%	1.8%	1.8%
Operatives	20.0%	17.2%	14.8%	10.7%
Laborers	0.9%	0.6%	1.0%	1.3%
Private household	8.9%	8.4%	3.9%	3.0%
Other services	12.6%	14.4%	16.3%	18.8%
Farm workers	3.7%	1.9%	0.8%	1.0%
Managers	0.7%	0.6%	0.2%	0.3%
Laborers	2.9%	1.3%	0.6%	0.7%

Source: "Major Occupation Groups of Employed Women, 1950-1980 (percent)," *Computer Chips and Paper Clips: Technology and Women's Employment*, Vol. 1, 1986, p. 18 (Washington, D.C., National Academy Press, 1986). Primary source: Bianchi, Suzanne M., and Daphne Spain, *American Women: Three Decades of Change*, Special Demographic Analyses, CDS-80-8. Washington, D.C.: U.S. Department of Commerce.

★ 522 ★

Medical School Enrollment

Total and first-year enrollment and percent of women in schools of medicine, according to race and ethnicity, academic years 1971-72, 1977-78, and 1987-88.

Race/ethnicity	Both sexes			Women		
	1971-72	1977-78	1987-88	1971-72	1977-78	1987-88
Total enrollment						
All races[1]	43,650	60,039	65,735	10.9%	23.7%	34.3%
White	-	31,974	51,728	-	22.4%	32.7%
Minority	3,072	6,728	13,487	19.0%	33.0%	40.3%
First-year enrollment						
All races[1]	12,361	16,136	16,713	13.7%	25.6%	36.5%
White	-	13,732	12,511	-	24.1%	34.7%
Minority	1,280	2,002	4,043	20.8%	35.2%	42.1%

Source: Selected from "Total and first-year enrollment and percent of women in schools of medicine, according to race and ethnicity: United States, academic years 1971-72, 1977-78, and 1987-88," *Health United States—1989*, p. 214. Primary source: Association of American Medical Colleges, Section for Student Services, Annual Fall Enrollment Surveys; unpublished data. Also in source: detailed breakdown of minority enrollment. *Note:* 1. Includes race/ethnicity unspecified.

★ 523 ★

Occupations of Hispanic American Women

Occupations of employed women, by Hispanic origin, March 1988.

Occupation	All Women	Hispanic Women			
		All Hispanic Women	Mexican Origin	Puerto Rican Origin	Cuban-Origin
Managerial and Professional Specialty	25.3%	15.7%	12.6%	20.5%	27.3%
Technical, Sales, and Administrative Support	45.1%	41.1%	41.7%	44.7%	41.8%
Service Occupations	17.7%	21.7%	21.9%	15.3%	13.0%
Precision, Production, Craft, and Repair	2.3%	3.5%	3.6%	3.6%	3.2%
Operators, Fabricators, and Laborers	8.8%	16.6%	18.0%	15.8%	14.7%
Farming, Fishing, and Forestry	0.9%	1.5%	2.1%	-	-

Source: U.S. Department of Commerce, Bureau of the Census, *The Hispanic Population in the United States: March 1988* (Advance Report).

★ 524 ★

Occupations with Largest Projected Growth: 1986-2000

Occupations with largest projected growth, 1986-2000, and percent female in occupation as of 1986.

Occupation	Expected number of new jobs 1986-2000	Percent female in 1986
Registered Nurse	612,000	93%
Truck Driver	525,000	3%
Office Clerk	462,000	80%
Janitor/Maid	604,000	28%
Nursing Aide	433,000	88%
Cashier	575,000	80%
Waiter/Waitress	752,000	79%
Retail Sales	1,200,000	69%
Food-Counter Worker	449,000	79%
General Manager	582,000	NA

Source: "So You Think You've Come a Long Way, Baby?," *Business Week* (February 29, 1988):48+. Primary source: Bureau of Labor Statistics, Census Bureau, and *Business Week* estimates. Also in source: average hourly pay by occupation (see *Income* chapter in this book under subhead "Wages and Salaries").

★ 525 ★

Physicians by Specialty

Physicians by age and selected specialties, 1988.

Specialty	Total physicians[1]		Under 35 years		35-44 years		45-54 years		55-64 years	
	Female	Male	Female	Male	Female	Male	Female	Male	Female	Male
Total physicians	86,670	482,490	37,188	103,735	30,397	139,522	12,158	95,482	6,457	75,098
Anesthesiology	4,189	20,069	1,327	5,654	1,454	6,121	877	3,980	377	3,183
Cardiovascular Disease	771	14,361	291	2,876	313	5,513	107	3,221	44	1,773
Dermatology	1,336	5,705	589	830	490	1,995	168	1,466	58	819

[Continued]

★ 525 ★

Physicians by Specialty
[Continued]

Specialty	Total physicians[1]		Under 35 years		35-44 years		45-54 years		55-64 years	
	Female	Male	Female	Male	Female	Male	Female	Male	Female	Male
Diagnostic Radiology	2,146	12,382	1,121	3,921	772	4,768	180	2,483	60	897
Emergency Medicine	1,745	11,180	765	2,986	722	5,424	177	1,508	69	895
Family Practice	7,062	37,882	3,861	11,615	2,240	12,947	580	5,001	253	5,527
Gastroenterology	358	6,510	154	1,376	160	2,919	32	1,423	8	543
General Practice	2,381	22,014	261	771	698	2,491	571	3,982	467	6,835
General Surgery	2,150	35,642	1,400	9,707	570	8,516	105	7,378	47	6,180
Internal Medicine	17,040	77,634	9,017	24,216	5,560	25,230	1,537	12,868	647	9,450
Neurology	1,304	7,359	502	1,688	529	2,914	183	1,696	69	787
Obstetrics/Gynecology	6,634	25,644	3,345	4,487	2,056	7,641	759	6,290	299	4,808
Ophthalmology	1,376	14,205	643	2,793	479	4,122	142	3,758	72	2,090
Orthopedic Surgery	348	17,886	196	4,373	116	5,408	15	4,509	14	2,477
Otolaryngology	361	7,451	184	1,519	136	2,152	20	2,137	14	964
Pathology	3,527	12,685	1,132	2,199	1,304	3,594	673	3,257	310	2,657
Pediatrics	14,032	24,199	6,149	6,160	4,868	7,953	1,867	4,847	784	3,503
Plastic Surgery	271	4,085	91	546	117	1,569	39	1,225	17	520
Psychiatry	7,375	26,304	2,198	3,812	2,424	7,179	1,391	6,628	865	5,587
Pulmonary Diseases	452	5,324	170	1,117	176	2,544	56	1,010	31	405
Radiology	710	7,665	133	362	277	1,388	184	2,773	90	2,184
Urological Surgery	118	9,037	72	1,586	34	2,622	9	2,608	2	1,478
Other	817	5,565	123	381	230	1,135	182	1,267	177	1,473

Source: "Physicians by Age, Sex, and Selected Specialties," *The World Almanac and Book of Facts 1991,* p. 845 (New York: Pharos Books, 1991). Primary source: American Medical Association, Jan 1., 1988. *Notes:* 1. Includes those 65 years and over, those living in U.S. possessions, APO's and FPO's, and those with addresses unknown.

★ 526 ★

Professional Choices of Doctorate Recipients: 1978 and 1988

Field	1978		1988	
	Women	Men	Women	Men
Academe	66%	53%	55%	46%
Industry	7%	18%	14%	25%
Government	9%	14%	9%	12%
Other and Unknown	18%	15%	23%	17%

Source: "Employment Sector Commitments of Doctorate Recipients, 1978 and 1988," *A Decade of Change: The Status of U.S. Women Doctorates, 1978-88,* p. 4 (Washington, D.C.: American Council on Education, 1990). Primary source: National Research Council, 1990 unpublished data. Data is for U.S. citizens and permanent residents.

★ 527 ★

Public School Employees

Total and female employees in public schools, by occupation, 1982 and 1986.

Occupation	1982		1986	
	Total	Female	Total	Female
	Numbers in thousands			
All occupations	3,082	2,019	2,733	1,898
Officials, administrators	41	10	39	11
Principals and assistant principals	90	19	79	21
Classroom teachers[1]	1,680	1,146	1,546	1,081
Elementary schools	798	669	748	635
Secondary schools	706	343	632	320
Other professional staff	235	144	192	136
Teachers aides[2]	215	200	244	206
Clerical, secretarial staff	210	206	191	185
Service workers[3]	611	295	482	256

Source: Selected from "Public School Employment, by Occupation, Sex, and Race: 1982 and 1986," *Statistical Abstract of the United States 1990*, 1990, p. 142. Primary Source: U.S. Equal Employment Opportunity Commission, *Elementary-Secondary Staff Information (EEO-5)*, biennial. Also in source: data by race. Covers full-time employment. 1982 excludes Hawaii, District of Columbia, and New Jersey. Based on sample survey of school districts with 250 or more students. 1986 based on sample survey of school districts with 100 or more employees. *Notes:* 1. Includes other classroom teachers, not shown separately. 2. Includes technicians. 3. Includes craftworkers and laborers.

★ 528 ★

Public School Teachers

Number of public elementary and secondary school teachers, in thousands, 1960-1988.

Year	Teachers (thousands)		
	Total	Elementary	Secondary
1960	1,355	834	521
1970	2,008	1,109	899
1975	2,171	1,169	1,001
1978	2,189	1,173	1,017
1979	2,199	1,189	1,010
1980	2,211	1,206	1,005
1981	2,192	1,196	996
1982	2,158	1,200	959
1983	2,134	1,182	952
1984	2,142	1,187	956
1985	2,174	1,208	966
1986	2,213	1,239	974

[Continued]

★ 528 ★

Public School Teachers
[Continued]

| Year | Teachers (thousands) | | |
	Total	Elementary	Secondary
1987	2,251	1,273	978
1988	2,283	1,306	977

Source: Selected from "Public Elementary and Secondary Schools-Number and Average Salary of Classroom Teachers, 1960 to 1989, and by State, 1989," *Statistical Abstract of the United States 1990,* 1990, p. 141. Primary source: National Education Association, Washington, DC, *Estimates of School Statistics, 1988-89* and earlier issues. Estimates for school year ending in June of year shown. Schools classified by type of organization rather than by grade-group; elementary includes kindergarten.

★ 529 ★

Public School Teachers, 1961-1986

Item	1961	1966	1971	1976	1981	1986
Number of teachers, in thousands	1,408	1,710	2,055	2,196	2,184	2,207
Sex						
Women	68.7%	69.0%	65.7%	67.0%	66.9%	68.8%
Men	31.3%	31.1%	34.3%	32.9%	33.1%	31.2%
Highest degree held						
Less than bachelor's	14.6%	7.0%	2.9%	0.9%	0.4%	0.3%
Bachelor's	61.9%	69.6%	69.6%	61.6%	50.1%	48.3%
Master's or specialist degree	23.1%	23.2%	27.1%	37.1%	49.3%	50.7%
Doctor's	0.4%	0.1%	0.4%	0.4%	0.3%	0.7%
Median years of teaching experience	11	8	8	8	12	15
Average number of hours in required school day	7.4	7.3	7.3	7.3	7.3	7.3
Average number of hours per week spent on all teaching duties						
All teachers	47	47	47	46	46	49
Elementary teachers	49	47	46	44	44	47
Secondary teachers	46	48	48	48	48	51

Source: Selected from "Selected characteristics of public school teachers: Spring 1961 to spring 1986," *Digest of Education Statistics,* p. 72 (Washington, D.C.: National Center for Education Statistics, 1989). Primary source: National Education Association, *Status of the American Public School Teacher 1985-86.* 1987. Washington, D.C.: NEA. Also in source: various other characteristics. Data are based upon sample surveys of public school teachers. Because of rounding, percents may not add to 100.0.

★ 530 ★

Registered Nurses

Characteristics of registered nursing personnel, 1988. Based on a sample of 1,402 U.S. hospitals registered and unregistered by the American Hospital Association.

Characteristic	Percent
Total full-time registered nurses per hospital (mean)...104	
Length of employment at hospital	
Full-time: Less than 1 year	17.9
1 to 2 years	13.7
2 to 5 years	22.3
5 years or more	46.2
Part-time: Less than 1 year	21.3
1 to 2 years	15.0
2 to 5 years	21.9
5 years or more	39.4
Educational attainment	
Associate degree in Nursing	41.7
Nursing diploma	33.2
Baccalaureate degree in Nursing	22.7
Master's degree in Nursing	2.3

Source: Selected from "Hospital Registered Nursing Personnel-Summary: 1988," *Statistical Abstract of the United States 1990*, 1990, p. 104. Primary source: American Hospital Association, Chicago, IL, *Report of the Hospital Nursing Personnel Survey, 1988*. Also in source: salary/wages (see *Income* chapter); other characteristics of registered nurses. See source for an explanation of "mean." Based on a sample of 1,402 (20%) U.S. hospitals registered and unregistered by the American Hospital Association, with a response rate of 58%.

★ 531 ★

Research and Development Managers

Proportions of men and women in management who are primarily engaged in research and development management, by field, 1986.

Field	Women	Men
Total	24%	32%
Scientists, total	22%	32%
Physical scientists	40%	60%
Mathematical scientists	35%	43%
Computer specialists	35%	38%
Environmental scientists	26%	35%
Life scientists	24%	28%
Psychologists	15%	14%
Social scientists	18%	16%

[Continued]

★ 531 ★

Research and Development Managers
[Continued]

Field	Women	Men
Engineers	33%	32%
Aeronautical/astronautical engineers	25%	68%
Chemical engineers	30%	37%
Civil engineers	5%	9%
Electrical/electronics engineers	48%	47%
Mechanical engineers	38%	34%

Source: "Proportions of men and women in management who are primarily engaged in R & D management, by field: 1986," *Women and Minorities in Science and Engineering*, 1990, p. 7 (Washington, D.C.: National Science Foundation, January 1990).

★ 532 ★

School Administrators

Some comparisons of female and male school administrators (results of various studies).

Characteristic	Female	Male
Married principals	59.8%	92%
Married superintendents	65%	93%
Member of ethnic or minority group, principals	21%	4%
Black administrator promoted prior to 1966	29.3%	70.7%
Black administrator promoted after 1966	24.3%	75.7%
Served in position 6 or more years	20.8%	60.5%
Modal age of principals	50	44
Number of years as teacher before seeking principalship	15	5

Source: Charol Shakeshaft, *Women in Educational Administration*, 1989, p. 62-63 (Newbury Park: Sage publications, 1989).

★ 533 ★

School Administrators-Public and Private Schools

Selected characteristics of school administrators: school year 1987-88.

Characteristics	Public schools		Private Schools	
	Number	Percent	Number	Percent
Total administrators	77,890	100%	25,401	100%
Sex				
Female	19,118	24.4%	13,243	52.1%
Male	58,585	75.2%	12,131	47.3%

Source: Selected from "Characteristics of School Administrators," *The Condition of Education 1990, Volume 1: Elementary and Secondary Education*, p. 94 (Washington, D.C.: National Center for Education Statistics, 1990). Primary Source: U.S. Department of Education, National Center for Education Statistics, Schools and Staffings survey, 1989. Also in source: characteristics by race/ethnicity, ethnic origin, and age. Details may not add to totals due to rounding or missing values in cells with too few sample cases, or item nonresponse. Cell entries may be underestimates due to item nonresponse.

★ 534 ★

Scientists and Engineers Worldwide

Number of scientists and engineers engaged in research and experimental development by field of study, number of females, by cou
latest available year. MF = total of males and females. See below for explanation of other codes.

Country, year	Sex	Type of Data	Total	Field of Study				
				Nat.Sci.	Eng./Tech.	Med.Sci.	Agri.Sci.	SocSci/H
Africa								
Congo-1984	MF	FT+PT	862	145	68	50	285	245
Egypt-1982	MF	FTE	19,939	4,322	3,850	4,180	4,070	3,517
	F	FT+PT	11,503	3,075	1,189	3,109	1,186	2,944
Libyan Arab Jamahiriya-1980	MF	FTE	1,100	230	198	130	221	321
Mauritius-1987	MF	FTE	234	4	29	1	160	39
	F	FTE	23	--	1	--	16	6
Seychelles-1981	MF	FT	2	2	--	--	--	--
	F	FTE	--	--	--	--	--	--
North America								
Cuba-1987	MF	FTE	11,225	907	2,927	2,456	2,549	1,213
Mexico-1984	MF	FTE	16,679	3,786	2,690	3,866	2,385	3,952
	F	FTE	4,319	980	697	1,001	618	1,023
Nicaragua-1987	MF	FT+PT	725	200	87	78	228	132
South America								
Argentina-1982	MF	FT+PT	18,929	6,381	3,218	2,612	2,992	2,445
	F	FT+PT	6,705	3,107	452	797	645	1,275
Brazil-1985	MF	FT+PT	52,863	11,768	7,765	6,107	7,607	11,007
Chile-1984	MF	PT	3,844	988	838	1,061	155	758
Colombia-1982	MF	PT	3,938	1,238	544	1,088	358	710
Guyana-1982	MF	FT	89	43	22	---	21	3
Venezuela-1983	MF	FT+PT	4,568	1,457	727	558	874	802
	F	FT+PT	1,479	438	134	302	171	375
Asia								
Indonesia-1983	MF	FT+PT	18,533	5,317	3,285	1,615	4,083	4,233
Israel-1984	MF	FTE	20,100	6,900	6,900	1,200	700	4,300
	F	FT+PT	10,400	3,300	800	1,300	300	4,600

[Continued]

★ 534 ★

Scientists and Engineers Worldwide
[Continued]

Country, year	Sex	Type of Data	Total	Field of Study				
				Nat.Sci.	Eng./Tech.	Med.Sci.	Agri.Sci.	SocSci/Hum.
Japan-1981	MF	FT	379,405	80,442	142,316	64,408	26,598	41,316
	F	FT	22,475	2,277	775	7,850	904	4,108
Jordan-1982	MF	FT+PT	1,241	310	340	118	92	381
Korea, Republic of-1983	MF	FT	30,309	4,706	16,371	3,964	3,589	---
Pakistan-1986	MF	FTE	9,325	2,635	1,325	1,316	3,289	---
	F	FTE	565	103	125	198	95	---
Philippines-1984	MF	FT+PT	4,830	576	1,419	421	1,272	1,011
	F	FT+PT	2,319	322	480	344	471	630
Qatar-1986	MF	FT+PT	229	160	53	2	5	---
	F	FT+PT	58	57	---	1	---	
Singapore-1987	MF	FT+PT	3,361	863	2,007	436	55	---
Sri Lanka-1985	MF	FTE	2,790	1,560	293	208	---	729
	F	FTE	667	416	27	74	---	150
Turkey-1983	MF	FTE	7,309	891	1,040	1,350	1,590	531
Europe								
Austria-1985	MF	FTE	4,591	1,500	739	590	282	1,480
Bulgaria-1987	MF	FTE	50,585	5,162	11,861	4,653	2,551	5,919
	F	FTE	22,268	2,185	3,463	2,163	720	2,906
Finland-1983	MF	FTE	10,951	2,291	5,211	890	572	1,947
German Democratic Republic-1987	MF	FTE	125,622	15,488	88,742	8,747	8,027	4,618
Hungary-1987	MF	FT+PT	38,232	3,983	18,155	3,735	2,935	9,130
	F	FT+PT	11,122	1,207	3,498	1,426	779	4,055
Malta-1987	MF	FTE	34	3	7	10	---	14
Norway-1985	MF	FTE	9,692	1,833	4,421	945	456	1,797
Poland-1987	MF	FTE	42,800	6,800	20,100	5,200	3,800	4,500
Portugal-1980	MF	FTE	2,663	808	416	251	383	430
Spain-1985	MF	FT+PT	31,362	5,498	9,485	5,239	1,746	9,394
	F	FTE	2,918	652	510	585	218	953
Yugoslovia-1980	MF	FT+PT	27,135	4,988	8,357	2,982	3,098	5,014

[Continued]

★ 534 ★

Scientists and Engineers Worldwide
[Continued]

Country, year	Sex	Type of Data	Total	Nat.Sci.	Eng./Tech.	Med.Sci.	Agri.Sci.	SocSci/Hum
Oceania								
Australia-1986	MF	FTE	33,768	7,625	4,498	3,049	3,720	6,683
French Polynesia-1983	MF	FT	17	8	1	7	---	1
New Caledonia-1985	MF	FT	77	48	8	3	14	3
Tonga-1981	MF	FT	9	---	---	---	9	---

Source: Selected from "Number of Scientists and Engineers Engaged in Research and Experimental Development by Their Field of Study," *Statistical Yearbook*, p. 5-24/5- (Paris: UNESCO, 1989). The figures selected are those representing the largest number of scientists and engineers. Also in source: data for males and for various permutation of types of data. FT=Full-Time; PT=Part-Time; FT+PT=Full-Time plus Part-Time; FTE=Full-Time Equivalent. Nat.Sci.=Natural Sciences; Engng./Tech.=Engineering a Technology; Med.Sci.=Medical Sciences; Agricul.Sci.=Agricultural Sciences; SocSci/Hum.=Social Sciences and Humanities.

★ 535 ★

Scientists and Engineers by Field
Employed scientist and engineers by field: 1988.

Field	Women	Men
Scientists and Engineers	867,900	4,417,400
Scientists	86%	41%
Physical scientists	5%	6%
Mathematical scientists	5%	3%
Computer specialists	25%	11%
Environmental scientists	1%	2%
Life scientists	15%	8%
Psychologists	15%	3%
Social scientists	19%	8%
Engineers	14%	59%
Aeronautical/astronautical engineers	1%	3%
Chemical engineers	1%	3%
Civil engineers	1%	8%
Electrical/electronics engineers	3%	14%
Industrial engineers	1%	4%
Materials engineers	[1]	1%
Mechanical engineers	2%	11%
Mining engineers	[1]	1%
Nuclear engineers	[1]	1%
Petroleum engineers	[1]	1%

Source: "Employed scientists and engineers, by field and gender: 1988," *Women and Minorities in Science and Engineering*, 1990, p. 4 (Washington, D.C.: National Science Foundation, January 1990). Details may not add to total because of rounding. *Note:* 1. Too few cases to estimate.

★ 536 ★

Scientists/Engineers by Race/Ethnicity and Field

Field distribution of women scientists and engineers by racial group, 1986.

Field	Total	White	Black	Asian	Native American
Scientists, total	86%	865	87%	80%	89%
Physical scientists	6%	5%	5%	12%	1
Mathematical scientists	5%	5%	7%	2%	4%
Computer specialists	23%	24%	21%	24%	15%
Environmental scientists	2%	2%	1	1%	4%
Life scientists	15%	15%	10%	15%	37%
Psychologists	16%	17%	17%	12%	19%
Social scientists	19%	19%	27%	14%	15%
Engineers, total	14%	14%	13%	20%	11%
Total scientists and engineers	-	608,900	34,500	36,300	2,700

Source: "Field distribution of women scientists and engineers, by racial group: 1986," *Women and Minorities in Science and Engineering*, 1990, p. 11, (Washington, D.C.: National Science Foundation, January 1990). Detail may not add to total because of rounding. *Note:* 1. Too few cases to estimate.

★ 537 ★

Secondary School Principals: 1965, 1977, and 1987

Selected characteristics of secondary school principals: 1965, 1977, and 1987.

Item	1965	1977	1987
Sex			
Female	10%	7%	12%
Male	89%	93%	88%
Race			
White	---	96%	94%
Black	---	3%	4%
Other	---	1%	3%
Highest degree held			
Less than bachelor's	0%	0%	0%
Bachelor's	10%	1%	1%
Master's	39%	14%	17%
Master's with additional courses	41%	56%	44%
Special degree or equivalent	6%	9%	16%
Master's plus all doctoral courses	6%	9%	8%
Doctor degree (Ph.D. or Ed.D.)	1%	9%	13%

Source: Selected from "Selected characteristics of secondary school principals: 1965, 1977, and 1987," *Digest of Education Statistics*, p. 72 (Washington, D.C.: National Center for Education Statistics, 1989). Primary source: National Association of Secondary School Principals, *High School Leaders and Their Schools*, Vol. 1, 1988. (This table was prepared November 1988.) Also in source: other characteristics of secondary school principals.

★ 538 ★

Teachers at the Third Level Worldwide

Teaching staff (number and percent female) at the third level, latest available year for countries where information is available.

Country	Year	Teaching Staff		
		Total	Female	% Female
Africa				
Benin	1986	1,031	105	10%
Botswana	1975	56	12	21%
Burkino Faso	1986	280	20	7%
Burundi	1986	462	30	6%
Central African Republic	1985	489	38	8%
Chad	1984	141	11	8%
Congo	1983	565	50	9%
Egypt[1]	1986	31,173	8,574	28%
Ethiopia	1987	1,395	106	8%
Gabon	1983	616	83	13%
Guinea	1987	873	22	3%
Liberia	1987	472	87	18%
Madagascar	1987	985	246	25%
Malawi[1]	1980	173	34	20%
Mauritius	1987	338	47	14%
Morocco	1987	8,353	1,613	19%
Mozambique	1987	368	95	26%
Niger	1986	349	44	13%
Rwanda	1986	442	23	5%
St. Helena	1981	9	5	56%
Senegal[1]	1985	701	88	13%
Seychelles	1980	28	16	57%
Sierra Leone	1975	289	38	13%
Sudan	1985	2,165	213	10%
Swaziland	1983	217	98	10%(sic)
Togo	1980	297	37	12%
Tunisia	1986	5,171	574	11%
Uganda	1982	640	45	7%
United Republic of Tanzania[1]	1981	893	21	3%
Zambia[1]	1985	613	78	13%
Zimbabwe[1]	1984	342	68	20%
North America				
Bahamas	1987	208	106	51%
Barbados	1983	446	122	27%
Bermuda	1982	110	40	36%

[Continued]

★ 538 ★

Teachers at the Third Level Worldwide
[Continued]

| Country | Year | Teaching Staff | | |
		Total	Female	% Female
Canada	1987	56,060	13,704	24%
Costa Rica[1]	1986	5,211	1,697	33%
Cuba	1987	22,492	9,768	43%
Dominica	1984	17	11	65%
El Salvador	1986	4,789	1,642	34%
Grenada	1983	53	16	30%
Haiti	1982	817	104	13%
Honduras	1985	2,662	917	34%
Jamaica[1]	1985	295	87	29%
Nicaragua	1984	1,887	613	32%
Panama	1986	3,581	1,079	30%
St. Kitts and Nevis	1985	28	8	29%
St. Lucia	1984	76	28	37%
St. Vincent and the Grenadines	1986	34	11	32%
United States	1980	395,992	104,663	26%
U.S. Virgin Islands	1986	221	103	47%
South America				
Argentina	1986	69,985	33,101	47%
Brazil	1983	122,697	52,935	43%
Chile	1984	15,131	3,350	22%
Colombia	1986	43,279	10,217	24%
Guyana	1985	527	119	23%
Peru	1975	11,598	1,669	14%
Suriname	1984	373	52	14%
Uruguay[1]	1980	3,847	1,141	30%
Asia				
Afghanistan	1979	1,448	101	7%
Bahrain	1984	466	135	29%
Bangladesh	1986	17,410	3,194	18%
Bhutan	1980	37	10	27%
Brunei Darussalam	1987	174	25	14%
China	1986	471,111	150,070	32%
Cyprus	1987	439	153	35%
Democratic Yemen	1981	403	45	11%
Hong Kong	1984	5,928	1,438	24%
India	1979	277,468	50,560	18%

[Continued]

★ 538 ★

Teachers at the Third Level Worldwide
[Continued]

Country	Year	Teaching Staff		
		Total	Female	% Female
Indonesia	1984	75,589	13,634	18%
Iran, Islamic Republic	1986	19,918	3,772	19%
Iraq	1987	10,365	2,606	25%
Israel[1]	1980	10,237	3,275	32%
Japan	1986	248,989	36,286	15%
Jordan	1985	2,307	468	20%
Korea, Republic of[1]	1986	28,655	4,593	16%
Kuwait	1987	1,653	301	18%
Lao People's Democratic Republic	1985	534	132	25%
Lebanon	1984	7,460	2,301	31%
Malaysia	1985	8,213	1,801	22%
Mongolia	1986	2,712	1,056	39%
Nepal	1980	2,918	480	16%
Pakistan	1986	3,948	564	14%
Philippines	1980	43,770	23,381	53%
Qatar	1987	452	150	33%
Saudi Arabia	1986	11,694	3,723	32%
Singapore	1983	3,141	653	21%
Sri Lanka[1]	1983	2,135	527	25%
Syrian Arab Republic[1]	1985	4,504	756	17%
Thailand	1975	9,070	5,121	56%
Turkey	1986	24,382	7,585	31%
United Arab Emirates	1984	599	76	13%
Viet-Nam	1980	17,242	3,857	22%
Yemen	1980	157	7	4%
Europe				
Albania	1987	1,625	410	25%
Austria	1987	12,518	2,642	21%
Belgium	1986	19,452	5,950	31%
Bulgaria	1987	16,900	6,323	37%
Czechoslovakia	1987	26,514	7,552	28%
France[1]	1987	45,797	10,426	23%
German Democratic Republic	1984	41,755	13,622	33%
Germany, Federal Republic	1986	183,528	38,368	21%
Greece	1986	12,350	3,685	30%
Holy See	1987	1,509	105	7%
Hungary	1987	15,302	4,816	31%
Iceland	1975	575	68	12%

[Continued]

★ 538 ★

Teachers at the Third Level Worldwide
[Continued]

Country	Year	Teaching Staff		
		Total	Female	% Female
Italy[2]	1983	481	77	16%
Luxembourg	1985	366	41	11%
Malta	1987	147	7	5%
Norway	1986	8,906	2,374	27%
Poland[1]	1987	58,398	20,787	36%
Portugal	1985	12,476	4,585	37%
Romania	1985	12,961	3,750	29%
Spain	1986	48,982	13,645	27%
Switzerland[1]	1980	5,942	457	8%
United Kingdom	1986	80,664	12,378	15%
Yugoslavia	1987	25,927	6,968	27%
Oceania				
Australia	1985	22,659	5,114	23%
Cook Islands	1980	41	10	24%
Fiji	1986	320	74	23%
French Polynesia	1982	12	4	33%
Guam	1986	257	106	41%
New Caledonia	1984	59	20	34%
New Zealand	1987	9,944	2,813	28%
Papua New Guinea	1986	902	188	21%
Samoa	1983	37	11	30%
Tonga	1981	64	25	39%
USSR				
USSR	1975	317,152	118,298	37%

Source: Selected from "Education at the third level: teachers and students by type of institution," *Statistical Yearbook*, 1989, p. 3-233/3-269 (Paris: UNESCO, 1989). See Introduction to this book for an explanation of levels of education. Also in source: data for other years; some data for other countries; number of students enrolled (see *Education: Enrollment*); extensive footnotes. *Notes:* 1. At universities and equivalent institutions. 2. Other third level institutions.

★ 539 ★

Teaching Staff Worldwide, First & Second Levels

Estimated female teaching staff in thousands by level of educational institution and percent female of total teaching staff, first and second levels, world summary, 1987.

Major areas	First Level		Second Level	
	Total Female Staff (thousands)	% of Total Staff	Total Female Staff (thousands)	% of Total Staff
World Total	11,545	54%	7,093	41%
Africa	702	37%	287	30%
America	3,217	79%	1,272	48%
Asia	4,785	41%	2,719	31%
Europe (Incl. USSR)	2,752	75%	2,749	57%
Oceania	88	66%	67	48%
Developed Countries	4,200	75%	3,492	52%
Developing Countries	7,345	46%	3,601	33%
Africa (Excl. Arab States)	428	33%	108	25%
Asia (Excl. Arab States)	4,558	40%	2,612	30%
Arab States	501	49%	286	37%
Northern America	1,128	81%	550	46%
Latin America and the Caribbean	2,089	77%	723	49%

Source: Selected from "Estimated Female Teaching Staff by Level of Education," *Statistical Yearbook,* p. 2-20/2-21 (Paris: UNESCO, 1989). Also in source: teaching staff in various years. The breakdown and percentage distribution by level of education are influenced by the length of schooling at each level, which, in turn, depends on the criteria applied in the national definitions of levels. Since these criteria vary from country to country, caution should be exercised in making comparisons between areas. See Introduction to this book for explanation of levels of education.

★ 540 ★

Women Managers

Women employed as executives, administrators, and managers, by industry, 1988 annual averages.

Industry	Employed women mgrs. (thousands)	Women as % of total	Percent of employed women mgrs.
Total	5,590	39.3%	100.0%
Agriculture	23	[1]	[1]
Mining	28	[1]	[1]
Construction	129	12.9%	2.3%
Manufacturing	647	26.3%	11.6%
Durable Goods	365	24.3%	6.5%
Nondurable Goods	282	29.4%	5.0%
Transportation and Public Utilities	274	29.9%	4.9%
Wholesale and Retail Trade	865	42.5%	15.5%
Wholesale Trade	167	32.5%	3.0%
Retail Trade	698	45.9%	12.5%
Finance, Insurance, and Real Estate	1,014	50.7%	18.1%
Services[2]	2,114	47.4%	37.8%
Professional Services	1,336	54.7%	23.9%
Public Administration	496	42.8%	8.9%

Source: Facts on Working Women, No. 89-4, December 1989, p. 5. *Notes:* 1. Percentage not shown where base is less than 35,000. 2. Includes business and repair services; personal services, except private household; entertainment and recreation services; professional and related services; and forestry and fisheries.

★ 541 ★

Women Writing for Television

Some statistics culled by the author from a 1989 study by the Writers Guild.

1. In 1987, women writers for film and television earned 63 cents for each dollar earned by white male writers; in 1982, the figure was 73 cents.

2. From 1982 to 1987, more than three-fourths of writers employed in television and film were white males.

3. From 1982 to 1987, minority writers comprised 2% of all writers employed in television and film.

Source: Sally Steenland, "Behind the Scenes: Women in Television," *The American Woman 1990-91,* 1990, p. 231+ (New York: W.W. Norton & Company, 1990). Also in source: a discussion of women producers and the television industry in general.

★ 542 ★

Women and Minorities in High Technology

Some statistics relating to Third World immigrant women production workers and their predominantly white male managers in the high-tech manufacturing industry in Silicon Valley, California.

Nearly 200,000 persons, 1 out of every 4 employees in the San Jose MSA labor force, work in the microelectronics industry. Women account for **18% of managers, 17% of professional employees, 25% of professionals,** and at least **68%** and possibly as many as **85 to 90%** of high-tech operative jobs. An estimated **50 to 80%** of operative jobs are held by minorities; the lower the skill and pay level of the job, the higher the percentage of Third World immigrant women who were employed in the job. Entry-level workers earn an average of **$4.50 to $5.50 an hour**; experienced workers earn **$5.50 to $8.50** per hour.

Source: Karen J. Hossfeld, "'Their Logic Against Them': Contradictions in Sex, Race, and Class in Silicon Valley," *Women Workers and Global Restructuring,* Cornell University Press, p. 153-155. Drawn from data collected from over 200 interviews conducted between 1982 and 1986 with Silicon Valley workers, family members, employers, managers, et al.

★ 543 ★

Women in Film

Some statistics on women's underrepresentation in feature films, as reported in *Rolling Stone.*

The author states that according to the Screen Actors Guild (SAG), men currently fill 71% of available roles in feature films, and their earnings are over double those of women. In an address to SAG, Meryl Streep stated that "if the trend continues, by the year 2000 we'll have **13%** of all roles, and by the year 2010 we'll be completely eliminated from movies."

Source: Peter Travers, "The Year in Movies," *Rolling Stone,* December 13-27, 1990, p. 20.

★ 544 ★

Women in Medical School

Some significant changes that have occurred with reference to women's representation in the medical field in the 1980s, according to the author.

1. Nearly one-third of medical degrees were awarded to women in 1985-86, up from a little over 10% in the early 1970s.

2. In 1970, less than 9% of applicants to medical school were women; by 1975, women were 20% of applicants; by 1988, nearly 40% of applicants were women.

3. Six out of 10 applicants to medical school are under age 23. Younger females are less likely to be accepted than younger males. However, in 1988, 34% of female applicants over the age of 34 were accepted, compared to 27% of male applicants over 34.

4. Of students who graduated in 1961, 14% of the women and 10% of the men are full-time medical school faculty members. However, as of 1987, women comprised only 19% of medical school faculties.

5. In 1988, women were 20% of all physicians; over 42% of them were under age 35, compared to 25% of men.

Source: Janet Bickel, "Women in Medical School," *The American Woman 1990-91*, 1990, p. 210+ (New York: W.W. Norton & Company, 1990). Also in source: a discussion of the proportion of students who are women in various medical schools; a discussion of medical school performance of women; career choices; women on medical school faculties; the future for women in medicine.

★ 545 ★

Women in Public Schools

Representation of women workers in public schools, 1972-1985.

Position	1972-73	1982-83	1984-85
Elementary school teachers	84.0%	83.0%	83.5%
Elementary principals	19.6%	23.0%	16.9%
Secondary teachers	46.0%	48.9%	50.1%
Secondary principals	1.4%	3.2%	3.5%
District superintendents	0.1%	1.8%	3.0%
School board members	12.0%	28.3%	38.3%

Source: Charol Shakeshaft, *Women in Educational Administration*, 1989, p. 20 (Newbury Park: Sage publications, 1989). Also in source: data for 1905, 1928, and 1950.

★ 546 ★

Women in Sales

Women as a percent of the sales force in 1981 and 1987, by industry.

Industry	% of Sales Force	
	1981	1987
Textile and apparel	21%	61%
Utilities	48%	59%
Banks and financial services	24%	58%
Housewares	37%	50%
Publishing	31%	49%
Food products	10%	40%
General machinery sales	1%	0%
Aerospace	1%	0%
Transportation equipment	2%	1%
Tools and hardware	4%	2%
Automotive parts	4%	2%
Fabricated metal products	4%	3%

Source: "'Pink Ghetto' in Sales for Women?", *Sales & Marketing Management*, July 1988, p. 80+.

★ 547 ★

Women in Television

Some highlights of a study of 555 characters on network television shows, as reported in the *New York Times* and the *Detroit Free Press*.

Women held **43%** of roles on prime-time shows. Female characters were rarely depicted beyond age **40.** About **3%** of female characters were over age **60,** compared with **14%** in the general population.

Women made up 15% of producers, 25% of writers, and 9% of directors of the shows surveyed. About 40% of shows surveyed hired no female producers, and 54% had no female directors.

Of the networks surveyed, Fox had the highest percentage of women producers **(26%)** writers **(33%),** and directors **(12%).**

Source: Andrea Adelson, "Study Attacks Roles of Women in Television," *New York Times,* November 19, 1990, p. B3; Deborah Hastings, "Women shortchanged on screen, behind scenes," *Detroit Free Press*, November 15, 1990, p. 8A. Primary source: "What's Wrong with This Picture," a study released by Women in Film (Los Angeles) and the National Commission on Working Women (Washington, D.C.). A year-long study that looked at 555 characters on 80 network shows and at employment statistics of the shows' creators.

★ 548 ★

Women in the Legal Profession

Justice Sandra Day O'Connor on the role of women in the legal profession, as reported in the *New York Times*.

Of 2,618 Federal judges, **216** are women

Of 1,133 state and appellate court judges, **115** are women

Women make up **20%** of attorneys, **6%** of partners in law firms, and **11%** of tenured law professors. **80%** of women lawyers entered the profession after 1970.

Source: Staci D. Kramer, "Enter O'Connor, Exit 'Mr. Justice'," *New York Times,* November 16, 1990, p. B11.

★ 549 ★

Worldwide Employment in Finance, Insurance, and Real Estate

Percentage of female employment in finance, insurance, and real estate, selected countries.

Country	Year	Percentage
United States	1982	53.2%
Sweden	1982	47.2%
Japan	1982	43.0%
Germany, Federal Republic	1982	47.8%
Norway	1982	45.3%
Venezuela	1981	37.8%
Hungary	1980	48.7%
Panama	1980	39.8%
Barbados	1982	51.4%
Korea, Republic of	1982	34.6%
Portugal	1981	36.6%
Sri Lanka	1981	20.4%
Indonesia	1980	16.9%
Bangladesh	1974	1.0%
Ghana	1970	19.7%

Source: "FIRE female employment in percentages," *World Survey on the Role of Women in Development,* 1986, p. 126 (New York: United Nations, 1986). Primary source: *Yearbook of Labour Statistics* (Geneva, International Labour Office), various issues.

★ 550 ★

Worldwide Energy Scientists and Engineers

Scientists and engineers in energy-related activities by major field, 1980.

Profession	Total	Women	% Women
Physical scientists	24,300	1,600	6.6%
Mathematical scientists	5,500	900	16.4%
Environmental scientists	34,700	2,100	6.1%
Engineers	279,700	8,000	2.9%

[Continued]

★ 550 ★

Worldwide Energy Scientists and Engineers
[Continued]

Profession	Total	Women	% Women
Life scientists	6,600	1,200	18.2%
Social scientists	10,800	2,800	25.9%
Total[1]	384,300	20,800	5.5%

Source: "Women scientists and engineers in energy-related activities by major field, 1980," *World Survey on the Role of Women in Development*, 1986, p. 205 (New York: United Nations, 1986). Primary source: *Women Scientists and Engineers Working in Energy-Related Activities by Major Field* (U.S. Department of Energy and Oak Ridge Associated Universities, 1980). "Information is not available on the number of women that receive an energy-related education and training in developing countries because information is not disaggregated by gender" (source). *Note:* 1. Including computer specialists and psychologists not shown here.

★ 551 ★

Worldwide Teachers at the Second Level

Total number of teachers, number and percent female, at the second level of education, by country, latest available year.

Country	Year	Teaching Staff		
		Total	Female	% Female
Africa				
Algeria	1985	84,676	30,305	36%
Benin	1986	3,657	-	-
Botswana	1986	2,050	803	39%
Burkino Faso	1975	818	-	-
Burundi	1986	1,908	385	20%
Cameroon	1983	10,439	2,167	21%
Central Africal Republic	1986	923	87	9%
Comoros	1980	449	91	20%
Congo	1975	2,413	266	11%
Djibouti	1975	148	57	39%
Egypt	1987	230,089	85,271	37%
Equatorial Guinea	1975	165	18	11%
Ethiopia (General Level)	1987	18,580	2,010	11%
Gabon	1987	2,278	425	19%
Gambia	1984	914	219	24%
Ghana	1987	53,514	12,508	23%
Guinea	1985	4,642	323	7%
Guinea-Bissau	1986	824	100	12%
Kenya	1987	26,025	7,785	30%
Lesotho	1984	1,746	889	51%

[Continued]

★ 551 ★

Worldwide Teachers at the Second Level
[Continued]

Country	Year	Teaching Staff		
		Total	Female	% Female
Libyan Arab Jamahiriya	1982	30,673	3,483	28%
Mali (General Level)	1987	4,601	691	15%
Mauritania (General Level)	1980	646	54	8%
Mauritius (General Level)	1987	3,683	1,529	42%
Morocco	1985	64,079	17,646	28%
Mozambique	1986	4,645	943	20%
Niger	1980	1,284	267	21%
Nigeria	1980	81,492	16,326	20%
Reunion	1983	3,713	1,641	44%
Rwanda	1987	3,616	341	21%
St. Helena	1985	54	37	69%
Sao Tome and Principe (General Level)	1987	331	103	31%
Senegal	1984	5,338	783	15%
Seychelles	1987	305	114	37%
Sierra Leone	1975	2,596	901	35%
Somalia	1985	2,887	299	10%
Sudan	1985	23,035	7,501	33%
Swaziland (General Level)	1987	1,767	850	48%
Togo	1987	4,374	522	12%
Tunisia	1987	28,036	8,457	30%
Uganda	1982	7,022	958	14%
United Republic of Tanzania	1987	6,678	1,580	24%
Zambia (General Level)	1984	5,043	1,229	24%
Zimbabwe	1986	19,507	5,596	29%
North America				
Antigua and Barbuda	1975	313	197	63%
Bahamas	1984	1,344	645	48%
Belize	1986	599	266	44%
Bermuda (General Level)	1984	418	218	52%
British Virgin Islands	1983	100	60	60%
Canada	1975	144,300	60,300	42%
Cayman Islands	1980	207	114	55%
Costa Rica (General Level)	1975	3,866	1,995	52%
Cuba	1987	104,741	53,417	51%
El Salvador	1984	3,590	1,097	31%
Grenada	1986	304	146	48%
Guadeloupe	1983	2,987	1,503	50%
Guatemala	1975	5,994	2,252	38%

[Continued]

451

★ 551 ★

Worldwide Teachers at the Second Level
[Continued]

Country	Year	Teaching Staff		
		Total	Female	% Female
Haiti (General Level)	1985	6,978	846	12%
Honduras	1984	6,313	3,043	48%
Jamaica	1983	8,193	5,419	66%
Martinique	1983	3,065	1,638	53%
Mexico	1975	169,781	55,218	33%
Nicaragua (General Level)	1987	3,794	2,300	61%
Panama	1986	9,873	5,244	53%
St. Kitts and Nevis	1984	235	159	68%
St. Lucia	1983	333	171	51%
St. Pierre and Miquelon	1986	71	33	46%
St. Vincent and the Grenadines	1975	243	104	43%
Trinidad and Tobago (General Level)	1987	4,891	2,579	53%
Turks and Caicos Islands	1984	51	34	67%
South America				
Argentina	1987	262,306	175,000	67%
Brazil	1980	198,087	105,945	53%
Chile	1987	41,657	23,151	56%
Colombia	1983	90,006	39,500	44%
Ecuador	1987	53,568	22,170	40%
Falkland Islands (Malvinas)	1980	11	4	36%
French Guiana	1983	578	302	52%
Guyana (General Level)	1981	3,797	1,697	45%
Peru (General Level)	1981	49,569	22,970	46%
Suriname	1975	1,793	901	50%
Venezuela	1985	60,112	32,957	55%
Asia				
Afghanistan (General Level)	1985	5,715	1,887	33%
Bahrain	1987	2,270	1,068	47%
Bangladesh	1985	112,700	9,575	8%
Brunei Darussalam	1987	1,521	565	37%
China	1987	3,264,700	953,100	29%
Cyprus	1987	3,407	1,531	45%
Democratic Yemen	1983	1,946	521	27%
Hong Kong	1987	20,183	9,843	49%
India (General Level)	1986	2,178,380	683,779	31%
Iran, Islamic Republic	1987	180,494	67,201	37%

[Continued]

★ 551 ★

Worldwide Teachers at the Second Level
[Continued]

Country	Year	Teaching Staff		
		Total	Female	% Female
Iraq	1987	50,138	26,562	53%
Israel	1987	41,036	25,372	62%
Japan	1986	632,432	178,391	28%
Jordan	1987	21,729	10,558	49%
Korea, Republic of	1988	158,569	49,982	32%
Kuwait	1986	19,270	9,917	51%
Lao People's Democratic Republic	1985	10,146	3,510	35%
Malaysia	1987	58,499	28,695	49%
Nepal	1984	17,069	1,490	9%
Oman	1987	4,326	1,545	36%
Pakistan	1986	170,449	53,102	31%
Philippines	1984	103,493	98,387	95%
Qatar	1987	2,809	1,583	56%
Saudi Arabia	1986	45,798	19,579	43%
Singapore	1984	9,644	5,092	53%
Syrian Arab Republic	1987	59,966	18,231	30%
Thailand (General Level)	1980	70,201	39,818	57%
Turkey	1987	144,543	53,630	37%
United Arab Emirates	1987	5,008	2,565	51%
Viet-Nam	1976	127,635	73,389	57%
Yemen (General Level)	1986	6,700	416	6%
Europe				
Albania	1987	8,442	3,318	39%
Austria	1987	70,490	39,022	55%
Belgium	1987	114,628	60,539	53%
Bulgaria	1987	27,862	16,082	58%
Czechoslovakia	1987	34,335	17,714	52%
France	1984	313,433	174,582	56%
German Democratic Republic	1987	159,138	83,761	53%
Germany, Federal Republic (General Level)	1986	349,939	155,401	44%
Gibraltar	1984	144	52	36%
Greece	1985	50,388	26,475	53%
Hungary (General Level)	1987	8,646	5,586	65%
Iceland	1975	2,387	699	29%
Ireland	1982	21,060	10,532	50%
Italy	1984	547,148	330,456	60%
Malta	1987	2,452	835	34%
Netherlands	1986	98,729	27,842	28%

[Continued]

★ 551 ★

Worldwide Teachers at the Second Level
[Continued]

Country	Year	Teaching Staff		
		Total	Female	% Female
Poland	1987	160,076	87,998	55%
Portugal	1980	32,028	18,963	59%
Romania	1985	50,333	23,998	48%
San Marino	1986	179	108	60%
Spain	1986	220,234	105,125	48%
Sweden	1983	51,466	24,019	47%
United Kingdom (General Level)	1986	305,000	154,000	50%
Yugoslavia	1987	135,888	70,150	52%
Oceania				
American Samoa	1987	231	92	40%
Australia	1987	102,436	49,192	48%
Fiji	1986	2,838	1,206	42%
French Polynesia	1986	1,240	540	44%
Guam	1983	720	451	63%
Kiribati	1988	182	51	28%
Nauru	1985	40	18	45%
New Caledonia (General Level)	1975	379	217	57%
New Zealand (General Level)	1987	19,541	9,472	48%
Niue	1988	28	11	39%
Pacific Islands	1981	445	143	32%
Papua New Guinea	1987	2,922	978	33%
Samoa (General Level)	1986	513	238	46%
Solomon Islands	1980	257	67	26%
Tokelau	1979	18	9	50%
Tonga	1986	799	431	54%
Vanuatu	1981	188	59	31%
USSR				
USSR (Vocational)	1975	218,428	109,214	50%

Source: Selected from "Education at the second level (general, teacher-training and vocational): teachers and pupils," *Statistical Yearbook*, p. 3-146/3-202 (Paris: UNESCO, 1989). Also in source: data for various years and by level; pupils enrolled, number and percent female. See Introduction to this book for an explanation of levels of education. In most cases, data include part-time teachers.

★ 552 ★

Worldwide Teaching Staff Preceding the First Level

Estimated teaching staff in thousands, number and percent female, for education preceding the first level, world summaries, 1987.

Major areas	Teaching Staff		
	Total	Female	% Female
World Total	4,313	4,078	95%
World Total (Excl. China)	3,662	3,515	96%
Africa	102	62	61%
America	687	665	97%
Asia	513	440	86%
Europe (Incl. USSR)	2,351	2,338	99%
Oceania	10	10	100%
Developed Countries	2,742	2,707	99%
Developing Countries	920	808	88%
Africa (Excl. Arab States)	52	49	94%
Asia (Excl. Arab States)	488	415	85%
Arab States	74	38	51%
Northern America	307	296	96%
Latin America and the Caribbean	380	369	97%

Source: Selected from "Estimated Teaching Staff and Enrolment by Sex for Education Preceding the First Level," *Statistical Yearbook*, p. 2-26/2-28 (Paris: UNESCO, 1989). Also in source: enrollment figures (see separate chart in *Education* chapter); data for various years. *Note:* See introduction to this book for an explanation of levels of education.

★ 553 ★

Worldwide Teaching Staff: First Level

Teaching staff, percent female, and number of schools at the first level, by country, latest available year.

Country, year	Schools	Teaching Staff		
		Total	Female	% Female
Africa				
Algeria-1988	12,240	139,917	56,543	40%
Angola-1982	6,308	32,004	-	-
Benin-1987	2,840	14,067	3,490	25%
Botswana-1986	537	7,324	5,699	78%
Burkina Faso-1986	1,964	5,780	1,460	25%
Burundi-1986	1,171	7,256	3,500	48%
Cameroon-1986	5,974	35,728	10,283	29%
Cape Verde-1986	545	1,791	1,085	65%
Central African Republic-1987	1,014	4,563	1,112	24%
Chad-1985	1,243	4,779	168	4%
Comoros-1985	257	1,901	393	21%

[Continued]

★ 553 ★

Worldwide Teaching Staff: First Level
[Continued]

Country, year	Schools	Teaching Staff		
		Total	Female	% Female
Congo-1986	1,589	7,818	2,533	32%
Cote D-Ivoire-1983	5,795	32,414	5,838	18%
Djibouti-1984	54	511	-	-
Egypt-1987	15,041	235,586	115,949	49%
Equatorial Guinea-1981	-	664	-	-
Ethiopia-1987	8,373	58,400	14,000	24%
Gabon-1986	986	4,083	1,416	35%
Gambia-1988	226	2,604	833	32%
Ghana-1987	10,181	66,147	26,107	39%
Guinea-1987	2,323	7,239	1,423	20%
Guinea-Bissau-1986	795	3,121	713	23%
Kenya-1987	-	149,151	51,992	35%
Lesotho-1984	1,133	5,648	4,313	76%
Liberia-1980	1,591	9,099	2,069	23%
Libyan Arab Jamahiriya-1982	2,729	42,696	22,627	53%
Madagascar-1988	12,406	37,439	19,672	53%
Malawi-1985	2,520	15,440	5,124	33%
Mali-1987	1,418	8,124	1,796	22%
Mauritania-1987	1,035	3,158	550	17%
Mauritius-1987	283	6,504	2,825	43%
Morocco-1987	3,752	83,787	28,791	34%
Mozambique-1986	-	20,756	4,479	22%
Niger-1986	1,976	7,690	2,661	35%
Nigeria-1985	35,433	292,821	-	-
Reunion-1986	351	3,917	2,781	71%
Rwanda-1987	1,633	16,975	7,974	47%
St. Helena-1985	8	32	7,974	47%
Sao Tome and Principe-1987	63	616	361	59%
Senegal-1987	2,420	11,985	3,265	27%
Seychelles-1987	25	681	564	83%
Sierra Leone-1982	1,219	10,451	2,290	22%
Somalia-1985	1,224	9,676	4,367	45%
Sudan-1985	6,775	50,089	22,038	44%
Swaziland-1987	477	4,241	3,365	79%
Togo-1987	2,388	10,217	2,127	21%
Tunisia-1987	3,633	43,490	18,180	42%
Uganda-1986	6,677	73,141	22,458	31%
United Republic of Tanzania-1987	10,428	95,503	37,701	39%
Zaire-1986	11,135	113,468	-	-
Zimbabwe-1986	4,297	58,257	24,787	43%

[Continued]

★ 553 ★

Worldwide Teaching Staff: First Level
[Continued]

Country, year	Schools	Teaching Staff		
		Total	Female	% Female
North America				
Antigua and Barbuda-1975	59	524	443	85%
Bahamas-1986	90	1,409	-	-
Barbados-1984	125	1,421	-	-
Belize-1986	-	1,611	1,186	74%
Bermuda-1984	22	309	278	90%
British Virgin Islands-1983	19	117	97	83%
Canada-1987	15,679	307,106	179,585	58%
Cayman Islands-1980	15	65	55	85%
Costa Rica-1987	3,170	12,490	-	-
Cuba-1987	9,617	73,874	57,320	78%
Dominica-1987	65	835	574	69%
Dominican Republic-1986	4,853	31,275	-	-
El Salvador-1987	3,994	22,358	14,090	63%
Grenada-1986	63	821	574	70%
Guadeloupe-1985	230	1,927	-	-
Guatemala-1987	8,481	31,441	-	-
Haiti-1983	3,406	18,483	9,197	50%
Honduras-1984	6,304	19,155	14,194	74%
Jamaica-1986	784	9,467	8,330	88%
Martinique-1983	224	2,004	1,505	75%
Mexico				
1975	55,618	255,939	159,055	62%
1987	79,677	463,115	-	-
Montserrat-1981	15	86	75	87%
Netherlands Antilles-1981	125	1,543	-	-
Nicaragua-1987	3,801	18,137	15,657	86%
Panama-1986	2,571	15,446	11,937	77%
Puerto Rico-1975	-	17,270	-	-
St. Kitts and Nevis-1986	32	266	197	74%
St. Lucia-1986	83	1,103	843	76%
St. Pierre and Miquelon-1986	5	37	25	68%
St. Vincent and the Grenadines-1987	65	1,374	930	68%
Trinidad and Tobabo-1987	469	7,686	5,409	70%
Turks and Caicos Islands-198	17	68	67	99%
United States-1985	-	1,371,000	-	-
U.S. Virgin Islands-1985	57	711	-	-

[Continued]

★ 553 ★
Worldwide Teaching Staff: First Level
[Continued]

Country, year	Schools	Teaching Staff		
		Total	Female	% Female
South America				
Argentina-1987	21,025	252,259	230,235	91%
Bolivia				
1980	-	48,894	23,293	48%
1987	12,639	48,133	-	-
Brazil				
1980	201,926	884,257	748,927	85%
1987	196,792	1,094,123	-	-
Chile-1987	-	68,905	51,409	75%
Colombia-1986	36,979	135,924	107,380	79%
Ecuador-1987	-	58,326	38,117	65%
Falkland Islands (Malvinas)				
1975	18	23	11	48%
1980	-	15	5	33%
French Guiana-1983	51	423	305	72%
Guyana-1981	423	3,493	2,433	70%
Paraguay-1986	4,101	23,407	-	-
Peru-1985	24,327	106,600	64,036	60%
Suriname				
1975	309	2,552	1,659	65%
1986	256	-	-	-
Uruguay-1986	2,613	16,212	-	-
Venezuela-1986	13,262	112,157	93,361	83%
Asia				
Afghanistan-1986	886	16,414	9,056	55%
Bahrain-1987	-	2,887	1,661	58%
Bangladesh-1987	44,432	191,507	15,568	8%
Bhutan-1986	147	1,321	-	-
Brunei Darussalam-1987	145	1,580	947	60%
Burma-1983	27,499	104,754	-	-
China-1987	807,406	5,433,800	2,225,300	41%
Cyprus-1987	379	2,574	1,358	53%
Democratic Yemen-1983	924	11,281	3,921	35%
Hong Kong-1984	-	19,625	14,619	74%
India-1986	537,399	1,522,108	416,584	27%
Indonesia-1986	165,033	1,078,597	-	-
Iran, Islamic Republic-1987	52,780	264,398	140,254	53%
Iraq-1987	7,954	119,280	79,907	67%
Israel-1987	1,599	37,623	30,550	81%

[Continued]

★ 553 ★

Worldwide Teaching Staff: First Level
[Continued]

Country, year	Schools	Teaching Staff		
		Total	Female	% Female
Japan-1987	24,933	448,977	253,840	57%
Jordan-1987	1,387	19,133	12,860	67%
Korea, Democratic People's Republic-1976	4,700	-	-	-
Korea, Republic of-1988	6,463	132,527	62,704	47%
Kuwait-1987	297	10,099	6,950	69%
Lao People's Democratic Republic-1985	8,011	21,033	6,744	32%
Lebanon-1984	2,130	-	-	-
Malaysia-1987	6,691	102,356	54,597	53%
Mongolia-1986	-	5,045	-	-
Nepal-1984	11,660	46,484	4,596	10%
Oman-1987	405	8,306	3,806	46%
Pakistan-1987	83,872	186,260	59,400	32%
Philippines-1984	33,074	286,246	272,129	95%
Qatar-1987	113	3,732	2,481	66%
Saudi Arabia-1986	8,012	90,535	41,235	46%
Singapore-1984	275	10,657	7,385	69%
Sri Lanka				
1975	-	99,067	51,526	52%
1986	9,325	146,356	-	-
Syrian Arab Republic-1987	9,323	83,722	52,934	63%
Thailand				
1980	-	299,473	145,950	49%
1987	34,073	349,210	-	-
Turkey-1987	50,457	220,943	91,870	42%
United Arab Emirates-1987	200 (1980)	7,220	3,966	55%
Viet-Nam-1985	12,511	235,791	165,825	70%
Yemen-1986	5,964	18,193	2,456	14%
Europe				
Albania-1987	1,668	27,297	14,437	53%
Andorra-1982	13	355	204	57%
Austria-1987	3,394	33,330	26,874	81%
Belgium-1987	4,263	71,064	53,114	75%
Bulgaria-1987	2,938	62,105	47,067	76%
Czechoslovakia-1987	6,236	97,733	80,742	83%
Denmark-1986	2,536	34,376	19,673	57%
Finland				
1975	-	24,494	14,990	61%
1980	4,245	25,949	-	-
France-1987	46,384	202,348	135,534	67%

[Continued]

★ 553 ★

Worldwide Teaching Staff: First Level
[Continued]

Country, year	Schools	Teaching Staff		
		Total	Female	% Female
German Democratic Republic-1987	5,683	57,158	50,973	89%
Germany, Federal Republic-1986	15,954	131,351	104,069	79%
Gibraltar-1984	13	183	141	77%
Greece-1985	8,675	37,994	18,594	49%
Hungary-1987	3,540	90,925	75,538	83%
Iceland-1975	183	-	-	-
Ireland-1985	3,334	15,674	11,907	76%
Italy-1984	28,244	276,553	245,808	89%
Luxembourg-1986	-	1,768	869	49%
Malta-1987	106	1,693	1,272	75%
Monaco-1982	6	-	-	-
Netherlands-1986	8,465	84,999	53,947	63%
Norway-1986	3,509	50,299	30,076	60%
Poland-1987	17,365	321,615	266,444	83%
Portugal-1985	12,741	73,343	60,800	83%
Romania-1985	14,076	147,147	103,470	70%
San Marino-1987	13	184	153	83%
Spain-1986	18,772	133,830	94,300	70%
Sweden-1987	-	92,664	63,081	68%
United Kingdom-1986	24,609	213,000	167,000	78%
Yugoslavia-1987	11,978	62,537	44,693	71%
Oceania				
American Samoa-1987	30	503	331	66%
Australia-1987	7,959	91,252	65,114	71%
Cook Islands-1988	28	137	95	69%
Fiji-1986	672	4,322	2,522	58%
French Polynesia				
1981	-	1,544	1,069	69%
1984	198	1,337	-	-
Guam-1983	39	672	609	91%
Kiribati-1988	113	459	264	58%
Nauru-1985	7	71	43	61%
New Caledonia-1987	202	1,190	-	-
New Zealand-1987	2,286	16,169	11,811	73%
Niue-1988	7	27	17	63%
Pacific Islands-1981	245	1,374	374	27%
Papua New Guinea-1987	2,584	12,294	4,021	33%
Samoa-1983	164	1,502	1,078	72%
Solomon Islands-1986	430	1,849	625	34%

[Continued]

★ 553 ★

Worldwide Teaching Staff: First Level
[Continued]

Country, year	Schools	Teaching Staff		
		Total	Female	% Female
Tokelau-1985	112	744	460	62%
Tonga-1985	112	744	603	62%
Tuvalu-1987	11	64	48	75%
Vanuatu-1981	289	1,076	422	39%
USSR				
USSR				
1980	130,000	2,321,000	1,653,000	71%
1987	127,000	2,807,000	-	-
Byelorussian SSR-1987	5,600	104,600	-	-
Ukrainian SSR-1987	20,500	447,800	-	-

Source: Selected from "Education at the first level: Institutions, teachers and pupils," *Statistical Yearbook*, p. 3-85/3-100 (Paris: UNESCO, 1989). Also in source: pupils enrolled and pupil/teacher ratio (see *Education, Enrollment*); data for various years. See Introduction to this book for explanation of levels of education. In general, data in this table cover both public and private schools, including primary classes attached to secondary schools. Figures on teaching staff refer in principle to both full-and part-time teachers. Data comparability may be affected as the proportion of part-time teachers varies greatly from one country to another.

Working Women Worldwide

★ 554 ★

Characteristics of the Labor Market: 10 Countries

Selected indicators of women's position in the labor market, selected countries, 1982.

Indicator	Belgium	Denmark	Fed. Rep. of Germany	France	Sweden	United Kingdom	Canada	United States
Women as percent of economically active population	30.7%[1]	45.7%[1]	33.9%	33.5%	46.3%	35.9%	41.2%	40.3%
Percent of women who are economically active	48.7%[2]	72.0%[2]	50.1%[2]	52.5%[2]	70.0%[3]	57.3%[2]	52.8k%[2]	-
Women as percent of total employees in employment	36.9%	44.8%[2]	38.6%	38.8%	46.1%	41.1%	41.2%	43.5%
Unemployment rate								
Total	13.8%	9.8%	7.5%	8.5%	3.1%	12.1%	11.0%	9.7%
Women	20.0%	10.4%	8.6%	10.8%	3.4%	7.8%	10.8%	9.4%
Women's wages in non-agricultural activities as percent of men's	73.6%	83.9%	72.7%	88.6%	-	69.1%	72.0%[1]	-
Percent of women in employment who work part-time (less than 30 hours per week)	29.0%[1]	42.0%[1]	24.0%[1]	20.0%[1]	51.5%[3]	46.0%[1]	24.0%[2]	
Union members as percent of all workers	72.5%	75.5%	42.0%	25.0%	-	52.5%	-	-

Source: "Selected indicators of women's position in the labor market for selected countries, 1982," *Computer Chips and Paper Clips: Technology and Women's Employment*, Vol. 2, 1987, p. 398-99 (Washington, D.C.: National Academy Press, 1987). Primary source: Compiled by the authors from data in ILO (1983), Berner (1984), Equal Opportunities Commission (1984), David-McNeil (1984), Department of Employment (UK)(1984), Boulet (1984), Liisa Rantalaiho (personal communication, 1985), Johannesson and Persson-Tanimura (1984), and Peitchinis (1984). *Notes:* 1. Data for 1980. 2. Data for 1981. 3. Data for 1983.

★ 555 ★

Economically Active Youth Worldwide

Total and economically active female youth population and percent economically active, 1987.

Country	Age group	Both sexes		Female	
		Total population	Economically active	Total population	Economically active
		Numbers in thousands			
Australia	15 to 24	2,693	1,852	1,329	856
Canada	15 to 24	4,058	2,809	1,996	1,323
Germany, Federal Republic	15 to 24	9,934	6,118	4,826	2,814
France	15 to 24	8,171	3,257	4,100	1,589
India	15 to 24	121,477	57,236	58,450	16,226
Israel	15 to 24	751	226	364	105
Italy	14 to 24	9,544	4,319	4,719	2,003
Japan	15 to 24	17,930	7,640	8,760	3,770
Norway	16 to 24	599	396	286	181
Sweden	16 to 24	1,066	707	520	346
United Kingdom	16 to 24	8,386	6,260	4,110	2,862
United States	16 to 24	34,713	22,964	17,196	11,015

Source: Selected from "Total and Economically Active Youth Population and Percent Economically Active, by Sex, Selected Countries: 1987," *Children's Well-Being: An International Comparison,* A Report of the Select Committee on Children, Youth, and Families, 101st Cong., 2d sess., March 1990, p. 115. Primary source: International Labour Office, 1988, Yearbook of Labour Statistics 1988, Geneva, table 1; United Kingdom Office of Population Censuses and Surveys, 1989, Population Trends, No. 58, London, table 6; and U.S. Bureau of the Census, 1989, *Statistical Abstract of the United States: 1989,* Washington, D.C., table 21. Data for India refer to 1981. Data for Federal Republic of Germany and United Kingdom refer to 1986.

★ 556 ★

Employment Status of Never-Married Women: 12 Countries

Employment status of never-married women by age group for 12 industrialized countries.

Country	Percent employed		Employed full-time	
	All never married	Older never married[1]	All never married	Older never married[1]
Austria	63.0%	70.1%	56.3%	63.6%
Denmark	63.6%	72.0%	43.4%	64.0%
Finland	71.6%	88.6%	45.5%	81.8%
Germany, Federal Republic	64.8%	60.8%	54.5%	55.0%
Great Britain	65.9%	59.9%	61.8%	55.4%
Israel	34.2%	70.7%	23.8%	48.1%
Japan	41.9%	79.5%	-	-
Netherlands	64.9%	84.6%	60.3%	76.9%
Northern Ireland	73.3%	69.5%	-	-
Norway	56.6%	77.8%	32.9%	74.1%

[Continued]

★ 556 ★

Employment Status of Never-Married Women: 12 Countries
[Continued]

Country	Percent employed		Employed full-time	
	All never married	Older never married[1]	All never married	Older never married[1]
Sweden	68.4%	83.3%	28.6%	62.5%
United States	60.9%	65.1%	49.4%	55.6%

Source: Patricia A. Roos, *Gender and Work: A Comparative Analysis of Industrial Societies*, p. 128 (Albany: State University of New York Press, 1985). Based on sample surveys in the 12 countries studied. *Notes:* 1. "Older never-married women" includes only those older than the age at which the average woman in the particular country marries. See source for additional details.

★ 557 ★

Employment Status of Women and Men: 12 Countries

Employment status of men and women (all ages) for 12 industrialized countries.

Country and sex of respondent	Employment status		
	Full time	Part time	Not employed
Austria			
Female	31.5%	9.1%	59.5%
Male	79.5%	0.5%	20.1%
Denmark			
Female	34.1%	22.3%	43.6%
Male	83.0%	7.0%	10.0%
Finland			
Female	55.0%	16.3%	28.7%
Male	70.9%	14.5%	14.7%
Germany, Federal Republic			
Female	18.7%	15.4%	65.9%
Male	72.9%	3.3%	23.8%
Great Britain			
Female	25.7%	17.8%	56.4%
Male	73.9%	4.9%	21.1%
Israel			
Female	16.0%	13.6%	70.4%
Male	54.4%	12.9%	32.6%
Japan			
Female	42.1%[1]	-	57.9%
Male	85.1%[1]	-	14.9%
Netherlands			
Female	25.0%	9.3%	65.7%
Male	68.5%	1.8%	29.7%
Northern Ireland			
Female	36.4%[1]	-	63.6%
Male	79.5%[1]	-	20.5%
Norway			

[Continued]

★ 557 ★

Employment Status of Women and Men: 12 Countries
[Continued]

Country and sex of respondent	Employment status		
	Full time	Part time	Not employed
Female	21.4%	21.9%	56.7%
Male	77.5%	10.1%	12.4%
Sweden			
Female	28.0%	37.7%	34.3%
Male	77.8%	14.3%	7.9%
United States			
Female	30.3%	11.9%	57.8%
Male	60.8%	8.8%	30.3%

Source: Patricia A. Roos, *Gender and Work: A Comparative Analysis of Industrial Societies*, p. 47 (Albany: State University of New York Press, 1985). Based on sample surveys in the 12 countries studied. *Note:* 1. Full-time/part-time status not available.

★ 558 ★

Employment Status of Women in 12 Countries
Employment status of women (all ages), by marital status, for 12 industrialized countries.

Country	Employment status		
	Full time	Part time	Not at work
Austria			
Ever married	27.3%	9.5%	63.2%
Never married	56.3%	6.7%	37.1%
Denmark			
Ever married	32.0%	22.9%	45.1%
Never married	43.4%	20.2%	36.4%
Finland			
Ever married	58.7%	12.6%	28.7%
Never married	45.5%	26.1%	28.4%
Germany, Federal Republic			
Ever married	13.2%	16.2%	70.6%
Never married	54.5%	10.3%	35.2%
Great Britain			
Ever married	19.7%	20.2%	60.1%
Never married	61.8%	4.1%	34.1%
Israel			
Ever married	13.4%	14.6%	71.9%
Never married	23.8%	10.4%	65.8%
Japan			
Ever married	42.1%[1]	-	57.9%
Never married	41.9%[1]	-	58.1%
Netherlands			
Ever married	13.2%	10.8%	76.0%
Never married	60.3%	4.6%	35.2%
Northern Ireland			

[Continued]

★ 558 ★

Employment Status of Women in 12 Countries
[Continued]

Country	Employment status		
	Full time	Part time	Not at work
Ever married	28.2%[1]	-	71.9%
Never married	73.3%[1]	-	26.7%
Norway			
Ever married	19.0%	21.6%	59.5%
Never married	32.9%	23.7%	43.4%
Sweden			
Ever married	27.7%	37.4%	34.9%
Never married	28.6%	39.8%	31.6%
United States			
Ever married	28.0%	11.8%	60.2%
Never married	49.4%	11.5%	39.0%

Source: Patricia A. Roos, *Gender and Work: A Comparative Analysis of Industrial Societies*, p. 127 (Albany: State University of New York Press, 1985). Based on sample surveys in the 12 countries studied. *Note:* 1. Full-time/part-time status not available.

★ 559 ★

Farming in Africa: Part 1
Answers to the question: "Who is primarily responsible for this task?"

Task	Self (Woman)	Husband	Children	Other Relatives
Preparing land	34.7%	54.6%	9.2%	1.5%
Fertilization	39.7%	47.2%	10.6%	2.5%
Plowing	24.4%	61.9%[1]	12.7%	1.0%
Planting	52.7%	35.8%	7.8%	3.7%
Hoeing	88.5%	1.9%	3.8%	5.8%
Weeding	91.0%	0%	3.8%	5.2%
Harvesting	92.4%	1.3%	0.4%	5.9%
Sorting and storing	88.7%	6.0%	1.0%	4.3%
Preservation of food	96.4%	0%	0%	3.6%
Sheep and goat care	47.3%	21.8%	27.3%	0%
Cattle care	46.7%	20.6%	32.7%	0%
Going to the cattle dip	34.6%	30.7%	33.9%	0.8%

Source: Ingrid Palmer, *The Impact of Male Out-Migration on Women in Farming*, 1985, p. 37 (West Hartford: Kumarian Press, 1985). Primary source: Government of Swaziland, 1978-79: 10. Based on a government survey of 30 women with and without migrant husbands. *Notes:* 1. "The highest percentage of men being primarily responsible for a task is in plowing (61.9%). This figure has to include some husbands who are not usually resident because the proportion of female-headed households in the country is higher than 38%" (source).

★ 560 ★

Farming in Africa: Part 2

Source of labor assistance to women who are primarily responsible for tasks.

Task	Source of assistance			
	Husband	Children	Relatives and friends	Hired labor
Preparing land	19.6%	37.3%	35.4%	9.8%
Fertilization	25.3%	47.4%	22.1%	5.3%
Plowing	21.1%	35.1%	26.3%	17.5%
Planting	30.4%	37.8%	25.9%	3.9%
Hoeing	22.6%	40.9%	29.6%	6.9%
Weeding	12.6%	40.8%	41.7%	4.3%
Harvesting	23.4%	48.1%	24.7%	3.9%
Sorting and storing	42.9%	23.5%	30.3%	3.4%
Preservation of food	3.2%	35.4%	61.3%	0%

Source: Ingrid Palmer, *The Impact of Male Out-Migration on Women in Farming*, 1985, p. 38 (West Hartford: Kumarian Press, 1985). Primary source: Government of Swaziland, 1978-79: 10. Based on a government survey of 30 women (with and without migrant husbands). These percentages do not represent share of labor input but frequency of any assistance coming from different people.

★ 561 ★

Female Labor Force Participation, Selected Countries

Percentage of women aged 25-34 in the labor force, 10 countries, 1970 and 1988.

Country	1970	1988
United States	44.7%	72.6%
Canada	41.2%[1]	74.9%
Japan	46.8%	54.5%
Denmark	NA	90.0%
France	52.2%	74.5%
Germany	47.6%	61.5%
Italy (ages 25-39)[2]	44.1%	60.8%
Netherlands	23.9%	55.4%
Sweden	60.7%	89.4%
United Kingdom	43.3%	66.0%

Source: Constance Sorrentino, "The changing family in international perspective," *Monthly Labor Review* 113:3 (March 1990), pp. 41+. *Notes:* 1. Bureau of Labor Statistics estimate. 2. 1977 data.

★ 562 ★

Labor Force Participation of Women: Selected Countries

Labor force participation rates of all women under age 60[1] and women with children under the ages of 18 and 3, eight countries, 1986 or 1988.

Country	All women	All women with children		Lone mothers[3] with children	
		Under 18	Under 3	Under 18	Under 3
United States	68.5%	65.0%	52.5%	65.3%	45.1%
Canada	66.8%	67.0%[4]	58.4%	63.6%[4]	41.3%
Denmark	79.2%	86.1%	83.9%	85.9%	80.9%
Germany	55.8%	48.4%	39.7%	69.7%	50.4%
France	60.1%	65.8%	60.1%	85.2%	69.6%
Italy	43.3%	43.9%	45.0%	67.2%	68.0%
Sweden	80.0%	89.4%[4]	85.8%[5]	[6]	[6]
United Kingdom	64.3%	58.7%	36.9%	51.9%	23.4%

Source: "Labor force particpation rates of all women under age 60 and women with children under the ages of 18 and 3, eight countries, 1986 or 1988," *Monthly Labor Review,* March 1990, p. 53. Primary source: Published data from U.S., Canadian, and Swedish labor force surveys; unpublished data for other countries provided by the Statistical Office of the European Communities from the European Community labor force surveys. *Notes:* 1. Women ages 60 to 64 are included in Canada and Sweden. Lower age limits are 16 for the U.S. and Sweden, 15 for Canada, and 14 for all other countries. For participation rates of women with children, no upper limit is applied for the United States or Canada. These differences do not distort the comparisons because very few women under 16 have children, while few women over 60 live with their children. 2. Data for the U.S. are for March 1988; Canada and Sweden—annual averages for 1988; data for all other countries are for spring 1986. 3. Includes divorced, separated, never-married, and widowed women. 4. Children under 16 years. 5. Children under 7 years. 6. Not available.

★ 563 ★

Managers and Secretaries

Percentage of women and men employed as managers and secretaries, by country.

Country	Managers		Secretaries	
	Women	Men	Women	Men
Germany, Federal Republic	1.3%	4.2%	34.0%	9.6%
Hungary	0.1%	0.2%	16.4%	3.5%
Norway	2.0%	6.6%	26.0%	2.5%
United States	3.8%	10.4%	27.9%	5.5%
Japan	0.4%	6.4%	18.2%	9.4%
Egypt	0.8%	0.9%	25.0%	6.5%
Bahrain	0.4%	1.1%	46.0%	5.8%
Singapore	1.2%	8.2%	14.9%	5.7%
Venezuela	1.6%	9.2%	16.7%	7.6%

Source: Eschel M. Rhoodie, *Discrimination Against Women: A Global Survey of the Economic, Educational, Social and Political Status of Women,* 1989, p. 42 (Jefferson, NC: McFarland & Company, 1989). Primary source: International Labour Organization, 1983 *Yearbook of Labour Statistics,* Geneva, 1984.

★ 564 ★

Managers, Laborers, and Clericals

Number of workers in management, labor, and clerical work, and percent occupation is dominated by one sex, by country.

Country	Managers			Laborers			Clericals		
	Female	Male	% Male	Female	Male	% Male	Female	Male	% Female
	Numbers in thousands								
Australia	45	290	87%	254	1,853	88%	750	329	70%
Canada	366	800	69%	446	2,712	86%	1,506	386	80%
New Zealand	4	42	91%	67	391	85%	148	67	69%
Sweden	19	76	80%	223	1,040	82%	429	101	81%
United States	3,070	7,063	70%	5,852	24,601	81%	12,997	3,854	77%

Source: "Occupational Sex Segregation in Selected Industrialized Countries," *A Comparable Worth Primer,* p. 78 (Lexington, MA: Lexington Books, 1986). Primary source: Adapted from international Labour Office, *Yearbook of Labour Statistics* (Geneva: International Labour Office, 1984), table 2B, 106-49. Because of differences in methodologies and data bases, strict comparisons between countries should not be made on the basis of these statistics.

★ 565 ★

United Nations Personnel

Representation of women in the United Nations, 1989.

Position	Number or % Female
Member, World Health Organization committee on breastfeeding	0
Doctor, World Health Organization (N=151)	6
Professional posts in International Labour Organization	20%
General services posts in United Nations (typists, secretaries, research assistants)	80%
Professional posts in United Nations (economists, scientists, information officers)	18%
Mid-professional level with doctoral degree (Men at mid-professional level with doctoral degree: 16%)	30%

Source: Chitra Subramaniam, "An Indifference Toward Women," *World Press Review,* October 1989, p. 65.

★ 566 ★

Women in the Labor Force: 1970-2000

Share of females in total labor force and female labor force distribution, 1970-2000.

Region	Share of females in labor force				Female labor force distribution			
	1970	1980	1985	2000	1970	1980	1985	2000
World	35.99%	36.86%	36.52%	35.50%	100%	100%	100%	100%
Developing countries	34.37%	34.96%	34.73%	33.78%	66.98%	68.59%	70.14%	73.89%
Africa	35.95%	35.62%	35.03%	33.40%	9.24%	9.34%	9.48%	10.88%
Asia (excl. China)	29.44%	28.51%	27.98%	26.70%	23.13%	21.88%	22.01%	23.37%
China	41.69%	43.18%	43.24%	43.47%	31.07%	32.75%	33.82%	33.84%
Latin America and the Caribbean	21.76%	26.36%	26.63%	27.74%	3.44%	4.51%	4.73%	5.68%

[Continued]

★ 566 ★

Women in the Labor Force: 1970-2000

[Continued]

Region	Share of females in labor force				Female labor force distribution			
	1970	1980	1985	2000	1970	1980	1985	2000
Developed countries	39.78%	41.83%	41.55%	41.51%	33.02%	31.41%	29.86%	26.11%
Centrally planned economies	48.58%	48.33%	47.57%	47.50%	14.50%	12.95%	12.12%	10.59%
Eastern Europe	44.27%	45.67%	45.73%	46.33%	4.18%	3.57%	3.36%	2.98%
Soviet union	50.57%	49.42%	48.32%	47.97%	10.32%	9.38%	8.76%	7.61%
Market economies	36.36%	39.30%	39.31%	39.36%	22.35%	21.62%	20.69%	18.09%
Europe	35.77%	38.51%	38.54%	38.81%	12.69%	11.63%	11.04%	9.46%
North America	36.14%	41.46%	41.36%	41.18%	6.04%	7.00%	6.78%	6.18%
Japan	39.03%	37.75%	37.82%	37.29%	3.62%	2.99%	2.86%	2.46%
Oceania (Australia and New Zealand)	30.94%	36.92%	37.24%	37.77%	0.35%	0.41%	0.42%	0.41%

Source: "Participation of Women in the Labour Force, 1970-2000," *1989 Report on the World Social Situation*, p. 9-10 (New York: United Nations, 1989). Primary source: ILO, *Economically Active Population-Estimates: 1950-1980, Projections: 1985-2025*, 3rd ed. (Geneva, 1986). Also in source: annual rate of growth.

★ 567 ★

Work Force in Selected Countries

Total labor force and percent female, selected European countries and USSR, 1990.

Country	Total labor force	Percent Female
Albania	1,591,000	41.2%
Austria	3,570,000	40.0%
Belgium	4,157,000	33.7%
Bulgaria	4,475,000	46.4%
Czechoslovakia	8,386,000	47.0%
Denmark	2,852,000	44.6%
East Germany	9,670,000	45.5%
Finland	2,552,000	47.0%
France	25,404,000	39.9%
Greece	3,852,000	26.7%
Hungary	5,276,000	44.9%
Iceland	136,000	42.6%
Ireland	1,481,000	29.4%
Italy	23,339,000	31.9%
Luxembourg	155,000	31.6%
Malta	146,000	23.3%
Netherlands	6,153,000	30.9%
Norway	2,128,000	41.2%
Poland	19,704,000	45.6%
Portugal	4,740,000	36.7%

[Continued]

★ 567 ★

Work Force in Selected Countries
[Continued]

Country	Total labor force	Percent Female
Romania	11,825,000	46.4%
Spain	14,456,000	24.4%
Sweden	4,319,000	44.6%
Switzerland	3,212,000	36.6%
United Kingdom	27,766,000	38.6%
USSR	146,634,000	48.0%
West Germany	29,311,000	37.2%
Yugoslavia	10,858,000	38.9%

Source: "Percentage of the Work Force That Is Female, 1990," *Market: Europe* 1:3 (October 1990), p. 2. Primary source: *Economically Active Population, 1950-2025,* Vol. IV, International Labour Office, Geneva.

★ 568 ★

Working Women Worldwide by Level of Education
Percentage of ever-married women aged 15-49 currently working, by level of education.

Region and country	Level of education				
	None	1-3 years	4-6 years	7-9 years	10+ years
Africa					
Benin	73.9%	77.0%	69.6%	62.5%	71.1%
Cameroon	67.6%	78.2%	65.3%	63.2%	53.0%
Egypt	14.5%	13.0%	9.5%	10.4%	61.9%
Ghana	88.6%	90.3%	88.1%	82.4%	83.2%
Ivory Coast	73.9%	56.9%	40.0%	35.3%	57.6%
Mauritania	31.3%	21.6%	31.0%	42.0%	-
Morocco	16.7%	12.9%	9.1%	23.0%	58.7%
Senegal	69.3%	43.4%	22.5%	26.9%	54.8%
Sudan	35.7%	10.9%	9.7%	23.4%	43.8%
Tunisia	18.6%	11.0%	6.7%	30.0%	35.2%
Colombia	23.3%	21.6%	25.6%	34.8%	49.1%
Costa Rica	17.8%	17.4%	15.5%	23.7%	33.4%
Dominican Republic	20.4%	17.2%	18.2%	28.3%	54.4%
Ecuador	32.4%	29.7%	25.2%	29.4%	43.3%
Guyana	36.5%	26.8%	27.1%	30.2%	67.0%
Haiti	67.3%	56.6%	40.4%	48.3%	42.9%
Jamaica	34.1%	42.4%	40.9%	38.8%	78.7%
Mexico	20.7%	17.5%	17.2%	24.2%	54.1%
Panama	20.7%	15.7%	24.7%	39.3%	63.5%

[Continued]

★ 568 ★

Working Women Worldwide by Level of Education
[Continued]

Region and country	Level of education				
	None	1-3 years	4-6 years	7-9 years	10+ years
Paraguay	43.1%	38.2%	27.0%	19.8%	24.9%
Peru	61.5%	51.2%	38.9%	34.8%	46.8%
Trinidad and Tobago	27.7%	17.1%	23.1%	31.7%	62.1%
Venezuela	16.7%	20.7%	20.9%	21.9%	44.1%
Asia and Oceania					
Bangladesh	14.0%	8.7%	2.6%	3.6%	19.8%
Fiji	9.2%	11.0%	15.2%	18.9%	42.8%
Indonesia	71.8%	64.95	52.4%	37.5%	45.7%
Jordan	9.5%	5.1%	5.3%	4.5%	32.5%
Malaysia	56.9%	49.3%	35.4%	26.7%	55.1%
Nepal	67.8%	52.8%	29.7%	25.5%	16.0%
Pakistan	17.9%	11.2%	9.6%	8.8%	18.2%
Philippines	47.1%	48.7%	41.7%	33.3%	50.7%
Korea, Republic of	74.6%	68.8%	47.9%	28.8%	24.0%
Sri Lanka	51.3%	44.6%	31.6%	19.6%	33.9%
Syrian Arab Republic	22.7%	7.7%	7.5%	5.7%	49.0%
Thailand	83.8%	81.1%	83.1%	55.0%	79.6%
Yemen[1]	47.3%	-	-	-	-

Source: "Percentage of ever-married women aged 15-49 currently working, by level of education," *Women's Employment and Fertility: A Comparative Analysis of World Fertility Survey Results for 38 Developing Countries,* 1985, p. 34 (New York: United Nations, 1985). Primary source: World Fertility Survey standard recode tapes. *Note:* 1. Of ever-married women, 98.2% have no education.

★ 569 ★

Working Women Worldwide, by Residence
Percentage of ever-married women aged 15-49 currently working, by type of place of residence.

Region and country	Place of residence		
	Major Urban	Other Urban	Rural
Africa			
Benin	70.7%	70.6%	74.5%
Cameroon	41.8%	42.1%	72.7%
Egypt	14.3%	15.3%	18.0%
Ghana	82.9%	84.9%	88.4%
Ivory Coast	40.1%	55.7%	82.1%
Mauritania	13.9%	23.9%	31.0%
Morocco	16.7%	14.7%	17.8%

[Continued]

★ 569 ★

Working Women Worldwide, by Residence
[Continued]

Region and country	Place of residence		
	Major Urban	Other Urban	Rural
Senegal	26.5%	37.4%	80.4%
Sudan	11.5%	12.0%	39.4%
Tunisia	10.2%	10.2%	25.0%
Latin America/Caribbean			
Colombia	36.9%	52.6%	22.4%
Costa Rica	26.0%	24.7%	14.2%
Dominican Republic	30.1%	28.6%	12.2%
Ecuador	32.3%	32.6%	28.0%
Guyana	42.6%	28.2%	26.6%
Haiti	40.3%	51.3%	71.7%
Jamaica	54.7%	45.4%	35.4%
Mexico	25.1%	22.0%	16.4%
Panama	48.6%	43.6%	18.7%
Paraguay	27.8%	27.3%	31.4%
Peru	36.7%	48.7%	60.0%
Trinidad and Tobago	46.9%	28.7%	24.2%
Venezuela	31.2%	24.3%	12.6%
Asia and Oceania			
Bangladesh	14.0%	13.4%	12.1%
Fiji	23.9%	19.3%	15.7%
Indonesia	30.5%	45.6%	70.8%
Jordan	8.5%	8.1%	13.3%
Malaysia	33.2%	34.4%	51.8%
Pakistan	14.5%	15.8%	17.7%
Philippines	43.3%	43.2%	44.9%
Korea, Republic of	30.5%	38.1%	71.3%
Sri Lanka	16.7%	19.4%	40.5%
Syrian Arab Republic	10.8%	8.9%	29.6%
Thailand	60.1%	63.7%	85.9%
Yemen	[1]	7.4%	52.0%

Source: "Percentage of ever-married women aged 15-49 currently working, by type of place of residence," *Women's Employment and Fertility: A Comparative Analysis of World Fertility Survey Results for 38 Developing Countries*, 1985, p. 30 (New York: United Nations, 1985). Primary source: World Fertility Survey standard recode tapes. *Note:* 1. No major urban category.

★ 570 ★

Working Women Worldwide: Currently Working
Percentage of ever-married women aged 15-49 currently working, by age group.

Region and country	Age group						
	15-19	20-24	25-29	30-34	35-39	40-44	45-49
Africa							
Benin	53.8%	69.2%	76.3%	75.3%	78.5%	74.3%	81.6%
Cameroon	44.5%	59.2%	63.0%	69.1%	70.3%	73.0%	79.5%
Egypt	9.7%	13.8%	19.2%	22.0%	17.3%	15.7%	12.7%
Ghana	61.1%	82.1%	87.0%	94.0%	92.5%	94.6%	91.8%
Ivory Coast	45.1%	56.6%	69.3%	78.6%	82.5%	90.7%	89.0%
Mauritania	22.6%	19.2%	27.2%	29.8%	28.5%	28.6%	33.7%
Morocco	10.6%	14.6%	18.5%	16.9%	19.7%	18.1%	17.1%
Senegal	59.4%	58.7%	61.7%	67.8%	71.2%	74.7%	75.9%
Sudan	17.5%	22.4%	32.8%	32.6%	37.2%	40.5%	38.2%
Tunisia	13.8%	13.4%	17.7%	20.2%	17.2%	20.5%	18.9%
Latin America/Caribbean							
Colombia	14.4%	20.0%	29.5%	26.9%	30.5%	26.5%	27.2%
Costa Rica	-	9.3%	21.5%	27.9%	26.4%	21.9%	23.0%
Dominican Republic	3.1%	12.0%	19.4%	24.2%	25.4%	25.8%	27.9%
Ecuador	14.2%	23.0%	29.5%	34.2%	32.8%	37.5%	37.3%
Guyana	15.2%	24.2%	29.9%	33.9%	35.2%	40.4%	41.9%
Haiti	33.6%	48.3%	58.9%	69.1%	72.7%	70.7%	71.3%
Jamaica	20.1%	34.5%	46.9%	46.8%	49.9%	53.4%	52.2%
Mexico	9.2%	15.4%	18.3%	22.1%	27.9%	24.1%	25.4%
Panama	-	38.0%	36.5%	36.3%	35.7%	36.5%	31.3%
Paraguay	3.8%	21.2%	36.1%	44.5%	52.5%	45.5%	48.4%
Peru	34.1%	38.6%	46.4%	49.7%	55.9%	56.2%	59.1%
Trinidad and Tobago	18.0%	26.1%	33.5%	34.1%	35.9%	39.9%	35.3%
Venezuela	16.2%	29.3%	28.3%	28.9%	26.5%	25.1%	-
Asia and Oceania							
Bangladesh	6.8%	9.6%	13.7%	16.2%	16.2%	14.7%	17.2%
Fiji	13.6%	13.9%	17.5%	17.9%	19.7%	20.8%	20.0%
Indonesia	51.4%	55.6%	60.3%	67.9%	74.5%	76.9%	74.9%
Jordan	7.1%	6.2%	11.4%	12.1%	10.2%	10.0%	9.6%
Malaysia	28.6%	30.9%	40.2%	52.0%	54.0%	53.3%	51.2%
Nepal	59.8%	66.5%	64.1%	68.2%	69.2%	70.4%	66.0%
Pakistan	12.8%	14.8%	16.4%	17.3%	19.2%	22.2%	18.1%
Philippines	22.8%	25.5%	40.5%	47.4%	51.9%	50.4%	52.1%
Korea, Republic of	23.6%	30.0%	32.5%	47.2%	61.4%	61.2%	64.7%
Sri Lanka	18.8%	27.0%	34.5%	36.8%	43.8%	41.7%	36.3%
Syrian Arab Republic	13.1%	16.5%	22.7%	20.9%	22.7%	20.3%	17.1%

[Continued]

★ 570 ★

Working Women Worldwide: Currently Working

[Continued]

Region and country	Age group						
	15-19	20-24	25-29	30-34	35-39	40-44	45-49
Thailand	70.3%	73.8%	81.7%	84.1%	88.4%	84.8%	87.0%
Yemen	46.7%	43.0%	49.8%	45.3%	47.6%	48.4%	49.0%

Source: "Percentage of ever-married women aged 15-49 currently working, by age group," *Women's Employment and Fertility: A Comparative Analysis of World Fertility Survey Results for 38 Developing Countries*, 1985, p. 28 (New York: United Nations, 1985). Primary source: World Fertility Survey standard recode tapes.

★ 571 ★

Working Women and Fertility Worldwide

Mean number of children ever born to ever-married women by most recent occupation since first marriage. See below for an explanation of types of occupations.

Region and country	Most recent occupation since first marriage				
	No work	Modern	Transitional	Mixed	Traditional
Africa					
Benin	3.16	3.63	3.77	3.95	4.09
Cameroon	2.83	3.17	3.04	3.07	3.80
Egypt	4.19	1.81	4.74	4.54	4.70
Ghana	2.08	2.29	3.05	3.66	4.21
Ivory Coast	2.36	3.35	2.95	3.84	4.44
Mauritania	3.64	3.73	3.78	5.03	4.25
Morocco	4.57	1.91	3.56	4.15	4.70
Senegal	3.45	2.92	3.94	5.21	4.15
Sudan	4.25	2.63	4.80	3.99	4.31
Tunisia	4.47	2.08	4.73	4.22	5.19
Latin America					
Colombia	4.45	2.33	4.39	4.00	5.99
Costa Rica	4.44	2.34	4.84	3.72	6.51
Dominican Republic	4.03	3.31	4.13	4.14	6.28
Ecuador	4.25	2.25	4.54	4.15	5.65
Guyana[1]	4.24	2.74	4.84	5.09	6.60
Haiti	2.66	2.72	2.33	3.75	4.08
Jamaica[1]	3.92	2.64	4.26	4.24	6.02
Mexico	4.50	2.63	5.22	4.58	6.08
Panama	4.39	2.50	4.46	3.70	6.25
Paraguay	3.75	2.29	2.96	3.76	5.23
Peru	4.18	2.64	4.51	4.66	5.54
Trinidad and Tobago[1]	3.99	2.55	4.14	3.68	6.19
Venezuela	3.69	2.48	5.00[2]	3.39	4.23

[Continued]

★ 571 ★

Working Women and Fertility Worldwide
[Continued]

Region and country	Most recent occupation since first marriage				
	No work	Modern	Transitional	Mixed	Traditional
Asia and Oceania					
Bangladesh	4.10	3.79	4.36	4.38	4.38
Fiji	3.96	2.39	2.98	4.15	4.48
Jordan	5.42	2.88	4.66	5.38	6.70
Malaysia	3.81	2.14	4.21	4.20	4.88
Nepal	3.21	2.39^2	3.16^2	3.79	3.31
Pakistan	4.09	3.87	5.83	4.69	4.33
Philippines	4.46	3.15	4.28	4.64	5.55
Korea, Republic of	2.79	2.00	3.22	3.42	4.82
Sri Lanka	3.79	2.41	4.07	4.02	4.46
Syrian Arab Republic	4.74	2.78	4.64^2	4.51	5.14
Thailand	2.99	2.24	3.17	3.58	4.28
Yemen	3.90	2.87^2	4.28^2	3.62	3.58

Source: "Mean number of children ever born to ever-married women, by most recent occupation since first marriage," *Women's Employment and Fertility: A Comparative Analysis of World Fertility Survey Results for 38 Developing Countries,* 1985, p. 60 (New York: United Nations, 1985). Primary source: World Fertility Survey standard recode tapes. "The modern occupational group includes women who were coded as professional or clerical workers by the World Fertility Survey (WFS). The transitional group (household and service workers in WFS) also generally work away from home for someone other than a family member but use traditional skills requiring little education (such as cleaning and washing clothes). Women in the mixed group (WFS codes for sales, skilled and unskilled workers) may work at home or away. They are often self-employed and perform jobs that require some level of training or skill (e.g., growing or making items for sale, trading in the market-place). The traditional group is comprised of women who work in agriculture. These women are often employed by a family member, have little education and live in rural areas" (source: p. 45). *Notes:* 1. Figures refer to ever-married women with one birth or more, by occupation since first birth. 2. Category contains fewer than 20 cases.

★ 572 ★

Working Women by Industry Worldwide

Youth and adult economically active population by broad industry group, circa 1981.

Country, year, and age	Number in thousands				Percent			
	Total	Agriculture	Industry	Service	Total	Agriculture	Industry	Service
Female								
China 1982:								
15 to 24 years	72,790	52,756	12,709	7,325	100%	72.5%	17.5%	10.1%
25+ years	107,149	84,545	13,056	9,549	100%	78.9%	12.2%	8.9%
Hungary 1980:								
15 to 24 years	366	29	159	178	100%	7.8%	43.4%	48.8%
25+ years	1,830	311	686	833	100%	17.0%	37.5%	45.5%
Japan 1980:								
15 to 24 years	3,383	50	800	2,533	100%	1.5%	23.6%	74.9%
25+ years	17,750	2,854	4,773	10,123	100%	16.1%	26.9%	57.0%
Norway 1980:								
16 to 24 years	187	6	29	152	100%	3.3%	15.5%	81.2%

[Continued]

★ 572 ★

Working Women by Industry Worldwide
[Continued]

Country, year, and age	Number in thousands				Percent			
	Total	Agriculture	Industry	Service	Total	Agriculture	Industry	Service
25+ years	649	45	89	516	100%	6.9%	13.7%	79.4%
United Kingdom 1981:								
16 to 24 years	1,989	13	488	1,488	100%	.7%	24.5%	74.8%
25+ years	7,084	77	1,527	5,480	100%	1.1%	21.6%	77.4%
United States 1980:								
16 to 24 years	9,851	117	1,598	8,137	100%	1.2%	16.2%	82.6%
25+ years	31,783	405	6,233	25,144	100%	1.3%	19.6%	79.1%
Male								
China 1982:								
15 to 24 years	86,426	54,877	18,011	13,538	100%	63.5%	20.8%	15.7%
25+ years	165,576	115,141	27,179	23,255	100%	69.5%	16.4%	14.0%
Hungary 1980:								
15 to 24 years	531	101	283	147	100%	19.1%	53.3%	27.7%
25+ years	2,318	499	1,085	735	100%	21.5%	46.8%	31.7%
Japan 1980:								
15 to 24 years	3,625	131	1,404	2,090	100%	3.6%	38.7%	57.6%
25+ years	30,991	3,076	12,109	15,807	100%	9.9%	39.1%	51.0%
Norway 1980:								
16 to 24 years	233	19	95	119	100%	8.3%	40.9%	50.8%
25+ years	955	94	387	475	100%	9.9%	40.5%	49.7%
United Kingdom 1981:								
16 to 24 years	2,415	80	1,143	1,193	100%	3.3%	47.3%	49.4%
25+ years	11,234	345	5,351	5,538	100%	3.1%	47.6%	49.3%
United States 1980:								
16 to 24 years	10,988	513	4,009	6,466	100%	4.7%	36.5%	58.8%
25+ years	45,016	1,878	18,215	24,923	100%	4.2%	40.5%	55.4%

Source: Selected from "Youth and Adult Economically Active Population, by Broad Industry Group and Sex, Selected Countries: Circa 1981," *Children's Well-Being: An International Comparison*, A Report of the Select Committee on Children, Youth, and Families, 101st Cong., 2d sess., March 1990, p. 116-117. Primary source: U.S. Bureau of the Census, Center for International Research, International Data Base. Also in source: data for "both sexes." Figures may not add to totals due to rounding.

★ 573 ★

Working Women by Occupation and Marital Status: 12 Countries
Occupational distribution of employed women (all ages), by marital status, in 12 industrialized countries.

Country and marital status	Occupational category						
	Professional /Technical	Adminis./ Managerial	Clerical & Related	Sales	Service	Agriculture	Production & Related
Austria							
Ever married	6.3%	0.7%	21.4%	12.3%	17.9%	23.2%	18.2%
Never married	10.8%	0.0%	30.1%	10.8%	14.5%	13.3%	20.5%
Denmark							
Ever married	15.5%	0.0%	27.7%	10.2%	18.4%	18.9%	9.2%

[Continued]

★ 573 ★

Working Women by Occupation and Marital Status: 12 Countries
[Continued]

Country and marital status	Occupational category						
	Professional /Technical	Adminis./ Managerial	Clerical & Related	Sales	Service	Agriculture	Production & Related
Never married	27.9%	0.0%	23.3%	2.3%	23.3%	11.6%	11.6%
Finland							
Ever married	12.6%	1.2%	17.3%	10.6%	14.6%	30.7%	13.0%
Never married	15.7%	1.4%	27.1%	5.7%	28.6%	11.4%	10.0%
Germany, Federal Republic							
Ever married	14.2%	0.0%	39.0%	16.3%	12.5%	3.2%	14.8%
Never married	15.4%	0.0%	46.4%	16.7%	5.5%	0.6%	15.4%
Great Britain							
Ever married	12.2%	1.1%	27.5%	12.9%	25.9%	1.3%	19.0%
Never married	25.9%	0.0%	38.8%	7.9%	9.4%	1.4%	16.5%
Israel							
Ever married	31.8%	1.2%	25.5%	9.9%	17.8%	3.2%	10.6%
Never married	22.9%	0.6%	36.7%	4.6%	13.6%	1.4%	20.3%
Japan							
Ever married	6.7%	0.9%	7.6%	11.0%	11.3%	45.4%	17.1%
Never married	9.9%	1.1%	45.8%	12.4%	8.8%	4.5%	17.5%
Netherlands							
Ever married	21.1%	0.9%	31.2%	20.2%	18.3%	3.7%	4.6%
Never married	28.1%	0.0%	35.4%	9.4%	18.8%	0.0%	8.3%
Northern Ireland							
Ever married	16.8%	1.3%	13.4%	8.1%	31.5%	2.7%	26.2%
Never married	17.6%	1.2%	30.6%	9.4%	14.1%	4.7%	22.4%
Norway							
Ever married	18.7%	1.4%	21.6%	14.4%	15.8%	19.4%	8.6%
Never married	21.9%	6.3%	25.0%	12.5%	28.1%	6.3%	0.0%
Sweden							
Ever married	24.8%	0.4%	29.0%	12.6%	23.5%	1.3%	8.4%
Never married	13.9%	0.0%	50.0%	5.6%	25.0%	0.0%	5.6%
United States							
Ever married	21.3%	3.4%	32.7%	6.9%	19.1%	0.5%	16.1%
Never married	27.6%	0.9%	35.9%	6.5%	19.8%	0.0%	9.2%

Source: Patricia A. Roos, *Gender and Work: A Comparative Analysis of Industrial Societies*, p. 138-139 (Albany: State University of New York Press, 1985). Based on sample surveys in the 12 countries studied.

★ 574 ★

Worldwide Administrative and Managerial Workers

Percentage of women in major group 02 of ISCO-68 administrative and managerial workers. (ISCO = International Standard Classification of Occupation.).

Country or area	Year	% Female
Egypt	1980	12.4%
Tunisia	1975	4.9%
El Salvador	1980	15.8%
Guatemala	1981	16.0%
Mexico[1]	1980	29.7%
Panama	1980	20.1%
Peru	1981	7.9%
Trinidad and Tobago	1975	48.3%
Uruguay	1975	18.0%
Venezuela	1981	10.4%
Bahrain	1981	3.8%
Hong Kong	1982	10.6%
Indonesia[1]	1980	10.3%
Kuwait	1980	2.1%
Nepal[1]	1975	19.1%
Philippines	1981	23.8%
Republic of Korea	1982	2.5%
Sri Lanka	1980	17.8%
Syrian Arab Republic[1]	1980	3.7%
Thailand	1980	17.8%
Finland	1980	16.1%
Germany, Federal Republic	1982	17.1%
Ireland[1]	1980	13.1%
Japan	1982	5.5%
Netherlands[1]	1980	4.9%
Norway	1982	17.1%
Portugal	1981	9.4%
Spain	1982	4.6%
Sweden	1982	19.3%

Source: Selected from "Percentage of women in major group 02 of ISCO-68 administrative and managerial workers," *World Survey on the Role of Women in Development,* 1986, p. 27 (New York: United Nations, 1986). Primary source: International Labour Office, *Yearbook of Labour Statistics,* various issues. Also in source: data for other years. *Note:* 1. Estimated value.

★ 575 ★

Worldwide Age at Marriage by Occupation Before Marriage

Mean age at marriage, by occupation before marriage, ever-married women aged 23 and over.
See below for an explanation of types of occupations.

Region and country	Mean age in years at marriage				
	No work	Modern	Transi-tional	Mixed	Traditional
Africa					
Benin	19.0	22.2[1]	18.2	18.7	18.6
Egypt	17.7	22.0	19.4	20.1	17.7
Ghana	18.2	21.2	19.5	18.7	18.7
Ivory Coast	17.5	20.3	19.6	17.9	18.6
Mauritania	15.6	17.2[1]	17.3	18.2	15.8
Morocco	16.9	19.7	18.1	16.9	17.3
Senegal	16.4	19.7	17.6	17.9	16.4
Sudan	16.5	20.5	18.0[1]	17.3	16.8
Tunisia	19.4	22.3	20.4	21.3	19.3
Average	17.5	20.6	18.6	18.6	17.7
Latin America and the Caribbean					
Colombia	19.1	21.8	20.7	21.2	20.7
Costa Rica	19.4	22.8	21.3	21.8	21.0
Dominican Republic	17.9	20.3	18.4	19.7	18.6
Ecuador	18.8	21.3	20.1	20.7	20.2
Haiti	19.1	21.6	20.0	20.5	20.9
Mexico	18.6	21.2	19.6	20.4	18.3
Panama	18.5	21.7	19.8	20.4	18.9
Paraguay	19.2	23.1	20.7	21.6	19.7
Peru	18.9	22.1	19.9	20.7	20.0
Venezuela	18.3	21.1	19.4	21.3	19.4
Average	18.8	21.7	20.0	20.8	19.8
Asia and Oceania					
Bangladesh	12.5	17.4[1]	12.3	13.6	15.0
Jordan	17.4	21.1	21.2[1]	20.0	18.1
Malaysia	17.9	21.5	21.4	21.1	18.6
Nepal	15.6	14.8[1]	15.7[1]	16.6	17.4
Pakistan	16.6	19.4	16.5	17.1	16.5
Philippines	19.9	23.9	21.7	21.8	19.9
Korea, Republic of	20.1	21.4	21.8	21.7	20.4

[Continued]

★ 575 ★

Worldwide Age at Marriage by Occupation Before Marriage
[Continued]

Region and country	Mean age in years at marriage				
	No work	Modern	Transi-tional	Mixed	Traditional
Sri Lanka	19.3	23.1	22.2	21.4	19.7
Syrian Arab Republic	18.7	21.8	23.0[1]	20.6	19.3
Thailand	19.0	21.3	21.1	20.6	19.7
Yemen	16.3	[1]	14.5[1]	18.4	16.6
Average	17.6	20.6	19.2	19.4	18.3

Source: "Mean age at marriage, by occupation before marriage, adjusted for education (Ever-married women aged 23 or over)" *Women's Employment and Fertility: A Comparative Analysis of World Fertility Survey Results for 38 Developing Countries,* 1985, p. 50 (New York: United Nations, 1985). Primary source: World Fertility Survey standard recode tapes. "The modern occupational group includes women who were coded as professional or clerical workers by the World Fertility Survey (WFS). The transitional group (household and service workers in WFS) also generally work away from home for someone other than a family member but use traditional skills requiring little education (such as cleaning and washing clothes). Women in the mixed group (WFS codes for sales, skilled and unskilled workers) may work at home or away. They are often self-employed and perform jobs that require some level of training or skill (e.g., growing or making items for sale, trading in the market-place). The traditional group is comprised of women who work in agriculture. These women are often employed by a family member, have little education and live in rural areas" (source: p. 45). *Note:* 1. Fewer than 20 cases.

★ 576 ★

Worldwide Contraceptive Use by Occupation

Percentage of women currently using any contraceptive method, by current occupation. See below for an explanation of types of occupations.

Region and country	Current occupation adjusted for demographic and socio-economic factors[1]				
	Modern	Transi-tional	Mixed	Traditional	No work
Africa					
Benin	29%	---	25%	33%	13%[2]
Egypt	27%	38%	36%	30%	32%
Ghana	26%	14%	13%	11%	8%[2]
Ivory Coast	17%	6%	4%	4%	3%[2]
Mauritania	3%	0%	2%	1%	1%
Morocco	37%	---	30%	23%	31%[2]
Sudan	16%	---	4%	5%	6%
Tunisia	52%	---	35%	37%	40%
Colombia	59%	57%	54%	3%	51%
Costa Rica	82%	79%	86%	75%	77%
Dominican Republic	46%	41%	44%	36%	42%

[Continued]

★ 576 ★

Worldwide Contraceptive Use by Occupation
[Continued]

Region and country	Current occupation adjusted for demographic and socio-economic factors[1]				
	Modern	Transi-tional	Mixed	Traditional	No work
Ecuador	53%	46%	44%	34%	43%[2]
Guyana	49%	37%	42%	34%	37%[2]
Haiti	7%	---	34%	23%	26%[2]
Jamaica	55%	60%	52%	37%	41%[2]
Mexico	46%	43%	44%	36%	42%
Panama	69%	64%	69%	65%	64%
Paraguay	54%	49%	51%	41%	46%
Peru	42%	46%	45%	35%	41%[2]
Trinidad and Tobago	67%	64%	62%	65%	58%
Asia and Oceania					
Bangladesh	3%	12%	11%	6%	10%
Fiji	59%	45%	50%	42%	53%[2]
Jordan	34%	---	39%	40%	37%
Malaysia	41%	61%	48%	40%	41%[2]
Philippines	53%	53%	54%	49%	45%[2]
Korea, Republic of	57%	43%	47%	47%	45%
Sri Lanka	41%	36%	42%	44%	42%
Thailand	59%	50%	50%	43%	45%

Source: "Percentage of exposed women currently using any contraceptive method, by current occupation, *Women's Employment and Fertility: A Comparative Analysis of World Fertility Survey Results for 38 Developing Countries*, 1985, p. 77 (New York: United Nations, 1985). Primary source: World Fertility Survey standard recode tapes. "The sample for the analysis is restricted to women exposed to the risk of conception, i.e., currently-married, fecund women who are not pregnant plus women who are contraceptively sterilized (counted as current contraceptive users)" (source, p. 76). "The modern occupational group includes women who were coded as professional or clerical workers by the World Fertility Survey (WFS). The transitional group (household and service workers in WFS) also generally work away from home for someone other than a family member but use traditional skills requiring little education (such as cleaning and washing clothes). Women in the mixed group (WFS codes for sales, skilled and unskilled workers) may work at home or away. They are often self-employed and perform jobs that require some level of training or skill (e.g., growing or making items for sale, trading in the market-place). The traditional group is comprised of women who work in agriculture. These women are often employed by a family member, have little education and live in rural areas" (source: p. 45). The symbol—- in a column indicates that the figure in the following column spans both columns. *Notes:* 1. Respondent's age, marital duration, type of place of residence, education, husband's occupation, number of living children and whether respondent wanted more children. 2. Occupation significant at the 0.05 level.

★ 577 ★

Worldwide Economically Active Population

Total and female economically active population by status.

Country, census year	Total active		Employers and own account workers		Employees		Unpaid family workers	
	Total	Female	Total	Female	Total	Female	Total	Female
Africa								
Algeria-1977	3,371,023	300,317	561,004	5,243	1,596,692	126,386	70,302	1,367
Burundi-1979	2,418,029	1,280,987	861,533	237,608	135,111	12,563	1,411,810	1,027,732
Cameroon-1976	2,757,899	1,101,732	1,659,783	646,348	392,523	38,748	512,946	360,165
Comoros-1980	99,463	26,231	47,314	11,858	25,486	6,133	-	-
Egypt-1976	11,037,093	983,546	2,885,072	64,814	6,601,354	568,520	616,611	55,399
Gambia-1983	325,618	150,762	254,076	111,988	1,777	358	46,601	29,779
Ghana-1984	5,580,104	2,855,623	3,777,675	2,127,058	874,528	206,028	679,422	431,347
Guinea-Bissau-1979	213,010	7,594	109,192	1,240	31,223	3,147	50,837	1,926
Lesotho-1976	423,882	136,831	31,930	12,123	211,710	32,274	155,851	81,403
Liberia-1984	704,321	288,630	415,987	194,513	152,075	20,489	101,268	66,005
Libyan Arab Jamahiriya-1973	541,174	36,910	128,032	1,444	376,660	20,967	22,510	13,567
Malawi-1977	2,288,351	1,056,539	1,827,969	1,002,514	406,520	38,164	7,233	3,595
Mali-1976	2,266,229	384,604	1,038,865	51,499	92,963	10,492	963,356	286,572
Maroc-1982	5,999,260	1,181,280	1,624,526	171,690	2,429,919	428,935	1,056,514	324,602
Mauritius-1972	260,749	51,735	26,857	3,630	192,232	39,851	2,397	1,117
Mozambique-1970	2,905,917	771,092	1,289,970	428,835	1,161,870	75,487	421,717	264,954
Reunion-1982	172,828	62,010	17,991	2,393	97,309	37,644	1,894	659
Rwanda-1978	2,661,359	1,371,474	1,033,341	343,803	192,643	28,981	1,431,319	998,049
Sao Tome and Principe-1981	30,607	9,927	4,840	1,266	24,317	7,890	26	14
Seychelles-1977	25,947	9,585	3,077	699	20,262	7,545	-	-
Sierra Leone-1963	937,737	333,564	384,932	50,215	101,756	6,067	421,459	274,940
South Africa-1980	8,689,726	2,806,703	350,989	64,034	7,761,589	2,430,418	-	-
Sudan-1973	3,473,278	694,485	2,012,781	410,814	905,942	67,506	327,912	209,558
Tanzania-1967	171,040	81,032	136,696	71,550	18,253	1,802	15,986	7,661
Togo-1981	901,543	395,194	633,629	306,421	94,009	14,114	101,711	54,775
Tunisia-1984	2,031,660	433,630	456,870	118,240	1,173,630	168,110	116,260	89,310
Zambia-1980	1,795,943	640,324	411,410	139,890	763,353	186,946	196,944	41,641
America								
Argentina								
1970	9,011,450	2,288,950	1,976,900	323,600	6,380,500	1,760,150	285,850	77,050
1980	10,033,798	2,755,764	2,515,391	-	7,147,327	-	326,472	-
Bahamas-1980	87,052	38,777	8,707	2,843	70,833	31,482	393	267
Barbados								
1960	92,200	38,699	15,450	7,268	69,099	27,256	453	340
1970	83,981	32,924	-	-	-	-	-	-
Belize								
1960	27,006	4,883	8,556	941	16,680	3,605	786	108
1980	47,327	10,742	-	-	-	-	-	-
Bermuda-1980	31,436	14,204	2,423	490	27,854	13,088	153	131
Bolivia-1976	1,501,391	336,772	733,595	141,070	573,025	134,813	137,264	51,753
Brazil-1980	43,796,763	12,038,930	11,825,146	1,954,133	28,605,051	8,926,871	2,270,679	786,551
Canada-1986	13,141,750	5,653,275	825,360	186,835	11,868,860	5,212,810	89,290	66,875
Colombia								
1964	5,134,125	1,032,062	1,702,979	227,933	2,940,289	737,330	420,685	54,707
1973	5,974,992	1,564,951	1,144,125	-	2,976,571	-	233,878	-
Costa Rica-1984	804,193	177,560	175,340	16,048	575,623	156,045	43,463	3,467
Cuba-1981	3,540,692	1,106,623	171,415	11,231	3,331,577	1,089,789	7,025	354
Chile-1982	3,680,277	959,455	687,152	124,560	2,746,687	775,230	139,265	21,134
Dominica-1981	25,333	8,635	7,455	1,708	12,610	4,816	486	166

[Continued]

★ 577 ★

Worldwide Economically Active Population
[Continued]

Country, census year	Total active		Employers and own account workers		Employees		Unpaid family workers	
	Total	Female	Total	Female	Total	Female	Total	Female
Dominican Republic-1981	1,915,388	554,279	698,443	138,051	982,704	348,736	63,654	27,384
Ecuador-1982	2,346,063	484,411	874,413	127,824	1,116,543	276,333	136,147	26,862
El Salvador-1971	1,166,479	252,155	302,928	49,188	616,397	136,372	106,016	10,271
Greenland-1976	21,378	7,144	2,700	57	17,644	7,011	77	75
Grenada-1960	27,314	10,922	7,659	2,800	17,066	6,931	439	218
Guadeloupe-1982	123,888	52,668	24,135	6,020	67,467	30,699	608	316
Guatemala-1981	1,696,464	247,406	715,700	57,789	795,277	163,544	114,237	8,772
Guyana								
1960	174,730	39,902	46,299	9,717	105,631	22,739	8,337	3,935
1980	239,331	59,247	-	-	-	-	-	-
French Guyana-1982	32,375	11,589	4,833	1,160	22,383	7,910	-	-
Haiti-1982	2,129,661	872,245	1,264,397	495,564	354,183	159,616	222,061	84,585
Honduras-1974	762,795	119,739	301,716	36,911	336,950	75,320	109,795	5,202
Jamaica-1982	708,442	275,130	154,882	38,056	314,632	129,693	8,316	3,691
Martinique-1982	130,500	58,293	16,062	3,570	74,862	36,406	365	192
Mexico-1980	22,066,084	6,141,278	5,958,692	1,484,327	9,766,511	2,640,863	1,464,996	479,921
Montserrat-1980	5,107	2,124	-	-	-	-	-	-
Netherlands Antilles-1981	96,193	38,055	2,976	615	74,613	28,073	133	106
Nicaragua-1971	505,445	110,478	149,246	28,559	293,682	72,693	45,366	4,145
Panama-1980	546,852	152,840	134,053	11,786	345,579	119,668	19,099	2,543
Paraguay-1982	1,039,258	204,950	448,190	68,199	392,271	76,613	95,927	10,791
Peru-1981	5,309,215	1,313,592	2,189,501	373,046	2,413,417	603,602	263,196	144,588
Puerto Rico-1980	865,719	321,480	57,553	7,201	674,569	260,410	1,800	985
St. Christopher and Nevis-1960	19,616	7,843	-	-	-	-	-	-
St. Lucia-1960	31,372	11,371	11,092	3,752	16,218	6,061	1,210	544
St. Pierre and Miquelon-1982	2,380	756	298	68	1,829	591	-	-
St. Vincent and the Grenadines-1980	34,739	12,546	-	-	-	-	-	-
Suriname-1980	80,821	22,730	9,049	1,747	67,001	19,137	1,685	938
Trinidad and Tobago-1980	374,713	108,121	42,224	8,458	296,068	88,627	5,729	1,083
Turks and Caicos Islands-1980	2,909	1,245	-	-	-	-	-	-
United States-1980	106,084,668	44,668,465	6,677,871	1,529,190	92,139,734	39,913,436	499,479	342,820
Uruguay-1985	1,176,808	390,864	262,793	67,632	833,658	293,681	20,793	8,390
Venezuela-1981	4,693,768	1,305,876	903,727	115,260	2,859,521	820,790	46,385	6,927
Virgin Islands (British)-1980	5,272	2,044	681	144	4,204	1,709	40	16
Virgin Islands (US)-1980	37,998	17,315	2,714	667	32,836	15,307	102	67
Asia								
Afghanistan-1979	3,945,591	313,436	-	-	-	-	-	-
Bahrain-1981	142,384	16,205	13,466	161	122,256	14,349	169	14
Bangladesh-1981	23,619,000	1,188,000	9,172,000	462,000	10,686,000	538,000	3,727,000	188,000
Brunei-1981	70,690	16,831	5,207	969	62,511	14,198	410	224
Cyprus-1960	241,823	80,195	73,523	13,032	118,759	26,581	42,481	37,385
Hong Kong-1986	2,753,848	1,037,437	284,489	57,434	2,309,706	899,074	49,078	37,077
India-1981	260,275,118	70,257,654	22,783,112	2,145,917	42,465,205	5,003,667	9,245,710	2,123,560
Indonesia-1980	52,421,245	17,322,443	27,516,419	7,874,743	14,546,661	3,939,339	9,197,968	5,007,972
Iran, Islamic Republic-1986	11,001,535	975,305	4,731,750	192,436	5,327,885	504,582	483,993	209,873
Iraq-1977	3,133,939	544,378	796,013	58,049	1,864,701	149,192	358,029	316,577
Israel-1983	1,442,570	556,495	161,720	26,200	1,191,225	485,650	11,850	7,910

[Continued]

★ 577 ★

Worldwide Economically Active Population
[Continued]

Country, census year	Total active		Employers and own account workers		Employees		Unpaid family workers	
	Total	Female	Total	Female	Total	Female	Total	Female
Japan-1980	57,231,120	21,584,454	9,543,307	2,438,889	39,763,743	13,506,790	6,494,911	5,211,054
Jordan-1979	446,316	33,334	101,613	1,296	300,177	28,001	3,458	139
Kampuchea, Democratic-1962	2,499,735	1,050,732	910,081	114,520	305,219	53,323	1,249,723	867,881
Korea, Republic of-1980	13,595,132	4,973,281	4,495,639	918,176	5,506,627	1,729,331	2,679,520	1,990,480
Kuwait-1985	670,385	132,128	39,873	325	619,722	129,137	900	37
Malaysia: Peninsular-1980	4,069,714	1,362,277	1,190,064	336,281	2,327,837	743,037	275,201	149,122
Malaysia: Sabah-1980	368,832	116,831	102,833	31,780	172,940	38,365	67,106	35,966
Malaysia: Sarawak-1980	485,210	178,826	120,457	38,659	175,063	38,741	161,672	88,489
Maldives: 1985	52,263	11,352	25,822	6,585	20,439	2,820	3,191	1,179
Myanmar-1983	12,199,979	4,935,292	-	-	-	-	-	-
Nepal-1981	6,850,886	2,370,942	5,907,387	2,141,289	621,432	91,062	172,789	95,443
Pakistan-1981	22,626,448	835,090	12,659,609	266,106	5,971,746	290,909	3,293,285	215,396
Philippines-1975	13,426,163	3,546,416	5,106,965	798,237	5,279,713	1,664,712	1,933,176	531,070
Qatar-1986	201,182	19,635	3,556	21	196,488	19,458	74	3
Singapore-1980	1,115,958	385,352	158,281	24,553	891,874	332,082	26,935	13,938
Sri Lanka-1981	5,016,513	1,280,345	1,240,876	122,976	2,769,469	707,647	108,920	40,214
Syrian Arab Republic-1981	2,049,887	174,925	583,238	20,740	1,231,832	106,952	161,542	39,482
Thailand-1980	23,841,359	11,461,125	7,092,158	1,615,284	4,692,642	1,736,231	11,320,602	7,805,502
United Arab Emirates-1980	559,960	28,267	38,113	237	518,969	27,581	289	25
Democratic Yemen-1973	409,742	75,788	122,189	19,164	140,123	5,455	61,734	30,450
Europe								
Austria-1981	3,411,521	1,376,751	398,539	152,321	2,945,180	1,173,957	67,802	50,473
Belgium-1981	3,971,843	1,435,167	482,800	124,059	2,961,129	994,994	84,815	64,819
Bulgaria-1985	4,686,140	2,234,969	14,015	3,824	4,603,052	2,184,370	-	-
Czechoslovakia-1980	7,848,867	3,664,386	10,431	4,073	7,160,387	3,334,070	663,893	317,536
Denmark-1985	2,825,581	1,291,199	255,146	49,170	2,318,230	1,071,387	54,232	53,458
Faeroe Islands-1977	17,585	4,777	2,095	377	15,147	4,244	-	-
Finland-1985	2,444,679	1,153,350	228,712	51,323	1,984,824	964,400	91,973	74,265
France-1982	23,551,176	9,617,932	3,513,680	1,243,240	17,958,104	7,230,160	-	-
Germany, Democratic Republic-1971	8,214,251	3,801,125	-	-	-	-	-	-
Germany, Federal Republic-1970	26,610,100	9,535,400	2,571,400	531,400	22,266,200	7,606,400	1,655,800	1,351,500
Gibraltar-1981	13,307	3,722	884	163	11,939	3,340	-	-
Greece-1981	3,543,797	959,215	1,265,998	124,510	1,730,298	504,574	394,008	270,112
Hungary-1980	5,068,840	2,202,046	99,676	26,537	4,247,660	1,848,699	100,059	95,117
Iceland-1960	68,140	18,683	11,673	741	49,521	14,745	3,437	1,941
Ireland-1981	1,271,122	358,627	231,705	22,173	877,424	301,549	28,698	5,435
Isle of Man-1981	27,564	10,537	3,869	745	21,995	9,127	-	-
Italy-1981	22,550,353	7,757,197	4,045,541	967,194	15,578,297	5,313,746	622,499	379,917
Luxembourg-1981	153,842	51,232	14,401	3,741	130,933	42,065	5,386	4,150
Malta-1967	102,253	21,999	20,787	4,613	70,798	15,187	2,782	788
Monaco-1968	10,325	4,270	2,155	638	7,695	3,310	243	200
Netherlands-1981	5,547,500	1,794,400	525,900	85,500	4,469,800	1,409,800	112,300	95,200
Norway-1980	2,041,642	844,206	177,325	33,968	1,761,208	755,929	44,230	33,231
Poland-1978	17,962,126	8,155,881	2,364,122	763,986	13,296,258	5,711,763	2,180,437	1,652,712
Portugal-1981	4,183,022	1,478,036	777,149	219,971	2,956,455	1,019,637	100,165	57,958
Romania-1977	10,793,602	4,926,719	700,956	470,349	6,945,851	2,369,807	3,114,848	2,071,417
St. Marin-1976	8,435	2,912	-	-	-	-	-	-
Spain-1981	12,797,020	3,168,130	2,261,251	354,352	8,785,927	2,079,142	492,255	214,061

[Continued]

★ 577 ★

Worldwide Economically Active Population
[Continued]

Country, census year	Total active		Employers and own account workers		Employees		Unpaid family workers	
	Total	Female	Total	Female	Total	Female	Total	Female
Sweden-1985	4,285,109	2,021,833	265,787	69,850	4,019,322	1,951,983	-	-
Switzerland-1980	3,091,694	1,117,937	298,799	40,394	2,792,895	1,077,543	-	-
Turkey-1985	21,579,996	7,647,265	4,855,129	361,817	6,978,181	1,072,481	8,721,860	6,058,365
United Kingdom-1981	26,035,370	10,110,270	1,972,070	388,540	21,468,430	8,965,120	-	-
Yugoslavia-1981	9,358,671	3,618,011	1,607,465	475,015	6,147,315	2,172,790	979,759	705,708
Oceania								
American Samoa-1980	8,308	3,265	-	-	-	-	-	-
Australia-1986	7,040,773	2,741,439	1,051,392	319,672	5,401,433	2,197,009	60,689	44,929
Cook Islands-1981	5,810	1,759	641	108	3,817	1,285	216	60
Fiji-1986	241,160	51,231	81,000	8,294	101,655	26,652	39,231	8,031
French Polynesia-1983	62,445	19,964	9,548	2,056	44,947	14,721	3,218	1,498
Guam-1980	31,807	12,361	959	285	29,419	11,415	23	16
New Caledonia-1976	50,469	17,178	10,345	2,289	29,664	9,324	6,445	4,141
New Zealand-1986	1,608,612	670,002	257,016	63,402	1,217,490	529,515	18,063	13,491
Samoa-1981	41,506	6,244	8,762	417	18,045	5,388	14,526	427
Tonga-1986	24,324	5,224	-	-	-	-	-	-

Source: Selected from "Economically Active Population," *Yearbook of Labour Statistics 1945-89: Retrospective Edition on Population Censuses*, p. 126-(Geneva: International Labour Office, 1989). Also in source: data broken down by industry; data for other censuses; data for men; data for "not classifiable by status."

★ 578 ★

Worldwide Employment in Finance, Insurance, and Real Estate

Total female workers and percentage female representation in ISCO groups 1, 2, and 3 of finance, insurance, and real estate employment, selected countries. (ISCO = International Standard Code of Occupation.).

Country	Total	Professional, technical, & related workers	Administrative & managerial workers	Clerical and related workers
Sweden	132,000	10.0%	1.2%	68.0%
Japan	1,410,000	1.4%	0.7%	61.0%
Germany, Federal Republic	738,000	8.4%	1.4%	71.8%
Norway	49,000	8.7%	4.3%	71.7%
Venezuela	80,422	8.7%	2.7%	67.2%
Hungary	97,000	9.3%	0.0%	37.1%
Panama	7,595	14.5%	9.3%	68.7%
Barbados	2,400	8.3%	8.3%	66.7%
Korea, Republic of	127,000	0.8%	0.0%	63.0%
Portugal	32,000	12.5%	0.0%	59.3%
Sri Lanka	13,394	4.0%	0.0%	91.6%
Indonesia	6,336	6.7%	0.0%	80.9%

[Continued]

★ 578 ★

Worldwide Employment in Finance, Insurance, and Real Estate
[Continued]

Country	Total	Professional, technical, & related workers	Administrative & managerial workers	Clerical and related workers
Bangladesh	565	17.9%	1.4%	29.2%
Ghana	1,877	3.4%	1.3%	87.4%

Source: "Occupational distribution of FIRE female employment," *World Survey on the Role of Women in Development*, 1986, p. 127 (New York: United Nations, 1986). Primary source: *Yearbook of Labour Statistics*, (Geneva, International Labour Office), various issues. "It can be concluded on the basis of the data available that although FIRE employs a large percentage of women, these women are concentrated at the bottom of the occupational ladder" (source).

★ 579 ★

Worldwide Female Labor Force in Trade

Economically active female population involved in trade and women's share in the total labor force involved in trade.

Country	Year	Active female population in trade	Women in the total labor force in trade
Algeria	1977	1.9%	2.7%
Brazil	1980	9.7%	28.4%
Bulgaria	1975	10.9%	64.3%
Czechoslovakia	1980	14.6%	70.1%
Germany, Federal Republic of	1982	12.4%	56.9%
Ghana	1970	2.6%	88.0%
Haiti	1980	-	91.2%
Hungary	1981	13.9%	64.5%
Kuwait	1980	3.0%	3.2%
Seychelles	1977	4.9%	38.6%
Sri Lanka	1980	4.9%	15.6%
Sweden	1982	15.0%	52.2%
Thailand	1980	9.6%	54.0%
United States	1982	6.6%	45.8%
Uruguay	1980	11.0%	26.6%

Source: "Female labour force in trade," *World Survey on the Role of Women in Development*, 1986, p. 165 (New York: United Nations, 1986). Primary source: *Yearbook of Labour Statistics* (Geneva, International Labour Office), various issues.

★ 580 ★

Worldwide Professional, Technical, and Related Workers

Percentage of women in major group 01 of ISCO-68 professional, technical and related workers. (ISCO = International Standard Classification of Occupation.).

Country or area	Year	% Female
Egypt	1980	28.4%
Tunisia	1980	14.2%
El Salvador	1980	44.1%
Guatemala	1981	39.0%
Mexico	1980	40.8%
Panama	1980	50.7%
Peru	1981	37.1%
Trinidad and Tobago	1981	49.9%
Uruguay	1975	58.5%
Venezuela	1981	55.1%
Bahrain	1981	30.8%
Hong Kong	1982	42.8%
Indonesia	1980	36.5%
Kuwait	1980	31.5%
Nepal[1]	1975	30.6%
Philippines	1981	59.7%
Republic of Korea	1982	32.8%
Sri Lanka	1980	47.1%
Syrian Arab Republic[1]	1980	25.3%
Thailand	1980	47.1%
Finland	1980	54.3%
Germany, Federal Republic	1982	39.3%
Ireland[1]	1980	46.4%
Japan	1982	45.9%
Netherlands	1980	35.6%
Norway	1981	53.4%
Portugal	1981	54.3%
Spain	1982	38.1%
Sweden	1982	54.1%

Source: Selected from "Percentage of women in major group 01 of ISCO-68 professional, technical and related workers," *World Survey on the Role of Women in Development,* 1986, p. 25 (New York: United Nations, 1986). Primary source: International Labour Office, *Yearbook of Labour Statistics,* various issues. Also in source: data for other years. "The data available indicate that in almost all countries, the share of women in professional occupations over the total population of economically active women is higher than the share of men. Women who work have more chances than men to be in the professional category" (source, p. 26). *Note:* 1. Estimated value.

THE MILITARY

Enlistees

★ 581 ★

Enlistees: 1989

Enlistees by branch, fiscal year 1989.

Branch	Female	Male	Total	% Female
U.S. Army	16,160	95,508	111,668	14.5%
U.S. Navy	10,864	78,515	89,379	12.2%
U.S. Marine Corps	2,119	30,911	33,030	6.4%
U.S. Air Force	9,327	34,124	43,451	21.5%
Department of Defense	38,470	239,058	277,528	13.9%

Source: Defense Advisory Committee on Women in the Services (DACOWITS) Fact Sheet, March 1990.

★ 582 ★

Reenlistment Rates

Reenlistment rates, fiscal year 1988.

Characteristic	Rate
First Term Women	54.5%
First Term Men	48.2%
Career Women	81.0%
Career Men	86.5%

Source: Defense Advisory Committee on Women in the Services (DACOWITS) Fact Sheet, March 1990.

Personnel

★ 583 ★

Active Duty Personnel: 1989

Numbers of officers and enlisted personnel on active duty and number who are female by branch, September 1989.

Branch	Total Officers	Total Enlisted	Female Officers	Female Enlisted	Total Female
U.S. Army	107,168	658,119	12,198	73,780	85,978
U.S. Navy	72,255	514,345	7,487	49,602	57,089
U.S. Air Force	103,699	462,831	13,403	63,175	76,578
U.S. Marine Corps	20,047	176,770	691	8,975	9,666
Department of Defense	303,169	1,812,065	33,779	195,532	229,311

Source: Defense Advisory Committee on Women in the Services (DACOWITS) Fact Sheet, March 1990.

★ 584 ★

Distribution of Enlisted Personnel by Race and Occupation

Occupational distribution of enlisted personnel by race/ethnicity, 1988.

Occupational group	White		Black		Hispanic	
	Female	Male	Female	Male	Female	Male
Managers and Professional	11.25%	6.94%	7.58%	7.45%	9.46%	6.75%
Executive, Administrative	4.75%	4.18%	4.92%	5.89%	5.40%	4.80%
Professional Speciality	6.51%	2.76%	2.66%	1.56%	4.07%	1.95%
T/S/A Supp.	49.06%	18.95%	64.61%	33.83%	54.07%	26.09%
Technical	14.95%	7.87%	13.27%	9.83%	13.00%	8.27%
Sales Occ.	0.23%	0.21%	0.26%	0.47%	0.39%	0.31%
Admin. Supp.	33.88%	10.87%	51.07%	23.54%	40.68%	17.51%
Service Occupations	12.48%	8.90%	10.75%	10.16%	10.67%	8.10%
Protective Service	4.28%	5.84%	1.95%	4.18%	2.30%	3.92%
Service except Protective Service	8.21%	3.07%	8.80%	6.00%	8.38%	4.18%
Prec. Prod.	18.21%	38.11%	9.36%	9.24%	14.09%	29.17%
Mech. & Rep.	16.11%	33.18%	8.47%	22.31%	12.09%	25.08%
Const. Trades	0.51%	1.91%	0.23%	1.66%	0.47%	2.42%
Prec. Prod.	1.59%	3.01%	0.66%	1.73%	1.52%	1.68%
Oper., Fab.	8.63%	14.06%	7.52%	24.43%	11.53%	14.98%
Mach. Oper.	2.71%	5.69%	1.59%	5.86%	2.16%	6.11%
Fabricators	0.52%	0.64%	0.12%	0.36%	0.26%	0.52%
Prod. Inspect.	0.10%	0.33%	0.05%	0.20%	0.02%	0.19%
Trans. & Mat.	5.26%	6.55%	5.63%	8.03%	9.04%	7.45%

[Continued]

★ 584 ★

Distribution of Enlisted Personnel by Race and Occupation
[Continued]

Occupational group	White		Black		Hispanic	
	Female	Male	Female	Male	Female	Male
Handlers	0.05%	0.85%	0.13%	0.98%	0.05%	0.70%
Military[1]	0.37%	13.04%	0.18%	14.88%	0.18%	14.91%

Source: Black Issues in Higher Education, 7:3 (April 12, 1990), p. 16. Primary source: Defense Manpower Data Center (DMDC). *Notes:* 1. Military Specific Occupations with which there are no comparable civilian occupations.

★ 585 ★

Military Women in the Persian Gulf

Characteristic of personnel in Persian Gulf	Number
Number of American forces stationed in Gulf region, Jan. '91	460,000
Number who were women	27,000

Source: Eric Schmitt, "War Puts U.S. Servicewomen Closer Than Ever to Combat," *New York Times*, January 22, 1991, p. 1+.

★ 586 ★

Recent Participation of Women in the Military

Statistics on women in the military, as reported to the House Subcommittee on Military Personnel and Compensation as part of a review of combat exclusion laws and other women-in-the-military issues.

In 1986, women comprised **10.1%** of U.S. overall forces, up from **2.5%** in 1973.

As of November 1987, there were **13** women on the firing crews of the Ground Launched Cruise Missile and **74** women serving on Minuteman missile firing crews.

Of the 1336 crew members of the *USS Acadia*, a destroyer tender that provided repair and logistics support to the *USS Stark* in the Persian Gulf in the spring of 1987, **240** were women.

By the 1990s, women are expected to represent over **11%** of all military personnel.

Source: "Combat Exclusion Laws for Women in the Military," Statement of Martin M. Ferber, Senior Associate Director, National Security and International Affairs Division, Before the Subcommittee on Military Personnel and Compensation, House Armed Services Committee, U.S. House of Representatives, released November 19, 1987. *The Labor Exchange*, November 1988.

★ 587 ★

Women Officers by Occupation

Officers'occupations and percent of jobs held by women, 1990.

Occupation	% Women
General and Executive	1.2%
Tactical Operations	7.0%
Intelligence	5.9%
Engineering, Maintenance	10.8%
Science, Professional	5.7%
Medical	39.6%
Administration	14.6%
Supplies, Logistics	8.3%
Other	6.9%

Source: Melinda Beck et al., "Our Women in the Desert: Sharing the duty—and danger—in a 'mom's war'," *Newsweek*, September 10, 1990, p. 22+. Primary source: Department of Defense; Sotoodeh-*Newsweek*.

★ 588 ★

Women in High Command Positions

Number of women in the highest offices of the Department of Defense.

Office	Total	No. of women
Secretary of Defense	28	1
Under Secretary for Defense Policy	8	0
Under Secretary of Defense for Acquisition[1]	15	1
Department of Defense Agencies[2]	14	0
Secretaries of Defense - 1947 to 1990	17	0
Joint Chiefs of Staff	7	0
Unified Commands	8	0
Specified Commands	2	0
Department of the Army	3	0
Department of the Air Force	3	0
Department of the Navy	5	0
Coast Guard	2	0
Senate Armed Services Committee	20	0
House Armed Services Committee	55	2

Source: Defense 90 Almanac, November/December 1990. *Notes:* 1. Three positions were vacant. 2. One position was vacant.

★ 589 ★

Women in Vietnam

Statistics on women in the military during the Vietnam war, as reported in the *New York Times*.

Number of women in the military during the Viet Nam war: **about 250,000**
Number of women who served in Viet Nam: **about 11,000**
Number of women killed in Viet Nam: **8**

Source: Irvin Molotsky, "A Memorial for Women in Vietnam," *New York Times*, November 12, 1990, p. B1.

★ 590 ★

Women in the Armed Forces

Number in the Armed Forces in the United States, September 1989 and September 1990.

	Number in Thousands	
	September 1989	September 1990
Women, 16 years and over		
Noninstitutional population	97,972	98,731
Resident Armed Forces	171	160

Source: Selected from "Employment status of the population, including Armed Forces in the United States, by sex," *Bureau of Labor Statistics News*, USDL 90-512, October 5, 1990. Figures are not adjusted for seasonal variation.

★ 591 ★

Women in the Coast Guard

Coast Guard personnel statistics as of May 31, 1989.

Position	Total	Number of Women	% Female
Total Active Duty	36,849	2,666	7.2%
Officers (incl. Reserves on Active Duty)	5,209	244	4.7%
Enlisted	29,220	2,411	8.0%
Assignments:			
Women Officers			
Ashore	-	174	-
Afloat	-	52	-
Pilots	-	18	-
Women Enlisted			
Ashore	-	2,267	-
Afloat	-	114	-

Source: Defense Advisory Committee on Women in the Services (DACOWITS) Fact Sheet, March 1990.

★ 592 ★

Women on Active Duty: 1981-1990

Percent of active duty forces who were women, 1981-1990.

Fiscal Year	% Female
1981	8.9%
1982	9.0%
1983	9.3%
1984	9.5%
1985	9.8%
1986	10.1%
1987	10.2%
1988	10.4%
1989	10.7%
1990	10.8%

Source: Defense Advisory Committee on Women in the Services (DACOWITS) Fact Sheet, March 1990.

Positions

★ 593 ★

Military Positions Opened to Women in 1988

Positions opened to women on recommendations of the 1987 DoD Task Force on Women in the Military.

Description	Number
Total new positions opened to women	11,138
Total enlisted military occupational specialties	368
Number women are authorized to serve in	319
Number of commissioned officers specialty codes	207
Number open to women	198
Number of warrant officer specialty codes	77
Number open to women	70

Source: Defense Advisory Committee on Women in the Services (DACOWITS) Fact Sheet, March 1990.

★ 594 ★

Military Skills/Positions Open to Women

Percent of skills and number and percent of positions open to women, by branch of service, September 1989.

Branch	Skills Open	Positions Open	% of Total Positions
U.S. Army	90.0%	398,000	52.0%
U.S. Navy	83.9%	298,900	59.0%
U.S. Marine Corps	80.0%	39,500	20.0%
U.S. Air Force	99.1%	547,800	97.0%
Department of Defense	87.0%	1,284,200	63.0%

Source: Defense Advisory Committee on Women in the Services (DACOWITS) Fact Sheet, March 1990.

Qualifying for Military Service

★ 595 ★

Armed Forces Qualifying Test Scores

Mean AFQT standard scores by race/ethnicity, youths aged 18-23 years.

Race/Ethnicity and Sex	Educational Level		
	Non-High School Grad.	GED Recipient	High School Diploma Grad.
White[1]	438	512	543
Female	437	513	539
Male	438	511	547
Black	337	412	431
Female	333	417	432
Male	341	407	430
Hispanic	359	442	481
Female	355	433	468
Male	358	451	495
All Groups	419	494	524
Female	418	495	520
Male	420	493	528

Source: Black Issues in Higher Education 7:3 (April 12, 1990), p. 26. Primary source: *Manpower for Military Occupations,* Office of the Assistant Secretary of Defense (Force Management and Personnel). Scores were standardized to a metric with a mean of 500 and a standard deviation of 100. American youth population includes all persons born between January 1, 1957 and December 31, 1962. *Notes:* 1. White category includes all racial/ethnic groups other than Black or Hispanic.

★ 596 ★

Average Ability to Qualify for Enlistment

Population subgroup arranged in order (from highest to lowest) by expected average ability to qualify for enlistment.

	Priority
White Male Graduates	1
White Female Graduates	2
White Male GEDS	3
White Female GEDS	4
Hispanic Male Graduates	5
Hispanic Female Graduates	6
Hispanic Male GEDS	7
White Male Nongraduates	8
White Female Nongraduates	9
Hispanic Female GEDS	10
Black Female Graduates	11
Black Male Graduates	12
Black Female GEDS	13
Black Male GEDS	14
Hispanic Male Nongraduates	15
Hispanic Female Nongraduates	16
Black Male Nongraduates	17
Black Female Nongraduates	18

Source: Black Issues in Higher Education 7:3 (April 12, 1990), p. 26. Primary source: *Manpower for Military Occupations,* Office of the Assistant Secretary of Defense (Force Management and Personnel). Author Mark Eithelberg used mean AFQT standard scores of American youths (18-23 years of age) to infer the probable effect the military's education and aptitude standards would have on persons with different backgrounds. Data on eligibility of persons who actually apply to the military would be drawn from a narrower, more eligible population, due to factors such as self-selection and pre-screening by recruiters. *Note:* 1. High school graduates.

★ 597 ★

Fitness Standards

Physical fitness standards for military women and men, by age.

Age and type of exercise	Women	Men
	In 2 minutes	
Sit-Ups		
27 to 31	40	42
32 to 36	35	38
37 to 41	30	33
42 and over	27	29
Pushups		
27 to 31	15	38
32 to 36	14	33
37 to 41	13	32
42 and over	12	26

[Continued]

★ 597 ★

Fitness Standards
[Continued]

Age and type of exercise	Women	Men
	Time-minutes/seconds	
1-1/2-Mile Run		
20 to 29	16:45	13:45
30 to 39	17:15	15:30
40 to 49	18:15	16:30
50 and over	19:00	17:00

Source: Philip Shenon, "O.K., Flabby Press Corps, 32 Pushups for Uncle Sam," *New York Times,* January 3, 1991, p. A5. Primary source: Defense Department. These standards were imposed by Pentagon officials on journalists who wished to be sent to cover the war with Iraq.

Sexual Harassment

★ 598 ★

Consequences of Response to Sexual Harassment in the Military
Work condition consequences of victims' response(s) to described experiences of sexual harassment in unweighted percentages.

Responses	Female	Male
Work assignments/conditions worse	14%	6%
Denied promotion/good fitness report	5%	2%
Transferred to another base	3%	3%
Was reassigned	3%	2%
Transferred to another work site	5%	2%
Working conditions better	8%	7%
Got promoted/good fitness report	1%	1%
No changes	74%	84%
Number of cases	5,406	1,512

Source: Melanie Martindale, Ph.D., *Sexual Harassment in the Military: 1988,* (Washington, D.C.: Defense Manpower Data Center, 1990). Related reading: Eric Schmitt, "2 Out of 3 Women in Military Study Report Sexual Harassment Incidents," *New York Times,* September 12, 1990, p. A12. Based on data compiled in 1988 and 1989 from 20,249 responses to a questionnaire distributed by the Defense Department. *Notes:* 1. Section II of the questionnaire instructs respondents: "Select the one experience of uninvited and unwanted sexual attention you experienced at work in the past year that had the greatest impact on you and answer in terms of that experience." 2. The data in this table are unweighted. Unweighted data describe only respondents and should not be generalized to the overall active military population. Unweighted statistics are generally presented when, for technical and conceptual reasons, respondents are not necessarily demographically or otherwise representative of the population from which they are drawn. Statistically adjusted to represent the active military population. *F 3. Percentages are rounded to the nearest whole number. Percentages of 0 may indicate less than 0.5 but not actually 0. Percentages will not add to 100 because respondents could select more than one answer.

★ 599 ★

Experiences of Sexual Harassment in the Military

Number of different types of sexual harassment experienced during the year prior to the survey by gender of victims in weighted percentages.

Number of different types	Female	Male
One	12%	27%
Two	17%	24%
Three	17%	22%
Four	18%	12%
Five	14%	8%
Six	11%	3%
Seven	6%	2%
Eight	3%	1%
Nine to Ten	2%	1%

Source: Melanie Martindale, Ph.D., *Sexual Harassment in the Military: 1988,* (Washington, D.C.: Defense Manpower Data Center, 1990). Related reading: Eric Schmitt, "2 Out of 3 Women in Military Study Report Sexual Harassment Incidents," *New York Times,* September 12, 1990, p. A12. Based on data compiled in 1988 and 1989 from 20,249 responses to a questionnaire distributed by the U.S. Defense Department. See table *Types of Sexual Harassment in the Military* for description of types. *Notes:* 1. The data in this table are weighted. Weighted data have been statistically adjusted to represent the active military population. Weighted statistics are estimates, within some error, of characteristics of the active military population. The weighting scheme used slightly underestimates the total Active Force. 2. Percentages are rounded to the nearest whole number. Percentages of 0 may indicate less than 0.5 but not actually 0. Percentages may not add to 100 due to rounding. 3. The number of different types was determined using a computerized counting algorithm. This algorithm when used with the weighting scheme results in an underestimate of victims.

★ 600 ★

Reasons for Tolerating Sexual Harassment in the Military

Reasons victims did not take formal action against perpetrator(s) of described experiences of sexual harassment in unweighted percentages.

Responses	Female	Male
Number of cases	5,021	1,479
Handled by self	64%	64%
Harasser(s) not colocated (sic)	6%	7%
Didn't know who did it	7%	5%
Someone else acted	16%	5%
Didn't know what to do	13%	8%
Saw no need to report	33%	49%
Didn't want to hurt harasser(s)	18%	19%
Too embarrassed	16%	12%
Didn't think anything would be done	27%	13%
Too much time/effort	8%	6%
Thought would be blamed	29%	13%

[Continued]

★ 600 ★

Reasons for Tolerating Sexual Harassment in the Military
[Continued]

Responses	Female	Male
Work would get unpleasant	38%	20%
Labelled troublemaker	33%	16%

Source: Melanie Martindale, Ph.D., *Sexual Harassment in the Military: 1988,* (Washington, D.C.: Defense Manpower Data Center, 1990). Related reading: Eric Schmitt, "2 Out of 3 Women in Military Study Report Sexual Harassment Incidents," *New York Times,* September 12, 1990, p. A12. Based on data compiled in 1988 and 1989 from 20,249 responses to a questionnaire distributed by the Defense Department. *Notes:* 1. Section II of the questionnaire instructs respondents: "Select the one experience of uninvited and unwanted sexual attention you experienced at work in the past year that had the greatest impact on you and answer in terms of that experience." 2. The data in this table are unweighted. Unweighted data describe only respondents and should not be generalized to the overall active military population. Unweighted statistics are generally presented when, for technical and conceptual reasons, respondents are not necessarily demographically or otherwise representative of the population from which they are drawn. statistically adjusted to represent the active military population. 3. Percentages are rounded to the nearest whole number. Percentages of 0 may indicate less than 0.5 but not actually 0. Percentages will not add to 100 because respondents could select more than one answer. .

★ 601 ★

Types of Sexual Harassment in the Military

Frequency of occurrence of types of sexual harassment for female victims (multiple responses) in weighted percentages.

Type of harassment	Once	Once a month or less	2-4 times a month	Once a week or more
Actual or attempted rape or sexual assault	91%	6%	1%	2%
Pressure for sexual favors	50%	27%	12%	10%
Touching, cornering	36%	33%	17%	13%
Looks, gestures	24%	30%	22%	24%
Letters, calls	51%	27%	14%	8%
Pressure for dates	37%	28%	21%	13%
Teasing, jokes	18%	29%	25%	29%
Whistles, calls	22%	36%	21%	21%
Attempts to get participation[3]	61%	27%	6%	6%

Source: Melanie Martindale, Ph.D., *Sexual Harassment in the Military: 1988,* (Washington, D.C.: Defense Manpower Data Center, 1990). Related reading: Eric Schmitt, "2 Out of 3 Women in Military Study Report Sexual Harassment Incidents," *New York Times,* September 12, 1990, p. A12. Based on data compiled in 1988 and 1989 from 20,249 responses to a questionnaire distributed by the Defense Department. *Notes:* 1. The data in this table are weighted. Weighted data have been statistically adjusted to represent the active military population. Weighted statistics are estimates, within some error, of characteristics of the active military population. The weighting scheme used slightly underestimates the total Active Force. 2. Percentages are rounded to the nearest whole number. Percentages of 0 may indicate less than 0.5 but not actually 0. Percentages will not add to 100 because respondents could select more than one answer. 3. "Attempts to get [respondent's] participation in any other kinds of sexually oriented activity."

POPULATION AND VITAL STATISTICS

Abortions

★ 602 ★

Abortions by Women's Age
Distribution of abortions by age of women having the abortions.

Age	Percentage
Under 15	1%
15-19	24%
20-24	33%
25-29	22%
30-34	12%
35-39	6%

Source: Scholastic Update 122:16 (April 20, 1990), p. 4-5. Primary source: Alan Guttmacher Institute. Since 1977, about 1.5 million legal abortions have been performed annually.

★ 603 ★

Legal Abortions by Selected Characteristics
Total number of legal abortions in thousands by selected characteristics: 1980 to 1985.

Characteristic	Number (1,000)						Percent Distribution		Abortion Ratio[1]	
	1980	1981	1982	1983	1984	1985	1980	1985	1980	1985
Total legal abortions	1,554	1,577	1,574	1,575	1,577	1,589	100.0%	100.0%	300	297
Age of woman:										
Less than 15 years old	15	15	15	16	17	17	1.0%	1.1%	607	624
15-19 years old	445	433	419	411	399	399	28.6%	25.1%	451	462
20-24 years old	549	555	552	548	551	548	35.4%	34.5%	310	328
25-29 years old	304	316	326	328	332	336	19.6%	21.2%	213	219
30-34 years old	153	167	168	172	176	181	9.8%	11.4%	213	203
35-39 years old	67	70	73	78	82	87	4.3%	5.4%	317	280
40 years old and over	21	21	21	21	20	21	1.3%	1.3%	461	409
Race of woman:										
White	1,094	1,108	1,095	1,084	1,087	1,076	70.4%	67.7%	274	265
Black	460	470	479	491	491	513	29.6%	32.3%	392	397
Marital status of woman:										
Married	320	299	300	295	287	266	20.6	16.7	98	84
Unmarried	1,234	1,279	1,274	1,280	1,290	1,323	79.4	83.3	649	607

[Continued]

499

★ 603 ★

Legal Abortions by Selected Characteristics
[Continued]

Characteristic	Number (1,000)						Percent Distribution		Abortion Ratio[1]	
	1980	1981	1982	1983	1984	1985	1980	1985	1980	1985
Number of prior live births:										
None	900	912	903	890	877	872	57.9%	54.9%	365	358
1	305	312	321	329	339	349	19.6%	22.0%	208	219
2	216	220	222	228	234	240	13.9%	15.1%	283	288
3	83	85	82	83	83	85	5.3%	5.3%	288	281
4 or more	51	49	46	45	44	43	3.3%	2.7%	251	230
Number of prior induced abortions:										
None	1,043	1,023	994	964	948	944	67.1%	59.5%	NA	NA
1	373	390	398	406	414	416	24.0%	26.2%	NA	NA
2 or more	138	165	182	205	216	228	8.9%	14.3%	NA	NA

Source: Selected from "Legal Abortions, by Selected Characteristics: 1973 to 1985," *Statistical Abstract of the United States 1990* Table 101, p. 71. Primary source: 1973-1983, S.K. Henshaw and J. Van Hort, eds., *Abortion Services in the United States, Each State and Metropolitan Area, 1984-1985,* The Alan Guttmacher Institute, New York, NY, 1988; 1985 and 1985, The Alan Guttmacher Institute, unpublished data. Also in source: Abortions by age of woman and other characteristics. Number of abortions from surveys conducted by source; characteristics from the U.S. Centers for Disease Control's (CDC) annual abortion surveillance summaries, with adjustments for changes in States reporting data to the CDC each year. Also in source: number of prior live births; number of prior induced abortions; weeks of gestation. *Notes:* 1. Number of abortions per 1,000 abortions and live births. Live births are those which occurred from July 1 of year shown through June 30 of the following year (to match time of conception with abortions).

★ 604 ★

Worldwide Legal Abortions, 1979-1987

Legally induced abortions, 1979-1987.

Country or area	Number								
	1979	1980	1981	1982	1983	1984	1985	1986	1987
Africa									
Botswana	-	-	-	-	-	17	-	-	-
Reunion	3,828	3,803	3,838	4,287	-	4,321	4,402	4,299	4,181
Seychelles	-	-	-	-	-	221[1]	188[1]	9	-
North America									
Bermuda	-	-	-	-	85	92	-	-	-
Canada	65,043	65,751	65,053	66,254	61,750	62,291	60,956	62,406	-
Cuba	106,549	103,974	108,559	126,745	116,956	139,588	138,671	160,926	-
Greenland	450	470	539	-	-	-	-	-	-
Guadeloupe	455	561	-	-	-	-	-	-	-
Martinique	-	-	1,846	2,211	2,455	2,321	1,753	-	-
Panama	11	26	11	12	-	-	-	-	-

[Continued]

★ 604 ★

Worldwide Legal Abortions, 1979-1987
[Continued]

Country or area	Number								
	1979	1980	1981	1982	1983	1984	1985	1986	1987
South America									
French Guiana	-	-	-	-	-	388	-	-	-
Asia									
India	-	346,327	388,405	500,624	492,696	561,033	583,704	-	-
Israel	15,925	14,708	14,514	16,829	15,593	18,948	18,406	17,469	-
Japan	-	-	-	590,299	568,363	568,916	550,127	527,900	497,756
Singapore	16,999	18,219	18,890	15,548	19,100	22,190	23,512	21,374	-
Europe									
Bulgaria	147,888	155,876	152,370	147,791	134,165	131,140	132,041	134,686	-
Czechoslovakia	94,486	100,170	103,517	107,638	108,662	113,802	119,325	124,188	158,451
Denmark	23,193	23,334	22,779	21,462	20,791	20,742	19,919	20,067	20,830
Finland	15,849	15,037	14,120	13,861	13,360	13,645	13,832	13,310	
France	156,810	171,218	180,695	181,122	182,862	180,789	173,335	166,797	161,036
Germany, Federal Rep.	82,788	87,702	87,353	91,064	86,529	86,298	83,538	84,274	88,540
Greece	137	117	109	-	220	193	180	-	-
Hungary	80,767	80,882	78,421	78,682	78,599	82,191	81,970	83,586	84,547
Iceland	556	523	597	613	687	-	-	-	-
Italy	187,752	207,644	216,755	231,308	321,061	228,377	210,192	196,969	
Netherlands	-	-	20,897	20,187	19,700	18,700	17,300	-	-
Norway	14,456	13,531	13,845	13,496	13,646	14,070	14,599	15,474	15,422
Poland	220,431	133,835	230,070	141,177	130,980	132,844	135,564	129,720	122,536
Sweden	34,709	34,887	33,294	32,604	31,014	30,755	30,838	33,090	34,707
United Kingdom	-	-	-	136,924	135,794	145,497	150,211	157,168	165,542
England and Wales	120,611	128,927	162,480	163,045	162,161	169,993	171,873	-	-
Scotland	7,754	7,855	8,975	8,372	8,459	9,109	9,110	-	-
Oceania									
New Zealand	-	5,945	6,758	6,903	7,198	7,275	7,130	8,056	8,789
USSR	7,009,000	7,003,000	7,834,000	6,912,000	6,765,000	6,780,000	7,034,000	7,116,000	
Byelorussian SSR	-	202,000	-	-	-	-	201,000	-	-
Ukrainian SSR	-	11,197,000	-	-	-	-	1,179,000	-	-

Source: "Legally Induced Abortions: 1979-1987," *1988 Demographic Yearbook*, 1990, p. 389 (New York: United Nations; 1990). *Note:* 1. Including spontaneous abortions.

★ 605 ★

Worldwide Legal Abortions by Age of Woman

Legally induced abortions by age of mother, latest available year.

Country or area, year	All ages	Age of Woman (in years)									
		-15	15-19	20-24	25-29	30-34	35-39	40-44	45-49	50+	Unknown
Africa											
Reunion-1987	4,140	22	574	1,303	955	683	451	134	-	17[1]	1
Seychelles-1985	188	1	24	58	61	25	14	4	1	-	-
North America											
Canada-1986	92	3	30	21	18	14	5	-	-	1	-
Panama-1982	12	-	1	-	7[1]	-	2	-	2[1]	-	2[1]
Asia											
India-1985	583,704	1,074	20,225	109,436	138,508	97,315	42,755	10,223	-	781[1]	163,387
Japan-1987	497,756	-	27,542[1]	81,178	86,633	117,866	131,514	48,262	4,408	105	248
Singapore-1986	21,374	27	1,755	5,851	6,056	4,547	2,492	567	-	79[1]	-
Europe											
Czechoslovakia-1985	119,325	34	8,103	24,773	31,419	29,545	19,145	5,898	375	22	11
Denmark-1987	20,830	57	2,788	6,096	4,551	3,428	2,546	1,232	132	-	-
Faeroe Islands-1975	26	-	4	2	3	8	6	3	-	-	-
Finland-1983	13,360	23	3,078	3,395	2,090	1,899	1,778	913	180	4	-
France-1986	166,797	-	17,075[1]	39,712	39,539	34,284	25,452	8,833	989	58	855
Germany, Federal Rep.-1987	88,540	81	7,098	21,960	21,746	17,366	13,277	5,524	976	58	454
Greece-1985	180	-	16	92	69	3	-	-	-	-	-
Hungary-1987	84,547	126	9,152	14,132	15,848	20,741	16,710	7,165	-	630[1]	43
Iceland-1983	687	4	160	203	125	91	67	-	37[1]	-	-
Italy-1984	228,377	267	18,318	47,867	51,420	48,247	41,884	17,507	1,857	129	881
Netherlands-1985	17,300	35	2,715	4,510	3,870	3,040	2,315	710	-	105[1]	-
Norway-1987	15,422	40	3,558	4,643	2,803	2,166	1,505	622	-	52[1]	3
Sweden-1987	34,707	150	5,775	9,324	6,694	5,361	4,782	2,371	250	-	-
United Kingdom-1987	165,542	977	40,626	52,210	32,954	20,030	13,327	4.997	383	24	14
England and Wales-1985	141,101	1,024	37,186	41,880	26,009	17,202	12,979	4,372	409	16	24
Scotland-1985	9,110	71	2,752	2,805	1,560	972	698	233	19	-	-
Oceania											
Cocos (Keeling) Islands-1978	2	-	-	-	1	-	1	-	-	-	-
New Zealand	8,789	52	1,921	2,535	2,067	1,289	666	230	27	2	-

Source: "Legally Induced Abortions by Age and Number of Previous Live Births of Woman: Latest Available Year," *1988 Demographic Yearbook*, 1990, p. 391-95 (New York: United Nations; 1990). *Note:* 1. Figures for adjacent blank column(s) combined here.

Births

★ 606 ★

Birth Rates by Educational Level and Race

Characteristic	Current Age of Woman						Total Number of Children (mil.)
	18-24 Years		25-34 Years		35-44 Years		
	Children Born per 1,000 Women	Percent Childless	Children Born per 1,000 Women	Percent Childless	Children Born per 1,000 Women	Percent Childless	
Total	429	71.7%	1,369	31.6%	2,089	15.6%	71.3
All Races							
Less than High School	885	49.0%	2,162	12.0%	2,919	8.8%	15.7
High School	478	66.9%	1,529	22.9%	2,138	12.2%	32.2
Some College	158	87.7%	1,241	33.7%	1,938	15.1%	13.5
College/More	79	93.6%	728	57.4%	1,611	26.6%	10.0
White							
Less than High School	837	50.9%	2,061	13.1%	2,760	9.0%	11.3
High School	427	69.6%	1,487	24.2%	2,114	12.1%	26.6
Some College	140	89.2%	1,204	35.1%	1,913	15.5%	11.1
College/More	60	94.8%	720	58.3%	1,577	28.2%	8.6
Black							
Less than High School	1,078	39.8%	2,553	8.3%	3,557	8.0%	3.7
High School	756	51.7%	1,777	15.0%	2,375	11.9%	4.8
Some College	286	76.6%	1,411	25.7%	2,124	11.1%	1.9
College/More	290	81.0%	878	43.7%	1,848	16.2%	.8
Hispanic[1]							
Less than High School	1,085	43.4%	2,381	11.9%	3,185	6.6%	4.1
High School	505	65.2%	1,732	18.6%	2,582	9.4%	2.4
Some College	235	81.9%	1,373	26.6%	2,166	9.2%	.8
College/More	[2]	[2]	621	63.0%	1,544	28.5%	[2]

Source: "Children Ever Born Per 1,000 Women and Percent Childless, by Education and Race/Hispanic Origin, June 1987," *U.S. Children and Their Families*, 1989, p. 12. Primary source: U.S. Bureau of the Census, Current Population Reports, *Fertility of American Women: June 1987*, Series P-20, No. 427, Table 2. *Notes:* 1. Persons of Hispanic origin may be of any race. 2. Population base too small to provide reliable estimates.

★ 607 ★

Births and Birth Rates: 1980-1987

Live births in thousands by age of parents; birth rate per 1,000 population by sex; birth rate per 1,000 women by race and age of mother, birth rate per 1,000 men by age of father, 1980-1987.

Item	1980	1981	1982	1983	1984	1985	1986	1987
Total live births[1]	3,612	3,629	3,681	3,639	3,669	3,761	3,757	3,809
Females	1,760	1,769	1,795	1,773	1,790	1,833	1,832	1,858
Males	1,853	1,860	1,886	1,866	1,879	1,928	1,925	1,951
Age of mother:								

[Continued]

★ 607 ★

Births and Birth Rates: 1980-1987
[Continued]

Item	1980	1981	1982	1983	1984	1985	1986	1987
Under 20 years	562	537	524	499	480	478	472	473
20-24 years	1,226	1,212	1,206	1,160	1,142	1,141	1,102	1,076
25-29 years	1,108	1,128	1,152	1,148	1,166	1,201	1,200	1,216
30-34 years	550	581	605	625	658	696	721	761
35-39 years	141	146	168	180	196	214	230	248
40 years or more	139	141	149	153	160	167	174	191
Age of father:								
Under 20 years	137	129	125	116	109	108	105	105
20-24 years	803	785	768	722	696	685	651	627
25-29 years	1,082	1,083	1,093	1,070	1,067	1,081	1,059	1,053
30-34 years	739	768	780	782	806	837	845	872
35-39 years	275	286	319	335	356	381	398	413
40 years or more	139	141	149	153	160	167	174	191
Birth rate per 1,000 population	15.9	15.8	15.9	15.5	15.5	15.8	15.6	15.7
Females	15.1	15.0	15.1	14.7	14.7	15.0	14.8	14.9
Males	16.8	16.7	16.7	16.4	16.3	16.6	16.4	16.5
Birth rate per 1,000 women[2]	68.4	67.4	67.3	65.8	65.4	66.2	65.4	65.7
White[1]	64.7	63.9	63.9	62.4	62.2	63.0	61.9	62.0
Black[1]	88.1	85.4	84.1	8.17	81.4	82.2	82.4	83.8
Age of mother:								
10-14 years old	1.1	1.1	1.1	1.1	1.2	1.2	1.3	1.3
15-19 years old	53.0	52.7	52.9	51.7	50.9	51.3	50.6	51.1
20-24 years old	115.1	111.8	111.3	108.3	107.3	108.9	108.2	108.9
25-29 years old	112.9	112.0	111.0	108.7	108.3	110.5	109.2	110.8
30-34 years old	61.9	61.4	64.2	64.6	66.5	68.5	69.3	71.3
35-39 years old	19.8	20.0	21.1	22.1	22.8	23.9	24.3	26.2
40-44 years old	3.9	3.8	3.9	3.8	3.9	4.0	4.1	4.4
45-49 years old	.2	.2	.2	.2	.2	.2	.2	.2
Birth rate per 1,000 men	57.0	56.3	56.4	55.3	55.0	55.7	54.9	55.0
Age of father:[3]								
15-19 years old	18.8	18.5	18.7	18.4	18.0	18.2	18.1	18.6
20-24 years old	92.0	88.0	86.1	83.5	81.9	82.8	82.3	83.0
25-29 years old	123.0	119.7	117.4	113.9	111.0	111.9	109.1	109.4
30-34 years old	91.0	88.6	90.4	88.7	88.8	89.7	88.7	89.3
35-39 years old	42.8	43.2	44.2	45.3	45.7	47.0	46.5	48.2
40-44 years old	17.1	16.9	17.6	17.2	17.8	18.1	18.4	19.1
45-49 years old	6.1	6.3	6.4	6.4	6.3	6.6	6.7	6.9
50-54 years old	2.2	2.3	2.4	2.3	2.4	2.5	2.5	2.5
55 years old and over	.4	.4	.4	.3	.4	.4	.4	.4

Source: Selected from "Births and birth rates: 1960 to 1987," *Statistical Abstract of the United States,* p. 63. Primary Source: U.S. National Center for Health Statistics, *Vital Statistics of the United States,* annual; and unpublished data. Also in source: data by other characteristics. *Notes:* 1. Includes other races, not shown separately. 2. Per 1,000 women, 15-44 years old in specified group. 3. Rates by age of father computed using frequencies with age not stated distributed among all age groups.

★ 608 ★

Births to Unmarried Women Worldwide

Percent of total births that were to unmarried women, 1960 to 1986.

Country	1960	1965	1970	1975	1980	1986
France	6.1%	5.9%	6.8%	8.5%	11.4%	21.9%
Germany, Federal Republic	6.3%	4.7%	5.5%	6.1%	7.6%	9.6%
Italy	2.4%	2.0%	2.2%	2.6%	4.3%	5.6%
Sweden	11.3%	13.8%	18.4%	32.4%	39.7%	48.4%
United Kingdom	5.2%	7.3%	8.0%	9.0%	11.5%	21.0%
United States	5.3%	7.7%	10.7%	14.2%	18.4%	23.4%

Source: "Percent of Total Births to Unmarried Women, Selected Countries: 1960 to 1986," *Children's Well-Being: An International Comparison*, A Report of the Select Committee on Children, Youth, and Families, 101st Cong., 2d sess., March 1990, p. 121. Primary source: U.S. Bureau of the Census, various years, *Statistical Abstract of the United States*; Statistical Office of the European Communities, 1989, Demographic Statistics, Luxembourg, and Statistics Sweden, various years, *Statistical Abstract of Sweden*, Stockholm.

★ 609 ★

Births to Unmarried Women: Selected Countries: 1960-1986

Births to unmarried women as a percent of all live births, 10 countries, 1960-1986.

Country	Births to unmarried women as % of live births			
	1960	1970	1980	1986
United States	5.3%	10.7%	18.4%	23.4%
Canada	4.3%	9.6%	11.3%	16.9%
Japan	1.2%	0.9%	0.8%	1.0%
Denmark	7.8%	11.0%	33.2%	43.9%
France	6.1%	6.8%	11.4%	21.9%
Germany	6.3%	5.5%	7.6%	9.6%
Italy	2.4%	2.2%	4.3%	5.6%
Netherlands	1.3%	2.1%	4.1%	8.8%
Sweden	11.3%	18.4%	39.7%	48.4%
United Kingdom	5.2%	8.0%	11.5%	21.0%

Source: "Births to unmarried women as a percent of all live births, 10 countries, selected years, 1960-86," *Monthly Labor Review*, March 1990, p. 45. Primary source: Statistical Office of the European Communities, *Demographic Statistics, 1988;* and various national sources.

★ 610 ★

Births: 1965 to 2080

Percent distibution of births, by age and race of mother: 1965 to 2080.

Year	Births to all women-		Births to White women		Births to Black women-		Births to other races women-	
	Under age 20	Age 35 and over	Under age 20	Age 35 and over	Under age 20	Age 35 and over	Under age 20	Age 35 and over
Estimates								
1965	15.9%	9.9%	14.3%	9.9%	25.1%	9.4%	11.1%	12.5%
1970	17.6%	6.3%	15.2%	6.2%	31.3%	6.5%	13.8%	9.2%
1975	19.0%	4.6%	16.3%	4.6%	33.1%	4.6%	14.1%	7.0%
1980	15.7%	4.6%	13.6%	4.6%	26.7%	4.1%	11.4%	8.0%
1985	12.8%	6.5%	10.9%	6.6%	23.0%	5.0%	9.2%	10.4%
Projections								
1987	12.1%	7.4%	10.4%	7.3%	21.5%	6.5%	8.2%	13.7%
1990	11.6%	8.4%	9.9%	8.2%	20.5%	7.5%	8.4%	14.5%
1995	11.7%	9.6%	10.1%	9.5%	20.0%	8.7%	8.6%	14.4%
2000	13.0%	9.8%	11.4%	9.7%	20.8%	8.9%	9.8%	13.6%
2005	13.0%	8.9%	11.7%	8.8%	20.0%	8.2%	9.0%	12.5%
2010	12.2%	8.0%	11.0%	7.8%	18.4%	7.6%	8.7%	12.0%
2020	11.2%	8.8%	10.2%	8.6%	16.1%	8.3%	9.3%	12.5%
2030	11.6%	9.0%	11.0%	8.9%	14.9%	8.4%	9.9%	10.7%
2040	11.0%	8.4%	10.7%	8.2%	12.8%	8.2%	10.0%	9.6%
2050	10.6%	8.6%	10.5%	8.7%	10.9%	8.4%	10.5%	8.7%
2080	10.7%	8.7%	10.7%	8.6%	10.8%	8.6%	10.5%	8.8%

Source: "Projections of the Population of the United States, by Age, Sex, and Race: 1988 to 2080," *Current Population Reports,* Series P-25, No. 1018, p. 12. Primary source: *Current Population Reports,* Series P-25, No. 952, and unpublished data. Projection data from middle series. Births adjusted for underregistration all years.

★ 611 ★

Fertility Rates of Young Women Worldwide

Age-specific fertility rates for women ages 15 to 19 and 20 to 24 and total fertility rates, various years.

Country	Year	Births per 1,000 women		Total (births per woman)
		Rate ages 15 to 19	Rate ages 20 to 24	
Australia	1985	22.4	94.0	1.9
Canada	1985	23.7	85.3	1.7
China	1981	15.3	182.1	2.6
France	1984	12.9	102.0	1.8
Germany, Federal Republic	1984	9.0	62.1	1.3
Hungary	1985	51.5	152.5	1.8
India	1980	93.1	259.9	4.7
Israel	1985	25.4	163.2	3.1
Italy	1981	18.0	93.4	1.5
Japan	1983	4.4	70.8	1.8

[Continued]

★ 611 ★

Fertility Rates of Young Women Worldwide
[Continued]

Country	Year	Births per 1,000 women		Total (births per woman)
		Rate ages 15 to 19	Rate ages 20 to 24	
Mexico	1981	106.1	203.0	4.4
Norway	1984	19.2	93.9	1.7
Soviet Union	1985	44.0	196.0	2.5
Sweden	1985	11.0	81.8	1.7
United Kingdom	1985	29.5	94.3	1.8
United States	1984	50.9	107.3	1.8

Source: "Age-Specific Fertility Rates for Women Ages 15 to 19 and 20 to 24 and Total Fertility Rates, Selected Countries: Selected Years, 1980 to 1985," *Children's Well-Being: An International Comparison,* A Report of the Select Committee on Children, Youth, and Families, 101st Cong., 2d sess., March 1990, p. 120. Primary source: U.S. Bureau of the Census, Center for International Research, International Data Base. Age-specific fertility rates are the number of live births per 1,000 women in a specific age group. The total fertility rate is the average number of live births a woman would have if she were to pass through her childbearing years conforming to the age-specific fertility rates of a given year.

★ 612 ★

Fertility of Jewish Women in Israel

Total fertility rates of Jewish women in Jerusalem and other locations, by region of birth, 1972 and 1983.

Region of birth	1972				1983			
	Jerusalem	Tel Aviv-Yafo	Haifa	Israel	Jerusalem	Tel Aviv-Yafo	Haifa	Israel
Total	3.28	2.50	2.72	3.19	3.65	2.13	2.37	2.83
Israel	3.16	2.33	2.77	2.96	3.94	2.12	2.32	2.85
Asia-Africa	3.70	3.40	3.62	3.85	3.23	2.46	2.75	3.13
Europe-America	3.06	2.13	2.43	2.71	3.44	2.04	2.26	2.83

Source: "Total fertility rates of Jewish women in Jerusalem and Other Locations, by Region of Birth, 1972 and 1983," *American Jewish Year Book,* 1987, Table 5, p. 86 (Scranton, PA.: American Jewish Committee and the Jewish Publication Society, 1987). *Total fertility rate* is the average number of children that a woman would bear during her lifetime if the age-specific fertility rates remained the same as in the year(s) under consideration. Under conditions of very low mortality the "replacement level" is 2.1 children per woman (regardless of marital status).

★ 613 ★

Live Births, Birth Rates, and Fertility Rates

Birth rates per 1,000 population and fertility rates per 1,000 women 15-44 years old, by month, 1988-1989.

	Number		Birth rate		Fertility rate	
	1989	1988	1989	1988	1989	1988
Total	4,021,000	3,913,000	16.2	15.9	68.8	67.3
January	311,000	306,000	14.8	14.8	62.9	62.2
February	296,000	302,000	15.6	15.5	66.1	65.5
March	330,000	320,000	15.7	15.4	66.6	65.1
April	317,000	297,000	15.6	14.8	66.0	62.3
May	352,000	332,000	16.7	16.0	70.9	67.4
June	327,000	333,000	16.1	16.5	68.2	69.9
July	372,000	353,000	17.6	17.0	74.9	71.6
August	358,000	359,000	17.0	17.2	72.1	72.8
September	348,000	342,000	17.0	17.0	72.4	71.7
October	348,000	336,000	16.4	16.1	69.9	68.2
November	322,000	311,000	15.7	15.4	66.9	65.2
December	341,000	323,000	16.1	15.5	68.5	65.5

Source: Selected from "Live births, birth rates, and fertility rates, by month: United States, 1988 and 1989," *Monthly Vital Statistics Report*: 38: No. 13, August 30, 1990. Data are provisional. Rates on an annual basis. Due to rounding, figures may not add to totals. Figures include revisions and, therefore, may differ from those previously published.

★ 614 ★

Worldwide Live Births

Live births by age of mother and sex, latest available year.

Area, Year	All ages	<15	15-19	20-24	25-29	30-34	35-39	40-44	45-49	50+	Unknown
AFRICA											
Algeria-1980	818,613	-	74,828	224,432	228,232	135,045	92,825	41,167	7,945	1,927	12,212
Cape Verde-1985	11,282	-	1,669[1]	3,812	2,772	1,753	663	377	-	106[2]	130
Female	5,577	-	830[1]	1,922	1,349	861	322	180	-	52[2]	61
Egypt-1982	1,601,265	-	67,935[1]	321,201	497,122	334,060	216,403	77,436	-	31,314[2]	55,794
Female	775,696	-	32,835[1]	155,175	241,377	161,906	104,650	37,676	-	15,300[2]	26,777
Libyan Arab Jamahiryia-1981	118,228	-	9,831[1]	29,757	28,228	21,957	13,823	5,515	1,817	97	7,203
Female	57,540	-	4,706[1]	14,381	13,691	10,705	6,879	2,676	918	43	3,541
Malawi-1977	267,805	1,049	36,853	71,119	64,160	38,803	28,348	13,708	7,830	5,533	402
Female	139,828	411	19,581	36,954	33,279	20,279	14,940	7,274	4,097	2,805	210
Mauritius-1987	19,152	19	1,886	6,657	5,680	3,055	1,295	245	20	3	292
Female	9,465	13	925	3,233	2,831	1,554	640	133	9	-	127
Rodrigues-1987	882	1	137	264	178	96	64	35	2	-	105
Female	456	-	69	144	88	42	32	18	1	-	62
Reunion-1986	12,797	25	1,640	4,176	3,465	2,207	955	294	-	26[2]	9
Rwanda-1978	261,268	-	14,187[1]	70,084	67,941	44,534	34,363	20,179	7,624	2,127	229
Sao Tome and Principe-1979	3,233	6	522	971	696	428	335	177	26	3	69
Seychelles-1987	1,684	9	234	604	482	234	96	23	2	-	-
Female	844	6	108	310	252	115	44	9	-	-	-
South Africa-1977											
Asiatic	18,881	4	1,474	6,366	5,851	3,381	1,393	370	40	2	-
Female	9,334	2	726	3,121	2,950	1,642	685	188	20	-	-
Colored	65,114	58	8,161	21,594	17,402	9,800	5,196	2,335	488	80	-

[Continued]

★ 614 ★

Worldwide Live Births

[Continued]

Area, Year	All ages	<15	15-19	20-24	25-29	30-34	35-39	40-44	45-49	50+	Unknown
Female	32,090	26	3,966	10,588	8,613	4,811	2,646	1,169	228	43	-
White	74,037	7	4,892	23,816	26,253	13,867	4,166	944	90	2	-
Female	36,188	3	2,417	11,618	12,942	6,714	1,992	464	37	1	-
Tunisia-1980	225,201	1,177	10,084	53,084	58,740	35,230	19,955	10,131	2,641	1,789	32,370
Female	109,552	657	4,923	25,949	28,440	17,025	9,740	4,871	1,274	935	15,738
Zimbabwe-1978											
Europeans	3,118	1	280	1,040	1,094	501	140	29	-	-	33
Female	1,492	1	132	505	518	241	63	16	-	-	16
NORTH AMERICA											
Antigua and Barbuda-1986	1,130	8	237	366	296	155	58	7	-	-	3
Female-1975	667	5	188	210	130	68	36	10	-	-	20
Bahamas-1986	4,770	6	780	1,447	1,324	738	270	57	5	-	143
Barbados-1986	4,043	17	603	1,247	1,163	690	260	50	7	-	6
Belize-1984	6,150	15	1,225	1,996	1,274	738	329	119	-	17[2]	437
Bermuda-1986	889	1	60	193	298	220	94	9	-	-	14
Female	417	-	33	89	140	104	40	5	-	-	6
British Virgin Islands-1986	213	1	31	41	51	51	19	-	5	-	14
Canada-1987	361,973	235	20,981	86,583	142,713	84,578	23,699	2,865	100	2	217
Female-1986	177,920	87	10,376	45,412	70,021	39,844	10,812	1,225	44	-	99
Cayman Islands-1987	359	2	55	113	99	679	20	1	-	-	-
Female	167	1	21	57	40	35	12	-	-	-	-
Costa Rica-1984	75,993	279	12,969	25,210	19,335	11,042	5,048	1,392	-	131[2]	587
Cuba-1986	166,049	1,396	44,492	62,180	33,659	16,210	6,140	992	174	263	543
Female	80,775	716	20,601	30,161	17,114	8,069	3,148	460	87	154	265
Dominican Republic-1982	106,235	920	7,361	18,721	17,787	14,137	9,497	6,661	4,561	5,770	20,820
Female	52,967	506	3,588	9,252	8,831	7,083	4,684	3,303	2,336	3,025	10,359
El Salvador-1985	139,514	538	27,131	44,265	29,791	17,644	10,664	4,259	943	89	4,190
Female	68,528	258	13,388	21,585	14,706	8,708	5,197	2,079	492	48	2,067
Greenland-1987	1,090	1	152	401	315	159	54	-	8[3]	-	
Female	535	-	84	192	151	81	25	-	2[3]	-	
Grenada-1978	2,521	11	677	847	493	272	124	47	3	-	47
Guadeloupe-1986	6,374	-	3	202	868	930	549	267	90	41	3,424
Female	3,133	-	3	94	418	459	273	130	51	15	1,690
Guatemala-1985	326,849	1,199	50,842	94,425	76,130	53,065	33,451	12,196	2,392	3,149	-
Female	159,405	570	24,708	45,596	37,185	26,125	16,352	6,024	1,179	1,666	-
Honduras-1983	158,419	1,471	22,206	55,190	32,281	20,268	12,476	4,945	-	1,063[3]	8,519
Jamaica-1984	57,240	358	14,554	18,875	12,471	6,449	2,990	1,012	108	9	414
Female-1982	29,034	160	7,684	9,565	5,858	3,340	1,660	550	50	4	163
Martinique-1986	5,961	10	584	1,713	1,778	1,209	535	121	6	1	4
Female	2,957	7	306	839	891	569	276	62	4	1	2
Mexico-1984	2,511,894	6,180	366,018	788,690	609,139	359,088	204,691	75,424	18,123	22,778	61,763
Female	1,241,420	3,017	179,486	387,683	300,264	178,199	101,814	37,362	8,952	12,455	32,188
Montserrat-1986	200	1	50	64	43	28	9	3	-	-	2
Panama-1987	57,647	380	11,121	18,680	14,358	7,632	3,410	953	137	21	955
Female	28,115	172	5,452	9,127	6,911	3,738	1,701	462	79	6	467
Puerto Rico-1985	63,629	254	10,724	21,645	17,550	9,032	3,591	753	47	2	31
Female	31,020	108	5,204	10,;615	8,515	4,435	1,734	367	24	-	18
St. Kitts and Nevis-1986	1,007	4	231	307	272	127	45	17	-	3[2]	1
St. Lucia-1986	3,907	12	958	1,309	881	434	240	71	-	2[3]	-
Female	1,954	2	476	679	423	226	112	36	-	-	-
St. Pierre and Miquelon-1977	105	1	15	43	24	13	7	2	-	-	-
Female	52	-	9	20	13	6	3	1	-	-	-
St. Vincent and Grenadines-1986	2,708	25	649	975	621	272	107	32	4	-	23

[Continued]

★ 614 ★

Worldwide Live Births
[Continued]

Area, Year	Age of mother (in years)										
	All ages	<15	15-19	20-24	25-29	30-34	35-39	40-44	45-49	50+	Unknown
Female	1,305	9	330	438	313	125	56	19	3	-	12
Trinidad and Tobago-1984	31,599	88	4,847	10,801	8,570	4,646	2,045	444	27	3	128
Female	15,546	43	2,463	5,205	4,192	2,324	1,031	204	15	2	67
United States-1986	3,756,547	10,176	461,905	1,102,119	1,199,519	721,395	230,335	29,847	-	1,251[2]	-
Female	1,831,679	4,968	224,677	537,821	584,981	351,372	112,492	14,733	-	635[2]	-
U.S. Virgin Islands-1982	2,509	-	493[1]	769	623	354	218	49	-	3[2]	
SOUTH AMERICA											
Argentina-1983	655,876	2,798	80,972	177,342	178,643	122,361	61,628	17,983	2,337	1,196	10,616
Bolivia-1977	142,277	106	14,779	39,220	36,251	24,989	16,778	6,804	2,443	907	-
Brazil-1986	2,779,253	6,037	392,889	885,607	746,564	420,112	204,538	66,670	10,598	1,026	45,212
Female	1,316,203	2,903	192,142	432,867	365,488	206,316	100,552	33,068	5,279	529	22,059
Chile-1987	129,548	597	35,633	84,674	75,416	45,037	19,282	4,742	383	10	-
Female	192,548	308	17,295	41,295	36,647	22,074	9,380	2,354	191	4	-
Colombia-1985	835,922	38,009	110,746	215,355	186,469	137,282	79,448	39,030	23,842	5,741	-
Ecuador-1987	204,475	322	27,563	61,291	50,216	33,641	19,686	8,182	1,380	291	1,903
Female	100,611	170	13,525	30,145	24,810	16,504	9,646	4,037	689	137	948
French Guiana-1985	2,472	20	325	696	692	452	196	48	3	2	38
Female	1,245	7	170	365	348	226	92	22	1	1	13
Paraguay-1986	36,891	30	4,252	10,278	9,160	6,147	3,964	1,420	-	352[2]	1,288
Female	18,027	9	2,053	4,939	4,481	3,065	1,952	719	-	188[2]	621
Peru-1982	526,999	848	69,327	156,695	130,713	83,886	54,513	20,107	3,802	328	6,780
Female	257,402	420	33,934	76,510	63,591	41,053	26,818	9,792	1,876	164	3,244
Uruguay-1985	53,766	146	6,442	14,984	15,126	9,874	5,180	1,536	-	138[2]	340
Female	26,146	64	3,036	7,236	7,362	4,888	2,584	756	-	74[2]	146
Venezuela-1987	516,773	3,532	91,440	155,598	128,957	83,198	39,302	10,852	1,599	437	1,858
Female	252,773	1,762	44,624	76,144	62,813	40,939	19,279	5,353	791	196	872
ASIA											
Afghanistan-1979	627,619	-	83,907[1]	163,116	151,167	106,756	71,654	35,011	-	16,008[2]	-
Bahrain-1986	12,893	14	563	3,292	4,283	2,775	1,224	489	183	58	12
Bangladesh-1982	3,247,470	-	618,784[1]	978,054	832,877	416,467	290,345	81,931	-	29,012[2]	-
Female	3,356	-	226	883	1,109	755	302	66	12	-	3
Brunei Darussalam-1986	6,920	4	456	1,826	2,299	1,509	640	153	20	-	13
Female	3,356	-	226	883	1,109	755	302	66	12	-	3
Cyprus-1987	10,337	-	701	3,491	3,579	1,809	577	96	3	-	81
Female	5,031	-	341	1,704	1,721	901	274	47	1	-	42
Hong Kong-1987	69,958	14	1,292	11,254	31,243	20,082	5,491	535	25	-	22
Female	33,977	6	662	5,448	15,207	9,631	2,711	290	13	-	9
Iraq-1977	289,522	854	25,017	77,821	74,458	52,112	31,117	11,740	4,455	1,797	10,151
Female	138,118	420	12,038	37,101	35,693	24,844	14,774	5,457	2,084	805	4,902
Israel-1987	99,022	18	4,072	25,724	32,393	23,164	11,203	1,986	99	26	337
Female	48,463	10	2,057	12,678	15,668	11,297	5,554	966	46	16	171
Japan-1987	1,346,658	28	17,530	225,098	634,440	364,838	95,776	8,682	229	1	36
Female	654,354	13	8,471	109,017	308,542	177,545	46,404	4,241	110	-	11
Jordan-1979	91,622	13	8,214	18,724	14,080	15,977	15,236	11,615	4,473	150	3,140
Korea, Rep. of-1986	613,703	-	16,705	206,126	320,042	59,962	8,749	1,644	381	9	85
Female	288,574	-	7,904	98,379	151,095	26,504	3,729	744	170	3	46
Kuwait-1986	53,485	-	3,319	13,108	16,056	11,728	6,565	1,748	-	335[2]	986
Female	26,523	-	1,576	6,476	7,938	5,755	3,257	851	-	159[2]	511
Macau-1987	7,565	-	112	1,413	3,382	2,175	437	42	3	1	-
Female	3,721	-	51	727	1,674	1,029	216	20	3	1	-
Malaysia-1987	391,815	137	14,522	91,483	133,244	90,821	46,239	13,161	1,148	84	976
Female	190,294	69	7,002	44,424	64,662	44,163	22,521	6,398	571	39	445
Sarawak-1986	41,702	105	4,563	12,059	12,256	7,716	3,231	933	138	33	668

[Continued]

★ 614 ★

Worldwide Live Births
[Continued]

Area, Year	All ages	<15	15-19	20-24	25-29	30-34	35-39	40-44	45-49	50+	Unknown
						Age of mother (in years)					
Female	19,541	51	2,118	5,557	5,811	3,656	1,517	445	64	16	306
Pakistan-1985	3,167,156	-	207,692	799,504	884,788	609,124	425,655	162,884	66,766	10,743	-
Female	1,540,939	-	101,858	389,728	422,567	305,339	200,120	82,207	31,853	7,267	-
Philippines-1986	1,493,995	432	127,715	441,066	432,710	272,088	147,430	47,382	8,223	1,977	14,972
Female-1984	1,540,939	-	101,858	389,728	422,567	305,339	200,120	82,207	31,853	7,267	-
Qatar-1987	9,919	3	584	2,782	3,338	2,000	982	154	20	12	44
Female	4,737	1	250	1,345	1,587	958	485	73	11	4	23
Singapore-1987	43,889	10	891	7,926	18,150	12,554	3,881	445	14	-	18
Female	21,154	7	414	3,793	8,795	6,049	1,881	201	6	-	8
Sri Lanka-1983	405,122	116	30,606	130,822	118,869	80,403	34,962	8,253	1,071	19	1
Female	198,478	58	15,005	64,148	58,249	39,238	17,158	4,084	528	10	-
Thailand-1987	884,043	1,195	117,771	307,419	233,428	128,531	54,898	20,216	7,070	3,843	9,672
Female	431,535	600	57,964	149,985	113,205	62,467	26,747	9,962	3,649	2,137	4,819
United Arab Emirates-1982	41,961	57	3,345	12,084	13,002	6,969	2,793	709	169	78	2,755
Female	20,585	21	1,627	5,947	6,492	3,345	1,364	336	71	36	1,346
EUROPE											
Albania-1987	79,696	-	2,371	24,123	30,419	15,448	5,712	1,261	167	28	167
Austria-1987	86,503	17	6,375	30,351	30,150	13,918	4,733	902	56	1	-
Female	42,218	8	3,102	14,871	14,653	6,803	2,300	449	31	1	-
Belgium-1983	117,145	18	5,915	39,633	46,689	19,020	5,026	780	51	6	7
Female	56,936	8	2,926	19,140	22,761	9,210	2,475	389	21	3	3
Bulgaria-1986	120,078	350	23,211	53,121	28,340	10,965	3,454	590	32	15	-
Female	58,728	162	11,358	26,090	13,816	5,328	1,673	277	19	5	-
Channel Islands-											
Guernsey-1986	671	-	42	147	250	166	57	9	-	-	-
Female	345	-	20	72	124	95	26	8	-	-	-
Jersey-1987	1,009	-	39	169	393	305	90	-	13[3]	-	-
Female	463	-	23	79	182	124	52	-	3[3]	-	-
Czechoslovakia-1986	220,494	31	26,535	100,668	58,604	25,778	7,842	1,001	35	-	-
Female	107,288	10	12,921	48,935	28,540	12,562	3,823	476	21	-	-
Denmark-1987	56,221	3	1,724	14,389	22,414	12,985	4,054	632	18	2	-
Female	27,142	3	865	6,833	10,884	6,276	1,968	302	9	2	-
Faeroe Islands-1987	777	-	58	204	267	161	71	16	-	-	-
Female	396	-	30	98	142	82	35	9	-	-	-
Finland-1986	60,632	3	2,138	13,060	22,207	15,375	6,647	1,147	54	1	-
Female	29,597	1	1,071	6,386	10,778	7,543	3,246	552	19	1	-
France-1987	767,828	66	20,998	184,197	301,937	180,307	67,8977	11,824	587	35	-
Female	374,597	27	10,294	90,034	147,001	87,950	33,187	5,785	300	19	-
German Democratic Rep.-1987	225,959	13	21,240	105,546	69,194	23,261	6,087	590	-	28[2]	-
Germany, Federal Rep.-1987	642,010	44	19,560	146,543	260,481	156,257	51,046	7,528	516	33	2
Female	311,351	21	9,612	71,035	126,282	75,703	24,782	3,644	253	18	1
Gibraltar-1980	550	-	53[1]	190	194	79	26	8	-	-	-
Greece-1985	116,481	93	13,391	41,288	35,956	17,846	6,418	1,286	131	26	46
Female	56,059	45	6,514	19,781	17,316	8,553	3,118	640	65	8	19
Hungary-1987	125,840	167	16,787	45,660	36,482	19,777	5,958	971	38	-	-
Female	61,261	80	8,213	22,131	17,740	9,641	2,977	466	13	-	-
Iceland-1984	4,113	1	403	1,346	1,258	764	297	44	-	-	-
Ireland-1985	62,245	5	2,616	12,176	20,045	16,283	8,110	1,946	119	3	942
Female	30,252	2	1,264	5,897	9,747	7,869	3,987	981	59	2	444
Italy-1983	601,928	21	35,099	179,235	203,854	122,652	48,082	9,513	577	68	2,827
Female	292,015	8	16,926	87,139	98,693	59,491	23,360	4,671	285	32	1,410
Liechtenstein-1986	351	-	7	60	139	102	34	7	2	-	-
Luxembourg-1987	4,238	-	141[1]	931	1,687	1,098	321	46	1	-	13
Female	2,079	-	72[1]	445	817	556	158	22	-	-	9
Malta-1987	5,314	-	141[1]	1,069	2,019	1,323	6067	155	1	-	-

[Continued]

★ 614 ★

Worldwide Live Births
[Continued]

Area, Year	All ages	<15	15-19	20-24	25-29	30-34	35-39	40-44	45-49	50+	Unknown
Netherlands-1986	184,513	-	4,051[1]	36,252	80,834	49,219	12,369	1,600	-	188[2]	-
Female	90,660	-	1,990[1]	17,811	39,677	24,141	6,157	785	-	99[2]	-
Norway-1987	54,027	5	2,877	14,569	20,141	12,178	3,652	578	27	-	-
Female	26,525	4	1,382	7,176	9,873	5,941	1,852	282	15	-	-
Poland-1987	605,492	101	40,558	217,454	194,342	104,471	41,203	6,974	376	13	-
Female	293,745	50	19,669	105,122	94,252	51,022	20,022	3,416	185	7	-
Portugal-1987	123,218	103	11,684	39,951	39,289	21,018	8,659	2,274	210	14	16
Female	59,646	49	5,643	19,227	19,108	10,194	4,169	1,139	102	7	8
Romania-1985	358,797	545	55,961	132,104	103,376	47,749	15,592	3,163	291	16	-
San Marino-1987	220	-	10	76	72	44	13	3	1	-	1
Female	106	-	6	37	32	19	8	3	-	-	1
Spain-1983	485,352	334	32,300	131,772	166,767	96,535	44,852	11,634	1,035	123	-
Female	223,767	160	15,489	63,550	80,152	46,597	21,668	5,590	509	52	-
Sweden-1987	104,699	10	2,990	25,203	37,769	26,797	10,029	1,846	55	-	-
Female	51,134	6	1,459	12,416	18,366	13,100	4,878	885	24	-	-
Switzerland-1987	76,505	7	1,366	15,558	32,177	20,513	6,008	837	38	1	-
Female	37,318	3	647	7,569	15,648	10,122	2,905	404	19	1	-
United Kingdom-1987	775,617	228	65,723	220,377	211,898	154,982	52,667	9,176	496	70	-
Female	377,714	115	31,703	107,164	132,724	75,594	25,655	4,487	250	22	-
England and Wales-1985	656,417	239	56,690	193,958	227,486	126,185	44,393	6,882	519	65	-
Female	319,582	104	27,672	94,037	111,086	61,460	21,538	3,392	262	31	-
Northern Ireland-1985	27,635	5	1,973	7,847	9,195	5,600	2,505	490	20	-	-
Female	13,451	4	961	3,809	4,534	2,667	1,227	239	10	-	-
Scotland-1985	66,676	19	6,499	20,778	23,477	11,583	3,687	511	23	1	98
Female	32,556	12	3,212	10,117	11,544	5,648	1,735	232	9	-	47
Yugoslavia-1987	359,338	216	35,331	134,991	112,366	53,082	18,361	3,546	421	96	928
Female	173,168	102	16,920	65,225	54,185	25,535	8,815	1,689	202	46	449
OCEANIA											
American Samoa-1982	1,160	1	92	403	341	217	90	15	1	-	-
Female	563	1	48	206	152	99	48	9	-	-	-
Australia-1986	243,408	522	13,804	59,045	94,561	56,187	17,021	2,146	-	87[2]	35
Female	118,494	242	6,823	28,713	46,220	27,236	8,181	1,021	-	42[2]	16
Cocos (Keeling) Islands-1986	10	-	-	2	6	2	-	-	-	-	-
Female	7	-	-	1	4	2	-	-	-	-	-
Cook Islands-1984	408	2	101	124	85	41	37	8	-	-	10
Female	216	1	54	62	52	16	19	5	-	-	7
Fiji-1985	19,464	2	2,156	7,720	5,432	2,595	1,110	302	44	7	96
Female	9,381	1	993	3,787	2,601	1,270	515	150	15	3	46
Guam-1986	3,309	3	459	1,144	920	531	208	42	2	-	-
Female	1,582	-	218	542	434	266	100	22	-	-	-
New Caledonia-1987	3,881	8	361	1,147	1,153	680	303	97	9	5	118
Female-1982	1,861	3	256	634	463	283	163	53	2	4	-
New Zealand-1987	55,254	184	4,617	14,441	20,452	11,824	3,267	44	-	25[2]	-
Female	26,660	94	2,339	7,002	9,813	5,592	1,591	214	-	15[2]	-
Norfolk Island-1988	29	-	1	5	11	11	1	-	-	-	-
Female	10	-	-	1	3	5	1	-	-	-	-
Pacific Islands-1982	3,066	1	455	939	799	583	210	74	5	-	-
Female-1979	1,996	2	295	651	538	294	153	54	7	-	2
Northern Mariana Islands-1985	698	6	97	210	210	121	50	4	-	-	-
Female	324	2	40	109	101	48	23	1	-	-	-
Samoa-1980	2,693	1	246	964	650	393	212	81	-	34[2]	112

[Continued]

★ 614 ★

Worldwide Live Births
[Continued]

Area, Year	Age of mother (in years)										
	All ages	<15	15-19	20-24	25-29	30-34	35-39	40-44	45-49	50+	Unknown
Female	1,234	1,	123	423	300	173	109	36	-	16[2]	53
Tokelau-1982	43	-	1	19	12	7	3	1	-	-	-
Female	24	-	-	9	7	4	3	1	-	-	-
USSR-1986	5,610,769	-	445,888[1]	2,139,407	1,767,433	376,759	324,490	45,749	7,936	991	2,116

Source: Selected from "Live Births by Age of Mother, Sex and Urban\Rural Residence: Latest Available Year, *1988 Demographic Yearbook*, 1990, Table 10, pp. 351-362 (New York: United Nations, 1990). *Notes:* 1. Figures for age -15 have been combined with this figure. 2. Figures for age 45-49 have been combined with this figure. 3. Figures for age 40-44 have been combined with this figure.

Characteristics of U.S. Adult Population

★ 615 ★

Adult Population by Census Region

Total and female and male adult population by census region, 1990.

Census Region	Number (thousands)		
	Total	Female	Male
All adults	180,974	94,667	86,307
North East	38,020	20,252	17,768
North Central	44,018	23,063	20,954
South	62,758	33,063	29,695
West	36,178	18,288	17,890

Source: Selected from *Mediamark Research Multimedia Audiences Report, Spring 1990* (New York: Mediamark Research Inc., 1990).

★ 616 ★

Adult Population by Race and Spanish Language

Total and female and male adult population by race and Spanish language, 1990.

Characteristic	Number (thousands)		
	Total	Female	Male
All adults	180,974	94,667	86,307
White	156,336	81,285	75,051
Black	20,257	11,075	9,182
Spanish Speaking	9,868	5,096	4,772

Source: Selected from *Mediamark Research Multimedia Audiences Report, Spring 1990* (New York: Mediamark Research Inc., 1990).

★ 617 ★

Adult Population by Residence

Total and male and female adult population by residence, 1990.

Area of residence	Number (thousands)		
	Total	Female	Male
All adults	180,974	94,667	86,307
MSA Central City	63,674	32,931	30,743
MSA Suburban	75,951	40,131	35,820
Non-MSA	41,349	21,606	19,743

Source: Selected from *Mediamark Research Multimedia Audiences Report, Spring 1990* (New York: Mediamark Research Inc., 1990). MSA = Metropolitan Statistical Area.

★ 618 ★

Age Distribution of Adults

Age distribution of persons over age 18, 1990.

Age	Number (thousands)		
	Total	Women	Men
Total adults	180,974	94,667	86,307
18-24	25,182	12,681	12,501
25-34	43,573	22,056	21,518
35-44	35,816	18,177	17,639
45-54	24,740	12,733	12,007
55-64	22,247	11,722	10,475
65 or over	29,414	17,248	12,166
18-34	68,756	34,736	34,019
18-49	117,909	59,765	58,144
25-54	104,130	52,966	51,164

Source: Selected from *Mediamark Research Multimedia Audiences Report, Spring 1990* (New York: Mediamark Research Inc., 1990).

★ 619 ★

Marital Status of the Adult Population

Total and female and male adult population, by marital status, 1990.

Marital Status	Number (thousands)		
	Total	Female	Male
All Adults	180,974	94,667	86,307
Single	38,207	16,895	21,312
Married	110,290	55,273	55,018
Other	32,477	22,500	9,977
Parents	60,095	34,261	25,834
Working Parents	45,282	21,544	23,738
Sole Parent	10,240	8,708	1,532

Source: Selected from *Mediamark Research Multimedia Audiences Report, Spring 1990* (New York: Mediamark Research Inc., 1990).

Contraception

★ 620 ★

Contraception in Africa

Contraceptive prevalence rate among women aged 15-49 in Africa.

Country	Year	Contraceptive prevalence rate
Cameroon	1977-78	3%
Ethiopia	1982	2%
Ghana	1979-80	10%
Kenya	1977-78	8%
Lesotho	1977	5%
Nigeria	1983	6%
Senegal	1978	4%
Sierra Leone	1982	4%
Zaire	1982	3%
Zimbabwe	1984	27%

Source: Eschel M. Rhoodie, *Discrimination Against Women: A Global Survey of the Economic, Educational, Social and Political Status of Women,* 1989, p. 104 (Jefferson, NC: McFarland & Company, 1989). Primary source: International Bank for Reconstruction and Development, *Population Growth and Policies in Sub-Saharan Africa,* Washington, D.C., August 1986, p. 50. "Africa is an essentially male dominated society and the value of a woman is stated mainly in terms of the number of children she can produce" (source).

★ 621 ★

Contraceptive Availability in Developing Countries

Percentage of developing countries where at least 80%, and percentage where at least 50% of the population was judged to have ready and easy access to family planning methods, by region, 1982.

Region	Number of countries	Percentage of countries						
--------	---------------------	At least one method	Sterilization Female	Sterilization Male	IUD	Pill[2]	Condom[3]	Induced Abortion
		% of countries where 80% or more have ready and easy access to family planning methods						
Africa	42	2%	-	-	-	2%	2%	-
Latin America	21	38%	10%	29%	5%	19%	10%	5%
Asia and Oceania	36	19%	11%	14%	6%	14%	14%	14%
Total	99	16%	6%	11%	3%	10%	8%	6%
		% of countries where 50% or more have ready and easy access to family planning methods						
Africa	42	12%	-	2%	5%	10%	12%	2%
Latin America	21	86%	24%	48%	38%	71%	76%	24%

[Continued]

★ 621 ★

Contraceptive Availability in Developing Countries
[Continued]

Region	Number of countries	At least one method	Sterilization		IUD	Pill[2]	Condom[3]	Induced Abortion
			Female	Male				
Asia and Oceania	36	44%	22%	28%	28%	39%	39%	22%
Total	99	39%	13%	21%	20%	33%	35%	14%

Source: "Percentage of developing countries where at least 80%, and percentage where at least 50% of the population was judged to have ready and easy access to family planning methods, by region, 1982," *Levels and Trends of Contraceptive Use as Assessed in 1988,* Table 14, p. 66 (New York: United Nations, 1989). "Ready and easy access" means that the recipient spends no more than an average of two hours per month to obtain contraceptive supplies and services, and that the cost of such supplies is not burdensome: a one-month supply of contraceptives should cost less than 1% of a month's wages to meet the criterion. For sterilization, the criterion implies that medically adequate voluntary sterilization services are legally and openly available and are readily accessible. Contraceptives supplied through community-based distribution and social marketing programs are not reflected in these scores. *Notes:* 1. For methods in columns 3 to 7. 2. If the availability of injectables is greater than that of pills, the data on injectables were used to score this item. 3. If the availability of female barrier methods is greater than that of condoms, data on female barrier methods were used to score this item.

★ 622 ★

Contraceptive Failure

Percentage of women experiencing contraceptive failure during the first 12 months of use, by method, marital status, race and age.

Marital status, race, and age	Method of contraception				
	Pill	Condom	Diaphragm	Rhythm	Spermicides
Unmarried					
White					
Less than 20 years	9.3%	13.3%	12.4%	28.8%	35.0%
20-24 years	5.9%	22.5%	22.5%	24.3%	38.7%
25-34 years	3.4%	12.4%	12.5%	14.2%	28.8%
35-44 years	2.2%	3.9%	12.0%	7.3%	11.0%
Nonwhite					
Less than 20 years	18.1%	22.3%	35.5%	34.1%	34.0%
20-24 years	11.7%	36.3%	57.0%	28.9%	37.6%
25-34 years	6.7%	20.9%	35.8%	17.2%	27.9%
35-44 years	4.5%	6.8%	34.7%	8.9%	10.6%
Married					
White					
Less than 20 years	8.0%	11.4%	10.6%	25.1%	30.6%
20-24 years	5.0%	19.5%	19.4%	21.1%	34.0%
25-34 years	2.9%	10.6%	10.7%	12.2%	25.1%
35-44 years	1.9%	3.3%	10.3%	6.2%	9.4%
Nonwhite					
Less than 20 years	15.6%	19.3%	31.1%	(29.8%)	29.7%
20-24 years	10.0%	31.8%	51.2%	25.2%	33.0%
25-34 years	5.8%	18.0%	31.3%	14.8%	24.3%
35-44 years	3.9%	5.8%	30.3%	7.6%	9.1%

Source: Elise E. Jones and Jacqueline Darroch Forrest, "Contraceptive Failure in the United States: Revised Estimates from the 1982 Survey of Family Growth," *Family Planning Perspectives* Table 2, 21:3 (May/June 1989):103+. The model included method, duration of use, age, race, marital status and the interactions of method with age and with race. Parentheses indicate cells for which there were no actual observations.

★ 623 ★

Contraceptive Methods by Age, Race, and Marital Status

Contraceptive use by women, 15-44 years old, by age, race, marital status, and method of contraception: 1982.

Contraceptive Status and Method	All women[1]	Age[3] 15-24 years	25-34 years	35-44 years	Race		Marital Status		
					White	Black	Never married	Currently married	Formerly married
All women (in thousands)	54,099	20,150	19,644	14,305	45,367	6,985	19,164	28,231	6,704

Percent Distribution

Sterile	27.2%	3.2%	27.9%	60.1%	27.7%	23.7%	3.2%	40.9%	38.0%
Surgically sterile	25.7%	2.6%	26.4%	57.3%	26.1%	22.2%	2.6%	38.9%	36.1%
Contraceptively sterile[2]	17.8%	2.2%	19.6%	37.4%	18.3%	14.9%	1.8%	27.8%	21.6%
Noncontraceptively sterily	7.8%	.3%	6.8%	19.9%	7.8%	7.3%	.8%	11.0%	14.5%
Nonsurgically sterile[3]	1.5%	.6%	1.5%	2.8%	1.6%	1.5%	.7%	2.0%	1.9%
Pregnant, postpartum	5.0%	6.3%	6.5%	1.0%	4.8%	5.6%	2.5%	7.2%	2.6%
Seeking pregnancy	4.2%	3.5%	6.2%	2.5%	4.0%	5.4%	1.2%	6.7%	2.1%
Other nonusers	26.9%	48.6%	14.2%	13.8%	26.2%	29.6%	59.7%	5.0%	25.6%
Not sexually active[4]	19.5%	39.4%	7.8%	7.8%	19.9%	16.1%	49.6%	.2%	15.1%
Sexually active[4]	7.4%	9.2%	6.5%	6.0%	6.4%	13.5%	10.1%	4.8%	10.4%
Nonsurgical contraceptors	36.7%	38.4%	45.2	22.6%	37.2%	35.7%	33.3%	40.1%	31.8%
Pill	15.6%	23.5%	17.1	2.3%	15.1%	19.8%	18.7%	13.4%	15.8%
IUD	4.0%	1.4%	6.5%	4.2%	3.9%	4.7%	1.9%	4.8%	6.4%
Diaphragm	4.5%	3.7%	6.8%	2.4%	5.0%	1.8%	4.7%	4.5%	3.7%
Condom	6.7%	5.5%	7.6%	7.0%	7.2%	3.2%	4.1%	9.8%	.8%
Foam	1.3%	.8%	1.5%	1.8%	1.4%	1.4%	.4%	2.0%	1.1%
Rhythm[5]	2.2%	1.2%	2.8%	2.6%	2.2%	1.6%	.9%	3.2%	1.4%
Other methods[6]	2.5%	2.3%	2.9%	2.2%	2.4%	3.1%	2.6%	2.3%	2.7%

Source: "Contraceptive use by women, 15-44 years old, by age, race, marital status, and method of contraception: 1982," *Statistical Abstract of the United States 1990*, p. 70. Primary source: U.S. National Center for Health Statistics, *Advance Data from Vital and Health Statistics*, No. 102 and unpublished data. Based on the 1982 National Survey of Family Growth. *Notes:* 1. Includes other races, not shown separately. 2. Includes sterility of the husband or a current partner. Persons who had sterilizing operation and who gave as one reason that they had already had all the children they wanted. 3. Persons sterile from illness, accident, or congenital conditions. 4. Those having intercourse in the last 3 months before the survey. 5. Periodic abstinence and natural family planning. 6. Withdrawal, douche, suppository and less frequently used methods.

★ 624 ★

Contraceptive Use in Developing Countries

Percentage of ever-married or currently married women (including consensual unions) who knew of any contraceptive method; percentage of currently married women (including consensual unions) who were currently using any method: developing countries, latest available year. (Estimates based on the most recent surveys available.).

Country	Year of survey	Age range	Knew of any method[1]	Were using a method[2]
Africa				
Eastern Africa				
Burundi	1987	15-49	78%	9%
Kenya	1984	15-49	84%	17%
Malawi	1984	15-49	4%[3]	7%[4]
Mauritius	1985	15-49	-	75%
Rwanda	1983	15-50	72%	10%
Zimbabwe	1984	15-49	90%	38%
Middle Africa				
Cameroon	1978	15-49	34%	2%

[Continued]

★ 624 ★

Contraceptive Use in Developing Countries
[Continued]

Country	Year of survey	Age range	Knew of any method[1]	Were using a method[2]
Northern Africa				
Egypt	1984	Under 50	85%	30%
Morocco	1987	15-49	98%	36%
Sudan (North)	1978-79	15-49	51%	5%
Tunisia	1983	15-49	97%	41%
Southern Africa				
Botswana	1984	15-49	80%	28%
Lesotho	1977	15-49	65%	5%
South Africa	1981-82	Under 50	-	48%
Western Africa				
Benin	1982	15-49	40%	9%
Cote D'Ivoire	1980-81	15-49	85%	3%
Ghana	1979	15-49	69%	10%
Liberia	1986	15-49	70%	6%
Mali	1987	15-49	43%	5%
Mauritania (sedentary population)	1981	15-49	8%	1%
Nigeria	1981-82	15-49	34%	5%
Senegal	1986	15-49	92%	12%
Sierra Leone	1969-70	15-49	78%[5]	--
Americas				
Caribbean				
Antigua	1981	15-44	93%[4]	39%
Barbados	1980-81	15-49	97%[4]	46%
Dominica	1981	15-44	90%[4]	49%
Dominican Republic	1986	15-49	99%	50%
Grenada	1985	15-44	92%[4]	31%
Guadeloupe	1976	15-49	-	44%
Haiti	1983	15-49	87%	7%[6]
Jamaica	1983	15-44	100%	52%
Martinique	1976	15-49	-	51%
Montserrat	1984	15-44	99%[4]	53%
Puerto Rico	1982	15-44	-	70%
St. Kitts and Nevis	1984	15-44	99%[4]	41%
St. Lucia	1981	15-44	92%[4]	43%
St. Vincent	1981	15-44	98%[4]	42%
Trinidad and Tobago	1987	15-49	99%	53%
Central America				
Costa Rica	1986	15-44	99%	70%
El Salvador	1985	15-49	93%	47%
Guatemala	1987	15-44	72%	23%
Honduras	1984	15-44	93%	35%
Mexico	1987	15-49	91%	53%

[Continued]

★ 624 ★

Contraceptive Use in Developing Countries
[Continued]

Country	Year of survey	Age range	Knew of any method[1]	Were using a method[2]
Nicaragua	1981	15-49	77%[4]	27%
Panama	1984	15-44	96%	58%[6]
Tropical South America				
Bolivia	1983	15-44	57%	26%
Brazil	1986	15-44	100%	66%
Colombia	1986	15-49	99%	65%
Ecuador	1987	15-49	90%[4]	44%
Guyana	1975	15-49	95%	31%
Paraguay	1987	15-44	96%[4]	45%
Peru	1986	15-49	89%	46%
Venezuela	1977	15-44	98%	49%
Asia and Oceania				
East Asia				
China	1985	15-49	-	74%
Hong Kong	1982	15-49	99%	72%
Republic of Korea	1985	15-44	100%	70%
South Asia				
Southeastern Asia				
Indonesia	1987	15-49	94%	48%
Malaysia (Peninsular)	1984	15-49	99%	51%
Philippines	1983	15-44[8]	94%	45%
Singapore	1982	15-44	100%	74%
Thailand	1987	15-49	100%	66%
Southern Asia				
Afghanistan	1972-73	15-44	4%	2%
Bangladesh	1985	Under 50	100%	25%
India	1980	15-49	95%[7]	34%
Nepal	1986	15-49	56%	14%
Pakistan	1984	15-49	61%	8%
Sri Lanka	1987	15-49	99%	62%
Western Asia				
Iraq	1974	15-49	-	14%
Jordan (Excl. West Bank)	1985	19-51[9]	97%	26%
Lebanon	1971	15-49	91%	53%
Syrian Arab Republic	1978	15-49	78%	20%
Turkey	1983	15-49	94%	51%
Yemen	1979	Under 50	25%	1%

[Continued]

★ 624 ★

Contraceptive Use in Developing Countries
[Continued]

Country	Year of survey	Age range	Knew of any method[1]	Were using a method[2]
Oceania Fiji	1974	15-49	100%	41%

Source: Selected from "Levels of knowledge, ever-use and current use of contraception in developing countries," *Levels and Trends of Contraceptive Use as Assessed in 1988,* p. 8-10 (New York: United Nations, 1989). Also in source: percent who knew of a source of family planning information or supplies; percent who had ever used contraception. Estimates are based on the most recent surveys available. Survey years range from 1970-1987. *Notes:* 1. Percentage of ever-married or currently married women (including consensual unions) who knew of any contraceptive method. 2. Percentage of currently married women (including consensual unions) who were currently using any contraceptive method. 3. Percentage who knew of the pill, the most widely known modern method; 14% knew of traditional medicine. 4. For all women of ages specified. 5. Currently married women and single women with children. 6. Excluding douche, abstinence and folk methods. 7. Percentage who knew of vasectomy, the most widely known method. 8. For 1978, ages 15-49. 9. Interviews in 1985 with husbands of women surveyed two years earlier, when they were aged 15-49.

★ 625 ★

Government Policies Regarding Contraception: 1976-1986
Number and percent of governments restricting access to modern methods of birth control; number and percent of governments providing direct, indirect, or no support to family planning.

Date of Assessment	Access to Modern Methods of Contraception				
	Total	Access Limited	Access Not Limited		
			No support provided	Indirect support	Direct support
Number of governments					
1976	158	15	28	18	97
1978	158	13	27	20	98
1980	165	11	27	22	105
1983	168	7	32	28	101
1986	170	6	18	24	122
Percentage of Governments					
1976	100%	9%	18%	11%	61%
1978	100%	8%	17%	13%	62%
1980	100%	7%	16%	13%	64%
1983	100%	4%	19%	17%	60%
1986	100%	4%	11%	14%	72%

Source: "Trends in government policies with respect to modern methods of fertility regulation, 1976-1986," *Levels and Trends of Contraceptive Use as Assessed in 1988,* p. 69 (New York: United Nations, 1989. Primary source: United Nations, 1979, table 20; 1982, table 42; 1985, table 101; and 1988, table 42.

★ 626 ★

Worldwide Contraceptive Prevalence

Trends in the percentage of women using contraception: developing and developed countries with two or more survey-based estimates.

Country or Area	Earlier Date		More Recent Date	
	Year	% currently using con-traception	Year	% currently using con-traception
Developing Countries				
Africa				
Eastern Africa				
Kenya	1977-78	7%	1984	17%
Mauritius	1975	46%	1985	75%
Northern Africa				
Egypt	1974-75	25%	1984	30%
Morocco	1980	20%	1985	36%
Tunisia	1978	31%	1983	41%
Western Africa				
Senegal	1978	4%	1986	11%
Americas				
Latin America				
Caribbean				
Dominican Republic	1975	32%	1986	50%
Haiti	1977	15%	1983	7%
Jamaica	1975-76	38%[1]	1983	51%[1]
Puerto Rico	1968	60%	1982	65%
Trinidad and Tobago	1977	52%	1987	53%
Central America				
Costa Rica	1976	70%[2]	1986	71%[2]
El Salvador	1975	22%	1985	48%
Guatemala	1978	19%	1987	23%
Honduras	1981	27%	1984	35%
Mexico	1976	30%	1987	53%
Panama	1976[1,2]	57%	1984	63%[1,2]
Tropical South America				
Colombia	1976	43%	1986	65%
Ecuador	1979	34%	1987	44%
Paraguay	1977	29%[1]	1987	38%[1]
Peru	1977	31%	1986	46%

[Continued]

★ 626 ★

Worldwide Contraceptive Prevalence
[Continued]

Country or Area	Earlier Date		More Recent Date	
	Year	% currently using con- traception	Year	% currently using con- traception
Asia				
East Asia				
China	1982	71%	1985	74%
Hong Kong	1972	50%	1982	72%
Republic of Korea	1975	37%	1985	70%
South Asia				
Southeastern Asia				
Indonesia	1976	18%	1987	48%
Malaysia (Peninsular)	1974-75	33%	1984	51%
Philippines	1978	38%	1986	46%
Singapore	1973	60%	1982	74%
Thailand	1978	54%	1987	68%
Southern Asia				
Bangladesh	1976	8%	1985	25%
India	1970	14%	1980	32%
Nepal	1976	2%	1986	14%
Pakistan	1975	5%	1984-85	8%
Sri Lanka	1975	34%	1987	62%
Western Asia				
Jordan	1972	22%	1983	26%[1]
Turkey	1973	38%	1983	53%
Developed Countries				
Americas				
Northern America				
United States	1973	70%	1982	68%
Asia				
Japan	1975	60%	1986	64%
Europe				
Eastern Europe				
Czechoslovakia	1970	66%	1977	95%
Hungary	1977	73%	1986	73%
Poland	1972	60%[3]	1977	75%[3]
Northern Europe				
Denmark	1970	67%[3]	1975	63%[3]
Finland	1971	77%	1977	80%
United Kingdom (Excl. N. Ireland)	1970	75%	1983	81%
Southern Europe				
Spain	1976	51%	1985	59%

[Continued]

★ 626 ★

Worldwide Contraceptive Prevalence
[Continued]

Country or Area	Earlier Date		More Recent Date	
	Year	% currently using con- traception	Year	% currently using con- traception
Yugoslavia	1970	59%[3]	1976	55%[3]
Western Europe				
Belgium (Flemish population)	1975-76	87%	1982/83	81%
France	1972	64%	1978	79%
Netherlands	1977	73%	1985	76%

Source: "Trends in the percentage of women using contraception: developing and developed countries with two or more survey-based estimates," *Levels and Trends of Contraceptive Use as Assessed in 1988,* Table 4, p. 18-19 (New York: United Nations, 1989). See also: *Sexuality: Contraception. Notes:* 1. Excluding use of douche, abstinence and folk methods. 2. Including sterilization for health reasons. 3. Excluding sterilization.

★ 627 ★

Worldwide Contraceptive Use by Method
Estimated number of users of specific contraceptive methods, in millions, for selected regions: 1987.

Method	World	More developed regions	Less developed regions	Africa	East Asia	South Asia	Latin America
	Number of users, in millions						
Female sterilization	113	13	99	1	56	30	13
Male sterilization	42	7	35	0	18	17	0.4
Pill	64	26	38	5	10	12	10
Injectables	7	0[1]	7	1	0[1]	5	1
IUD	82	11	71	2	59	7	3
Condom	42	25	17	0.5	5	10	1
Vaginal barrier methods	7	5	3	0.2	1	1	0.5
Rhythm	31	17	14	1	2	8	3
Withdrawal	36	26	10	1	1	7	2
Other	13	3	10	2	0.3	6	1
Total	437	133	304	14	151	103	36

Source: "Estimated number of users of specific contraceptive methods, for selected regions, 1987 (Millions)," *Levels and Trends of Contraceptive Use as Assessed in 1988,* Table 13, p. 62 (New York: United Nations, 1989). Also in source: number of users based on prevalence extrapolated to 1987. Based on prevalence from most recent surveys (applied to estimated number of married women in 1987). *Notes:* 1. Users of injectables in these regions were usually not shown separately for countries in these regions; combined with oral pill.

Deaths

★ 628 ★

Death Rates by Selected Causes: 1970-1987

Age-adjusted death rates per 100,000 resident population for selected causes of death, by race: 1970-1987.

Race and Cause of Death	Deaths per 100,000 resident population							Rank		
	1970	1980	1983	1984	1985	1986	1987	1985	1986	1987
All races										
All causes	714.3	585.8	550.5	545.9	546.1	541.7	535.5	1	1	1
Diseases of heart	253.6	202.0	188.8	183.6	180.5	175.0	169.6			
Ischemic heart disease	-	149.8	135.2	129.7	125.5	118.8	113.9			
Cerebrovascular diseases	66.3	40.8	34.4	33.4	32.3	31.0	30.3	3	3	3
Malignant neoplasms	129.8	132.8	132.6	133.5	133.6	133.2	132.9	2	2	2
Respiratory system	28.4	36.4	37.9	38.4	38.8	39.0	39.7			
Colorectal	16.8	15.5	14.9	15.0	14.8	14.4	14.3			
Prostate[1]	13.3	14.4	14.6	14.5	14.6	15.0	14.9			
Breast[2]	23.1	22.7	22.7	23.2	23.2	23.1	22.9			
Chronic obstructive pulmonary diseases	13.2	15.9	17.4	17.7	18.7	18.8	18.7	5	5	5
Pneumonia and influenza	22.1	12.9	11.8	12.2	13.4	13.5	13.1	6	6	6
Chronic liver disease and cirrhosis	14.7	12.2	10.2	10.0	9.6	9.2	9.1	9	9	9
Diabetes mellitus	14.1	10.1	9.9	9.5	9.6	9.6	9.8	7	7	7
Accidents and adverse effects	53.7	42.3	35.3	35.0	34.7	35.2	34.6	4	4	4
Motor vehicle accidents	27.4	22.9	18.5	19.1	18.8	19.4	19.5			
Suicide	11.8	11.4	11.4	11.6	11.5	11.9	11.7	8	8	8
Homicide and legal intervention	9.1	10.8	8.6	8.4	8.3	9.0	8.6	12	12	12
Human immunodeficiency virus infection	-	-	-	-	-	-	5.5	19	16	15
White Female										
All causes	501.7	411.1	392.7	391.3	390.6	387.7	384.1			
Diseases of heart	167.8	134.6	126.7	124.0	121.7	119.0	116.3	1	1	1
Ischemic heart disease	-	97.4	89.0	86.0	82.9	79.5	76.9			
Cerebrovascular diseases	56.2	35.2	29.6	28.9	27.9	27.1	26.3	3	3	3
Malignant neoplasms	107.6	107.7	108.5	109.9	110.3	110.1	109.7	2	2	2
Respiratory system	10.1	18.2	21.0	21.6	22.6	23.1	23.8			
Colorectal	15.3	13.3	12.5	12.8	12.3	12.0	11.8			
Breast	23.4	22.8	22.7	23.1	23.3	23.0	22.8			
Chronic obstructive pulmonary diseases	5.3	9.2	11.3	11.8	12.9	13.3	13.7	5	5	5
Pneumonia and influenza	15.0	9.4	8.6	8.8	9.8	9.9	9.7	4	4	4
Chronic liver disease and cirrhosis	8.7	7.0	6.0	5.9	5.6	5.4	5.1	10	11	11
Diabetes mellitus	12.8	8.7	8.6	8.0	8.1	8.1	8.1	7	7	7
Accidents and adverse effects	27.2	21.4	18.3	18.5	18.4	18.4	18.6	6	6	6
Motor vehicle accidents	14.4	12.3	10.3	10.9	10.8	11.0	11.4			
Suicide	7.2	5.7	5.6	5.6	5.3	5.4	5.3	12	12	12
Homicide and legal intervention	2.2	3.2	2.8	2.9	2.9	2.9	2.9	17	17	16
Human immunodeficiency virus infection	-	-	-	-	-	-	0.6			24

[Continued]

★ 628 ★

Death Rates by Selected Causes: 1970-1987
[Continued]

Race and Cause of Death	Deaths per 100,000 resident population							Rank		
	1970	1980	1983	1984	1985	1986	1987	1985	1986	1987
Black Female										
All causes	814.4	631.1	590.4	585.3	589.1	588.2	586.2			
Diseases of heart	251.7	201.1	191.5	186.6	186.8	185.1	180.8	1	1	1
Ischemic heart disease	-	116.1	106.8	102.6	100.8	97.0	93.6			
Cerebrovascular diseases	107.9	61.7	53.8	51.8	50.3	47.6	46.7	3	3	3
Malignant neoplasms	123.5	129.7	129.8	131.0	130.4	132.1	132.0	2	2	2
Respiratory system	10.9	19.5	22.0	21.4	22.5	23.3	24.3			
Colorectal	16.1	15.3	15.1	15.3	16.1	15.2	15.5			
Breast	21.5	23.3	24.4	26.1	25.3	25.8	26.5			
Chronic obstructive pulmonary diseases	-	6.3	7.6	8.1	8.7	8.9	9.5	11	11	11
Pneumonia and influenza	29.2	12.7	10.2	11.3	12.4	13.1	12.2	7	6	6
Chronic liver disease and cirrhosis	17.8	14.4	10.8	10.3	10.1	9.3	9.1	12	12	12
Diabetes mellitus	30.9	22.1	21.1	20.5	21.1	21.4	21.3	4	4	4
Accidents and adverse effects	35.3	25.1	21.9	20.1	20.7	21.0	21.0	5	5	5
Motor vehicle accidents	13.8	8.4	7.5	7.6	8.2	8.5	8.7			
Suicide	2.9	2.4	2.1	2.3	2.1	2.4	2.1	19	19	19
Homicide and legal intervention	15.0	13.7	11.2	11.0	10.8	11.8	12.3	9	9	10
Human immunodeficiency virus infection	-	-	-	-	-	-	4.7			16

Source: Selected from "Age-adjusted death rates for selected causes of death, according to sex and race: United States, selected years 1950-87," *Health United States, 1989*, Table 24, p. 121-124 (Hyattsville: National Center for Health Statistics, 1990. Primary source: Unpublished data from the Division of Vital Statistics; *Vital Statistics of the United States*, Vol. II, Mortality, Part A, for data years 1950-87. Public Health Service. Washington. U.S. Government Printing Office; Data computed by the Division of Analysis from data complied by the Division of Vital Statistics and from table 1 (source). Also in source: data for 1950 and 1960; data broken down for white and black males. Data are based on the National Vital Statistics System. *Notes:* 1. Male only. 2. Female only.

★ 629 ★

Death Rates: 1970-1988

Death rates per 1,000 population by sex and race: 1970-1988.

Sex and Race	1970	1975	1980	1981	1982	1983	1984	1985	1986	1987	1988|2|[1]
Female	8.1	7.6	7.9	7.8	7.7	7.9	7.9	8.1	8.1	8.1	8.3
Male	10.9	10.0	9.8	9.5	9.4	9.4	9.4	9.5	9.4	9.3	9.4
White	9.5	8.9	8.9	8.8	8.7	8.8	8.9	9.0	9.0	9.0	9.1
Female	8.1	7.8	8.1	8.0	8.0	8.2	8.2	8.4	8.4	8.5	8.6
Male	10.9	10.0	9.8	9.7	9.5	9.6	9.5	9.6	9.5	9.5	9.6
Black	10.0	8.8	8.8	8.4	8.2	8.3	8.3	8.5	8.5	8.6	8.5
Female	8.3	7.3	7.3	7.1	6.9	7.1	7.1	7.3	7.3	7.4	7.3
Male	11.9	10.6	10.3	9.9	9.6	9.6	9.6	9.8	9.9	9.9	9.9

Source: Selected from "Deaths and death rates, by sex and race: 1960 to 1988," *Statistical Abstract of the United States, 1990*, p. 75. Primary source: U.S. National Center for Health Statistics, *Vital Statistics of the United States*, annual; and unpublished data. Also in source: deaths (see separate table); age-adjusted death rates; data for 1960. *Notes:* 1. Preliminary. Includes deaths of nonresidents of the U.S. 2. Based on a 10% sample of deaths.

★ 630 ★

Deaths Due to HIV Infection

Deaths and death rates per 100,000 population, due to human immunodeficiency virus infection, by race and age: 1988 and 1989.

	All races[1]				White				Black			
	1989		1988		1989		1988		1989		1988	
	Number	Rate	Number	Rate	Number	Rate	Number	Rate	Number	Rate	Number	Rate
Total	21,360	8.6	16,210	6.6	14,730	7.0	10,720	5.2	6,470	21.1	5,300	17.5
Female	2,300	1.8	1,910	1.5	970	0.9	880	0.8	1,330	8.3	1,010	6.4
Under 15 years	140	0.5	160	0.6	70	0.3	70	0.3	70	1.7	90	2.2
15-24 years	80	0.4	110	0.6	50	0.3	60	0.4	30	1.1	50	1.8
25-34 years	910	4.2	720	3.3	360	2.0	280	1.5	550	18.7	440	15.1
35-44 years	760	4.1	600	3.4	270	1.7	250	1.7	490	22.6	350	16.9
45-54 years	210	1.6	150	1.2	80	0.7	80	0.8	130	9.0	70	5.0
55 years and over	180	0.6	160	0.5	140	0.5	140	0.5	40	1.5	10	0.4
Male	19,060	15.8	14,300	11.9	13,750	13.5	9,840	9.7	5,140	35.3	4,290	29.9
Under 15 years	110	0.4	200	0.7	70	0.3	120	0.5	40	1.9	80	1.9
15-24 years	420	2.3	570	3.0	270	1.8	370	2.4	150	5.6	180	6.6
25-34 years	6,490	29.6	4,980	22.8	4,450	24.0	3,190	17.3	1,990	75.6	1,720	66.2
35-44 years	7,860	43.6	5,490	31.6	5,790	37.2	3,850	25.6	1,990	109.5	1,600	92.2
45-54 years	2,780	23.0	2,110	18.0	2,090	19.8	1,580	15.4	670	57.3	510	44.5
55 years and over	1,390	6.1	930	4.1	1,070	5.3	730	3.6	300	15.0	190	9.6

Source: Selected from "Estimated deaths and death rates for Human immunodeficiency virus infection by age, race, and sex and age-adjusted rates by race and sex: United States, 1988 and 1989," *Monthly Vital Statistics Report,* Vol. 38, No. 13, August 30, 1990. Data are provisional, estimated from a 10% sample of deaths. Figures may differ from those previously published. Due to rounding of estimates, figures may not add to totals. *Notes:* 1. Includes races other than white and black. 2. Figures for age not stated are included in "All Ages."

★ 631 ★

Deaths and Death Rates

Total deaths and rate per 100,000 population, by age and race: 1989.

	All races			White			Black		
	Total	Female	Male	Total	Female	Male	Total	Female	Male
All ages	2,155,000	1,039,530	1,115,410	1,866,700	911,300	955,400	260,030	116,830	143,200
Under 1 year	38,900	17,150	21,750	25,910	11,140	14,770	11,760	5,500	6,260
1-4 years	6,480	2,950	3,530	4,640	2,080	2,560	1,580	730	850
5-14 years	9,350	3,530	5,820	6,900	2,510	4,390	2,110	870	1,240
15-24 years	37,790	9,730	28,060	28,460	7,530	20,930	8,120	1,820	6,300
25-34 years	61,240	16,620	44,620	43,690	11,570	32,120	15,960	4,570	11,390
35-44 years	80,670	26,280	54,390	59,590	19,040	40,550	19,350	6,610	12,740
45-54 years	119,280	43,200	76,080	93,170	33,690	59,480	23,670	8,590	15,080
55-59 years	102,830	39,000	63,830	83,900	31,450	52,450	17,030	6,750	10,280
60-64 years	158,430	62,140	96,290	133,830	51,830	82,000	22,230	9,390	12,840
65-69 years	217,050	88,060	128,990	186,700	75,070	111,630	27,950	12,130	15,820
70-74 years	260,810	113,390	147,420	230,720	99,620	131,100	27,310	12,600	14,710
75-79 years	302,000	145,680	156,320	269,770	129,920	139,850	28,910	14,450	14,460
80-84 years	300,000	162,880	137,120	274,290	149,150	125,140	22,810	12,520	10,290
85 years and over	458,830	308,420	150,410	424,160	286,340	137,820	30,940	20,170	10,770

[Continued]

★ 631 ★

Deaths and Death Rates
[Continued]

	All races			White			Black		
	Total	Female	Male	Total	Female	Male	Total	Female	Male
Rate per 100,000 population									
All ages[1]	868.1	816.9	922.0	893.3	853.8	934.6	848.1	725.0	984.5
Under 1 year[2]	986.0	890.9	1,076.7	819.2	722.9	910.0	1,899.8	1,803.3	1,993.6
1-4 years	43.8	40.8	46.6	39.0	35.9	42.0	69.6	65.4	73.6
5-14 years	26.6	20.6	32.3	24.5	18.3	30.3	38.5	32.3	44.5
15-24 years	103.5	53.9	152.0	95.8	51.4	139.0	150.1	66.5	235.7
25-34 years	139.7	75.9	203.3	119.1	63.8	173.4	286.5	155.4	432.9
35-44 years	221.0	142.2	301.7	191.1	122.0	260.4	485.4	304.6	701.2
45-54 years	479.1	337.9	628.2	434.1	308.7	563.8	904.1	593.2	1,288.9
55-59 years	958.7	695.8	1,246.4	901.2	651.1	1,170.8	1,526.0	1,110.2	2,023.6
60-64 years	1,457.9	1,073.6	1,895.8	1,398.6	1,022.1	1,823.0	2,147.8	1,656.1	2,749.5
65-69 years	2,134.2	1,590.1	2,785.4	2,067.8	1,532.4	2,702.9	3,051.3	2,355.3	3,935.3
70-74 years	3,255.2	2,492.6	4,255.8	3,207.6	2,445.3	4,201.9	4,131.6	3,264.2	5,368.6
75-79 years	5,005.8	3,993.4	6,554.3	4,968.1	3,958.6	6,513.7	5,948.6	4,832.8	7,732.6
80-84 years	8,047.2	6,725.0	10,499.2	8,046.1	6,718.5	10,524.8	8,910.2	7,587.9	11,307.7
85 years and over	15,083.2	14,070.3	17,695.3	15,362.5	14,317.0	18,110.4	13,110.2	12,224.2	14,958.3

Source: Selected from "Estimated deaths and death rates, by age, race, and sex: United States: 1989, *Monthly Vital Statistics Report* 38:13, August 30, 1990. Data are provisional, estimated from a 10% sample of deaths. *Notes:* 1. Figures for age not stated are included in "All ages" but are not distributed among age groups. 2. Death rates under 1 year (based on population estimates) differ from infant mortality rates (based on live births).

★ 632 ★

Deaths of Young Adults Worldwide
Total and female deaths, ages 15 to 24 years, circa 1986.

Country	Year	Total youth deaths	
		Both sexes	Female
Australia	1986	2,398	626
Canada	1986	3,422	845
Germany, Federal Republic	1987	6,163	1,636
France	1986	7,212	1,907
Hungary	1987	1,095	294
Italy	1987	5,730	1,405
Israel	1986	388	120
Japan	1987	8,699	2,363
Mexico	1983	22,070	6,419
Norway	1986	496	103
Sweden	1986	648	163

[Continued]

★ 632 ★

Deaths of Young Adults Worldwide
[Continued]

| Country | Year | Total youth deaths | |
		Both sexes	Female
United Kingdom	1987	5,084	1,347
United States	1986	39,929	10,095

Source: Selected from "Violent Deaths to Youth Ages 15 to 24 Years, by Cause and Sex, Selected Countries: Circa 1986," *Children's Well-Being: An International Comparison*, A Report of the Select Committee on Children, Youth, and Families, 101st Cong., 2d sess., March 1990, p. 111. Primary source: World Health Organization, 1988, 1988 *World Health Statistics Annual*, Geneva, table 10. Also in source: violent deaths by cause (see separate tables).

★ 633 ★

Deaths of Young Adults-Motoring Accidents-Worldwide
Total and female motor-vehicle-accident deaths, ages 15-24 years, circa 1986.

Country	Year	Both sexes	Female
Australia	1986	1,040	249
Canada	1986	1,283	290
Germany, Federal Republic	1987	2,495	536
France	1986	2,914	660
Hungary	1987	279	42
Italy	1987	2,234	397
Israel	1986	100	24
Japan	1987	3,258	432
Mexico	1983	3,003	520
Norway	1986	170	37
Sweden	1986	219	39
United Kingdom	1987	1,641	303
United States	1986	15,038	3,738

Source: Selected from "Violent Deaths to Youth Ages 15 to 24 Years, by Cause and Sex, Selected Countries: Circa 1986," *Children's Well-Being: An International Comparison*, A Report of the Select Committee on Children, Youth, and Families, 101st Cong., 2d sess., March 1990, p. 111. Primary source: World Health Organization, 1988, 1988 *World Health Statistics Annual*, Geneva, table 10. Also in source: total and violent deaths by cause (see separate tables).

★ 634 ★

Deaths: 1970-1988

Deaths, in thousands, 1970-1988.

Sex and Race	1970	1975	1980	1981	1982	1983	1984	1985	1986	1987	1988[1]
Deaths	1,921	1,893	1,990	1,978	1,975	2,019	2,039	2,086	2,105	2,123	2,171
Females	843	842	915	914	918	947	963	989	1,001	1,015	1,040
Males	1,078	1,051	1,075	1,064	1,056	1,072	1,077	1,098	1,104	1,108	1,131
White	1,682	1,660	1,739	1,731	1,729	1,766	1,782	1,819	1,831	1,843	1,887
Females	740	743	805	806	810	834	847	869	879	890	913
Males	942	918	934	925	919	932	935	950	953	953	974
Black	226	218	233	229	227	233	236	244	250	255	258
Females	98	94	103	101	101	105	107	111	113	115	116
Males	128	124	130	127	126	128	129	134	137	140	142

Source: Selected from "Deaths and death rates, by sex and race: 1960 to 1988," *Statistical Abstract of the United States, 1990,* p. 75. Primary source: U.S. National Center for Health Statistics, *Vital Statistics of the United States,* annual; and unpublished data. Also in source: data by other characteristics; death rates (see separate table); data for 1960. *Notes:* 1. Preliminary. Includes deaths of nonresidents of the U.S. Based on a 10% sample of deaths.

★ 635 ★

Homicide Deaths of Young Adults Worldwide

Total and female homicide deaths, ages 15-24, circa 1986.

Country	Year	Both sexes	female
Australia	1986	61	28
Canada	1986	99	37
Germany, Federal Republic	1987	119	70
France	1986	91	32
Hungary	1987	17	6
Italy	1987	166	30
Israel	1986	18	4
Japan	1987	85	38
Mexico	1983	3,171	251
Norway	1986	13	2
Sweden	1986	19	5
United Kingdom	1987	119	29
United States	1986	5,452	1,181

Source: Selected from "Violent Deaths to Youth Ages 15 to 24 Years, by Cause and Sex, Selected Countries: Circa 1986," *Children's Well-Being: An International Comparison,* A Report of the Select Committee on Children, Youth, and Families, 101st Cong., 2d sess., March 1990, p. 111. Primary source: World Health Organization, 1988, 1988 *World Health Statistics Annual,* Geneva, table 10. Also in source: total and violent deaths by cause (see separate tables).

★ 636 ★

Suicide Among Young Adults Worldwide

Total and female suicides, ages 15-24 years, circa 1986.

Country	Year	Both sexes	Female
Australia	1986	361	71
Canada	1986	679	109
Germany, Federal Republic	1987	1,074	211
France	1986	888	193
Hungary	1987	242	69
Italy	1987	309	60
Israel	1986	41	16
Japan	1987	1,634	569
Mexico	1983	335	80
Norway	1986	81	12
Sweden	1986	162	45
United Kingdom	1987	566	105
United States	1986	5,120	844

Source: Selected from "Violent Deaths to Youth Ages 15 to 24 Years, by Cause and Sex, Selected Countries: Circa 1986," *Children's Well-Being: An International Comparison,* A Report of the Select Committee on Children, Youth, and Families, 101st Cong., 2d sess., March 1990, p. 111. Primary source: World Health Organization, 1988, 1988 *World Health Statistics Annual,* Geneva, table 10. Also in source: violent deaths by cause (see separate tables).

★ 637 ★

Violent Deaths of Young Adults Worldwide

Total and female violent deaths, circa 1986.

Country	Year	Total violent deaths	
		Both sexes	Female
Australia	1986	1,769	391
Canada	1986	2,609	527
Germany, Federal Republic	1987	4,233	922
France	1986	5,046	1,112
Hungary	1987	718	144
Italy	1987	3,613	642
Israel	1986	223	57
Japan	1987	5,785	1,186
Mexico	1983	13,103	1,790
Norway	1986	357	63
Sweden	1986	491	109

[Continued]

★ 637 ★

Violent Deaths of Young Adults Worldwide
[Continued]

| Country | Year | Total violent deaths | |
		Both sexes	Female
United Kingdom	1987	3,166	601
United States	1986	31,082	6,640

Source: Selected from "Violent Deaths to Youth Ages 15 to 24 Years, by Cause and Sex, Selected Countries: Circa 1986," *Children's Well-Being: An International Comparison,* A Report of the Select Committee on Children, Youth, and Families, 101st Cong., 2d sess., March 1990, p. 111. Primary source: World Health Organization, 1988, 1988 *World Health Statistics Annual,* Geneva, table 10. Also in source: total and violent deaths by cause (see separate tables). Total violent deaths include accidents of all types, suicide, homicide, and deaths classified as other violent deaths.

★ 638 ★

Worldwide Deaths

Deaths by sex by country, latest available year.

Country or area, year	Female	Male
Africa		
Algeria-1982	101,065	107,962
Cape Verde-1985	1,350	1,385
Egypt-1981	204,767	227,497
Libyan Arab Jamahiriya-1981	6,982	8,961
Malawi-1977	65,818	72,876
Mali-1976	54,514	60,016
Mauritius-1987	2,820	3,761
Rodrigues-1987	89	83
Reunion-1987	1,243	1,831
St. Helena-1986	23	30
Sao Tome and Principe-1979	409	450
Seychelles-1987	226	279
Tunisia-1980	15,453	20,992
Zimbabwe-1982	7,429	12,613
Europeans	922	1,327
North America		
Antigua and Barbuda-1986	195	189
Bahamas-1986	569	838
Barbados-1986	1,108	1,052
Belize-1983	325	394
Bermuda-1986	170	245
British Virgin Islands-1986	31	51
Canada-1987	83,701	101,252

[Continued]

★ 638 ★

Worldwide Deaths
[Continued]

Country or area, year	Female	Male
Cayman Islands-1987	53	53
Costa Rica-1984	4,324	5,607
Cuba-1986	27,387	35,758
Dominica-1982	193	213
Dominican Republic-1985	12,596	15,248
El Salvador-1985	11,246	15,979
Greenland-1987	164	281
Grenada-1978	400	365
Guadeloupe-1986	1,020	1,218
Guatemala-1985	31,560	37,895
Honduras-1983	8,427	10,877
Jamaica-1982	5,444	5,417
Martinique-1986	973	1,131
Mexico-1985	178,699	232,238
Montserrat-1986	58	65
Netherlands Antilles-1981	449	444
Panama-1986	3,753	5,189
Puerto Rico-1985	9,747	13,446
St. Kitts and Nevis-1986	222	239
St. Lucia-1986	411	432
St. Vincent and the Grenadines-1986	327	328
Trinidad and Tobago-1984	3,498	4,321
Turks and Caicos Islands-1979	23	11
United States-1986	1,001,356	1,104,005
South America		
Argentina-1983	109,279	141,565
Bolivia-1977	16,835	18,548
Brazil-1986	339,343	495,584
Chile-1987	32,473	38,086
Colombia-1986	60,812	85,534
Ecuador-1987	23,332	28,235
Falkland Islands (Malvinas)-1983	5	13
French Guiana-1985	204	280
Guyana-1987	2,800	3,451
Paraguay-1986	5,345	6,174
Peru-1983	44,614	48,676
Suriname-1981	1,174	1,171
Uruguay-1986	13,132	15,639
Venezuela-1986	33,633	44,014

[Continued]

★ 638 ★

Worldwide Deaths
[Continued]

Country or area, year	Female	Male
Asia		
Afghanistan-1979	142,420	148,554
Bahrain-1986	588	835
Bangladesh-1982	539,210	572,569
Brunei Darussalam-1986	290	433
Cyprus-1987	2,442	2,470
Hong Kong-1987	11,915	14,998
Iran (Islamic Rep.)-1986	58,042	132,019
Iraq-1977	21,943	28,615
Israel-1985	13,179	14,914
Japan-1987	343,078	408,094
Jordan-1980	2,377	3,941
Korea, Rep. of-1986	97,692	137,730
Kuwait-1986	1,659	2,731
Macau-1987	634	687
Malaysia-1987	28,487	36,795
Sabah-1986	1,936	3,178
Malaysia-1986	2,016	3,168
Maldives-1987	689	836
Pakistan-1985	381,113	458,134
Philippines-1987	137,979	197,275
Qatar-1987	263	525
Singapore-1987	5,760	7,410
Sri Lanka-1983	38,806	56,368
Syrian Arab Republic-1984	14,855	17,224
Thailand-1987	99,789	133,179
Europe		
Albania-1987	7,547	9,572
Austria-1987	45,705	39,202
Belgium-1984	53,766	57,307
Bulgaria-1986	46,518	57,521
Channel Islands-		
Guernsey-1986	315	299
Jersey-1987	418	427
Czechoslovakia-1987	86,269	92,773
Denmark-1987	27,914	30,222
Faeroe Islands-1987	140	227

[Continued]

★ 638 ★

Worldwide Deaths
[Continued]

Country or area, year	Female	Male
Finland-1986	23,155	23,980
France-1987	252,106	275,360
German Democratic Rep.-1987	119,789	94,083
Germany, Fed. Rep.-1987	362,790	324,629
Gibraltar-1984	126	126
Greece-1985	44,434	48,452
Hungary-1987	67,684	74,917
Iceland-1984	731	853
Ireland-1985	15,012	18,201
Isle of Man-1987	457	468
Italy-1984	248,869	277,696
Liechtenstein-1986	86	102
Luxembourg-1987	1,965	2,047
Malta-1987	1,410	1,498
Monaco-1983	203	245
Netherlands-1986	58,654	66,653
Norway-1987	20,951	24,008
Poland-1987	177,630	200,735
Portugal-1987	45,595	49,828
Romania-1985	116,492	130,178
San Marino-1987	57	97
Spain-1983	144,194	158,375
Sweden-1987	43,969	49,338
Switzerland-1987	28,771	30,740
United Kingdom-1987	326,060	318,282
England and Wales-1985	298,407	292,327
Northern Ireland-1985	7,867	8,088
Scotland-1985	32,820	31,147
Yugoslavia-1987	101,707	112,959
Oceania		
American Samoa-1982	50	99
Australia-1986	52,771	62,210
Cocos (Keeling) Islands-1985	-	1
Cook Islands-1984	50	52
Fiji-1985	1,476	2,204
Guam-1986	165	286
Nauru-1978	12	46
New Caledonia-1982	376	538
New Zealand-1987	12,952	14,467

[Continued]

★ 638 ★

Worldwide Deaths
[Continued]

Country or area, year	Female	Male
Niue-1975	9	15
Norfolk Island-1988	3	6
Pacific islands-1979	258	357
Northern Mariana Islands-1985	39	56
Samoa-1980	189	286
Tokelau-1982	11	5

Source: Selected from "Deaths by Age, Sex and Urban/Rural Residence: Latest Available Year," *1988 Demographic Yearbook*, p. 434-455 (New York: United Nations, 1990).

★ 639 ★

Worldwide Suicide Ratios, Selected Countries

Comparative suicide ratios and percent change since 1970, selected countries: 1979-1981.

Country	Female/Male Suicide Ratio	Percent change since 1970	
		Female	Male
Argentina	3/2	-10.4%	-36.6%
Australia	8/2	-28.0%	-2.9%
Austria	6/2	+3.5%	+16.8%
Barbados	2/5	-37.5%	-18.7%
Belgium	9/1	+48.5%	+30.6%
Bulgaria	3/2	+9.2%	+19.8%
Canada	1/3	+9.5%	+30.7%
Chile	2/5	-28.0%	-7.0%
Costa Rica	1/4	+183.3%	+48.9%
Czechoslovakia	1/3	-23.8%	-15.8%
Denmark	8/1	+29.4%	+30.9%
Ecuador	7/1	+90.9%	+2.9%
El Salvador	2/3	+142.1%	+10.5%
Finland	0/4	+5.3%	+13.5%
France	6/2	+28.2%	+21.8%
West Germany	0/2	-3.4%	+4.3%
Greece	2/2	0.0	-6.4%
Guatemala	0/9	-85.7%	-66.0%
Hong Kong	2/1	+18.1%	+15.4%
Hungary	3/2	+37.2%	+26.8%
Iceland	8/2	+32.5%	+45.0%
Ireland	4/2	+270.0%	+171.9%
Israel	9/1	-26.8%	+4.0%
Italy	3/2	+22.9%	+23.7%

[Continued]

★ 639 ★

Worldwide Suicide Ratios, Selected Countries

[Continued]

Country	Female/Male Suicide Ratio	Percent change since 1970	
		Female	Male
Japan	7/1	-0.8%	+29.8%
Luxembourg	3/2	+40.8%	+5.9%
Mauritius	8/2	+110.0%	+61.1%
Mexico	7/3	+133.3%	+85.7%
Netherlands	5/1	+30.6%	+28.1%
New Zealand	5/2	-10.6%	+20.8%
Norway	7/2	+63.4%	+46.8%
Panama	5/5	-25.0%	-31.2%
Paraguay	2/1	+71.4%	+76.5%
Poland	4/5	-2.4%	+14.7%
Portugal	8/2	+32.4%	-3.1%
Puerto Rico	4/5	-44.9%	-2.7%
Singapore	2/1	+11.2%	-4.4%
Spain	1/3	0.0	-1.5%
Sri Lanka	9/1	+80.7%	+50.2%
Sweden	3/2	-8.7%	-11.6%
Switzerland	3/2	+44.2%	+32.7%
Thailand	1/1	+109.1%	+68.2%
United Kingdom			
England and Wales	7/1	-2.9%	+11.1%
Northern Ireland	3/2	-11.4%	+29.1%
Scotland	8/1	+24.6%	+41.1%
United States	3/3	-12.3%	+12.7%
Venezuela	0/4	-53.7%	-20.0%
Yugoslavia	4/2	+15.8%	+3.4%

Source: "Suicide Rates for Males and Females for Nations of the World for 1979-1981," *Why Women Kill Themselves,* Table 1, p. 17 (Springfield: Charles C. Thomas, 1988). Primary source: calculated by the author from WHO publications. Also in source: male/female suicide rates; rates for other countries with data missing for 1970; and data from other sources.

Estimates and Projections of Population

★ 640 ★

Children, Worldwide: 1990-2010

Number of children ages 0 to 14 per 100 persons ages 15 to 64 years, selected countries, 1990, 2000, and 2010.

Region and country	1990	2000	2010
World	52.8	50.3	44.5
Africa	85.4	82.8	75.6
Asia	53.2	49.7	41.8
Europe	29.4	28.3	26.3
Latin America	60.5	50.9	43.3
North America	32.6	30.2	26.7
Oceania	41.0	39.0	35.6
Soviet Union	40.4	37.5	34.9
Australia	33.5	32.2	29.5
Canada	30.9	27.9	24.3
China	40.1	40.4	30.3
Germany, Federal Republic	21.5	24.4	23.1
France	30.3	28.8	25.5
Hungary	30.2	28.1	29.1
India	60.2	52.0	43.0
Israel	51.9	45.9	42.2
Italy	24.7	25.5	25.1
Japan	26.6	26.1	28.5
Mexico	66.8	57.9	48.9
Norway	28.5	27.6	25.0
Sweden	26.7	26.3	24.7
United Kingdom	28.7	28.7	24.7
United States	32.8	30.5	27.0

Source: "Child Dependency Ratio, by Region and Selected Countries: 1990, 2000, and 2010," *Children's Well-Being: An International Comparison*, A Report of the Select Committee on Children, Youth, and Families, 101st Cong., 2d sess., March 1990, p. 100. Primary source: U.S. Bureau of the Census, Center for International Research, International Data Base. Child dependency ratio is defined as the number of persons ages 0 to 14 years per 100 persons ages 15 to 64 years.

★ 641 ★

Elderly Females: 1985-2020

Female proportion of elderly population, 1985-2020.

Age	1985	2000	2020
Total 65+	60.1%	60.1%	57.6%
65-74 years	56.5%	55.1%	53.3%
75-84 yers	63.0%	61.9%	60.0%
85+	72.0%	73.3%	72.0%

Source: Personnel for Health Needs of the Elderly Through Year 2020, September 1987 Report to Congress, U.S. Department of Health and Human Services. Primary source: Social Security Administration, 1985.

★ 642 ★

Female Population 18 To 34 Years Old: 1960 to 2080

Women 18 to 34 years old, in thousands, by race: 1960 to 2080.

Year	Total	White	Black	Other races
Estimates				
1960	19,625	17,179	2,233	213
1965	21,415	18,709	2,438	269
1970	25,048	21,745	2,922	382
1975	29,704	25,501	3,607	596
1980	33,905	28,642	4,359	905
1985	35,284	29,357	4,791	1,136
1987	35,191	29,134	4,848	1,211
Projections				
1990	34,772	28,569	4,908	1,296
1995	32,375	26,189	4,759	1,426
2000	30,948	24,634	4,713	1,601
2005	31,195	24,530	4,851	1,816
2010	32,096	25,073	5,053	1,969
2020	31,799	24,417	5,181	2,200
2030	30,624	22,964	5,169	2,491
2040	31,031	22,994	5,275	2,760
2050	30,403	22,237	5,217	2,948
2080	28,783	20,579	4,841	3,363

Source: "Projections of the Population of the United States by Age, Sex, and Race: 1988 to 2080," *Current Population Reports,* Series P-25, No. 1018, p. 12. Primary source: *Current Population Reports,* Series P-25, Nos. 519,917, 1022; table 4; and unpublished data. Projection data from middle series. As of July 1. Includes Armed Forces oversease.

★ 643 ★

Population by Age Group and Region

Percent distribution of the U.S. population by age group and region.

Region	Age Groups								
	0-6	6-11	12-17	18-24	25-34	35-44	45-54	55-64	65+
New England									
Female	3.7%	3.9%	4.1%	5.4%	8.7%	7.4%	5.3%	5.0%	8.7%
Male	3.9%	4.1%	4.3%	5.4%	8.6%	7.2%	5.0%	4.4%	5.1%
Middle Atlantic									
Female	3.9%	3.9%	4.0%	5.0%	8.4%	7.7%	5.7%	5.3%	8.5%
Male	4.0%	4.0%	4.2%	5.0%	8.2%	7.2%	5.2%	4.5%	5.2%
East N. Central									
Female	4.5%	4.3%	4.1%	5.4%	8.6%	7.4%	5.2%	4.6%	7.4%
Male	4.7%	4.4%	4.3%	5.5%	8.7%	7.2%	4.9%	4.1%	4.7%
West N. Central									
Female	4.5%	4.1%	4.0%	5.4%	8.3%	7.1%	4.9%	4.5%	8.6%
Male	4.7%	4.2%	4.2%	5.6%	8.6%	7.0%	4.7%	4.0%	5.5%
South Atlantic									
Female	4.1%	4.1%	4.0%	5.2%	8.7%	7.7%	5.2%	4.9%	7.9%
Male	4.2%	4.2%	4.1%	5.5%	8.6%	7.4%	4.8%	4.1%	5.3%
East S. Central									
Female	4.6%	4.4%	4.2%	5.3%	8.4%	7.5%	5.1%	4.5%	7.6%
Male	4.8%	4.6%	4.4%	5.5%	8.4%	7.1%	4.7%	3.9%	4.9%
West S. Central									
Female	4.9%	4.5%	4.1%	5.4%	8.8%	7.4%	4.9%	4.1%	6.9%
Male	5.1%	4.7%	4.3%	5.8%	9.0%	7.2%	4.7%	3.7%	4.5%
Mountain									
Female	5.2%	4.4%	4.0%	5.5%	9.1%	7.4%	4.6%	4.0%	6.0%
Male	5.4%	4.6%	4.2%	5.8%	9.6%	7.5%	4.6%	3.7%	4.4%
Pacific									
Female	4.4%	3.9%	3.7%	5.3%	9.4%	7.7%	5.0%	4.4%	6.8%
Male	4.6%	4.1%	3.9%	5.8%	9.8%	7.8%	4.8%	4.0%	4.5%
U.S. Total									
Female	4.4%	4.1%	4.0%	5.3%	8.7%	7.5%	5.5%	4.7%	7.6%
Male	4.6%	4.3%	4.2%	5.5%	8.8%	7.3%	4.8%	4.1%	4.9%

Source: Melissa Campanelli, "Where the Boys Aren't (Demographics in Action)," *Sales & Marketing Management*, May 1990, p. 32. Primary source: Sales & Marketing Management 1989 *Survey of Buying Power Data Service.* Also in source: a discussion of the significance of this type of data to marketing personnel and others. Assumes a total population of 247.9 million; 127.5 million females and 120.4 million males.

★ 644 ★

Projections of U.S. Population by Race, 1989-2010

Population in thousands by race and sex, projections 1989-2010.

	1989	1990	1995	2000	2005	2010
Total	248,251	250,410	260,138	268,266	275,604	282,575
Female	127,092	128,167	133,016	137,076	140,746	144,241
Total White	209,178	210,616	216,820	221,514	225,424	228,978
Female	106,730	107,432	110,455	112,739	114,639	116,368
Total Black	30,719	31,148	33,199	35,129	37,003	38,833
Female	16,094	16,313	17,359	18,342	19,296	20,231
Total Other Races	8,354	8,645	10,119	11,624	13,177	14,764
Female	4,267	4,422	5,202	5,995	6,811	7,642

Source: "Projections of the Total Population by Age, Sex, and Race: 1989 to 2010," *Statistical Abstract*, 1990, p. 16. Primary source: U.S. Bureau of the Census, *Current Population Reports*, series P-25, No. 1018. As of July 1. Includes Armed Forces overseas. Also in source: Projections by age, sex, and race.

★ 645 ★

Worldwide Population Estimates and Projections

Population in thousands for the world and by level of development, estimates 1970 and 1980, and medium-variant fertility projections for 1990-2020.

	1970	1980	1990	2000	2010	2020
World total	3,697,918	4,450,210	5,292,178	6,251,055	7,190,762	8,062,274
Female	1,845,159	2,213,510	2,628,249	3,101,566	3,568,794	4,007,611
More developed regions	1,049,273	1,136,406	1,205,193	1,262,482	1,307,469	1,340,063
Female	543,553	587,178	620,454	646,792	667,247	682,697
Less developed regions	2,648,644	3,313,804	4,086,985	4,988,573	5,883,293	6,722,211
Female	1,301,606	1,626,332	2,007,795	2,454,774	2,901,547	3,324,915
Least developed countries	254,734	328,738	424,643	565,037	728,810	896,330
Female	126,790	163,819	211,590	281,160	362,321	445,508

Source: Selected from "Population by Sex and Age for the World, Major Areas and Regions, 1950-2025, Estimates and Medium-, High-, and Low-Variant Projections," *Global Estimates and Projections of Population by Sex and Age: The 1988 Revision*, pp. 4-8,62 (New York: United Nations, 1989). Also in source: estimates and projections by sex and age and high-and low-variant fertility levels.

★ 646 ★

Worldwide Population Estimates and Projections by Country

Population in thousands by country, 1970-1980 estimates, and medium-variant fertility projections for 1990-2020.

Country or Area	1970	1980	1990	2000	2010	2020
Afghanistan	13,623	16,063	16,557	26,608	32,765	38,440
Female	6,627	7,819	8,042	12,995	16,003	18,779
Albania	2,138	2,671	3,245	3,795	4,316	4,792
Female	1,058	1,293	1,575	1,848	2,108	2,349
Algeria	13,746	18,666	25,364	33,247	40,685	47,502
Female	7025	9,402	12,678	16,548	20,217	23,592
Angola	5,588	7,723	10,020	13,295	17,561	22,438
Female	2,847	3,928	5,085	6,725	8,860	11,299
Argentina	23,963	28,237	32,322	36,238	40,193	43,837
Female	11,944	14,192	16,320	18,334	20,350	22,216
Australia	12,552	14,695	16,746	16,610	20,344	21,966
Female	6,227	7,357	8,391	9,321	10,184	11,008
Austria	7,447	7,549	7,492	7,461	7,339	7,173
Female	3,952	3,982	3,908	3,854	3,766	3,676
Bahrain	220	374	515	682	823	937
Female	102	145	210	278	342	400
Bangladesh	66,671	88,219	115,593	150,589	188,196	220,119
Female	32,085	42,727	56,033	73,066	91,402	107,053
Barbados	239	249	261	285	311	336
Female	127	131	136	148	160	171
Belgium	9,656	9,852	9,938	10,034	10,040	9,974
Female	4,930	5,037	5,080	5,114	5,104	5,065
Benin	2,708	3,494	4,741	6,561	8,987	11,691
Female	1,380	1,780	2,407	3,320	4,537	5,893
Bhutan	1,045	1,245	1,516	1,906	2,388	2,861
Female	512	605	732	918	1,150	1,380
Bolivia	4,325	5,570	7,314	9,724	12,820	16,401
Female	2,191	2,826	3,709	4,924	6,482	8,280
Botswana	623	902	1,265	1,804	2,441	3,068
Female	339	477	671	933	1,253	1,567
Brazil	95,847	121,286	150,368	179,487	207,454	233,817
Female	47,863	60,679	75,376	90,164	104,442	118,004
Bulgaria	8,490	8,862	9,010	9,071	9,059	8,985
Female	4,246	4,446	4,546	4,597	4,594	4,555
Burkino Faso	5,593	6,959	9,007	12,025	16,001	20,520
Female	2,828	3,515	4,546	6,061	8,055	10,323
Burma	27,102	33,821	41,675	51,129	60,567	68,743
Female	13,558	16,883	20,942	25,625	30,304	34,376
Burundi	3,456	4,100	5,451	7,283	9,598	11,998
Female	1,787	2,106	2,780	3,694	4,851	6,052
Cameroon	6,761	8,623	11,245	14,787	19,286	24,016
Female	3,452	4,386	5,701	7,481	9,739	12,114
Canada	21,324	23,941	26,525	28,508	30,197	31,587

[Continued]

★ 646 ★

Worldwide Population Estimates and Projections by Country
[Continued]

Country or Area	1970	1980	1990	2000	2010	2020
Female	10,639	12,062	13,393	14,404	15,263	15,993
Cape Verde	271	296	379	518	673	818
Female	142	160	201	268	344	414
Central African Republic	1,875	2,298	2,913	3,765	4,878	6,186
Female	977	1,190	1,495	1,919	2,473	3,124
Chad	3,625	4,477	5,678	7,337	9,491	12,013
Female	1,859	2,274	2,878	3,709	4,786	6,046
Chile	9,504	11,145	13,173	15,272	17,182	18,973
Female	4,814	5,646	6,668	7,728	8,702	9,627
China	830,675	996,134	1,135,496	1,285,894	1,382,463	1,459,753
Female	403,327	482,837	551,124	626,049	675,734	717,100
Colombia	20,803	25,793	31,819	37,998	43,840	49,259
Female	10,423	12,869	15,840	18,908	21,828	24,565
Comoros	271	381	519	710	951	1,205
Female	137	193	262	357	478	606
Congo	1,201	1,529	1,994	2,635	3,474	4,470
Female	611	776	1,010	1,331	1,752	2,251
Costa Rica	1,731	2,285	3,015	3,711	4,366	4,977
Female	858	1,132	1,491	1,836	2,164	2,472
Cote D'Ivoire	5,510	8,327	12,596	18,547	26,486	35,406
Female	2,734	4,105	6,211	9,193	13,185	17,670
Cuba	8,571	9,732	10,324	11,189	11,710	11,958
Female	4,177	4,769	5,076	5,524	5,800	5,943
Cyprus	615	629	701	765	826	882
Female	311	315	352	384	413	441
Czechoslovakia	14,334	15,311	15,667	16,179	16,715	17,061
Female	7,350	7,848	8,032	8,276	8,527	8,700
Democratic Kampuchea	6,938	6,400	8,246	10,046	11,539	13,266
Female	3,465	3,223	4,138	5,027	5,769	6,631
Democratic Yemen	1,497	1,861	2,491	3,430	4,584	5,801
Female	750	943	1,259	1,721	2,288	2,885
Denmark	4,929	5,123	5,120	5,139	5,117	5,038
Female	2,483	2,594	2,600	2,611	2,600	2,568
Djibouti	167	300	406	552	747	966
Female	82	148	202	275	374	484
Dominican Republic	4,423	5,697	7,170	8,621	9,902	11,001
Female	2,178	2,803	3,526	4,239	4,869	5,412
East Timor	605	581	737	876	978	1,096
Female	297	285	363	432	484	543
Ecuador	6,051	8,123	10,782	13,939	17,403	21,064
Female	3,014	4,039	5,358	6,927	8,651	10,479
Egypt	33,053	41,520	54,059	66,710	78,456	89,025
Female	16,323	20,453	26,617	32,821	38,622	43,909
El Salvador	3,588	4,525	5,252	6,739	8,491	10,348

[Continued]

★ 646 ★

Worldwide Population Estimates and Projections by Country
[Continued]

Country or Area	1970	1980	1990	2000	2010	2020
Female	1,784	2,292	2,677	3,430	4,309	5,236
Equatorial Guinea	291	352	440	561	715	898
Female	149	180	224	285	361	453
Ethiopia	30,623	38,750	46,743	61,206	79,974	101,631
Female	15,379	19,448	23,550	30,949	40,436	51,318
Fiji	520	629	749	834	905	948
Female	256	312	373	417	453	476
Finland	4,606	4,780	4,975	5,076	5,132	5,148
Female	2,381	2,469	2,561	2,602	2,626	2,640
France	50,772	53,880	56,173	58,196	59,430	60,229
Female	25,980	27,568	28,748	29,749	30,352	30,769
Gabon	504	806	1,171	1,620	2,085	2,639
Female	257	410	594	817	1,047	1,322
Gambia	464	641	858	1,116	1,421	1,719
Female	235	325	435	565	718	869
German Democratic Republic	17,066	16,737	16,649	16,618	16,618	16,363
Female	9,212	8,890	8,689	8,537	8,463	8,314
Germany, Federal Republic	60,651	61,566	60,539	59,818	57,907	55,389
Female	31,784	32,149	31,436	30,722	29,561	28,290
Ghana	8,611	10,734	15,020	20,418	27,071	33,888
Female	4,347	5,411	7,564	10,270	13,603	17,021
Greece	8,793	9,643	10,017	10,193	10,249	10,139
Female	4,501	4,909	5,098	5,157	5,171	5,094
Guadeloupe	320	327	340	354	381	410
Female	163	167	174	182	195	209
Guatemala	5,246	6,916	9,197	12,221	15,827	19,706
Female	2,588	3,416	4,550	6,054	7,848	9,782
Guinea	4,388	5,407	6,876	8,879	11,451	14,353
Female	2,212	2,734	3,479	4,491	5,786	7,248
Guinea-Bissau	526	809	987	1,244	1,577	1,972
Female	272	417	507	635	802	1,000
Guyana	709	865	1,040	1,197	1,352	1,504
Female	357	433	518	596	673	750
Haiti	4,500	5,413	6,504	7,837	9,292	10,785
Female	2,297	2,758	3,312	3,985	4,719	5,475
Honduras	2,627	3,662	5,138	6,846	8,668	10,558
Female	1,307	1,816	2,546	3,396	4,302	5,244
Hong Kong	3,942	5,039	5,841	6,449	6,737	6,913
Female	1,937	2,414	2,828	3,107	3,267	3,381
Hungary	10,353	10,711	10,552	10,531	10,459	10,291
Female	5,334	5,523	5,463	5,455	5,396	5,293
Iceland	204	228	253	274	291	305

[Continued]

★ 646 ★

Worldwide Population Estimates and Projections by Country

[Continued]

Country or Area	1970	1980	1990	2000	2010	2020
Female	101	113	126	136	145	152
India	554,911	688,856	853,373	1,042,530	1,225,305	1,374,470
Female	267,905	332,191	412,328	505,136	595,680	671,223
Indonesia	120,280	150,958	180,514	208,329	231,956	253,560
Female	60,722	75,904	90,517	104,287	116,036	126,842
Iran	28,397	38,900	56,585	74,460	94,691	113,550
Female	14,076	19,130	27,801	36,491	46,419	55,721
Iraq	9,356	13,291	18,920	26,339	35,323	45,080
Female	4,597	6,528	9,278	12,926	17,371	22,210
Ireland	2,954	3,401	3,720	4,086	4,462	4,808
Female	1,469	1,691	1,853	2,035	2,220	2,393
Israel	2,974	3,878	4,581	5,280	6,009	6,653
Female	1,475	1,940	2,292	2,633	2,988	3,303
Italy	53,822	56,434	57,332	57,881	57,290	55,785
Female	27,497	28,962	29,453	29,701	29,330	28,521
Jamaica	1,869	2,173	2,521	2,886	3,227	3,579
Female	957	1,102	1,268	1,445	1,609	1,782
Japan	104,331	116,807	123,457	129,105	131,677	129,916
Female	53,126	59,339	62,758	65,539	66,810	65,946
Jordan	2,299	2,923	4,270	6,329	8,941	11,728
Female	1,118	1,410	2,078	3,097	4,390	5,771
Kenya	11,498	16,632	25,130	37,581	53,466	69,635
Female	5,748	8,317	12,555	18,755	26,666	34,733
Korea	45,815	56,149	66,519	76,176	84,701	91,488
Female	22,945	27,985	33,281	38,072	42,294	45,719
Dem. People's Rep. of Korea	13,892	18,025	22,937	28,165	33,115	37,600
Female	7,080	9,120	11,539	14,096	16,520	18,744
Republic of Korea	31,923	38,124	43,582	48,012	51,586	53,888
Female	15,865	18,865	21,742	23,976	25,774	56,975
Kuwait	744	1,375	2,090	2,782	3,451	4,072
Female	322	587	897	1,217	1,555	1,890
Lao People's Dem. Rep.	2,713	3,205	4,071	5,134	6,234	7,259
Female	1,343	1,593	2,025	2,554	3,099	3,608
Lebanon	2,469	2,669	2,965	3,603	4,170	4,691
Female	1,227	1,358	1,525	1,839	2,117	2,371
Lesotho	1,064	1,339	1,774	2,354	3,096	3,904
Female	557	695	921	1,221	1,601	2,012
Liberia	1,369	1,856	2,554	3,543	4,884	6,466
Female	679	916	1,263	1,759	2,431	3,223
Libyan Arab Jamahiriya	1,986	3,043	4,544	6,500	8,977	11,571
Female	945	1,433	2,163	3,135	4,378	5,685
Luxembourg	339	364	367	368	363	355

[Continued]

★ 646 ★

Worldwide Population Estimates and Projections by Country
[Continued]

Country or Area	1970	1980	1990	2000	2010	2020
Female	173	186	188	188	185	181
Madagascar	6,742	8,777	11,980	16,562	22,594	29,588
Female	3,426	4,448	6,049	8,331	11,327	14,798
Malawi	4,518	6,091	8,428	11,706	15,972	20,605
Female	2,345	3,131	4,279	5,890	7,986	10,264
Malaysia	10,853	13,763	17,339	20,870	23,692	26,556
Female	5,375	6,853	8,602	10,347	11,747	13,177
Mali	5,685	7,023	9,362	12,658	16,992	21,855
Female	2,948	3,642	4,809	6,453	8,617	11,048
Malta	326	364	353	366	379	388
Female	170	186	179	185	190	194
Martinique	326	326	331	352	376	400
Female	166	168	170	180	192	203
Mauritania	1,221	1,551	2,024	2,685	3,545	4,508
Female	619	786	1,024	1,356	1,788	2,272
Mauritius	849	957	1,103	1,240	1,358	1,447
Female	424	485	558	626	685	729
Mexico	52,770	70,416	88,598	107,233	125,166	142,135
Female	26,328	35,168	44,393	53,892	63,090	71,863
Mongolia	1,248	1,663	2,227	2,996	3,894	4,916
Female	625	830	1,110	1,492	1,938	2,445
Morocco	15,310	19,382	25,139	31,366	36,977	41,953
Female	7,638	9,680	12,556	15,651	18,439	20,915
Mozambique	9,398	12,100	15,663	20,445	26,198	31,856
Female	4,787	6,147	7,937	10,337	13,225	16,072
Namibia	1,042	1,371	1,876	2,567	3,479	4,472
Female	527	691	942	1,285	1,738	2,233
Nepal	11,488	14,858	19,143	24,084	28,900	33,080
Female	5,672	7,258	9,318	11,701	14,025	16,044
Netherlands	13,032	14,150	14,752	15,207	15,318	15,225
Female	6,528	7,128	7,455	7,672	7,728	7,703
New Zealand	2,820	3,113	3,379	3,632	3,842	4,006
Female	1,410	1,564	1,705	1,831	1,937	2,022
Nicaragua	2,053	2,771	3,871	5,261	6,824	8,435
Female	1,030	1,389	1,931	2,615	3,383	4,177
Niger	4,146	5,311	7,109	9,750	13,266	17,114
Female	2,096	2,681	3,585	4,911	6,676	8,612
Nigeria	57,221	80,555	113,016	159,149	216,235	274,114
Female	28,988	40,725	57,009	80,134	108,746	137,796
Norway	3,877	4,086	4,212	4,331	4,416	4,485
Female	1,949	2,061	2,131	2,187	2,225	2,259
Oman	654	984	1,468	2,057	2,882	3,835

[Continued]

★ 646 ★

Worldwide Population Estimates and Projections by Country
[Continued]

Country or Area	1970	1980	1990	2000	2010	2020
Female	323	472	698	990	1,402	1,882
Pakistan	65,706	85,299	122,666	162,467	205,472	248,112
Female	31,699	40,520	58,798	78,165	99,205	120,332
Panama	1,531	1,956	2,418	2,893	3,324	3,701
Female	749	957	1,188	1,427	1,646	1,839
Papua New Guinea	2,422	3,086	4,011	5,141	6,456	7,897
Female	1,158	1,471	1,930	2,489	3,139	3,853
Paraguay	2,351	3,147	4,277	5,538	6,928	8,423
Female	1,176	1,559	2,111	2,736	3,426	4,177
Peru	13,193	17,295	22,332	27,952	33,479	38,647
Female	6,544	8,581	11,083	13,870	16,616	19,197
Philippines	37,540	48,317	62,409	77,447	92,038	105,289
Female	18,629	24,085	31,046	38,482	45,714	52,334
Poland	32,526	35,574	38,423	40,366	42,553	44,333
Female	16,730	18,242	19,661	20,632	21,701	22,581
Portugal	9,044	9,766	10,285	10,587	10,809	10,912
Female	4,754	5,043	5,320	5,460	5,551	5,579
Puerto Rico	2,718	3,199	3,709	4,192	4,615	5,008
Female	1,384	1,641	1,903	2,148	2,359	2,552
Qatar	111	229	367	499	632	783
Female	39	83	138	197	267	349
Reunion	441	508	595	685	768	843
Female	216	262	307	353	396	435
Rwanda	3,728	5,163	7,232	10,144	13,556	16,633
Female	1,888	2,613	3,657	5,125	6,845	8,401
Romania	20,360	22,201	23,272	24,346	25,013	25,521
Female	10,361	11,248	11,781	12,310	12,632	12,871
Saudi Arabia	5,745	9,372	14,131	20,686	29,551	39,667
Female	2,790	4,297	6,450	9,605	14,007	19,096
Senegal	4,008	5,672	7,369	9,668	12,431	15,155
Female	2,023	2,864	3,722	4,879	6,270	7,645
Sierra Leone	2,656	3,263	4,151	5,399	7,014	8,809
Female	1,356	1,664	2,112	2,739	3,550	4,452
Singapore	2,075	2,415	2,702	2,950	3,117	3,220
Female	1,013	1,182	1,328	1,456	1,545	1,604
Somalia	3,668	5,352	7,555	9,803	13,247	17,086
Female	1,856	2,810	3,952	5,026	6,737	8,640
South Africa	22,459	28,283	35,248	43,332	51,827	59,799
Female	11,242	14,205	17,731	21,806	26,081	30,102
Soviet Union	242,959	265,546	287,991	307,737	326,415	343,212
Female	130,887	141,425	151,660	160,056	168,148	175,687
Spain	33,779	37,542	39,333	40,812	41,831	42,366

[Continued]

★ 646 ★

Worldwide Population Estimates and Projections by Country
[Continued]

Country or Area	1970	1980	1990	2000	2010	2020
Female	17,290	19,112	19,964	20,630	21,086	21,315
Sri Lanka	12,514	14,819	17,209	19,385	21,458	23,554
Female	6,011	7,266	8,575	9,757	10,849	11,914
Sudan	13,859	18,681	25,195	33,610	44,007	54,618
Female	6,927	9,316	12,540	16,697	21,830	27,073
Suriname	372	355	403	469	535	598
Female	187	179	204	237	270	301
Swaziland	420	564	789	1,116	1,542	1,992
Female	214	287	400	563	775	1,001
Sweden	8,043	8,310	8,339	8,322	8,275	8,205
Female	4,027	4,193	4,226	4,219	4,197	4,169
Switzerland	6,267	6,327	6,521	6,553	6,434	6,247
Female	3,152	3,248	3,338	3,347	3,286	3,196
Syrian Arab Republic	6,258	8,800	12,501	17,611	23,646	29,518
Female	3,049	4,309	6,176	8,719	11,713	14,640
Thailand	35,745	46,718	55,702	63,670	71,594	78,118
Female	17,945	23,290	27,751	31,726	35,696	39,007
Togo	2,020	2,554	3,455	4,727	6,432	8,484
Female	1,028	1,296	1,747	2,383	3,236	4,261
Trinidad and Tobago	955	1,095	1,283	1,480	1,663	1,840
Female	484	549	643	743	836	927
Tunisia	5,127	6,384	8,169	9,821	11,273	12,625
Female	2,590	3,150	4,036	4,859	5,581	6,254
Turkey	35,321	44,438	55,616	66,622	76,641	85,432
Female	17,435	21,894	27,072	32,597	37,680	42,190
Uganda	9,806	13,119	18,442	26,285	36,932	49,203
Female	4,961	6,624	9,295	13,219	18,536	24,667
United Arab Emirates	223	1,015	1,588	1,950	2,286	2,578
Female	84	314	518	690	883	1,075
United Kingdom	55,632	56,330	56,926	57,509	57,560	57,630
Female	28,568	28,894	29,148	29,360	29,344	29,406
United Rep. of Tanzania	13,513	18,867	27,328	39,572	56,271	75,368
Female	6,885	9,587	13,816	19,929	28,261	37,794
United States of America	205,051	227,757	249,235	266,194	281,221	295,420
Female	104,697	116,869	127,668	136,151	143,522	150,727
Uruguay	2,808	2,908	3,128	3,364	3,581	3,782
Female	1,412	1,473	1,590	1,711	1,821	1,922
Venezuela	10,604	15,024	19,736	24,716	30,007	35,395
Female	5,239	7,421	9,781	12,289	14,966	17,708
Viet Nam	42,729	53,700	67,171	83,030	98,045	111,226
Female	21,964	27,655	34,265	42,021	49,380	55,870
Yemen	4,835	5,995	8,017	11,145	15,540	20,720
Female	2,468	3,155	4,188	5,727	7,861	10,369
Yugoslavia	20,371	22,299	23,849	25,026	25,822	26,211

[Continued]

★ 646 ★

Worldwide Population Estimates and Projections by Country
[Continued]

Country or Area	1970	1980	1990	2000	2010	2020
Female	10,370	11,296	12,051	12,625	13,000	13,176
Zaire	19,481	26,377	35,990	49,349	67,440	88,854
Female	10,008	13,393	18,188	24,849	33,868	44,548
Zambia	4,189	5,738	8,456	12,197	17,152	22,743
Female	2,113	2,931	4,285	6,142	8,596	11,359
Zimbabwe	5,270	7,138	9,721	13,135	16,984	20,876
Female	2,654	3,600	4,903	6,622	8,563	10,536

Source: Selected from: "Population by Sex and Age, for Countries and Areas, 1950-2025, Estimates and Medium-, High-, and Low-Variant Projections," *Global Estimates and Projections of Population by Sex and Age: The 1988 Revision*, 1989, pp. 77-382 (New York: United Nations, 1989). Also in source: Estimates and projections by age and high-and low-variant fertility.

Fertility

★ 647 ★

Fertility Rates by Race and Age Group: 1990 to 2010
Projected fertility rates by race and age group: 1990 to 2010.

Age Group	All Races			White			Black			Other Races		
	1990	2000	2010	1990	2000	2010	1990	2000	2010	1990	2000	2010
Total fertility rate	1,850	1,846	1,849	1,781	1,780	1,791	2,170	2,095	2,040	2,175	2,110	2,059
Birth rates (live births per 1,000 women in age group indicated):												
10-14 years old	.8	.9	.8	.4	.5	.5	3.0	2.8	2.3	.4	.5	.5
15-19 years old	49.3	46.6	45.2	41.5	40.3	40.0	90.8	80.2	71.6	39.9	39.0	38.9
20-24 years old	105.5	104.1	102.2	102.2	100.4	99.2	132.0	124.6	118.4	98.6	97.5	96.9
25-29 years old	110.9	113.0	115.0	111.4	113.3	115.2	104.6	107.5	110.5	124.9	124.7	124.5
30-34 years old	72.3	73.9	75.4	71.6	72.9	74.3	67.3	69.4	71.4	108.8	104.5	100.1
35-39 years old	26.0	26.2	26.7	24.4	24.7	25.1	29.5	29.0	28.6	48.9	45.3	41.9
40-44 years old	5.0	4.3	4.2	4.5	3.8	3.8	6.8	5.4	5.1	12.6	9.6	8.4
45-49 years old	.2	.2	.2	.1	.1	.1	.2	.2	.2	1.0	.9	.7

Source: "Projected fertility rates, by race and age group: 1990 to 2010," *Statistical Abstract of the United States 1990*, Table 87, p. 65. Primary source: U.S. Bureau of the Census, *Current Population Reports*, Series P-25, No. 1018. The *total fertility rate* is the number of births that 1,000 women would have in their lifetime if, at each year of age, they experienced the birth rates occurring in the specified year. *Birth rates* represent live births per 1,000 women in the age group indicated.

★ 648 ★

Fertility Rates in Selected Countries

Average number of children born to each female: 1966-1986.

Country/Area	1966-1970	1971-1975	1976-1980	1981-1986
Brazil	5.60	5.00	4.35	3.79
Chile	3.67	3.14	2.50	2.46
China	5.91	4.54	2.76	2.27
Colombia	6.26	4.70	4.23	3.38
Costa Rica	5.91	4.34	3.79	3.61
Cuba	4.12	3.31	2.07	1.77
Cyprus	3.01	2.28	2.33	2.44
Dominican Republic	7.09	5.71	4.72	3.80
Ecuador	6.87	6.23	5.36	4.34
El Salvador	-	5.89	5.59	4.44
Fiji	4.25	3.57	3.40	3.30
Guatemala	6.13	6.02	6.07	6.48
Hong Kong	3.37	3.24	2.29	1.71
Indonesia	5.57	5.20	4.66	3.77
Israel	3.77	3.77	3.35	3.13
Jamaica	5.93	5.00	3.64	3.35
Korea, Republic of	4.73	4.28	2.86	2.19
Malaysia	5.10	4.65	4.02	3.83
Mauritius	4.49	3.32	3.04	2.27
Mexico	6.97	6.18	5.06	4.03
Morocco	-	6.86	5.91	4.80
Panama	5.09	4.65	3.84	3.27
Peru	6.80	6.31	5.57	4.46
Philippines	6.13	5.56	5.08	4.90
Reunion	6.41	4.12	3.21	2.87
Singapore	3.52	2.69	1.89	1.65
Sri Lanka	4.73	4.01	3.83	3.18
Thailand	6.20	4.75	3.86	2.36
Trinidad and Tobago	3.69	3.38	3.14	3.14
Tunisia	6.43	5.81	5.46	5.09
Turkey	-	5.46	4.31	4.05
Venezuela	5.72	4.97	4.50	3.88

Source: "Correlates of Fertility in Selected Developing Countries," *Population Bulletin of the United Nations,* No. 28 (1989):95+, 1990. "The total fertility rate refers to the average number of children that would be born to each female if the fertility patterns of a given period were to stay unchanged. This measure gives the approximate total number of children an average woman will bear in her lifetime, assuming no mortality" (according to *Compendium of Statistics and Indicators on the Situation of Women* [New York: United Nations, 1989).

★ 649 ★

Worldwide Fertility Rates: 1989 to 2020

Average number of children that would be born per woman if all women lived to the end of their childbearing years and bore children according to a given fertility rate at each year.

Country or Area	Total Fertility Rates							
	1989	1990	1995	2000	2005	2010	2015	2020
Sub-Saharan Africa	6.54	6.53	6.26	5,89	5.47	5.01	4.55	4.12
Angola	6.72	6.72	6.42	6.05	5.63	5.18	4.71	4.25
Benin	7.87	7.87	7.52	7.09	6.57	5.99	5.39	4.79
Botswana	5.06	4.84	3.91	3.20	2.75	2.49	2.35	2.28
Burkina	6.56	6.56	6.25	5.89	5.49	5.06	4.61	4.18
Burundi	6.95	6.95	6.65	6.25	5.74	5.15	4.53	3.94
Cameroon	5.76	5.70	5.36	5.00	4.63	4.26	3.92	3.61
Cape Verde	6.69	6.69	6.23	5.69	5.10	4.52	3.98	3.52
Central African Republic	5.63	5.63	5.37	5.07	4.74	4.40	4.05	3.73
Chad	5.33	5.33	5.33	5.08	4.80	4.49	4.18	3.86
Comoros	7.05	7.05	6.73	6.34	5.89	5.40	4.88	4.38
Congo	6.85	6.85	6.54	5.17	5.74	5.27	4.79	4.32
Djibouti	6.44	6.44	6.14	5.80	5.40	5.00	4.60	4.21
Equatorial Guinea	5.56	5.56	5.45	5.22	4.97	4.70	4.42	4.14
Ethiopia	7.03	7.03	6.71	6.33	5.88	5.40	4.90	4.41
Gabon	3.99	3.98	3.94	3.73	3.53	3.33	3.15	2.99
Gambia	6.40	6.40	6.11	5.76	5.37	4.95	4.52	4.11
Ghana	6.44	6.44	6.13	5.79	5.43	5.07	4.70	4.35
Guinea	6.07	6.07	5.79	5.46	5.10	4.71	4.32	3.95
Guinea-Bissau	5.85	5.85	5.43	5.00	4.57	4.17	3.80	3.48
Ivory Coast	6.69	6.69	6.39	6.03	5.61	5.16	4.70	4.25
Kenya[1]	7.81	7.75	7.34	6.86	6.32	5.75	5.16	4.60
Lesotho	4.96	4.87	4.40	3.94	3.53	3.18	2.91	2.70
Liberia	6.61	6.61	6.30	5.95	5.57	5.18	4.78	4.39
Madagascar	6.94	6.94	6.62	6.25	5.82	5.35	4.87	4.41
Malawi	7.68	7.68	7.27	6.79	6.24	5.66	5.07	4.52
Mali	6.59	6.59	6.29	5.93	5.51	5.06	4.59	4.14
Mauritania	7.25	7.25	6.92	6.53	6.06	5.55	5.03	4.51
Mauritius	2.21	2.19	2.09	2.00	2.00	2.00	2.00	2.00
Mayotte	6.83	6.81	6.72	6.33	5.89	5.40	4.90	4.41
Mozambique	6.49	6.49	6.19	5.84	5.44	5.02	4.58	4.16
Namibia	6.64	6.64	6.33	5.97	5.56	5.11	4.65	4.20
Niger	6.80	6.80	6.49	6.12	5.72	5.28	4.84	4.41
Nigeria	6.54	6.54	6.40	5.99	5.51	4.97	4.44	3.96
Reunion	2.67	2.64	2.44	2.25	2.25	2.24	2.24	2.23
Rwanda	8.49	8.49	8.12	7.65	7.08	6.43	5.74	5.06
St. Helena	1.82	NA	NA	NA	NA	NA	NA	NA
Sao Tome and Principe	5.38	5.33	5.04	4.73	4.41	4.09	3.78	3.50

[Continued]

★ 649 ★

Worldwide Fertility Rates: 1989 to 2020
[Continued]

Country or Area	Total Fertility Rates							
	1989	1990	1995	2000	2005	2010	2015	2020
Senegal	6.56	6.51	6.26	6.00	5.73	5.46	5.18	4.90
Seychelles	3.21	3.18	3.03	2.89	2.80	2.71	2.62	2.53
Sierra Leone	6.18	6.18	5.90	5.57	5.19	4.79	4.39	4.00
Somalia	7.29	7.28	6.96	6.54	6.03	5.45	4.84	4.25
South Africa	4.52	4.50	4.39	4.28	4.12	3.88	3.64	3.42
Sudan	6.52	6.52	6.05	5.52	4.96	4.41	3.90	3.47
Swaziland	6.10	6.03	5.66	5.27	4.88	4.49	4.13	3.79
Tanzania	7.09	7.09	6.77	6.39	5.94	5.44	4.94	4.44
Togo	6.64	6.64	6.34	5.98	5.57	5.12	4.67	4.22
Uganda	7.02	7.02	6.69	6.32	5.91	5.49	5.06	4.64
Zaire	6.22	6.22	5.94	5.60	5.23	4.82	4.42	4.02
Zambia	7.00	7.00	6.68	6.30	5.86	5.38	4.88	4.39
Zimbabwe	5.92	5.76	4.94	4.15	3.49	3.00	2.68	2.48
Near East and North Africa	5.07	5.00	4.55	4.16	3.84	3.58	3.35	3.16
Algeria	5.57	5.42	4.55	3.78	3.19	2.77	2.51	2.34
Bahrain	3.47	3.38	3.03	2.77	2.58	2.46	2.38	2.33
Cyprus	2.39	2.37	2.32	2.28	2.26	2.24	2.23	2.22
Egypt	4.78	4.68	4.23	3.82	3.47	3.18	2.94	2.75
Gaza Strip	7.16	7.05	6.42	5.77	5.15	4.57	4.06	3.63
Iraq	7.14	7.31	6.56	5.81	5.31	4.81	4.26	3.78
Israel	2.97	2.94	2.80	2.69	2.59	2.50	2.44	2.39
Jordan	6.34	6.23	5.69	5.16	4.65	4.20	3.82	3.49
Kuwait	3.90	3.81	3.72	3.78	3.86	3.92	3.95	3.94
Lebanon	3.78	3.69	3.31	3.00	2.76	2.59	2.47	2.38
Libya	5.34	5.19	4.47	3.84	3.31	2.93	2.67	2.49
Morocco	4.55	4.43	3.90	3.46	3.10	2.84	2.64	2.50
Oman	6.54	6.47	6.05	5.58	5.08	4.58	4.12	3.70
Qatar	4.72	4.67	4.40	4.15	3.91	3.69	3.49	3.31
Saudi Arabia	6.84	6.79	6.62	6.46	6.23	5.94	5.62	5.30
Syria	6.79	6.73	6.38	6.00	5.61	5.20	4.81	4.43
Tunisia	3.97	3.85	3.37	3.01	2.74	2.56	2.44	2.36
Turkey	3.74	3.64	3.22	2.90	2.67	2.50	2.40	2.33
United Arab Emirates	4.98	4.92	4.58	4.25	3.93	3.63	3.36	3.13
West Bank	5.05	4.96	4.52	4.12	3.78	3.48	3.23	3.02
Western Sahara	7.25	NA	NA	NA	NA	NA	NA	NA
Yemen (Aden)	7.10	7.02	6.55	6.00	5.41	4.81	4.25	3.76
Yemen (Sanaa)								

[Continued]

★ 649 ★

Worldwide Fertility Rates: 1989 to 2020

[Continued]

Country or Area	Total Fertility Rates							
	1989	1990	1995	2000	2005	2010	2015	2020
Asia	3.42	3.33	3.04	2.76	2.66	2.59	2.49	2.41
Afghanistan	6.47	6.40	6.01	5.58	5.12	4.66	4.23	3.83
Bangladesh	5.83	5.72	5.11	4.50	3.94	3.47	3.10	2.82
Bhutan	5.07	5.00	4.66	4.30	3.97	3.65	3.38	3.13
Brunei	3.09	2.94	2.64	2.45	2.34	2.27	2.24	2.22
Burma	4.22	4.15	3.81	3.51	3.24	3.02	2.83	2.69
Cambodia	4.59	4.53	4.24	3.96	3.70	3.47	3.26	3.07
China								
Mainland	2.50	2.38	2.13	1.85	1.95	2.12	2.12	2.12
Taiwan	1.77	1.75	1.72	1.71	1.70	1.70	1.70	1.70
Hong Kong	1.40	1.41	1.49	1.56	1.57	1.59	1.60	1.62
India	3.87	3.78	3.35	3.00	2.72	2.52	2.36	2.25
Indonesia	3.39	3.29	2.89	2.59	2.38	2.24	2.15	2.10
Iran	6.18	6.32	5.81	5.31	4.81	4.31	3.91	3.56
Japan	1.74	1.76	1.81	1.85	1.84	1.83	1.83	1.84
Korea, North	3.25	3.44	3.11	2.84	2.63	2.46	2.33	2.24
Korea, South	2.20	2.17	2.12	2.11	2.10	2.10	2.10	2.10
Laos	5.22	5.12	4.55	3.98	3.48	3.08	2.79	2.58
Macau	2.24	2.19	1.95	1.70	1.71	1.72	1.73	1.74
Malaysia	2.95	2.87	2.61	2.45	2.35	2.29	2.25	2.23
Maldives	6.99	6.95	6.71	6.44	6.13	5.79	5.43	5.06
Mongolia	4.72	4.65	4.29	3.94	3.62	3.34	3.09	2.89
Nepal	5.70	5.61	5.15	4.68	4.24	3.84	3.48	3.19
Pakistan	6.51	6.46	6.13	5.77	5.39	5.00	4.61	4.23
Philippines	4.62	4.57	4.34	4.12	3.89	3.69	3.46	3.27
Singapore	1.62	1.62	1.62	1.62	1.62	1.62	1.62	1.62
Sri Lanka	2.45	2.41	2.27	2.22	2.21	2.20	2.20	2.20
Thailand	2.20	2.12	1.92	1.85	1.82	1.81	1.80	1.80
Vietnam	4.27	4.16	3.67	3.27	2.95	2.71	2.54	2.42
Latin America and the Caribbean	3.38	3.30	2.99	2.74	2.57	2.44	2.36	2.29
Anguilla	3.16	3.15	3.05	2.96	2.86	2.77	2.67	2.58
Antigua and Barbuda	1.70	1.71	1.76	1.80	1.81	1.82	1.83	1.84
Argentina	2.81	2.77	2.62	2.50	2.41	2.35	2.31	2.28
Aruba	1.77	1.76	1.72	1.69	1.67	1.65	1.64	1.63
Bahamas	2.55	2.51	2.36	2.26	2.18	2.13	2.09	2.06
Barbados	2.01	2.00	2.00	2.00	2.00	2.00	2.00	2.00
Belize	4.95	4.81	4.11	3.50	3.02	2.67	2.43	2.27
Bolivia	4.75	4.65	4.17	3.75	3.42	3.10	2.90	2.69

[Continued]

★ 649 ★

Worldwide Fertility Rates: 1989 to 2020

[Continued]

Country or Area	Total Fertility Rates							
	1989	1990	1995	2000	2005	2010	2015	2020
Brazil	3.22	3.13	2.82	2.60	2.44	2.33	2.25	2.20
British Virgin Islands	2.19	NA	NA	NA	NA	NA	NA	NA
Cayman Islands	1.59	NA	NA	NA	NA	NA	NA	NA
Chile	2.46	2.44	2.32	2.21	2.21	2.21	2.21	2.21
Colombia	2.96	2.90	2.57	2.25	2.18	2.10	2.10	2.10
Costa Rica	3.34	3.28	3.02	2.82	2.65	2.52	2.42	2.34
Cuba	1.71	1.71	1.73	1.74	1.76	1.78	1.79	1.81
Dominica	2.72	2.63	2.43	2.32	2.26	2.23	2.22	2.21
Dominican Republic	3.29	3.19	2.82	2.57	2.40	2.29	2.22	2.17
Ecuador	3.91	3.79	3.36	2.93	2.78	2.64	2.49	2.35
El Salvador	4.05	3.97	3.58	3.25	2.99	2.78	2.63	2.51
French Guiana	3.52	3.47	3.22	3.00	2.81	2.66	2.53	2.43
Grenada	4.86	4.86	4.18	3.50	3.30	3.10	2.90	2.70
Guadeloupe	2.27	2.23	2.12	2.06	2.03	2.02	2.01	2.00
Guatemala	5.07	4.91	4.14	3.50	3.02	2.70	2.50	2.38
Guyana	2.77	2.69	2.47	2.34	2.27	2.24	2.22	2.21
Haiti	4.21	4.01	3.60	3.26	2.98	2.76	2.59	2.46
Honduras	4.98	4.84	4.11	3.50	3.05	2.73	2.53	2.40
Jamaica	3.05	3.02	2.87	2.75	2.65	2.56	2.50	2.44
Martinique	1.91	1.87	1.75	1.69	1.65	1.63	1.62	1.61
Mexico	3.63	3.56	3.25	3.00	2.80	2.65	2.53	2.44
Montserrat	1.88	NA	NA	NA	NA	NA	NA	NA
Netherlands Antilles	2.02	1.98	1.87	1.79	1.73	1.69	1.66	1.64
Nicaragua	4.96	4.84	4.27	3.77	3.35	3.03	2.78	2.60
Panama	3.13	3.07	2.80	2.60	2.45	2.34	2.27	2.21
Paraguay	4.88	4.81	4.22	3.50	3.13	2.84	2.63	2.49
Peru	3.75	3.62	3.08	2.70	2.46	2.31	2.22	2.17
Puerto Rico	2.20	2.18	2.12	2.05	2.05	2.04	2.04	2.03
St. Kitts and Nevis	2.71	2.66	2.48	2.36	2.29	2.25	2.23	2.22
St. Lucia	3.87	3.81	3.52	3.27	3.06	2.88	2.74	2.62
St. Vincent and the Grenadines	2.87	2.86	2.78	2.71	2.63	2.55	2.48	2.40
Suriname	3.00	2.93	2.67	2.50	2.39	2.32	2.27	2.25
Trinidad and Tobago	3.15	3.12	2.98	2.87	2.77	2.68	2.60	2.54
Turks and Caicos Islands	3.85	NA	NA	NA	NA	NA	NA	NA
Uruguay	2.29	2.27	2.19	2.11	2.11	2.11	2.11	2.11
Venezuela	3.69	3.63	3.36	3.12	2.93	2.77	2.65	2.55
Virgin Islands	2.48	NA	NA	NA	NA	NA	NA	NA

[Continued]

★ 649 ★

Worldwide Fertility Rates: 1989 to 2020
[Continued]

Country or Area	Total Fertility Rates							
	1989	1990	1995	2000	2005	2010	2015	2020
North America, Europe, Soviet Union	1.96	1.96	1.93	1.92	1.92	1.92	1.92	1.91
Albania	2.99	2.89	2.50	2.20	2.17	2.14	2.11	2.08
Andorra	1.14	NA	NA	NA	NA	NA	NA	NA
Austria	1.53	1.54	1.62	1.70	1.71	1.72	1.73	1.74
Belgium	1.59	1.60	1.65	1.70	1.71	1.72	1.73	1.74
Bermuda	1.79	NA	NA	NA	NA	NA	NA	NA
Bulgaria	1.92	1.92	1.91	1.90	1.90	1.90	1.90	1.90
Canada	1.69	1.69	1.69	1.70	1.71	1.72	1.73	1.74
Czechoslovakia	2.02	2.01	1.96	1.90	1.90	1.90	1.90	1.90
Denmark	1.52	1.54	1.62	1.70	1.71	1.72	1.73	1.74
Faroe Islands	2.22	2.21	2.16	2.10	2.10	2.10	2.10	2.10
Finland	1.66	1.67	1.68	1.70	1.71	1.72	1.73	1.74
France	1.79	1.79	1.74	1.70	1.71	1.72	1.73	1.74
East Germany	1.80	1.81	1.80	1.89	1.91	1.91	1.89	1.89
West Germany	1.40	1.43	1.56	1.70	1.71	1.72	1.73	1.74
Gibraltar	2.44	2.44	NA	NA	NA	NA	NA	NA
Greece	1.69	1.69	1.69	1.70	1.71	1.72	1.73	1.74
Greenland	2.23	2.22	2.16	2.10	2.10	2.10	2.10	2.10
Guernsey	1.64	NA	NA	NA	NA	NA	NA	NA
Hungary	1.85	1.86	1.88	1.90	1.90	1.90	1.90	1.90
Iceland	1.87	1.85	1.78	1.70	1.71	1.72	1.73	1.74
Ireland	2.27	2.25	2.12	2.00	1.98	1.96	1.94	1.92
Isle of Man	1.78	NA	NA	NA	NA	NA	NA	NA
Italy	1.48	1.50	1.60	1.70	1.71	1.72	1.73	1.74
Jersey	1.31	NA	NA	NA	NA	NA	NA	NA
Liechtenstein	1.48	1.50	1.60	1.70	1.71	1.72	1.73	1.74
Luxembourg	1.49	1.51	1.61	1.70	1.71	1.72	1.73	1.74
Malta	1.80	1.80	1.75	1.70	1.71	1.72	1.73	1.74
Monaco	1.22	1.22	NA	NA	NA	NA	NA	NA
Netherlands	1.56	1.57	1.64	1.70	1.71	1.72	1.73	1.74
Norway	1.69	1.69	1.69	1.70	1.71	1.72	1.73	1.74
Poland	2.24	2.21	2.05	1.90	1.90	1.90	1.90	1.90
Portugal	1.82	1.81	1.76	1.70	1.71	1.72	1.73	1.74
Romania	2.22	2.19	2.04	1.90	1.90	1.90	1.90	1.90
St. Pierre and Miquelone	2.18	NA	NA	NA	NA	NA	NA	NA
San Marino	1.26	1.26	NA	NA	NA	NA	NA	NA
Soviet Union	2.42	2.39	2.30	2.27	2.24	2.20	2.17	2.14
Spain	1.73	1.73	1.72	1.70	1.71	1.72	1.73	1.74
Sweden	1.73	1.72	1.71	1.70	1.71	1.72	1.73	1.74
Switzerland	1.56	1.58	1.64	1.70	1.71	1.72	1.73	1.74

[Continued]

★ 649 ★

Worldwide Fertility Rates: 1989 to 2020
[Continued]

Country or Area	Total Fertility Rates							
	1989	1990	1995	2000	2005	2010	2015	2020
United Kingdom	1.77	1.76	1.73	1.70	1.71	1.72	1.73	1.74
United States	1.87	1.87	1.86	1.86	1.86	1.87	1.88	1.87
Yugoslavia	2.02	2.01	1.96	1.90	1.90	1.90	1.90	1.90
Oceania	2.58	2.53	2.45	2.37	2.29	2.23	2.17	2.13
American Samoa	5.44	NA	NA	NA	NA	NA	NA	NA
Australia	1.93	1.93	1.93	1.93	1.93	1.93	1.93	1.93
Cook Islands	3.54	NA	NA	NA	NA	NA	NA	NA
Federated States of Micronesia	4.97	NA	NA	NA	NA	NA	NA	NA
Fiji	3.12	3.05	2.79	2.60	2.46	2.37	2.31	2.27
French Polynesia	3.38	3.29	2.96	2.71	2.54	2.43	2.35	2.30
Guam	2.76	NA	NA	NA	NA	NA	NA	NA
Kiribati	4.19	NA	NA	NA	NA	NA	NA	NA
Marshall Islands	5.88	NA	NA	NA	NA	NA	NA	NA
Nauru	2.49	NA	NA	NA	NA	NA	NA	NA
New Caledonia	3.01	2.95	2.73	2.57	2.46	2.38	2.32	2.28
New Zealand	1.88	1.87	1.85	1.85	1.85	1.85	1.85	1.85
Northern Mariana Islands	5.64	NA	NA	NA	NA	NA	NA	NA
Papua New Guinea	5.11	5.01	4.50	4.02	3.61	3.26	2.98	2.77
Solomon Islands	6.41	6.30	5.59	4.81	4.07	3.46	3.01	2.70
Tonga	3.96	NA	NA	NA	NA	NA	NA	NA
Trust Territory of the Pacific Islands	3.32	NA	NA	NA	NA	NA	NA	NA
Tuvalu	2.80	2.80	2.80	2.80	2.73	2.66	2.59	2.52
Vanuatu	5.60	5.49	4.79	4.05	3.41	2.93	2.62	2.44
Wallis and Futuna	3.86	NA	NA	NA	NA	NA	NA	NA
Western Samoa	4.76	4.63	4.02	3.50	3.10	2.80	2.60	2.46

Source: "Total Fertility Rates, by Country or Area: 1989 to 2020," *World Population Profile: 1989,* p. 53-57. Primary source: U.S. Bureau of the Census, International Data Base. *Total fertility rate* is the average number of children that would be born per woman if all women lived to the end of their childbearing years and bore children according to a given fertility rate at each year. *Notes:* 1. Based on information just received from the 1989 Demographic and Health Survey in Kenya, it appears that the total fertility rates presented here may be too high. A preliminary evaluation of the new data suggests a total fertility rate of 6.7 in 1989.

Fetal and Infant Deaths

★ 650 ★

10 Worst Cities for Infant Mortality

10 worst cities for infant mortality and number of infants per 1,000 born who died within 1 year of birth.

City	Rank	No. of infant deaths per 1,000 births
New Haven, CT	1	20.2
Detroit	2	19.7
Washington	3	19.3
Baltimore	4	19.2
Savannah, GA	5	19.0
Richmond, VA	6	17.9
Syracuse, NY	7	17.8
Portsmouth, VA	8	17.7
Memphis, TN	9	17.7
Flint, MI	10	17.6

Source: "Detroit ranks 2nd-worst nationwide," *Detroit Free Press*, February 19, 1991, p. 4A. Primary source: National Center for Health Statistics information gathered for 1987, the latest year for which official figures were available.

★ 651 ★

Fetal and Infant Deaths in Developing Countries

Neonatal and post-neonatal mortality rates and as proportions of infant mortality, per 1,000 live births, selected developing countries.

Country	Neonatal mortality		Post-natal mortality		Infant Mortality Rate-Total
	Rate	Percentage	Rate	Percentage	
Sierra Leone	79.1	51.4%	74.7	48.6%	153.8
Afghanistan	40.4	34.6%	76.2	65.4%	116.6
Pakistan	53.7	61.7%	33.3	38.3%	87.0
Guatemala	18.1	25.9%	51.7	74.1%	69.8
Mexico	19.8	38.1%	32.2	61.9%	52.0
Sudan	11.5	26.6%	31.8	73.4%	43.2
Sri Lanka	25.9	60.9%	16.6	39.1%	42.5
Argentina	22.2	54.4%	18.6	45.6%	40.8
Mauritius	18.4	57.0%	13.9	43.0%	32.3
Thailand	20.5	70.4%	8.6	29.6%	29.1

Source: "Neonatal and Post-Neonatal Mortality in Selected Developing Countries: Rates, and as Proportions of Infant Mortality," *Women, Health, and Development*, Table 3, p. 39 (1985). Primary source: special surveys and national data, about 1980.

★ 652 ★

Infant Mortality Rates by Race: 1960, 1970, and 1980-87

Infant mortality rates per 1,000 live births by race: 1960, 1970, and 1980-87.

Year	All races			White			All other					
							Total			Black		
	Both sexes	Female	Male	Both sexes	Female	Male	Both sexes	Female	Male	Both sexes	Female	Male
1987	10.1	8.9	11.2	8.6	7.6	9.6	15.4	13.9	16.9	17.9	16.0	19.6
1986	10.4	9.1	11.5	8.9	7.8	10.0	15.7	14.0	17.3	18.0	16.0	20.0
1985	10.6	9.3	11.9	9.3	8.0	10.6	15.8	14.4	17.2	18.2	16.5	19.9
1984	10.8	9.6	11.9	9.4	8.3	10.5	16.1	14.8	17.3	18.4	16.9	19.8
1983	11.2	10.0	12.3	9.7	8.6	10.8	16.8	15.2	18.3	19.2	17.2	21.1
1982	11.5	10.2	12.8	10.1	8.9	11.2	17.3	15.5	18.9	19.6	17.7	21.5
1981	11.9	10.7	13.1	10.5	9.2	11.7	17.8	16.3	19.2	20.0	18.3	21.7
1980	12.6	11.2	13.9	11.0	9.6	12.3	19.1	17.5	20.7	21.4	19.4	23.3
1970	20.0	17.5	22.4	17.8	15.4	20.0	30.9	27.5	34.2	32.6	29.0	36.2
1960	26.0	22.6	29.3	22.9	19.6	26.0	43.2	38.5	47.9	44.3	39.4	49.1

Source: "Infant mortality rates, by race and sex: United States, 1960, 1970, and 1980-89," *Monthly Vital Statistics Report*, Vol 38, No. 13, August 30, 1990, p. 25. Also in source: scant data for 1988-1989.

★ 653 ★

Infant Mortality in the 1990s

Highlights of a report issued by the United Nations Childrens Fund on December 19, 1990, reported in the *New York Times*.

Large increases in population will continue. The total number of world births will rise to **149 million in the year 2000** compared to **142 million in 1990**, before declining to **144 million by 2020**.

An additional **$20 billion a year** will need to be spent on child care, family planning, and educational programs in poor countries over the next 10 years. Fertility rate declines are greatest in countries with strong family planning and female education programs.

The majority of the developing countries now have under-5 child mortality rates of about **140 per 1,000 births**. The country with the highest child mortality rate is Mozambique, where for every 1,000 births, **297 children die before reaching age 5.** The United States rate is **12 per 1,000**.

Source: Paul Lewis, "Falling Infant Mortality Rates Give Unicef Hope," *New York Times*, December 19, 1990, p. A4.

★ 654 ★

Neonatal and Fetal Deaths By Race: 1970-1987

Fetal and neonatal deaths per 1,000 live births, 1970-1987.

Item	1970	1975	1978	1979	1980	1981	1982	1983	1984	1985	1986	1987
Fetal deaths[1]	14.2	10.7	9.7	9.4	9.2	9.0	8.9	8.4	8.2	7.9	7.7	NA
White	12.4	9.5	8.5	8.4	8.2	8.0	7.9	7.4	7.4	7.0	6.8	NA
Black and other	22.6	16.0	14.7	13.8	13.4	12.8	12.7	12.2	11.5	11.3	11.2	NA
Neonatal deaths[2]	15.1	11.6	9.5	8.9	8.5	8.0	7.7	7.3	7.0	7.0	6.7	6.5
White	13.8	10.4	8.4	7.9	7.5	7.1	6.8	6.4	6.2	6.1	5.8	5.5
Black and other	21.4	16.8	14.0	12.9	12.5	11.8	11.3	10.8	10.2	10.3	10.1	10.0
Black	22.8	18.3	15.5	14.3	14.1	13.4	13.1	12.4	11.8	12.1	11.7	11.7

Source: Selected from "Infant, Maternal, and Neonatal Mortality rates, and Fetal Mortality Ratios, by Race: 1960 to 1987," *Statistical Abstract of the United States 1990*, p. 77. Also in source: infant and maternal mortality rates (see separate tables); data for 1960. *Notes:* 1. Beginning 1970, includes only those deaths with stated or presumed period of gestation of 20 weeks or more. 2. Represents deaths of infants under 28 days old, exclusive of fetal deaths.

★ 655 ★

Worldwide Fetal Deaths and Fetal Death Ratios

Late fetal deaths and late fetal death ratios per 1,000 live births: 1983-1987.

Country or area	Number					Ratio				
	1983	1984	1985	1986	1987	1983	1984	1985	1986	1987
Africa										
Algeria	-	-	16,851	-	-	-	-	19.9	-	-
Mauritius	379	388	368	342	344	-	-	-	-	-
Rodrigues	24	16	15	23	19	-	-	-	-	-
Reunion	232	216	170	189	-	-	-	-	-	-
Seychelles	-	15	-	-	-	-	-	-	-	-
Sierra Leone	2,596	3,024	3,701	3,898	-	42.5	44.4	48.8	46.4	-
North America										
Antigua and Barbuda	8	-	-	-	-	-	-	-	-	-
Bahamas	69	42	54	58	31	-	-	-	-	-
Barbados	50	47	41	41	-	-	-	-	-	-
British Virgin Islands	8	8	7	2	-	-	-	-	-	-
Canada	1,828	1,678	1,629	1,574	1,584	4.9	4.4	4.3	4.2	4.3
Cayman Islands	1	3	2	3	1	-	-	-	-	-
Cuba	1,913	1,933	1,918	2,001	-	11.6	11.6	10.5	12.0	
El Salvador	961	864	832	-	-	-	-	-	-	-
Greenland	5	11	4	5	6	-	-	-	-	-
Guadeloupe	125	83	85	-	-	-	-	-	-	-
Guatemala	6,316	6,363	6,796	-	-	20.6	20.4	20.8	-	-
Jamaica	467	276	-	-	-	-	-	-	-	-

[Continued]

558

★ 655 ★

Worldwide Fetal Deaths and Fetal Death Ratios
[Continued]

Country or area	Number					Ratio				
	1983	1984	1985	1986	1987	1983	1984	1985	1986	1987
Martinique	78	71	81	30	-	-	-	-	-	-
Mexico	22,255	28,541	27.993	-	-	8.5	11.4	10.5	-	-
Panama	457	442	428	421	471	-	-	-	-	-
Puerto Rico	710	673	657	-	-	-	-	-	-	-
St. Kitts and Nevis	20	16	28	14	-	-	-	-	-	-
Trinidad and Tobago	564	372	-	-	-	-	-	-	-	-
United States	21,306	20,670	10,167	19,353	-	5.9	5.6	5.4	5.2	-
South America										
Brazil	43,684	40,453	39,057	38,460	-	16.1	15.8	14.9	13.8	-
Chile	1,542	1,612	1,522	1,746	1,823	5.9	6.1	5.8	6.4	6.5
Colombia	-	-	5,797	6,177	-	-	-	6.9	-	-
Ecuador	3,891	3,723	3,597	4,265	4,067	18.8	18.1	17.1	20.7	19.9
French Guiana	23	55	67	67	-	-	-	-	-	-
Uruguay	649	-	-	-	-	-	-	-	-	-
Venezuela	6,850	7,107	6,409	6,520	6,514	13.3	14.1	12.8	12.9	12.6
Asia										
Hong Kong	386	330	295	292	291	-	-	-	-	-
India	-	-	-	-	-	-	10.4	-	-	-
Israel	618	549	576	-	-	-	-	-	-	-
Japan	9,464	8,724	7,733	6,902	6,252	6.3	5.9	5.4	5.0	4.6
Kuwait	667	551	588	522	-	-	-	-	-	-
Macau	45	62	33	-	35	-	-	-	-	-
Peninsular Malaysia	4,856	4,439	4,516	4,218	3,702	13.2	11.4	11.1	10.5	9.4
Sabah	215	211	222	179	-	-	-	-	-	-
Sarawak	144	159	117	131	-	-	-	-	-	-
Maldives	188	202	161	137	165	-	-	-	-	-
Philippines	13,811	11,145	8,517	7,977	9,679	9.2	7.5	5.9	5.3	-
Qatar	136	-	84	95	71	-	-	-	-	-
Singapore	223	243	227	201	206	-	-	-	-	-
Sri Lanka	2,552	-	-	-	-	6.3	-	-	-	-
Thailand	861	809	640	749	-	-	-	-	-	-
Europe										
Austria	481	381	391	385	289	-	-	-	-	-

[Continued]

★ 655 ★

Worldwide Fetal Deaths and Fetal Death Ratios
[Continued]

Country or area	Number					Ratio				
	1983	1984	1985	1986	1987	1983	1984	1985	1986	1987
Belgium	824	780	764	-	-	-	-	-	-	-
Bulgaria	863	840	785	716	-	-	-	-	-	-
Channel Islands- Jersey	2	5	5	-	-	-	-	-	-	-
Czechoslovakia	1,176	1,148	1,097	1,194	1,016	5.1	5.0	4.9	5.4	4.7
Denmark	264	228	236	242	258	-	-	-	-	-
Faeroe Islands	8	2	4	3	3	-	-	-	-	-
Finland	268	260	241	193	-	-	-	-	-	-
France	5,723	5,835	5,658	5,615	5,304	7.6	7.7	7.4	7.2	6.9
German Democratic Rep.	1,317	1,236	1,187	1,041	1,117	5.6	5.4	5.2	4.7	4.9
Germany, Federal Rep.	2,790	2,567	2,414	2,506	2,485	4.7	4.4	4.1	4.0	3.9
Greece	963	990	846	-	-	-	-	-	-	-
Hungary	902	799	808	828	882	-	-	-	-	-
Iceland	14	17	-	-	-	-	-	-	-	-
Ireland	581	542	516		-	-	-	-	-	-
Isle of Man	2	8	2	1	5	-	-	-	-	-
Italy	4,361	4,160	3,833	3,658	3,455	7.3	7.1	6.7	6.6	6.3
Luxembourg	24	20	22	20	23	-	-	-	-	-
Netherlands	1,002	1,036	1,054	1,060	-	5.9	5.9	5.9	5.7	-
Norway	303	261	279	268	237	-	-	-	-	-
Poland	4.397	4,201	3,897	3,703	3,475	6.1	6.0	5.8	5.8	5.7
Portugal	1,517	1,405	1,270	1,169	1,045	10.5	9.8	9.7	9.2	8.5
Romania	2,605	2,988	2,824	-	-	8.1	8.5	7.9	-	-
San Marino	1	1	-	1	-	-	-	-	-	-
Spain	3,151	-	-	-	6.5	-	-	-	-	
Sweden	340	381	388	423	412	-	-	-	-	-
Switzerland	361	352	345	334	337	-	-	-	-	-
United Kingdom	4,214	4,186	4,189	4,065	3,931	5.8	5.7	5.6	5.4	5.1
England and Wales	3,631	3,643	3,645	3,550	3,420	5.8	5.7	5.6	5.4	4.4
Northern Ireland	204	164	178	125	171	-	-	-	-	-
Scotland	379	379	366	390	-	-	-	-	-	-
Yugoslavia	2,482	2,334	2,253	2,231	2,238	6.6	6.2	6.1	6.2	6.2
Oceania										
American Samoa	18	22	15	-	-	-	-	-	-	-
Australia	1,233	1,193	1,128	1,180	-	5.1	5.1	4.6	4.8	-
Fiji	86	74	101	-	-	-	-	-	-	-
Guam			16	4						
New Caledonia	57			46						
New Zealand	269	261	254	249	265					

[Continued]

★ 655 ★

Worldwide Fetal Deaths and Fetal Death Ratios
[Continued]

Country or area	Number					Ratio				
	1983	1984	1985	1986	1987	1983	1984	1985	1986	1987
Pacific Islands- Northern Mariana Islands	-	-	9	-						

Source: "Late foetal deaths and late foetal death ratios, by urban/rural residence:1983-1987," *1988 Demographic Yearbook*, 1990, p. 384-385 (New York: United Nations, 1990). Also in source: late fetal deaths and ratios by urban/rural residence. Late fetal deaths are those of 28 or more completed weeks of gestation. Data include fetal deaths of an unknown gestational age. Ratios are the number of late fetal deaths per 1,000 live births and are shown only for countries or areas having at least a total of 1,000 late fetal deaths in a given year.

★ 656 ★

Worldwide Infant Deaths

Infant deaths by age, latest available year.

Country or Area, Year	Age (in days)				
	-365	-1	1-6	7-27	28-364
AFRICA					
Algeria-1980	83,449	21,336	-	-	56,749[1]
Botswana-1983	291	-	-	40[1]	251
Female	143	-	-	22[1]	121
Egypt-1979	124,318	18	7,776	11,565	104,959
Female	61,658	7	3,156	5,139	53,356
Mali-1976	132,981	-	-	14,890[1]	18,091
Female	14,691	-	-	6,262[1]	8,429
Mauritius-1987	463	60	183	91	129
Female	180	29	72	28	51
Rodrigues-1987	41	8	8	6	19
Female	26	4	6	4	12
Reunion-1987	124	-	52	10	62
Female	51	-	27	2	22
St. Helen-1986	3	-	1	1	-
Female	1	-	-	1	-
Sao Tome and Principe-1979	231	-	52[1]	50	129
Female	108	-	22[1]	23	63
Seychelles-1986	30	15	10	1	4
Female	10	5	3	-	2
Tunisia-1982	8,011	-	1,690[1]	-	6,351[1]
Female	3,628	-	663[1]	-	2,965[1]
Zimbabwe-1978	46	18	11	2	15
Female	21	7	7	-	7
NORTH AMERICA					
Antigua and Barbuda-1975	52	10	12	1	22
Female	15	1	3	-	10
Bahamas-1986	169	-	102[1]	14	53

[Continued]

★ 656 ★

Worldwide Infant Deaths
[Continued]

Country or Area, Year	Age (in days)				
	-365	-1	1-6	7-27	28-364
Female	72	-	46[1]	6	20
Barbados-1986	51	31	8	3	9
Female	18	13	4	-	1
Bermuda-1986	12	-	6	1	5
Female	5	-	3	-	2
British Virgin Islands-1986	5	2	1	1	1
Female	2	1	-	1	-
Canada-1986	2,938	1,085	492	332	1,029
Female	1,278	446	212	151	469
Cayman Islands-1983	4	2	1	-	1
Female	3	1	1	-	1
Costa Rica-1984	1,440	438	303	153	541
Female	618	188	121	66	242
Cuba	2,262	509	657	285	811
Female	933	211	253	118	351
Dominican Republic-1982	6,276	596	1,542	1,228	2,910
Female	2,785	263	659	548	1,315
El Salvador-1985	4,540	405	682	555	2,898
Female	2,075	159	300	254	1,362
Greenland-1987	29	9	8	1	11
Female	16	6	6	-	4
Guadeloupe-1986	98	8	32	28	30
Female	42	2	14	9	17
Guatemala-1985	18,292	1,338	2,070	2,709	12,175
Female	8,135	593	838	1,185	5,519
Honduras-1979	3,919	231	419	617	2,652
Female	1,693	89	155	269	1,180
Jamaica-1982	590	39	114	57	379
Female	269	14	49	20	186
Martinique-1984	59	4	17	18	20
Female	25	1	5	8	11
Mexico-1984	73,238	5,368	16,321	10,017	41,532
Female	32,409	2,398	6,775	4,352	18,884
Montserrat-1982	2	1	1	-	-
Female	2	1	1	-	-
Panama-1986	1,117	235	300	128	454
Female	477	91	122	58	206
Puerto Rico-1985	947	306	312	149	179
Female	429	132	138	74	85
St. Kitts and Nevis-1986	40	16	13	-	11
Female	19	5	7	-	7
St. Lucia-1986	84	15	37	4	28
Female	36	7	14	3	12
Trinidad and Tobago-1984	434	124	108	55	146

[Continued]

★ 656 ★

Worldwide Infant Deaths
[Continued]

Country or Area, Year	Age (in days)				
	-365	-1	1-6	7-27	28-364
Female	193	56	42	27	67
United States-1986	38,891	14,585	6,468	4,159	13,679
Female	16,667	6,430	2,654	1,854	5,729
SOUTH AMERICA					
Argentina-1983	19,478	4,222	4,552	2,137	8,567
Female	8,399	1,785	1,881	917	3,816
Brazil-1986	131,697	18,957	22,426	16,622	73,692
Female	56,411	7,987	9,066	7,057	32,301
Chile-1987	5,182	1,193	935	563	2,491
Female	2,275	530	394	254	1,097
Colombia-1986	16,185	2,428	3,210	2,097	8,450
Female	7,099	1,073	1,301	934	3,791
Ecuador-1987	9,761	916	1,454	1,407	5,984
Female	4,345	374	594	635	2,742
Paraguay-1985	2,060	-	543[1]	270	1,247
Female	914	-	221[1]	118	575
Peru-1982	21,578	2,788	-	6,221[1]	12,569
Suriname-1981	269	42	81	43	103
Female	112	22	25	18	47
Uruguay-1987	1,275	334	270	164	502
Female	552	139	119	62	232
Venezuela-1987	12,247	-	-	7,458[1]	4,789
Female	5,307	-	-	3,147	2,160
ASIA					
Brunei Darussalam-1982	76	14	19	11	32
Female	36	7	8	6	15
Hong Kong-1987	515	36	219	85	175
Female	231	16	99	43	73
Iraq-1977	8,868	-	2,240[1]	1,460	5,168
Female	3,672	-	843[1]	534	2,295
Israel-1985	1,183	294	328	161	400
Female	531	141	134	68	188
Japan-1987	6,711	1,575	1,490	868	2,778
Female	2,977	688	651	388	1,250
Jordan-1980	1,052	-	-	192[1]	860
Female-1979	571	-	-	84[1]	860
Kuwait-1986	841	292	191	62	296
Female	388	120	78	29	161
Macau-1987	52	28	11	1	12
Female	23	11	5	-	7
Malaysia-1987 (Peninsular Malaysia)	5,625	-	2,820[1]	743	2,062

[Continued]

★ 656 ★

Worldwide Infant Deaths
[Continued]

Country or Area, Year	Age (in days)				
	-365	-1	1-6	7-27	28-364
Female	2,474	-	1,211[1]	330	933
Sabah-1984	1,064	-	603[1]	103	358
Female	489	-	257[1]	58	174
Sarawak-1986	426	-	220[1]	68	138
Female	173	-	89[1]	21	63
Maldives-1987	417	13	158	74	172
Female	183	7	61	31	84
Pakistan-1985	367,096	9,169	111,809	73,075	169,511
Female	160,783	2,779	37,856	36,416	81,539
Philippines-1987	50,803	7,178	8,958	5,245	29,422
Female	21,436	2,970	3,536	2,223	12,707
Qatar-1987	133	18	37	29	49
Female	68	9	16	17	26
Singapore-1987	324	-	191[1]	55	78
Female	130	-	80[1]	18	32
Sri Lanka-1983	11,492	2	5,094	1,869	4,527
Female	5,213	-	2,272	837	2,104
Thailand-1987	9,358	390	1,910	1,143	5,522
Female	3,992	161	799	506	2,350
EUROPE					
Albania-1987	2,247	108	291	253	1,595
Austria-1987	850	216	154	125	355
Female	375	103	62	59	151
Belgium-1983	1,235	355	260	144	476
Female	512	163	110	47	192
Bulgaria-1986	1,760	129	579	293	759
Female	734	60	208	136	330
Channel Islands					
Guernsey-1986	2	1	-	-	1
Female	1	1	-	-	-
Jersey-1987	9	1	3	1	4
Female	4	-	1	-	3
Czechoslovakia-1985	3,165	924	846	402	993
Female	1,339	381	352	172	434
Denmark-1987	467	138	71	59	199
Female	177	54	23	24	76
Faeroe Islands-1987	4	3	-	-	1
Female	2	2	-	-	-
Finland-1986	353	79	115	48	111
Female	140	28	46	19	47
France-1987	6,017	845	1,476	792	2,904
Female	2,445	351	584	348	1,162
German Democratic Rep.-1987	1,969	364	623	302	680

[Continued]

★ 656 ★

Worldwide Infant Deaths
[Continued]

Country or Area, Year	Age (in days)				
	-365	-1	1-6	7-27	28-364
Female-1983	1,001	-	-	668[1]	332
Germany, Federal Rep.-1987	5,318	946	1,289	742	2,341
Female	2,236	428	525	309	974
Greece-1985	1,647	385	505	339	418
Female	687	165	209	130	183
Hungary-1987	2,178	661	650	321	546
Female	900	273	252	137	238
Iceland-1984	25	1	7	7	10
Female	11	1	3	4	3
Ireland-1985	553	179	92	68	214
Female	240	77	36	33	94
Isle of Man-1987	4	2	-	-	2
Female	1	-	-	-	1
Italy-1983	7,397	2,335	2,469	955	1,638
Female	3,276	992	1,067	456	761
Luxembourg-1987	40	9	13	4	14
Female	17	2	5	2	8
Malta-1987	39	-	19	8	12
Female	17	-	8	3	6
Netherlands-1986	1,428	329	412	144	543
Female	625	148	173	58	246
Norway-1987	453	87	107	55	204
Female	202	47	42	22	91
Poland-1987	10,601	2,222	3,870	1,499	3,010
Female	4,451	927	1,602	647	1,275
Portugal-1987	1,755	668	369	181	537
Female	756	313	136	71	236
Romania-1985	9,191	-	1,677[1]	-	7,514[1]
Female-1980	5,028	191	784	817	3,236
San Marino-1987	3	1	1	1	-
Female	-	-	-	-	-
Spain-1983	5,285	1,631	1,147	888	1,619
Female	2,296	718	444	380	754
Sweden-1987	641	133	195	73	240
Female	283	63	92	27	101
Switzerland-1987	524	164	104	57	199
Female	233	79	41	25	88
United Kingdom-1987	7,077	1,765	1,279	851	3,182
Female	2,972	727	535	371	1,339
England and Wales-1985	6,141	1,634	1,219	678	2,610
Female	2,631	698	510	318	1,105
Northern Ireland-1985	265	72	58	25	110
Female	114	30	28	8	48
Scotland-1985	624	164	126	74	260

[Continued]

★ 656 ★

Worldwide Infant Deaths
[Continued]

Country or Area, Year	Age (in days)				
	-365	-1	1-6	7-27	28-364
Female	282	84	58	36	104
Yugoslavia-1987	9,036	1,870	2,219	1,100	3,847
Female	4,140	825	919	509	1,887
OCEANIA					
American Samoa-1976	22	4	5	3	10
Female	8	-	2	-	6
Australia-1986	2,154	728	339	255	832
Female	910	296	145	109	360
Cook Islands-1977	4	-	1	1	2
Female	1	-	-	1	-
Fiji-1985	361	-	182[1]	48	131
Female	176	-	80[1]	26	70
Guam-1986	31	17	5	2	7
New Caledonia-1981	70	12	19	7	32
Female-1977	40	5	5	3	27
New Zealand-1987	554	91	82	55	326
Female	252	44	28	25	155
Niue-1986	2	-	1	-	1
Female	2	-	1	-	1
Pacific Islands-1979	128	31	33	9	55
Female	64	13	17	5	29
Northern Mariana Islands-1985	14	7	3	-	4
Female	4	1	2	-	1
Samoa-1980	35	-	9	5	21
Female	13	-	3	4	6

Source: Selected from "Infant Deaths and Infant Mortality Rates by Age, Sex and Urban/Rural Residence: Latest Available Year," *1988 Demographic Yearbook*, 1990, Table 16, pp. 405-416 (New York: United Nations, 1990). Also in source: Infant mortality rates by age, sex, and residence. Data exclude fetal deaths. *Note:* 1. Combined with age in previous column(s).

Life Expectancy

★ 657 ★

Countries with the Lowest Female Life Expectancy

A comparison of vital statistics in the 15 countries with the lowest female life expectancy: 1980.

Country	Life Expectancy years	Total Fertility rate[1]	Infant Mortality rate[2]	Women's Illiteracy rate[3]
World Average (140 countries)	64	3.6	81	34%
Afghanistan	41	6.9	205	94%
Chad	42	5.9	143	92%
Ethiopia	43	6.7	143	95%
Gambia	44	6.4	193	88%
Nepal	44	6.2	144	94%
Yemen, Arab Rep.	45	6.8	153	98%
Upper Volta	45	6.5	204	95%
Somalia	45	6.1	143	97%
Senegal	45	6.5	141	86%
Niger	45	7.1	140	94%
Mauritania	45	6.9	137	-
Mali	45	6.7	148	92%
Burundi	45	6.1	117	85%
Angola	45	6.4	148	81%
Bangladesh	47	6.2	133	80%

Source: Selected from "15 Countries with the Lowest Female Life Expectancy, 1980," *Women... a world survey,* 1985, p. 26 (Washington, D.C.: World Priorities, 1985). *Notes:* 1. The number of children who would be born per woman through her childbearing years if she were to have children at prevailing age-specific fertility rates. 2. Deaths of infants under one year of age per 1,000 live births. 3. The United Nations defines illiteracy percentages as the illiterate population 15 years of age and over per 100 total population of corresponding sex-age group, excluding population of unknown literacy.

★ 658 ★

Life Expectancy at Birth: 1950-1989

"The expectation of life at birth in 1989 reached a new record high of 75.2" (source).

Year	All races			White			Black		
	Total	Female	Male	Total	Female	Male	Total	Female	Male
1989	75.2	78.5	71.8	75.9	79.1	72.6	69.7	74.0	65.2
1988	74.9	78.3	71.4	75.5	78.9	72.1	69.5	73.8	65.1
1987	75.0	78.4	71.5	75.6	78.9	72.2	69.4	73.6	65.2
1986	74.8	78.3	71.3	75.4	78.8	72.0	69.4	73.5	65.2
1985	74.7	78.2	71.2	75.3	78.7	71.9	69.5	73.5	65.3
1984	74.7	78.2	71.2	75.3	78.7	71.8	69.7	73.7	65.6

[Continued]

★ 658 ★

Life Expectancy at Birth: 1950-1989
[Continued]

Year	All races			White			Black		
	Total	Female	Male	Total	Female	Male	Total	Female	Male
1983	74.6	78.1	71.0	75.2	78.7	71.7	69.6	73.6	65.4
1982	74.5	78.1	70.9	75.1	78.7	71.5	69.4	73.7	65.1
1981	74.2	77.8	70.4	74.8	78.4	71.1	68.9	73.2	64.5
1980	73.7	77.4	70.0	74.4	78.1	70.7	68.1	72.5	63.8
1979	73.9	77.8	70.0	74.6	78.4	70.8	68.5	72.9	64.0
1978	73.5	77.3	69.6	74.1	78.0	70.4	68.1	72.4	63.7
1977	73.3	77.2	69.5	74.0	77.9	70.2	67.7	72.0	63.4
1976	72.9	76.8	69.1	73.6	77.5	69.9	67.2	71.6	62.9
1975	72.6	76.6	68.8	73.4	77.3	69.5	66.8	71.3	62.4
1970	70.8	74.7	67.1	71.7	75.6	68.0	64.1	68.3	60.0
1960	69.7	73.1	66.6	70.6	74.1	67.4	-	-	-
1950	68.2	71.1	65.6	69.1	72.2	66.5	-	-	-

Source: "Average length of life in years, by race and sex: United States, 1950, 1960, 1970, 1975-89," *Monthly Vital Statistics Report* 38: No. 13: August 30, 1990. Data for 1988 and 1989 are provisional, estimated from a 10% sample of deaths.

★ 659 ★

Worldwide Expectation of Life at Birth

Expectation of life at birth by sex, latest available year.

Country or area, year	Age (in years)	
	Female	Male
AFRICA		
Algeria-1983	63.32	61.57
Angola-1985-1990	46.11	42.94
Benin-1985-1990	48.14	44.90
Botswana-1981	59.70	52.32
Burkina Faso-1985-1990	48.89	45.60
Burundi-1985-1990	50.68	47.36
Cameroon-1985-1990	53.00	49.00
Cape Verde-1979-1982	61.04	58.95
Central African Republic-1985-1990	47.12	43.93
Comoros-1985-1990	53.77	50.28
Congo-1985-1990	50.17	46.88
Cote d'Ivoire-1985-1990	54.20	50.80
Djibouti-1985-1990	48.65	45.40
Egypt-1985-1990	61.97	59.29
Equatorial Guinea-1985-1990	48.13	44.90
Ethiopia-1985-1990	42.60	39.45
Gabon-1985-1990	53.18	49.86

[Continued]

★ 659 ★

Worldwide Expectation of Life at Birth
[Continued]

Country or area, year	Age (in years)	
	Female	Male
Gambia-1985-1990	44.62	41.43
Ghana-1985-1990	55.81	52.24
Guinea-1985-1990	43.81	40.63
Guinea-Bissau-1985-1990	46.63	43.41
Kenya-1985-1990	60.46	56.50
Lesotho-1985-1990	60.50	51.50
Liberia-1985-1990	56.00	53.00
Libyan Arab Jamahiriya-1985-1990	62.46	59.05
Madagascar-1985-1990	55.00	52.00
Malawi-1977	41.16	38.12
Mali-1976	49.66	46.91
Mauritania-1985-1990	47.64	44.41
Mauritius-1984-1986	71.88	64.45
Rodrigues-1981-1985	68.95	64.47
Morocco-1985-1990	62.46	59.05
Mozambique-1985-1990	48.14	44.90
Namibia-1985-1990	57.50	55.00
Niger-1985-1990	46.13	42.92
Nigeria-1985-1990	52.23	48.82
Reunion-1985-1990	75.46	66.98
Rwanda-1978	47.70	45.10
Senegal-1985-1990	47.44	44.21
Seychelles-1981-1985	74.05	65.26
Sierra Leone-1985-1990	42.60	39.45
Somalia-1985-1990	46.60	43.41
South Africa-1985-1990	63.48	57.51
Sudan-1985-1990	51.00	48.60
Swaziland-1976	49.50	42.90
Togo-1985-1990	54.79	51.26
Tunisia-1985-1990	66.11	64.55
Uganda-1985-1990	52.69	49.36
United Rep. of Tanzania-1985-1990	54.70	51.30
Zaire-1985-1990	54.22	50.83
Zambia-1980	52.46	50.36
Zimbabwe-1985-1990	60.13	56.52
NORTH AMERICA		
Aruba-1972-1978	75.40	68.30
Barbados-1980	72.46	67.15
Bermuda-1980	76.28	68.81

[Continued]

★ 659 ★

Worldwide Expectation of Life at Birth
[Continued]

Country or area, year	Age (in years)	
	Female	Male
Canada-1984-1986	79.78	73.00
Costa Rica-1985-1990	77.04	72.41
Cuba-1983-1984	76.10	72.66
Dominican Republic-1985-1990	68.06	63.86
El Salvador-1985	63.89	50.74
Greenland-1981-1985	66.30	60.40
Guadeloupe-1975-1979	72.40	66.40
Guatemala-1979-1980	59.43	55.11
Haiti-1985-1990	56.41	53.09
Honduras-1985-1990	66.07	61.94
Jamaica-1985-1990	76.67	71.34
Martinique-1975	73.50	67.00
Mexico-1979	66.00	62.10
Netherlands Antilles-1970	65.70	58.90
Nicaragua-1985-1990	64.61	61.98
Panama-1980-1985	72.85	69.20
Puerto Rico-1983-1985	77.28	70.26
St. Kitts and Nevis-1985	69.67	65.99
St. Lucia-1986	74.80	68.00
Trinidad and Tobago-1980-1985	71.62	66.88
United States-1986	78.30	71.30
SOUTH AMERICA		
Argentina-1975-1980	72.12	65.43
Bolivia-1985-1990	55.41	50.85
Brazil-1985-1990	67.60	62.30
Chile-1985-1990	75.05	68.05
Colombia-1980-1985	69.23	63.39
Ecuador-1985	67.59	63.39
Guyana-1985-1990	72.30	67.30
Paraguay-1980-1985	68.51	64.42
Peru-1980-1985	66.50	56.77
Suriname-1985-1990	72.10	67.05
Uruguay-1984-1986	74.88	68.43
Venezuela-1985	72.80	66.68
ASIA		
Afghanistan-1985-1990	42.00	41.00

[Continued]

★ 659 ★

Worldwide Expectation of Life at Birth
[Continued]

Country or area, year	Age (in years)	
	Female	Male
Bahrain-1981-1986	68.90	65.90
Bangladesh-1984	54.70	54.90
Bhutan-1985-1990	47.10	48.60
Brunei Darussalam-1981	72.69	70.13
China-1985-1990	70.94	67.98
Cyprus-1983-1987	77.82	73.90
Democratic Kampuchea-1985-1990	49.90	47.00
Democratic Yemen-1985-1990	52.37	49.40
East Timor-1985-1990	43.44	41.65
Hong Kong-1987	79.72	74.24
India-1976-1980	52.10	52.50
Indonesia-1985-1990	57.40	54.60
Iran (Islamic Rep. of)-1976	55.04	55.75
Iraq-1985-1990	64.82	62.98
Israel-1985	76.99	73.53
Japan-1987	81.39	75.61
Jordan-1985-1990	67.84	64.16
Korea, Dem. People's Rep.-1985-1990	72.68	66.16
Korea, Republic of-1978-1979	69.07	62.70
Kuwait-1985-1990	74.97	70.75
Lao People's Dem. Rep.-1985-1990	50.00	47.00
Lebanon-1985-1990	69.00	65.10
Malaysia-1985-1990	71.58	67.52
Peninsular Malaysia-1987	73.00	68.83
Maldives-1985	69.48	62.20
Mongolia-1985-1990	65.60	61.50
Myanmar-1978	63.66	58.93
Nepal-1981	48.10	50.88
Oman-1985-1990	56.75	54.08
Pakistan-1976-1978	59.20	59.04
Philippines-1987	65.50	61.90
Qatar-1985-1990	71.80	66.93
Saudi Arabia-1985-1990	65.20	61.70
Singapore-1980	74.00	68.70
Sri Lanka-1981	71.66	67.78
Syran Arab Republic-1976-1979	64.70	63.77
Thailand-1985-1986	68.85	63.82
Turkey-1985-1990	65.77	62.50
United Arab Emirates-1985-1990	72.92	68.57
Viet Nam-1979	67.89	63.66
Yemen-1985-1990	52.40	49.50

[Continued]

★ 659 ★

Worldwide Expectation of Life at Birth
[Continued]

Country or area, year	Age (in years)	
	Female	Male
EUROPE		
Albania-1986-1986	73.94	68.48
Austria-1987	78.13	71.53
Belgium-1979-1982	76.79	70.04
Bulgaria-1978-1980	73.55	68.35
Czechoslovakia-1985	74.71	67.25
Denmark-1986-1987	77.60	71.80
Faeroe Islands-1981-1985	79.60	73.30
Finland-1986	78.72	70.49
France-1987	80.27	72.03
German Democratic Rep.-1986-1987	75.74	69.73
Germany, Federal Rep.-1985-1987	78.37	71.81
Greece-1980	76.35	72.15
Hungary-1987	73.74	65.67
Iceland-1983-1984	80.20	73.96
Ireland-1980-1982	75.62	70.14
Italy-1983	78.14	71.43
Liechtenstein-1980-1984	72.94	66.07
Luxembourg-1980-1982	76.70	70.00
Malta-1987	77.01	72.54
Netherlands-985-1986	79.55	72.95
Norway-1987	79.55	72.75
Poland-1987	75.20	66.81
Portugal-1979-1982	75.20	68.35
Romania-1976-1978	72.06	67.42
San Marino-1977-1986	79.12	73.16
Spain-1980-1982	78.61	72.52
Sweden-1987	80.15	74.16
Switzerland-1986-1987	80.50	73.80
United Kingdom-1984-1987	77.51	71.22
England and Wales-1983-1985	77.74	71.80
Northern Ireland-1983	75.65	69.25
Scotland-1985	75.83	70.05
Yugoslavia-1984-1985	73.55	68.13
OCEANIA		
Australia-1986	79.13	72.77

[Continued]

★ 659 ★

Worldwide Expectation of Life at Birth
[Continued]

Country or area, year	Age (in years)	
	Female	Male
Cook Islands-1974-1978	67.09	63.17
Fiji-1976	63.90	60.75
Guam-1979-1981	75.59	69.53
New Zealand-1986-1988	77.27	71.03
Papua New Guinea-1985-1990	54.84	53.18
Samoa-1976	64.30	61.00
Solomon Islands-1980-1984	61.40	59.90
USSR		
USSR-1985-1986	73.27	64.15
Byelorussian SSR-1985-1986	75.52	66.66
Ukrainian SSR-1985-1986	74.45	65.90

Source: Selected from "Expectation of Life at Specified Ages for Each Sex: Latest Available Year," *1988 Demographic Yearbook,* p 522-49 (New York: United Nations, 1990). Also in source: expectation of life by age.

Marital Status

★ 660 ★

Marital Status of Young Adults Worldwide

Marital status of young adults, ages 20-24, circa 1981.

Country	Year	Percent single		Percent married		Percent separated or divorced	
		Female	Male	Female	Male	Female	Male
Australia	1981	54.5%	77.4%	41.6%	21.2%	3.8%	1.4%
Canada	1981	51.1%	71.9%	48.0%	27.8%	.8%	.3%
China	1982	46.5%	72.0%	53.3%	27.8%	.2%	.2%
Germany, Federal Republic	1982	65.3%	86.6%	33.6%	13.0%	1.0%	.3%
France	1982	64.6%	85.1%	34.4%	14.6%	.9%	.3%
Hungary	1981	30.9%	66.1%	66.0%	32.9%	3.0%	1.0%
Israel	1980	45.3%	77.9%	54.7%	22.1%	NA	NA
Japan	1980	77.8%	91.8%	21.9%	8.1%	.3%	.1%
Mexico	1982	53.0%	NA	42.5%	NA	4.1%	NA
Norway	1982	67.1%	86.9%	31.0%	12.5%	1.8%	.5%
Sweden	1981	84.8%	95.0%	14.2%	4.7%	1.0%	.3%

[Continued]

★ 660 ★

Marital Status of Young Adults Worldwide
[Continued]

Country	Year	Percent single		Percent married		Percent separated or divorced	
		Female	Male	Female	Male	Female	Male
United Kingdom	1981	53.7%	74.3%	44.5%	25.0%	1.7%	.6%
United States	1980	51.2%	68.2%	44.4%	29.5%	4.2%	2.2%

Source: "Marital Status of Young Adults, Ages 20-24, by Sex, Selected Countries: Circa 1981," *Children's Well-Being: An International Comparison,* A Report of the Select Committee on Children, Youth, and Families, 101st Cong., 2d sess., March 1990, p. 119. Primary source: U.S. Bureau of the Census, Center for International Research, International Data Base. Percents may not add to 100 since widowhood data are not shown. Percent single for Mexico includes 13% reported living in consensual unions.

★ 661 ★

Young Adults Never Married, Worldwide
Percent of youth population never married, 1980 or 1981.

Country	Year	Ages 15 to 19		Ages 20 to 24	
		Female	Male	Female	Male
Canada	1980	95.6%	99.1%	55.2%	76.1%
Germany, Federal Republic	1980	96.4%	99.6%	60.1%	84.2%
France	1980	95.4%	99.6%	51.4%	74.3%
Hungary	1981	85.7%	98.2%	30.9%	66.1%
Israel	1980	92.5%	99.3%	45.3%	77.9%
Japan	1980	99.0%	99.6%	77.8%	91.8%
Norway	1981	97.9%	99.8%	64.6%	85.7%
Sweden	1981	99.3%	99.9%	84.8%	95.0%
United Kingdom	1981	95.5%	98.9%	53.7%	74.3%
United States	1981	92.0%	97.8%	51.9%	69.5%

Source: "Percent of Youth Population Never Married, by Age and Sex, Selected Countries: 1980 or 1981, *Children's Well-Being: An International Comparison,* A Report of the Select Committee on Children, Youth, and Families, 101st Cong., 2d sess., March 1990, p. 119. Primary source: U.S. Bureau of the Census, Center for International Research, International Data Base, and Youth Data Base.

Marriages and Divorces

★ 662 ★

Divorcees' Incidence of Remarriage

Percentage of women divorced from their first husband who had remarried by the survey date, by age at divorce from first marriage: June 1985.

Age at divorce from first husband	% remarried by Jun '85
All ages	64.9%
Under 25	81.5%
25-29	67.4%
30-34	56.8%
35-39	52.0%
40-44	39.7%
45 +	28.7%

Source: "How Many Women Remarry?", *Census and You,* Vol 26, No. 2, Februry 1991, p. 4. Primary source: *Studies in Household and Family Formation,* Current Population Reports, Series P-23, No. 169.

★ 663 ★

Divorces and Divorce Rates

Divorces, and divorce rates on an annual basis per 1,000 population, by month, 1988 and 1989.

Month	Number		Rate	
	1989	1988	1989	1988
Total	1,163,000	1,183,000	4.7	4.8
January	98,000	93,000	4.7	4.5
February	89,000	84,000	4.7	4.3
March	98,000	100,000	4.7	4.8
April	89,000	92,000	4.4	4.6
May	99,000	108,000	4.7	5.2
June	108,000	104,000	5.3	5.2
July	90,000	100,000	4.3	4.8
August	97,000	106,000	4.6	5.1
September	93,000	98,000	4.6	4.8
October	96,000	98,000	4.6	4.7
November	98,000	91,000	4.8	4.5
December	107,000	108,000	5.1	5.2

Source: "Divorces and divorce rates, by month: United States, 1988 and 1989," *Monthly Vital Statistics Report* 138: No. 13, August 30, 1990, p. 4. Data are provisional. Includes reported annulments. Rates on an annual basis per 1,000 population. Data are estimated for some States. Due to rounding, figures may not add to totals. Figures include revisions and, therefore, may differ from those previously published.

★ 664 ★

Divorces/Annulments: 1960 to 1986

Divorces/annulments in thousands and rate per 1,000 population: 1960 to 1986.

Year	Divorces/Annulments		
	Number	Rate	
		Total	Married women 15 and over
1960	393	2.2	9.2
1965	479	2.5	10.6
1970	708	3.5	14.9
1975	1,036	4.8	20.3
1980	1,189	5.2	22.6
1981	1,213	5.3	22.6
1982	1,170	5.0	21.7
1983	1,158	4.9	21.3
1984	1,169	5.0	21.5
1985	1,190	5.0	21.7
1986	1,178	4.9	21.2

Source: Selected from "Marriages and Divorces: 1960 to 1986," *Statistical Abstract of the United States 1990*, p. 86. Also in source: marriages (see separate table).

★ 665 ★

Marital Status and Religion in Israel

Population of Jerusalem and Israel, by marital status and religion, 1972 and 1983 (ages 15 and over, in percent).

Marital status and sex	Jerusalem total 1983	Jews				Non-Jews, Jerusalem	
		Jerusalem		Israel		Muslims	Christians
		1972	1983	1972	1983	1983	1983
			Percent				
Women							
Total	100	100	100	100	100	100	100
Single	27.6	28.3	26.6	22.9	20.8	28.4	42.4
Married	59.0	58.8	59.5	63.7	64.1	60.4	42.9
Divorced	3.0	2.1	3.5	1.9	3.2	1.5	1.7
Widowed	10.3	10.7	10.4	11.5	11.9	9.7	13.0
Men							
Total	100	100	100	100	100	100	100
Single	36.6	35.4	34.6	31.5	28.9	41.8	46.9
Married	60.2	61.4	61.7	65.1	66.8	56.6	50.0
Divorced	1.4	1.0	1.7	0.9	1.6	0.5	0.9
Widowed	1.8	2.2	2.0	2.5	2.6	1.1	2.2

Source: "Population of Jerusalem and Israel, by Religion, Sex, and Marital Status, 1972 and 1983 (percent)," *American Jewish Year Book*, 1987, Table 12, p. 94 (Scranton, PA: American Jewish Committee and Jewish Publication Society, 1987).

★ 666 ★

Marriages and Marriage Rates

Marriages, and marriage rates on an annual basis per 1,000 population, by month, 1988 and 1989.

Month	Number		Rate	
	1989	1988	1989	1988
Total	2,404,000	2,389,000	9.7	9.7
January	117,000	120,000	5.6	5.8
February	126,000	121,000	6.7	6.3
March	159,000	175,000	7.6	8.4
April	185,000	181,000	9.1	9.0
May	228,000	223,000	10.8	10.7
June	291,000	277,000	14.3	13.8
July	217,000	226,000	10.3	10.9
August	245,000	243,000	11.6	11.6
September	231,000	229,000	11.3	11.3
October	210,000	218,000	9.9	10.5
November	188,000	176,000	9.2	8.7
December	208,000	200,000	9.8	9.6

Source: "Marriages and marriage rates, by month: United States, 1988 and 1989," *Monthly Vital Statistics Report* 138: No. 13, p. 4, August 30, 1990. Data are provisional. Due to rounding, figures may not add to totals. Figures include revisions and, therefore, may differ from those previously published.

★ 667 ★

Marriages and Marriage Rates: 1960 to 1986

Marriages in thousands and rate per 1,000 population, 1960 to 1986.

Year	Marriages[1]					
	Number	Rate per 1,000 population				
		Total	Women 15 years old and over	Men 15 years old and over	Unmarried women	
					15 years old and over	15-44 years old
1960	1,523	8.5	24.0	25.4	73.5	148.0
1965	1,800	9.3	26.0	27.9	75.0	144.3
1970	2,159	10.6	28.4	31.1	76.5	140.2
1975	2,153	10.0	25.6	27.9	66.9	118.5
1980	2,390	10.6	26.1	28.5	61.4	102.6
1981	2,422	10.6	26.1	28.4	61.7	103.1
1982	2,456	10.6	26.1	28.4	61.4	101.9
1983	2,446	10.5	25.7	28.0	59.9	99.3
1984	2,477	10.5	25.8	28.1	59.5	99.0
1985	2,413	10.1	24.8	26.9	57.0	94.9
1986	2,407	10.0	24.5	26.5	56.2	93.9

Source: Selected from "Marriages and Divorces: 1960 to 1986," *Statistical Abstract of the United States 1990*, p. 86. Also in source: divorces/annulments (see separate table). *Note:* 1. Beginning 1980 includes nonlicensed marriages registerd in California.

★ 668 ★

Median Age at First Marriage: 1970-1989

Year	Median age	
	Women	Men
1989	23.8	26.2
1985	23.3	25.5
1980	22.0	24.7
1975	21.1	23.5
1970	20.8	23.2

Source: Current Population Reports, Series P-20, No. 445, "Marital Status and Living Arrangements: March 1989, 1990, p. 1.

★ 669 ★

Median Age at Marriage: Selected Countries

Median age at marriage, selected countries, selected years.

Country	Year	Median age at marriage	
		Female	Male
Australia	1981	23.0	25.0
Canada	1981	22.0	25.0
China	1982	22.2	24.5
France	1982	23.8	26.2
Germany, Federal Republic	1982	24.0	28.0
Hungary	1981	20.0	24.0
India	1981	17.9	23.3
Israel	1980	21.8	25.3
Japan	1980	25.0	28.0
United States	1982	23.0	25.0

Source: Selected from "Median Age at Marriage and Median Age of Mother at First Birth, Selected Countries: Selected Years, 1980 to 1985," *Children's Well-Being: An International Comparison,* A Report of the Select Committee on Children, Youth, and Families, 101st Cong., 2d sess., March 1990, p. 120. Primary source: U.S. Bureau of the Census, Center for International Research, International Data Base; and United Nations, 1988, *Demographic Yearbook 1986,* table 26. Also in source: Median age of mother at first birth (see separate table). The median age at marriage is the age at which 50% of the population is married. Median age at marriage calculated at the U.S. Bureau of the Census based on reported distributions of persons by marital status.

★ 670 ★

Widows' Incidence of Remarriage

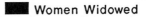
Women Widowed

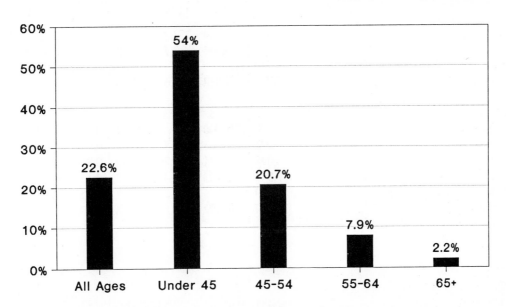

Percentage of women widowed from their first marriage who had remarried by the survey date, by age at widowhood from first marriage: June 1985.

Age at widowhood from first marriage	% remarried by Jun '85
All ages	22.6%
Under 45	54.0%
45-54	20.7%
55-64	7.9%
65+	2.2%

Source: "How Many Women Remarry?", *Census and You*, Vol. 26, No. 2, February 1991, p. 5. Primary source: *Studies in Household and Family Formation*, Series P-23, No. 169.

★ 671 ★

Worldwide Divorce

Divorces and crude divorce rates by country: 1984-1987. Rates are the number of final divorce decrees granted under civil law per 1,000 mid-year population.

Country or Area	Number				Rate			
	1984	1985	1986	1987	1984	1985	1986	1987
Asia								
Indonesia	175,630	-	-	-	1.10	-	-	-
Iran (Islamic Republic of)	35,178	-	38,983	33,697	0.76	-	0.79	0.66
Israel	4,834	4,911	5,806	5,128	1.16	1.16	1.18	1.19

[Continued]

★ 671 ★

Worldwide Divorce
[Continued]

Country or Area	Number				Rate			
	1984	1985	1986	1987	1984	1985	1986	1987
Japan	178,746	166,640	166,054	158,227	1.49	1.38	1.37	1.29
Jordan	2,652	3,687	3,446	3,709	0.79	1.05	0.94	0.98
Korea, Republic of	33,305	34,640	33,835	-	0.82	0.85	0.82	
Kuwait	2,548	2,739	2,834	2,697	1.56	1.60	1.58	1.44
Macau	40	42	32	37	-	-	-	-
Mongolia	600	700	1,000	-	0.32	0.37	0.51	-
Qatar	305	291	308	337	1.07	0.97	0.98	1.03
Singapore	2,028	2,048	2,271	2,708	0.80	0.80	0.88	1.04
Sri Lanka	2,612	2,344	3,103	4,429	0.17	0.15	0.19	0.27
Syrian Arab Republic	5,788	6,679	6,776	7,249	0.58	0.65	0.64	0.66
Thailand	30,057	30,057	36,602	0.59	0.58	0.69	-	
Turkey	16,987	18,571	18,774	18,305	0.35	0.38	0.37	0.36
Europe								
Albania	2,335	2,451	2,383	2,537	0.80	0.83	0.79	0.82
Austria	14,869	15,460	14,679	14,639	1.97	2.04	1.94	1.93
Belgium	18,645	18,437	18,316	-	1.89	1.87	1.85	-
Bulgaria	13,227	14,361	10,042	12,552	1.48	1.60	1.12	1.40
Channel Islands	364	313	382	358	2.76	2.36	2.81	2.63
Guernsey	170	140	192	153	3.19	2.63	3.46	2.76
Jersey	194	173	190	205	2.48	2.18	2.37	2.55
Czechoslovakia	37,422	38,289	37,885	39,522	2.42	2.47	2.44	2.54
Denmark	14,490	14,385	14,490	14,381	2.83	2.81	2.83	2.80
Faeroe Islands	29	34	26	45	-	-	-	-
Finland	9,644	9,063	9,742	10,363	1.97	1.85	1.98	2.10
France	104,012	107,505	108,380	106,527	1.89	1.95	1.96	1.91
German Democratic Rep.	50,320	51,240	52,234	50,640	3.02	3.08	3.14	3.04
Germany, Federal Rep.	130,744	128,124	122,443	129,850	2.14	2.10	2.00	2.12
Greece	8,672	7,568	8,650	-	0.88	0.76	0.87	-
Hungary	28,696	29,302	29,545	29,846	2.69	2.75	2.78	2.81
Iceland	449	520	500	500	1.87	2.15	2.05	2.03
Isle of Man	124	146	128	305	1.94	2.32	2.02	4.75
Italy	15,065	15,650	16,857	0.26	0.27	0.29	-	
Luxembourg	631	665	680	739	1.72	1.81	1.85	2.01
Netherlands	34,068	34,044	29,836	27,809	2.36	2.35	2.05	1.90
Norway	7,974	8,206	7,891	8,417	1.93	1.98	1.89	2.01
Poland	52,948	49,095	50,580	49,707	1.43	1.32	1.35	1.32
Portugal	7,034	8,988	8,411	8,948	0.70	0.88	0.82	0.87
Romania	32,853	32,587	-	-	1.45	1.43	-	-
San Marino	5	3	10	22	-	-	-	-

[Continued]

★ 671 ★

Worldwide Divorce
[Continued]

Country or Area	Number				Rate			
	1984	1985	1986	1987	1984	1985	1986	1987
Sweden	20,377	19,763	19,107	18,426	2.44	2.37	2.28	2.19
Switzerland	11,219	11,415	11,395	11,552	1.74	1.76	1.75	1.76
United Kingdom	157,211	174,666	167,309	164,208	2.78	3.08	2.95	2.88
England and Wales	143,746	159,693	-	-	2.89	3.20	-	-
Northern Ireland	1,553	1,602	-	-	1.00	1.03	-	-
Scotland	11,915	13,371	-	-	2.31	2.60	-	-
Yugoslavia	22,260	23,952	22.093	20,807	0.97	1.03	0.95	0.89
Oceania								
Australia	43,124	39,830	39,417	-	2.77	2.52	2.46	-
Guam	550	876	1,023	1,279	4.59	7.65	8.26	10.12
New Caledonia	116	168	158	166	0.78	1.11	1.02	1.05
New Zealand	9,167	8,551	8,746	8,702	2.84	2.63	2.69	2.65
Pacific Islands								
Northern Mariana Islands	21	35	62	-	-	-	-	-
Tonga	88	63	-	-	-	-	-	-
USSR								
USSR	932,305	933,097	941,329	950,709	3.39	3.36	3.36	3.36
Byelorussian SSR	30,825	31,197	30,297	30,507	3.11	3.13	3.02	3.02
Ukrainian SSR	186,629	183,373	180,366	184,720	3.68	3.60	3.53	3.60

Source: Selected from "Divorces and Crude Divorce Rates: 1984-1988," *1988 Demographic Yearbook,* p. 568-71 (New York: United Nations, 1990). Also in source: scant data for 1988. Data exclude annulments and legal separations. Rates are shown only for countries or areas having at least a total 100 divorces in a given year.

★ 672 ★

Worldwide Marriages by Age of Bride

Marriages by age of bride and legal age of marriage for women: latest available year.

Country or area, year	Age	Age of bride (in years)											
		All ages	<15	15-19	20-24	25-29	30-34	35-39	40-44	45-49	50-54	55-59	60+
AFRICA													
Algeria-1980	-	128,424	283	54,867	45,276	16,722	4,631	1,934	1,403	869	5	13	-
Egypt-1981	16	385,095	-	-	116,357	46,669	16,356	6,478	3,967	2,454	1,788	956	1,386
Mauritius-1987	16	11,201	5	2,484	4,494	2,246	1,002	507	236	99	60	26	42
Reunion-1987	-	3,001	-	444	1,343	662	258	119	56	48	32	19	20
South Africa-1977													
Asiatic	16	7,831	-	1,974	3,162	1,259	598	322	195	124	89	57	51
Colored	16	18,611	-	2,400	7,803	4,161	1,667	971	601	398	256	117	237

[Continued]

581

★ 672 ★

Worldwide Marriages by Age of Bride

[Continued]

Country or area, year	Age	Age of bride (in years)										
		All ages	<15	15-19	20-24	25-29	30-34	35-39	40-44	45-49	50-54	55-59	60+
White	16	38,537	-	9,995	16,810	4,911	2,195	1,269	860	726	599	432	740
Tunisia-1980	17	39,558	-	15,775[2]	16,568	5,213	865	212	140	73	37	42	632
Zimbabwe-1977													
Europeans	-	2,432	-	507	966	377	183	89	79	71	44	22	24
NORTH AMERICA													
Bahamas-1986	15	1,784	-	124	643	485	245	129	75	38	24	7	9
Barbados-1986	16	1,461	-	32	376	476	299	120	57	40	25	10	25
Canada-1987	2	182,151	6	11,332	71,068	49,624	21,217	11,010	6,471	4,046	2,455	1,777	3,145
Costa Rica-1982	15	18,542	119	6,584	6,766	2,704	1,058	494	283	157	108	53	114
Cuba-1986	14	84,014	1,154	22,851	30,896	10,472	4,950	3,354	2,514	1,951	1,573	1,314	2,316
Dominican Republic-1984	15	30,985	9	831	6,336	8,273	5,414	3,226	2,120	1,454	898	598	755
El Salvador-1985	14	18,142	200	4,247	5,810	3,328	1,719	997	635	426	249	148	148
Guadeloupe-1986	19	1,692	-	-	653	443	187	93	48	36	-	-	-
Guatemala-1985	14	38,489	1.163	14,802	10,264	4,373	2,598	1,646	1,163	879	621	416	564
Honduras-1983	12	19,875	760	4,798	9,229	2,407	1,244	627	350	199	129	63	69
Martinique-1984	-	1,297	1	64	460	384	150	79	48	29	-	-	-
Mexico-1984	14	498,698	8,051	179,407	176,353	69,115	24,849	11,908	6,660	4,584	-	-	-
Panama-1987	12	11,188	138	1,852	3,752	2,463	1,165	634	391	244	161	114	136
Puerto Rico-1985	12	30,306	419	7,068	10,340	5,244	2,607	1,641	979	692	477	-	-
Trinidad and Tobago-1987	2	7,602	48	1,506	2,769	1,689	718	319	187	114	92	55	101
United States-1986	2	1,854,744	56,654	186,143	612,901	427,787	234,121	-	-	-	-	-	18,866
SOUTH AMERICA													
Argentina-1981	14	161,422	1,128	39,937	65,075	30,103	10,024	4,128	2,232	1,667	1,589	1,348	2,163
Bolivia-1977	-	28,233	160	7,203	10,564	5,089	2,234	1,169	677	461	283	-	-
Brazil-1986	-	1,007,474	7,276	334,513	370,409	156,096	61,223	31,382	17,840	12,392	7,405	4,442	4,496
Chile-1987	12	95,531	417	19,518	42,317	20,641	6,719	2,499	1,203	732	507	390	588
Colombia-1980	12	102,448	691	31,578	40,571	17,333	5,817	2,351	1,181	665	421	264	296
Ecuador-1987	12	61,301	1,112	19,975	21,961	9,804	4,034	1,911	975	593	326	247	325
French Guiana-1984	-	309	-	21	81	90	46	20	19	11	-	-	-
Paraguay-1985	12	18,370	273	5,386	5,792	3,060	1,558	887	516	332	192	127	247
Peru-1977	14	38,297	409	9,518	12,871	6,828	3,091	1,700	1,142	818	-	-	-
Uruguay-1987	12	21,812	-	-	7,668	4,148	1,700	900	-	-	-	-	-
Venezuela-1987	18	105,058	2,695	31,908	34,807	19,100	8,469	4,007	1,777	1,057	539	343	356
ASIA													
Bahrain-1986	-	2,708	-	-	997	957	337	135	50	38	-	-	-
Brunei Darussalam-1986	2	1,673	12	181	523	534	312	82	9	13	2	2	3
Cyprus-1987	15	5,954	-	1,110	2,737	1,306	377	185	101	57	33	24	24
Hong Kong-1987	16	48,561	-	1,589	16,439	18,938	5,150	1,737	876	802	1,019	994	1,017
Iraq-1987	18	47,408	-	-	13,959	8,415	5,185	3,066	-	-	-	-	440
Israel-1987	17	30,116	-	-	14,191	5,549	1,794	807	306	126	89	56	159
Japan-1987	16	630,333	-	21,079	252,669	254,677	55,381	24,847	9,825	5,858	3,357	1,585	1,052
Jordan-1987	16	23,208	2	10,241	9,092	2,674	645	235	141	71	50	15	25
Korea, Republic of-1986	16	353,477	-	-	190,598	116,147	13,792	4,468	2,413	1,588	906	-	-
Kuwait-1987	-	9,842	79	3,360	3,925	1,451	571	234	129	48	30	7	4
Macau-1987	-	2,472	-	47	785	1,076	427	97	16	6	10	4	4

[Continued]

★ 672 ★

Worldwide Marriages by Age of Bride
[Continued]

Country or area, year	Age	Age of bride (in years)											
		All ages	<15	15-19	20-24	25-29	30-34	35-39	40-44	45-49	50-54	55-59	60+
Malaysia													
Peninsular Malaysia-1979	14	19,075	9	1,507	8,923	5,756	1,676	641	262	161	74	38	28
Philippines-1987	14	400,760	1,798	111,659	158,646	80,855	26,874	10,389	4,367	2,532	-	-	-
Qatar-1987	-	1,349	-	87	504	456	159	53	28	22	15	8	9
Singapore-1987	2	23,404	-	1,355	10,173	8,200	2,455	802	228	114	37	17	23
Sri Lanka-1983	-	123,731	368	20,137	66,064	23,618	9,120	2,577	826	455	265	166	135
Turkey-1987	15	436,065	1,244	154,468	185,341	62,478	17,746	6,244	3,009	1,735	1,437	939	1,392
EUROPE													
Albania-1987	-	27,370	-	-	15,366	5,150	916	212	66	35	-	-	-
Austria-1987	16	76,205	-	8,281	36,184	19,314	6,191	2,588	1,600	1,107	407	235	298
Belgium-1985	15	57,551	-	-	31,873	10,039	3,393	1,771	946	670	-	-	-
Bulgaria-1986	18	64,965	-	24,301	24,903	7,563	3,580	2,004	1,004	553	353	311	393
Czechoslovakia-1985	16	119,583	-	33,825	54,527	14,244	6,998	3,891	2,487	1,499	980	543	589
Denmark-1987	15	31,132	1	827	8,617	9,897	4,718	2,555	1,896	1,063	493	233	295
Finland-1986	17	25,820	1	1,657	9,661	7,815	3,195	1,634	802	485	252	144	174
France-1987	15	265,177	6	13,252	116,470	72,080	29,004	15,341	8,054	4,230	2,899	1,742	2,099
German Democratic Rep.-1987	18	141,283	-	15,856	71,453	26,768	10,792	5,978	3,645	3,512	1,785	783	711
Germany, Federal Rep.-1986	16	372,112	4	27,326	156,719	103,311	37,180	17,706	10,710	9,384	4,393	2,298	3,081
Greece-1985	14	63,709	342	16,089	24,476	12,870	4,645	2,209	1,005	808	515	373	374
Hungary-1987	14	66,082	19	19,289	26,394	7,932	4,740	2,618	1,695	1,242	724	611	818
Iceland-1984	18	1,413	-	107	657	385	128	61	35	17	11	7	5
Ireland-1985	12	18,791	-	-	9,226	5,896	1,454	398	128	91	51	30	40
Italy-1983	16	303,663	-	53,321	149,454	66,376	17,475	6,613	3,470	2,283	1,712	1,240	1,719
Luxembourg-1987	15	1,958	-	160	796	558	232	100	49	32	15	11	5
Malta-1987	14	2,437	-	239	1,192	732	162	64	26	14	4	1	3
Netherlands-1986	18	87,337	-	-	41,777	22,884	8,493	4,144	2,128	1,341	789	441	821
Norway-1987	18	20,285	-	1,216	8,324	6,080	2,358	1,076	607	307	159	67	91
Poland-1987	18	252,819	-	49,411	128,013	39,309	14,841	7,467	3,463	2,832	2,609	1,977	2,897
Portugal-1987	16	71,656	1,595	13,944	33,611	13,519	3,447	1,686	947	761	737	568	841
Romania-1985	16	161,094	-		56,873	20,765	9,762	4,570	2,574	2,454	1,700	1,142	1,375
Spain-1983	12	196,155	320	33,245	102,816	40,287	8,797	3,465	1,639	1,384	1,244	1,047	1,911
Sweden-1987	18	43,530	-	1,065	10,093	13,207	7,427	3,948	2,665	1,407	727	319	365
Switzerland-1987	17	43,063	-	1,293	14,990	15,194	5,883	2,473	1,507	832	434	253	204
United Kingdom-1987	16	397,937	-	-	170,147	90,911	36,643	21,634	15,344	9,424	5,577	3,190	6,076
England and Wales-1985	16	346,389	-	41,927	149,174	70,495	30,055	20,079	12,217	8,439	5,110	2,858	6,035
Northern Ireland-1985	16	10,343	-	1,611	5,179	2,217	623	287	145	102	61	48	70
Scotland-1985	16	36,385	-	4,900	16,855	7,393	2,746	1,670	982	717	463	255	404
Yugoslavia-1987	18	163,469	4	40,793	72,060	29,029	9,793	4,205	1,811	1,552	1,338	1,003	1,673
OCEANIA													
Australia-1986	18	114,913	-	9,809	48,518	27,394	11,922	6,878	3,920	2,475	1,370	999	1,627
Fiji-1985	16	6,593	-	2,166	2,776	928	344	184	86	65	25	11	8
Guam-1987	17	1,512	1	43	538	447	252	135	49	19	19	5	4
New Zealand-1987	16	24,443	-	1,751	10,199	6,018	2,516	1,410	903	652	368	233	393
USSR													
USSR-1984	18	2,634,144	-	-	1,188,116	365,704	157,187	71,986	43,595	49,624	30,906	29,997	37,131

[Continued]

★ 672 ★

Worldwide Marriages by Age of Bride
[Continued]

Country or area, year	Age	Age of bride (in years)											
		All ages	<15	15-19	20-24	25-29	30-34	35-39	40-44	45-49	50-54	55-59	60+
Byelorussian SSR-1986	18	99,358	-	-	45,194	15,213	6,403	3,576	1,381	1,726	1,160	1,040	1,458
Ukrainian SSR-1986	17	483,366	-	-	181,782	65,423	32,370	18,744	8,703	12,862	6,643	6,662	9,98

Source: Selected from "Marriages by Age of Bridegroom and by Age of Bride: Latest Available Year," *1988 Demographic Yearbook,* p. 557-567 (New York: United Nation 1990). Also in source: marriages by age of bridegroom. Data are for legal (recognized) marriages performed and registered. "Unknown" figures not included. Some figures hav been combined with other age groups; see source for detail. *Notes:* 1. Age below which marriage is unlawful or invalid without dispensation by competent authority. 2. Varie among major civil divisions, or ethnic or religious groups.

Maternal Deaths

★ 673 ★

Maternal Mortality Rates: 1970-1987
Maternal deaths per 100,000 live births.

	1970	1975	1978	1979	1980	1981	1982	1983	1984	1985	1986	1987
Maternal deaths	21.5	12.8	9.6	9.6	9.2	8.5	7.9	8.0	7.8	7.8	7.2	6.6
White	14.4	9.1	6.4	6.4	6.7	6.3	5.8	5.9	5.4	5.2	4.9	5.1
Black and other	55.9	29.0	23.0	22.7	19.8	17.3	16.4	16.3	16.9	18.1	16.0	12.0
Black	59.8	31.3	25.0	25.1	21.5	20.4	18.2	18.3	19.7	20.4	18.8	14.2

Source: Selected from "Infant, Maternal, and Neonatal Mortality Rates, and Fetal Mortality Ratios, by Race: 1960 to 1987," *Statistical Abstract of the United States 1990,* p. 77. Also in source: infant and neonatal mortality rates and fetal mortality ratios (see separate tables). *Notes:* 1. Per 100,000 live births from deliveries and complications of pregnancy, childbirth, and the puerperium.

★ 674 ★

Worldwide Maternal Deaths
Number of maternal deaths (caused by deliveries and complications of pregnancy, childbirth, and the puerperium) per 100,000 live births.

Country or Area	1980	1981	1982	1983	1984	1985	1986	1987
Africa								
Cape Verde	107.4	-	-	-	-	-	-	-
Egypt	93.1	-	78.5	-	-	-	-	-
Mauritius	110.4[1]	68.5[1]	98.9[1]	55.5[1]	93.6[1]	104.1 1[1]	26.2[1]	99.2[1]
Sao Tome	-	-	-	-	-	152.9[1]	-	-
North America								
Bahamas	-	37.1[1]	18.9[1]	18.9[1]	19.3[1]	17.9[1]	-	-
Barbados	24.1[1]	-	-	-	71.2[1]	-	-	-

[Continued]

★ 674 ★

Worldwide Maternal Deaths
[Continued]

Country or Area	1980	1981	1982	1983	1984	1985	1986	1987
Canada	7.6[1]	6.2[1]	1.9[1]	5.4[1]	3.2[1]	4.0[1]	3.0[1]	-
Costa Rica	24,2[1]	38.4[1]	29.5[1]	26.0[1]	23.7[1]	34.4[1]	-	-
Cuba	59.9	51.4	55.7	45.4	46.3	46.1	52.4	-
Dominican Republic	-	51.0	60.3	58.4	61.4	-	-	-
El Salvador	70.6	61.8	84.8	74.2	69.6	-	-	-
Guatemala	91.0	105.7	-	-	75.6	-	-	-
Mexico	93.9	86.9	90.5	81.8	-	-	-	-
Panama	72.2	61.3	89.9	59.8	49.4[1]	56.9	62.4	-
Puerto Rico	8.2[1]	16.8[1]	11.5[1]	6.1[1]	9.5[1]	12.6[1]	-	-
Trinidad and Tobago	-	-	43.0[1]	54.2[1]	-	-	-	-
United States	9.2	8.5	7.9	8.0	7.8	7.8	7.2	-
South America								
Argentina	69.5	69.4	69.9	60.2	-	-	-	-
Brazil	92.1	88.6	77.1	78.1	76.7	-	47.3	-
Chile	74.9	43.8	51.8	40.3	34.7	50.0	47.3	-
Colombia	-	19.5	-	-	-	-	-	
Ecuador	-	185.9	181.8	-	186.2	189.1	160.4	173.6
Paraguay	-	439.8	467.3	502.1	382.9	365.3	379.5	-
Peru	160.6	141.4	109.3	88.7	-	-	-	-
Suriname	81.3[1]	-	-	-	-	-	-	-
Uruguay	-	59.3	37.2[1]	39.3[1]	37.5[1]	42.8[1]	26.1[1]	-
Venezuela	64.7	53.3	50.3	58.9	-	-	-	-
Asia								
Bahrain	-	-	-	-	-	16.2[1]	-	-
Hong Kong	4.7[1]	8.1[1]	1.2[1]	7.2[1]	6.5[1]	5.3[1]	2.8[1]	4.3[1]
Israel	5.3[1]	-	3.1[1]	2.0[1]	5.1[1]	8.1[1]	6.0[1]	-
Japan	20.5	19.2	18.4[1]	15.5	15.3	15.8	13.5	12.0
Korea, Rep. of	-	-	[1]	-	-	16.9	15.7	9.7
Kuwait	7.8[1]	7.7[1]	18.4[1]	12.6[1]	14.1	3.6[1]	5.6[1]	2.0[1]
Macau	-	47.5[1]	-	-	-	-	-	-
Maldives	-	-	-	-	-	-	684.9	645.6
Philippines	-	105.5	-	-	-	-	-	-
Singapore	4.9[1]	4.7[1]	11.7[1]	14.8[1]	12.0[1]	4.7[1]	13.0[1]	6.9[1]
Europe								
Austria	7.7[1]	13.8[1]	16.9[1]	11.1[1]	4.5[1]	6.9[1]	6.9[1]	4.6[1]

[Continued]

★ 674 ★

Worldwide Maternal Deaths
[Continued]

Country or Area	1980	1981	1982	1983	1984	1985	1986	1987
Belgium	5.6[1]	9.7[1]	7.5[1]	5.1[1]	8.6[1]	-	3.4[1]	-
Bulgaria	21.1[1]	24.1[1]	17.7[1]	22.0[1]	17.2[1]	12.6[1]	25.0[1]	19.9[1]
Czechoslovakia	9.2	13.5[1]	8.1[1]	10.0[1]	9.7[1]	8.0[1]	10.9[1]	-
Denmark	1.7[1]	3.8[1]	11.4[1]	3.9[1]	7.7[1]	1.9[1]	3.6[1]	-
Finland	1.6[1]	4.7[1]	4.5[1]	3.0[1]	1.5[1]	6.4[1]	6.6[1]	-
France	12.9	15.5	13.8	15.1	14.2	12.0	10.9	-
German Democratic Rep.	17.5	14.7	12.5[1]	15.8	18.4	16.7	13.0	12.4
Germany, Federal Rep.	20.6	20.0	17.7	11.4	10.8	10.7	8.0[1]	8.7
Greece	17.6[1]	11.4[1]	11.7[1]	14.3[1]	8.7[1]	6.9[1]	8.0	-
Hungary	10.9	17.5[1]	27.7	14.9[1]	15.2[1]	26.1	14.8[1]	13.5[1]
Iceland	-	-	-	-	-	-	-	24.1[1]
Ireland	6.8[1]	4.2[1]	5.6[1]	11.9[1]	6.2[1]	6.4[1]	4.9[1]	-
Italy	13.1	13.2	9.6	9.2	9.2	8.2	-	-
Malta	-	18.3[1]	32.9[1]	-	-	35.8[1]	-	-
Netherlands	8.8[1]	7.8[1]	6.4[1]	5.3[1]	9.7[1]	4.5[1]	8.1[1]	-
Norway	11.8[1]	2.0[1]	-	4.0[1]	2.0[1]	2.0[1]	3.8[1]	5.6[1]
Poland	11.7	14.6	14.2	16.2	14.2	11.1	13.1	15.5
Portugal	19.6	19.1[1]	22.5	15.9[1]	15.4[1]	10.0[1]	8.7[1]	12.2[1]
Romania	132.1	139.9	174.8	170.1	148.8	-	-	-
Spain	13.4	-	10.5	7.6	5.2[1]	4.4[1]	-	-
Sweden	8.2[1]	4.3[1]	4.3[1]	-	2.1[1]	5.1[1]	2.9[1]	-
Switzerland	5.4[1]	6.8[1]	12.0[1]	5.4[1]	1.3[1]	5.4[1]	3.9[1]	6.5[1]
United Kingdom								
England and Wales	10.7	9.0	6.7	8.6	8.2	7.0	6.8	5.9
Northern Ireland	7.0[1]	3.7[1]	7.4[1]	14.7[1]	10.8[1]	-	-	3.6[1]
Scotland	14.5[1]	18.8[1]	9.1[1]	12.3[1]	12.3[1]	13.5[1]	10.6[1]	3.0[1]
Yugoslavia	17.8	26.6	22.4	16.8	17.2	16.4	-	10.6
Oceania								
Australia	9.8[1]	10.6[1]	10.4[1]	6.2[1]	7.7[1]	4.4[1]	6.2[1]	-
Fiji	10.6[1]	326.7	-	131.3[1]	41.0[1]	41.1[1]	-	-
New Zealand	13.8[1]	7.4[1]	12.0[1]	19.8[1]	5.8[1]	13.5[1]	18.9[1]	-
USSR								
USSR	-	-	-	-	-	-	13.9	-
Byelorussian SSR	-	-	-	-	-	-	4.1[1]	-
Ukrainian SSR	-	-	-	-	-	-	10.3	-

Source: Selected from "Maternal Deaths and Maternal Mortality Rates: 1978-1987," *1988 Demographic Yearbook*, 1990, pp. 420-423 (New York: United Nations, 1990). *Note:* 1. Rates based on 30 or fewer maternal deaths.

Population Estimates and Projections

★ 675 ★

Worldwide Population Estimates and Projections

Population in thousands for major areas of the world, 1970-1980 estimates, and medium-variant fertility projections for 1990-2020.

	1970	1980	1990	2000	2010	2020
Africa	362,788	481,034	647,518	872,234	1,148,497	1,441,285
Female	183,169	242,341	325,615	437,913	575,992	722,482
Eastern Africa	108,193	144,040	194,823	269,185	365,851	471,764
Female	54,718	72,882	98,420	135,668	184,003	236,930
Middle Africa	39,427	52,269	69,564	93,498	125,128	161,769
Female	20,198	26,581	35,231	47,191	62,984	81,285
Northern Africa	83,158	107,811	142,649	181,481	220,655	257,629
Female	41,484	53,501	70,677	89,824	109,206	127,595
Southern Africa	25,609	32,458	40,972	51,172	62,385	73,235
Female	12,878	16,355	20,664	25,806	31,448	36,916
Western Africa	106,402	144,455	199,511	276,898	374,479	476,887
Female	53,890	73,022	100,623	139,424	188,351	239,756
Latin America	285,127	361,756	448,096	539,697	630,855	719,032
Female	142,305	180,785	224,277	270,518	316,676	361,593
Caribbean	24,881	29,260	33,640	38,566	43,022	47,021
Female	12,412	14,612	16,806	19,276	21,512	23,529
Central America	69,665	92,677	117,670	145,125	172,925	200,157
Female	34,705	46,241	58,866	72,761	86,872	100,762
South America	190,580	239,820	296,787	356,007	414,907	471,854
Female	95,187	119,932	148,605	178,481	208,293	237,303
Northern America	226,480	251,808	275,880	294,830	311,555	327,153
Female	115,389	128,988	141,122	150,621	158,854	166,794
Asia	2,101,102	2,582,836	3,108,476	3,697,849	4,226,018	4,680,433
Female	1,027,362	1,260,146	1,517,573	1,808,013	2,070,960	2,301,157
Eastern Asia	986,255	1,176,115	1,334,018	1,501,277	1,610,251	1,693,806
Female	482,081	573,562	651,335	734,580	790,425	834,995
South-Eastern Asia	286,709	360,063	440,831	523,814	600,138	668,733
Female	144,377	181,028	221,110	262,121	299,965	334,192
Southern Asia	754,468	948,413	1,202,858	1,502,312	1,799,526	2,054,594

[Continued]

★ 675 ★

Worldwide Population Estimates and Projections
[Continued]

	1970	1980	1990	2000	2010	2020
Female	364,642	457,590	581,732	728,368	874,904	1,002,645
Western Asia	73,670	98,244	130,769	170,447	216,102	263,300
Female	36,263	47,965	63,396	82,944	105,666	129,325
Europe	460,132	484,436	497,741	508,569	513,637	513,811
Female	236,514	248,504	254,818	259,425	261,315	261,240
Eastern Europe	103,128	109,397	113,573	117,112	120,417	122,554
Female	53,233	56,197	58,172	59,807	61,313	62,314
Northern Europe	80,457	82,494	83,794	84,995	85,523	85,899
Female	41,086	42,136	42,773	43,282	43,494	43,731
Southern Europe	128,339	138,806	144,535	148,768	150,807	150,707
Female	65,673	70,846	73,691	75,659	76,494	76,285
Western Europe	148,209	153,740	155,839	157,694	156,890	154,650
Female	76,522	79,325	80,182	80,676	80,012	78,909
Oceania	19,329	22,794	26,476	30,139	33,787	37,349
Female	9,533	11,320	13,182	15,017	16,848	18,657
Australia-New Zealand	15,371	17,808	20,124	22,242	24,186	25,972
Female	7,638	8,922	10,096	11,152	12,121	13,030
Melanesia	3,300	4,196	5,417	6,832	8,421	10,109
Female	1,582	2,015	2,624	3,329	4,121	4,964
Micronesia	252	316	379	436	485	522
Female	118	152	187	223	257	286
Polynesia	407	473	555	630	694	746
Female	196	232	275	314	348	376
USSR	242,959	265,546	287,991	307,737	326,415	343,212
Female	130,887	141,425	151,660	160,056	168,148	175,687

Source: Selected from "Population by Sex and Age for the World, Major Areas and Regions, 1950-2025, Estimates and Medium-, High-, and Low-Variant Projections," *Global Estimates and Projections of Population by Sex and Age: The 1988 Revision*, 1989, pp. 10-60,358 (New York: United Nations, 1989). Also in source: estimates and projections by sex and age and low-and high variant fertility levels.

Refugee/Immigrant Population

★ 676 ★

Americans in Canada/Canadians in America

Canadians in the U.S. in 1980 and Americans in Canada in 1981, in thousands, by period of immigration.

Period of immigration	Canadians in the U.S. in 1980		Americans in Canada in 1981	
	Females (thousands)	Males (thousands)	Females (thousands)	Males (thousands)
All periods	494.4	348.5	168.3	133.4
Before 1960	332.8	212.5	78.2	55.2
1960 to 1964	51.5	41.8	10.8	8.6
1965 to 1969	42.3	34.1	20.5	19.0
1970 to 1974	25.0	20.1	28.8	26.2
1975 to 1980(81)	42.8	40.0	30.0	24.4

Source: Selected from "Sex Composition of Canadians in the United States in 1980 and Americans in Canada in 1981, by Period of Immigration," *Current Population Reports Special Studies*, Series P-23, No. 161, p. 21, 1990. Primary source: special tabulations from the 1980 census of the United States and the 1981 census of Canada. Also in source: ratio of males to females.

★ 677 ★

Cuban Refugee Population

Total Cuban entrant population and percent distribution by age: March 1981.

Age	Female		Male		Total	
	Number	Percent	Number	Percent	Number	Percent
0-5 years	2,620	2.1%	2,995	2.4%	5,615	4.5%
6-12 years	4,617	3.7%	5,241	4.2%	9,858	7.9%
13-15 years	1,248	1.0%	1,497	1.2%	2,745	2.2%
16-17 years	2,121	1.7%	2,246	1.8%	4,367	3.5%
18-24 years	5,366	4.3%	15,224	12.2%	20,590	16.5%
25-29 years	3,993	3.2%	15,973	12.8%	19,966	16.0%
30-34 years	3,744	3.0%	13,228	10.6%	16,972	13.6%
35-44 years	5,366	4.3%	16,597	13.3%	21,963	17.6%
45-64 years	5,990	4.8%	11,106	8.9%	17,096	13.7%
65+ years	2,621	2.1%	2,246	1.8%	4,867	3.9%
Unknown	125	0.1%	499	0.4%	750	0.6%
Total	37,811	30.3%	86,852	69.6%	124,789	100%

Source: Selected from "Percent Distribution of Total Cuban Entrant Population, by Age and Sex: March 1981," p. 73 (Washington, D.C.: American Association of Community and Junior Colleges, January 1985). Primary source: Cuban-Haitian Task Force, "Monthly Entrant Data Report" for March 1981, Office of Refugee Resettlement, U.S. Department of Health and Human Services, Table 7.

★ 678 ★

Haitian Refugee Population

Total Haitian entrant population and percent distribution by age: January 1981.

Age	Female		Male		Total	
	Number	Percent	Number	Percent	Number	Percent
0-5 years	270	1.1%	370	1.5%	691	2.8%
6-12 years	266	1.1%	295	1.2%	603	2.4%
13-15 years	94	0.4%	96	0.4%	195	0.8%
16-17 years	281	1.1%	375	1.5%	662	2.7%
18-24 years	1,960	7.9%	4,155	16.8%	6,167	24.9%
25-29 years	2,257	9.1%	5,642	22.8%	7,968	32.2%
30-34 years	1,078	4.4%	2,459	9.9%	3,578	14.5%
35-44 years	999	4.0%	2,477	10.0%	3,509	14.2%
45-64 years	300	1.2	811	3.3	1,129	4.5%
65+ years	20	0.1%	26	0.1%	46	0.2%
Unknown	25	0.1%	52	0.2%	204	0.8%
Total	7,550	30.5%	16,758	67.7%	24,743	100%

Source: "Percent Distribution of Haitian Entrant Population, by Age and Sex: January 1981," p. 84 (Washington, D.C.: American Association of Community and Junior Colleges, January 1985). Primary source: Cuban-Haitian Task Force, "Monthly Entrant Data Report" for January 1981, Office of Refugee Resettlement, U.S. Department of Health and Human Services (Washington: 1983), Table 3.

★ 679 ★

Southeast Asian Refugees

Total Southeast Asian refugee population and percent distribution by age: January 1976 and January 1981.

Age	January 1976			January 1981		
	Female	Male	Total	Female	Male	Total
0-5 years	14.8%	14.2%	14.5%	9.3%	8.2%	8.7%
6-11 years	14.7%	14.6%	14.7%	17.2%	15.8%	16.4%
12-17 years	13.3%	13.5%	13.4%	15.2%	16.6%	16.0%
18-24 years	16.9%	19.6%	18.3%	17.4%	19.7%	18.7%
25-34 years	18.2%	18.3%	18.2%	19.8%	20.6%	20.3%
35-44 years	9.1%	9.5%	9.3%	10.4%	10.3%	10.3%
45-62 years	7.4%	7.0%	7.2%	8.0%	7.5%	7.7%
63+ years	5.6%	3.2%	4.4%	2.7%	1.3%	1.9%
Total	56,221	57,919	114,140	100,829	122,579	223,408

Source: "Southeast Asian Refugee Population, by Age and Sex: January 1976 and January 1981," *In America and in Need: Immigrant, Refugee, and Entrant Women,* p. 16 (Washington, D.C.: American Association of Community and Junior Colleges, January 1985). Primary source: Office of Refugee Resettlement, *Refugee Resettlement Program: Report to Congress,* U.S. Department of Health and Human Services (Washington: 1983), Table 8. Figures may not add to totals due to rounding.

Vital Statistics

★ 680 ★

Fertility, Abortion & Pregnancy Rates of Young Women Worldwide

Pregnancy, abortion, and birth rates per 1,000 women for women ages 15 to 19, circa 1983. 1983.

Country	Year	Age-specific fertility rate	Abortion rate	Pregnancy rate
Canada	1983	24.4	14.7	39.1
Hungary	1984	52.7	27.7	80.4
Japan	1983	4.3	6.2	10.5
Norway	1984	19.2	21.0	40.2
Sweden	1983	11.7	17.9	29.5
United Kingdom	1982	NA	NA	44.7
United States	1982	53.9	44.4	98.0

Source: "Fertility, Abortion and Pregnancy Rates for Women Ages 15 to 19, Selected Countries: Circa 1983, *Children's Well-Being: An International Comparison*, A Report of the Select Committee on Children, Youth, and Families, 101st Cong., 2d sess., March 1990, p. 121. Primary source: United Nations Department of international Economic and Social Affairs, 1986, Adolescent Reproductive Behaviour; Evidence from Developed Countries, Vol. 1, Population Studies, No. 109, New York, tables 6 and A2.

★ 681 ★

Never-Married Women, 1970-1989

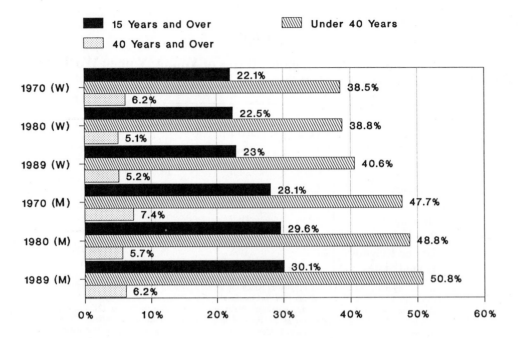

Percent of women never married, by age, 1970-1989.

Age	Women never married		
	1989	1980	1970[1]
Total, 15 years and over	23.0%	22.5%	22.1%
Under 40 years	40.6%	38.8%	38.5%
40 years and over	5.2%	5.1%	6.2%
15 to 17 years	98.6%	97.0%	97.3%
18 years	93.8%	88.0%	82.0%
19 years	87.2%	77.6%	68.8%
20 to 24 years	62.5%	50.2%	35.8%
25 to 29 years	29.4%	20.9%	10.5%
30 to 34 years	16.9%	9.5%	6.2%
35 to 39 years	9.9%	6.2%	5.4%
40 to 44 years	6.3%	4.8%	4.9%
45 to 54 years	5.4%	4.7%	4.9%
55 to 64 years	4.4%	4.5%	6.8%
65 years and over	5.0%	5.9%	7.7%

Source: "Percent Never Married, by Age and Sex: 1989, 1980, 1970, and 1960," *Current Population Reports,* Series P-20, No. 445, "Marital Status and Living Arrangements: March 1989, 1990, p. 2. Also in source: data for men; data by single year of age. *Note:* 1. Figures for 1970 include persons 14 years of age.

★ 682 ★

Ratio of Males to Females

Number of males per 100 females in the total resident population by age group, 1970, 1980, and 1985; by race and age group, 1988.

Age	1970	1980	1985	1988				
				Total	White	Black	Other races	Hispanic
All ages	94.8	94.5	94.8	95.0	95.7	90.2	95.7	101.2
Under 14 years	103.9	104.6	104.9	104.9	105.4	103.2	102.7	104.0
14-24 years	98.7	101.9	102.2	102.4	103.0	98.0	107.6	106.0
25-44 years	95.5	97.4	98.5	98.9	100.9	87.0	93.7	106.1
45-64 years	91.6	90.7	91.5	92.0	93.5	81.8	85.6	90.3
65 years and over	72.1	67.6	67.9	68.6	68.5	67.0	77.8	71.4

Source: Selected from "Ratio of Males to Females, by Age Group, 1940 to 1988," *Statistical Abstract of the United States 1990*, 1990, p. 17. Primary source: *Current Population Reports*, Series P-25, No. 1045. Also in source: data for 1940-1960. 1970 and 1980 as of April 1. 1985 and 1988 as of July 1. Persons of Hispanic origin may be of any race.

★ 683 ★

Status of Women in Islamic Nations

Indicators of the status of women in Islamic nations compared with other developing nations in the same geographic region.

Geographic region and indicator	Islamic Nations Ratio	Other Developing Nations Ratio
Ratio of girls per 100 boys enrolled in secondary schools		
North Africa	72	[1]
Sub-Saharan Africa	45	63
Western Asia	65	126
South Asia	36	56
Southeast Asia	86	91
Ratio of female life expectancy at birth to male life expectancy at birth (x 100)		
North Africa	106	[1]
Sub-Saharan Africa	106	107
Western Asia	105	105
South Asia	98	99
Southeast Asia	105	106

Source: John R. Weeks, "The Demography of Islamic Nations, *Population Bulletin* 43:4 (December 1988), Table 8. Primary source: United Nations, *Demographic Yearbook*, various years; John A. Ross et al., *Family Planning and Child Survival: 100 Developing Countries* (New York: Columbia University, Center for Population and Family Health, 1988). *Note:* 1. All North African countries are Islamic.

★ 684 ★

Vital Statistics Rates: 1982-89

Vital statistics rates per 1,000 population except for infant mortality, which is per 1,000 live births: 1982-1989.

	1989[1]	1988[1]	1987	1986	1985	1984	1983	1982
Birth	16.2	15.9	15.7	15.6	15.8	15.5	15.5	15.9
Death	8.7	8.8	8.7	8.7	8.7	8.6	8.6	8.5
Natural increase	7.5	7.1	7.0	6.9	7.1	6.9	6.9	7.4
Marriage	9.7	9.7	9.9	10.0	10.1	10.5	10.5	10.6
Divorce	4.7	4.8	4.8	4.9	5.0	5.0	4.9	5.0
Infant Mortality	9.7	9.9	10.1	10.4	10.6	10.8	11.2	11.5

Source: "Vital statistics rates: United States, 1982-89," *Monthly Vital Statistics Report* 38:13, August 30, 1990. *Note:* 1. Provisional.

★ 685 ★

Vital Statistics in Selected Developed Countries

Extra-marital births, divorce and remarriage in selected developing countries. Births as a percentage of total births. Divorces per 1,000 population. Remarriages as a percentage of total marriages.

Country	Births to unmarried women circa 1985	Divorce rate circa 1985	Remarriages circa 1980
Japan	1.0	1.38	16.9
Belgium	5.7	1.86	15.0
France	19.6	1.95	11.4
Germany, Federal Republic of	9.4	2.10	17.4
Ireland	7.8	-	1.5
Italy	4.4	0.29	2.1
Netherlands	8.3	2.35	16.6
Portugal	12.3	0.88	4.9
Spain	3.9[1]	0.57	1.1
Sweden	46.4	2.37	20.6
Switzerland	5.6	1.76	12.7
United Kingdom	19.2	3.20	23.7
Canada	12.1[2]	2.44	17.9
United States	21.0	4.96	32.5

Source: "Extra-marital births, divorce and remarriage in selected developed countries, *1989 Report on the World Social Situation,* 1989, Table 3, p. 4. Primary source: *Demographic Yearbook* (United Nations publication, 1981, 1982, and 1986). *Notes:* 1. 1980. 2. 1973.

★ 686 ★

Worldwide Vital Statistics: 1983-2025

Estimates and projections of population; number of women and number of married women 15-49, and number of contraceptive users in millions: 1983-2025.

	1983	1987	1990	2000	2010	2025
World population (in millions)	4,709	5,025	5,292	6,251	7,191	8,467
Women aged 15-49 (in millions)						
World	1,142	1,253	1,320	1,569	1,811	2,102
More developed regions	292	299	302	310	303	291
Less developed regions	850	954	1,018	1,259	1,508	1,811
Africa	120	136	146	201	274	419
East Asia[1]	279	313	333	370	392	361
South Asia and Oceania[2]	356	399	426	547	675	837
Latin America	95	106	113	141	167	194
Married women aged 15-49 (in millions)						
World	789	863	907	1,070	1,223	1,398
More developed regions	184	188	190	196	191	183
Less developed regions	605	675	717	874	1,032	1,215
Africa	90	102	109	146	193	277
East Asia[1]	183	205	217	239	252	232
South Asia and Oceania[2]	275	304	323	404	487	590
Latin America	57	64	68	85	100	116
Contraceptive users (in millions)[3]						
World	403	459	498	639	769	1,011
More developed regions	130	134	135	139	134	128
Less developed regions	273	325	357	493	657	883
Africa	13	16	19	40	81	184
East Asia[1]	135	152	163	186	197	184
South Asia and Oceania[2]	93	119	134	210	308	429
Latin America	32	38	41	57	71	86

Source: "Estimated and projected total population, number of women aged 15-49, number of married women aged 15-49 and number of contraceptive users (millions)," *Levels and Trends of Contraceptive Use as Assessed in 1988*, Table 8, p. 36 (New York: United Nations, 1989). *Notes:* 1. Excluding Japan. 2. Excluding Australia and New Zealand. 3. Excluding users not in a marital union.

Women and Children

★ 687 ★

Childless Women and Children Born: 1980 to 1988

Percent childless women among women ever married, and children ever born per 1,000 women ever married, 1980 and 1985; by race, 1988.

Age	Percent childless among women ever married						Children ever born per 1,000 women ever married					
	1980	1985	1988				1980	1985	1988			
			Total[1]	White	Black	Hispanic[2]			Total[1]	White	Black	Hispanic[2]
Total	18.8%[3]	20.3%	19.6%	20.3%	13.6%	17.2%	1,965[3]	1,785	1,769	1,727	2,099	2,086
18-19 years old	46.6%[4]	50.9%	55.7%	56.3%	48.2%	41.7%	628[4]	587	559	548	613	829
20-24 years old	40.4%	40.9%	41.7%	43.1%	29.7%	29.5%	930	916	935	890	1,342	1,137
25-29 years old	25.3%	28.7%	29.1%	30.0%	17.5%	25.1%	1,397	1,351	1,340	1,299	1,748	1,628
30-34 years old	13.7%	18.3%	16.6%	17.5%	11.2%	13.3%	1,970	1,775	1,773	1,738	1,980	2,027
35-39 years old	8.0%	11.6%	11.9%	12.4%	7.6%	11.7%	2,572	2,130	2,092	2,045	2,527	2,638
40-44 years old	6.6%	8.0%	10.2%	10.0%	12.5%	5.5%	3,105	2,548	2,280	2,257	2,436	3,047

Source: "Childless Women and Children Ever Born, by Age of Woman: 1980 to 1988," *Statistical Abstract of the United States 1990*, Table 95, p. 69. Primary source: U.S. Bureau of the Census, *Current Population Reports*, Series P-20, No. 436 and earlier reports. As of June. *Notes:* 1. Includes other races not shown separately. 2. Hispanic persons may be of any race. 3. Women, 15-44 years old 4. Women, 15-19 years.

★ 688 ★

Children of Single Women

Children ever born to single women, by age and race of woman, 1980 and 1988.

Item	All single women[1]			White single women			Black single women		
	Total, 18-44 years	18-29 years	30-44 years	Total, 18-44 years	18-29 years	30-44 years	Total, 18-44 years	18-29 years	30-44 years
1980									
Single women (in thousands)	12,500[2]	10,693	1,807[3]	9,862[2]	8,557	1,305[3]	2,327[2]	1,888	439[3]
Percent by number of children born:									
None	85.7%	87.3%	76.4%	93.5%	93.9%	90.5%	52.2%	56.7%	32.6%
One	8.6%	8.5%	9.0%	4.9%	4.7%	5.9%	24.5%	26.0%	18.5%
Two or more	5.7%	4.2%	14.6%	1.6%	1.3%	3.6%	23.3%	17.3%	49.0%
Children ever born (in thousands)	3,142[2]	2,022	1,120[3]	898[2]	666	232[3]	2,199[2]	1,325	874
Rate per 1,000 women	251	189	620	91	78	178	945	702	1,991
1988									
Single women (in thousands)	15,739	12,410	3,328	11,960	9,605	2,355	3,225	2,343	881
Percent by number of children born:									
None	81.0%	84.1%	69.5%	89.4%	90.8%	83.5%	48.9%	55.6%	31.2%
One	10.5%	9.3%	15.0%	6.5%	6.0%	8.5%	26.1%	23.6%	32.7%
Two or more	8.4%	6.5%	15.4%	4.2%	3.2%	8.0%	25.0%	20.8%	36.2%
Children ever born (in thousands)	5,270	3,264	2,004	2,047	1,339	709	3,121	1,857	1,264
Rate per 1,000 women	335	263	602	171	139	301	968	793	1,435

Source: "Children ever born to single women, by age and race of woman: 1980 and 1988," *Statistical Abstract of the United States 1990*, Table 96, p. 69. Primary source: U.S. Bureau of the Census, *Current Population Reports*, Series P-20, Nos. 375 and 436. As of June. Covers civilian noninstitutional population. Refers to women never-married at time of survey. *Notes:* 1. Includes other races not shown separately. 2. Covers single women, 18-49 years old. 3. Covers single women, 30-49 years old.

★ 689 ★

Distribution of Women by Age at First Birth

Distribution of women, by age at first birth: 1960-85.

Year	Number of first births (thousands)	Percent	Mother's age at first birth			
			Under 20	20-24	25-29	30 or older
1985	1,555	100%	23.7%	35.6%	26.9%	13.8%
1980	1,546	100%	28.2%	39.2%	24.1%	8.6%
1975	1,319	100%	35.1%	39.2%	20.4%	5.3%
1970	1,431	100%	35.6%	45.6%	14.8%	4.0%
1965	1,157	100%	38.0%	44.6%	12.1%	5.3%
1960	1,090	100%	37.0%	43.2%	13.0%	6.8%

Source: Martin O'Connell, "Maternity Leave Arrangements: 1961-85," *Work and Family Patterns of American Women*, Current Population Reports Special Studies Series P-23, No. 165, 1990, p. 11+. Primary source: National Center for Health Statistics, Vital Statistics of the United States, annual issues.

★ 690 ★

Median Age of Mother at First Birth, Worldwide

Median age of mother at first birth, various years.

Country	Year	Median age
Australia	1983	25.3
Canada	1985	25.4
Hungary	1985	22.4
Italy	1981	24.6
Japan	1985	26.6
Mexico	1980	22.3
Sweden	1985	25.8
United States	1984	23.4

Source: Selected from "Median Age at Marriage and Median Age of Mother at First Birth, Selected Countries: Selected Years, 1980 to 1985," *Children's Well-Being: An International Comparison*, A Report of the Select Committee on Children, Youth, and Families, 101st Cong., 2d sess., March 1990, p. 120. Primary source: U.S. Bureau of the Census, Center for International Research, International Data Base; and United Nations, 1988, *Demographic Yearbook 1986*, table 26. Also in source: median age at marriage (see separate table). Median age of mother at first birth calculated at the U.S. Bureau of the Census based on age-and order-specific birth rates.

★ 691 ★

Total, Child, and Youth Population Worldwide: 1990-2010

Projections of total population and percent children and youth, by region and selected countries, 1990, 2000, and 2010. 1990, 2000, and 2010.

Region and country	Total, all ages (millions)			Children ages 0 to 14 years			Youth, ages 15 to 24 years		
	1990	2000	2010	1990	2000	2010	1990	2000	2010
World	5,332	6,290	7,253	32.5%	31.2%	28.6%	19.2%	17.2%	17.5%
Developing countries	4,121	5,020	5,938	35.7%	34.0%	30.7%	20.5%	18.0%	18.4%
Developed countries	1,211	1,270	1,315	21.5%	20.3%	19.1%	14.8%	13.7%	13.3%
Africa	661	890	1,177	44.7%	43.9%	41.7%	19.2%	19.5%	20.0%

[Continued]

★ 691 ★

Total, Child, and Youth Population Worldwide: 1990-2010
[Continued]

Region and country	Total, all ages (millions)			Children ages 0 to 14 years			Youth, ages 15 to 24 years		
	1990	2000	2010	1990	2000	2010	1990	2000	2010
Asia	3,128	3,712	4,255	33.1%	31.3%	27.6%	20.6%	17.3%	17.8%
Europe	499	510	513	19.6%	18.8%	17.5%	14.9%	12.9%	12.5%
Latin America	450	540	630	36.0%	31.9%	28.3%	20.3%	19.2%	17.8%
North America	277	296	312	21.5%	20.2%	18.2%	14.5%	13.5%	13.5%
Oceania	26	29	32	26.4%	25.3%	23.6%	17.3%	15.4%	15.3%
Soviet Union	291	312	334	26.0%	24.1%	22.8%	14.5%	15.7%	15.1%
Australia	17	18	20	22.3%	21.5%	19.9%	16.2%	13.8%	13.8%
Canada	27	28	29	20.9%	19.0%	16.6%	14.4%	13.2%	12.8%
China	1,130	1,292	1,398	27.0%	26.8%	21.3%	22.1%	14.6%	16.8%
Germany, Federal Republic	61	61	59	14.9%	16.3%	14.9%	13.6%	9.8%	11.2%
France	56	58	58	20.0%	18.9%	17.0%	15.2%	12.9%	12.7%
Hungary	11	10	10	20.1%	18.9%	19.3%	14.2%	14.2%	12.2%
India	850	1,013	1,166	36.3%	32.8%	28.6%	20.2%	19.0%	18.6%
Israel	4	5	6	31.0%	28.6%	27.1%	17.5%	17.5%	16.2%
Italy	58	58	58	16.9%	16.9%	16.4%	15.6%	11.4%	11.1%
Japan	124	129	133	18.5%	17.3%	17.8%	15.3%	12.3%	10.8%
Mexico	88	109	131	38.4%	34.9%	31.0%	22.2%	19.4%	18.6%
Norway	4	4	4	18.5%	18.3%	16.8%	15.4%	12.1%	12.2%
Sweden	8	8	8	17.3%	17.2%	15.9%	13.5%	11.5%	11.8%
United Kingdom	57	58	57	18.8%	18.8%	16.6%	14.8%	12.1%	13.0%
United States	250	268	282	21.6%	20.3%	18.4%	14.5%	13.5%	13.6%

Source: "Total, Child, and Youth Population, by Region and Selected Countries: 1990, 2000, and 2010," *Children's Well-Being: An International Comparison*, A Report of the Select Committee on Children, Youth, and Families, 101st Cong., 2d sess., March 1990, p. 99. Primary source: U.S. Bureau of the Census, Center for International Research, International Data Base. Also in source: numbers of children.

★ 692 ★

Women Having a Child in the Last Year: 1976 to 1988
Women who have had a child in the last year, by age and labor force status, 1976 to 1988.

Year	Total, 18 to 44 years old				18 to 29 years old				30 to 44 years old			
	All women, percent in labor force	Women who have had a child in the last year			All women, percent in labor force	Women who have had a child in the last year			All women, percent in labor force	Women who have had a child in the last year		
		Number (thousands)	In the labor force			Number (thousands)	In the labor force			Number (thousands)	In the labor force	
			Number (thousands)	Percent			Number (thousands)	Percent			Number (thousands)	Percent
1976	59.7%	2,797	865	30.9%	NA	2,220	706	31.8%	NA	577	159	27.6%
1980	66.1%	3,247	1,233	38.0%	68.3%	2,476	947	38.2%	63.7%	770	287	37.3%
1982	68.3%	3,433	1,508	43.9%	69.7%	2,445	1,040	42.5%	66.7%	988	469	47.5%
1983	69.1%	3,625	1,563	43.1%	70.6%	2,682	1,138	42.4%	67.6%	942	425	45.1%
1984	70.2%	3,311	1,547	46.7%	71.5%	2,375	1,058	44.5%	68.9%	936	489	52.2%
1985	70.8%	3,497	1,691	48.4%	71.3%	2,512	1,204	47.9%	70.3%	984	488	49.6%
1986	72.2%	3,625	1,805	49.8%	72.8%	2,452	1,185	48.3%	71.6%	1,174	620	52.8%
1987	72.7%	3,701	1,881	50.8%	73.0%	2,521	1,258	49.9%	72.5%	1,180	623	52.8%
1988	73.3%	3,667	1,866	50.9%	73.9%	2,384	1,177	49.4%	72.8%	1,283	688	53.6%

Source: "Women who have had a child in the last year, by age and labor force status: 1976 to 1988," *Statistical Abstract of the United States 1990*, Table 94, p. 69. Primary source: U.S. Bureau of the Census, *Current Population Reports*, series P-20, No. 436 and earlier reports.

PUBLIC LIFE

Politics and Government

★ 693 ★

Candidates for Congress: 1970-1990

Women candidates for Congress, 1970-1990.

Year	U.S. Senate		U.S. House	
	Candidates	Winners	Candidates	Winners
1990	8	1	70[1]	29[1]
1988	2	0	59	25
1986	6	1	64	23
1984	10	1	65	22
1982	3	0	55	21
1980	5	1	52	19
1978	2	1	46	16
1976	1	0	54	18
1974	3	0	44	18
1972	2	0	32	14
1970	1	0	25	12

Source: Center for the American Woman and Politics (CAWP), National Information Bank on Women in Public Office, Eagleton Institute of Politics, Rutgers University. Includes major party nominees for the general elections, not those running in special elections. *Notes:* 1. Includes a Democratic candidate for non-voting delegate of Washington, D.C.

★ 694 ★

Candidates for Governor: 1970-1990

Number of women candidates for governor and number of winners, 1970-1990.

Year	Women Candidates	Women Winners
1990	8	3
1988	2	1
1986	8	1
1984	1	1
1983	1	1
1982	2	0
1980	0	0
1978	1	1

[Continued]

599

★ 694 ★

Candidates for Governor: 1970-1990
[Continued]

Year	Women Candidates	Women Winners
1976	2	1
1974	3	1
1972	0	0
1970	0	0

Source: Center for the American Woman and Politics (CAWP), National Information Bank on Women in Public Office, Eagleton Institute of Politics, Rutgers University.

★ 695 ★

Judicial Nominees: 1977-1987

Number of female and male nominees to federal courts during the Carter and Reagan administrations.

Level	Reagan Administration		Carter Administration	
	Women	Men	Women	Men
Total, Supreme, Circuit, and District Courts	31	336	40	218
Supreme Court	1	4	0	0
Circuit Courts	7	78	11	45
District Courts	23	254	29	173

Source: "The Performance of the Reagan Administration in Nominating Women and Minorities to the Federal Bench," report of a hearing before the U.S. Senate, Committee on the Judiciary, Washington, D.C., Tuesday, February 2, 1988, p. 3.

★ 696 ★

Local Elected Officials

Number of elected officials and number and percent female, by type of government, 1987.

Type of government	Total	Female	Not reported	% Female of reported
Local governments	485,691	87,379	59,830	20.5%
County	59,932	12,475	71	20.8%
Municipal	137,688	23,239	11,801	18.5%
Township	120,790	24,566	14,457	23.1%
School district	86,772	20,648	8,950	26.5%
Special district	80,509	6,451	24,551	11.5%

Source: "Local Elected Officials by Sex and Type of Government: 1987," *1987 Census of Governments*, December 1989, p. 4.

★ 697 ★

Members of Congress: 1975-1991

Female and male members of Congress, 1975 to 1991.

Members of Congress and Year	Female	Male
Representatives		
94th Congress, 1975	19	416
95th Congress, 1977	18	417
96th Congress, 1979	16	417
97th Congress, 1981	19	416
98th Congress, 1983	21	413
99th Congress, 1985	22	412
100th Congress, 1987	23	412
101st Congress, 1989	25	408
102nd Congress, 1991	30	505
Senators		
94th Congress, 1975	0	100
95th Congress, 1977	0	100
96th Congress, 1979	1	99
97th Congress, 1981	2	98
98th Congress, 1983	2	98
99th Congress, 1985	2	98
100th Congress, 1987	2	98
101st Congress, 1989	2	98
102nd Congress, 1991	2	98

Source: Selected from "Members of Congress-Selected Characteristics: 1975 to 1989," *Statistical Abstract of the United States 1990,* p. 257. Primary source: Compiled by U.S. Bureau of the Census from data published in *Congressional Directory,* biennial. 1991 figures are from the Center for the American Woman and Politics (CAWP), National Information Bank on Women in Public Office, Eagleton Institute of Politics, Rutgers University. As of beginning of first session of each Congress. Figures for Representatives exclude vacancies.

★ 698 ★

Voting and Registration

Females who reported registration and voting in the election of November 1988, by age.

Age	All persons	Reported registered	Reported voted	Reported that they did not vote[1]	
				Total	Registered
			Numbers in thousands		
Total, 18 years and over	93,568	63,450	54,519	39,048	8,931
20 to 24 years	9,406	4,972	3,730	5,676	1,242
25 to 29 years	10,812	6,117	4,973	5,8739	1,144
30 to 34 years	10,907	6,954	5,906	5,001	1,048
35 to 44 years	17,980	12,883	11,381	6,599	1,502
45 to 54 years	12,512	9,231	8,337	4,175	895
55 to 64 years	11,421	8,789	7,874	3,547	914

[Continued]

★ 698 ★

Voting and Registration
[Continued]

Age	All persons	Reported registered	Reported voted	Reported that they did not vote[1]	
				Total	Registered
65 to 74 years	9,773	7,806	6,986	2,787	820
75 years and over	7,082	5,026	4,069	3,012	957

Source: "Reported Voting and Registration, by Single Years of Age and Sex," *Current Population Reports*, "Voting and Registration in the Election of November 1988, Series P-20, No. 440, p. 15. Also in source: data for both sexes and males by single years of age. *Notes:* 1. Includes persons reported as "did not vote," "do not know," and "not reported" on voting.

★ 699 ★

Voting and Registration by Race/Ethnicity

Females reporting registration and voting in the election of November 1988 by race/origin.

Race	All persons	Reported registered	Reported voted	Reported that they did not vote[1]	
				Total	Registered
	Numbers in thousands				
White females, 18 years and over	79,730	54,994	47,695	32,035	7,300
Black females, 18 years and over	10,915	7,356	5,911	5,004	1,445
Hispanic females, 18 years and over	6,495	2,431	1,958	4,538	473

Source: "Reported Voting and Registration, by Race, Hispanic Origin, Sex, and Age, for the United States and Regions," *Current Population Reports*, "Voting and Registration in the Election of November 1988, Series P-20, No. 440, p. 16-17. Also in source: breakdown by single years of age by race, Hispanic origin, and sex, U.S. and regions. *Notes:* 1. Includes persons reported as "did not vote," "do not know," and "not reported" on voting.

★ 700 ★

Women Governors

Women state governors: 1991.

Name	Party	State
Total Number of States: 50		
Total Number of Women Governors: 4[1]		
Women Governors		
Joan Finney	D	KS
Rose Mofford	D	AZ
Ann Richards	D	TX
Barbara Roberts	D	OR

Source: Center for the American Woman and Politics (CAWP), National Information Bank on Women in Public Office, Eagleton Institute of Politics, Rutgers University. *USA Today*, February 28, 1991. *Notes:* 1. Mofford, who was serving as secretary of state, became governor in April 1988 following the impeachment and conviction by the legislature of Gov. Evan Mecham (R). In a runoff election held on February 26, 1991, Fife Symington (R) was elected governor.

★ 701 ★

Women Lieutenant Governors/Attorneys General

Women serving as lieutenant governors and attorneys general, 1991.

Name	Party	State
Total Number of States: 50		
Total Number of Women Lieutenant Governors: 6		
Total Number of Women Attorneys General: 4		
Women Lieutenant Governors		
Connie Binsfeld	R	MI
Joy Corning	R	IA
Joanell Dyrstad	R	MN
Eunice Groark	IND	CT
Maxine Moul	D	NE
Sue Wagner	R	NV
Women Attorneys General		
Gale Norton	R	CO
Bonnie Campbell	D	IA
Frankie Sue del Papa	D	NV
Mary Sue Terry	D	VA

Source: Center for the American Woman and Politics (CAWP), National Information Bank on Women in Public Office, Eagleton Institute of Politics, Rutgers University.

★ 702 ★

Women Mayors

Women mayors among the 100 largest cities in the U.S. by order of city population (according to 1988 Census Bureau data), January 1991.

Mayor and City	City Rank
Kathy Whitmire, Houston, TX	4
Maureen O'Connor, San Diego, CA	6
Annette Strauss, Dallas, TX	8
Lila Cockrell, San Antonio, TX	9
Susan Hammer, San Jose, CA	12
Sharon Pratt Dixon, Washington, DC	17
Suzie Azar, El Paso, TX	23
Sophie Masloff, Pittsburgh, PA	38
Sue Myrick, Charlotte, NC	42
Meyera Oberndorf, Virginia Beach, VA	43
Anne Rudin, Sacramento, CA	48
Karen Humphrey, Fresno, CA	51
Sandra Freedman, Tampa, FL	56
Peggy Rubach, Mesa, AZ	57
Betty Turner, Corpus Christi, TX	59
Terry Frizzel, Riverside, CA	74
Joan Darrah, Stockton, CA	80

[Continued]

★ 702 ★

Women Mayors
[Continued]

Mayor and City	City Rank
Sharron Priest, Little Rock, AR	89
Sheri Barnard, Spokane, WA	95

Source: Center for the American Woman and Politics (CAWP), National Information Bank on Women in Public Office, Eagleton Institute of Politics, Rutgers University.

★ 703 ★

Women in County and Municipal Government
Statistics on women holding county and municipal offices.

Office	No. of women	Year
County governing boards (47 states have 18,483 seats)[1]	1,653	1988
Mayor (of 100 largest cities in U.S.)	19	1991
Mayor (of 900 cities with population over 30,000)[2]	150	1991

Source: Center for the American Woman and Politics (CAWP), National Information Bank on Women in Public Office, Eagleton Institute of Politics, Rutgers University. *Notes:* 1. Between 1975 and 1988, the number of women serving at the county governing board level more than tripled, rising from 456 in 1975. 2. United States Conference of Mayors 3. Includes data from Washington DC. States for which data were incomplete and therefore not included are: IL, IN, KY, MO, PA, WI.

★ 704 ★

Women in Elective Offices
Percentages of women in elective offices, 1975-1991.

Level of Office	1975	1977	1979	1981	1983	1985	1987	1989	1991
U.S. Congress	4%	4%	3%	4%	4%	5%	5%	5%	6%
Statewide Elective[1]	10%	8%	11%	11%	13%	14%	15%	14%[3]	18%
State Legislatures	8%	9%	10%	12%	13%	15%	16%	17%	18%
County Governing Boards[2]	3%	4%	5%	6%	8%	8%	9%	9%	NA
Mayors and Municipal/Township Governing Boards	4%	8%	10%	10%	NA	14%[4]	NA	NA	NA

Source: Center for the American Woman and Politics (CAWP), National Information Bank on Women in Public Office, Eagleton Institute of Politics, Rutgers University. *Notes:* 1. These numbers do not include: officials in appointive state cabinet-level positions; officials elected to executive posts by the legislature; members of the judician branch; or elected members of university Boards of Trustees or Boards of Education. 2. The three states without county governing boards are CT, RI, and VT. 3. Although there was an increase in the number of women serving between 1987 and 1989, the percentage decrease reflects a change in the base used to calculate these figures. 4. Includes data from Washington DC. States for which data were incomplete and therefore not included are: IL, IN, KY, MO, PA, WI.

★ 705 ★

Women in Government Worldwide

Number of women and men in national legislative bodies, by country, 1970 and 1980.

Country	1970 Female	1970 Male	1980 Female	1980 Male
Australia	4	187	19	170
Austria	23	213	30	206
Barbados	1	23	1	26
Belgium	26	368	34	360
Bulgaria	78	322	83	317
Burundi	-	-	6	59
Byelorussia	159	271	130	305
Canada	15	360	39	343
Chile	15	185	3	77
China	853	2,232	632	2,346
Costa Rica	5	55	4	55
Cuba	105	376	113	386
Cyprus	0	35	1	34
Czechoslovakia	99	251	99	251
Denmark	30	149	42	137
Dominica	1	20	1	20
Dominican Republic	15	103	8	139
Ecuador	-	-	4	134
Egypt	-	-	43	615
El Salvador	-	-	10	50
Equatorial Guinea	-	-	2	58
Finland	46	154	62	138
France	-	-	38	770
Germany, Democratic Republic	168	332	162	338
Germany, Federal Republic	38	480	51	469
Greece	7	293	14	286
Guyana	9	44	16	55
Honduras	-	-	6	76
Hungary	101	251	109	243
Iceland	3	57	9	51
India	19	523	28	514
Indonesia	31	429	42	418
Ireland	11	197	20	206
Israel	8	112	8	112
Italy	23	828	86	886
Ivory Coast	11	99	8	139
Japan	25	701	26	733
Kenya	4	168	3	169
Korea, Republic of	8	213	8	268

[Continued]

★ 705 ★

Women in Government Worldwide
[Continued]

Country	1970 Female	1970 Male	1980 Female	1980 Male
Luxembourg	3	56	6	53
Malawi	4	83	10	96
Malaysia	6	148	8	146
Mauritius	3	67	4	96
Mexico	-	-	54	110
Mongolia	-	-	23	77
Nepal	-	-	7	128
Netherlands	23	202	43	182
New Zealand	4	83	8	84
Norway	24	131	40	115
Philippines	12	166	7	165
Poland	95	365	114	346
Portugal	20	230	18	232
Romania	66	275	122	247
Rwanda	-	-	9	61
St. Lucia	2	18	2	26
Samoa	1	46	1	46
Senegal	8	92	13	107
Spain	27	600	32	571
Sri Lanka	6	161	7	147
Sweden	75	274	98	251
Switzerland	15	229	25	221
Turkey	7	627	12	387
United Kingdom	75	1,715	87	1,762
Ukrainian SSR	-	-	234	416
Uruguay	3	96	-	-
United States	19	516	23	511
USSR	475	1,025	492	1,008
Venezuela	-	-	12	219
Viet Nam	132	358	108	389
Yugoslavia	13	86	17	83
Zambia	8	127	4	131
Zimbabwe	-	-	11	122

Source: Eschel M. Rhoodie, *Discrimination Against Women: A Global Survey of the Economic, Educational, Social and Political Status of Women,* 1989, p. 38-39 (Jefferson, NC: McFarland & Company, 1989). Primary source: *Women: A World Report,* Debbie Taylor (ed.) (New York: Oxford University Press, 1985), p. 375-376.

★ 706 ★

Women in Government Worldwide

Percentage of government seats held by women, 1975 and latest year.

Region	Lower chamber of bicameral assembly		Upper chamber of bicameral assembly	
	1975	Latest yr.	1975	Latest yr.
Africa	4.08%	6.30%	-	4.92%
Asia	13.16%	12.84%	6.87%	6.93%
Latin America and the Caribbean	3.41%	10.61%	4.18%	6.50%
North America	3.58%	6.97%	2.94%	7.35%
Oceania	1.87%	4.93%	9.38%	22.37%
Europe	13.15%	17.62%	6.41%	8.21%
Soviet Union	32.13%	34.53%	30.51%	31.07%

Source: "Percentage of women in parliament," *1989 Report on the World Social Situation,* 1989, p. 13 (New York: United Nations, 1989). Primary source: United Nations Women's Indicators and Statistical Data Base (WISTAT), 1988, based on data compiled by the Inter-Parliamentary Union, "Distribution of seats between men and women in the 144 National Parliaments in existence as at 30 June 1987."

★ 707 ★

Women in State Legislatures: Part 1

Ten states with lowest percentage of women state legislators, 1991.

State	% Female Legislators
Louisiana	2.1%
Kentucky	5.1%
Alabama	5.7%
Arkansas	6.7%
Mississippi	6.9%
Oklahoma	8.7%
Pennsylvania	9.5%
New Jersey	10.0%
South Carolina	10.0%
Tennessee	11.4%

Source: Center for the American Woman and Politics (CAWP), National Information Bank on Women in Public Office, Eagleton Institute of Politics, Rutgers University.

★ 708 ★

Women in State Legislatures: Part 2

Ten states with the highest percentages of women state legislators, 1991.

State	% Female Legislators
Arizona	35.6%
Maine	32.8%
New Hampshire	32.1%
Vermont	31.7%
Washington	31.3%

[Continued]

★ 708 ★

Women in State Legislatures: Part 2
[Continued]

State	% Female Legislators
Colorado	31.0%
Idaho	27.8%
Hawaii	27.6%
Kansas	26.7%
South Dakota	24.8%

Source: Center for the American Woman and Politics (CAWP), National Information Bank on Women in Public Office, Eagleton Institute of Politics, Rutgers University.

★ 709 ★

Women in State Legislatures: Part 3
Number of state legislative seats held by women, 1991.

Office	Total
State Legislators, Total	7,461
Women, Total	1,351
Women State Senators	299
Women State Representatives	1,052

Source: Center for the American Woman and Politics (CAWP), National Information Bank on Women in Public Office, Eagleton Institute of Politics, Rutgers University. The number of women serving in state legislatures has more than quadrupled since 1969, when 301, or 4.0% of all state legislators were women.

★ 710 ★

Women in State and Local Government
Women holding state and local public offices, by office and state, 1989.

State	Statewide elective executive office[1,2] 1989	State legislature,[1] 1989	County governing boards, 1988	Mayors and municipal council 1985
U.S.	45	1,261	1,653	14,672
Alabama	1	8	7	281
Alaska	-	13	17	233
Arizona	3	27	8	87
Arkansas	2	10	71	365
California	1	18	56	465
Colorado	2	29	18	315
Connecticut	1	41	-	240
Delaware	1	10	2	57

[Continued]

★ 710 ★

Women in State and Local Government
[Continued]

State	Statewide elective executive office[1,2] 1989	State legis-lature,[1] 1989	County governing boards, 1988	Mayors and municipal council 1985
District of Columbia	-	-	-	7
Florida	1	27	51	311
Georgia	-	24	28	251
Hawaii	-	18	8	3
Idaho	1	31	14	141
Illinois	-	33	152	-
Indiana	2	22	10	-
Iowa	2	25	35	732
Kansas	1	42	24	445
Kentucky	1	7	17	-
Louisiana	1	3	32	183
Maine	-	57	3	243
Maryland	-	41	21	133
Massachusetts	1	35	5	217
Michigan	1	22	123	2,779
Minnesota	2	37	37	542
Mississippi	-	10	8	176
Missouri	1	29	17	-
Montana	2	27	18	110
Nebraska	1	10	27	241
Nevada	1	13	10	15
New Hampshire	-	136	8	113
New Jersey	-	11	15	451
New Mexico	1	15	17	86
New York	-	24	131	797
North Carolina	-	25	45	337
North Dakota	2	24	11	174
Ohio	1	16	25	1,129
Oklahoma	-	13	5	312
Oregon	2	18	20	344
Pennsylvania	2	17	35	-
Rhode Island	1	23	-	30
South Carolina	-	15	36	184
South Dakota	2	20	16	149
Tennessee	-	12	117	144
Texas	1	19	30	786
Utah	-	12	2	137
Vermont	1	55	-	87
Virginia	1	14	49	211
Washington	1	42	15	341

[Continued]

★ 710 ★

Women in State and Local Government
[Continued]

State	Statewide elective executive office[1,2] 1989	State legis-lature,[1] 1989	County governing boards, 1988	Mayors and municipal council 1985
West Virginia	-	24	11	202
Wisconsin	-	35	241	-
Wyoming	2	22	5	86

Source: "Women Holding State and Local Public Offices, by Office and State: 1975 to 1989," *Statistical Abstract of the United States 1990*, p. 261. Primary source: Center for the American Woman and Politics, Eagleton Institute of Politics, Rutgers University, New Brunswick, NJ, information releases. *Notes:* 1. As of May. 2. Excludes women elected to the judiciary, women appointed to State cabinet-level positions, women elected to executive posts by the legislature, and elected members of university Board of Trustees or Board of Education.

★ 711 ★

Women in Statewide Elective Offices
States where women hold elective executive offices, 1991.

Office	No. of states
Secretary of State	10
State Treasurer	14
State Auditor	5
Comptroller	1
Tax Commissioner	1
Chief Education Official[1]	8
Commissioner of Labor	1
Commissioner of Agriculture	1
Railroad Commissioner[2]	1
Corporation Commissioner	1
Public Utilities Commissioner	1
Public Service Commissioner	1

Source: Center for the American Woman and Politics (CAWP), National Information Bank on Women in Public Office, Eagleton Institute of Politics, Rutgers University. *Notes:* 1. Office titles vary by state. 2. In Texas, where railroad commissioners are elected statewide, a woman has been appointed to fill a vacancy.

★ 712 ★

Women in the House

Women in the U.S. House of Representatives: 1991.

Name	Party	State
Number of Seats in House: 435		
Number Held by Women: 28 (6.4%)		
Party Affiliation: 20 Democrats, 9 Republicans		
Women in the House		
Helen Delich Bentley	R	MD
Barbara Boxer	D	CA
Beverly Byron	D	MD
Barbara-Rose Collins	D	MI
Cardiss Collins	D	IL
Rosa DeLauro	D	CT
Joan Kelly Horn	D	MO
Nancy Johnson	R	CT
Marcy Kaptur	D	OH
Barbara Kennelly	D	CT
Marilyn Lloyd	D	TN
Jill Long	D	IN
Nita Lowey	D	NY
Jan Meyers	R	KS
Patsy Takemoto Mink	D	HI
Susan Molinari	R	NY
Constance Morella	R	MD
Eleanor Holmes Norton[1]	D	DC
Mary Rose Oakar	D	OH
Elizabeth Patterson	D	SC
Nancy Pelosi	D	CA
Ileana Ros-Lehtinen	R	FL
Marge Roukema	R	NJ
Patricia Schroeder	D	CO
Louise Slaughter	D	NY
Olympia Snowe	R	ME
Jolene Unsoeld	D	WA
Barbara Vucanovich	R	NV
Maxine Waters	D	CA

Source: Center for the American Woman and Politics (CAWP), National Information Bank on Women in Public Office, Eagleton Institute of Politics, Rutgers University. *Note:* 1. Norton is non-voting Democratic delegate from Washington, D.C.

★ 713 ★

Women in the Senate

Women in the U.S. Senate, 1991.

Name	Party	State
Total Number of Senate Seats: 100 **Number Held by Women: 2 (2%)** Nancy Landon Kassebaum Barbara Mikulski	R D	KS MD

Source: Center for the American Woman and Politics (CAWP), National Information Bank on Women in Public Office, Eagleton Institute of Politics, Rutgers University.

★ 714 ★

Women of Color in Elective Office: Part 1

Women of color holding congressional elective offices, October 1990. There were 31 women serving in Congress.

Officer	Party	State
Representative Cardiss Collins	D	IL
Representative Patsy Takemoto Mink	D	HI
Representative Ileana Ros-Lehtinen	R	FL
Representative Patricia Saiki	R	HI

Source: Center for the American Woman and Politics (CAWP), National Information Bank on Women in Public Office, Eagleton Institute of Politics, Rutgers University. "We use 'women of color'... when referring to Black, Hispanic, Asian/Pacific Islander, and Native American women as a group. We understand that both the terms 'women of color' and 'minority women' are problematic, but know of no preferable inclusive term" (source).

Volunteerism

★ 715 ★

Characteristics of Volunteer Workers

Total and female unpaid volunteer workers by age, race, and Hispanic origin, marital status, and educational attainment, May 1989.

Characteristic	Total	Women
	Thousands	
Total, 16 years and over	38,042	21,361
16 to 19 years	1,902	1,023
20 to 24 years	2,064	1,129
25 to 34 years	8,680	5,002
35 to 44 years	10,337	5,655
45 to 54 years	5,670	3,069
55 to 64 years	4,455	2,468
65 years and over	4,934	3,016

[Continued]

★ 715 ★

Characteristics of Volunteer Workers
[Continued]

Characteristic	Total	Women
Race and Hispanic Origin		
White	34,823	19,550
Black	2,505	1,423
Hispanic origin	1,289	702
Marital Status		
Single, never married	6,327	3,225
Married, spouse present	26,344	14,213
Married, spouse absent	765	489
Divorced	2,510	1,602
Widowed	2,096	1,831
Educational Attainment		
Less than 4 years of high school	2,939	1,644
4 years of high school	11,105	6,985
1 to 3 years of college	7,572	4,531
4 years of college or more	12,459	6,049

Source: Selected from "Unpaid volunteer workers by selected characteristics, May 1989," *Bureau of Labor Statistics News*, USDL 90-154, March 29, 1990, Table 1. Data on volunteer workers relate to persons who performed unpaid work for an organization or institution during the year ended May 1989. Detail for race and Hispanic-origin groups will not add to totals because data for the "other races" group are not presented and Hispanics are included in both the white and black population groups.

★ 716 ★

Employment Status of Volunteers

Total and female unpaid volunteer workers by employment status, May 1989.

Employment status	Total both sexes		Women	
	Total	Volunteers	Total	Volunteers
	Numbers in thousands			
Civilian noninstitutional population	186,181	38,042	97,525	21,361
In labor force	123,293	27,284	55,792	13,190
Employed	117,157	26,439	52,903	12,705
Full time	96,935	21,182	39,309	8,641
Part time	20,222	5,257	13,594	4,064
Unemployed	6,136	845	2,888	485
Not in labor force	62,888	10,758	41,734	8,171

Source: Selected from "Unpaid volunteer workers by employment status and sex, May 1989," *Bureau of Labor Statistics News*, USDL 90-154, March 29, 1990, Table 2. Data on volunteer workers relate to persons who performed unpaid work for an organization or institution during the year ended May 1989.

★ 717 ★

Involvement in Charitable Activities

Questions: Do you happen to be involved in any charity or social service activities...? Number surveyed: women = 616; men = 614.

Characteristic of respondent	Personal involvement	
	Yes	No
U.S. Total	41%	59%
Sex:		
Female	46%	54%
Male	36%	64%
Age:		
18-29 years	30%	70%
30-49 years	44%	56%
50 and older	45%	55%

Source: George Gallup, Jr., *The Gallup Report,* Report No. 290 (Princeton, NJ: The Gallup Poll, November 1989), p. 19. Also in source; other characteristics of respondents; opinions on the involvement of others in the community; trends of personal involvement since 1977.

★ 718 ★

Types of Volunteer Work

Percent distribution of female and male unpaid volunteers by type of organization for which work was performed, May 1989.

Sex	Total (thousands)	Percent distribution by type of organization					
		Hospital/ Health Org.	School/Other educational instit.	Social or welfare org.	Civic or political org.	Sport or recreation. org.	Church or other relig. org.
Women	21,361	13.1%	18.5%	9.7%	10.1%	4.6%	38.5%
Men	16,681	7.0%	10.5%	10.1%	17.2%	11.8%	35.9%

Source: Selected from "Unpaid volunteer workers by type of organization for which work was performed and seledcted characteristics, May 1989," *Bureau of Labor Statistics News,* USDL 90-154, March 29, 1990, Table 3.

★ 719 ★

Volunteer Hours

Question: In the past 30 days, roughly how many hours, if any, did you spend on volunteer activities? Number surveyed: women = 287; men = 255.

Characteristic of respondent	Hours spent in last month			
	15 or more	6-14	Less than 6	None
U.S. Total	23%	24%	20%	29%
Sex:				
Female	265	23%	17%	29%
Male	17%	24%	25%	30%
Age:				

[Continued]

★ 719 ★

Volunteer Hours
[Continued]

Characteristic of respondent	Hours spent in last month			
	15 or more	6-14	Less than 6	None
18-29 years	14%	20%	21%	43%
30-49 years	23%	25%	23%	27%
50 and older	26%	25%	19%	23%

Source: George Gallup, Jr., *The Gallup Report*, Report No. 290 (Princeton, NJ: The Gallup Poll, 1989), p. 21. Also in source: other characteristics of respondents; opinions on level of enjoyment of volunteer work.

Women's Groups

★ 720 ★

Membership of Feminist Groups
Membership in feminist groups, 1985 and 1987.

Group	Membership	
	1985	1987
NARAL	100,000	115,000
NOW	156,000	260,000
NWPC	77,000	75,000

Source: "Feminist Groups' Membership (1985)," *Women and Public Policies,* 1987, p. 26 (Princeton, NJ: Princeton University Press, 1987). Primary source: Annual reports of the groups, telephone interviews, and the *Washington Post,* July 14, 1985. 1987 figures are from *Encyclopedia of Associations,* 1987 (Detroit: Gale Research Inc., 1987). NARAL = National Abortion Rights Action League; NOW = National Organization for Women; NWPC = National Women's Political Caucus.

★ 721 ★

Membership of Traditional Women's Groups
Membership of traditional women's groups, 1980 and 1990.

Group	Membership	
	1980	1990
American Association of University Women	190,000	140,000
B'nai Brith Women	120,000	120,000
League of Women Voters	115,000	110,000
General Federation of Women's Clubs	600,000	400,000
National Federation of Business and		▲

[Continued]

★ 721 ★

Membership of Traditional Women's Groups
[Continued]

Group	Membership	
	1980	1990
Professional Women's Clubs	154,000	125,000
National Council of Jewish Women	100,000	100,000

Source: "Membership of Traditional Women's Groups (1980)," *Women and Public Policies* 1987, p. 25 (Princeton, NJ: Princeton University Press, 1987). Primary source: Telephone survey, July 15, 1981. 1990 figures are from *Encyclopedia of Associations*, 1991 (Detroit: Gale Research Inc., 1991).

★ 722 ★

Peace Organizations
Membership of national women's peace groups, 1988.

Group	Membership
Grandmothers for Peace	500
Mothers Embracing Nuclear Disarmament (MEND)	1,600
Peace Links	30,000
Women for a Meaningful Summit (WMS)	[1]
Women's Action for Nuclear Disarmament (WAND)	11,000
Women's Encampment for a Future of Peace and Justice	[2]
Women's International League for Peace and Freedom	15,000
Women's Peace Initiative	NA
Women Strike for Peace (WSP)	10,000

Source: Kate McGuinness, "Women and the Peace Movement," *The American Woman 1990-91*, 1990, p. 300+ (New York: W.W. Norton & Company, 1990). Also, *Peace Resource Book* (Cambridge, Mass: Ballinger Publishing, 1988). *Notes:* 1. An ad hoc coalition made up primarily of women's peace groups to create a voice for women at the 1985 summit meeting with Soviet leaders. The board of directors represents a worldwide grassroots network with four million members in the United States. 2. Organized in 1983 as a response to the deployment of Cruise and Pershing II missiles in Europe. In 1983, more than 12,000 women visited the camp for actions at the U.S. Army Depot in Seneca, NY. Women's Encampment maintains a mailing list of 8,000 people.

★ 723 ★

Rise of Women's Services: 1970-1988

Some interesting facts about women's groups culled by the author from Susanna Downie's *Decade of Achievement*.

1. No one had heard of a battered women's shelter in 1970, but by 1988 there were at least 1,200 such establishments;

2. No one had heard of a "women's center" in 1970, but according to the National Association of Women's Centers, there were at least 4,000 such centers by 1988;

3. Few had heard of a rape crisis center in 1970; by 1988 there were 600 such centers;

4. The need for displaced homemakers groups, programs, or services, first recognized in the early 1970s, had resulted in the formation of more than 1,000 such groups, programs, or services by 1988.

Source: Sarah Harder, "Flourishing in the Mainstream: The U.S. Women's Movement Today," *The American Woman 1990-91*, 1990, p. 273+. Also: Downie, Susanna (editor). *Decade of Achievement: 1977-1987—A Report of a Survey Based on the National Plan of Action for Women.* Beaver Dam, Wisconsin: National Women's Conference Committee, 1988.

RELIGION

Religious Practices, Preferences, and Attitudes

★ 724 ★

Attendance at Religious Services

Response to the question: Do you attend regular religious services?

Sex	% Yes
Female	52.5%
Male	41.9%

Source: World Almanac and Book of Facts 1990, p. 34 (New York: Pharos Books, 1990). Based on a survey conducted by ICR Survey Research Group of 1,006 respondents (half female and half male).

★ 725 ★

Church Positions on Abortion

U.S. religious denominations that have taken official positions on abortion, and number of U.S. members.

Denomination and position	U.S. members (thousands)
Pro-choice denominations	
Disciples of Christ	NA
Episcopal Church	2,462
Moravian Church in America	NA
Reform Judaism	NA
Reorganized Church of Latter Day Saints	192
Presbyterian Church (U.S.A.)	2,986
Unitarian Universalist	173
United Church of Christ	1,663
United Methodist Church	9,125
Anti-abortion denominations	
Assemblies of God	2,161
Church of Jesus Christ of Latter Day Saints (Mormons)	4,000
Greek Orthodox	1,950
Jehovah's Witnesses	773
Lutheran Church-Missouri Synod	2,614

[Continued]

★ 725 ★

Church Positions on Abortion
[Continued]

Denomination and position	U.S. members (thousands)
Roman Catholic	53,497
Southern Baptist	14,723

Source: Kate DeSmet, "Theologians Campaign for Choice," *Detroit News*, January 20, 1991, p. 1C+. U.S. membership figures from *Statistical Abstract of the United States 1990*, 1990, p. 56-57. Also in source: a discussion of the emerging pro-choice theology; a discussion of the views of various other faiths.

★ 726 ★

Importance of Religion

Responses to the question: "How important would you say religion is in your own life—very important, fairly important, or not very important?"

Year	Very important		Fairly important		Not very important	
	Women	Men	Women	Men	Women	Men
1983	62%	49%	28%	32%	9%	17%
1982	63%	48%	28%	32%	8%	19%
1980	62%	48%	27%	34%	10%	17%
1978	58%	46%	29%	35%	11%	18%

Source: Religion in America 1984: Commentary on the State of Religion in the U.S. Today, p. 32 (Princeton, NJ: American Institute of Public Opinion; 1984). 1983 figures are based on an average of three surveys conducted during 1983.

★ 727 ★

Influences on Religious Development

Mean ratings of 10 influences on religious development of women and men aged 65 to 88.

Variable	Rank
Mother	1
Church	2
Father	3
Reading	4
Habit	5
Personal experience	6
Relatives	7
School	8
Friends	9
Media	10

Source: Bruce Hunsberger, "Religion, Age, Life Satisfaction, and Perceived Sources of Religiousness: A Study of Older Persons," *Journal of Gerontology* 40:5 (1985), p. 615-620. Based on a study of 52 women and 33 men aged 65 to 88. The study "supported previous findings of a tendency toward increased religiosity in older age."

★ 728 ★

Religious Preferences

Percentage of persons in 1983 survey expressing a preference for three religious denominations or expressing no religious preference.

Sex	Protestant	Catholic	Jewish	No preference
National	56%	29%	2%	9%
Women	59%	29%	2%	7%
Men	54%	28%	2%	12%

Source: Religion in America 1984: Commentary on the State of Religion in the U.S. Today, p.67 (Princeton, NJ: American Institute of Public Opinion; 1984). Based on national sample, 1983 surveys).

★ 729 ★

Religious Television Programs

Gender makeup of viewers of particular religious television shows (N = >100).

Sex	Religious television programs				
	Billy Graham	Jimmy Swaggart	Oral Roberts	Pat Robertson	Local Programs
Women	62%	56%	57%	59%	58%
Men	38%	44%	43%	41%	42%

Source: Selected from "Profiles of Audiences of Leading Religious TV Programs," *The People's Religion: American Faith in the 90's,* p. 153 (New York: Macmillan Publishing Company, 1990). Also in source: other characteristics of viewers.

★ 730 ★

Support Networks of Black Church Members

Type of support received from church members by older black Americans who received support (n = 259).

Type of support	Percentage
Advice and encouragement	12.0%
Companionship	15.1%
Goods and services	5.8%
Financial assistance	7.7%
Transportation	5.4%
Help during sickness	32.0%
Prayer	16.6%
Total support	5.4%

Source: Robert Joseph Taylor, PhD and Linda M. Chatters, PhD, "Church-based Information Support Among Elderly Blacks," *Gerontologist* 26:6 (1986), p. 637+. Based on a survey of 581 older black Americans (366, or 63% of whom were women).

★ 731 ★

Worldwide Religious Preferences

Total population, number of females, population by religion and number of females by religion for the largest denominations, by country and year.

Country or area, census date, religion	Total	Female
Africa		
Egypt-1986	48,205,049	23,549,752
Moslem	45,368,453	22,169,912
Christian	2,829,349	1,377,959
Mauritius-1983	964,762	484,614
Hindu	297,555	149,818
Islam	123,999	61,758
Sanatanist	99,535	49,901
Rodrigues-1983	33,082	16,530
Catholic	31,518	15,847
St. Helena-1987	5,500	2,831
Church of England	4,756	2,423
Jehovah Witness	268	155
South Africa-1980	25,016,525	12,296,077
Nederduitsc	3,782,510	1,862,250
Catholic	2,406,699	1,170,545
Other religions	4,674,704	2,383,002
Unknown	4,405,311	2,089,306
North America		
Bahamas-1980	209,505	107,731
Baptist	67,193	35,431
Catholic	39,397	19,539
Barbados-1980	244,228	128,457
Anglican	96,894	52,653
No religion	42,721	15,354
Belize-1980	142,847	70,948
Catholic	88,587	43,945
Methodist	8,632	4,340
Bermuda-1980	54,050	27,700
Anglican	20,163	10,531
Catholic	7,458	3,668
British Virgin Islands-1980	10,985	5,368
Methodist	4,997	2,426
Anglican	2,302	1,106

[Continued]

★ 731 ★

Worldwide Religious Preferences
[Continued]

Country or area, census date, religion	Total	Female
Dominica-1981	73,795	37,041
Catholic	56,770	28,789
Methodist	3,663	1,796
Grenada-1981	89,088	46,145
Catholic	52,820	27,340
Anglican	15,226	7,724
Haiti-1982	5,053,792	2,605,422
Catholic	4,057,496	2,076,958
Baptist	491,329	257,744
Jamaica-1982	2,172,879	1,109,417
Church of God	400,379	225,239
No religion	385,517	141,326
Mexico-1980	66,846,833	33,807,526
Catholic	61,916,757	31,443,532
Protestant	2,201,609	1,140,245
Montserrat-1980	11,519	5,983
Anglican	3,676	1,873
Methodist	2,742	1,440
Netherlands Antilles-1981	231,932	119,784
Catholic	197,115	NA
Protestant	7,369	NA
St. Kitts and Nevis-1980	43,309	22,469
Anglican	14,111	7,135
Methodist	12,473	6,495
St. Lucia-1980	113,409	58,900
Catholic	97,075	50,616
Seventh Day Adventist	4,909	2,645
St. Vincent and the Grenadines-1980	97,845	50,436
Agnostic	40,682	20,617
Methodist	20,454	10,370
Trinidad and Tobago-1980	1,055,763	529,529
Catholic	347,740	175,003
Hindu	262,917	129,447
Turks and Caicos Islands-1980	4,510	2,375
Baptist	1,807	967
Methodist	864	432

[Continued]

★ 731 ★

Worldwide Religious Preferences
[Continued]

Country or area, census date, religion	Total	Female
Brazil-1980	119,011,052	59,868,219
Catholic	114,606,475	57,821,375
No religion	1,953,096	749,277
Guyana-1980	758,619	382,778
Hindu	281,119	140,118
Agnostic	108,787	55,320
Peru-1981	17,005,210	8,515,343
Catholic	15,150,572	7,574,319
Asia		
Bangladesh-1981	87,119,965	42,200,774
Moslem	75,486,980	36,557,601
Hindu	10,570,245	5,125,589
India-1981	665,287,849	321,357,426
Hindu	549,724,717	265,359,428
Moslem	75,571,514	36,551,871
Israel-1983	4,037,620	2,026,030
Jews	3,349,997	1,687,272
Moslem	526,639	257,995
Jordan-1979	2,132,997	1,017,156
Moslem	2,036,407	971,945
Korea, Republic of-1985	40,419,652	20,192,088
Buddhist	8,059,624	4,318,727
No religion	23,216,356	10,944,809
Macau-1981	222,525	NA
Buddhist	100,350	NA
No religion	102,209	NA
Malaysia-1980	10,886,713	5,463,099
Moslem	6,106,105	3,107,834
Buddhist	2,064,949	1,036,915
Sabah-1980	950,556	455,061
Islam	487,627	231,957
Sarawak-1980	1,233,103	615,103
Christian	351,361	176,968
Moslem	324,575	161,901

[Continued]

★ 731 ★

Worldwide Religious Preferences
[Continued]

Country or area, census date, religion	Total	Female
Pakistan-1981	84,253,644	40,020,967
Moslem	81,450,057	NA
Sri Lanka-1981	14,846,750	7,278,496
Buddhist	10,288,325	5,040,259
Hindu	2,297,806	1,118,928
Europe		
Austria-1981	7,555,338	3,982,912
Catholic	6,398,192	3,417,261
Finland-1985	4,910,664	2,532,884
Lutheran	4,381,534	2,311,562
Ireland-1981	3,443,405	1,714,051
Catholic	3,203,574	1,599,550
Liechtenstein-1982	26,380	13,376
Catholic	22,467	NA
Portugal-1981	7,836,504	NA
Catholic	6,352,705	NA
United Kingdom		
Northern Ireland-1981	1,481,959	756,742
Catholic	414,532	211,315
Other Christians	281,472	143,915
Oceania		
Australia-1981	14,576,330	7,309,254
Church of England	3,810,469	1,965,652
Catholic	3,786,505	1,924,361
Fiji-1986	715,375	352,807
Christian	378,452	186,021
Hindu	273,088	135,275
New Zealand-1986	3,263,283	1,646,616
Anglican	791,850	423,384
Presbyterian	587,517	307,407
Papua New Guinea-1980	2,079,128	989,933
Catholic	718,352	339,832
Lutheran	548,973	262,586

[Continued]

★ 731 ★

Worldwide Religious Preferences
[Continued]

Country or area, census date, religion	Total	Female
United Church	272,469	129,775
Samoa-1981	156,349	75,322
Other Christians	74,031	35,728
Catholic	33,997	16,523
Vanuatu-1979	111,251	52,177
Presbyterians	40,843	19,169
Anglican	16,778	7,872

Source: Selected from "Population by Religion and Sex: Each Census, 1979-1988," *1988 Demographic Yearbook,* p. 671-81 (New York: United Nations, 1990). Also in source: total population for relevant census year; male population and male religious preferences; religious preferences for other denominations.

Women Clergy

★ 732 ★

Black Women Ministers

Some statistics on black women in the ministry, according to a book entitled *The Black Church in the African Experience*.

The authors conducted a 10-year study of over 1,800 black clergy in the Baptist, Methodist, and Pentecostal communities. Only **3.7%** of the ministers studied were women, and the authors estimate the total proportion of female ministers in the black church to be about **5%**.

Source: C. Eric Lincoln and Lawrence H. Mamiya, *The Black Church in the African American Experience* (Durham, NC: Duke University Press, 1990).

★ 733 ★

Heads of Pastoral Staff and Congregations

Total women clergy, number and percent of heads of pastoral staff, and number and percent serving in congregations, by denominations with more than 100 women clergy, 1986.

Denomination	Total Women Clergy	Heads of Pastoral Staff	%	Total in Congregation	%
American Baptist Churches	429	156	36%	259	60%
American Lutheran Church	306	89	29%	237	77%
Assemblies of God	3,718	276	7%	NA	NA
Christian Church (Disciples of Christ)	743	196	26%	363	49%
Christian Congregation	290	289	99%	289	99%

[Continued]

★ 733 ★

Heads of Pastoral Staff and Congregations
[Continued]

Denomination	Total Women Clergy	Heads of Pastoral Staff	%	Total in Congregation	%
Church of God (Anderson, Inc.)	275	64	23%	129	47%
Church of the Brethren	120	38	32%	68	57%
Church of the Nazarene	355	36	10%	70	20%
Episcopal Church	796	220	28%	NA	NA
Lutheran Church in American	484	268	55%	375	77%
Presbyterian Church (U.S.A.)	1,519	389	26%	923	61%
Reorganized Church of Jesus Christ of Latter Day Saints	860	21	2%	849	98%
Salvation Army	3,220	568	18%	1,161	36%
United Church of Christ[1]	1,460	277	19%	486	33%
United Methodist Church	1,891	NA	NA	1,344	71%

Source: Yearbook of American and Canadian Churches 1989, p. Table 2 (Nashville: Abingdon Press, 1989). Also in source: "Women Clergy in Canada, 1986: Percentage and Functional Categories by Denomination," Table 3, p. 266. Based on a questionnaire sent to over 300 Canadian and American denominations that appear in the *Yearbook*. *Notes:* 1. Estimated from "Women Clergy Still Experiencing Discrimination, UCC Survey Finds," Office of Communication, United Church of Christ, Dec. 18, 1986.

★ 734 ★

Women Clergy by Denomination
Numbers of female clergy in 1977 and 1986 by denomination.

Denomination	No. of women clergy	
	1977	1986
American Baptist Churches	157	429
American Lutheran Church[1]	18	306
Assemblies of God	1,572	3,718
Christian Church (Disciples of Christ)	388	743
Christian Congregation	125	290
Church of God (Anderson, Inc.)	272	275
Church of the Brethren	27	120
Church of the Nazarene	426	355
Episcopal Church	94	756
Free Methodist Church	11	69
International Church of the Foursquare Gospel	804	666
Lutheran Church in American[1]	55	484
Mennonite Church	4	48
Mennonite Church, General Conference	4	33
Moravian Church (Unitas Fratrum)	3	16
Presbyterian Church (U.S.A.)[3]	370	1,519
Reformed Church in America	1	42

[Continued]

★ 734 ★

Women Clergy by Denomination
[Continued]

Denomination	No. of women clergy	
	1977	1986
Salvation Army	3,037	3,220
United Church of Christ	400	1,460
United Methodist Church	319	1,891
Wesleyan Church	384	255
Total	8,741	16,735

Source: Yearbook of American and Canadian Churches 1989, Table 1 (Nashville: Abingdon Press, 1989). Based on a questionnaire sent to over 300 Canadian and American denominations that appear in the *Yearbook. Notes:* 1. This body and the Association of Evangelical Churches merged to form The Evangelical Lutheran Church in America which began operations on January 1, 1988. 2. The totals presented are actual statistics reported by the various denominations but the total of all women clergy in the U.S., estimated to be 20,730, is derived by taking the estimated total of women clergy from the 1977 study (10,470) and increasing it by the average increase of women clergy over the decade reported by 21 denominations in 1986 (98%) making a total of 20,730. 3. Data for 1977 are for two bodies that merged in 1983. These were The United Presbyterian Church in the U.S.A. and the Presbyterian Church in the United States.

★ 735 ★

Women Clergy: An Overview
A summary of trends in the ordination of women since 1977.

Characteristic	Number or %
Estimated female clergy in the U.S. in 1986:	20,730
Approximate increase since 1977:	100%
% female of total clergy in demoninations that ordain women:	7.9%
Increase in number of women enrolled in ordination programs in seminaries, 1977-1986:	110%
Results of a 1986 survey of 221 religious groups in the U.S.	
Number that ordained women:	84
Number that did not ordain women:	82
Uncertain:	49
No clergy:	6

Source: Gary L. Ward, "A Survey of the Women's Ordination Issue," *The Churches Speak On: Women's Ordination,* 1991, p. xiii (Detroit: Gale Research Inc., 1991).

★ 736 ★

Women in Theological Schools

Some statistics on women in ordination programs, as reported in the *Yearbook of American and Canadian Churches*.

Women enrolled in ordination programs have increased from **2,905 (11.5% of total enrollment)** in 1976 to **6,108** in 1987 (**22.4% of total enrollment**).

Source: Yearbook of American and Canadian Churches 1989, p. 264 (Nashville: Abingdon Press, 1989). Primary source: *Fact Book on Theological Education*, academic year 1987-1988 (Association of Theological Schools in the United States and Canada).

★ 737 ★

Women in the Ministry

Numbers of women clergy in denominations represented in the *Yearbook of American and Canadian Churches*.

According to the author, and based on a questionnaire sent to more than 300 Canadian and American denominations that appear in the *Yearbook*, the number of women ordained to the full ministry in the United States is estimated to have increased from **4.0%** of clergy in those denominations that ordained women in 1977 to **7.9%** in 1986, an increase over the decade of **98%**. In Canada, surveyed for the first time in 1987, **908 female clergy** were reported in those denominations that ordain women, out of a total of 12,493. Total numbers of female clergy were estimated to be **10,470** in 1977 and **20,730** in 1987.

It was estimated in 1977 that 87 denominations in the United States did not ordain women while 76 did. The estimate in 1987 (based on a survey of 221 bodies) was that **84 denominations ordained women and 82 did not.**

Source: Yearbook of American and Canadian Churches 1989, p. 261, 264 (Nashville: Abingdon Press, 1989).

★ 738 ★

Women in the Rabbinate

Total rabbis, number and percent women, by branch, 1987.

Branch	Total Rabbis	Women Rabbis	% Women Rabbis
Reformed	1,450	101	7.0%
Reconstructionist	110	27	24.5%
Conservative	1,000	4	0.4%
Orthodox	850	0	-
Total	3,410	132	3.9%

Source: Yearbook of American and Canadian Churches 1989, p. 264 (Nashville: Abingdon Press, 1989). Also in source: number of members by branch. Related reading: Ari L. Goldman, "A Bar to Women as Cantors Is Lifted," *New York Times*, September 19, 1990, p. A15.

Youth

★ 739 ★

Born-Again Teenagers

Percent of teenagers in a national survey who said they had had a "born again" experience.

Sex	Percent
National total	19%
Girls	22%
Boys	16%

Source: Religion in America 1984: Commentary on the State of Religion in the U.S. Today, p. 67 (Princeton, NJ: American Institute of Public Opinion; 1984). Also in source: other characteristics of evangelical teenagers.

★ 740 ★

Importance of Religion to Teens

Percentage of teenagers in a national survey who said religion was very important or the most important influence on their lives.

Sex	Very Important	Most Important
National total	40%	22%
Girls	42%	21%
Boys	39%	23%

Source: Religion in America 1984: Commentary on the State of Religion in the U.S. Today, p. 67-68 (Princeton, NJ: American Institute of Public Opinion; 1984).

★ 741 ★

Teenagers' Belief in God

Responses of teenagers in a national survey on their belief in God and belief in a personal God.

Sex	Believe in God	Believe in a personal God
National total	95%	75%
Girls	96%	77%
Boys	94%	74%

Source: Religion in America 1984: Commentary on the State of Religion in the U.S. Today, p. 69 (Princeton, NJ: American Institute of Public Opinion; 1984).

SEXUALITY

Adolescents

★ 742 ★

Sex, Drugs, and Alcohol

Cumulative percentages of adolescents who participated in selected activities prior to given ages by gender (number of respondents approximately 12,200).

Age	Females					Males				
	Sexual intercourse	Monthly alcohol use[1]	Weekly alcohol use[1]	Marijuana use	Other drug use	Sexual intercourse	Monthly alcohol use[1]	Weekly alcohol use	Marijuana use	Other drug use
14	3.3%	2.4%	0.7%	7.7%	1.3%	10.2%	5.4%	1.7%	12.0%	2.0%
15	8.4%	4.5%	1.7%	14.6%	2.7%	17.2%	9.6%	3.2%	19.9%	3.4%
16	17.6%	9.2%	3.4%	24.5%	5.5%	29.1%	19.2%	7.2%	31.4%	5.8%
17	33.2%	22.3%	6.7%	34.6%	9.0%	48.4%	38.0%	15.1%	43.0%	10.4%
18	50.9%	35.2%	11.7%	43.8%	12.8%	64.8%	54.1%	25.2%	53.0%	15.6%
19	67.6%	59.7%	28.0%	51.2%	16.5%	78.2%	77.8%	49.4%	61.5%	21.6%
N	5,450	5,474	5,471	5,464	5,430	5,396	5,444	5,434	5,410	5,389

Source: Frank L. Mott and R. Jean Haurin, "Linkages Between Sexual Activity and Alcohol and Drug Use Among American Adolescents," *Family Planning Perspectives*, 20(3), May/June 1988, Table 1, p. 130. Also in source: data by race/ethnicity. Sample consists of respondents interviewed in 1983 and 1984 who were at least 19 years of age in 1983, and percentages are weighted to represent the U.S. population. *Notes:* 1. For monthly alcohol use, respondents who had consumed alcohol less than monthly were grouped with those who never used alcohol; similarly, in the analysis of weekly alcohol use, those who had consumed alcohol less than weekly were grouped with those who had never used it.

★ 743 ★

Sexually Active Teens

Some statistics on teen sexual behavior in the United States and some comparisons to other countries.

Each Year:
- **1 out of 10** teenage women in the U.S. becomes pregnant
- About **30,000** pregnancies occur to girls under the age of 15

Each Day:
- More than **3,000** girls become pregnant
- **1,300** babies are born to teen-age girls
- **500** girls have induced abortions
- **26** 13-and 14-year-old girls have their first child
- **13** 16-year-olds have their second child

Sexual Activity:
- **1 of 5** 15-year-old girls are having intercourse
- **5 million** teenage females are sexually active
- **one third** of sexually active girls report using contraceptives consistently
- **one half** of unintended teen pregnancies occur during the first six months after the initiation of sexual activity

Comparative Statistics:
American teen sexual activity is similar to that in other developed countries, but American girls are **twice as likely** to become pregnant.

Teenage birth, abortion, and pregnancy rates in the U.S. are the highest in the world.

The teenage pregnancy rate in the U.S. is:
- Two times that of Canada, England, Wales, New Zealand, and Norway
- Three times that of Denmark, Finland, and Sweden
- Seven times that of the Netherlands

Source: Hutzel Hospital, "Statistics," mimeographed (Detroit, Michigan).

★ 744 ★

Sexually Active Teens Worldwide

Percentage of adolescents reported to have experienced premarital coitus, selected countries.

Country	Age group	Females	Males
Australia	By age 20	47%	58%
Germany, Federal Republic of	By age 16	30%	35%
Israel	14-19	11%	42%
Japan	16-21	7%	15%

[Continued]

★ 744 ★

Sexually Active Teens Worldwide
[Continued]

Country	Age group	Females	Males
Nigeria	14-19	43%	68%
Korea, Republic of	12-21	4%	17%

Source: Herbert L. Friedman, "The Health of Adolescents and Youth: A Global Overview," *World Health Statistics Quarterly*, 38(3) 1985, p. 256-266. Primary source: Adapted from Hoffman, A.D., *Contraception in adolescence: a review. 1. Psychological aspects. Bulletin of the World Health Organization* 62(1):151-162 (1984).

Prostitution

★ 745 ★

Number of Prostitutes in Selected Asian Countries
Estimated number of prostitutes in selected Asian countries, 1950-1980.

Country	Year			
	1950	1960	1970	1980
Thailand	20,000	-	300,000	500-700,000
Philippines	-	20,000	200,000	-
Korea, Republic of	-	-	-	260,000

Source: "Estimated number of prostitutes in selected countries," *Virtue, Order, Health and Money: Towards a Comprehensive Perspective on Female Prostitution in Asia*, 1986, Table 4, p. 25. Primary source: M.G. Fox, "Problem of Prostitution in Thailand," - Memorandum dated 26 February 1957 from Fox as UN Social Welfare Adviser, to the Director-General, Dept. of Public Welfare, Thailand, published in *Social Service in Thailand*, May 1960, Department of Public Welfare, Ministry of Interior, Bangkok, Thailand; K. Choonhavan, "Thailand: economic development and rural provery-a country report" (1984); The Thailand National Commission on Women's Affairs, Summary of Long-term Women's Development Plan (1982-2001), December 1981, p. 23; A.J. Akut, "Metro Manila by night" (1971); L. Neumann, "Hospitality girls in the Philippines" (1979); J. Gay, "The Patriotic Prostitute," *Progressive*, February 1985. Since the American withdrawal from Viet Nam, the tourist market in Thailand has been replaced by Europeans, Japanese, Malaysians, Singaporeans, Australians, and more recently by visitors from the Middle East, 90% of whom came for the "night life" (source).

★ 746 ★

Prostitution Income Compared to Other Employment

Gross income per year from prostitution and from alternative forms of employment, selected countries, different years in the period 1974-1978.

Country	Earnings Range-U.S. $	
	From	To
Republic of Korea		
Garment industry	$135	$480
Prostitution in Seoul	$4,500	$9,000
Philippines		
Spinning and weaving	$580	-
Prostitution in Manila	$850	$3,200
Prostitution in Olongapo	$3,375	$5,000
Thailand		
Restaurant waitress	$250	-
Battery factory	$312	-
Garment industry	$450	
Prostitution in Bangkok	$1,875[1]	$1,800[2]
Netherlands		
Textile industry	$15,000	-
Prostitution	$30,000[3]	-

Source: "Gross income per year from prostitution and from alternative forms of employment; different years in the period 1974-1978," *Virtue, Order, Health and Money: Towards a Comprehensive Perspective on Female Prostitution in Asia,* 1986, Table 1, p. 20. Primary source: T.D. Truong, "The dynamics of sex tourism; the case of South East Asia," *Development and Change,* V. 14, 1983. Compiled by H.L. Theuns. Up to 75% of the young women working in the Asian "entertainment industry" come from depressed rural areas. The size of their families (or households) averages 6 children, excluding other dependents. Entry into prostitution in these cases forms a part of the family's strategy for survival (source). *Notes:* 1. Excluding "bonded" girls who may make only about $625. 2. For a "star-masseuse." 3. Assuming a gross income of 60% of gross revenue.

Sex Partners

★ 747 ★

Fidelity

Percent of currently married respondents reporting that they have been chaste since age 18 (N=682). "Chaste" refers to reporting no more sex partners since age 18 than marriage partners.

Respondent	Percent
All	48.1%
Women	64.8%
Men	30.0%

Source: Tom W. Smith, "Adult Sexual Behavior in 1989: Number of Partners, Frequency, and Risk," paper presented to the American Association for the Advancement of Science, February 1990, New Orleans. "Chaste" respondents may or may not have had sexual relations with a future marriage partner before or between marriage(s). Those respondents who are not "chaste" may have always been faithful within marriage, since their "extra" partners may have been pre-or intermarital relationships.

★ 748 ★

Gender of Sex Partners

Response to the question: Have your sex partners in the last 12 months been exclusively male, both male and female, or exclusively female?

Number of Respondents/Sex/Year	Gender of Sex Partner		
	Exclusively Male	Both Male and Female	Exclusively Female
543 Females/1988	100%	0%	0%
476 Males/1988	3%	0%	97%
560 Females/1989	98%	0%	1%
499 Males/1989	1%	0%	98%

Source: Selected from *An American Profile—Opinions and Behavior, 1972-1989*, p. 963 (Detroit: Gale Research Inc., 1990). Primary source: General Social Survey. Also in source: data breakdown by totals, race, and age.

★ 749 ★

Number of Sex Partners in Last Year

Responses to the question: "How many sex partners have you had in the last 12 months?" (1988-1989).

Number and Sex of Respondents/Year	Number of Sex Partners in Last Year in Percent								
	1	2	3	4	5-10	11-20	21-100	Over 100	More than 1
568 Females, 1988	86%	8%	4%	1%	1%	0%	0%	0%	1%
576 Females, 1989	89%	7%	2%	1%	0%	0%	0%	0%	0%
504 Males, 1988	77%	7%	6%	4%	4%	1%	1%	0%	1%
512 Males, 1989	77%	9%	6%	3%	4%	0%	0%	0%	1%

Source: Selected from *An American Profile—Opinions and Behavior, 1972-1989*, p. 950 (Detroit: Gale Research Inc., 1990). Primary source: General Social Survey. Also in source: data for various years.

★ 750 ★

Sex Partners in Last Year

Number of persons responding "Yes" to questions about their sex partners in the last 12 months: 1988 and 1989.

Question	Sex	Total Respondents/Percent "Yes" and Year			
		Number	1988	Number	1989
Was one of your sex partners in the last 12 months your husband or wife or regular sex partner?	F	562	94%	569	93%
	M	499	89%	509	90%
Was one of your sex partners in the last 12 months a close personal friend?	F	65	66%	60	73%
	M	105	65%	100	67%
Was one of your sex partners in the last 12 months a neighbor, co-worker, or a long-term acquaintance?	F	65	32%	60	37%
	M	105	34%	100	30%
Was one of your sex partners in the last 12 months a casual date or pickup?	F	65	15%	60	10%
	M	105	36%	100	36%
Was one of your sex partners in the last 12 months a person you paid or paid you for sex?	F	65	0%	60	2%
	M	105	4%	100	3%

Source: Selected from *An American Profile—Opinions and Behavior, 1972-1989*, p. 953,955,957,959,961 (Detroit: Gale Research Inc., 1990). Primary source: General Social Survey. Also in source: data by total population, by race, and by age.

★ 751 ★

Sex and AIDS

Responses of *Glamour* magazine readers to questions on AIDS and sex partners.

Question	Percent Yes
Should it be a criminal offense for known AIDS-virus carriers to have sex without first informing their partners?	98%
Would making AIDS-virus transmission a crime reduce risky behavior by infected individuals?	75%
Do you trust prospective sex partners to tell you the truth about their possible past exposure to the AIDS virus?	23%

Source: "This Is What You Thought: 98 Percent Say It Should Be a Crime to Knowingly Spread AIDS," *Glamour*, December 1987, p. 81-82. Also in source: readers' responses to questions on other aspects of AIDS. *Glamour* magazine is aimed at college and young working women.

★ 752 ★

That *Cosmopolitan* Woman

Results of a survey of 100 women between the ages of 19 and 45 conducted in late 1987 by *Cosmopolitan* magazine.

Question	Response
As well as you can remember, how many different sex partners did you have in 1985, 1986, and so far in 1987?	
1985	
One	42%
Two	25%
More than three	20%
None	6%
1986	
One	46%
Two	18%
More than three	16%
None	6%
1987	
One	49%
Two	25%
More than three	8%
None	9%
In previous years, how soon did you sometimes go to bed with a new lover?[1]	
First meeting	13%
First date	25%
Second or third date	41%
Later than the third date	53%
More than three	16%

[Continued]

★ 752 ★

That *Cosmopolitan* Woman
[Continued]

Question	Response
How soon would you go to bed with a new lover now?	
First meeting or date	1%
Third or fourth date	71%
Later than third or fourth date	37%
If you currently have fewer sex partners than in previous years, are you enjoying sex more, less, or about the same?	
More	57%
Just as much as before	32%
Less than before	13%
If you wait longer than in the past to begin having sex with a new man (possibly for fear of AIDS), do you find this waiting helps you know each other better, makes sex more exciting, makes sex less exciting, or doesn't make any difference?	
Helps to know the man better	72%
Makes sex more exciting	52%
Makes no difference	14%
Makes sex less exciting	0%
How do you feel about not participating in the sort of varied, active sex life with new lovers you may previously have enjoyed?	
It's a relief	68%
It's quiet and boring	24%
Both answers apply	8%

Source: *Cosmo's Private Sex Survey*, July, 1988, p. 140-144. *Notes:* 1. Some women checked more than one answer, so the numbers don't add up to 100.

Sexual Practices, Preferences, and Attitudes

★ 753 ★

Bisexuality in Marriage

Answers of psychiatrists and sex therapists to questions about bisexuality in marriage.

Question/Incidence	Total (N=63)	Years in Practice				Size of Community		
		Less than 5	5 to 15	16 to 25	More than 25	Under 200,000	200,000 to 1,000,000	Over 1,000,000
What percentage of married women do you estimate are bisexual or homosexual?								
Less than 5%	29%	0%	28%	35%	10%	39%	26%	24%
5-9%	16%	51%	17%	18%	0%	17%	13%	19%

[Continued]

★ 753 ★

Bisexuality in Marriage
[Continued]

Question/Incidence	Total (N=63)	Years in Practice				Size of Community		
		Less than 5	5 to 15	16 to 25	More than 25	Under 200,000	200,000 to 1,000,000	Over 1,000,000
10-20%	29%	50%	21%	12%	80%	11%	39%	29%
21% or more	13%	0%	24%	6%	0%	6%	13%	19%
No response	14%	0%	10%	29%	10%	28%	9%	9%
What percentage of married bisexual or homosexual men keep their bisexuality or homosexuality a secret from their wives?								
Less than 40%	19%	0%	21%	23%	10%	28%	13%	19%
40-75%	13%	50%	14%	12%	10%	6%	9%	24%
76-100%	52%	50%	55%	35%	60%	39%	70%	43%
No response	16%	0%	10%	29%	20%	28%	9%	14%

Source: The Bisexual Spouse: Different Dimensions in Human Sexuality, 1987, p. 230-231 (McLean, VA: Barlina Books, 1987). Based on a random sample of psychiatrists and sex therapists located throughout the country.

★ 754 ★

Date Rape

Answers of female college students on 32 campuses to a question whether they had experienced sexual assault in the previous 12 months.

	Number	Number "Yes"	% "Yes"
Female college students	3,187	207	7%

Source: William Celis 3d, "Growing Talk of Date Rape Separates Sex from Assault," *New York Times,* January 2, 1991, p. 1+. Primary source: A study conducted in 1984/1985 by Mary P. Koss and associates with financing from the National Institute of Mental Health. The poll defined assault as intercourse by physical force, intercourse as a result of intentionally getting the woman intoxicated, or forcible oral or anal penetration.

★ 755 ★

Elderly Lesbians: Part 1

Answers of lesbians over 60 to the question: "Over the last year, how often were you physically sexual with another woman?"

Response	Percent
Daily	3%
About once a week	15%
About once a month	8%
A few times a year	16%
Never	53%

Source: Monika Kehoe, PhD, "Lesbians Over 60 Speak for Themselves," *Journal of Homosexuality* 16(3-4), p. 73. Results of a nationwide study of 50 lesbians over the age of 65 begun in 1980.

★ 756 ★

Elderly Lesbians: Part 2

Answers of lesbians over 60 to the question: "How satisfied have you been with your sex life over the last year?"

Response	Percent
Very satisfied	16%
Somewhat satisfied	17%
Neither satisfied nor unsatisfied	20%
Somewhat unsatisfied	21%
Very unsatisfied	26%

Source: Monika Kehoe, PhD, "Lesbians Over 60 Speak for Themselves," *Journal of Homosexuality* 16(3-4), p. 73. Results of a nationwide study of 50 lesbians over the age of 65 begun in 1980.

★ 757 ★

Frequency of Intercourse

Respondents' answer to a question on frequency of sexual intercourse during the last year (N = 1,361).

Respondent	Mean
All	57.4
Women	50.6
Men	66.4

Source: Tom W. Smith, "Adult Sexual Behavior in 1989: Number of Partners, Frequency, and Risk," paper presented to the American Association for the Advancement of Science, February 1990, New Orleans.

★ 758 ★

Knowledge About Sex

Some questions and answers testing Americans' knowledge about sex.

Question	Correct Answer(s)	% Answering Correctly
Of every 10 American women, how many would you estimate have had anal (rectal) intercourse? A. Fewer than 1 of 10 B. One C. Two D. Three E. Four F. Five G. Six H. Seven I. Eight J. Nine K. More than nine L. Don't know	D or E	21%

[Continued]

★ 758 ★

Knowledge About Sex
[Continued]

Question	Correct Answer(s)	% Answering Correctly
A woman or teen-age girl can get pregnant during her menstrual flow (her "period"). True False Don't know	True	51%

Source: Natalie Angier, "Americans Sex Knowledge Is Lacking, Poll Says," *New York Times*, September 6, 1990, p. A15. Primary source: Kinsey Institute. Based on the Kinsey Institute and Roper Organization poll of 1,974 adult Americans on their basic knowledge of sex and reproduction.

★ 759 ★

Lack of Male Friends Among Elderly Women

Percentage of friendships of each type (N=678) and percentage of respondents with each type of friendship (N=70).

Friendships with...	Percentage of friendships	Percentage of respondents with one or more
Male[1]	3.6%	17.1%
Couple[2]	6.1%	20.0%
Male closest	0.4%	4.3%
Equal	3.3%	14.3%
Female closest	2.4%	7.1%
Female	90.6%	95.7%[3]

Source: Rebecca G. Adams, PhD, "People Would Talk: Normative Barriers to Cross-Sex Friendships for Elderly Women," *Gerontologist* 25(6), 1985, p. 605+. A follow-up study is reported in *Gerontologist* 27(2), 1987, p. 222+, "Patterns of Network Change: A Longitudinal Study of Friendships of Elderly Women," (it was found that "Because the women had acquired more new friends than they had eliminated or lost, they averaged more friends in 1984. In other ways, however, the average respondent's friendship network had tended to contract"). Based on interviews with 70 mon-married, white, elderly women who lived in a middle-class Chicago suburb. *Notes:* 1. Some of the males were married, but the respondent did not identify their wives as friends. 2. A couple friendship is one in which the respondent considered both members as friends. 3. All of the women who named at least one friend named at least one female friend.

★ 760 ★

Norplant

The state of birth control in America, as reported in the *New York Times Magazine*.

Norplant, introduced in late 1990 and said to be the "first substantially new contraceptive brought out in the United States in 25 years," is expected to be the most effective contraceptive ever introduced other than sterilization. A five-year dose will cost about $200 to $300. At the time of Norplant's introduction, sterilization was the contraceptive of choice of **28%** of women and 12% of men who used some form of contraception. Other popular methods were the pill (31%) and the condom (15%). Abortion was the method of birth control for **1.6 million** women annually.

Source: Philip J. Hilts, "Birth-Control Backlash: Years of litigation and agitation have left America in the dark ages of contraception," *New York Times Magazine*, December 16, 1990, p. 41+. Also in source: a discussion of contraceptive use and abortion rates among young and low-income American women as compared to women in other countries.

★ 761 ★

Patient-Therapist Sex

A discussion of the problem of patient-therapist sex prompted by the meeting of the American Psychological Association's panel on sexual impropriety to draw up new professional guidelines, reported in the *New York Times*.

The author discusses a study to be published in 1991 in the journal *Psychotherapy* based on a survey of 1,320 clinical psychologists in which half of the respondents indicated they had treated patients who had had sex with a previous therapist. Studies indicate that the frequency of such contact may be decreasing or, alternatively, that therapists are increasingly unwilling to discuss the topic. A 1977 survey of psychologists found that 12% of the men and **3%** of the women admitted sexual contact with patients; a 1989 survey of mental health workers found only 0.9% of men and **0.2%** of women admitting sexual contact.

About **50%** of complaints filed by therapy patients with state licensing boards concern sexual misconduct by therapists. In a 1986 survey of 1,000 psychologists, 87% admitted having occasionally felt a sexual attraction toward a patient.

Source: Daniel Goleman, "New Guidelines Issued on Patient-Therapist Sex," *New York Times*, December 20, 1990, p. B7. Also in source: a discussion of the new movement to deal with the problem of patient-therapist sex; a discussion of personality types of 150 therapists who admitted having sex with patients; some warning signs of trouble in a therapy situation.

★ 762 ★

Sexual Desire and the Monthly Cycle

Answers to the question, "Do you notice an increase in sexual desire at certain times of the month?"

Answer	Number
Yes, before and during menstruation	320
During and after menstruation	24
After menstruation	30
During ovulation	62
"Yes" (did not say when)	99
Total	571

Source: The Hite Report: A Nationwide Study on Female Sexuality, 1981, p. 433 (New York: MacMillan Publishing Co., Inc., 1981). Also in source: Numerous results of a series of surveys on "how women view their own sexuality."

SPORTS AND RECREATION

Adult Participation/Attitudes

★ 763 ★

Athletes' Body Image

Female athletes' answers to questions about body image.

Question/Responses	%
When you were an adolescent, how did you feel about your body? (N=1,641)	
Very positively	15%
Somewhat positively	32%
Indifferently	20%
Somewhat negatively	26%
Very negatively	7%
Compared to 5 years ago, how do you feel now about your body? (N=1,666)	
Much more positively	29%
More positively	33%
About the same	23%
More negatively	13%
Much more negatively	2%

Source: Miller Lite Report on Women in Sports, December 1985, p. 5 Based on a random sample of 7,000 members of the Women's Sports Foundation.

★ 764 ★

Business and Pleasure Trips

Total business and pleasure trips in millions and percent female travelers, 1980-1988.

Characteristic	Business trips					Pleasure trips				
Total trips, in millions	97.1	133.3	140.0	157.5	155.6	342.8	384.4	415.2	444.9	455.3
Female travelers, in percent	NA	33%	33%	32%	31%	NA	52%	49%	53%	50%

Source: "Characteristics of Business Trips and Pleasure Trips: 1980 to 1988," Statistical Abstract of the United States 1990, p. 238. Primary source: US Travel Data Center, Washington, DC, National Travel Survey, annual. Also in source: other characteristics of travelers. Represents trips to places 100 miles or more from home by one or more household members traveling together. Based on a monthly telephone survey of 1,500 U.S. adults.

★ 765 ★

Members of Sports Groups

Persons responding "Yes" to the question: "Are you a member of any sports group?"

Sex	Year										
	1974	1975	1977	1978	1980	1983	1984	1986	1987	1988	1989
Female	14%	13%	13%	15%	13%	16%	17%	16%	14%	14%	16%
Number Surveyed	784	806	829	879	811	906	862	845	813	556	574
Male	23%	26%	25%	25%	23%	29%	28%	28%	25%	27%	29%
Number Surveyed	680	658	688	641	634	687	591	616	636	433	432

Source: Selected from *An American Profile—Opinions and Behavior, 1972-1989*, p. 888 (Detroit: Gale Research Inc., 1990). Primary source: General Social Survey. Also in source: "No" responses.

★ 766 ★

Sports Participation

Frequency of participation, by activity.

Activity	Participation Level			
	Every day or almost every day	About once or twice a week	About once a month or less	Never
Walking	49%	27%	14%	10%
Jogging/running	32%	23%	24%	21%
Calisthenics/aerobics	22%	33%	18%	27%
Weightlifting	15%	31%	16%	38%
Softball or baseball	17%	26%	21%	36%
Bicycling	15%	28%	36%	21%
Swimming	12%	26%	41%	21%
Volleyball	11%	21%	30%	38%
Basketball	11%	16%	29%	44%
Tennis, squash, badminton or other racquet sports	6%	24%	45%	25%

Source: Miller Lite Report on Women in Sports, December 1985, p. 5. Also in source: other activities. Based on a random sample of 7,000 members of the Women's Sports Foundation.

★ 767 ★

Women and Golf

Some statistics on women in golf, according to *Business Week*, October 1990.

1. "Upscale" women now make up **40%** of beginning golfers.
2. About **50%** of Mazda owners are women. Mazda sponsors the Mazda LPGA (Ladies Professional Golf Assn.) Championship.
3. LPGA prize money grew from $13 million in 1989 to $17.1 million in 1990.
4. Only 5 LPGA tournaments were televised on the three major networks in 1990, compared to 37 for the regular PGA Tour.

Source: William C. Symonds, "Golf: The Ladies Tour Slices Into the Rough," *Business Week*, October 1, 1990, p. 134.

★ 768 ★

Women's Favorite Activities

Ten most popular activities of women, 1987 and 1988.

Activity	1987	1988
Swimming	40%	34%
Bicycling	32%	25%
Aerobics, dancerize (sic)	24%	23%
Bowling	23%	20%
Fishing	20%	17%
Running, jogging	15%	16%
Camping	19%	16%
Hiking	21%	13%
Weight training (net)	15%	12%
Calisthenics	17%	11%

Source: George Gallup, Jr., *The Gallup Report*, Report No. 281 (Princeton, NJ: The Gallup Poll, February 1989), p. 29. Also in source: men's top activities; long-term trends 1959-1988. The 1988 results are based on interviews with 2,019 adults, age 18 and older, in over 300 scientifically selected localities across the nation in two surveys during the periods Nov. 11-14 and Dec. 9-12.

College

★ 769 ★

College Athletic Administrators

Percentage of women's intercollegiate athletic programs with male head directors and percentage of schools having no female representation in administrative structure, 1990 and 1984.

Division	1990	1984
Male head director of women's athletic programs		
All Divisions	84.1%	83.0%
Division I	92.9%	90.0%
Division II	84.8%	84.1%
Division III	75.2%	78.8%
No female representation in administration		
All Divisions	30.2%	31.6%
Division I	21.8%	21.4%
Division II	39.8%	36.9%
Division III	32.7%	36.9%

Source: Selected from R. Vivian Acosta and Linda Jean Carpenter, "Perceived Causes of the Declining Representation of Women Leaders in Intercollegiate Sports, 1988 Update," 1990, Department of Physical Education, Brooklyn College, Brooklyn, NY 11210. Also in source: data for intervening years. Information gathered in an on-going national study of all four-year college and university members of the NCAA with intercollegiate athletic programs for women.

★ 770 ★

College Basketball

Number of women's college basketball teams and attendance in thousands, 1982-1988.

Teams and Attendance	1982	1983	1984	1985	1986	1987	1988
College Basketball Teams	1,095	1,114	1,147	1,166	1,188	1,188	1,190
Attendance (in thousands)	2,397	2,502	2,870	2,944	3,020	3,121	3,301

Source: Selected from "Selected Spectator Sports: 1980 to 1988," *Statistical Abstract of the United States 1990*, 1990, p. 229. Primary source: National Basketball Assn., New York, NY. Also in source: data for numerous other sports, including salaries, not by gender. Season ending in year shown. Attendance total excludes double-headers with men's teams.

★ 771 ★

College Coaches

Number of coaching jobs in women's college athletic programs and number held by women, 1990 and 1978.

Year	Number jobs	Held by women
1990	5,718	2,706
1978	4,208	2,449

Source: Selected from R. Vivian Acosta and Linda Jean Carpenter, "Perceived Causes of the Declining Representation of Women Leaders in Intercollegiate Sports, 1988 Update," 1990, Department of Physical Education, Brooklyn College, Brooklyn, NY 11210. Also in source: data for intervening years. Information gathered in an on-going national study of all four-year college and university members of the NCAA with intercollegiate athletic programs for women.

★ 772 ★

College Expenditures on Athletics

Total budget and per capita expenditures on athletics at AIAW and NCAA Colleges, by sex, and percent difference between budgets.

Membership	Total Budget		Per capita expendit.		Difference
	Women	Men	Women	Men	
All AIAW Colleges	$141,000	$717,000	$1,382	$3,013	-80.3%
All AIAW & NCAA Div. I	276,000	1,650,000	2,156	5,257	-83.3%
NCAA Div. II	120,000	418,000	1,143	1,883	-71.3%
NCAA Div. III	24,000	79,000	218	315	-69.6%
All NCAA	199,000	1,042,000	1,686	3,755	-80.9%

Source: "Athletes, Budgets, and Per Capita Expenditures (PCE) at AIAW and NCAA Colleges (1978)," *Women and Public Policies*, 1987, Table 6, p. 103 (Princeton, NJ: Princeton University Press, 1987). Primary source: *AIAW Competitive Division Structure Implementation Study: Final Data Summary*, Association for Intercollegiate Athletics for Women, Fall 1978, Table XIV.

★ 773 ★

College Sports Coached by Women

Intercollegiate sports coached by women, 1977-78 and 1989-90.

Sport	1989/1990	1977/1978
Archery	80%	83.4%
Badminton	50%	75.0%
Basketball	59%	79.4%
Bowling	0%	42.9%
Crew	39.1%	11.9%
Cross Country	20.6%	35.2%
Fencing	28.9%	51.7%
Field Hockey	97.8%	99.1%
Golf	41.4%	54.6%
Gymnastics	57.5%	69.7%
Ice Hockey	12.5%	37.5%
Lacrosse	95.1%	98.7%
Riding	85.7%	75.0%
Riflery	12.5%	17.4%
Sailing	12.5%	7.1%
Skiing	21.9%	22.7%
Soccer	23.1%	29.4%
Softball	63.8%	83.5%
Squash	68.2%	71.4%
Swimming/Diving	26.4%	53.6%
Synchronized Swimming	100.0%	85.0%
Tennis	49.8%	72.9%
Track	19.6%	52.3%
Volleyball	68.4%	86.6%

Source: Selected from R. Vivian Acosta and Linda Jean Carpenter, "Perceived Causes of the Declining Representation of Women Leaders in Intercollegiate Sports, 1988 Update," 1990, Department of Physical Education, Brooklyn College, Brooklyn, NY 11210. Also in source: data for intervening years. Information gathered in an on-going national study of all four-year college and university members of the NCAA with intercollegiate athletic programs for women.

★ 774 ★

Declining Representation of Women Leaders - College Sports

Responses of college athletic administrators to a survey on women leaders in intercollegiate sports.

Some perceived causes of the declining representation of women leaders in intercollegiate sports, in decreasing order of importance, 1988.

1. Success of "old boys club" network
2. Lack of support systems for females
3. Failure of "old girls club" network
4. Females "burn out" and leave coaching and/or administration sooner than males
5. Failure of females to apply for job openings
6. Lack of qualified female administrators
7. Lack of qualified female coaches
8. Time constraints on females due to family duties
9. Unconscious discrimination in the selection/hiring process
10. Conscious discrimination in the selection/hiring process

Source: Selected from R. Vivian Acosta and Linda Jean Carpenter, "Perceived Causes of the Declining Representation of Women Leaders in Intercollegiate Sports, 1988 Update," 1990, Department of Physical Education, Brooklyn College, Brooklyn, NY 11210. Responses to 400 questionnaires mailed to males and females involved in athletic administration in colleges and universities in 1988; over 60% of questionnaires were returned and compared to data from a similar study conducted in 1984.

★ 775 ★

Intercollegiate Sports: An Overview

Some findings from an ongoing national study of four-year college and university members of the NCAA with intercollegiate athletic programs for women.

Finding	Number or %
Average number of sports offered for women per school, 1990	7.24
Average number of sports offered for women per school, 1977	5.61
Percent of coaches of women's teams who are women, 1990	47.3%
Percent of coaches of women's teams who were women, 1972	90%
Percent of coaches of men's teams who are male, 1990	99%
Number of jobs as head coaches of women's NCAA teams, 1990	5,718
Number of those jobs held by women, 1990	2,706
Number of jobs as head coaches of women's NCAA teams, 1988	5,757
Number of those jobs held by women, 1988	2,780
Percent of women's programs headed by a female administrator, 1990	15.9%
Percent of women's programs headed by a female administrator, 1972	90%
Number of women's programs in which no females are involved in the administration	30.3%

Source: Selected from R. Vivian Acosta and Linda Jean Carpenter, "Perceived Causes of the Declining Representation of Women Leaders in Intercollegiate Sports, 1988 Update," 1990, Department of Physical Education, Brooklyn College, Brooklyn, NY 11210.

★ 776 ★

Most Popular Collegiate Sports

24 most popular sports among college women.

	Rank
Basketball	1
Volleyball	2
Tennis	3
Cross-Country	4
Softball	5
Track	6
Swim/Diving	7
Soccer	8
Field Hockey	9
Golf	10
Lacrosse	11
Gymnastics	12
Crew	13
Fencing	14
Skiing	15
Sailing	16
Riflery	17
Squash	18
Riding	19
Ice Hockey	20
Badminton	21
Bowling	22
Archery	23
Synchronized Swimming	24

Source: Selected from R. Vivian Acosta and Linda Jean Carpenter, "Perceived Causes of the Declining Representation of Women Leaders in Intercollegiate Sports, 1988 Update," 1990, Department of Physical Education, Brooklyn College, Brooklyn, NY 11210. Also in source: rank in various years; percent of schools offering sport; percent of teams coached by women; percent coached by women in 1990. Information gathered in an ongoing national study of all four-year college and university members of the NCAA with intercollegiate athletic programs for women.

★ 777 ★

Results of Title IX Legislation

A comparison of the percentage of women participating in NCAA-sanctioned sports and the percentage of athletic budgets spent on female athletes in four Michigan universities, 1980 and 1990.

Institution	Women participating in NCAA-sanctioned sports		Portion of athletic budget spent on female athletes	
	1980	1990	1980	1990
University of Michigan	27%	12%	29%	11%
Michigan State University	31%	21%	30%	29%
Central Michigan University	39%	28%	41%	34%
Western Michigan University	28%	21%	28%	NA

Source: Michelle Kaufman, "Title IX makes headway, but women's programs still struggle," *Detroit Free Press*, November 26, 1990, p. 1D+. Primary source: University of Michigan, Michigan State University, Central Michigan University, Western Michigan University. Also in source: an analysis of athlete/coach ratios by gender for each institution. Title IX prohibits sex discrinination in educational programs, including sports, that receive federal funding.

★ 778 ★

Sports Offered to Women in College

Percent of NCAA schools with intercollegiate atheltic programs for women offering these sports to women, 1989/1990 and 1977/1978.

Sport	1989/1990	1977/1978
Archery	0.8%	3.0%
Badminton	1.0%	5.9%
Basketball	96.2%	90.3%
Bowling	0.8%	3.4%
Crew	10.5%	6.9%
Cross Country	82.1%	29.4%
Fencing	7.4%	9.8%
Field Hockey	29.4%	36.3%
Golf	25.8%	19.9%
Gymnastics	15.5%	25.9%
Ice Hockey	2.6%	1.3%
Lacrosse	16.9%	13.0%
Riding	3.5%	2.0%
Riflery	2.6%	3.8%
Sailing	4.0%	2.3%
Skiing	5.3%	3.6%
Soccer	41.3%	2.8%
Softball	70.9%	48.4%
Squash	3.6%	2.3%
Swimming/Diving	53.6%	41.0%
Synchronized Swimming	0.5%	3.3%
Tennis	88.8%	80.0%

[Continued]

★ 778 ★

Sports Offered to Women in College
[Continued]

Sport	1989/1990	1977/1978
Track	68.6%	46.1%
Volleyball	90.6%	80.1%

Source: Selected from R. Vivian Acosta and Linda Jean Carpenter, "Perceived Causes of the Declining Representation of Women Leaders in Intercollegiate Sports, 1988 Update," 1990, Department of Physical Education, Brooklyn College, Brooklyn, NY 11210. Also in source: Data for intervening years. Information gathered in an on-going national study of all four-year college and university members of the NCAA with intercollegiate athletic programs for women.

★ 779 ★

Women in NCAA-Sanctioned Sports: 1981-1988
Women participating in NCAA-sanctioned sports, 1981-1988.

Year	Number (thousands)
1981	74.2
1982	80.0
1983	84.7
1984	91.6
1985	95.3
1986	91.1
1987	89.8
1988	91.4

Source: Michelle Kaufman, "Title IX makes headway, but women's programs still struggle," *Detroit Free Press*, November 26, 1990, p. 1D+. Primary source: NCAA.

General Participation

★ 780 ★

Participation in Sports Activities
Total participation in sports activities by sport, rank, and percent participation by sex, 1988.

Activity	All persons		Female	Male
	Number	Rank		
Total (in thousands)	216,837	-	111,963	104,876
Percent participated in:				
Aerobic exercising[1]	11.2%	8	18.4%	3.5%
Backpacking/wilderness camping	4.2%	24	2.8%	5.6%
Baseball	6.2%	18	2.3%	10.3%
Basketball	10.7%	9	5.9%	15.7%
Bicycle riding[1]	24.8%	3	24.8%	24.9%

[Continued]

★ 780 ★

Participation in Sports Activities
[Continued]

Activity	All persons		Female	Male
	Number	Rank		
Bowling	17.5%	6	16.7%	18.2%
Calisthenics[1]	6.3%	17	7.2%	5.3%
Camping (vacation/overnight)	19.5%	4	18.0%	21.1%
Exercise walking[1]	28.7%	2	36.8%	20.1%
Exercising with equipment[1]	13.3%	7	12.7%	14.0%
Fishing-fresh water	18.3%	5	11.9%	25.2%
Fishing-salt water	6.0%	19	3.4%	8.7%
Football	5.7%	20	1.4%	10.3%
Golf	10.5%	11	4.9%	16.4%
Hiking	9.2%	14	8.9%	9.5%
Hunting with firearms	7.9%	16	1.8%	14.4%
Racquetball	4.3%	23	2.6%	6.2%
Running/jogging[1]	10.6%	10	8.5%	12.7%
Skiing-alpine/downhill	5.7%	20	4.3%	7.2%
Skiing-cross country	2.7%	26	2.6%	2.7%
Soccer	4.0%	25	2.9%	5.2%
Softball	9.5%	13	7.6%	11.6%
Swimming[1]	32.8%	1	34.5%	30.9%
Target shooting	4.7%	22	1.9%	7.6%
Tennis	8.0%	15	6.8%	9.2%
Volleyball	10.1%	12	10.2%	10.0%

Source: Selected from "Participation in Sports Activities, by Selected Characteristics: 1988," *Statistical Abstract of the United States 1990*, 1990, p. 231. Primary source: National Sporting Goods Association, Mt. Prospect, IL, *Sports participation in 1988: Series 1*. Also in source: Participation by age and household income. For persons 7 years of age or older. Except as indicated, a participant plays a sport more than once in the year. Based on a sampling of 10,000 households. *Note:* 1. Participant engaged in activity at least six times in the year.

★ 781 ★

Quitting Sports: Reasons
Reasons for discontinuing or never participating in sports, by age.

Reason	Total Daughters	Age 7-10	Age 11-14	Age 15-18
Interested in other things	88%	88%	88%	88%
Got tired of it - it was boring	58%	73%	58%	49%
More interested in boys	39%	20%	40%	47%
Too hard to get to activity	31%	38%	28%	30%
Sport no longer offered	30%	29%	32%	29%
Didn't have enough money	26%	42%	22%	20%
Didn't have enough time	59%	62%	58%	58%
Got a job	19%	4%	11%	33%

[Continued]

★ 781 ★

Quitting Sports: Reasons
[Continued]

Reason	Total Daughters	Age 7-10	Age 11-14	Age 15-18
Felt I wasn't good enough at sport	49%	47%	47%	51%
Got hurt/didn't want to get hurt	39%	49%	44%	29%
Too old for sports/that sport	20%	295	24%	12%
Didn't want boys to see me play sports	16%	18%	14%	16%
Sports aren't good for girls	12%	22%	10%	8%
Sports aren't ladylike/feminine	10%	16%	11%	6%
Friends don't play	33%	36%	39%	28%
Friends, family, others discouraged me	15%	20%	18%	10%

Source: The Wilson Report: Moms, Dads, Daughters and Sports, 1988. Results of interviews conducted by telephone in 1987 with a random sample of 1,004 mothers and fathers, and 513 of their 7-to 18-year-old daughters.

★ 782 ★

Tenpin Bowling

Total and female participants in tenpin bowling, and membership in Women's Bowling Congress, 1970 to 1988.

	1970	1975	1980	1983	1984	1985	1986	1987	1988
Total participants, in millions	51.8	62.5	72.0	NA	67.0	67.0	67.0	68.0	68.0
Female	27.0	32.6	38.0	NA	35.0	35.0	35.0	34.9	34.9
Membership, Women's Bowling Congress, in thousands	2,988	3,692	4,118	3,947	3,866	3,714	3,551	3,351	3,189

Source: Selected from "Selected Recreational Activities: 1970 to 1988," *Statistical Abstract of the United States 1990,* 1990, p. 230. Primary source: National Bowling Council, Washington, DC. Data regarding numerous other recreational activities, not by gender. For season ending in year shown. Persons 5 years old and over.

★ 783 ★

Youth Physical Fitness

Physical fitness performance (averages) of school-age population, by sex, age, and fitness test, 1958, 1965, 1975, and 1985.

Sex, age, and fitness test	1958	1965	1975	1985
Girls				
10-year-olds				
50-yard dash (seconds)	9.2	8.5	8.7	8.9
Standing long jump (inches)	50.7	55.6	56.0	54.2
Shuttle run (seconds)	12.9	11.9	11.9	12.2
Flexed arm-hangs (seconds)	-	-	12.7	12.5
17-year-olds				

[Continued]

★ 783 ★

Youth Physical Fitness
[Continued]

Sex, age, and fitness test	1958	1965	1975	1985
50-yard dash (seconds)	9.0	8.4	7.9	8.2
Standing long jump (inches)	60.4	64.7	65.4	64.4
Shuttle run (seconds)	11.8	11.4	11.4	11.1
Flexed arm-hangs (seconds)	-	-	11.6	12.0
Boys				
10-year-olds				
50-yard dash (seconds)	8.9	8.3	8.4	8.6
Standing long jump (inches)	53.7	60.3	59.1	59.2
Shuttle run (seconds)	12.1	11.3	11.4	11.7
Pull ups (seconds)	1.5	2.9	2.3	2.8
17-year-olds				
50-yard dash (seconds)	6.8	6.7	6.7	6.7
Standing long jump (inches)	82.5	86.5	84.9	87.1
Shuttle run (seconds)	10.4	10.0	9.9	9.6
Pull-ups (seconds)	6.3	8.1	7.2	8.3

Source: "Physical fitness performance of school-age population, by sex, age, and fitness test: 1958, 1965, 1975, and 1985," *Youth Indicators 1988: Trends in the Well-Being of American Youth,* Volume 1, August 1988, p. 92. Primary source: U.S. Department of Health and Human Services, Office of the Assistant Secretary for Health, *The President's Council on Physical Fitness and Sports 1985, National School Population Fitness Survey,* and unpublished data.

Girl Scouts

★ 784 ★

Girl Scout Membership

The state of Girl Scout membership, as of September 30, 1989, according to the Girl Scouts' *Annual Report*.

Girl Scout membership reached **3,165,802**, an increase of **3.7%** over 1988, and the largest total membership in 15 years.

Girl membership reached **2,415,099**, the highest in 10 years. **One in 9 girls ages 5-17, 1 in four girls ages 6-8, and 1 in 6 girls ages 9-11** in the U.S. is a member of the Girl Scout movement.

Racial/ethnic minority membership increased **5.3%**, reaching a total of **430,228**, or **13.7%** of girl and adult members.

Adult membership reached **750,703**, an increase of **6.2%** over the previous year, and the highest adult membership in over 25 years. Volunteers make up more than **99%** of total adult membership.

Source: Girl Scouts of the U.S.A. 1989 Annual Report, p. 15.

★ 785 ★

Girl Scout Membership: 1970-1985

Girl Scout membership, 1970 to 1985.

Year	Females 6 to 17 years of age, in thousands	Girl Scout membership, in thousands	Percent of female population participating
1970	23,958	3,248	13.6%
1975	23,285	2,723	11.7%
1978	22,467	2,511	11.2%
1979	22,007	2,389	10.9%
1980	21,543	2,250	10.4%
1981	21,125	2,276	10.8%
1982	20,703	2,247	10.9%
1983	20,423	2,281	11.2%
1984	20,242	2,247	11.1%
1985	20,216	2,111	10.4%

Source: Selected from "Boy Scout and Girl Scout Membership: 1950 to 1985," *Youth Indicators 1988: Trends in the Well-Being of American Youth*, 1988, p. 106. Primary source: Girl Scouts of the United States of America, *Annual Report*. U.S. Dept. of Commerce, Bureau of the Census, *Current Population Reports*, Series P-25, no. 519, 917, and 985. Also in source: data for 1950 to 1965; Boy Scout membership.

★ 786 ★

Girl Scout Membership: 1970-1988

Girl Scout membership as of September 30, in thousands, 1970-1988.

Item	1970	1975	1980	1981	1982	1983	1984	1985	1986	1987	1988
					Numbers in thousands						
Membership	3,922	3,234	2,784	2,829	2,819	2,888	2,871	2,802	2,917	2,947	3,052
Girls[1]	3,248	2,723	2,250	2,276	2,247	2,281	2,247	2,172	2,248	2,274	2,345
Daisies (5 yr. old)	-	-	-	-	-	-	-	61	114	137	162
Brownies (6-8 yr. old)	1,259	1,160	1,115	1,110	1,120	1,163	1,172	1,128	1,166	1,167	1,243
Juniors (9-11 yr. old)	1,509	1,188	894	916	874	847	801	735	725	705	739
Cadettes (12-14 yr. old)	395	301	172	170	169	176	170	151	143	132	144
Seniors (14-17 yr. old)	85	74	46	45	41	40	40	40	41	38	43
Adults	674	511	534	553	572	607	624	630	669	673	707
Total units (troops, groups)	164	159	154	157	160	165	166	166	174	180	189

Source: Selected from Boy Scouts and Girl Scouts-Membership and Units: 1960 to 1988," *Statistical Abstract of the United States 1990*, p. 235, 1990. Primary Source: Girl Scouts of the United States of America, New York, NY, *Annual Report*. Also in source: Boy Scout membership; data for 1960. *Notes:* 1. Beginning 1980, includes girls registered in other categories, not shown separately.

High School

★ 787 ★

College Attendance Rate for Former High School Athletes

Percent of former athletes and nonathletes who attended a four-year college in 1984 by race, gender, and high school location.

Race, gender, and high school location	Number	Former Athletes	Former Nonathletes
Rural Hispanic Females	172	42%	9%
Rural Hispanic Males	192	18%	4%
Urban Hispanic Males	155	31%	15%
Rural White Females	1,258	44%	23%
Suburban White Females	1,977	53%	26%
Rural White Males	1,193	42%	18%
Suburban White Males	1,747	49%	25%
Urban White Males	442	44%	21%

Source: The Women's Sports Foundation Report: Minorities in Sports, August 15, 1989, p. 28. Based on the U.S. Department of Education's *High School and Beyond* study, a data base generated by the National Center for Education Statistics, Washington, D.C. The term athlete refers to those individuals who reported participating on athletic teams both in their sophomore year (1980) and in their senior year (1982).

★ 788 ★

Degree Goals of High School Athletes

Percent of former athletes and nonathletes aiming at a bachelor's degree, 1986, by race, gender, and high school location.

Race, gender, and high school location	Number	Former Athletes	Former Nonathletes
Rural Hispanic Females	166	31%	7%
Urban Hispanic Females	125	35%	10%
Urban Hispanic Males	140	21%	10%
Urban Black Males	151	26%	7%
Suburban White Females	1,889	27%	15%
Rural White Males	1,139	45%	18%
Suburban White Males	1,679	51%	27%

Source: The Women's Sports Foundation Report: Minorities in Sports, August 15, 1989, p. 29. Based on the U.S. Department of Education's *High School and Beyond* study, a data base generated by the National Center for Education Statistics, Washington, D.C. The term athlete refers to those individuals who reported participating on athletic teams both in their sophomore year (1980) and in their senior year (1982).

★ 789 ★

Educational Progress of High School Athletes

Percent of former athletes and nonathletes having made educational progress toward a bachelor's degree by 1986 by race, gender, and high school location.

Race, gender, and high school location	Number	Former Athletes	Former Nonathletes
Rural Hispanic Females	174	49%	9%
Suburban Hispanic Females	200	28%	13%
Rural White Females	1,251	48%	24%
Suburban White Females	1,967	55%	31%
Urban White Males	466	39%	23%

Source: The Women's Sports Foundation Report: Minorities in Sports, August 15, 1989, p. 30. Based on the U.S. Department of Education's *High School and Beyond* study, a data base generated by the National Center for Education Statistics, Washington, D.C. The term athlete refers to those individuals who reported participating on athletic teams both in their sophomore year (1980) and in their senior year (1982).

★ 790 ★

High School Athletes by Race/Ethnicity

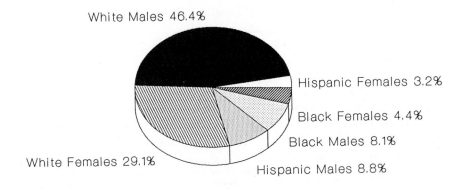

White Males 46.4%

Hispanic Females 3.2%

Black Females 4.4%

Black Males 8.1%

Hispanic Males 8.8%

White Females 29.1%

Composition of high school athletes by race and gender.

Race and gender	Percent
White Males	46.4%
White Females	29.1%
Hispanic Males	8.8%
Black Males	8.1%
Black Females	4.4%
Hispanic Females	3.2%

Source: The Women's Sports Foundation Report: Minorities in Sports, August 15, 1989, p. 23. Based on the U.S. Department of Education's *High School and Beyond* study, a data base generated by the National Center for Education Statistics, Washington, D.C. The term athlete refers to those individuals who reported participating on athletic teams both in their sophomore year (1980) and in their senior year (1982).

★ 791 ★

High School Seniors' Extracurricular Activities

Participation of high school seniors in extracuricular activities, 1972 and 1982.

Student characteristics	Percent of seniors participating in activities								
	Athletics	Debating, drama,band, chorus[2]	Subject-matter club	Vocational education clubs	Newspaper, magazine, yearbook clubs	Student council, government, politics	Hobby clubs	Cheerlead, pep clubs, majorettes	Honorary clubs
All 1972 seniors	44.5%	32.9%	25.8%	23.0%	20.4%	19.6%	18.7%	17.3%	14.8%
Sex									
Female	32.1%	39.8%	31.2%	29.8%	26.7%	21.0%	13.3%	29.6%	19.4%
Male	58.2%	26.9%	20.4%	16.0%	14.7%	18.6%	23.7%	5.3%	11.1%
All 1982 seniors	51.5%	34.6%	20.6%	23.6%	18.3%	16.3%	20.0%	13.7%	15.6%
Sex									

[Continued]

★ 791 ★

High School Seniors' Extracurricular Activities
[Continued]

Student characteristics	Percent of seniors participating in activities								
	Athletics	Debating, drama,band, chorus[2]	Subject-matter club	Vocational education clubs	Newspaper, magazine, yearbook clubs	Student council, government, politics	Hobby clubs	Cheerlead, pep clubs, majorettes	Honorary clubs
Female	41.8%	42.9%	24.6%	26.7%	23.1%	19.3%	16.7%	22.8%	18.8%
Male	61.7%	25.8%	16.4%	20.2%	13.3%	13.1%	23.5%	4.1%	12.1%

Source: Selected from "Participation of high school seniors in extracurricular activities, by selected student characteristics: 1972 and 1982," *Digest of Education Statistics,* p. 132 (Washington, D.C.: National Center for Education Statistics, 1989). Primary source: U.S. Department of Education, National Center for Education Statistics, "National longitudinal Study of 1972" and High School and Beyond surveys. (This table was prepared August 1987.) Also in source: other student characteristics. *Notes:* 1. In 1972, includes participation i team athletics, intramurals, letterman's clubs, and sports clubs. In 1982, includes varsity athletic teams and other athletic teams - in or out of school. 2. In 1972, includes debating, drama, band, and chorus. In 1982, includes debating, drama, band, orchestra, chorus, and dance.

★ 792 ★

Influence of Significant Others on Sports Participation
Summary of a study on parental and peer influence on adolescent athletes.

The study was designed to examine the influence of significant others on continuing involvement in sport by adolescent females. It was determined that "the degree to which involvement in sports is maintained is positively related to the source, amount, and type of influence received from significant others, and varied by the participation context. Overall, the socializing influence accounted for **11%** of the variance in intramural activity, **20%** of the variance in interschool sport, and **10%** of the variance in community-based activity.

Source: Barbara A. Brown, B. Gail Frankel, and Marilyn P. Fennell, "Hugs or Shrugs: Parental and Peer Influence on Continuity of Involvement in Sport by Female Adolescents," *Sex Roles* 20:7/8, April 1989, p. 397-412. Based on questionnaires administered to 376 female high school students in a mid-sized Canadian city.

★ 793 ★

Sport Participation and Community Leadership
Percent of former athletes and nonathletes who aspire to be community leaders by race and gender.

Race and gender	Total	Athletes	Nonathletes
Hispanic Females[1]	499	38%	44%
Hispanic Males	565	58%	49%
Black Females[1]	572	42%	51%
Black Males	423	72%	56%
White Females	3,656	48%	29%
White Males	3,290	60%	39%

Source: The Women's Sports Foundation Report: Minorities in Sports, August 15, 1989, p. 32. Based on the U.S. Department of Education's *High School and Beyond* study, a data base generated by the National Center for Education Statistics, Washington, D.C. The term athlete refers to those individuals who reported participating on athletic teams both in their sophomore year (1980) and in their senior year (1982). *Notes:* 1. Regression analysis shows the differences are not directly owed to athletic participation; the findings are not statistically significant.

★ 794 ★

Sports and Achievement Test Performance

Percent of athletes and nonathletes scoring in the top quartile range of achievement tests measuring mathematics, reading, and vocabulary, by race and gender.

Race and gender	Total	Athletes	Nonathletes
Hispanic Females	116	39%	23%
Hispanic Males	126	27%	25%
Black Females	132	26%	24%
Black Males	108	28%	23%
White Females	785	32%	21%
White Males	713	29%	20%

Source: The Women's Sports Foundation Report: Minorities in Sports, August 15, 1989, p. 25. Based on the U.S. Department of Education's *High School and Beyond* study, a data base generated by the National Center for Education Statistics, Washington, D.C. The term athlete refers to those individuals who reported participating on athletic teams both in their sophomore year (1980) and in their senior year (1982).

★ 795 ★

Sports and Achievement Test Scores of Minorities

Percent of minority athletes and nonathletes scoring in the top quartile range on achievement tests.

Sex/ethnicity	Total	Athletes	Nonathletes
Rural Hispanic Females	116	43%	14%
Urban Black Males	108	28%	22%

Source: The Women's Sports Foundation Report: Minorities in Sports, August 15, 1989, p. 26. Based on the U.S. Department of Education's *High School and Beyond* study, a data base generated by the National Center for Education Statistics, Washington, D.C. The term athlete refers to those individuals who reported participating on athletic teams both in their sophomore year (1980) and in their senior year (1982).

★ 796 ★

Sports and Grades by Race

Percent of high school athletes and nonathletes reporting high grades, by race and gender.

Race and gender	Total	Athletes	Nonathletes
Hispanic Females	594	20%	9%
Hispanic Males	675	22%	20%
Black Females	676	12%	10%
Black Males	532	20%	16%
White Females	4,266	10%	6%
White Males	3,939	20%	11%

Source: The Women's Sports Foundation Report: Minorities in Sports, August 15, 1989, p. 24. Based on the U.S. Department of Education's *High School and Beyond* study, a data base generated by the National Center for Education Statistics, Washington, D.C. The term athlete refers to those individuals who reported participating on athletic teams both in their sophomore year (1980) and in their senior year (1982).

★ 797 ★

Sports and High School Grades of Minorities

Percent of athletes and nonathletes reporting high grades.

Sex	Athletes	Nonathletes
Rural Hispanic Females	26%	10%
Suburban Black Males	22%	11%

Source: The Women's Sports Foundation Report: Minorities in Sports, August 15, 1989, p. 25. Based on the U.S. Department of Education's *High School and Beyond* study, a data base generated by the National Center for Education Statistics, Washington, D.C. The term athlete refers to those individuals who reported participating on athletic teams both in their sophomore year (1980) and in their senior year (1982).

★ 798 ★

Sports and School Dropouts

Percent of athletes and nonathletes dropping out of school by senior year by race, gender, and high school location.

Race, gender, and high school location	Number	Athletes	Nonathletes
Rural Hispanic Females	221	5%	15%
Suburban Hispanic Males	330	8%	22%
Rural Black Males	148	8%	37%
Rural White Females	1,600	8%	13%
Suburban White Females	2,493	5%	10%
Rural White Males	1,546	6%	16%
Suburban White Males	2,333	6%	14%

Source: The Women's Sports Foundation Report: Minorities in Sports, August 15, 1989, p. 27. Based on the U.S. Department of Education's *High School and Beyond* study, a data base generated by the National Center for Education Statistics, Washington, D.C. The term athlete refers to those individuals who reported participating on athletic teams both in their sophomore year (1980) and in their senior year (1982).

Leisure

★ 799 ★

Book Readership

Percent of persons who read and didn't read books, 1983.

Characteristic	Book reader	Non-book reader	Non-reader
All persons	50%	44%	6%
Female	57%	37%	6%
Male	42%	52%	6%

Source: Selected from "Selected Characteristics of Readers-Percent Distribution: 1983," *Statistical Abstract of the United States 1990*, 1990, p. 228. Primary source: Book Industry Study Group, Inc., New York, NY, *1983 Consumer Research Study on Reading and Book Purchasing*. Also in source: data by race, age, educational attainment, household income, and region. Covers persons 16 years old and over. Book reader is one who read one or more books in the six months prior to the survey; a nonbook reader read newspapers or magazines but no books in the previous six months; and a nonreader did not read a book, newspaper, or magazine. Based on a sample survey of 1,429 respondents.

★ 800 ★

Favorite Television Programs

Percent of television households and percent persons in television households watching 10 favorite network and syndicated programs.

Program	TV households	Women	Men
Network Programs			
Bill Cosby Show	23.2%	17.1%	11.8%
Cheers	23.1%	17.1%	13.8%
Roseanne	22.1%	16.9%	11.9%
A Different World	21.6%	15.9%	10.6%
America's Funniest Home Videos	20.8%	15.9%	14.7%
Golden Girls	20.7%	17.9%	10.7%
Wonder Years	19.7%	13.9%	-
Empty Nest	19.6%	16.8%	-
60 Minutes	18.9%	14.7%	13.5%
Unsolved Mysteries	18.2%	14.5%	11.7%
L.A. Law	18.2%	14.0%	11.6%
Syndicated Programs			
Wheel of Fortune	15.9%	13.4%	9.3%
Jeopardy	14.2%	11.6%	7.9%
Oprah Winfrey Show	11.0%	9.2%	3.3%
Star Trek Next Generation	10.5%	6.4%	8.6%
Cosby Show	10.2%	7.3%	5.1%
PM Magazine	9.5%	7.3%	5.6%
Current Affair	9.5%	7.2%	5.8%

[Continued]

★ 800 ★

Favorite Television Programs
[Continued]

Program	TV house-holds	Women	Men
Entertainment Tonight	9.4%	7.3%	5.3%
Inside Edition	7.5%	5.6%	4.3%
Cheers	7.3%	4.9%	5.0%

Source: Selected from "America's Favorite Television Programs: 1989," and "Favorite Syndicated Programs," *World Almanac and Book of Facts 1991,* p. 317 (New York: Pharos Books, 1991). Primary source: Nielsen Media Research. Also in source: data for teens, and children. Regularly scheduled network programs as of February 1990.

★ 801 ★

High School Seniors' Leisure Activities
Daily leisure activities of female high school seniors, by type of activity, 1976 to 1985.

Activity	Percent participating in activity each day						
	1976	1980	1981	1982	1983	1984	1985
Watch television	71	72	72	73	75	73	72
Females	71	73	69	72	73	69	69
Males	71	72	75	76	77	76	74
Read books, magazines, or newspapers	59	59	59	56	55	53	51
Females	62	59	60	57	55	54	52
Males	58	59	58	56	55	52	50
Get together with friends	52	51	49	48	47	48	47
Females	48	47	44	43	44	43	43
Males	55	55	54	52	50	51	52
Participate in sports and exercise	44	47	48	46	46	44	43
Females	36	38	39	37	36	33	34
Males	52	57	56	56	56	54	53
Spend at least one hour of leisure time alone	40	42	44	44	44	44	42
Females	41	44	45	46	44	45	45
Males	39	40	42	42	44	42	40
Work around house, yard, or car	41	40	40	42	42	41	35
Females	49	49	48	51	50	47	42
Males	33	30	32	34	34	35	28
Ride around in a car for fun	-	33	32	33	34	34	35
Females	-	28	27	29	30	27	31
Males	-	38	36	37	38	40	39
Play a musical instrument or sing	28	29	31	28	28	30	29
Females	35	34	34	32	33	37	35
Males	22	25	27	24	24	24	24

[Continued]

★ 801 ★

High School Seniors' Leisure Activities
[Continued]

Activity	Percent participating in activity each day						
	1976	1980	1981	1982	1983	1984	1985
Do art or craft work	12	13	14	12	12	12	11
Females	13	14	15	12	10	10	10
Males	10	12	13	13	13	14	12
Do creative writing	6	5	6	5	5	6	6
Females	6	6	7	6	6	6	7
Males	4	4	4	5	3	6	4

Source: "Daily leisure activities of high school seniors, by type of activity and sex of student: 1976 to 1985," *Youth Indicators 1988: Trends in the Well-Being of American Youth*, Volume 1, August 1988, p. 108. Primary source: U.S. House of Representatives, Select Committee on Children, Youth, and Families, *U.S. Children and Their Families: Current Conditions and Recent Trends, 1987.* University of Michigan, Institute for Social Research, *Monitoring the Future*, various years.

★ 802 ★

Hobbies of Retired Persons
Comparison of the hobby types chosen by retired women and men in the People's Republic of China.

Sex	Reading	Physical Exercise	Productive Hobbies	Visual-Auditory Hobbies	Recreational
Retired Women	25.7%	20.5%	13.7%	24.5%	15.4%
Retired Men	33.3%	16.1%	6.0%	12.6%	31.8%

Source: Jun-Chen Hu, Ph.D., "Hobbies of Retired Poeple in the People's Republic of China: A Preliminary Study," *International Journal of Aging and Human Development* 31(1)31-44, 1990. Based on a study of over 500 retired individuals in the People's Republic of China.

★ 803 ★

Newspaper Readership
Daily and Sunday newspaper readership, in thousands, 1990.

	All Adults	Females	Males
Total	180,974	94,667	86,307
Daily newspapers: read any	104,220	53,600	50,621
Read one daily	82,253	44,183	38,070
Read two or more dailies	21,968	9,417	12,551
Sunday newspapers: read any	117,846	61,402	56,444
Read one Sunday	104,283	54,668	49,615
Read two or more Sundays	13,563	6,734	6,830

Source: Selected from *Mediamark Research Multimedia Audiences Report, Spring 1990*, p. 2 (New York: Mediamark Research Inc., 1990).

★ 804 ★

Participation Rates, Arts Performances and Leisure Activities

Attendance rates for various arts performances and leisure activities, 1985.

Characteristic	Attended at least once						Visited at least once- art museum or gallery	Read-novel, short stor- ies, poetry, or plays
	Jazz per- formance	Classical music per- formance	Opera per- formance	Musical plays	Plays	Ballet per- formance		
Average	10%	13%	3%	17%	12%	4%	22%	56%
Female	9%	14%	3%	19%	12%	5%	23%	63%
Male	10%	11%	2%	15%	11%	3%	21%	48%

Source: "Participation Rates for Various Arts Performances and Leisure Activities by Selected Characteristics: 1985," *Statistical Abstract of the United States 1990,* 1990, p. 235. Primary source: U.S. National Endowment for the Arts, *1985 Survey of Public Participation in the Arts.* Also in source: Other characteristics of attendees. Represents percent of population 18 years old and over who participated at least once in the 12 months prior to the survey. Based on a survey conducted by the Bureau of the Census for the National Endowment for the Arts.

★ 805 ★

Radio Format Preferences

Number of persons, in thousands, who listen to a station with a specified format any time during an average week.

Radio Format	All Adults	Women	Men
Adult Contemporary	31,401	16,774	14,657
All News	9,408	4,069	5,339
Album-Oriented Radio/Progressive Rock	19,401	7,737	11,664
Black	1,569	855	714
CHR/Rock	26,445	14,053	12,392
Classic Rock	6,780	2,447	4,333
Classical	3,573	2,025	1,548
Country	28,743	14,219	14,524
Easy Listening	9,602	5,589	4,013
Golden Oldies	11,240	5,182	6,058
Jazz	2,246	1,007	1,239
MOR/Nostalgia	6,208	2,936	3,271
News/Talk	16,348	6,929	9,419
Religious/Gospel	5,425	3,380	2,045
Soft Contemporary	5,141	2,793	2,348
Urban Contemporary	9,995	5,247	4,748

Source: Selected from *Mediamark Research Multimedia Audiences Report, Spring 1990,* p. 3 (New York: Mediamark Research Inc., 1990). Reprinted by permission.

★ 806 ★

Television Viewing Time

Hours and minutes per week spent watching television, by age.

Age	Hours and minutes of viewing time				
	Mon-Fri 10am-4:30pm	Mon-Fri 4:30pm-7:30pm	Mon-Sun 8-11 pm	Sat 7am-1pm	Mon-Fri 11:30pm-1am
Total women age 18+	5:55	4:44	9:49	:38	1:18
18-24	4:55	3:18	6:43	:32	:57
25-54	5:06	3:52	9:18	:39	1:20
55+	7:52	6:55	12:06	:38	1:22
Female Teens 12-17	2:40	3:30	6:27	:46	:36
Total men age 18+	3:31	3:46	9:05	:40	1:20
18-24	2:56	2:35	5:55	:33	1:14
25-54	2:56	3:05	8:46	:41	1:20
55+	5:37	6:07	11:46	:41	1:23
Male Teens 12-17	2:20	3:35	7:16	:55	:49

Source: "Average Television Viewing Time," *World Almanac and Book of Facts 1991,* p. 317 (New York: Pharos Books, 1991). Primary source: Nielsen Media Research. Also in source: data for men and children. As of February 1990.

Olympic Games

★ 807 ★

Summer Olympics

Number of competitors in the Summer Olympics, 1968-1988.

Olympic Year/Place	Competitors	
	Women	Men
1968/Mexico City, Mexico	781	4,750
1972/Munich, Germany	1,299	5,848
1976/Montreal, Canada	1,251	4,834
1980/Moscow, USSR	1,088	4,265
1984/Los Angeles, U.S.	1,620	5,458
1988/Seoul, South Korea	9,593 (total)	

Source: The Universal Almanac 1990, p. 585 (Kansas City: Andrews and McMeel, 1990). Primary Source: David Wallechinsky, *The Complete Book of the Olympics* (1988); U.S. Olympic Committee. Also in source: data for other years.

★ 808 ★

Winter Olympics

Number of competitors in the Winter Olympics, 1968-1988.

Olympics Year/Place	Competitors	
	Women	Men
1968/Grenoble, France	212	1,081
1972/Sapporo, Japan	217	1,015
1976/Innsbruck, Austria	228	900
1980/Lake Placid, U.S.	234	833
1984/Sarajevo, Yugoslavia	276	1,002
1988/Calgary, Canada	1,445 (total)	

Source: The Universal Almanac 1990, p. 583 (Kansas City: Andrews and McMeel, 1990). Primary Source: David Wallechinsky, *The Complete Book of the Olympics* (1988); U.S. Olympic Committee. Also in source: data for other years.

Parental Influence/Attitudes

★ 809 ★

Benefits of Sports Participation

What white and black parents perceive to be the benefits of girls participating in sports.

Benefit	White Parents	Black Parents
Physical/health factors	58%	37%
Character benefits	42%	31%
Social factors	29%	17%
Career/travel opportunities	7%	18%

Source: The Wilson Report: Moms, Dads, Daughters and Sports, 1988. Results of interviews conducted by telephone in 1987 with a random sample of 1,004 mothers and fathers, and 513 of their 7-to 18-year-old daughters.

★ 810 ★

Parents' Perceptions of Sports' Importance

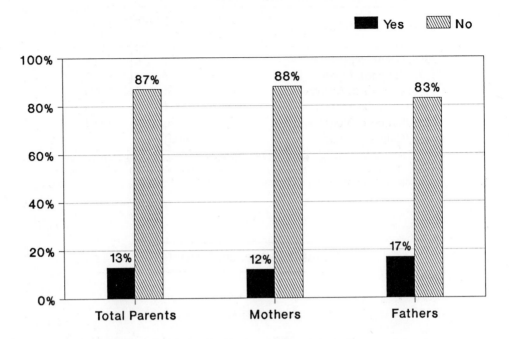

Parents' responses to the question: "Are sports more important for boys than girls?" by race.

Parents	Yes	No
Total white parents	13%	87%
Mothers	12%	88%
Fathers	17%	83%
Total black parents	30%	70%

Source: The Wilson Report: Moms, Dads, Daughters and Sports, 1988. Results of interviews conducted by telephone in 1987 with a random sample of 1,004 mothers and fathers, and 513 of their 7-to 18-year-old daughters.

★ 811 ★

Reasons Sports Are Important

Reasons parents believe sports are equally important for boys and girls.

Reason	% of parents who agree
Sexes are equal/should have equal opportunity	60%
Both sexes need the exercise	16%
Both sexes enjoy/have fun with sports	4%
Both sexes need the social interaction/competition	4%
Both sexes need the mental development	3%

Source: The Wilson Report: Moms, Dads, Daughters and Sports, 1988. Results of interviews conducted by telephone in 1987 with a random sample of 1,004 mothers and fathers, and 513 of their 7-to 18-year-old daughters.

Popularity

★ 812 ★

Girls' Attitudes Toward Sports and Popularity

Attitudes toward sports and popularity by age.

Attitude	Total Daughters	Age 7-10	Age 11-14	Age 15-18
Girls who play sports are...				
not at all popular	19%	35%	15%	4%
a little popular	40%	39%	41%	41%
real popular	42%	27%	45%	55%
Do boys make fun of girls who play sports?				
no	64%	50%	66%	78%
sometimes/depends	24%	28%	24%	18%
yes	12%	22%	10%	3%
Do girls like boys who play sports?				
no	7%	15%	5%	1%
sometimes/depends	19%	32%	18%	6%
yes	73%	54%	77%	92%
Do boys like girls who play sports?				
no	16%	23%	17%	7%
sometimes/depends	30%	30%	31%	28%
yes	54%	47%	51%	65%

Source: The Wilson Report: Moms, Dads, Daughters and Sports, 1988. Results of interviews conducted by telephone in 1987 with a random sample of 1,004 mothers and fathers, and 513 of their 7-to 18-year-old daughters.

★ 813 ★

Girls' Attitudes Toward Sports and Popularity by Race

Attitudes toward sports and popularity by race.

Attitude	White Girls	Black Girls
Girls who play sports are...		
not at all popular	17%	23%
a little popular	41%	45%
real popular	42%	32%
Do boys make fun of girls who play sports?		
yes	11%	25%
sometimes/depends	23%	25%
no	66%	50%

Source: The Wilson Report: Moms, Dads, Daughters and Sports, 1988. Results of interviews conducted by telephone in 1987 with a random sample of 1,004 mothers and fathers, and 513 of their 7-to 18-year-old daughters.

★ 814 ★

Sports and Popularity by Race

Percent of high school athletes and nonathletes reporting high popularity by race and gender (N=9,181).

Race and gender	Number	Athletes	Nonathletes
Hispanic Females	505	93%	71%
Hispanic Males	526	86%	67%
Black Females	532	91%	68%
Black Males	345	94%	71%
White Females	3,856	87%	73%
White Males	3,417	92%	70%

Source: The Women's Sports Foundation Report: Minorities in Sports, August 15, 1989, p. 23. Based on the U.S. Department of Education's *High School and Beyond* study, a data base generated by the National Center for Education Statistics, Washington, D.C. The term athlete refers to those individuals who reported participating on athletic teams both in their sophomore year (1980) and in their senior year (1982).

LIST OF SOURCES CONSULTED

Acosta, R. Vivian, and Carpenter, Linda Jean, "Perceived Causes of the Declining Representation of Women Leaders in Intercollegiate Sports," 1988 Update, "Women in Intercollegiate Sport: A Longitudinal Study - Thirteen Year Update 1977-1990," Department of Physical Education, Brooklyn College, Brooklyn, NY 11210. (718)780-5879 or (718)780-5514 (message).

Advisory Commission on Intergovernmental Relations (ACIR), *Changing Public Attitudes on Governments and Taxes 1988*. Annual. ACIR Rpt. S-17. Seventeenth annual report presenting results of public opinion surveys on taxes, spending, and other government issues. Advisory Commission on Intergovernmental Relations, Washington, DC 20575.

AIChE 1990 Salary Survey Report. 1990. American Institute of Chemical Engineers, 345 East 47th Street, New York, NY 10017. (212)705-7524.

Alsalam, Nabeel, ed., *The Condition of Education 1990: Volume 2: Postsecondary Education*. 1990. NCES-90-684. National Center for Education Statistics, Washington, DC 20208-5650. For sale by the Superintendent of Documents, U.S. Government Printing Office, Washington, D.C. 20402. (202)783-3238.

American Demographics. Monthly magazine focusing on consumer trends and demographics. P.O. Box 68, Ithaca, NY 14851-0068. (607)273-6343.

American College of Obstetricians and Gynecologists, *Vaginal Birth After Cesarean Section: Report of a 1990 Survey of ACOG's Membership*. August 1990. American College of Obstetricians and Gynecologists, 409 12th Street, S.W., Washington, DC 20024-2188. (202)638-5577.

American College Testing Program, *ACT High School Profile Report: H S Graduating Class 1990*. Iowa City, IA.

American Institute of Physics, "AIP Report." AIP Pub. No. R-207-22. September 1990. Education & Employment Statistics Division, 335 East 45th Street, New York, NY 10017-3483. (212)661-9404.

American Jewish Committee and Jewish Publication Society. *American Jewish Year Book*. 1987. Special supplement, volume 87. ISBN 0-8276-0290-1. c/o Inst. of Human Relations, 165 E. 56th Street, New York, NY 10022.

American Library Association, *Academic and Public Librarians: Data by Race, Ethnicity and Sex*. 1986. ISBN 8389-7061-3. Study conducted to obtain current national statistics on the library profession to be used in affirmative action planning. American Library Association, Office for Library Personnel Resources, 50 East Huron St., Chicago, IL 60611.

Amnesty International Publications, *Women in the Front Line: Human Rights Violations Against Women*. March 1991. ISBN 0-939994-64-X. Amnesty International Publications, 322 Eighth Avenue, New York, NY 10001. (212)807-8400.

Ando, Faith, and Associates, *Minorities, Women, Veterans and the 1982 Characteristics of Business Owners Survey, A Preliminary Analysis*. September 1988. Haverford, Pennsylvania, and U.S. Small Business Administration. For information contact Office of Women's Business Ownership in the U.S. Small Business Administration at (202)653-8000.

Automotive News. Weekly. Tabloid reporting on all facets of the automotive and truck industry. Crain Communications, Inc., 1400 Woodbridge Ave., Detroit, MI 48207. (313)446-6000.

Biden, Joseph R., Jr., Senator, *Fighting Crime in America: An Agenda for the 1990's*. A Majority Staff Report Prepared for the Use of the Committee on the Judiciary, United States Senate, One Hundred Second Congress, First Session, March 12, 1991. U.S. Senate Judiciary Committee, Dirksen Senate Office Building, Room 224, Washington, DC 20510.

Black Issues in Higher Education. Semimonthly. Focuses on education and factors related to the status of education. Individual issues frequently contain in-depth statistical reports. Cox, Matthews & Associates, Inc., 10520 Warwick Ave., Ste. B-8, Fairfax, VA 22030.

Bose, Christine E., *Jobs and Gender: A Study of Occupational Prestige.* 1985. ISBN 0-03-071692-6. Praeger Publishers, 521 Fifth Avenue, New York, NY 10175.

British Medical Journal. Quarterly and annual cumulative indexes. British Medical Association, Tavistock Square, London WC1H 9JP, England. Telephone 1 3874499.

Bulletin of the World Health Organization. Bimonthly. ISSN 0043-9686. Presents original research findings selected on the basis of their immediate or potential relevance to problems of human health. WHO, Distribution and Sales, 1211 Geneva 27, Switzerland.

Business Week. Published weekly, except for one issue in January. ISSN 0007-7135. McGraw-Hill Building, 1221 Avenue of the Americas, New York, NY 10020. (212)512-2000.

Camp, Sharon L., ed., *Country Rankings of the Status of Women: Poor, Powerless, and Pregnant.* 1988. One of a series of publications designed to inform policymakers, opinion leaders, and the general public on world population issues.Population Crisis Committee, Washington, D.C.

Canadian Journal of Psychiatry. 9X/Yr. ISSN 0008-4824. Journal reporting on clinical developments in the field of psychiatry. Canadian Psychiatric Assn., 294 Albert St., Ste. 204, Ottawa, ON, Canada K2G 4T1. (613)234-2815.

Center for the American Woman and Politics (CAWP), National Information Bank on Women in Public office, Eagleton Institute of Politics, Rutgers University, New Brunswick, NJ 08901. (908)828-2210. FAX (908)932-6778.

Chicago Tribune. Daily newspaper. 435 N. Michigan Ave., Chicago, IL 60611. (312)222-3232.

Children's Well-Being: An International Comparison. A Report of the Select Committee on Children, Youth, and Families. One Hundred First Congress, Second Session, together with Additional Minority Views. March 1990. For sale by the Superintendent of Documents, U.S. Government Printing Office, Washington, D.C. 20402. (202)783-3238.

Chronicle of Higher Education. 48X/Yr. ISSN 0009-5982. 1225 23rd St., NW, No. 700, Washington, DC 20037. (202)466-1000.

College Board, *College Bound Seniors: 1990 Profile of SAT and Achievement Test Takers.* National data describing those students from each high school graduating class that participate in the Admissions Testing Program; information is based on the latest test scores and background these graduating seniors have provided. College Entrance Examination Board, 45 Columbus Avenue, New York, NY 10023.

College Placement Council, Inc. (CPC). *Salary Survey: A Study of Beginning Offers.* Annual. CPC provides services to career planning and placement directors at two- and four-year colleges and universities in the U.S. and to employers who hire graduates of these institutions. Compiles statistics and publishes *Journal of Career Planning and Employment*, a quarterly college career planning, placement, and recruitment magazine. College Placement Council, Inc., 62 Highland Avenue, Bethlehem, PA 18017. (215)868-1421.

Committee on the Judiciary, *Hearing before the Committee on the Judiciary, United States Senate, One Hundred First Congress, Second Session, On Legislation to Reduce the Growing Problem of Violent Crime Against Women*, June 20, 1990, Part 1, Serial No. J-101-80. For sale by the Superintendent of Documents, U.S. Government Printing Office, Washington, D.C. 20402. (202)783-3238.

Conetta, Carl, ed., *Peace Resource Book.* 1988. Ballinger Publishing, Cambridge, MA 02138.

Corporate Giving Watch. Monthly. ISSN 0747-8003. The Taft Group, 12300 Twinbrook Parkway, Suite 450, Rockville, MD 20852.

Counts, Dorothy, Ph.D., Brown, Judith K., Ph.D., Campbell, Jacquelyn C., Ph.D., R.N., F.A.A.N., eds., *Sanctions and Sanctuary: Cultural Perspectives on the Beating of Wives.* Bouldor, CO, Westview Press, forthcoming.

COYOTE/National Task Force on Prostitution. As part of its mission to inform the public about the reality of prostitution, publishes *Prostitutes Prevent AIDS: A Manual for Health Educators; Patterns of Prostitution in North America and Europe*; and *Role of Prostitutes in Prevention of HIV Transmission: Education + Empowerment = AIDS Prevention.* Contact CAL-PEP, 333 Valencia Street, Room 101, San Francisco, CA 94103. (415)558-0450.

CWI Newsletter. 9X/Yr. Forum for the exchange and dissemination of educational information and materials on issues related to discrimination on the basis of sex and marital status, with particular emphasis on public policies affecting the economic and educational status of women. Clearinghouse on Women's Issues, P.O. Box 70603, Friendship Heights, MD 20813. (301)871-6106 or (202)363-9795.

Deaux, Kay, and Ullman, Joseph C., *Women of Steel: Female Blue-Collar Workers in the Basic Steel Industry.* ISBN 0-03-062008-2. Praeger Publishers, 521 Fifth Avenue, New York, NY 10175.

Defense 90. Bimonthly. Department of Defense publication intended to provide official and professional information to commanders and key personnel on matters related to defense policies, programs, and interests. American Forces Information Service, 601 N. Fairfax St., Room 312, Alexandria, VA 22314-2007. (703)274-4849.

Developmental Psychology. Bimonthly journal focusing on topical research, cross-cultural studies, and socially important topics of interest to the field of developmental psychology. ISSN 0012-1649. American Psychological Assn., 1200 17th St., NW, Washington, DC 20036. (202)955-7600.

Dickinson, Eleanor, *Statistics: Gender Discrimination in the Art Field: Incomplete and Random Statistics of Number of Artists, Art Faculty, Art Criticism, Art Exhibitions, etc. Which May Be Useful in Indicating Patterns and Trends.* 1990. Copies may be obtained through sponsors of this study: Artists Equity Association National Office, P.O. Box 28068, Central Station, Washington, D.C. 20005. (202)628-9633. Women's Caucus for Art National Office, 20th and Parkway, Philadelphia, PA 19103. (215)854-0922. Coalition of Women's Art organizations, 123 East Beutel Road, Port Washington, WI 53074. (414)284-4458. California Lawyers for the Arts, Bldg. C, Fort Mason, San Francisco, CA 94123. (415)775-7200.

Downie, Susanna, ed., *Decade of Achievement: 1977-1987 — A Report of a Survey Based on the National Plan of Action for Women.* 1988. National Women's Conference Committee, Beaver Dam, WI 53916.

Equal Employment Opportunity Commission, *Job Patterns for Minorities and Women in Private Industry, 1989.* Annual report on employment of women and minorities in private industry, by occupational group. U.S. Equal Employment Opportunity Commission, 1801 L Street, N.W., Washington, D.C. 20507.

Family Circle. Every third week. Women's magazine. The Family Circle, Inc., 110 Fifth Ave., New York, NY 10011.

Family Planning Perspectives. Bimonthly. ISSN 0014-7354. Family planning magazine. Alan Guttmacher Institute, 111 Fifth Avenue, New York, NY 10003. (212)254-5656.

Federal Bureau of Investigation, *Uniform Crime Reports 1989: Crime in the United States.* Annual. Release date August 5, 1990. Presents data on crime trends, crime rate, public safety, employment data, and arrests. Preliminary crime data is available in a quarterly release, *Uniform Crime Reporting.* For sale by the Superintendent of Documents, U.S. Government Printing Office, Washington, D.C. 20402. (202)783-3238.

Fernandez, John P., *The Politics and Reality of Family Care in Corporate America.* 1990. ISBN 0-669-21562-7. Lexington Books, Lexington, MA.

Fortune. 27X/Yr. Business and industry magazine printed in regional and demographic editions. Time and Life Bldg., 1271 Avenue of the Americas, New York, NY 10020. (212)586-1212.

Gallup, George, Jr., and Castelli, Jim, *The People's Religion: American Faith in the 90's.* 1989. ISBN 0-02-542381-9. Macmillan Publishing Company, 866 Third Avenue, New York, NY 10022.

Gannon, Martin J., "Preferences of temporary workers: time, variety and flexibility." *Monthly Labor Review* 107(8):26-28, 1984.

Garfinkel, Irwin, and McLanahan, Sara S., *Single Mothers and Their Children: A New American Dilemma.* 1986. The Changing Domestic Priorities Series. The Urban Institute Press, Washington, DC

Gelb, Joyce, and Palley, Marian Lief, *Women and Public Policies.* 1982. Princeton University Press, Fine Hall, Washington Rd., Princeton, NJ 08544. (609)452-4191.

Gerald, Debra E., Horn, Paul J., and Hussar, William J., *Projection of Education Statistics to 2000: 1998, 1996, 1994, 1992, 1990.* December 1989. Nineteenth report in a series begun in 1964. NCES 89-648. National Center for Education Statistics, Washington, DC 20208-5650.

Gerontologist. Bimonthly. Magazine featuring science and the study of aging. Gerontological Society of America, 1411 K St., N.W., Suite 300, Washington, DC 20005. (202)393-1411.

Girl Scouts of the U.S.A. 1989 Annual Report. Girl Scouts of the U.S.A., 830 Third Avenue, New York, NY 10022.

Glamour. Monthly fashion magazine. ISSN 0017-0747. 350 Madison Avenue, New York, NY 10017. (212)880-8700. FAX (212)880-8336.

Gottfried, Frances, *The Merit System and Municipal Civil Service: A Fostering of Social Inequality.* 1988. Contributions in political science, ISSN 0147-1066; no. 201. Greenwood Press, Inc., 88 Post Road West, Westport, CT 06881.

Hartmann, Heidi I., Kraut, Robert E., and Tilly, Louise A., eds., *Computer Chips and Paper Clips: Technology and Women's Employment*, Volume 1. 1986. ISBN 0-309-03688-7. National Academy Press, 2101 Constitution Ave., NW, Washington, DC 20418.

Hess, Jennifer, et al., *A Decade of Change: The Status of U.S. Women Doctorates, 1977-88.* ACE Research Briefs, Vol. 1, No. 6, 1990. One of a collection of analytical papers exploring timely and pertinent issues in higher education. The series is published 8 times a year. Division of Policy Analysis and Research, American Council on Education, One Dupont Circle NW, Washington, DC 20036. (202)939-9450.

Hite, Shere, *The Hite Report: A Nationwide Study on Female Sexuality.* 1984 printing. Macmillan Publishing Co., Inc., 866 3rd Avenue, New York, NY 10022.

Hill, Ivan, ed., *The Bisexual Spouse: Different Dimensions in Human Sexuality.* ISBN 0-937525-01-4. Barlina Books, Inc., P.O. Box 7425, McLean, VA 22106.

Hoffman, Mark S., ed. *The World Almanac and Book of Facts.* 1991. Annual (November). ISBN 0-88687-578-1 (softcover). ISBN 0-88687-580-3 (hardcover). Pharos Books, 200 Park Avenue, New York, NY 10166.

Howard, Christian, *The Ordination of Women to the Priesthood: Further Report: A Background Paper.* 1984. ISBN 0 7151 3699 2. A report to the General Synod of the Church of England. CIO Publishing, Church House, Dean's Yard, London SWlP 3NZ.

Hunt, H. Allan, and Hunt, Timothy L., *Clerical Employment and Technological Change: A Review of Recent Trends and Projections.* Paper prepared for the Panel on Technology and Women's Employment, Committee on Women's Employment and Related Social Issues, National Research Council,

Washington, D.C. July 1985. Office of Public Affairs, 2101 Constitution Ave., Washington, DC 20418. (202)334-2000.

Hutzel Hospital, 4707 St. Antoine Blvd., Detroit, MI 48201.

Information Please Almanac, Atlas and Yearbook. 1990. ISSN 0073-7860. Houghton Miffline Company, Boston, MA.

International Criminal Police Organization (INTERPOL), *International Crime Statistics*, 26 rue Armengaud, 92210 Saint Cloud, France.

International Journal of Aging and Human Development. 8X yr. ISSN 0091-4151. Baywood Publishing Co., Inc., 26 Austin Ave., P.O. Box 337, Amityville, NY 11701. (516)691-1270.

International Labour Office, *World Labour Report 1-2.* 1987. ISBN 0-19-828561-2. Oxford University Press, Walton Street, Oxford OX2 6DP.

International Labour Office. *Yearbook of Labour Statistics* (also known as *Year Book of Labour Statistics), 1945-1989.* Retrospective edition on population censuses. 1990. Statistical data from more than 180 countries and territories are provided on such subjects as population, employment, hours of work, wages, consumer prices, household budgets, etc. Information is given in English, French, and Spanish. The *Yearbook* is supplemented by the *Bulletin of Labour Statistics,* published quarterly with eight supplements. International Labour Office, Geneva, Switzerland.

International Labour Office, *Yearbook of Labour Statistics: Retrospective Edition on Population Censuses: 1945-89.* 1989. International Labour Office, Geneva.

Jacquet, Constant H., ed., *Yearbook of American & Canadian Churches 1989.* Annual. Fifty-seventh in a series begun in 1916. ISBN 0-687-46644-X. ISSN 0195-9034. Abingdon Press, Nashville, TN. The full survey entitled "Women Ministers in 1986 and 1977: A Ten-Year View," can be obtained by writing to:

Communication Unit, National Council of Churches, 475 Riverside Dr., New York, NY 10115.

Jamison, Ellen, *World Population Profile: 1989.* September 1989. U.S. Bureau of the Census, Center for International Research. For sale by the Superintendent of Documents, U.S. Government Printing Office, Washington, D.C. 20402. (202)783-3238.

Jaynes, Gerald David, and Williams, Robin M., Jr., *A Common Destiny: Blacks and American Society.* Committee on the Status of Black Americans, Commission on Behavioral and Social Sciences and Education, National Research Council, 1989. ISBN 0-309-03998-3. A report summarizing and interpreting a large body of data and research analyses concerning the position of blacks in American society since World War II. National Academy Press, 2101 Constitution Avenue, NW, Washington, DC 20418.

Journal of Consulting and Clinical Psychology. Bimonthly. ISSN 0095-8891. Psychology journal. American Psychological Assn., 1200 17th St., N.W., Washington, DC 20036. (202) 955-7600.

Journal of Family Issues. 4X/Yr. ISSN 0192-513X. Focuses on family studies. Sage Publications, Inc., 211 W. Hillcrest Dr., Newbury park, CA 91320. (805)499-0721.

Journal of Gerontology. Bimonthly technical publication emphasizing the study of aging from the biological, medical, and psychological disciplines. The Gerontological Society of America, 1411 K St., NW, Ste. 300, Washington, DC 20006. (202)393-1411.

Journal of Homosexuality. Quarterly. ISSN 0091-8369. Journal devoted to theoretical, empirical, and historical research on homosexuality, heterosexuality, sexual identity, social sex roles, and the sexual relationships of both men and women. Haworth Press, Inc., 12 W. 32 St., New York, NY 10001-3813. (212)228-2800.

Juster, F. Thomas, and Stafford, Frank P., *The Allocation of Time: Empirical Findings, Behavioral Models, and Problems of Measurement.* For a copy, contact Peter Seidman, Information Officer, News and Information Services, The University of Michigan, 412 Maynard, Ann Arbor, MI 48109- 1399. (313)747-4416.

Kinsella, Kevin, *Aging in the Third World.* September 1988. International Population Reports Series P-95, No. 79. U.S. Bureau of the Census. For sale by the Superintendent of Documents, U.S. Government Printing Office, Washington, D.C. 20402. (202)783-3238.

Koziara, Karen Shallcross, et al., eds., *Working Women: Past, Present, and Future.* 1987. ISBN 0-87179-547-7. ISBN 0-913447-34-X(soft). Industrial Relations Research Association Series. Bureau of National Affairs, Inc., Washington, DC.

Lancet. Weekly medical journal. North American Edition, Little Brown and Co., 34 Beacon St., Boston, MA 02106. (617)227-0730.

Leonard, K.E., and Jacob, T., "Alcohol, Alcoholism, and Family Violence," pp. 383-406. In *Handbook of Family Violence*, Vincent B. Van Hasselt, et al., eds., 1988. New York, Plenum Press.

Lester, David, Ph.D., ed., *Why Women Kill Themselves.* 1988. Includes case studies of Virginia Woolf, who killed herself, and Dorothy Parker, who attempted suicide. Charles C. Thomas Publisher, Springfield, IL.

Levine, Sumner N., *The Dow Jones-Irwin Business and Investment Almanac.* 1990 (14th ed.). ISSN 0733-2610. Dow Jones-Irwin, Homewood, IL 60430.

Lopata, Helena Znaniecka, and Brehm, Henry P., *Widows and Dependent Wives: From Social Problem to Federal Program.* 1986. ISBN 0-03-046301-7. Praeger Publishers Division, Westport, CT. Order from CBS International Publishing, 383 Madison Ave., New York, NY 10175

Los Angeles Times. Newspaper published Mon-Sun (morning). Times Mirror Square, Los Angeles, CA 90053.

Management Accounting. Monthly journal reporting on corporate finance, accounting, cash management, and budgeting. May 1990 reprint entitled "NAA Salaries: CMAs earn more than those without a professional designation," by Karl E. Reichardt, CMA, and David L. Schroeder. National Assn. of Accountants, Ten Paragon Drive, Montvale, NJ 07645-1760. (201)573-9000.

Mann, R.D., ed., *Oral Contraceptives and Breast Cancer: The Implications of the Present Findings for Informed Consent and Informed Choice.* 1990. The Parthenon Publishing Group, 120 Mill Road, Park Ridge, NJ.

Martindale, Melanie, Ph.D., *Sexual Harassment in the Military: 1988.* September 1990. Defense Manpower Data Center, 1600 Wilson Boulevard, Arlington, VA 22209.

Mediamark Research Multimedia Audiences Report, Spring 1990, Mediamark Research Inc., 708 Third Avenue, 8th Floor, New York, NY 10017. (212)476-0216.

Melton, J. Gordon, Gary L. Ward, contributing editor. *The Churches Speak on: Women's Ordination.* 1991. ISBN 0-8103-7647-4. ISSN 1043-9609. Gale Research Inc., 835 Penobscot Bldg., Detroit, MI 48226-4094.

Midgley, Jane, *The Woman's Budget.* Third Edition. 1989. Proposals for the transfer of government funds from the military budget to support of human needs. Women's International League for Peace and Freedom, 1213 Race Street, Philadelphia, PA 19107.

Michel, Jean et al., *Women in Engineering Education.* 1988. Monograph. (Studies in Engineering Education No. 12). Report examining status of women in engineering education worldwide. Includes data on female engineering enrollment and graduates, with enrollment compared to total higher education; professional employment, by selected occupation and engineering branch; and total labor force participation; with some comparisons to men, by selected country, world region, or economic grouping, varying periods, 1954-1984/85. ISBN 92-3-102490-6. United Nations Educational, Scientific and Cultural Organization, 7 place de Fontenoy, 75700 Paris.

Military Women in the Department of Defense. Irregular. Publication designed to provide current data on the status of women in all components of the Armed Forces. Available from the Superintendent of Documents, U.S. Government Printing Office, Washington, D.C. 20402. (202)783-3238.

Miller, Dorothy C., *Helping the Strong: An Exploration of the Needs of Families Headed by Women.* 1987. National Association of Social Workers, 7981 Eastern Ave., Silver Spring, MD 20910. (310)565-0333.

Miller Lite Report on Women in Sports: In Cooperation with the Women's Sports Foundation. A survey conducted in September and October, 1985, addressing a range of questions about sports/fitness activities. Women's Sports Foundation, 342 Madison Avenue, Suite 728, New York, NY 10173.

Mishel, Lawrence, and Simon, Jacqueline, *The State of Working America.* 1988. ISBN 0-944826-04-0. Order #6-04-0. Economic Policy Institute, 1730 Rhode Island Ave. NW, Suite 812, Washington, DC 20036. Orders for publications should be addressed to EPI Reports, M.E. Sharpe, Inc., 80 Business Park Drive, Armonk, NY 10504. (800)541-6563.

Monthly Labor Review. "Special Issue on the Family." March 1990 113(3). The *Review* contains statistical information on fluctuations in the cost of living, wage rates, hours of labor, industrial relations, output per man- hours, wholesale and retail prices, etc. Includes research summaries and foreign labor developments. Other BLS periodicals include: *Current Wage Developments, Employment and Earnings; Occupational Outlook Quarterly.* BLS makes its current news releases available through the on-line "BLS Electronic News Release Service." U.S. Department of Labor, Bureau of Labor Statistics, Washington, DC 20402. For sale by the Superintendent of Documents, U.S. Government Printing Office, Washington, D.C. 20402. (202)783-3238.

Mosher, William D., Ph.D., and Pratt, William F., Ph.D., *Fecundity and Infertility in the United States, 1965-88*. 1990. Advance Data from Vital and Health Statistics of the National Center for Health Statistics, No. 192, December 4, 1990. Hyattsville, MD: National Center for Health Statistics.

MS Magazine. Monthly women's general editorial magazine. ISSN 047-8318. 119 W. 40th Street, New York, NY 10018. (212)719-9800.

National Center for Education Statistics. *Digest of Education Statistics*. Annual. 1990. Provides an abstract of statistical information covering the entire field of American education from kindergarten through graduate school. Listed are figures pertaining to such topics as schools, enrollments, teachers, graduates, attainment, and expenditures. A companion volume, published annually, *Projections of Education Statistics*, shows trends for the past 10 years and projects data for the next 10 years. A related publication, *The Condition of Education*, provides an overview of trends and current issues. Washington, DC. For sale by the Superintendent of Documents, U.S. Government Printing Office, Washington, D.C. 20402. (202)783-3238.

National Center for Education Statistics, "Higher Education Enrollment: Fall 1987 to Fall 1993," (July 1989), CS 89-644, and "Early Estimates: National Higher Education Statistics: Fall 1989," by Elaine Kroe (December 1989), DR-IPEDS-89/90-1, NCES 90-379. Crosscutting Education Statistics and Analysis Division, National Center for Education Statistics, 555 New Jersey Avenue, NW, Washington, DC 20208-5650. (202)357-6581.

National Center for Health Statistics. "Annual Summary of Births, Marriages, Divorces, and Deaths: United States, 1989." Provisional data. Monthly vital statistics report; vol. 38, No. 13, August 30, 1990. DHHS Publication No. (PHS)90-1120. Centers for Disease Control, 6525 Belcrest Road, Hyattsville, MD. To receive this publication regularly, contact the National Center for Health Statistics, (301)436-8500.

National Center for Health Statistics. *Health, United States, 1989*. Hyattsville, Maryland: Public Health Service. 1990. DHHS Pub. No. (PHS) 90-1232. For sale by the Superintendent of Documents, U.S. Government Printing Office, Washington, D.C. 20402.

National Center for Health Statistics, Kathryn A. London. 1989. Children of Divorce. *Vital and Health Statistics.* Series 21, No. 46. DHHS Pub. No. (PHS)89-1924. Public Health Service, Washington; U.S. Government Printing Office.

National Chamber Foundation, *Determinants of Employee Absenteeism.* A study prepared by Carole E. Bonilla. 1989. National Chamber Foundation, 1615 H Street, N.W., Washington, D.C. 20062. (202) 463-5552.

National Committee on Pay Equity, *Briefing Paper #1: The Wage Gap.* April 1989. Also: *Newsnotes.* National Committee on Pay Equity, 1201 Sixteenth Street, NW, Suite 420, Washington, DC 20036. (202)822-7304.

National Education Association, *Estimates of School Statistics 1989-90,* as provided by the State Departments of Education. 1990. NEA Professional Library, P.O. Box 509, West Haven, CT 06516.

National Education Association, *Status of the American Public School Teacher 1985-86.* 1987. NEA, 1201 16th St., NW, Washington, DC 20036-3290. (202)822-7400.

National Research Council. *Summary Report 1988: Doctorate Recipients From United States Universities.* The Survey of Earned Doctorates has been conducted each year since 1958 by the National Research Council's Office of Science and Engineering Personnel. Questionnnaires are filled out by the graduates as they complete all requirements for their doctorates. Published by National Academy Press, Washington, DC. Inquiries regarding the survey should be addressed to: Doctorate Recipients Project, Office of Science and Engineering Personnel, National Research Council, 2101 Constitution Avenue, NW, Washington, DC 20418. (202)334-3161.

National Science Board. *Science and Engineering Indicators — 1989.* Washington, DC: U.S. Government Printing Office, 1989. (NSB 89-1). For sale by the Superintendent of Documents, U.S. Government Printing Office, Washington, D.C. 20402. (202)783-3238.

National Science Foundation, *Women and Minorities in Science and Engineering.* January 1990. NSF 90-301. National Science Foundation, Washington, DC 20550.

National Women's Health Network's Network News. Bimonthly. ISSN 8755-867X. Newsletter covering network activities and women's health issues for members. The Women's Health Information Service is a clearinghouse for women's lifetime wellness, offering information on health issues affecting women, by topic. National Women's Health Network, 1325 G Street, N.W., Washington, DC 20005. (202)347-1140.

New England Journal of Medicine. Weekly (Thursday) journal for the medical profession. Massachusetts Medical Society, 1440 Main St., Waltham, MA 02154-1649. (617)893-3800.

New York Times. Daily. 229 W. 43rd St., New York, NY 10036. (212)556-1234.

Nolen-Hoeksema, Susan, *Sex Differences in Depression.* 1990. Stanford University Press, Stanford, CA 94305.

Northrup, Herbert R., *The Changing Role of Women in Research and Development.* 1988. ISBN 0-89546-072-06. Manpower and Human Resources Studies No. 11A. University of Pennsylvania, The Wharton School, Industrial Research Unit, Philadelphia, PA 19104-6358.

Norwood, Janet L., "Working Women: Where Have We Been? Where Are We Going?" April 1990, Report 785. U.S. Department of Labor, Bureau of Labor Statistics, Washington, DC 20212.

Nuss, Shirley, in collaboration with Ettore Denti and David Viry, *Women in the world of work: Statistical analysis and projections to the year 2000.* Number 18 in the series *Women, Work and Development.* ISBN 92-2-106507-3. ISSN

0253-2042. 1989. ILO Publications, International Labour Office, CH-1211 Geneva 22, Switzerland.

Oakes, Jeannie, *Lost Talent: The Underparticipation of Women, Minorities, and Disabled Persons in Science*. February 1990. ISBN 0-8330-1008-5. RAND Corporation, 1700 Main Street, P.O. Box 2138, Santa Monica, CA 90406-2138.

O'Connell, Martin, and Bachu, Amara, *Who's Minding the Kids? Child Care Arrangements: Winter, 1986-87*. U.S. Bureau of the Census. Current Population Reports, Household Economic Studies, Series P-70, No. 20. Child care statistics for children under the age of 15 whose parents or guardians were employed in the labor force or attending school during September to November, 1987. For sale by the Superintendent of Documents, U.S. Government Printing Office, Washington, D.C. 20402. (202)783-3238.

OECD. *Labour Force Statistics*. Annual. Contains historical time series on the evolution of the population and labor force for the OECD's 24 member countries. A section of general tables is provided in addition to sections for each country. Time series cover a 10-year period. Quarterly supplement, *Quarterly Labour Force Statistics*, is also available, beginning with 1978. Organisation for Economic Cooperation and Development (OECD), Publications and Information Center, 2001 L Street, NW, Ste. 700, Washington, DC 20036. (202)785-6323.

OECD Observer. 6X/Yr. ISSN 0029-7054. Magazine covering economic affairs, science, and technology. Organization for Economic Cooperation & Development, 2001 L St., N.W. Suite 700, Washington, DC 20036-4905.

Office of Educational Research and Improvement, U.S. Department of Education, *Youth Indicators 1988: Trends in the Well-Being of American Youth*. 1988. For sale by the Superintendent of Documents, U.S. Government Printing Office, Washington, D.C. 20402. (202)783-3238.

Office of Women in Development, Bureau for Program and Policy Coordination, Agency for International Development, *Planning for the Next Decade: A*

Perspective of Women in Development: A Report to Congress. Submitted to the House Committee on Appropriations and the Senate Committee on Appropriations, March 1, 1989. Washington, DC.

Ogle, Laurence T., ed., *The Condition of Education 1990: Volume 1: Elementary and Secondary Education.* 1990. NCES-90-681. National Center for Education Statistics, Washington, DC 20208-5650. For sale by the Superintendent of Documents, U.S. Government Printing Office, Washington, D.C. 20402. (202)783-3238.

Palmer, Ingrid, *Women's Roles & Gender Differences in Development: The Impact of Male Out-Migration on Women in Farming.* 1985. ISBN 0-931816-22-X. Kumarian Press, 29 Bishop Road, West Hartford, CT 06119.

Palmore, Erdman B., Ph.D., Burchett, Bruce M., Ph.D., Fillenbaum, Gerda G., Ph.D., George, Linda K., Ph.D., and Wallman, Laurence M., M.A., *Retirement: Causes and Consequences.* 1985. Some results of the first and second Duke University longitudinal study on aging. New York: Springer Publishing Company.

Parsons, Michael H., *Part-Time Occupational Faculty: A Contribution to Excellence.* 1985. Information Series No. 300. National Center Publications, National Center for Research in Vocational Education, 1960 Kenny Road, Columbus, OH 43210-1090 (Order No. IN300).

Population Reference Bureau, Inc., *America in the 21st Century: Human Resource Development.* December 1989. Circulation Department, Population Reference Bureau, Inc., P.O. Box 96152, Washington, DC 20090-67152. (800)877-9881.

Population Today. 11X/Yr. ISSN 0749-2448. Magazine covering US and world population data, trends, policy, and analysis, including family planning programs and technology. Population Reference Bureau, 777 14th St., N.W., Suite 800, Washington, DC 20005-3201. (202)639-8040.

Psychology Today. Monthly magazine covering psychology for the layperson. One Park Ave., New York, NY 10016. (212)481-0200.

Public Health Reports. Journal of the U.S. Public Health Service. Bimonthly. PHS 90-50193. U.S. Dept. of Health and Human Services, Room 13C-26 Parklawn Bldg., 5600 Fishers Lane, Rockville, MD 20857.

Radical America. 4X/Yr. Socialist-feminist journal of politics and culture specializing in radical, labor, women's history and theory, grassroots and community organizing, peace and disarmament issues, and Afro-American and Third World issues. ISSN 0033-7617. Alternative Education Project, One Summer Street, Somerville, MA 02143. (617)628-6585.

Research Triangle Institute, P.O. Box 12194, Research Triangle Park, NC 27709. (919)541-6000. Research results are published in reports to clients and technical journals.

Reviews of Infectious Diseases. 6X/Yr. Medical journal. University of Chicago Press, 5720 S. Woodlawn Ave., Chicago, IL 60637. (312)702-7600.

Rhoodie, Eschel M., *Discrimination Against Women: A Global Survey of the Economic, Educational, Social and Political Status of Women*. ISBN-0-89950-448-5. McFarland & Company, Inc., Bbox 611, Jefferson, NC 28640.

Ricardo-Campbell, Rita, and Lazear, Edward P., eds., *Issues in Contemporary Retirement*. 1988. ISBN 0-8179-8701-0. Hoover Institution Press, Stanford University, Stanford, CA 94305.

Ries, Peter W., *Health of Black and White Americans, 1985-87*. National Center for Health Statistics. Vital Health Stat 10(171). 1990. DHHS Pub. No. (PHS)90-1599.

Rix, Sara E., ed. *The American Woman 1990-91: A Status Report*. 1990. ISBN 0-393-02840-2. ISBN 0-393-30686-0 (paperback). W.W. Norton & Company, Inc., 500 Fifth Avenue, New York, NY 10110.

Rolling Stone. Magazine published every other week and featuring contemporary culture, politics, arts, and music. Straight Arrow Publishers, Inc., 745 Fifth Avenue, New York, NY 10151. (212)758-3800.

Roos, Patricia A., *Gender and Work: A Comparative Analysis of Industrial Societies*. 1985. ISBN 0-88706-031-5. ISBN 0-88706-032-3 (Pbk.). State University of New York Press, State University Plaza, Albany, NY 12246.

Rose, Stephen, and Fasenfest, David, *Family Incomes in the 1980s: New Pressure on Wives, Husbands, and Young Adults*. Working Paper No. 103, November 1988. Economic Policy Institute, 1730 Rhode Island Ave. NW, Suite 812, Washington, DC 20036. (202)775-8810.

Sales & Marketing Management. 16X/Yr. ISSN 0163-7517. Marketing magazine for sales, marketing, and management executives. Bill Communications, 633 Third Ave., New York, NY 10017. (212)986-4800.

Scholastic Update. 18X/Yr. Social studies magazine for grades 8-12 (high school network comprised of: *Scholastic Update, Choices, Voice, Scope* and *Science World*). Scholastic, Inc., 730 Broadway, New York, NY 10003. (212) 505-3000.

Sex Roles. Monthly journal focusing on sex roles in children and adults. ISSN 0360-0025. Plenum Publishing Corp., 233 Spring St., New York, NY 10013. (212)620-8000.

Shakeshaft, Charol, *Women in Educational Administration*. 1989. ISBN 0-8039-3612-5. ISBN 0-8039-3550-1 (paperback). Sage Publications, Inc., 2111 West Hillcrest Drive, Newbury Park, CA 91320.

Silvestri, George T., and Lukasiewicz, John M., "Occupational employment projections: the 1984-95 outlook," *Monthly Labor Review* 108(11):42-59, 1985.

Sivard, Ruth Leger, *Women ... A World Survey*. 1985. ISBN 0-918281-00-8. World Priorities, Box 25140, Washington, DC 20007.

Smith, Tom W., *Adult Sexual Behavior in 1989: Number of Partners, Frequency, and Risk*. GSS Topical Report No. 18. Paper presented to the American Association for the Advancement of Science, February, 1990, New Orleans. Research done for the General Social Survey Project directed by James A. Davis and Tom W. Smith. NORC, University of Chicago, Chicago, IL.

Social Forces. Quarterly. Magazine highlighting sociological inquiry and exploring realms shared with social psychology, anthropology, political science, history, and economics. ISSN 0037-7732. University of North Carolina Press, Department of Sociology, Hamilton Hall 070A, CB #3210, Chapel Hill, NC 27599. (919)962-5502.

Social Science Quarterly. Quarterly. ISSN 0038-4941. Journal featuring articles about current research in political science, history, sociology, economics, and women's studies. University of Texas Press, Box 7819, Austin, TX 78713. (512)471-4531.

SR Studies in Religion/Sciences Religieuses. Quarterly. ISSN 0008-4298. Magazine covering the study of religion (French and English). Canadian Corporation for Studies in Religion, Wilfrid laurier University, Waterloo ON, Canada N2L 3C5. (416)978-6221.

Time special issue, *Women: The Road Ahead*. Fall 1990, Vol. 136, No. 19. Weekly with an extra issue in October. ISSN 0040-781X. Time & Life Building, Rockefeller Center, New York, NY 10020-1393.

UNESCO, *Statistical Yearbook*. 1989. Annual (irregular). This work contains tables grouped according to various subjects: population, education, science and technology, libraries and museums, book production, newspapers and other periodicals, paper consumption, film and cinema, radio broadcasting, television and cultural expenditure. The information has been supplied by over 200 countries or territories in reply to UNESCO questionnaires, as well as from official reports and publications. In English, French, and Spanish. A briefer publication, the *Statistical Digest*, is also available (1981). ISBN 92-3-002630-1. 7, place de Fontenoy, 75700, Paris.

United Nations, *Compendium of Statistics and Indicators on the Situation of Women: 1986*. 1989. Sales No. E/F.88.XVII.6. United Nations Publishing Division, United Nations, New York, NY 10017. (212)963-8302.

United Nations, *1988 Demographic Yearbook*. ISBN 92-1-051073-9. Annual. 1990. A central source for demographic data from approximatley 220 countries. Topics center around population changes throughout the world: rate of increase, birth and death rates, population by sex, urban population, international migration, marriage and divorce. United Nations Publishing Division, United Nations, New York, NY 10017. (212)963-8302.

United Nations, Department of International Economic and Social Affairs, *Global Estimates and Projections of Population by Sex and Age: The 1988 Revision*. 1989. Based on the eleventh round of the revision of the population estimates and projections undertaken by the United Nations Secretariat begun in 1986. Free. A magnetic tape and a set of diskettes containing the major results of the present estimates and projections can be provided upon request for a nominal fee. Address inquiries to the Director of the Population Division, Department of International Economic and Social Affairs, United Nations, New York, NY 10017.

United Nations. Department of International Economic and Social Affairs. *Levels and Trends of Contraceptive Use as Assessed in 1988*. 1989. Population Studies, No. 110. ST/ESA/SER.A/110. United Nations Publishing Division, United Nations, New York, NY 10017. (212)963-8302.

United Nations. Department of International Economic and Social Affairs. *Population and Vital Statistics Report: Data Available as of 1 April 1990*. Statistical Papers, Series A, Vol. XLII, No. 2. ST/ESA/STAT/SER.A/173. United Nations Publishing Division, United Nations, New York, NY 10017. (212)963-8302.

United Nations, Department of International Economic and Social Affairs, *Women's Employment and Fertility: Comparative Analysis of World Fertility Survey Results for 38 Developing Countries*. 1985. ISBN 92-1-151152-6. Population Studies, No. 96. Sales No. E.85.XIII.5. One of a series dealing with findings from the World Fertility Survey; it includes the 38 developing countries for which data were available by late 1984. United Nations Publishing Division, United Nations, New York, NY 10017. (212)963-8302.

United Nations, *The Economic Role of Women in the ECE Region.* Sales No. E.80.II.E.6. United Nations Publishing Division, United Nations, New York, NY 10017. (212)963-8302.

United Nations, *Virtue, Order, Health and Money: Towards a Comprehensive Perspective on Female Prostitution in Asia.* 1986. ST/ESCAP/388. Paper prepared by Truong Thanh-Dam of the Institute of Social Studies, The Hague, Netherlands, Consultant, for the Workshop of Experts on Prevention and Rehabilitation Schemes for Young Women in Prostitution and Related Occupations, 17-21 June 1985, Bangkok, Thailand. United Nations Economic and Social Commission for Asia and the Pacific, United Nations Building, Rajadamnern Avenue, Bangkok 10200, Thailand.

United Nations, *World Survey on the Role of Women in Development.* 1986. ISBN 92-1-130109-2. Prepared by the Secretary-General at the request of the UN General Assembly for a comprehensive and detailed outline for an interdisciplinary and multisectoral world survey on the role of women in overall development. UN Sales No. E.86.IV.3. United Nations Publishing Division, United Nations, New York, NY 10017. (212)963-8302.

The Universal Almanac 1990. 1989. ISBN 0-8362-7977-8. ISBN 0-8362-7949-2(Pbk.). Andrews and McMell, 4900 Main Street, Kansas City, MO 64112.

U.S. Congress. House. *U.S. Children and Their Families: Current Conditions and Recent Trends, 1989.* A Report Together with Additional Views of the Select Committee on Children, Youth, and Families. 101st Cong., 1st Sess., Washington, DC. U.S. Government Printing Office, 1989.

U.S. Bureau of the Census, 1987 Census of Governments, *Popularly Elected Officials in 1987.* Preliminary report GC87-2(P), issued December 1988. For sale by the Superintendent of Documents, U.S. Government Printing Office, Washington, D.C. 20402. (202)783-3238.

U.S. Bureau of the Census, *Statistical Abstract of the United States: 1990.* (110th edition.) Presents the most important statistical information gathered by all branches of the federal government, covering vital statistics, political data, economic life, and many cultural subjects. Most of the data are presented in tabular form and are well organized for reference. Washington, DC, 1990. For sale by Superintendent of Documents, U.S. Government Printing Office, Washington, DC 20402, Tel. (202)783-3238.

U.S. Bureau of Labor Statistics. *Handbook of Labor Statistics.* August 1989 (reported to be annual; previous edition, 1985). All the major statistical series compiled by the Bureau are included. U.S. Department of labor, Bureau of Labor Statistics, Washington, DC 20212. For sale by the Superintendent of Documents, U.S. Government Printing Office, Washington, D.C. 20402. (202)783-3238.

U.S. Bureau of the Census. *1987 Economic Censuses: Women-Owned Businesses.* WB87-1. Issued August 1990. Superintendent of Documents No. C3.250. For sale by the Superintendent of Documents, U.S. Government Printing Office, Washington, D.C. 20402. (202)783-3238.

U.S. Bureau of the Census. Current Housing Report, Series H-121, No. 19. *Housing in America 1985/86.* 1989. First biennial report presenting a wide variety of data collected in 1985 and 1986 in current surveys dealing with housing and the demographic, social, and economic characteristics of its occupants. U.S. Government Printing Office, Washington, DC.

U.S. Bureau of the Census. Current Population Reports, Consumer Income, Series P-60, No. 168. *Money Income and Poverty Status in the United States 1989.* Advance data from the March 1990 Current Population Survey. Issued September 1990. For sale by the Superintendent of Documents, U.S. Government Printing Office, Washington, D.C. 20402. (202)783-3238.

U.S. Bureau of the Census. Current Population Reports, Series P-20, No. 447. *Household and Family Characteristics: 1990 and 1989.* For sale by the Superintendent of Documents, U.S. Government Printing Office, Washington, D.C. 20402. (202)783-3238.

U.S. Bureau of the Census. Current Population Reports, Series P-70, No. 19. *The Need for Personal Assistance with Everyday Activities: Recipients and Caregivers.* For sale by the Superintendent of Documents, U.S. Government Printing Office, Washington, D.C. 20402. (202)783-3238.

U.S. Bureau of the Census. Current Population Reports, Series P-70, No. 21. *What's It Worth? Educational Background and Economic Status: Spring 1987.* For sale by the Superintendent of Documents, U.S. Government Printing Office, Washington, D.C. 20402. (202)783-3238.

U.S. Bureau of the Census. Current Population Reports, Series P-70, No. 22. *Household Wealth and Asset Ownership: 1988.* For sale by the Superintendent of Documents, U.S. Government Printing Office, Washington, D.C. 20402. (202)783-3238.

U.S. Bureau of the Census. Current Population Reports, Special Studies, Series P-23, No. 161. *Migration Between the United States and Canada.* For sale by the Superintendent of Documents, U.S. Government Printing Office, Washington, D.C. 20402. (202)783-3238.

U.S. Bureau of the Census. Current Population Reports, Special Studies Series P-23, No. 165. *Work and Family Patterns of American Women. The Family Life Cycle: 1985. Maternity Leave Arrangements: 1961-85.* Papers focusing on some of the social, demographic, and economic consequences of the expanding roles for women. For sale by the Superintendent of Documents, U.S. Government Printing Office, Washington, D.C. 20402. (202)783-3238.

U.S. Bureau of the Census. *Illustrative Statistics on Women in Selected Developing Countries.* Washington, DC, 1980. Charts intended to give a general overview of some basic aspects of women's participation in selected developing countries. For sale by the Superintendent of Documents, U.S. Government Printing Office, Washington, D.C. 20402. (202)783-3238.

U.S. Bureau of the Census. Current Population Reports, Household Economic Studies, Series P-70, No. 13. *Who's Helping Out? Support Networks Among American Families.* For sale by the Superintendent of Documents, U.S. Government Printing Office, Washington, D.C. 20402. (202)783-3238.

U.S. Bureau of the Census. Current Population Reports, Population Characteristics, Series P-20, No. 440. *Voting and Registration in the Election of November 1988.* Issued October 1989. Biennial report presenting sociodemographic characteristics of persons by self-reported voter registration and voting status, for the November 1988 presidential election. For sale by the Superintendent of Documents, U.S. Government Printing Office, Washington, D.C. 20402. (202)783-3238.

U.S. Department of Health and Human Services, *Personnel for Health Needs of the Elderly Through Year 2020.* September 1987 Report to Congress. National Institute on Aging, Bethesda, MD 20892.

U.S. Department of Health and Human Services, *Seventh Special Report to the U.S. Congress on Alcohol and Health from the Secretary of Health and Human Services, January 1990.* 1990. DHHS Publication No. (ADM)90-1656. Public Health Service, Alcohol, Drug Abuse, and Mental Health Administration, National Institute on Alcohol Abuse and Alcoholism, 5600 Fishers Lane, Rockville, MD 20857.

U.S. Department of Health and Human Services, Social Security Administration, *Fast Facts & Figures About Social Security.* 1989. SSA Pub. No. 13-11785. Office of Research and Statistics, 4301 Connecticut Ave, NW, Ste. 209, Washington, DC 20008.

U.S. Department of Justice, Bureau of Justice Statistics, *Sourcebook of Criminal Justice Statistics.* 1989. Annual. Recent criminal justice data for the U.S. are presented. Data are displayed by regions, states, and cities to increase their value for comparative analyses. For sale by the Superintendent of Documents, U.S. Government Printing Office, Washington, D.C. 20402. (202)783-3238.

U.S. Department of Labor, Bureau of Labor Statistics, *Errata for Handbook of Labor Statistics*. Bulletin 2340, March 1990.

U.S. Department of Labor, Bureau of Labor Statistics, *Occupational Projections and Training Data*. Bulletin 2351, April 1990. Biennial since 1974. Statistical and research supplement to the 1990-91 edition of the *Occupational Outlook Handbook*; tenth in a series dating back to 1971. Presents statistics and technical data underlying the qualitative information presented in the *Handbook*. Washington, DC 20212.

U.S. Department of Labor, Bureau of Labor Statistics, *White-Collar Pay: Private Goods-Producing Industries, March 1990*. Bulletin 2374, issued October 1990. Summarizes the results of the Burea's March 1990 survey. For sale by the Superintendent of Documents, U.S. Government Printing Office, Washington, D.C. 20402. (202)783-3238.

U.S. Department of Labor News. Monthly. U.S. Dept. of Labor, Bureau of Labor Statistics, Washington, DC 20212.

U.S. Department of Labor, Women's Bureau, *In America and in Need: Immigrant, Refugee, and Entrant Women*, by Abby Spero. January 1985. Published by the American Association of Community and Junior Colleges, One Dupont Circle, NW, Ste. 410, Washington, DC 20036.

U.S. Department of Justice, *Compendium of Federal Justice Statistics, 1986*. November 1990. NCJ-125617. Justice Statistics Clearinghouse/NCJRS, U.S. Department of Justice, Box 6000, Rockville, MD 20850.

Ward, Kathryn, ed., *Women Workers and Global Restructuring*. 1990. ILR Press, School of Industrial and Labor Relations, Cornell University, Ithaca, NY 14851-0952.

Wider Opportunities for Women in conjunction with The Center for National Policy Review, *A Territorial Issue: A Study of Women in the Construction Trades.* 1982. One of a series of publications designed to expand employment opportunities for women. Wider Opportunities for Women (WOW), 1325 G St., N.W., Lower level, Washington, DC 20005. (202)638-3143.

Willborn, Steven L., *A Comparable Worth Primer.* 1986. Lexington Books, Lexington, MA 02173.

The Wilson Report: Moms, Dads, Daughters and Sports. Presented by: Wilson Sporting Goods Co. in cooperation with the Women's Sports Foundation, June 7, 1988. Women's Sports Foundation, 342 Madison Avenue, Suite 728, New York, NY 10173.

Wolfe, Linda, *The Cosmo Report.* 1981. Based on a survey made by *Cosmopolitan* magazine, 1980. Arbor House, New York, NY.

Women and Criminal Justice. Biannual. ISSN 0897-4454. Journal aiming to provide a single forum in which members of the academic community and representatives of governmental and private institutions and agencies throughout the world can explore and exchange information on issues associated with women and criminal justice from an interdisciplinary perspective. Haworth Press, Inc., 10 Alice Street, Binghamton, NY 13904-1580.

Women's Sports Foundation, *The Women's Sports Foundation Report: Minorities in Sports: The Effect of Varsity Sports Participation on the Social, Educational, and Career Mobility of Minority Students with Policy Recommendations from The Center for the Study of Sport in Society, Northeastern University.* August 15, 1989. Third major research project on sports funded by Miller Lite. Women's Sports Foundation, 342 Madison Avenue, Suite 728, New York, NY 10173.

Women Studies Abstracts. Quarterly with an annual index in the fourth issue. ISSN 0049-7835. Magazine providing abstracts of journal articles. Rush Publishing Co., P.O. Box 1, Rush, NY 14543-0001. (716)624-4418.

Women's Studies International Forum. Bi-monthly. ISSN 0277-5395. Journal focusing on women's studies. Pergamon Journals Inc., Maxwell House, Fairview Park, Elmsford, NY 10523. (914)592-7700.

Women's Studies Quarterly. Quarterly feminist journal focusing on education. ISSN 0732-1562. Feminist Press City University of NY, 311 E. 94 St., New York, NY 10128-5603. (212)360-5790.

Women's Sports and Fitness. 11X/Yr. Membership publication of Women's Sports Foundation, 342 Madison Avenue, Suuite 728, New York, NY 10173.

Wood, Floris W., ed. *An American Profile — Opinions and Behavior, 1972- 1989*. Opinion Results on 300 High-Interest Issues. Derived from the General Social Survey Conducted by the National Opinion Research Center. 1990. ISBN 0-8103-7723-3. Gale Research Inc., 835 Penobscot Bldg., Detroit, MI 48226-4094.

World Health Organization, *Women, Health and Development*. 1985. ISBN 92 4 170090 4. ISSN 0303-7878. WHO Offset Publication No. 90, intended to make generally available material that for economic, technical, or other reasons cannot be included in WHO's regular publications program. World Health Organization Publications Center USA, 49 Sheridan Avenue, Albany, NY 12219 or United Nations Bookshop, New York, NY 10017 (retail only).

World Health Statistics Quarterly. ISSN 0043-8510. Contains articles in either French or English with a summary in both languages. World Health Organization, 1211 Geneva 27, Switzerland.

World Press Review. Monthly foreign press digest. ISSN 0195-8895. 200 Madison Ave., New York, NY 10016. (212)889-5155.

SUBJECT AND GEOGRAPHIC INDEX

The *Subject and Geographic Index* indexes general table topics as well as "line items" within tables. The primary reference numbers appearing after subject index terms are page numbers; reference numbers in brackets are entry numbers. All subject terms in this index apply to the United States unless modified by *worldwide*; e.g., *Athletes, adolescent* applies to the United States. Tables filed under the term *United States* in this index are international in scope and include the United States. All subject headings in this index, e.g., *Golf*, apply to women unless otherwise indicated. Many of the tables indexed also include comparative data for men.

The *Library of Congress Subject Headings* was used as a general guide for the selection of subject headings in this index but was not followed in all cases.

Adult contemporary radio 665 [805]

Advertising

— periodicals 30 [45]

Advertising and sales occupations 352, 357, 404 [416], [423], [485]

Aerobic exercising 645, 651 [768], [780]

Aerobics *See:* Calisthenics and aerobics

Aeronautical and astronautical engineering occupations 434, 438 [531], [535]

Aerospace engineering occupations 343 [399]

Afghanistan

— birth control 517 [624]

— births 508 [614]

— childbirth 291 [321]

— deaths 531 [638]

— education, enrollment 150, 187, 194, 208 [191], [196], [200], [202]

— educational attainment 231 [226]

— employment 482 [577]

— fertility 508, 550, 567 [614], [649], [657]

— fetal and infant deaths 556, 567 [651], [657]

— life expectancy 567, 568 [657], [659]

— literacy 235, 567 [227], [657]

— population 541 [646]

— teachers 440, 450, 455 [538], [551], [553]

Africa

See also: Central African Republic; Eastern Africa; Middle Africa; Near East and North Africa; Northern Africa; South Africa; Southern Africa; Sub-Saharan Africa; Western Africa

— agriculture 465, 466 [559], [560]

— birth control 515, 523, 595 [621], [627], [686]

— birth weight 280 [301]

— childbirth 280 [301]

— children 280, 537, 597 [301], [640], [691]

— clitoridectomy 257, 258, 259, [258], [259], [260], [261]

— early childhood education 142 [182]

— education, enrollment 142, 148, 192, 193, 280 [182], [190], [197], [198], [301]

— education, enrollment, science 194 [199]

— employment 468 [566]

— fetal and infant deaths 280 [301]

— literacy 280 [301]

— married women 280 [301]

— politicians 607 [706]

— population 280, 537, 587, 597 [301], [640], [675], [691]

— pregnancy, complications of 296 [322]

— status of Muslim women 593 [683]

— teachers 444, 455 [539], [552]

— vital statistics 595 [686]

— youth, population 597 [691]

African-Americans

— abortions 499 [603]

— absenteeism 272 [284]

African-Americans continued:

— academic achievement 227, 240, 241 [221], [231], [232]

— acute conditions 261 [265]

— adoption 95 [122]

— adult population 513 [616]

— aged 272 [284]

— agriculture employment 378 [455]

— AIDS 261 [264]

— alcohol and drug use during pregnancy 297, [323], [324]

— amniocentesis 289 [318]

— anemia in pregnancy 298 [326]

— arrestees 48 [67]

— athletes 657, 658, 660, 670 [788], [790], [796], [814]

— attitudes toward community problems 10 [15]

— birth control 517 [623]

— births 300, 503, 506, 548, [330], [606], [607], [610], [647]

— business owners 32, 37 [49], [54]

— cancer 253, 254 [250], [251]

— child support 310 [344]

— childless 596 [687]

— children 96, 596 [123], [687]

— cholesterol 271 [283]

— chronically ill 271 [282]

— cigarette smokers 255 [254]

— convicted offenders 45, 46 [63], [64]

— criminals 81 [102]

— deaths 524, 525, 526, 529 [628], [629], [631], [634]

— deaths, HIV 526 [630]

— elevated blood pressure 262 [267]

— employment 363, 378, 379, 402, 409 [430], [455], [456], [483], [489]

— engineers 361, 439 [428], [536]

— enrolled in school 145 [186]

— executives 26, 28, 419 [37], [41], [506]

— family income 321 [362]

— fertility 548 [647]

— fetal and infant deaths 557, 558 [652], [654]

— government employment 425 [514]

— high school dropouts 218 [206]

— high school students, courses 218 [205]

— home owners 106 [137]

— households 108 [141]

— hypertension 265, [271], [272]

— income 323, 326 [365], [368]

— labor force projections 391 [470]

— librarians 428 [520]

— male/female ratio 593 [682]

— mathematics achievement 219 [207]

— military personnel 489 [584]

— military test scores 494 [595]

— mothers 596 [688]

— mothers, heads of household 102 [132]

— mothers, mortality 584 [673]

— overweight 268, 269 [277], [278]

African-Americans continued:
— physics students 222 [213]
— police 74 [91]
— politicians 612 [714]
— population 513, 538, 540, 593 [616], [642], [644], [682]
— poverty 104, 118, 374 [133], [150], [449]
— pregnancy, alcohol and drug use 297, [323], [324]
— prenatal care 300, 302 [330], [334]
— rape 83 [105]
— religion 620 [730]
— renters 106 [137]
— school administrators 435, 439 [532], [537]
— school dropouts 661 [798]
— scientists 361, 439 [428], [536]
— sick 261, 271 [265], [282]
— soldiers 489 [584]
— sports 659, 660, 661, 668, [793], [794], [797], [798], [810]
— sports, attitudes 670 [813]
— sports, benefits 667 [809]
— teachers 424 [513]
— test scores 242, 660 [235], [795]
— unemployment 378, 402, 409 [455], [483], [489]
— victims of crimes 79, 81, 83, 85, [100], [102], [103], [105], [108]
— volunteers 612 [715]
— voters 602 [699]
— wages 349, 354, 372, [409], [417], [418], [446]
Age distribution
— adults 514 [618]
Aged and aging 272, 275 [284], [291]
— care 89, 95, 412 [113], [121], [494]
— friendship 640 [759]
— hobbies 664 [802]
— in poverty 377 [453]
— income 329, 375 [374], [450]
— lesbians 638, 639 [755], [756]
— living alone, worldwide 105 [135]
— living arrangements 116 [148]
— old age homes 117 [149]
— osteoporosis 268 [276]
— population 538 [641]
— religion 619 [727]
— support networks 620 [730]
— worldwide 92 [117]
Agricultural scientists 436 [534]
Agricultural services
— women-owned firms 39, 40 [57], [58]
Agriculture
— Africa 465, 466 [559], [560]
— employment 380, 381, 423 [457], [458], [511]
— employment, worldwide 475, 476 [572], [573]
— executives 445 [540]
Agriculture education
— worldwide 155, 163, 168, 176, 194 [192], [193], [194], [195],

Agriculture education continued:
  [199]
Agriculture occupations 357, 404, 429, 445 [423], [485], [521], [540]
— African-Americans 378 [455]
— Hispanic Americans 389, 430 [468], [523]
— wages 323, 325, 357, 372 [364], [367], [423], [445]
— wages, worldwide 368 [441]
AIDS 260, 261, 272, 636, [262], [263], [264], [284], [751]
— maternal-fetus exchange, worldwide 267 [275]
— pediatric, worldwide 267 [275]
— research 332 [378]
Alabama
— politicians 607, 608 [707], [710]
Alaska
— Indians of North America business owners 38 [56]
— politicians 608 [710]
Albania
— births 508 [614]
— deaths 531 [638]
— divorces 579 [671]
— education, enrollment 150, 176, 187, 194, 208 [191], [195], [196], [200], [202]
— employment 469 [567]
— fertility 508, 550 [614], [649]
— fetal and infant deaths 561 [656]
— life expectancy 568 [659]
— marriages 581 [672]
— population 541 [646]
— teachers 440, 450, 455 [538], [551], [553]
Album-oriented radio 665 [805]
Albuquerque, NM
— breast cancer 249 [244]
Alcohol
— and adolescents 247, 630 [241], [742]
— and pregnancy 68, 290, 297, 300, [82], [319], [323], [324], [329]
Alcohol use and abuse 21, 58, 249, 274 [30], [79], [243], [289]
Algebra education 218 [205]
Algeria
— births 508 [614]
— childbirth 291 [321]
— deaths 531 [638]
— education, enrollment 150, 155, 187, 194, 197 [191], [192], [196], [200], [201]
— educational attainment 231 [226]
— employment 482, 486 [577], [579]
— engineering education 155 [192]
— fertility 508, 550 [614], [649]
— fetal and infant deaths 558, 561 [655], [656]
— life expectancy 568 [659]
— literacy 235 [227]
— marriages 581 [672]
— population 541 [646]

Algeria continued:
—teachers 450, 455 [551], [553]
Aliens 70 [85]
Allergies
—in infants 298 [325]
All-news radio 665 [805]
American Association of University Women
—membership 615 [721]
American Civil Liberties Union
—Reproductive Freedom Project 318, 332 [356], [379]
—Women's Rights Project 318, 332 [356], [379]
American College Testing scores 239 [228]
American Indians *See:* Indians of North America
American Samoa
—births 508 [614]
—deaths 531 [638]
—education, enrollment 150, 187, 208 [191], [196], [202]
—educational attainment 231 [226]
—employment 482 [577]
—fertility 508, 550 [614], [649]
—fetal and infant deaths 558, 561 [655], [656]
—teachers 450, 455 [551], [553]
Amniocentesis 289 [318]
Andorra
—education, enrollment 187, 208 [196], [202]
—fertility 550 [649]
—teachers 455 [553]
Anemia
—and alcohol abuse 249 [243]
—by race/ethnicity 298 [326]
Anesthesiology occupations 430 [525]
Angiocardiography 287 [314]
Angola
—childbirth 291 [321]
—education, enrollment 187, 197 [196], [201]
—employment 397 [480]
—fertility 550, 567 [649], [657]
—fetal and infant deaths 567 [657]
—life expectancy 567, 568 [657], [659]
—literacy 567 [657]
—population 541 [646]
—teachers 455 [553]
—unemployment 397 [480]
Anguilla
—fertility 550 [649]
Antigua
—birth control 517 [624]
Antigua and Barbuda
—births 508 [614]
—childbirth 291 [321]
—deaths 531 [638]
—education, enrollment 187, 197 [196], [201]
—educational attainment 231 [226]
—fertility 508, 550 [614], [649]

Antigua and Barbuda continued:
—fetal and infant deaths 558, 561 [655], [656]
—teachers 450, 455 [551], [553]
Arab physics students in the United States 222 [213]
Arab States
—early childhood education 142 [182]
—education, enrollment 142, 148, 192, 193 [182], [190], [197], [198]
—teachers 444 [539]
Archery 649, 650 [776], [778]
Architects 343 [399]
—wages 343 [399]
Architecture education
—worldwide 155, 163, 168, 176 [192], [193], [194], [195]
Archivists
—wages 352 [414]
Argentina
—arrests 50 [71]
—astronomy and astronomers 418 [505]
—births 508 [614]
—crime 58 [80]
—deaths 531 [638]
—education, enrollment 150, 187, 194, 197 [191], [196], [200], [201]
—educational attainment 231 [226]
—employment 397, 482 [480], [577]
—engineers 436 [534]
—fertility 508, 550 [614], [649]
—fetal and infant deaths 556, 561 [651], [656]
—imprisonment 50 [71]
—life expectancy 568 [659]
—literacy 229, 235 [224], [227]
—marriages 581 [672]
—mothers, mortality 584 [674]
—population 229, 541 [224], [646]
—rural population 229 [224]
—scientists 436 [534]
—suicides 535 [639]
—teachers 440, 450, 455 [538], [551], [553]
—unemployment 397 [480]
Arizona
—employee benefits 305 [338]
—Hispanic American business owners 37 [55]
—politicians 602, 603, 607, 608 [700], [702], [708], [710]
Arkansas 603, 607, 608 [702], [707], [710]
Armed Forces personnel *See:* Military personnel; Veterans
Armed Forces Qualifying Test 494 [595]
Arrests 44, 48 [62], [68]
—drug 47, 68 [66], [82]
—worldwide 50 [71]
Arson
—arrests 44, 48 [62], [68]
Art and artists 31, 330, 338, 343 [47], [375], [388], [399]
Artist printmakers 343 [399]

Australia continued:
— politicians 605 [705]
— population 537, 541, 597 [640], [646], [691]
— religious denominations 621 [731]
— scientists 436 [534]
— secretaries 468 [564]
— suicides 530, 535 [636], [639]
— teachers 440, 450, 455 [538], [551], [553]
— unemployment 397 [480]
— wages 341, 342, 347, 350, 367, 368, 369, 373 [396], [397], [405], [412], [440], [441], [442], [448]
— welfare recipients 314 [349]
— youth, population 597 [691]
Austria
— arrests 50 [71]
— births 508 [614]
— childbirth 291 [321]
— crime 58 [80]
— deaths 531 [638]
— divorces 579 [671]
— education, enrollment 150, 176, 187, 194, 208 [191], [195], [196], [200], [202]
— educational attainment 231 [226]
— employment 397, 462, 463, 464, 469, 476, 482 [480], [556], [557], [558], [567], [573], [577]
— engineering education 143 [183]
— engineers 436 [534]
— fertility 508, 550 [614], [649]
— fetal and infant deaths 558, 561 [655], [656]
— imprisonment 50 [71]
— labor unions 410 [492]
— life expectancy 568 [659]
— marriages 581 [672]
— mothers, mortality 584 [674]
— pay equity 367 [440]
— politicians 605 [705]
— population 541 [646]
— religious denominations 621 [731]
— science education 143 [183]
— scientists 436 [534]
— suicides 535 [639]
— teachers 440, 450, 455 [538], [551], [553]
— unemployment 397 [480]
— wages 367, 368, 373 [440], [441], [448]
Automobile accidents 281 [302]
Automotive industry 29 [44]
Azar, Suzie 603 [702]
Bachelors' degrees 131, 132 [165], [166]
Backpacking 651 [780]
Badminton 644, 649, 650 [766], [776], [778]
Bahamas
— arrests 50 [71]
— births 508 [614]
— childbirth 291 [321]

Bahamas continued:
— deaths 531 [638]
— education, enrollment 150, 187, 197 [191], [196], [201]
— employment 397, 482 [480], [577]
— fertility 508, 550 [614], [649]
— fetal and infant deaths 558, 561 [655], [656]
— imprisonment 50 [71]
— marriages 581 [672]
— mothers, mortality 584 [674]
— religious denominations 621 [731]
— teachers 440, 450, 455 [538], [551], [553]
— unemployment 397 [480]
Bahrain
— arrests 50 [71]
— births 508 [614]
— childbirth 291 [321]
— deaths 531 [638]
— education, enrollment 150, 187, 194, 208 [191], [196], [200], [202]
— educational attainment 231 [226]
— employment 482 [577]
— executives 467 [563]
— fertility 508, 550 [614], [649]
— imprisonment 50 [71]
— life expectancy 568 [659]
— literacy 235 [227]
— marriages 581 [672]
— mothers, mortality 584 [674]
— occupations 478, 487 [574], [580]
— police 421 [509]
— population 541 [646]
— public prosecutors 421 [509]
— secretaries 467 [563]
— teachers 440, 450, 455 [538], [551], [553]
Ballet
— attendance 665 [804]
Baltimore, MD
— fetal and infant deaths 556 [650]
— police 73 [90]
Bangkok
— Thailand, prostitution 633 [746]
Bangladesh
— aged 92 [117]
— arrests 50 [71]
— birth control 480, 517, 521 [576], [624], [626]
— births 508 [614]
— childbirth 291 [321]
— children 92 [117]
— deaths 531 [638]
— education, enrollment 150, 168, 187, 194, 208 [191], [194], [196], [200], [202]
— educational attainment 231 [226]
— employment 449, 470, 471, 473, 482, 485 [549], [568], [569], [570], [577], [578]

Business owners 36, 39, 40, 41, [52], [57], [59], [60], [61]
— African-Americans 32, 37 [49], [54]
— Asian Americans 31, 37 [48], [53]
— by industry 40 [58]
— Hispanic Americans 34, 37 [50], [55]
— Indians of North America 35, 38 [51], [56]
— male 40 [60]
Business travel 643 [764]
Buyers
— wages 352 [416]
Byelorussian SSR
— abortions 500 [604]
— divorces 579 [671]
— education, enrollment 187, 194, 208 [196], [200], [202]
— educational attainment 231 [226]
— life expectancy 568 [659]
— marriages 581 [672]
— mothers, mortality 584 [674]
— politicians 605 [705]
— teachers 455 [553]
Byron, Beverly 611 [712]
Caicos Islands *See:* Turks and Caicos Islands
California
— African-American business owners 37 [54]
— automobile accidents 281 [302]
— employee benefits 305 [338]
— Hispanic American business owners 37 [55]
— Indians of North America, business owners 38 [56]
— politicians 603, 608 [702], [710]
— sexual harassment 55 [74]
— Silicon Valley 446 [542]
Calisthenics and aerobics 644, 651 [766], [780]
Cambodia
— fertility 550 [649]
Cameroon
— birth control 515, 517 [620], [624]
— childbirth 291 [321]
— education, enrollment 155, 187, 197 [192], [196], [201]
— educational attainment 231 [226]
— employment 470, 471, 473, 482 [568], [569], [570], [577]
— fertility 474, 550 [571], [649]
— life expectancy 568 [659]
— literacy 235 [227]
— population 541 [646]
— teachers 450, 455 [551], [553]
Campbell, Bonnie 603 [701]
Camping
— participation 651 [780]
Canada 311, 466, 467 [345], [561], [562]
— abortions 500, 502, 591 [604], [605], [680]
— academic achievement 225 [218]
— arrests 50 [71]
— births 505, 506, 508, 594 [609], [611], [614], [685]
— childbirth 291, 597 [321], [690]

Canada continued:
— children 97, 104, 537, 597 [124], [134], [640], [691]
— children, economic status 314 [349]
— crime 58 [80]
— deaths 531 [638]
— deaths, young adults 527, 528, 530 [632], [633], [637]
— divorces 594 [685]
— education, enrollment 150, 163, 187, 194, 197 [191], [193], [196], [200], [201]
— educational attainment 231 [226]
— employment 388, 397, 461, 467, 468, 482 [467], [480], [554], [562], [564], [577]
— employment, youth 462 [555]
— executives 468 [564]
— family income 314, 317 [349], [355]
— fertility 506, 508, 550, 591 [611], [614], [649], [680]
— fetal and infant deaths 558, 561 [655], [656]
— homicides 529 [635]
— households 111, 112, 113, 114 [142], [144], [145], [147]
— households with children 98 [126]
— imprisonment 50 [71]
— life expectancy 568 [659]
— marital status 573, 574 [660], [661]
— marriages 578, 581, 594 [669], [672], [685]
— mothers, mortality 584 [674]
— pay equity 347 [405]
— politicians 605 [705]
— population 537, 541, 597 [640], [646], [691]
— pregnancy 591, 631 [680], [743]
— secretaries 468 [564]
— suicides 530, 535 [636], [639]
— teachers 440, 450, 455 [538], [551], [553]
— unemployment 397 [480]
— wages 347 [405]
— welfare recipients 314 [349]
— youth, population 597 [691]
Canadian immigrants 589 [676]
Cancer
— and oral contraceptives 250, 251 [246], [247]
— breast *See:* Breast cancer
— cervical 257 [256]
— deaths 252, 255, 524 [249], [253], [628]
— rates by race and cite 253, 254 [250], [251]
— recovery rates 289 [317]
Cape Verde
— births 508 [614]
— deaths 531 [638]
— education, enrollment 187, 197 [196], [201]
— fertility 508, 550 [614], [649]
— life expectancy 568 [659]
— literacy 235 [227]
— mothers, mortality 584 [674]
— population 541 [646]
— teachers 455 [553]

Cosmetologists
— wages 362 [429]
Cost and rate clerks 336 [387]
Costa Rica
— aged 92 [117]
— arrests 50 [71]
— birth control 480, 517, 521 [576], [624], [626]
— births 508 [614]
— childbirth 291 [321]
— children 92 [117]
— deaths 531 [638]
— education, enrollment 187, 197 [196], [201]
— educational attainment 231 [226]
— employment 397, 470, 471, 473, 482 [480], [568], [569], [570], [577]
— fertility 474, 508, 549, 550 [571], [614], [648], [649]
— fetal and infant deaths 561 [656]
— imprisonment 50 [71]
— life expectancy 568 [659]
— literacy 235 [227]
— marriages 479, 581 [575], [672]
— mothers, mortality 584 [674]
— politicians 605 [705]
— population 541 [646]
— suicides 535 [639]
— teachers 440, 450, 455 [538], [551], [553]
— unemployment 397 [480]
— wages 373 [448]
Cote D'Ivoire *See:* Ivory Coast
Counselors 357, 365, 404 [423], [434], [485]
Counterfeiting
— worldwide 58 [80]
Country music
— radio 665 [805]
Craft artists 343 [399]
Crafts education
— worldwide 155, 163, 168, 176 [192], [193], [194], [195]
Crew (Sports) 647, 650 [773], [778]
Crime
— worldwide 58 [80]
Crime and criminals 44, 45, 46, 56, 58 [62], [63], [64], [77], [79]
— arrestees 47, 48 [66], [67]
— juvenile delinquents 46 [65]
— murder 78 [99]
— victims 86 [109]
Crime victims *See:* Victims of crimes
Cross-country skiing 647, 649, 650 [773], [776], [778]
Cuba
— abortions 500 [604]
— births 508 [614]
— childbirth 291 [321]
— deaths 531 [638]
— education, enrollment 150, 163, 187, 194, 197 [191], [193],

Cuba continued:
[196], [200], [201]
— educational attainment 231 [226]
— employment 482 [577]
— engineers 436 [534]
— fertility 508, 549, 550 [614], [648], [649]
— fetal and infant deaths 558, 561 [655], [656]
— life expectancy 568 [659]
— literacy 235 [227]
— marriages 581 [672]
— mothers, mortality 584 [674]
— politicians 605 [705]
— population 541 [646]
— scientists 436 [534]
— teachers 440, 450, 455 [538], [551], [553]
Cuban Americans
— employment 393 [474]
Cuban refugees 589 [677]
Curators
— wages 352 [414]
CWPS *See:* Center for Women Policy Studies
Cyprus
— births 508 [614]
— childbirth 291 [321]
— deaths 531 [638]
— education, enrollment 150, 168, 187, 194, 208 [191], [194], [196], [200], [202]
— educational attainment 231 [226]
— employment 397, 482 [480], [577]
— fertility 508, 549, 550 [614], [648], [649]
— life expectancy 568 [659]
— literacy 235 [227]
— marriages 581 [672]
— pay equity 342, 371 [397], [444]
— police 421 [509]
— politicians 605 [705]
— population 541 [646]
— public prosecutors 421 [509]
— teachers 440, 450, 455 [538], [551], [553]
— unemployment 397 [480]
— wages 341, 342, 350, 368, 371, 373 [396], [397], [412], [441], [444], [448]
Cystoscopy 287 [314]
Czechoslovakia
— abortions 500, 502 [604], [605]
— arrests 50 [71]
— birth control 521 [626]
— births 508 [614]
— child care 124 [157]
— childbirth 291 [321]
— deaths 531 [638]
— divorces 579 [671]
— education, enrollment 150, 187, 194, 208 [191], [196], [200], [202]

Czechoslovakia continued:
— educational attainment 231 [226]
— employment 469, 482, 486 [567], [577], [579]
— fertility 508, 550 [614], [649]
— fetal and infant deaths 558, 561 [655], [656]
— imprisonment 50 [71]
— life expectancy 568 [659]
— marriages 581 [672]
— mothers, mortality 584 [674]
— pay equity 371 [444]
— police 421 [509]
— politicians 605 [705]
— population 541 [646]
— public prosecutors 421 [509]
— suicides 535 [639]
— teachers 440, 450, 455 [538], [551], [553]
— time allocation 124 [157]
— wages 369, 371 [442], [444]
D & C *See:* Dilatation and curettage
Dallas, TX 48 [67]
— police 73 [90]
Darrah, Joan 603 [702]
Data-entry keyers 336 [387]
Date rape 638 [754]
Day care *See:* Child care
Day care centers *See:* Child care centers
Deaths
— by age and race 525, 526, 529, [629], [630], [631], [634]
— cancer 255 [253]
— causes 395, 524 [476], [628]
— fetal and infant 557 [652]
— fetal and infant, worldwide 556 [651]
— homicides, worldwide 529 [635]
— pregnancy-related, worldwide 296 [322]
— suicides *See:* Suicides
— worldwide 531 [638]
— young adults, worldwide 527, 528, 530 [632], [633], [637]
Degrees
— academic 131, 132, 133, 134, 135, 136, 137, 226, 360, 431, [165], [166], [167], [168], [170], [171], [172], [174], [219], [426], [526]
— academic, African-Americans 133 [167]
— academic, Asian Americans 133 [167]
— academic, Hispanic Americans 133 [167]
— academic, Indians of North America 133 [167]
— academic, life sciences 226 [219]
— academic, nursing 434 [530]
— bachelors' *See:* Bachelors' degrees
— doctors' *See:* Doctors' degrees
— masters' *See:* Masters' degrees
Del Papa, Frankie Sue 603 [701]
DeLauro, Rosa 611 [712]
Delaware
— employee benefits 305 [338]

Delaware continued:
— politicians 608 [710]
Delinquents
— juvenile 46, 49, 117 [65], [69], [149]
Democratic Kampuchea *See:* Kampuchea, Democratic
Democratic People's Republic of Korea
　　See: Korea, Democratic People's Republic
Democratic Yemen *See:* Yemen, Democratic
Denmark 466, 467 [561], [562]
— abortions 500, 502 [604], [605]
— arrests 50 [71]
— birth control 521 [626]
— births 505, 508 [609], [614]
— childbirth 291 [321]
— deaths 531 [638]
— divorces 579 [671]
— education, enrollment 150, 176, 187, 194, 208 [191], [195], [196], [200], [202]
— employment 397, 461, 462, 463, 464, 467, 469, 476, 482 [480], [554], [556], [557], [558], [562], [567], [573], [577]
— engineering education 143 [183]
— fertility 508, 550 [614], [649]
— fetal and infant deaths 558, 561 [655], [656]
— households 113 [145]
— imprisonment 50 [71]
— labor unions 410 [492]
— life expectancy 568 [659]
— marriages 581 [672]
— mothers, mortality 584 [674]
— pay equity 367, 371 [440], [444]
— police 421 [509]
— politicians 605 [705]
— population 541 [646]
— pregnancy 631 [743]
— public prosecutors 421 [509]
— science education 143 [183]
— suicides 535 [639]
— teachers 455 [553]
— unemployment 397 [480]
— wages 367, 369, 370, 371, 373 [440], [442], [443], [444], [448]
Dental assistants 362 [429]
Dental care
— utilization 279 [300]
Dentistry education 137, 426 [173], [516]
Dentists
— wages 355 [420]
Denver, CO
— police 73 [90]
Depression
— mental 283, 284, 285 [305], [306], [308]
Dermatology
— occupations 430 [525]
Designers 343 [399]

Detroit, MI 48 [67]
— police 73 [90]
— fetal and infant deaths 556 [650]
Developed countries
— birth control 521 [626]
— birth weight 280 [301]
— childbirth 280 [301]
— children 280, 597 [301], [691]
— early childhood education 142 [182]
— education, enrollment 148, 193, 280 [190], [198], [301]
— employment 468 [566]
— enrollment 142 [182]
— fetal and infant deaths 280 [301]
— households 108 [140]
— literacy 280 [301]
— married women 280 [301]
— population 280, 597 [301], [691]
— teachers 444, 455 [539], [552]
— youth, population 597 [691]
Developing countries
— birth control 521 [626]
— birth weight 280 [301]
— childbirth 280 [301]
— children 280, 597 [301], [691]
— early childhood education 142 [182]
— education, enrollment 148, 193, 280 [190], [198], [301]
— employment 406, 468 [486], [566]
— enrollment 142 [182]
— fetal and infant deaths 280 [301]
— households 108 [140]
— literacy 280 [301]
— married women 280 [301]
— population 597 [691]
— teachers 444, 455 [539], [552]
— youth, population 597 [691]
Diabetes 269, 524 [280], [628]
Diagnostic radiology occupations 430 [525]
Diagnostic services 287 [314]
Diaphragm 517 [623]
Diet
— maternal, effects on infants 298 [325]
— weight-reducing 274, [287], [288]
Dilatation and curettage 288 [316]
Directors
— wages 343 [399]
Disabled 404 [484]
Disease
— cardiovascular, and oral contraceptives 262 [266]
— death from 524 [628]
— liver 249 [243]
— of the homeless 263 [269]
— pelvic inflammatory 269 [279]
— sexually transmitted 260, 269, 273 [262], [279], [285]
Dispatchers 336, 404 [387], [485]

Displaced homemakers 617 [723]
Distribution clerks 336 [387]
District of Columbia
— fetal and infant deaths 556 [650]
— politicians 603, 608 [702], [710]
Diving 650 [778]
Divorce 100, 575, 576 [128], [663], [664]
— children of divorced parents 98 [125]
— worldwide 579 [671]
Divorcees
— mothers 121 [152]
— remarriage 122, 575 [155], [662]
Dixon, Sharon Pratt 603 [702]
Djibouti
— childbirth 291 [321]
— education, enrollment 187, 197 [196], [201]
— fertility 550 [649]
— life expectancy 568 [659]
— population 541 [646]
— teachers 450, 455 [551], [553]
Doctors' degrees 133, 134, 226, 431, [167], [168], [169], [170], [219], [526]
Domestic violence *See:* Family violence
Dominica
— birth control 517 [624]
— deaths 531 [638]
— education, enrollment 150, 187, 197 [191], [196], [201]
— educational attainment 231 [226]
— employment 482 [577]
— fertility 550 [649]
— literacy 235 [227]
— politicians 605 [705]
— religious denominations 621 [731]
— teachers 440, 455 [538], [553]
Dominican Republic
— birth control 480, 517, 521 [576], [624], [626]
— births 508 [614]
— childbirth 291 [321]
— deaths 531 [638]
— education, enrollment 187, 197 [196], [201]
— educational attainment 231 [226]
— employment 470, 471, 473, 482 [568], [569], [570], [577]
— fertility 474, 508, 549, 550 [571], [614], [648], [649]
— fetal and infant deaths 561 [656]
— life expectancy 568 [659]
— literacy 235 [227]
— marriages 479, 581 [575], [672]
— mothers, mortality 584 [674]
— politicians 605 [705]
— population 541 [646]
— teachers 455 [553]
Drafting occupations 357, 366, 404 [423], [437], [485]
Dropouts 218, 392, 661 [206], [471], [798]
Drug arrests 48 [68]

Education continued:
[239], [240], [338]
— secondary, teachers 447 [545]
— secondary, working students 220 [208]
Education science and teacher training
— worldwide 155, 163, 168, 176 [192], [193], [194], [195]
Educational attainment
See also: Academic achievement
— adults 138 [175]
— worldwide 231 [226]
— young adults 407 [487]
Educational science and teacher training
— worldwide 194 [199]
Egypt
— birth control 480, 517, 521 [576], [624], [626]
— births 508 [614]
— childbirth 291 [321]
— deaths 531 [638]
— education, enrollment 150, 155, 187, 194, 197 [191], [192], [196], [200], [201]
— educational attainment 231 [226]
— employment 397, 470, 471, 473, 482 [480], [568], [569], [570], [577]
— engineers 436 [534]
— executives 467 [563]
— fertility 474, 508, 550 [571], [614], [649]
— fetal and infant deaths 561 [656]
— life expectancy 568 [659]
— literacy 229, 235 [224], [227]
— marriages 479, 581 [575], [672]
— mothers, mortality 584 [674]
— occupations 478, 487 [574], [580]
— pay equity 342 [397]
— politicians 605 [705]
— population 229, 541 [224], [646]
— religious denominations 621 [731]
— rural population 229 [224]
— scientists 436 [534]
— secretaries 467 [563]
— teachers 440, 450, 455 [538], [551], [553]
— unemployment 397 [480]
— wages 341, 342, 373 [396], [397], [448]
El Salvador
— birth control 517, 521 [624], [626]
— births 508 [614]
— childbirth 291 [321]
— deaths 531 [638]
— education, enrollment 150, 163, 187, 194, 197 [191], [193], [196], [200], [201]
— educational attainment 231 [226]
— employment 482 [577]
— fertility 508, 549, 550 [614], [648], [649]
— fetal and infant deaths 558, 561 [655], [656]
— life expectancy 568 [659]

El Salvador continued:
— literacy 235 [227]
— marriages 581 [672]
— mothers, mortality 584 [674]
— occupations 478, 487 [574], [580]
— pay equity 371 [444]
— politicians 605 [705]
— population 541 [646]
— suicides 535 [639]
— teachers 440, 450, 455 [538], [551], [553]
— wages 341, 350, 369, 371, 373 [396], [412], [442], [444], [448]
Elderly *See:* Aged and aging
Elections 600, 611 [696], [712]
— by state 608 [710]
— state government 599 [694]
— U.S. Congress 599, 601 [693], [697]
Electrical and electronic engineers 343, 434, 438 [399], [531], [535]
Electrical and electronic repairers 357 [423]
Electrical repairers 404 [485]
Electrical technicians 366 [437]
Elementary school students
— attitudes 22 [32]
— reading difficulties 230 [225]
Elementary teachers 357 [423]
Eligibility clerks
— social welfare 336 [387]
Emergency medicine occupations 430 [525]
Employee benefits 305, 306 [338], [339]
Employment 382, 386, [459], [463], [464]
— absenteeism 412, 415, [494], [495], [499]
— African-Americans 378 [455]
— agriculture, worldwide 406 [486]
— by employment classification 386 [464]
— by household status 382 [459]
— by industry 388, 402 [466], [482]
— by industry, United States 475 [572]
— by industry, worldwide 406, 475 [486], [572]
— by level of education, worldwide 470 [568]
— by marital status, United States 476 [573]
— by marital status, worldwide 464, 476 [558], [573]
— by occupation 423 [511]
— by occupation, United States 476 [573]
— by occupation, worldwide 476 [573]
— by occupational class 404 [485]
— by presence of children 382, 383, 385 [460], [461], [462]
— by race and marital status 402 [483]
— by status, worldwide 482 [577]
— Cuban Americans 393 [474]
— effects of technological innovations on 394 [475]
— finance, insurance, and real estate, worldwide 485 [578]
— government 425, [514], [515]
— Hispanic Americans 389 [468]

Netherlands continued:
— marriages 581, 594 [672], [685]
— mothers, mortality 584 [674]
— occupations 478, 487 [574], [580]
— pay equity 342, 371 [397], [444]
— politicians 605 [705]
— population 541 [646]
— pregnancy 631 [743]
— prostitution 633 [746]
— science education 143 [183]
— suicides 535 [639]
— teachers 450, 455 [551], [553]
— unemployment 397 [480]
— wages 341, 342, 369, 370, 371, 373, 633 [396], [397], [442], [443], [444], [448], [746]
Netherlands Antilles
— deaths 531 [638]
— education, enrollment 187, 197 [196], [201]
— employment 397, 482 [480], [577]
— fertility 550 [649]
— life expectancy 568 [659]
— literacy 235 [227]
— religious denominations 621 [731]
— teachers 455 [553]
— unemployment 397 [480]
— wages 368, 369 [441], [442]
Neurology
— occupations 430 [525]
Nevada
— politicians 603, 608 [701], [710]
Nevis *See:* St. Kitts and Nevis
New Caledonia
— births 508 [614]
— deaths 531 [638]
— divorces 579 [671]
— education, enrollment 150, 176, 187, 194, 208 [191], [195], [196], [200], [202]
— educational attainment 231 [226]
— employment 397, 482 [480], [577]
— engineers 436 [534]
— fertility 508, 550 [614], [649]
— fetal and infant deaths 558, 561 [655], [656]
— literacy 235 [227]
— scientists 436 [534]
— teachers 440, 450, 455 [538], [551], [553]
— unemployment 397 [480]
New Hampshire
— politicians 607, 608 [708], [710]
New Haven, CT
— fetal and infant deaths 556 [650]
New Jersey
— employee benefits 305 [338]
— politicians 607, 608 [707], [710]

New Mexico
— Hispanic American Business owners 37 [55]
— politicians 608 [710]
New Orleans, LA 48, 73 [67], [90]
New York 48 [67]
— African-American business owners 37 [54]
— breast cancer 249 [244]
— employee benefits 305 [338]
— fetal and infant deaths 299 [327]
— Hispanic American business owners 37 [55]
— police 73 [90]
— politicians 608 [710]
— sexual harassment 55 [74]
New Zealand
— abortions 500, 502 [604], [605]
— arrests 50 [71]
— births 508 [614]
— childbirth 291 [321]
— crime 58 [80]
— deaths 531 [638]
— divorces 579 [671]
— education, enrollment 150, 176, 187, 194, 208 [191], [195], [196], [200], [202]
— educational attainment 231 [226]
— employment 397, 468, 482 [480], [564], [566], [577]
— executives 468 [564]
— fertility 508, 550 [614], [649]
— fetal and infant deaths 558, 561 [655], [656]
— hours of labor 390 [469]
— imprisonment 50 [71]
— life expectancy 568 [659]
— marriages 581 [672]
— mothers, mortality 584 [674]
— pay equity 347, 371 [405], [444]
— police 421 [509]
— politicians 605 [705]
— population 541, 587 [646], [675]
— pregnancy 631 [743]
— public prosecutors 421 [509]
— religious denominations 621 [731]
— secretaries 468 [564]
— suicides 535 [639]
— teachers 440, 450, 455 [538], [551], [553]
— unemployment 397 [480]
— wages 347, 368, 369, 370, 371, 373 [405], [441], [442], [443], [444], [448]
Newark, NJ
— police 73 [90]
News/talk radio 665 [805]
Newspaper reading 664 [803]
See also: Reading interests
Nicaragua
— birth control 517 [624]
— childbirth 291 [321]

Northern Ireland continued:
— suicides 535 [639]
Northern Mariana Islands
— births 508 [614]
— deaths 531 [638]
— divorces 579 [671]
— fertility 508, 550 [614], [649]
— fetal and infant deaths 558, 561 [655], [656]
Norton, Eleanor Holmes 611 [712]
Norton, Gale 603 [701]
Norway
— abortions 500, 502, 591 [604], [605], [680]
— AIDS, maternal-fetus exchange 267 [275]
— AIDS, pediatric 267 [275]
— arrests 50 [71]
— births 506, 508 [611], [614]
— childbirth 291 [321]
— children 104, 537, 597 [134], [640], [691]
— crime 58 [80]
— deaths 531 [638]
— deaths, young adults 527, 528, 537 [632], [633], [640]
— divorces 579 [671]
— education, enrollment 150, 176, 187, 194, 208 [191], [195], [196], [200], [202]
— educational attainment 231 [226]
— employment 397, 449, 462, 463, 464, 469, 475, 476, 482, 485 [480], [549], [556], [557], [558], [567], [572], [573], [577], [578]
— employment, youth 462 [555]
— engineering education 143 [183]
— engineers 436 [534]
— executives 467 [563]
— family income 317 [355]
— fertility 506, 508, 550, 591 [611], [614], [649], [680]
— fetal and infant deaths 558, 561 [655], [656]
— homicides 529 [635]
— households 112 [144]
— imprisonment 50 [71]
— labor unions 410 [492]
— life expectancy 568 [659]
— marital status 573, 574 [660], [661]
— marriages 581 [672]
— mothers, mortality 584 [674]
— occupations 478, 487 [574], [580]
— pay equity 371 [444]
— politicians 605 [705]
— population 537, 541, 597 [640], [646], [691]
— pregnancy 591, 631 [680], [743]
— scientists 436 [534]
— secretaries 467 [563]
— suicides 530, 535 [636], [639]
— teachers 440, 455 [538], [553]
— unemployment 397 [480]
— wages 350, 368, 369, 371, 373 [412], [441], [442], [444],

Norway continued:
[448]
— youth, population 597 [691]
NOW *See:* National Organization for Women (NOW)
Nuclear engineers 438 [535]
Nurses 145, 404, 430, 434 [185], [485], [524], [530]
— enrollment in nursing school 426 [516]
— job growth projections 426, 427 [517], [518]
— registered 426 [517]
— temporary employment 395 [477]
— wages 338, 348, 355, 359, 366 [389], [407], [419], [424], [437]
Nurses' aides 338, 362, 426, 427, 430 [389], [429], [517], [518], [524]
Nursing
See also: Nurses
— education 226 [220]
— enrollment 426 [516]
— faculty salaries 352 [415]
— students 145, 226 [185], [220]
Nursing home care 275, [291], [292]
Nutritional disorders
— and alcohol abuse 249 [243]
O'Connor, Maureen 603 [702]
O'Connor, Sandra Day 449 [548]
Oakar, Mary Rose 611 [712]
Oberndorf, Meyera 603 [702]
Obesity 249, 268, 269 [243], [277], [278]
Obstetrics
— surgery 288 [316]
Obstetrics and gynecology
— occupations 430 [525]
Occupational therapy technology 352 [415]
Occupations
— expected at age 30 by 8th graders 424 [512]
— job growth projections 426, 427 [517], [518]
— major groups 429 [521]
— worldwide 487 [580]
Oceania
— arrests 50 [71]
— birth control 515, 517, 595 [621], [624], [686]
— birth weight 280 [301]
— births 508 [614]
— childbirth 280 [301]
— children 280, 537, 597 [301], [640], [691]
— early childhood education 142 [182]
— education, enrollment 142, 148, 192, 193, 194, 280 [182], [190], [197], [198], [200], [301]
— employment 397, 468 [480], [566]
— fertility 508, 550 [614], [649]
— fetal and infant deaths 280 [301]
— households 108 [140]
— imprisonment 50 [71]
— literacy 280 [301]

Panama continued:
— birth control 480, 517, 521 [576], [624], [626]
— births 508 [614]
— childbirth 291 [321]
— deaths 531 [638]
— education, enrollment 150, 187, 197 [191], [196], [201]
— educational attainment 231 [226]
— employment 397, 449, 470, 471, 473, 482, 485 [480], [549], [568], [569], [570], [577], [578]
— fertility 474, 508, 549, 550 [571], [614], [648], [649]
— fetal and infant deaths 558, 561 [655], [656]
— illiteracy 229 [224]
— imprisonment 50 [71]
— life expectancy 568 [659]
— literacy 229, 235 [224], [227]
— marriages 479, 581 [575], [672]
— mothers, mortality 584 [674]
— occupations 478, 487 [574], [580]
— population 229, 541 [224], [646]
— rural population 229 [224]
— suicides 535 [639]
— teachers 440, 450, 455 [538], [551], [553]
— unemployment 397 [480]
Papua New Guinea
— childbirth 291 [321]
— education, enrollment 176, 187, 194, 208 [195], [196], [200], [202]
— educational attainment 231 [226]
— fertility 550 [649]
— life expectancy 568 [659]
— literacy 235 [227]
— population 541 [646]
— religious denominations 621 [731]
— teachers 440, 450, 455 [538], [551], [553]
Paraguay
— birth control 480, 517, 521 [576], [624], [626]
— births 508 [614]
— childbirth 291 [321]
— deaths 531 [638]
— education, enrollment 187, 197 [196], [201]
— educational attainment 231 [226]
— employment 470, 471, 473, 482 [568], [569], [570], [577]
— fertility 474, 508, 550 [571], [614], [649]
— fetal and infant deaths 561 [656]
— life expectancy 568 [659]
— literacy 235 [227]
— marriages 479, 581 [575], [672]
— mothers, mortality 584 [674]
— population 541 [646]
— suicides 535 [639]
— teachers 455 [553]
Parental leave benefits
  See: Employee benefits (see also under individual State)

Parents
— working 514 [619]
Pathology occupations 430 [525]
Patterson, Elizabeth 611 [712]
Pay equity 343, 354, 356, 357, 363, 373 [398], [417], [421], [423], [430], [447]
— labor union members 367 [439]
— United States 347, 367 [405], [440]
— worldwide 342, 347, 350, 367, 371, 373 [397], [405], [412], [440], [444], [448]
Payroll and timekeeping clerks 336 [387]
Peace Links 616 [722]
Pediatrics occupations 430 [525]
Pelosi, Nancy 611 [712]
Pelvic inflammatory disease
  See: Disease, pelvic inflammatory
Peninsular Malaysia *See:* Malaysia
Pennsylvania
— employee benefits 305 [338]
— politicians 603, 607, 608 [702], [707], [710]
Pensions 327 [369]
Periodicals 30, [45], [46]
Personnel clerks 336 [387]
Personnel managers 352 [416]
Peru
— aged 92 [117]
— arrests 50 [71]
— birth control 480, 517, 521 [576], [624], [626]
— births 508 [614]
— childbirth 291 [321]
— children 92 [117]
— crime 58 [80]
— deaths 531 [638]
— education, enrollment 150, 187, 197 [191], [196], [201]
— educational attainment 231 [226]
— employment 397, 470, 471, 473, 482 [480], [568], [569], [570], [577]
— fertility 474, 508, 549, 550 [571], [614], [648], [649]
— fetal and infant deaths 561 [656]
— fuel gathering 127 [161]
— imprisonment 50 [71]
— life expectancy 568 [659]
— literacy 235 [227]
— marriages 479, 581 [575], [672]
— mothers, mortality 584 [674]
— occupations 478, 487 [574], [580]
— population 541 [646]
— religious denominations 621 [731]
— teachers 440, 450, 455 [538], [551], [553]
— time allocation 127 [161]
— unemployment 397 [480]
— wages 350 [412]
Petroleum engineers 438 [535]
Pharmacists 348 [407]

Polynesia
— French *See:* French Polynesia
— population 587 [675]
Population
— adult, age distribution 514 [618]
— adult, by census region 513 [615]
— adult, by marital status 514 [619]
— adult, by race 513 [616]
— adult, by residence 514 [617]
— African-American adults 513 [616]
— American, in Canada 589 [676]
— by age 539 [643]
— by age and race 538 [642]
— by region 539 [643]
— Canadian immigrants 589 [676]
— institutionalized 117 [149]
— male/female ratio 593 [682]
— projections by race 540 [644]
— refugee 589, 590, [677], [678], [679]
— Spanish speaking adults 513 [616]
— United States 541 [646]
— worldwide 229, 540, 541, 597 [224], [645], [646], [691]
Population estimates and projections
— worldwide 587 [675]
Pornography
— opinions 14 [21]
Portland, OR 48 [67]
Portsmouth, VA
— fetal and infant deaths 556 [650]
Portugal
— arrests 50 [71]
— births 508, 594 [614], [685]
— childbirth 291 [321]
— crime 58 [80]
— deaths 531 [638]
— divorces 579, 594 [671], [685]
— education, enrollment 150, 176, 187, 194, 208 [191], [195], [196], [200], [202]
— educational attainment 231 [226]
— employment 397, 449, 469, 482, 485 [480], [549], [567], [577], [578]
— engineering education 143 [183]
— engineers 436 [534]
— fertility 508, 550 [614], [649]
— fetal and infant deaths 558, 561 [655], [656]
— imprisonment 50 [71]
— life expectancy 568 [659]
— literacy 235 [227]
— marriages 581, 594 [672], [685]
— mothers, mortality 584 [674]
— occupations 478, 487 [574], [580]
— police 421 [509]
— politicians 605 [705]
— population 541 [646]

Portugal continued:
— public prosecutors 421 [509]
— religious denominations 621 [731]
— science education 143 [183]
— scientists 436 [534]
— suicides 535 [639]
— teachers 440, 450, 455 [538], [551], [553]
— unemployment 397 [480]
— wages 368 [441]
Postal clerks 357 [423]
Poverty
— children 97, 374 [124], [449]
Precision production
— craft and repair occupations 372, 423, 430 [445], [511], [523]
Pregnancy
— adolescent, Canada 631 [743]
— adolescent, Denmark 631 [743]
— adolescent, England 631 [743]
— adolescent, Finland 631 [743]
— adolescent, Netherlands 631 [743]
— adolescent, New Zealand 631 [743]
— adolescent, Norway 631 [743]
— adolescent, Sweden 631 [743]
— adolescent, United States 631 [743]
— adolescent, Wales 631 [743]
— adolescent, worldwide 591 [680]
— complications 290 [319]
— complications, worldwide 296 [322]
— miscarriage of 299 [328]
Pregnancy and alcohol 297, 300, [323], [324], [329]
Pregnancy and anemia 298 [326]
Pregnancy and drugs 297, 299, [323], [324], [327]
Pregnancy and family violence 290 [320]
Pregnancy and hard work 303 [335]
Premenstrual syndrome 270 [281]
Premenstrual tension 270 [281]
Prenatal care 300, 302 [330], [334]
Preventive health services 287 [314]
Priest, Sharron 603 [702]
Principals
  See also: School administrators
— by race 439 [537]
Principe *See:* Sao Tome and Principe
Prisoners *See:* Imprisonment
Production coordinators 336 [387]
Professional degrees 137, [173], [174]
  See also: Doctors' degrees
Professional schools
— enrollment 147 [188]
Professional services occupations 445 [540]
Professional speciality occupations 343 [399]
Professional Women's Clubs
— membership 615 [721]

Saudi Arabia continued:
—teachers 440, 450, 455 [538], [551], [553]
Savannah, GA
—fetal and infant deaths 556 [650]
Scheduling clerks 336 [387]
Scheduling supervisors/clerks 357 [423]
Scholastic Aptitude Test 241, 242, [232], [233], [234]
Scholastic Aptitude Test scores 243 [236]
School administrators 352, 432, 435, 439, 447, [416], [527], [532], [533], [537], [545]
School board members 447 [545]
School dropouts 661 [798]
Schools
—personnel *See:* School administrators
—volunteer work in 614 [718]
Schroeder, Patricia 611 [712]
Science
—doctors, income 329 [373]
Science and engineering enrollment 143, 227 [183], [222]
—worldwide 194, [199], [200]
Science education 143, 227, 239 [183], [222], [229]
—college graduates, worldwide 225 [218]
Science technicians 366 [437]
Scientists 221, 361, 434, 438, 439 [212], [428], [531], [535], [536]
—faculty 423 [510]
—worldwide 436, 449 [534], [550]
Scotland
—abortions 500, 502 [604], [605]
—births 508 [614]
—childbirth 291 [321]
—deaths 531 [638]
—divorces 579 [671]
—fertility 508 [614]
—fetal and infant deaths 558, 561 [655], [656]
—life expectancy 568 [659]
—marriages 581 [672]
—mothers, mortality 584 [674]
—suicides 535 [639]
Sculptors 343 [399]
Seattle, WA
—police 73 [90]
Secretarial faculty salaries 352 [415]
Secretaries 325, 336, 426 [367], [387], [517]
—health problems of 263 [268]
—job growth projections 419, 426, 427 [507], [517], [518]
—worldwide 467, 468 [563], [564]
Security
—attitudes 6 [8]
Senegal
—arrests 50 [71]
—birth control 515, 517, 521 [620], [624], [626]
—childbirth 291 [321]
—crime 58 [80]

Senegal continued:
—education, enrollment 150, 187, 194, 197 [191], [196], [200], [201]
—employment 397, 470, 471, 473 [480], [568], [569], [570]
—fertility 474, 550, 567 [571], [649], [657]
—fetal and infant deaths 567 [657]
—fuel gathering 127 [161]
—imprisonment 50 [71]
—life expectancy 567, 568 [657], [659]
—literacy 567 [657]
—marriages 479 [575]
—politicians 605 [705]
—population 541 [646]
—teachers 440, 450, 455 [538], [551], [553]
—time allocation 127 [161]
—unemployment 397 [480]
Servants 355, 362 [420], [429]
Service occupations 323, 325, 362, 372, 388, 402, 423, 430 [364], [367], [429], [445], [466], [482], [511], [523]
—executives 445 [540]
—Hispanic Americans 430 [523]
—worldwide 475, 476 [572], [573]
Service trades education 155, 163, 168, 176 [192], [193], [194], [195]
Services 445 [540]
—women-owned firms 39, 40 [57], [58]
Sewing-machine operators 355, 357, 404 [420], [423], [485]
Sex 634, 635, 636, 639, [747], [748], [749], [750], [752], [757]
—patient-therapist 641 [761]
Sex research 639 [758]
Sex roles
—elderly 640 [759]
Sexual assault 53, 79 [72], [100]
Sexual behavior
—adolescents 630, 631 [742], [743]
—adolescents, worldwide 631 [744]
Sexual behavior surveys 634, 635, 636, 639, [747], [748], [749], [750], [751], [752], [757], [758]
Sexual cycle 642 [762]
Sexual excitement 642 [762]
Sexual harassment 55, 496, 497, 498, [74], [598], [599], [600], [601]
Sexually transmitted diseases 260, 269, 273 [262], [279], [285]

Seychelles
—abortions 500, 502 [604], [605]
—births 508 [614]
—childbirth 291 [321]
—deaths 531 [638]
—education, enrollment 150, 187, 208 [191], [196], [202]
—educational attainment 231 [226]
—employment 397, 482, 486 [480], [577], [579]

Spain continued:
— teachers 440, 450, 455 [538], [551], [553]
— unemployment 397 [480]
Spalding University 224 [215]
Spanish speaking adults 513 [616]
Sporting goods
— purchases 334 [382]
Sports 328, 644, 651, 652, 667, 668, 669, 670, [372], [765], [780], [781], [809], [810], [811], [812], [813]
   See also: Athletes; Recreation; names of specific sports
— adolescents 659, 661 [792], [798]
— adults 644, 645 [766], [768]
— and body image 643 [763]
— college 646, 647, 648, 649, 650, 651, [770], [773], [774], [775], [776], [777], [778], [779]
— college administrators 645 [769]
— college coaches 646 [771]
— college expenditures 646 [772]
— high school 657, 658 [788], [791]
— minorities 659, 660, 661 [793], [794], [797]
— Olympic games 666, 667 [807], [808]
— opinions on women in 4 [6]
Spouse abuse 80, 128 [101], [162]
   See also: Abused women; Wife abuse
— worldwide 130 [164]
Squash 644, 649, 650 [766], [776], [778]
Sri Lanka
— arrests 50 [71]
— birth control 480, 517, 521 [576], [624], [626]
— births 508 [614]
— childbirth 291 [321]
— crime 58 [80]
— deaths 531 [638]
— divorces 579 [671]
— education, enrollment 150, 168, 187, 194, 208 [191], [194], [196], [200], [202]
— educational attainment 231 [226]
— employment 449, 470, 471, 473, 482, 485, 486 [549], [568], [569], [570], [577], [578], [579]
— engineers 436 [534]
— fertility 474, 508, 549, 550 [571], [614], [648], [649]
— fetal and infant deaths 556, 558, 561 [651], [655], [656]
— illiteracy 229 [224]
— imprisonment 50 [71]
— life expectancy 568 [659]
— literacy 229, 235 [224], [227]
— marriages 479, 581 [575], [672]
— occupations 478, 487 [574], [580]
— pay equity 342, 371 [397], [444]
— police 421 [509]
— politicians 605 [705]
— population 229, 541 [224], [646]
— public prosecutors 421 [509]
— religious denominations 621 [731]

Sri Lanka continued:
— rural population 229 [224]
— scientists 436 [534]
— suicides 535 [639]
— teachers 440, 455 [538], [553]
— wages 342, 368, 369, 371, 373 [397], [441], [442], [444], [448]
Stanford University 224 [216]
Statistical clerks 336 [387]
STDs *See:* Sexually transmitted diseases; AIDS; HIV; Syphilis
Steel industry and trade 417, 418, [502], [503], [504]
Stenographers 336 [387]
Sterility 266 [273]
Sterilization 517 [623]
— worldwide 523 [627]
Stock and inventory clerks 336, 357 [387], [423]
Stock handlers 357 [423]
Stock handlers and baggers 357 [423]
Strauss, Annette 603 [702]
Streep, Meryl 446 [543]
Student nurses 226 [220]
Students
— attitudes 22 [32]
— drug use 67, 69, [81], [83], [84]
— employment and unemployment 404 [484]
— expected occupations 424 [512]
— school satisfaction 23 [33]
Sub-Saharan Africa
— fertility 550 [649]
Sudan
— birth control 480, 517 [576], [624]
— childbirth 291 [321]
— crime 58 [80]
— education, enrollment 150, 155, 187, 194, 197 [191], [192], [196], [200], [201]
— employment 397, 470, 471, 473, 482 [480], [568], [569], [570], [577]
— fertility 474, 550 [571], [649]
— fetal and infant deaths 556 [651]
— life expectancy 568 [659]
— marriages 479 [575]
— population 541 [646]
— teachers 440, 450, 455 [538], [551], [553]
— unemployment 397 [480]
Suicides 524 [628]
— United States 535 [639]
— worldwide 530, 535 [636], [639]
Supervisors 336 [387]
Support (domestic relations) 307, 308, 309, 310, [340], [341], [342], [343], [344]
— for graduate students 329 [373]
Suriname
— arrests 50 [71]

Suriname continued:
— deaths 531 [638]
— education, enrollment 150, 163, 187, 194, 197 [191], [193], [196], [200], [201]
— employment 397, 482 [480], [577]
— fertility 550 [649]
— fetal and infant deaths 561 [656]
— imprisonment 50 [71]
— life expectancy 568 [659]
— literacy 235 [227]
— mothers, mortality 584 [674]
— population 541 [646]
— teachers 440, 450, 455 [538], [551], [553]
— unemployment 397 [480]
Surveyors 343 [399]
— wages 343, 366 [399], [437]
Swarthmore College 224 [216]
Swaziland
— childbirth 291 [321]
— education, enrollment 150, 155, 187, 194, 197 [191], [192], [196], [200], [201]
— educational attainment 231 [226]
— fertility 550 [649]
— life expectancy 568 [659]
— literacy 235 [227]
— population 541 [646]
— teachers 440, 450, 455 [538], [551], [553]
— wages 369 [442]
Sweden 466, 467 [561], [562]
— abortions 500, 502, 591 [604], [605], [680]
— AIDS, maternal-fetus exchange 267 [275]
— AIDS, pediatric 267 [275]
— arrests 50 [71]
— births 505, 506, 508, 594, [608], [609], [611], [614], [685]
— childbirth 291, 597 [321], [690]
— children 97, 104, 314, 537, 597 [124], [134], [349], [640], [691]
— deaths 531 [638]
— deaths, young adults 527, 528, 530 [632], [633], [637]
— divorces 579, 594 [671], [685]
— education, enrollment 150, 176, 187, 194, 208 [191], [195], [196], [200], [202]
— educational attainment 231 [226]
— employment 388, 397, 449, 461, 462, 463, 464, 467, 468, 469, 476, 482, 485, 486 [467], [480], [549], [554], [556], [557], [558], [562], [564], [567], [573], [577], [578], [579]
— employment, youth 462 [555]
— executives 468 [564]
— family income 314, 317 [349], [355]
— fertility 506, 508, 550, 591 [611], [614], [649], [680]
— fetal and infant deaths 558, 561 [655], [656]
— homicides 529 [635]
— households 111, 112, 113, 114 [142], [144], [145], [147]
— households with children 98 [126]

Sweden continued:
— imprisonment 50 [71]
— labor unions 410 [492]
— life expectancy 568 [659]
— marital status 573, 574 [660], [661]
— marriages 581, 594 [672], [685]
— mothers, mortality 584 [674]
— mothers, unmarried 505 [608]
— occupations 478, 487 [574], [580]
— pay equity 347, 367, 371 [405], [440], [444]
— police 421 [509]
— politicians 605 [705]
— population 537, 541, 597 [640], [646], [691]
— pregnancy 591, 631 [680], [743]
— public prosecutors 421 [509]
— secretaries 468 [564]
— suicides 530, 535 [636], [639]
— teachers 450, 455 [551], [553]
— time allocation 126 [160]
— unemployment 397 [480]
— wages 341, 347, 367, 368, 369, 371, 373 [396], [405], [440], [441], [442], [444], [448]
— welfare recipients 314 [349]
— youth, population 597 [691]
Swimming 644, 649, 650, 651 [766], [776], [778], [780]
Switzerland
— births 508, 594 [614], [685]
— childbirth 291 [321]
— crime 58 [80]
— deaths 531 [638]
— divorces 579, 594 [671], [685]
— education, enrollment 150, 176, 187, 194, 208 [191], [195], [196], [200], [202]
— educational attainment 231 [226]
— employment 397, 469, 482 [480], [567], [577]
— engineering education 143 [183]
— fertility 508, 550 [614], [649]
— fetal and infant deaths 558, 561 [655], [656]
— hours of labor 390 [469]
— households 111 [142]
— labor unions 410 [492]
— life expectancy 568 [659]
— marriages 581, 594 [672], [685]
— mothers, mortality 584 [674]
— pay equity 342, 371 [397], [444]
— politicians 605 [705]
— population 541 [646]
— science education 143 [183]
— suicides 535 [639]
— teachers 440 [538]
— unemployment 397 [480]
— wages 341, 342, 368, 369, 371, 373 [396], [397], [441], [442] [444], [448]
Synchronized swimming 650 [778]

Unemployed continued:
— adults 386 [464]
— African-Americans 378 [455]
— Cuban-Americans 393 [474]
— Mexican-Americans 393 [474]
— Puerto-Rican Americans 393 [474]
Unemployment 386 [463]
— by age and race 402 [483]
— Hispanic Americans 389 [468]
— male 397 [479]
— young adults 407 [487]
— youth 409 [489]
United Arab Emirates
— arrests 50 [71]
— births 508 [614]
— childbirth 291 [321]
— education, enrollment 150, 168, 187, 194, 208 [191], [194], [196], [200], [202]
— educational attainment 231 [226]
— employment 482 [577]
— fertility 508, 550 [614], [649]
— imprisonment 50 [71]
— life expectancy 568 [659]
— literacy 235 [227]
— police 421 [509]
— population 541 [646]
— public prosecutors 421 [509]
— teachers 440, 450, 455 [538], [551], [553]
United Kingdom 311, 466, 467 [345], [561], [562]
— abortions 500, 502, 591 [604], [605], [680]
— AIDS, maternal-fetus exchange 267 [275]
— AIDS, pediatric 267 [275]
— arrests 50 [71]
— birth control 521 [626]
— births 505, 506, 508, 594, [608], [609], [611], [614], [685]
— children 104, 537, 597 [134], [640], [691]
— children, economic status 97, 314 [124], [349]
— crime 58 [80]
— deaths 531 [638]
— deaths, young adults 527, 528, 530 [632], [633], [637]
— divorces 579, 594 [671], [685]
— education, enrollment 150, 176, 187, 194, 208 [191], [195], [196], [200], [202]
— employment 388, 397, 461, 467, 469, 475, 482 [467], [480], [554], [562], [567], [572], [577]
— employment, youth 462 [555]
— engineering education 143 [183]
— family income 314, 317 [349], [355]
— fertility 506, 508, 550, 591 [611], [614], [649], [680]
— fetal and infant deaths 558, 561 [655], [656]
— homicides 529 [635]
— hours of labor 390 [469]
— households 112, 113, 114 [144], [145], [147]
— households with children 98 [126]

United Kingdom continued:
— imprisonment 50 [71]
— labor unions 410 [492]
— life expectancy 568 [659]
— marital status 573, 574 [660], [661]
— marriages 581, 594 [672], [685]
— mothers, mortality 584 [674]
— mothers, unmarried 505 [608]
— pay equity 342, 347, 367, 371 [397], [405], [440], [444]
— police 421 [509]
— politicians 605 [705]
— population 537, 541, 597 [640], [646], [691]
— pregnancy 591 [680]
— public prosecutors 421 [509]
— science education 143 [183]
— suicides 530, 535 [636], [639]
— teachers 440, 450, 455 [538], [551], [553]
— unemployment 397 [480]
— wages 341, 342, 347, 367, 368, 369, 370, 371, 373 [396], [397], [405], [440], [441], [442], [443], [444], [448]
— welfare recipients 314 [349]
— youth, population 597 [691]
United Nations officials and personnel 468 [565]
United Rep. of Tanzania
— childbirth 291 [321]
— education, enrollment 150, 155, 187, 194, 197 [191], [192], [196], [200], [201]
— fuel gathering 127 [161]
— life expectancy 568 [659]
— literacy 235 [227]
— pay equity 342 [397]
— population 541 [646]
— teachers 440, 450, 455 [538], [551], [553]
— time allocation 127 [161]
— wages 341, 342, 369, 373 [396], [397], [442], [448]

United States—Note: Most subject terms in this index, e.g., *Mothers, mortality*, refer to U.S. coverage. The following references appearing under the term *United States* indicate international tables which include the United States as one of the countries.

United States 311, 466 [345], [561]
— abortions 591 [680]
— academic achievement 225 [218]
— AIDS, maternal-fetus exchange 267 [275]
— AIDS, pediatric 267 [275]
— arrests 50 [71]
— astronomy and astronomers 418 [505]
— birth control 521 [626]
— births 506, 508, 594 [611], [614], [685]
— births to single women 505 [609]
— births to unmarried women 505 [608]
— child care 124 [157]
— childbirth 291, 597 [321], [690]